The Lessons of the Temporal Cycle and the Principal Feasts of the Sanctoral Cycle According to the Monastic Breviary

Compiled and Adapted
for the
Office of the Brothers of St. Meinrad's Abbey

Copyright 1943
by
St. Meinrad's Abbey
St. Meinrad, Indiana
1943

IMPRIMI POTEST

☩ IGNATIUS ESSER, O.S.B.
Abbot

NIHIL OBSTAT

PATRICK SHAUGHNESSY, O.S.B., S.T.D.
Censor Deputatus

IMPRIMATUR

☩ JOSEPH E. RITTER, D.D.
Bishop of Indianapolis

August 10, 1941

The portions of the New Testament contained in this book are reproduced with the permission of the Confraternity of Christian Doctrine, Washington, D. C., owner of the copyright of the revision of the Challoner-Rheims Version of *The New Testament of Our Lord and Savior Jesus Christ*.

Second Printing
All rights reserved

The present translation is lovingly dedicated to those devout souls who are desirous of reading and meditating upon the words of the Fathers of the Church, but who have been hindered from so doing by an insufficient knowledge of Latin. In this translation the Latin idioms have been rather closely adhered to for the purpose of comparative study.

The feast of Saint Lawrence

August 10, 1941

Ut In Omnibus Glorificetur Deus

THE TEMPORAL CYCLE

I SUNDAY IN ADVENT

I Nocturn
Beginning of the Prophecy of Isaias, c. 1, 1 - 11

II Nocturn
Sermon of St. Leo, Pope

When our Savior was instructing His disciples about the coming of the kingdom of God and about the end of the world and of time, teaching His entire Church in the person of the apostles, He said, "Beware lest perhaps your hearts be weighed down by gluttony and drunkenness and worldly thoughts." Indeed, we know, most dearly beloved, that that command pertains more especially to us, to whom the foretold day, even though it be hidden, cannot be doubted to be close at hand.

It behooves every man to be prepared for its coming lest he be found either given up to gluttony or entangled in the cares of the world. For, most dearly beloved, it is proved by daily experience that keenness of mind is dulled by drunkenness, and that the strength of the heart is weakened by over-eating, so that the pleasure of eating is injurious to the health of the body unless the principle of temperance resists the enticement, and, because it would become a burden, withdraws from the pleasure.

For although the flesh desires nothing without the soul, and gets it feelings from the same source as it takes its movements, it is nevertheless the duty of the same soul to deny certain things to the substance subject to itself and by an interior judgment to restrain the exterior from unbecoming things, that being more often free from bodily desires, it may devote itself to divine wisdom in the chamber of the mind where, all noise of earthly cares being silenced, the soul may rejoice in holy meditations and eternal delights.

But although in this life it is difficult that such a state be continuous, it can nevertheless be frequently taken up anew, that we may be occupied oftener and for longer periods with spiritual matters rather than with carnal. And while we give more time to better pursuits, even temporal actions are changed into incorruptible riches.

℟. I look from afar, and, behold I see the power of God coming, and a cloud covering all the earth. * Go ye out to meet Him, and say: Tell us if Thou art He, who shall rule over the people of Israel. ℣. Both the earth-born and the sons of men, rich and poor together. ℟. Go ye out to meet Him and say. ℣. Give ear, O Thou who rulest Israel, Thou who leadest Joseph like a sheep. ℟. Tell us if Thou art He. ℣. Lift up your gates, O ye princes, and be ye lifted up, O eternal gates, and the King of Glory shall enter in. ℟. Who shall rule over the people of Israel. ℣. Glory be to the Father, and to the Son, and to the Holy Ghost. *Then is repeated.* ℟. I look from afar, and behold I see the power of God coming, and a cloud covering all the earth. Go ye out to meet Him, and say: Tell us if Thou art He who shall rule over the people of Israel.

III Nocturn

The reading of the holy Gospel according to St. Luke

At that time Jesus said to His disciples: "There will be signs in the sun and moon and stars, and upon the earth distress of nations." And so forth.

Homily of St. Gregory, Pope

Our Lord and Redeemer, desiring to find us prepared, proclaims the evils which shall follow the last stages of the world in order thereby to restrain us from the love of it. He makes known to us how great afflictions will precede this world's approaching close, so that if we will not with a tranquil mind fear God, at least we may fear His approaching judgment, having been humbled by these very afflictions.

Indeed, to this Gospel lesson, which your fraternity has just heard, the Lord had shortly before prefixed the following: "Nation shall rise against nation, and kingdom against kingdom. And there shall be great earthquakes in divers places, and pestilences and famines." Then, having said a few other things, He added this which you have just heard: "There will be signs in the sun and moon and stars, and upon the earth distress of nations, bewildered by the roaring of the sea and waves." Of all these things we have certainly seen some accomplished, while the others, we fear, are soon to come.

Now of nation rising against nation and of their suffering distress throughout the land, we have seen already in our own time more than we have read of in the Scriptures. You know how often we have heard from other parts of the world of earthquakes destroying innumerable cities. Pestilences without end do we suffer. But the signs in the sun and moon and stars we as yet in no way clearly see; but that even these things are not far distant we may gather from the very change in our atmospheric conditions.

There has not yet arisen any new disturbance of the sea and of the waves. But since many prophecies have already been fulfilled, there is no doubt but that the few which remain will also follow, for the accomplishment of that which has gone before is our certitude of that which is to follow. For this reason do we speak these things, dearest brethren, that your minds may be alert and zealous for your safety, lest, feeling secure, they remain inactive, and on account of ignorance they become weak. But in all things let fear, on the one hand, rouse them up, and on the other hand, let solicitude for doing good strengthen them.

℟. I beseech thee, O Lord, send whom Thou wilt send: behold the affliction of Thy people: * As Thou hast spoken, come, and deliver us. ℣. Give ear, O Thou who rulest Israel, Thou who leadest Joseph like a sheep, Thou who sittest upon the Cherubim. As. Glory. As.

Here is said the Hymn Te Deum

✛ Continuation of the holy Gospel according to St. Luke.— At that time Jesus said to his disciples: "And there will be signs in the sun and moon and stars, and upon the earth distress of nations bewildered by the roaring of sea and waves; men fainting for fear and for expectation of the things that are coming on the world; for the powers of heaven will be shaken. And then they will see the Son of Man coming upon a cloud with great power and majesty. But when these things begin to come to pass, look up, and lift up your heads, because your redemption is at hand."

And he spoke to them a parable. "Behold the fig tree, and all the trees. When they now put forth their buds, you know that summer is near. Even so, when you see these things coming to pass, know that the kingdom of God is near. Amen I say to you, this generation will not pass away till all things have been accomplished. Heaven and earth will pass away, but my words will not pass away."

LET US PRAY

Arouse Thy power and come, we beseech Thee, O Lord, that Thou mayest protect and save us from the threatening dangers of our sins, who livest and reignest with God the Father, in the unity of the Holy Ghost, one God, world without end. ℟. Amen.

II SUNDAY IN ADVENT

I Nocturn

From Isaias the Prophet, c. 11, 1 - 13

II Nocturn

From the Exposition of St. Jerome, Priest, on Isaias the Prophet

"And a rod shall come forth from the root of Jesse." Up to the begining of the vision, or of the burden of Babylon, which Isaias, the son of Amos, saw, this whole prophecy concerns Christ. We wish to explain it part by part, lest, being set forth and explained all at once, it confuse the memory of the reader. The Jews interpret the rod and the flower of the root of Jesse to be the Lord Himself, in that in the rod is signified the power of the ruler, and in the flower His beauty is designated.

We, however, may understand the rod of the root of Jesse to be the Virgin Mary, who had no branch cleaving to her, of whom we read above: "Behold a Virgin shall conceive and shall bring forth a son." And the flower we understand to be our Lord the Savior, who says in the Canticle of Canticles: "I am the flower of the field and the lily of the valley."

Upon this flower, which shall unexpectedly come forth from the stem and root of Jesse by means of the Virgin Mary, the Spirit of the Lord will rest, for in Him all the fullness of the Godhead was pleased to dwell bodily. The Spirit was not poured out upon Him by measure, as upon the other saints, but as the Nazarenes read in their Gospel, which is written in the Hebrew tongue, "The whole fountain of the Holy Spirit shall be poured forth upon him." "The Lord is a spirit, and where the Spirit of the Lord is, there is liberty."

In the same Gospel of St. Matthew we read: "Behold my Son whom I have chosen; my elect in whom my soul is well pleased; I shall place my Spirit over him and he will mete out judgment to the Gentiles." This is to be understood of the Savior, on whom the Spirit of the Lord rested, that is, remained eternally.

℟. Behold there cometh the Lord, our defender, the Holy One of Israel, * Wearing the royal crown upon His head. ℣. And His power shall be from sea to sea, and from the rivers even to the ends of the earth. Wearing. Glory. Wearing.

II Sunday In Advent

III Nocturn

The reading of the holy Gospel according to St. Matthew

At that time when John had heard in prison of the works of Christ, he sent two of his disciples to say to him, "Art thou he who is to come, or shall we look for another?" And so forth.

Homily of St. Gregory, Pope

Having seen so many signs and such great wonders, one should not have been easily moved to take offense, but to admire. Yet the mind of unbelievers did take grave scandal at Him, when, after such miracles, they saw Him die. Wherefore Paul says: "But we preach Christ crucified, to the Jews a stumbling-block indeed, but to the Gentiles foolishness."

It seemed foolish indeed to men that for men the very Author of life should die. And hence man took scandal against Him from the very circumstance whence he ought to have become more a debtor. For the more God suffered disgraceful things for men, so much the more worthily ought He to be honored by men.

Why did He say, "Blessed is he who is not scandalized in Me," except to designate in clear words the abjection and humility of His death? As if He would openly say: "I do indeed wonderful things, but I do not disdain to suffer indignities. Thus, because I am like to you in death, men must take care that they, who reverence My miracles, do not despise death in Me."

But now that the disciples of John have been sent away, let us hear what He says to the multitudes concerning this same John. "What went you out into the desert to see? A reed shaken by the wind?" This He says not to affirm it, but to deny it. As soon as a breeze blows, it bends the reed the other way. And what is designated by the reed save a carnal mind which, as soon as it is touched by applause or blame, is immediately bent in any direction whatsoever?

℟. Jerusalem, thou shalt plant a vineyard in thy mountains: Thou shalt rejoice, for the day of the Lord will come: arise, O Sion, and turn unto the Lord thy God: rejoice and be glad, O Jacob: * For thy Savior cometh from the midst of the nations. ℣. Rejoice greatly, O daughter of Sion: shout with gladness, O daughter of Jerusalem. For. Glory. For.

✠ Continuation of the holy Gospel according to St. Matthew.—At that time, when John had heard in prison of the works of Christ, he sent two of his disciples to say to him, "Art thou he who is to come, or shall we look for another?" And Jesus answering said to them, "Go and report to John what you have heard and seen: the blind see, the lame walk, the lepers are cleansed, the deaf hear, the dead rise, the poor have the gospel preached to them. And blessed is he who is not scandalized in me."

But as these were going, Jesus began to say to the crowds concerning John, "What did you go out to the desert to see? A reed shaken by the wind? But what did you go out to see? A man clothed in soft garments? Behold, those who wear soft garments are in the houses of kings. But what did you go out to see? A prophet? Yes, I tell you, and more than a prophet. This is he of whom it is written, 'Behold, I send my messenger before thy face, who shall make ready the way before thee.'"

Let Us Pray

Arouse our hearts, O Lord, to prepare the way for Thy only begotten Son, that by His coming we may be worthy to serve Thee with minds that have been purified, who liveth and reigneth with Thee in the unity of the Holy Ghost, one God, world without end.

III SUNDAY IN ADVENT

I Nocturn

From Isaias the Prophet, c. 26, 1 - 14

II Nocturn

Sermon of St. Leo, Pope

Since the season of the year and the custom of our devotion advises, dearly beloved, we announce to you with pastoral solicitude that the fast of the tenth month is to be celebrated, by which, for the plentiful harvest of all the fruits, a libation of continence is most fittingly offered to God, their donor.

For what can be more efficacious than fasting, by the practice of which we draw near to God, and, resisting the devil, overcome seductive vices? For fasting has always been food for the strong. Moreover, from abstinence proceed chaste thoughts, rational desires, and sound counsels; and by voluntary afflictions the flesh dies to its concupiscences and the spirit is renewed in strength.

But because the salvation of our souls is not acquired by fasting alone, let us supplement our fasting with works of mercy towards the poor. Let us spend for virtue what we have subtracted from pleasure. Let the abstinence of the one fasting be food for the poor. Let us be zealous for the defense of widows, for the assistance of orphans, for the consolation of those who mourn, for the peace of dissenters. Let the stranger be taken in, the oppressed helped, the naked clothed, the sick cared for, so that whoever of us shall have offered of his good works a sacrifice of such piety to God, the Author of all good things, may deserve to receive the reward of the heavenly kingdom from the same God.

On Wednesday and Friday, therefore, let us fast; on Saturday, however, let us celebrate the vigil at the tomb of the Apostle Peter, by whose merits may we be able to obtain what we ask through our Lord Jesus Christ, who with the Father and the Holy Spirit liveth and reigneth forever and ever. Amen.

℞. Behold the Lord shall appear upon a white cloud, * And thousands of His Saints with Him: and He shall have on His vesture, and on His thigh written: King of kings, and Lord of lords. ℣. He shall appear at the end, and shall not lie; though He tarry, wait for Him, because He will surely come. And thousands. Glory. And thousands.

III Nocturn

The reading of the holy Gospel according to St. John

At that time the Jews sent to him from Jerusalem priests and Levites to ask him, "Who art thou?" And so forth.

Homily of St. Gregory, Pope

By the words of today's lesson, dearest brethren, the humility of John is recommended to us, who, though he was a man of such great virtue that he could be believed to be the Christ, chose to remain and be considered what he really was, lest he should be foolishly rapt above himself by the opinion of men. "For he acknowledged and did not deny, and he acknowledged: 'I am not the Christ.'" But he who said, "I am not," plainly denied himself to be what he was not, but did not deny what he was; so that, speaking the truth, he might become a member of Him whose name he had not deceitfully usurped.

Since, then, he had no desire to take to himself the name of Christ, he was made a member of Christ. For whilst he endeavored humbly to acknowledge his own littleness, he merited in reality to obtain the greatness of Christ. But since this lesson brings another sentence of our Redeemer to mind, a very perplexing question presents itself to us from the words of this lesson. For in another place, when questioned by His disciples concerning the coming of Elias, the Lord answered: "Elias is already come and they knew him not, but they did unto him whatsoever they had a mind"; and, "if you will know it, John himself is Elias."

But John, when questioned, answers: "I am not Elias." How is it, dearest brethren, that what Truth affirms, the prophet of Truth denies? Indeed there is a vast difference between "He is" and "I am not." How then is he a prophet? Is he of the Truth if he is not in accord with the words of that same Truth? But if the truth itself be accurately sought after, it is found how those things which sound contradictory to one another are in reality not so.

Indeed the angel said to Zachary concerning John: "He shall go before him in the spirit and power of Elias." Now he is said to come in the spirit and power of Elias because as Elias shall come before the second advent of the Lord so John came before the first. As the former is to come as precursor of the Judge, so the latter, as the precursor of the Redeemer. Therefore John was Elias in spirit, but in his person he was not Elias. What therefore the Lord affirmed of the spirit, John denied of the person.

℞. Bethlehem, city of the most high God, out of thee shall come forth the Ruler of Israel, whose going forth is from the beginning of the days of eternity, and He shall be magnified in the midst of the whole earth: * And there shall be peace in our land when He cometh. ℣. He shall speak peace unto the Gentiles, and shall have dominion from sea to sea. And. Glory. And.

✠ Continuation of the holy Gospel according to St. John.— At that time the Jews sent to him from Jerusalem priests and Levites to ask him, "Who art thou?" And he acknowledged and did not deny; and he acknowledged, "I am not the Christ." And they asked him, "What then? Art thou Elias?" And he said, "I am not." "Art thou the Prophet?" And he answered, "No."

They therefore said to him, "Who art thou? that we may give an answer to those who sent us. What hast thou to say of thyself?" He said, "I am the voice of one crying in the desert, 'Make straight the way of the Lord,' as said Isaias the prophet."

And they who had been sent were from among the Pharisees. And they asked him, and said to him, "Why, then, dost thou baptize, if thou art not the Christ, nor Elias, nor the Prophet?" John said to them in answer, "I baptize with water; but in the midst of you there has stood one whom you do not know. He it is who is to come after me, who has been set above me, the strap of whose sandal I am not worthy to loose."

These things took place at Bethany, beyond the Jordan, where John was baptizing.

Let Us Pray

We beseech Thee, O Lord, listen to our prayers, and by the grace of Thy visit to us enlighten the darkness of our minds, who livest and reignest with God the Father.

WEDNESDAY IN EMBER WEEK

The reading of the holy Gospel according to St. Luke

At that time the angel Gabriel was sent from God to a town of Galilee called Nazareth, to a virgin betrothed to a man named Joseph, of the house of David, and the virgin's name was Mary. And so forth.

Homily of St. Ambrose, Bishop

The divine mysteries are truly hidden, nor can any man easily know the counsel of God, according to the saying of the prophet; nevertheless, from other acts and mandates of the Lord our Savior we are able to understand that it was of even more deliberate design that she who was espoused to a man was especially chosen to give birth to our Lord. But why was she not made pregnant before she was espoused? Perhaps it was lest it be said that she had conceived in adultery.

"And the angel being come in." Study the virgin in her manners; study her in her modest reserve; study her in her conversation; study her in this mystery. It is proper for virgins to tremble and to be afraid at every approach of a man, to fear all conversations with a man. Let women strive to imitate this example of self-respect. She is alone in her chamber; only the angel shall find her whom no man shall behold; she, alone without companion, alone without witness, is saluted by the angel so that she be not dishonored by any shameful greeting.

For the mystery of such a great message was not to be uttered by the mouth of a man, but of an angel. It is first heard today: "The Holy Ghost shall come upon thee." It is both heard and believed. To conclude—"Behold the handmaid of the Lord," she says, "be it done unto me according to thy word." See her humility; behold her devotion. She, who is chosen as Mother of God, calls herself "the handmaid of the Lord," nor is she suddenly elated by the promise.

FRIDAY IN EMBER WEEK

The reading of the holy Gospel according to St. Luke

At that time Mary arose and went with haste into the hill country, to a town of Juda. And so forth.

Homily of St. Ambrose, Bishop

All who ask to be believed are expected to give reasons why they should be believed. Therefore, when the angel had announced what should come to pass, he made known to the Virgin Mary, as a reason for believing in him, that an aged and sterile woman had conceived. This he did to assure her that whatever was pleasing to God was also possible. When Mary heard this, she set out for the hill country, not because she did not believe the announcement, or was incredulous of the messenger, or doubted the example of Elizabeth, but cheerfully, as if to fulfill a vow; with devotion, as to a religious duty, in haste for very joy. Whither, indeed, if not to greater heights, should she who was now full of God make her way with haste? The grace of the Holy Spirit knows no languid efforts.

Do you also, O holy women, learn what attention you ought to bestow on your kinsfolk when they are with child. The virgin modesty of Mary did not hold her back from mixing with the crowd, though till then she had lived alone in strictest privacy; nor did the roughness of the mountain ways abate her zeal, nor the length of the journey keep her back from doing a kindness. The Virgin set out in haste into the hill country, a Virgin mindful of her duty, unmindful of mishaps, urged on by affection, heedless of the delicacy of her sex, leaving her home behind her. Learn, O virgins, not to run about to the houses of strangers, not to loiter in the streets, not to spend time talking with others in public. Mary, who moved quietly about her own home, in haste only on the public roads, abode three months with her kinswoman.

You have learned, O virgins, the modesty of Mary; learn also her humility. She went as a relative to her relative, the younger to the elder; and not only did she come, but she first saluted Elizabeth. For the more chaste a virgin is, the more humble she should be. She will know how to submit to her elders. She who professes chastity should be mistress of humility. For humility is the root of piety, and the very rule of its teaching. It is to be noted, that the superior comes to the inferior, that the inferior may be assisted, Mary comes to Elizabeth, Christ to John.

SATURDAY IN EMBER WEEK

The reading of the holy Gospel according to St. Luke

In the fifteenth year of the reign of Tiberius Caesar, when Pontius Pilate was procurator of Judea. And so forth.

Homily of St. Gregory, Pope

The ruler of the Roman Empire and the kings of Judea having been named, mention is made of the time when the precursor of our Redeemer took up his office of preaching. For because he came to preach Him who was to redeem some of the Jews and many of the Gentiles, the time of his preaching is designated by naming the ruler of the Gentiles and the princes of the Jews. That the Gentile world was to be chosen and that the Jews were to be rejected for their sin of infidelity is shown by the description of the earthly dominion—for in the Roman Empire one man is shown to be ruler and in the kingdom of Judea several ruled by reason of its four-fold division.

By the voice of our Redeemer it is declared: "Every kingdom divided against itself shall be brought to desolation." It is plain, therefore, that Judea had come to the end of her rule, she who lay divided among so many kings. Likewise, it is fittingly shown not only what kings were in power, but also what priests; and because John the Baptist would preach Him who was to be at once King and Priest, the Evangelist Luke pointed out the period of his preaching through reference to the government and the priesthood.

"And he came into all the country about the Jordan, preaching the baptism of penance for the remission of sins." It is clear to all who read that John not only *preached* the baptism of penance, but that he also gave it to certain ones; but, nevertheless, he was not able to bestow *his own* baptism for the remission of sins. For the remission of sins is granted to us in the baptism of Christ alone. Consequently, it must be noted that it is said: "*Preaching* the baptism of *penance* for the remission of sins"; for, because he could not bestow it, he was *preaching* the baptism which absolved sins, so that, as he preceded the Incarnate Word of the Father by the word of his preaching, so by his baptism through which sins could not be loosed, he preceded the baptism of penance by which sins are absolved.

IV SUNDAY IN ADVENT

I Nocturn

From Isaias the Prophet, c. 35, 1 - 10; c. 41, 1 - 4

II Nocturn

Sermon of St. Leo, Pope

If we, dearly beloved, with faith and prudence understand the beginning of our creation, we shall find that man was formed to the likeness of God in order that he might be an imitator of his Maker, and that this is a dignity natural to our race that the form of the Divine Majesty shines in us as in a kind of mirror. To which dignity daily the grace of the Savior truly restores us, since what fell in the first Adam is raised up in the second.

There is no cause for our restoration, however, except the mercy of God, whom we would not love unless He first loved us and scattered the darkness of our ignorance by the light of His truth. Foretelling this through the holy Isaias, the Lord said: "I will lead the blind into the way which they know not, and in the paths of which they were ignorant I will make them walk; I will make darkness light before them, and crooked things straight. These things have I done to them, and have not forsaken them." And again: "I was found by them that did not seek me: I appeared openly to those who made no inquiry of me."

How this is accomplished the Apostle John teaches, saying: "We know that the Son of God is come, and he hath given us understanding that we may know the true God, and may be in his true Son." And again: "Let us therefore love God, because God first hath loved us."

So, by loving us God reforms us to His own likeness, and, in order to find the image of His own goodness in us, He grants us that by which we ourselves may work what He works, namely, lighting the lamps of our minds, and inflaming us with the fire of His love, so that we may love not only Him, but likewise what He loves.

℟. Blow ye the trumpet in Sion, call together the nations, tell it among the people and say: * Behold God our Savior cometh. ℣. Tell it, and make it to be heard; speak aloud, and cry. Behold. Glory. Behold.

IV Sunday In Advent

III Nocturn

The reading of the holy Gospel according to St. Luke

In the fifteenth year of the reign of Tiberius Caesar, when Pontius Pilate was procurator of Judea. And so forth.

From a Homily of St. Gregory, Pope

John said to the multitudes that went forth to be baptized by him: "Ye offspring of vipers, who hath showed you to flee from the wrath to come?" The *wrath to come* is a reference to the last judgment which the sinner will not be able to escape then if he does not have recourse now to expressions of penance. Now it must be noted that wicked children who imitate the actions of their evil parents are called the offspring of vipers for this reason, because they envy the good and persecute them; because they render evil to some and seek to injure their neighbors; for in all these actions they follow the paths of their carnal-minded forebears, as poisoned children born of poisoned parents.

But because we have already sinned and have become involved in evil practices, let John tell us what we must do that we may be able to flee the wrath to come. Here is what he tells us: "Bring forth therefore fruits worthy of penance." It must be observed in these words that the friend of the Spouse not only admonishes us to bring forth fruits of penance, but fruits *worthy* of penance. For it is one thing to bring forth fruits of penance; quite another to bring forth fruits worthy of penance.

Speaking of fruits worthy of penance it ought to be known that whoever has committed no illicit acts, to him is it rightly permitted to use licit things, and so to perform works of piety without giving up the things of this world. But if anyone has fallen into the sin of fornication—or what is worse, adultery—he must so much the more abstain from licit things, the more he is conscious of having done that which is illicit.

Nor should the fruit of good works be equal in one who has sinned less and in one who has sinned more; likewise in him who has never fallen and in him who has fallen a few times and in him who has fallen many times. By this saying, then, "Bring forth fruits worthy of penance," the conscience of each one is bound to acquire through penance so much the greater riches of good works the more serious the losses it has brought upon itself through its own fault.

℞. I must decrease, but He must increase: He it is who, coming after me, is preferred before me: * The latchet of whose shoe I am not worthy to loose. ℣. I have baptized you in water:

He shall baptize you in the Holy Ghost. The latchet. Glory. The latchet.

✠ Continuation of the holy Gospel according to St. Luke.—Now in the fifteenth year of the reign of Tiberius Caesar, when Pontius Pilate was procurator of Judea, and Herod tetrarch of Galilee, and Philip his brother tetrarch of the district of Iturea and Trachonitis, and Lysanias tetrarch of Abilina, during the high priesthood of Annas and Caiphas, the word of God came to John, the son of Zachary, in the desert. And he went into all the region about the Jordan, preaching a baptism of repentance for the forgiveness of sins, as it is written in the book of the words of Isaias the prophet, "The voice of one crying in the desert, 'Make ready the way of the Lord, make straight his paths. Every valley shall be filled, and every mountain and hill shall be brought low, and the crooked shall be made straight, and the rough ways smooth; and all mankind shall see the salvation of God.'"

LET US PRAY

Arouse, we beseech Thee, O Lord, Thy power and come; assist us by Thy great strength that through the help of Thy grace what our sins keep back from us may be quickly granted by Thy goodness and mercy, who livest and reignest with God the Father.

VIGIL OF THE NATIVITY

The reading of the holy Gospel according to St. Matthew

When Mary his mother had been betrothed to Joseph, she was found, before they came together, to be with child by the Holy Spirit. And so forth.

Homily of St. Jerome, Priest

Why was He not conceived of a simple virgin, but of a virgin who was espoused? First, in order that through Joseph's lineage the descent of Mary might be shown; secondly, lest she be stoned as an adulteress by the Jews; thirdly, so that when fleeing into Egypt, she might have a companion. The martyr Ignatius has also added a fourth reason why He was conceived of one espoused, saying: "In order that His birth might be hidden from Satan, since the latter thought that Jesus was begotten not of a virgin, but of one in wedlock."

"Before they came together she was found with child of the Holy Ghost." She was not found by any other except Joseph, who already possessed a husband's privilege to know all that concerned her. But because it is said here, "*Before* they came together," it does not follow that they came together afterwards; the Scripture shows that this did not happen.

"Whereupon, Joseph, her husband, being a just man and not willing to expose her publicly, was minded to put her away privately." If anyone be joined to one guilty of fornication, he is made one body with the fornicator, and it is commanded in the law that not only those guilty, but also those having knowledge of the crime are liable to the punishment of the sin. How can Joseph, since he concealed the crime of his wife, be described as a just man? But this testimony is Mary's—that Joseph, *knowing* her chastity and marvelling at what had happened, kept secret the mystery of which he was ignorant.

"Joseph, son of David, fear not to take unto thee Mary thy wife." We have already stated above that spouses are called wives, as our book against Helvidius more fully sets forth. Indeed, in the attitude of one paying respect the angel speaks to Joseph in a dream in order to confirm the justice of his silence. And at the same time it is to be noted that Joseph is said to be the son of David so that Mary, too, might be shown to be from the family of David.

NATIVITY OF OUR LORD
I Nocturn
The four following Lessons from Isaias are read without a title
Chapter 9, 1 - 6

At the first time the land of Zabulon, and the land of Nephtali was lightly touched: and at the last the way of the sea beyond the Jordan of the Galilee of the Gentiles was heavily loaded. The people that walked in darkness have seen a great light: to them that dwelt in the region of the shadow of death, light is risen. Thou hast multiplied the nation, and hast not increased the joy. They shall rejoice before Thee as they that rejoice in the harvest, as conquerors rejoice after taking a prey, when they divide the spoils. For the yoke of their burden, and the rod of their shoulder, and the scepter of their oppressor Thou hast overcome, as in the day of Madian. For every violent taking of spoils, and tumult, and garment mingled with blood, shall be burnt, and be fuel for the fire. For a Child is born to us, and a Son is given to us, and the government is upon His shoulder: and His name shall be called Wonderful, Counsellor, God the Mighty, the Father of the world to come, the Prince of Peace.

℟. This day the King of heaven was pleased to be born to us of a Virgin, that He might bring back to heaven man who was lost: * There is joy among the hosts of Angels: because eternal salvation hath appeared unto men. ℣. Glory to God in the highest, and on earth peace to men of good will. ℟. There is joy among the hosts of Angels: because eternal salvation hath appeared unto men. ℣. Glory be to the Father and to the Son and to the Holy Ghost. ℟. This day the King of heaven was pleased to be born to us of a Virgin that He might bring back to heaven man who was lost: There is joy among the hosts of Angels: because eternal salvation hath appeared unto men.

Chapter 40, 1 - 3

Be comforted, be comforted, My people, saith your God. Speak ye to the heart of Jerusalem, and call her: for her evil is come to an end, her iniquity is forgiven: she hath received of the hand of the Lord double for all her sins. The voice of one crying in the desert: Prepare ye the way of the Lord, make straight in the wilderness the paths of our God.

℟. This day is the true peace come down to us from heaven: * This day throughout the whole world the skies drop down honey. ℣. This day is the daybreak of our new redemption, of the restoring of the old, of everlasting joy. * This day throughout the whole world the skies drop down honey.

Chapter 40, 4 - 8

Every valley shall be exalted, and every mountain and hill shall be made low, and the crooked shall become straight, and the rough ways plain. And the glory of the Lord shall be revealed and all flesh together shall see that the mouth of the Lord hath spoken. The voice of one, saying: Cry. And I said: What shall I cry? All flesh is grass, and all the glory thereof as the flower of the field. The grass is withered, and the flower is fallen, because the spirit of the Lord hath blown upon it. Indeed the people is grass: The grass is withered, and the flower is fallen: but the Word of our Lord endureth for ever.

℟. Whom have you seen, O shepherds? Speak, and tell us, Who has appeared on earth? * We saw the newborn Child, and the choirs of Angels loudly praising the Lord. ℣. Speak, what have ye seen? And tell us of the Birth of Christ. * We saw.

Chapter 52, 1 - 6

Arise, arise, put on thy strength, O Sion, put on the garments of thy glory, O Jerusalem, the city of the Holy One: for henceforth the uncircumcised and unclean shall no more pass through thee. Shake thyself from the dust, arise, sit up, O Jerusalem: loose the bonds from off thy neck, O captive daughter of Sion. For thus saith the Lord God: My people went down into Egypt at the beginning to sojourn there: and the Assyrian hath oppressed them without any cause at all. And now what have I here, saith the Lord: for My people is taken away gratis? They that rule over them treat them unjustly, saith the Lord, and My name is continually blasphemed all the day long. Therefore My people shall know My name in that day: for I Myself that spoke, behold I am here.

℟. The true God, begotten of the Father, descended from heaven and entered into the womb of a Virgin, so that He might appear visibly to us, clothed with human flesh as were the first parents: * And He, being God-Man, the Light, Life and Maker of the world, came forth from a closed door. ℣. As a bridegroom coming forth from the bride chamber. And He. Glory. And He.

II Nocturn
Sermon of St. Leo, Pope

Our Savior is born today, dearly beloved, let us rejoice! For it is not right that place be given to sadness when it is the birthday of life, which, having taken away the fear of death, fills us with joy by reason of the eternal life which it promises. No one is shut out from a share in this happiness. All have one common cause of joy, for, as our Lord, the destroyer of sin and death, finds no one free from guilt, so He comes to liberate everyone.

℟. O great mystery and wonderful sacrament, that animals should see the newborn Lord lying in a manger: * Blessed is that Virgin whose womb deserved to bear Christ our Lord. ℣. Hail, Mary, full of grace: the Lord is with thee. * Blessed.

Let the just man exult, for he draws near to the palm; let the sinner rejoice, for he is invited to forgiveness; let the Gentile take courage for he is summoned unto life. For the Son of God, according to the fullness of time, which the inscrutable depth of the divine counsel ordained, took upon Himself the nature of the human race in order to reconcile it to its Maker, so that the inventor of death, the devil, might be overcome through that very nature which he had conquered.

℟. Blessed is Mary, the Mother of God, who remained a Virgin undefiled: * This day she hath brought forth the Savior of the ages. ℣. Blessed is she that hath believed: because all those things are accomplished which were told her by the Lord. * This day.

In this conflict, entered into for our sakes, He fights with a great and admirable insistence on fairness, since the Almighty Lord meets the most terrible enemy not in His own majesty, but in our lowliness, pitting against him the same form, the same nature, partaker in every way of our mortality, yet free from all sin. Truly incongruous with this birth is that which is declared of all men: "No man is clean from stain, neither an infant whose life upon earth is but one day!" Nothing, then, of the concupiscence of the flesh found place in this singular nativity, nothing of the law of sin. A royal virgin from the root of David is chosen, who, about to be made pregnant with the Sacred Offspring, conceives the Child, divine and human, first in her mind rather than in her body. And lest, unaware of the divine plan, she be frightened at the unusual tidings, she learns from the words of an angel what is to be effected in her by the Holy Spirit; nor does she believe it to be a loss of her virginity that she is about to become the Mother of God.

℟. O holy and spotless virginity, how to proclaim thy praises, I know not: * For thou hast borne in thy bosom Him whom the heavens cannot contain. ℣. Blessed are thou amongst women, and blessed is the fruit of thy womb. * For.

Therefore, dearly beloved, let us give thanks to God the Father through His Son, in the Holy Spirit, who, because of His great charity with which He hath loved us, has had mercy on us; and, when we were dead in our sins, He revivified us in Christ so that we might be in Him a new creature and a new image. So let us put off the old man with his works, and having obtained a participation in the generation of Christ, let us renounce the works of the flesh. Recognize, O Christian, thy dignity! And being made partaker of the divine nature, do not return to thy old wretchedness by an evil manner of life. Be mindful of whose head and body thou art a member! Remember that, being torn from the power of darkness, thou hast been born into the light and kingdom of God.

℟. The angel said to the shepherds: I announce to you a great joy which is for all people; because today is born for us the Savior, * Who is Christ, in the city of David. ℣. You shall find the Infant wrapped in swaddling clothes, and laid in a manger. Who is. Glory. Who is.

III Nocturn

The reading of the holy Gospel according to St. Matthew

The book of the origin of Jesus Christ, the Son of David, the son of Abraham. Abraham begot Isaac, Isaac begot Jacob. And so forth.

Homily of St. Jerome, Priest

In Isaias we read: "His generation who shall declare?" Let us not think that the Evangelist contradicts the Prophet when he begins to narrate what the Prophet had declared impossible of narration, for the Prophet spoke of the generation of His divine nature while St. Matthew spoke of His Incarnation. He begins therefore with that which is carnal so that through man we may begin to know God. "The son of David, the son of Abraham." An inverted order, but necessarily so changed. For if Abraham had been placed first and David afterwards, it would have been necessary to again repeat Abraham in order to form the exact genealogical order.

℟. Behold the Lamb of God, behold Him who taketh away the sins of the world, behold Him of whom I spoke to you: He who cometh after me was made before me: * The latchet of whose shoe I am not worthy to loose. ℣. He who is of the earth speaks of the earth: He who cometh from heaven is above all. * The latchet.

The reading of the holy Gospel according to St. Luke

At that time there went forth a decree from Caesar Augustus that a census of the whole world should be taken. And so forth.

Homily of St. Gregory, Pope

Since by the goodness of God we are to celebrate thrice today the solemn ceremonies of the Mass, we cannot speak long on the Gospel lesson; but the birthday of our Redeemer forces us to say something, even though briefly. Now why is it that the world is enrolled when the Lord is about to be born, unless to plainly show that He had appeared in the flesh who would enroll His elect in eternity? While on the other hand it is said of the reprobate through the Prophet: "Let them be blotted out of the book of the living; and with the just let them not be written." And well is He born in Bethlehem. For Bethlehem means the *house of bread*. And He it is who said: "I am the living bread which came down from heaven."

The place therefore where the Lord is born was called beforehand the house of bread, because He was to appear there in the flesh who was to satiate the minds of the elect with an eternal abundance. And He is not born in the home of His parents, but along the way, unquestionably in order to show that by the humanity which He had assumed He had been born out of His proper sphere.

℟. Blessed is the womb of the Virgin Mary which bore the Son of the eternal Father, and blessed are the breasts that nursed Christ the Lord: * Who this day hath been pleased to be born of a Virgin for the salvation of the world. ℣. This day which is dawning for us is holy: O come ye Gentiles and adore the Lord. * Who this day.

The reading of the holy Gospel according to St. Luke

At that time the shepherds were saying to one another, "Let us go over to Bethlehem and see this thing that has come to pass, which the Lord has made known to us." And so forth.

Homily of St. Ambrose, Bishop

Behold the beginning of the newborn Church. Christ is born, and the shepherds began to watch, in order to gather into the sheepfold of the Lord the flocks of the nations who were formerly living after the manner of wild beasts, lest they suffer from the attacks of any spiritual beasts during the overshadowing darkness of the nights. And well do those shepherds whom the Lord instructs keep watch. For the flock is the people; the night is the world; and the shepherds are the priests. Or perchance he also may be signified by the shepherd to whom it was said: "Be watchful and strengthen." For the Lord not only appointed bishops, but He also destined angels to guard His flock.

℟. In the beginning was the Word and the Word was with God and the Word was God: * This was in the beginning with God. ℣. All things were made by Him and without Him was made nothing. * This was.

The reading of the holy Gospel according to St. John

In the beginning was the Word, and the Word was with God, and the Word was God. And so forth.

Homily of St. Augustine, Bishop

That you may not consider worthless what I have to say, as you generally do when you hear the words of men, hear what you should think: "The Word was God." There may come forward I know not what unbelieving Arian and say that the Word of God was made. But how can it be that the Word of God was made when God made all things through the Word? If the Word of God Himself was made, by what other word was He made? If you say that this is the word of the Word, through whom that Word was made, I say then that this word is the only Son of God. But if you do not speak of a word of the Word, concede that He, by whom all things were made, was not made. For He by whom all things were made could not be made by Himself. Therefore believe the Evangelist.

℟. The Word was made flesh and dwelt with us: * And we saw His glory, the glory as of the only begotten of the Father, full of grace and truth. ℣. In the beginning was the Word and the Word was with God and the Word was God. And we saw. Glory. And we saw.

✠ Beginning of the holy Gospel according to St. Matthew.— The book of the origin of Jesus Christ, the Son of David, the son of Abraham. Abraham begot Isaac, Isaac begot Jacob, Jacob begot Judas and his brethren. Judas begot Phares and Zara of Thamar, Phares begot Esron, Esron begot Aram. And Aram begot Aminadab, Aminadab begot Naasson, Naasson begot Salmon. Salmon begot Booz of Rahab. Booz begot Obed of Ruth, Obed begot Jesse, Jesse begot David the king.

And David the king begot Solomon of the former wife of Urias. Solomon begot Roboam, Roboam begot Abia, Abia begot Asa. And Asa begot Josaphat, Josaphat begot Joram, Joram begot Ozias. And Ozias begot Joatham, Joatham begot Achaz,

Achaz begot Ezechias. And Ezechias begot Manasses, Manasses begot Amon, Amon begot Josias. And Josias begot Jechonias and his brethren at the time of the carrying away to Babylon.

And after the carrying away to Babylon Jechonias begot Salathiel, Salathiel begot Zorobabel. And Zorababel begot Abiud, Abiud begot Eliachim, Eliachim begot Azor. And Azor begot Sadoc, Sadoc begot Achim, Achim begot Eliud. And Eliud begot Eleazar, Eleazar begot Matthan, Matthan begot Jacob. And Jacob begot Joseph, the husband of Mary, and of her was born Jesus who is called Christ.

Let Us Pray

Grant, we beseech Thee, O almighty God, that the new birth of Thy Son as man may deliver those whom the old servitude held under the yoke of sin. Through the same Jesus Christ.

December 26

ST. STEPHEN, THE FIRST MARTYR

I Nocturn

From the Acts of the Apostles, c. 6, 1 - 10; c. 7, 54 - 60

II Nocturn

Sermon of St. Fulgentius, Bishop

Yesterday we celebrated the temporal birth of our Eternal King; today we celebrate the triumphant passion of His soldier. For yesterday our King, clothed in the garb of our flesh and coming from the palace of the virginal womb, deigned to visit the world; today the soldier, leaving the tent of the body, has gone to heaven in triumph. The One, while preserving the majesty of the Everlasting God, putting on the servile girdle of flesh, entered into the field of this world ready for the fray. The other, laying aside the perishable garment of the body, ascended to the palace of heaven to reign eternally. The One descended, veiled in flesh; the other ascended, crowned with blood.

The latter ascended while the Jews were stoning him, because the former descended while the angels were rejoicing. "Glory to God in the highest," sang the exulting Angels yesterday; today, rejoicing, they received Stephen into their company! Yesterday the Lord came forth from the womb of the Virgin; today the soldier of Christ has passed from the prison of the flesh.

Yesterday Christ was wrapped in swathing bands for our sake; today Stephen is clothed by Him in the robe of immortality. Yesterday the narow confines of the crib held the Infant Christ; today the immensity of heaven has received the triumphant Stephen. The Lord descended alone that He might raise up many; our King has humbled Himself that He might exalt His soldiers. It is necessary for us, nevertheless, brethren, to acknowledge with what arms Stephen was girded and able to overcome the cruelty of the Jews that thus he merited so happily to triumph.

Stephen, therefore, that he might merit to obtain the *crown* his name signifies, had as his weapon charity, and by means of that he was completely victorious. Because of love for God, he did not flee the raging Jews; because of his love of neighbor, he interceded for those stoning him. Because of love he convinced the erring of their errors that they might be corrected; because of love, he prayed for those stoning him that they might not be punished. Supported by the strength of charity, he overcame Saul who was so cruelly raging against him; and him whom he had as a persecutor on earth, he deserved to have as a companion in heaven.

℟. Blessed Stephen, looking up to heaven, saw the glory of God, and said: * Behold, I see the heavens opened, and the Son of man standing on the right hand of God. ℣. But he, being full of the Holy Ghost, looking up steadfastly to heaven, saw the glory of God, and said. Behold. Glory. Behold.

III Nocturn

The reading of the holy Gospel according to St. Matthew

At that time Jesus said to the scribes and Pharisees: "Behold I send you prophets and wise men and scribes; and some of them you will put to death and crucify." And so forth.

Homily of St. Jerome, Priest

That which we said before, namely, that the text, "Fill ye up the measure of your fathers," pertains to the person of our Lord, because He would be killed by them, can also refer to His disciples, concerning whom He now says: "Behold, I send to you prophets and wise men and scribes." And likewise observe, according to the Apostle, writing to the Corinthians, that the disciples of Christ have various gifts: some are prophets, who foretell future events; some are wise men, who know when they should speak; some are scribes, most learned in the law, from among whom Stephen was stoned, Paul killed, Peter crucified, the disciples scourged, as related in the Acts of the Apostles.

We inquire who this Zacharias the son of Barachias may be, because we read of many named Zacharias. And lest a chance for error might be unintentionally given us, it is added: "Whom you killed between the temple and the altar." In various writings I have read different interpretations and I must set forth the opinions of each. Some consider him to be that Zacharias the son of Barachias who was the eleventh among the twelve prophets —and the name of the father agrees in that case, but that he was killed between the temple and the altar, Scripture does not say; moreover, at his time scarcely the ruins of the temple were existing.

Others believe that it is Zachary, the father of John, showing from certain dreams of apocryphal writers that he was killed because he predicted the coming of the Savior. Others consider him to be that Zacharias who was killed by Joas, King of Juda, between the temple and the altar, as the history of the Kings narrates. But it must be observed that the latter Zacharias is not the son of Barachias, but the son of Joiada the priest, whence Holy Scripture declares: "Joas did not remember the kindness that Joida, his father, had done to him."

Therefore, since we hold this Zacharias to be meant, and since the place of the killing is in accord, we ask why he is called the son of Barachias and not of Joiada? In our language Barachias means *Blessed of the Lord*, and the justice of Joiada the priest is demonstrated by the Hebrew name. In the Gospel which the Nazarenes use, instead of "the son of Barachias" we find written "the son of Joiada."

℞. With one accord they ran violently upon him, and cast him out of the city, invoking, and saying: * Lord Jesus, receive my spirit. ℣. And the witnesses laid down their garments at the feet of a young man whose name was Saul: and they stoned Stephen, invoking, and saying. Lord. Glory. Lord.

✠ Continuation of the holy Gospel according to St. Matthew.— At that time Jesus said to the Scribes and Pharisees: "Behold, I send you prophets, and wise men, and scribes; and some of them you will put to death, and crucify, and some you will scourge in your synagogues, and persecute from town to town; that upon you may come all the just blood that has been shed on the earth, from the blood of Abel the just, unto the blood of Zacharias the son of Barachias, whom you killed between the temple and the altar. Amen I say to you, all these things will come upon this generation.

ST. JOHN, APOSTLE AND EVANGELIST 25

"Jerusalem, Jerusalem! thou who killest the prophets, and stonest those who are sent to thee! How often would I have gathered thy children together, as a hen gathers her young under her wings, but thou wouldst not! Behold, your house is left to you desolate. For I say to you, you shall not see me henceforth until you shall say, 'Blessed is he who comes in the name of the Lord!'"

LET US PRAY

Grant us, we beseech Thee, O Lord, to imitate the example we honor that we also might learn to love our enemies, for we celebrate the heavenly birthday of him who knew how to pray even for his persecutors to Jesus Christ, Thy Son, who liveth and reigneth with Thee.

December 27

ST. JOHN, APOSTLE AND EVANGELIST

I Nocturn

From the first Epistle of St. John, the Apostle, c. 1, 1 - 10; c. 2, 1 - 5

II Nocturn

From the Book of St. Jerome, Priest, on Ecclesiastical Writers

John the Apostle, whom Jesus greatly loved, the son of Zebedee, and the brother of the Apostle James, whom Herod beheaded after the Passion of the Lord, wrote his Gospel the last of all, being called upon by the Bishops of Asia to write against Cerinthus and other heretics, and especially the then rising teaching of the Ebionites, who claimed that Christ did not exist before Mary. Hence John found it necessary to proclaim publicly His divine nativity.

Therefore in the fourteenth year, the second after the persecution of Nero, having been exiled by Domitian, he was confined to the island of Patmos where he wrote the Apocalypse, on which Justin the Martyr and Irenæus commented.

Domitian having been killed and his decrees having been revoked by the senate because of their exceeding cruelty, John returned to Ephesus under the emperor Nerva, and, staying there until the time of the Emperor Trajan, he founded and erected churches in the whole of Asia. Having grown old, John died in the sixty-eighth year after the passion of the Lord, and was buried near the same city.

From the Commentaries of St. Jerome on the
Epistle to the Galatians

Since St. John remained at Ephesus up to a very old age and, scarcely able to be carried to the Church in the arms of his disciples, was not able to raise his voice in many words, he was accustomed to say nothing else to those gathered together except this: "Little children, love one another." Finally the disciples and brethren who were present, becoming weary of always hearing the same thing, said: "Master, why do you always say this?" To which he responded with the saying worthy of John: "Because it is the precept of the Lord, and if only this be done, it is sufficient!"

℟. Most worthy of honor is blessed John who leaned upon the Lord's breast at the supper: * To whom Christ on the cross committed His Mother, a Virgin to a virgin. ℣. A virgin is is chosen by the Lord and beloved above all the rest. To whom. Glory. To whom.

III Nocturn

The reading of the holy Gospel according to St. John

At that time Jesus said to Peter, "Follow me." Turning round, Peter saw following them the disciple whom Jesus loved. And so forth.

Homily of St. Augustine, Bishop

The Church is acquainted with two different lives divinely preached and commended to her: one is the life of faith, the other the life of vision; one the life of this pilgrimage, the other the life of the eternal mansions: one the life of labor, the other the life of rest; one the life of the journey, the other the life of home; one the life of action, the other the life of contemplation.

The one avoids evil and does good, the other has no evil from which to turn away; but only a great good to enjoy. The one fights against the foe; the other reigns, having no foe. One comes to the aid of the needy; the other is there where no needy are found. One forgives the sins of others that its own may be forgiven; the other suffers nothing it could forgive, nor does anything that calls for forgiveness.

One is scourged with evils lest it be lifted up by prosperity; the other enjoys such a fullness of grace that it is free from every evil, and cleaves so firmly to the Highest Good that it has no temptation to pride. Hence the one life is good, but yet full of sorrows; the other is better and perfectly blessed. Of the first of these lives the Apostle Peter is the type; of the other, John.

The one labors here even to the end, and finds its end hereafter; the other reaches out into the hereafter and in eternity finds no end. Therefore to Peter it is said, "Follow me," but of John, "If I wish him to remain until I come, what is it to thee? Do thou follow me." But what is this? How little do I understand, how little do I grasp it! What is the meaning of this? Is it "Follow me, imitating me in bearing earthly sorrow; let him remain until I come to bestow everlasting rewards"?

℟. He that shall overcome I will make him a pillar in My temple, saith the Lord: * And I will write upon him My name and the name of the city, the new Jerusalem. ℣. To him that overcometh I will give to eat of the tree of life, which is in the paradise of my God. And. Glory. And.

✠ Continuation of the holy Gospel according to St. John.— At that time Jesus said to Peter: "Follow me."

Turning round, Peter saw following them the disciple whom Jesus loved, the one who, at the supper, had leaned back upon his breast and said, "Lord, who is it that will betray thee?" Peter therefore, seeing him, said to Jesus, "Lord, and what of this man?" Jesus said to him, "If I wish him to remain until I come, what is it to thee? Do thou follow me." This saying therefore went abroad among the brethren, that that disciple was not to die. But Jesus had not said to him, "He is not to die"; but rather, "If I wish him to remain until I come, what is it to thee?"

This is the disciple who bears witness concerning these things, and who has written these things, and we know that his witness is true.

LET US PRAY

O Lord, mercifully enlighten Thy Church, that illumined by the teachings of blessed John, Thy Apostle and Evangelist, It may attain the eternal rewards. Through our Lord.

December 28
THE HOLY INNOCENTS, MARTYRS
I Nocturn
From Jeremias the Prophet, c. 31, 15 - 23
II Nocturn
Sermon of St. Augustine, Bishop

Today, dearly beloved brethen, we honor the birthday of those infants whom the text of the Gospel relates to have been slain by

Herod, that most cruel king. And therefore let the earth rejoice with the greatest exultation as the fruitful parent of this heavenly throng and of such great virtues. Behold this wicked enemy could never have so greatly benefited the blessed children by honor as he did by hate.

For as today's most sacred feast shows, as much as iniquity did abound against the blessed children, so much the more did the grace of benediction flow out upon them. Blessed art thou, O Bethlehem in the land of Juda, who endured the cruelty of King Herod in the slaughter of thy children; who deserved to offer to God at one time a snow white army of defenseless infants.

Fittingly, indeed, do we celebrate the birthday of those whom the world brought forth unto eternal life more happily than did birth from their mothers' wombs. Indeed, they possessed the dignity of eternal life before they partook of the enjoyment of the present.

The precious death of the other martyrs indeed merits praise by its testimony; the death of these infants is pleasing in its very consummation. For, in the first moments of their life, the same disaster which put an end to their present life bestowed the beginning of their glory on them whom Herod's wickedness snatched away while suckling at their mothers' breasts. They are rightly called "the flowers of the martyrs" who, springing up as the first buds of the Church, having been born in the midst of the cold of infidelity, were made to whither by the frost of persecution.

℟. I beheld a Lamb standing upon mount Sion, and thousands of His Saints with Him: * And they had His name, and the name of His Father, written on their foreheads. ℣. These are they who, bearing their cross, follow the Lamb wherever He goeth. And they had. Glory. And they had.

III Nocturn

The reading of the holy Gospel according to St. Matthew

At that time an angel of the Lord appeared in a dream to Joseph, saying, "Arise, and take the child and his mother, and flee into Egypt, and remain there until I tell thee. And so forth.

Homily of St. Jerome, Priest

When Joseph took the Child and His Mother to flee into Egypt, he took them in the night and in the darkness, because he left the night of ignorance to those infidels from whom he fled. But when he returned into Judea, neither night nor darkness are mentioned in the Gospel, because at the end of the world the Jews shall be enlightened, receiving faith as if receiving Christ returning from Egypt.

"In order that it might be fulfilled which was spoken by the Lord through His Prophet, saying: 'Out of Egypt I have called my Son.'" Let those who deny the truth of the books of the Hebrews answer where this is written by the interpreters in the Septuagint version. When they have not found it, we shall tell them that it is written in the Prophet Osee, as the versions which we have recently produced can prove.

"Then was fulfilled that which was spoken by Jeremias the Prophet, saying: 'A voice in Rama was heard, lamentation and great mourning: Rachel bewailing her children.'" Of Rachel was born Benjamin, in whose tribe there is no Bethlehem. Therefore, it is asked how Rachel can bewail the children of Juda, that is, of Bethlehem, as her own.

We shall answer shortly that she was buried in Ephrata near Bethlehem, and from the resting place of her body she receives the name of mother. Or, because the two tribes of Juda and Benjamin were joined together, and Herod had commanded not only all the children in Bethlehem to be slain, but also those within all its neighborhood.

℟. They shall walk with Me clothed in white garments: * And I will not blot out their names from the book of life. ℣. These are they who were not defiled with women, for they are virgins. And I. Glory. And I.

✠ Continuation of the holy Gospel according to St. Matthew.— At that time an angel of the Lord appeared in a dream to Joseph, saying, "Arise, and take the child and his mother, and flee into Egypt, and remain there until I tell thee. For Herod will seek the child to destroy him." So he arose, and took the child and his mother by night, and withdrew into Egypt, and remained there until the death of Herod; that there might be fulfilled what was spoken by the Lord through the prophet, saying, "Out of Egypt I called my son."

Then Herod, seeing that he had been tricked by the Magi, was exceedingly angry; and he sent and slew all the boys in Bethlehem and all its neighborhood who were two years old or under, according to the time that he had carefully ascertained from the Magi. Then was fulfilled what was spoken through Jeremias the prophet, saying, "A voice was heard in Rama, weeping and loud lamentation; Rachel weeping for her children, and she would not be comforted, because they are no more."

LET US PRAY

O God, whose praises the Innocent Martyrs have this day confessed, not by their words, but by their death, mortify within us all our evil habits, that the actions of our lives may show forth Thy faith which our lips profess. Through our Lord.

SUNDAY WITHIN THE OCTAVE OF THE NATIVITY

I Nocturn

From the Epistle of St. Paul the Apostle to the Romans, c. 1, 1 - 19

II Nocturn

Sermon of St. Leo, Pope

The greatness of the divine work, beloved, surpasses and goes far beyond the capability of human speech; and thence arises the difficulty of speaking, whence is the reason for not remaining silent. For in Christ Jesus, the Son of God, what is said by the Prophet, "Who shall declare his generation?" refers not alone to the divine essence, but also to the human nature.

That both substances should come together in one person, except faith believe, words do not explain. And so there never lacks matter for praise, because the praiser's stock never suffices. Let us, therefore, rejoice that we are unequal to speak plainly of so great a sacrament of mercy; and since we are unable to expound the heights of our salvation, let us realize that it is good for us to fail.

For no one more nearly approaches knowledge of the truth than he who understands that in divine things, though he be much advanced, what he seeks is ever beyond him. For he who presumes that he has attained that for which he strives, does not find what he seeks, but has failed in the search. Nor let us be disturbed at the want and poverty of our weakness; the words of the Gospels and prophets help us. By them we are so stirred up and instructed that we seem to recall the Lord's Nativity, by which "the Word was made flesh," not so much as a thing for us past and gone, as to look upon as present.

For what the angel announced to the shepherds keeping watch over their flocks has also filled our ears. And therefore are we over the Lord's sheep because in the ear of our heart we keep the words divinely given, as in today's festivity it is said: "Behold I bring you good tidings of great joy, that shall be to all the people; for this day is born to you a Savior, who is Christ the Lord, in the city of David."

℟. Whom have you seen, O shepherds? speak and tell us who has appeared on earth? * We saw the newborn Child and choirs of Angels loudly praising the Lord. ℣. Speak, what have you seen? And tell us of the Birth of Christ. We saw. Glory. We saw.

III Nocturn

The reading of the holy Gospel according to St. Luke

At that time his father and mother were marvelling at the things spoken concerning him. And so forth.

Homily of St. Ambrose, Bishop

You see grace abounding for all, poured out through the birth of the Lord, and prophesying denied to the incredulous, not to the just. And behold, Simeon prophesies that our Lord Jesus Christ has come for the rise and fall of many that he may decide the merits of the just and unjust, and, being a true and just Judge, may mete out either punishments or rewards according to the quality of our deeds.

"And thy own soul a sword shall pierce." Neither literature nor history teach that Mary departed this life by suffering a violent physical death. For not the soul, but the body is pierced by a material sword. And therefore it shows that Mary was not unaware of the heavenly mystery.

For the Word of God, living and powerful and more piercing than the sharpest sword, penetrating even to the division of the soul and spirit, of the joints and marrow, searching out the thoughts of the heart and the secrets of the soul, for all things are naked and open to the Son of God, whom the hidden things of the conscience do not deceive.

Thus Simeon prophesied; the Virgin had prophesied; she who was joined in marriage (Elizabeth) had prophesied; the widow now had to prophesy so that no class or sex be wanting. And so Anna is introduced with the marks of her widowhood and as such a one in habit that she might be believed worthy to announce that the Redeemer of all men had come. Since we have described her merits elsewhere, where we gave exhortation to widows, we do not think that in this place they must be repeated, because we are hastening on to other things.

℟. O King of heaven who is served by such fitting homage: He who holds the world in His hand is laid in a stable: * He lieth in a manger and reigneth in heaven. ℣. Unto us is born this day a Savior in the city of David, who is Christ the Lord. He lieth. Glory. He lieth.

✠ Continuation of the holy Gospel according to St. Luke.—
At that time his father and mother were marvelling at the things spoken concerning him. And Simeon blessed them, and said to Mary his mother, "Behold, this child is destined for the fall and for the rise of many in Israel, and for a sign that shall be contradicted. And thy own soul a sword shall pierce, that the thoughts of many hearts may be revealed."

And there was Anna, a prophetess, daughter of Phanuel, of the tribe of Aser. She was of a great age, having lived with her husband seven years from her maidenhood, and by herself as a widow to eighty-four years. She never left the temple, worshipping with fastings and prayers night and day. And coming up at that very hour, she began to give praise to the Lord, and spoke of him to all who were awaiting the redemption of Jerusalem.

And when they had fulfilled all things as prescribed in the Law of the Lord, they returned into Galilee, to their own town of Nazareth. And the child grew and became strong. He was full of wisdom and the grace of God was upon him.

Let Us Pray

Almighty and eternal God, guide our actions according to Thy own good pleasure, that we may merit to abound in good works in the name of Thy dearly beloved Son, who liveth and reigneth with Thee in the unity of the Holy Ghost, one God, world without end.

December 29

FIFTH DAY WITHIN THE OCTAVE OF THE NATIVITY

The reading of the holy Gospel according to St. Luke

At that time the shepherds were saying to one another, "Let us go over to Bethlehem and see this thing that has come to pass, which the Lord has made known to us." So they went with haste. And so forth.

Homily of St. Bede the Venerable, Priest

With happy joy, indeed, did these shepherds hasten to see that which they had heard, and because they instantly sought the Savior with an ardent and faithful love, they merited to find Him whom they sought. But they also have shown by their words as well as by their deeds with what effort of mind the shepherds of intelligent flocks, yea, all the faithful must seek Christ. "Let us go over to Bethlehem," they say, "and let us see this word that is come to pass." Therefore, dearest brethren, let us also go over in thought to Bethlehem, the city of David, and in love recall to our minds that there the Word was made flesh, and let us celebrate His Incarnation with honors worthy of Him. Having thrown off carnal desires, let us with all the desire of our mind go over to the heavenly Bethlehem, that is, the house of living bread, not made by hands, but eternal in heaven, and in love let us recall that the Word was made flesh. Thither He has ascended in the flesh; there He sits on the right hand of God the Father. Let us follow Him with the whole force of our strength and by careful mortification of heart and body let us merit to see Him reigning on the throne of His Father, Him whom they saw crying in the manger.

"And they came with haste; and they found Mary and Joseph, and the Infant lying in the manger." The shepherds came in haste and found God born as man, together with the ministers of His nativity. Let us hasten too, my brethren, not with footsteps, but by the advances of good works, to see the same glorified humanity together with the same ministers remunerated with a reward worthy of their services; let us hasten to see Him refulgent with the divine Majesty of His Father and of Himself. Let us hasten, I say, for such happiness is not to be sought with sloth and torpor, but the footsteps of Christ must be eagerly followed. For, offering His hand, He desires to help our course and delights to hear from us: "Draw us, we will run after thee in the odor of thy ointments." Therefore, let us follow swiftly with strides of virtue that we may merit to possess. Let no one be tardy in converting to the Lord; let no one put it off from day to day; let us beseech Him through all things and before all things that He direct our steps according to His word and let not injustice dominate over us.

"And seeing, they understood the word that had been spoken to them concerning this Child." Let us also, most dearly beloved brethren, hasten in the meantime to perceive by a loving faith and to embrace with complete love those things that are said to us concerning our Savior, true God and Man, so that by this we may be able to comprehend Him perfectly in the future vision of knowledge. For this is the only and the true life of the blessed, not only of men, but even of the angels, to look continually upon the face of their Creator, which was so ardently desired by the Psalmist who said: "My soul hath thirsted after the living God; when shall I come and appear before the face of God? The Psalmist has shown that the vision of Him alone, and no abundance of the things of earth, could satisfy his desire when he said: "I shall be satisfied when thy glory shall appear." But since neither the idle nor the slothful, but those who perspire in works of virtue, are worthy of divine contemplation, he carefully premised these words: "But as for me, I will appear before thy sight in justice."

December 30

SIXTH DAY WITHIN THE OCTAVE OF THE NATIVITY

The reading of the holy Gospel according to St. Luke

At that time the shepherds were saying to one another, "Let us go over to Bethlehem and see this thing that has come to pass, which the Lord has made known to us." So they went with haste. And so forth.

Homily of St. Ambrose, Bishop

Behold the shepherds hastening! For no one seeks for Christ with tepidity. See that the shepherds have believed an angel, and do you not wish to believe the Father, the Son, the Holy Spirit, the angels, the prophets, and the apostles? Look how precisely the Scripture measures the weight of every word! "They *hasten*," it says, "to see the Word." For when the body of the Lord is seen, the Word, which is the Son, is beheld.

Let not this example of faith seem of little worth to you because the person of the shepherds is lowly. Surely the poorer a person is with regard to prudence so much the more precious is he in his faith. Not the schools packed with assemblies of wise men did our Lord seek out, but the simple people who knew not how to dress up and embellish the things they heard. For simplicity is looked for; ambition is not desired.

Neither think that they must be despised as the rude words of shepherds. For Mary received her faith from them. By them the people were brought to the adoration of God. "And all that heard wondered at those things which were told them by the shepherds. But Mary kept all these words, pondering them in her heart." Let us study in all things the chastity of the holy Virgin, who, with her mouth not less chaste than her body, preserved the arguments of faith in her heart.

January 1
CIRCUMCISION OF OUR LORD
AND OCTAVE OF THE NATIVITY

I Nocturn
*From the Epistle of St. Paul the Apostle
to the Romans, c. 4, 1 - 17*

II Nocturn
Sermon of St. Leo, Pope

Dearly beloved, he is a true venerator and loving observer of today's feast who thinks nothing false in reference to our Lord's Incarnation, nor anything unworthy of His Divinity. For the evil is of equal danger whether the reality of our nature be denied Him or the equality to the glory of His Father. Therefore, when we attempt to understand the mystery of Christ's Nativity, by which He was born of a Virgin Mother, let the darkness of our human minds be driven far away, and let the fog of worldly wisdom depart from the eye of illumined faith.

For divine is the authority in which we believe; divine is the teaching which we follow. Because, whether we turn our interior attention to the testimony of the law, or to the utterances of the prophets, or to the clarion of the Gospel, that is true which John, filled with the Holy Spirit, intoned: "In the beginning was the Word, and the Word was with God, and the Word was God. The same was in the beginning with God. All things were made by Him, and without Him was made nothing."

And similarly is that true which the same teacher added: "And the Word was made flesh, and dwelt among us: and we saw His glory, as it were the glory of the only begotten of the Father." In both natures, therefore, it is the same Son of God, taking to Himself the things that are ours and not losing. His own, renewing man by man, but remaining immutable in Himself.

For His divinity, which is common to Him and the Father, suffered no loss of omnipotence, nor did His form of servant dishonor His form of God, because the supreme and eternal Essence, who lowered Himself for the salvation of the human race, has indeed translated us into His own glory, but He did not cease to be that which He had been. Wherefore, when the only begotten Son of God confesses that He was less than the Father, to whom He says that He is equal, He demonstrates the reality of both forms in Himself: so that the inequality proves the human form, and the equality declares the divine form.

℟. Behold the Lamb of God, behold Him who taketh away the sins of the world: behold Him of whom I said to you: He that cometh after me is preferred before me: * The latchet of whose shoe I am not worthy to loose. ℣. He that is of the earth speaketh of the earth: He that cometh from heaven is above all. The latchet. Glory. The latchet.

III Nocturn

The reading of the holy Gospel according to St. Luke

At that time when eight days were fulfilled for his circumcision, his name was called Jesus. And so forth.

Homily of St. Ambrose, Bishop

So the Child is circumcised. Who is this Child but He of whom it is said: "A child is born to us, and a son is given to us"? For He was made flesh under the law that He might gain them that were under the law. "That they might present him to the Lord." Here I might explain what it means to be presented to the Lord in Jerusalem if I had not already done so in my commentary on Isaias. Now he who is circumcised from his vices is judged worthy of the benign gaze of his Lord, for "the eyes of the Lord are upon the just."

You see that the entire order for the old Law was a type of the new; hence circumcision signifies the purgation from our sins. But because of a certain strong inclination to sin, the frailty of our human flesh and spirit is involved in inextricable vices; therefore by the eighth day, which was that of circumcision, there was prefigured the cleansing from all sin which will be ours at the time of our resurrection. This is the meaning of the words: "Every male opening the womb shall be called holy to the Lord." By these words of the Law a virgin birth was promised. And truly He that opened her womb was holy, for He was spotless.

Then too, that it is He who was meant by the Law, the words repeated by the Angel in this same sense evidently show: "The holy which shall be born of thee," he said, "shall be called the Son of God." For among all those born of woman the Lord Jesus alone is holy, who, because of the uniqueness of His virgin birth, never felt the touch of human corruption; He kept it afar off by reason of His heavenly majesty.

Now if we were to follow the letter of the Law, how could we say that every male is holy when it is not unknown that many have been very wicked? Was Achab holy? Were the false prophets holy whom the heavenly avenger, the destroying fire, consumed at the prayer of Elias? But this One is holy whom the pious ceremonies of the divine Law, themselves prefiguring future mysteries, signified; hence He alone might open the secret womb of spotless fecundity of the holy Virgin, the Church, in order to beget the people of God.

℟. A holy day dawns upon us: come, ye Gentiles, and adore the Lord: * Because today a great light has come down upon the earth. ℣. This is the day which the Lord hath made; let us rejoice and be glad therein. Because. Glory. Because.

✠ Continuation of the holy Gospel according to St. Luke.— At that time when eight days were fulfilled for his circumcision, his name was called Jesus, the name given him by the angel before he was conceived in the womb.

LET US PRAY

O God, who hast given the reward of eternal salvation to the human race by the fruitful virginity of the Blessed Mary, grant, we beseech Thee, that we may be assisted by her intercession through whom we have received the Author of life, Jesus Christ, Thy Son our Lord, who liveth and reigneth with Thee in the unity of the Holy Ghost, God, world without end.

Sunday within the Octave of the Circumcision or,
if there is no Sunday, January 2

THE MOST HOLY NAME OF JESUS

I Nocturn

From the Acts of the Apostles, c. 3, 1 - 16; 4, 5 - 12

II Nocturn

Sermon of St. Bernard, Abbot

The Holy Spirit does not without purpose compare the Name of the Spouse to oil, since He so teaches the espoused to cry to her Spouse: "Thy name is as oil poured out!" For oil gives light, it nourishes, and it anoints. It sustains the fire; it nourishes the flesh; it soothes pain—light, food, medicine. See, now, the same thing with regard to the name of the Spouse. It enlightens him who is instructed; It nourishes him who meditates; It anoints and christens him who is called. Let us also consider these three things individually. Whence do you think was so great and so sudden a light of faith over the whole world but from the preaching of the name of Jesus? Has not God in the light of this Name called us into His own admirable Light; to whom, when enlightened and beholding the Light in this light, Paul rightly says: "You were heretofore darkness, but now light in the Lord."

Finally, this Name the same Apostle was commanded to carry before Kings and nations and the children of Israel; and he bore the Name as a light, and he enlightened his native country and cried everywhere: "The night is passed, and the day is at hand. Let us therefore cast off the works of darkness and put on the armour of light. Let us walk honestly as in the day." And he showed to all the "light upon a candlestick," announcing in every place Jesus, and Him crucified.

How did this light shine and dazzle the eyes of all who saw, when, as lightning proceeding from the mouth of Peter, it healed the bodily feet and soles of the one who was lame and enlightened many who were spiritually blind? Did Peter not spread forth fire when he declared: "In the name of Jesus Christ of Nazareth, arise, and walk"?

Nor is the name of Jesus light only, but it is also food. Are you not strengthened as often as you recall It? What so enriches the mind which thinks of It? What so revives the exhausted senses, builds up power, gives growth to good and upright habits, fosters chaste affections? All food is coarse to the soul if it be not sated with this oil. All food is tasteless if it be not seasoned with this salt. If you write, it does not appeal to me unless I read there *Jesus*. If you are arguing or discussing anything, it means nought to me unless *Jesus* is uttered. *Jesus* is honey to the mouth, melody to the ear, joy to the heart. Still, it is likewise a medicine. Is any of us saddened? Let the Name of Jesus come into his heart and thence It will leap into his mouth. And lo! at the dawning of the light of His Name, every cloud flies away; calm returns. Has one fallen into crime? Does he, moreover, run in despair to the trap of death? Will he not, if he invokes the name of Life, immediately return to life?

℞. Behold thou shalt conceive and bring forth a Son and thou shalt call His name Jesus: * For He shall save His people from their sins. ℣. His name was called Jesus, which was so named by the Angel before He was conceived in the womb. For. Glory. For.

III Nocturn

The reading of the holy Gospel according to St. Luke

At that time when eight days were fulfilled for his circumcision, his name was called Jesus. And so forth.

Homily of St. Bernard, Abbot

Great and wonderful mystery! The Child is circumcised and is called Jesus. What does this connection signify? It seems that circumcision is more for the sake of one who needs salvation than for the Savior; and it is more proper that the Savior should circumcise than be circumcised. But recognize here the mediator of God and men, who from the very beginning of His birth associated the human with the divine, the lowest with the most sublime. He is born of a woman, but of one in whom the fruit of fecundity so ripens that the flower of virginity fades not. He is wrapped in swaddling clothes, but these very clothes are honored by the praises of the angels. He is hidden in a manger, but proclaimed abroad by a radiant star from heaven. So too the circumcision proves the truth of His assumed humanity, and His Name which is above every name indicates the glory of His majesty. As a true son of Abraham He is circumcised; as the true Son of God He is called Jesus.

Not like other men does my Jesus bear this name, vainly and without reason. In Him it is not the shadow of a great name, but the truth. Indeed the Evangelist testifies that from heaven came the name by which He was called by the Angel before He was conceived in the womb. And mark the depth of these words: "After Jesus was born." He is then called Jesus by men, who was so called by the Angel before He was conceived in the womb. Indeed the same Jesus is Savior both of angels and of men: of angels from the beginning of creation; but of men from the time of His Incarnation.

"His name," the Evangelist says, "was called Jesus, which was called by the angel." In the mouth, then, of two or three witnesses every word stands; and that very Word which in the Prophet was shortened, in the Gospel is more clearly read as the Word made Flesh.

Rightly indeed is the Child who is born to us called Savior when He is circumcised, because, you see, from this very time He began to labor for our salvation, shedding His immaculate blood for us. Truly it is not for Christians to ask now why Christ our Lord wished to be circumcised. He was circumcised for the same reason for which He was born, and for which He suffered: none of these things on account of Himself, but all for His chosen ones. He was neither begotten in sin nor freed from sin by circumcision, nor did He die for His own sin, but rather in atonement for our crimes. "Which was called," says the Evangelist, "by the angel before he was conceived in the womb." By His own very nature He is the Savior. With this name was He born; it was not given Him by any creature, human or angelic.

℟. Blessed is Thy name, O God of our fathers, for in Thy wrath Thou wilt remember mercy, * And in the time of tribulation Thou dost forgive sins. ℣. And blessed be the name of Thy majesty forever, Thou who alone dost wonderful things. And in. Glory. And in.

✠ Continuation of the holy Gospel according to St. Luke.— At that time, when eight days were fulfilled for his circumcision, his name was called Jesus, the name given him by the angel before he was conceived in the womb.

LET US PRAY

O God, who didst appoint Thy only-begotten Son as Savior of the human race and didst command His name to be called Jesus, mercifully grant that we, who honor His holy name on earth, may enjoy the vision of Him in heaven. Through the same Jesus Christ.

January 5

VIGIL OF THE EPIPHANY

The reading of the holy Gospel according to St Matthew

At that time, when Herod was dead, behold an Angel of the Lord appeared in a dream to Joseph in Egypt saying, "Arise and take the Child and His Mother and go into the land of Israel." And so forth.

Homily of St. Jerome, Priest

From this passage we understand that not only Herod, but also the priests and scribes had meditated upon the killing of our Lord. "Who arose and took the Child and his mother." It does not say, "He took his child and his wife," but "the Child and his mother," as protector rather than husband.

"But hearing that Archelaus reigned in Judea in the place of Herod his father, he was afraid to go thither." Many fall into error through their ignorance of history, thinking that this was the same Herod by whom our Lord was mocked during His Passion, and who is now reported to have died. Thus, that Herod who afterwards made friends with Pilate is the son of this Herod, the brother of Archelaus.

"That he shall be called a Nazarene." If the Evangelist had given a certain example from the Scriptures, he would never have said: "Which was said by the *prophets*"; but simply: "Which was said by the *prophet*." But by now calling upon the *prophets*, he shows that he has not taken the *words* from the Scriptures, but the *thought*. Nazarene is interpreted as "the holy one." And all the Scripture makes mention of the Lord who was to come as Holy. We can even state in a different way that which is written in the same words, according to the Hebrew text, in Isaias: "There shall come forth a rod out of the root of Jesse, and the *Nazarene* shall rise up out of his root."

January 6

THE EPIPHANY OF THE LORD

I Nocturn

From Isaias the Prophet, c. 55, 1 - 4; c. 60, 1 - 6; c. 61, 10 - 11; c. 62, 1

II Nocturn

Sermon of St. Leo, Pope

Rejoice in the Lord, beloved! again I say, rejoice! for in but a brief time after the solemnity of Christ's Nativity, the feast of His manifestation has shone upon us; and Him whom on that day the Virgin bore, on this, the world acknowledged. For the Word made flesh so disposed the beginnings of our redemption that while the Infant Jesus was manifest to believers He was hidden from persecutors.

Then verily did the heavens show forth the glory of God and unto all the earth the sound of truth went forth, when to the shepherds there appeared a host of angels telling of the Savior's birth and the Magi were led by a guiding star to worship Him, that from the rising of the sun to its setting the true King's generation should shine forth, since the kingdoms of the East would learn the truth of things through the Magi, and the Roman Empire also would not be left without this knowledge.

The very cruelty of Herod, striving to crush at His birth this King whom he feared, was made a blind means to help carry out this dispensation of mercy. While he was intent on his awful crime and pursued the unknown child by an indiscriminate murder of infants, his infamous act served to spread wider abroad the heaven-told news of the birth of the Lord. Not only the novelty of the heavenly message but also the bloody impiety of the persecutor proclaimed loudly these glad tidings. Then the Savior was taken into Egypt that that nation, given up to ancient errors, might be marked by a hidden grace for its approaching salvation; and that she who had not yet cast out of her mind superstition and error, might receive Truth as a guest.

Let us then, beloved, acknowledge in the Magi, the adorers of Christ, the first-fruits of our calling and faith; and let us, with exultant soul, celebrate the beginnings of a blessed hope. For then we began to enter into an eternal inheritance when the secrets of the Scriptures—speaking to us of Christ—were laid open, and the truth, whom the Jews' blindness receives not, gave forth its light to all nations. Let that most holy day be honored by us, on which the author of our salvation appeared. Him whom the Magi revered in His cradle, let us adore—almighty in heaven. And as they from their treasures offered the Lord mystic semblances for gifts, so let us from our hearts bring gifts which are worthy of God.

℟. This day when the Lord was baptized in the Jordán, the heavens were opened and the Spirit in the form of a dove rested upon Him and the voice of the Father was heard saying: * This is My beloved Son in whom I am well pleased. ℣. The Holy Ghost descended in a bodily shape as a dove upon Him and a voice came from heaven. This is. Glory. This is.

III Nocturn

The reading of the holy Gospel according to St. Matthew

When Jesus was born in Bethlehem of Judea, in the days of King Herod, behold, there came Magi from the East to Jerusalem saying, "Where is the newly born king of the Jews?" And so forth.

Homily of St. Gregory, Pope

Dearly beloved brethren, as you have heard in the Gospel lesson, when the King of heaven was born, an earthly king was troubled; for in very truth every earthly eminence is brought to confusion when the heights of heaven are revealed. But let us now ask why, when the Redeemer was born, an angel appeared to the shepherds in Judea, while not an angel, but a star, led the Magi from the East to adore Him.

For it seems that to the Jews, as rational creatures, it was fitting that a rational creature, that is, an angel, should preach, while the Gentiles, who knew not how to use their reason, are led to know their Lord not by the rational word, but by signs. Hence it is said through Paul: "Prophecies are given to believers, not to unbelievers; but signs to unbelievers, not to believers." For this reason to the Jews, as to believers, were given prophecies, while to the Gentiles, as to unbelievers, were given signs.

We should also note that to these same Gentiles the Apostles preach our Redeemer when He had advanced to a perfect age, but when He was a child and could not as yet speak, a star proclaimed Him to these nations. For right reason indeed required that on the one hand the silent elements should proclaim to us their Lord before He Himself began to speak, and on the other hand that preachers should make known their Lord by speech, once He Himself had begun to speak. But in all these signs which were shown at the birth and death of our Lord we should consider how very great was the hardness of heart of some of the Jews who would acknowledge Him neither in the fulfillment of the prophecies nor in His miracles.

Indeed all the elements testified that their Maker had come. Let me reckon them after the manner of men. The heavens recognized Him as their God, and sent a star to shine over where He lay. The sea knew Him, for it offered itself as a solid basis for His feet. The earth knew Him, for when He died it quaked. The sun knew Him, for it hid the rays of its light. The rocks and walls knew Him, for at the time of His death they were rent asunder. The lower world knew Him, for it gave up the dead that it held captive. But despite all this, the hearts of the unbelieving Jews still in no way recognize as their God Him whom all nature discerned as its Lord, and, harder to rend than the very rocks, they refuse to be brought to penance.

℟. The kings of Tharsis and the islands shall offer presents: * The kings of the Arabians and of Saba shall bring gifts to the Lord. ℣. All they from Saba shall come, bringing gold and frankincense. The kings. Glory. The kings.

✠ Continuation of the holy Gospel according to St. Matthew.— When Jesus was born in Bethlehem of Judea, in the days of King Herod, behold, there came Magi from the East to Jerusalem, saying, "Where is the newly born king of the Jews? For we have seen his star in the East and have come to worship him."

But when King Herod heard this, he was troubled, and so was all Jerusalem with him. And gathering together all the chief priests and Scribes of the people, he inquired of them where the Christ was to be born. And they said to him, "In Bethlehem of Judea; for thus it is written through the prophet, 'And thou, Bethlehem, of the land of Juda, art by no means least among the princes of Juda; for from thee shall come forth a leader who shall rule my people Israel.'"

Then Herod summoned the Magi secretly, and carefully ascertained from them the time when the star had appeared to them. And sending them to Bethlehem, he said, "Go and make careful inquiry concerning the child, and when you have found him, bring me word, that I too may go and worship him."

Now they, having heard the king, went their way. And behold, the star that they had seen in the East went before them, until it came and stood over the place where the child was. And when they saw the star they rejoiced exceedingly. And entering the house, they found the child with Mary his mother, and falling down they worshipped him. And opening their treasures they offered him gifts of gold, frankincense and myrrh. And being warned in a dream not to return to Herod, they went back to their own country by another way.

LET US PRAY

O God, who on this day by the guidance of a star didst reveal Thy only-begotten Son to the Gentiles, mercifully grant that we, who already know Thee by faith, may be led to behold the beauty of Thy majesty. Through the same Jesus Christ.

SECOND DAY WITHIN THE OCTAVE OF THE EPIPHANY

The reading of the holy Gospel according to St. Matthew

When Jesus was born in Bethlehem of Judea, in the days of King Herod, behold, there came Magi from the East to Jerusalem, saying, "Where is the newly born king of the Jews?" And so forth.

Homily of St. Gregory, Pope

When the nativity of our King became known, Herod turned to cunning arguments, and, that he might not be deprived of a terrestrial kingdom, he asks that it be announced to him where the Christ might be found. In order that he might kill Him, if he could find Him, he makes it appear that he wishes to adore Him. How great is human malice against the counsels of the Divinity? It is written indeed: "There is no wisdom, there is no prudence, there is no counsel against the Lord." For that star which appeared leads the Magi; they find the newborn King, they offer gifts; and they are admonished in their sleep that they should not return to Herod. And so it happens that Herod cannot find Jesus, whom he seeks. By Herod's person who else are designated but hypocrites, who, as long as they seek Him falsely, will never deserve to find God?

But in these matters it must be noted, that the Priscillianist heretics think that every man is born under the influence of the stars, and in defense of their error they bring up the fact that a new star went forth when the Lord appeared in the flesh, and they say that this star ruled over His destiny. But if we consider the words of the Gospel in which it says concerning the same star, "Until it came and stood over where the Child was," it can be said that the Child ruled the star instead of that the star ruled the Child, since the Child did not hasten to the star, but the star hastened to the Child.

But may it never enter the hearts of the faithful to say that there is any such thing as fate. For that Maker alone who has created it directs the life of men. For man was not made because of the stars, but the stars because of man, and if the star is called the ruler of man's destiny, man is forced to submit to its ministry. Certainly, when Jacob, coming forth from the womb, held the heel of the elder brother with his hand, the elder by no means could come forth entirely unless the one following had begun to come forth, and, although the mother brought both forth at the same time and the same moment, the manner of life of both was not the same.

THIRD DAY WITHIN THE OCTAVE OF THE EPIPHANY

The reading of the holy Gospel according to St. Matthew

When Jesus was born in Bethlehem of Judea, in the days of King Herod, behold, there came Magi from the East to Jerusalem, saying, "Where is the newly born king of the Jews?" And so forth.

Homily of St. Gregory, Pope

The Magi offer gold, frankincense, and myrrh. Gold indeed is fitting for a king; incense is offered in sacrifice to God, while the bodies of the deceased are embalmed with myrrh. Therefore the Wise Men proclaim also by their mystic gifts Him whom they adore: by the gold they proclaim Him King; by frankincense, God; by myrrh, a mortal man. However, there are some heretics who believe that He is God, but by no means believe that He reigns over all. These indeed offer Him frankincense, but they do not wish to offer Him gold too. And there are some who recognize Him as King, but deny that He is God. Hence these offer Him gold, but will not offer incense.

And there are some who acknowledge Him both as God and King, but they deny that He assumed mortal flesh. These, of course, offer Him gold and frankincense, but they refuse to offer the myrrh of assumed mortality. Let us, therefore, offer gold to our newborn Lord, that we may confess that He reigns over all; let us offer frankincense, that we may believe that He who has appeared in time, existed as God before all times; let us offer myrrh in order that we may believe that He whom we know to be immortal in His divinity also became mortal in our flesh.

However, in the gold, frankincense, and myrrh something else can also be understood. For by gold wisdom is designated, as Solomon testifies, who says: "A desirable treasure abideth in the mouth of the wise." But by frankincense, which is burned unto God, the power of prayer is expressed, as the Psalmist testifies, who says: "Let my prayer be directed as incense in thy sight." And by myrrh the mortification of our flesh is symbolized. From this Holy Church says of her laborers who strive for God even unto death: "My hands have dropped myrrh."

FOURTH DAY WITHIN THE OCTAVE OF THE EPIPHANY

The reading of the holy Gospel according to St. Matthew

When Jesus was born in Bethlehem of Judea, in the days of King Herod, behold, there came Magi from the East to Jerusalem, saying, "Where is the newly born king of the Jews?" And so forth.

Homily of St. Gregory, Pope

The wise men indicate to us something important in that they returned to their own country by a different way. For by the fact that they did what they were advised, they undoubtedly intimate to us what we should do. Our homeland, to be sure, is Paradise, whither, when we have known Jesus, we are forbidden to return by the way which we came. From our country we have departed by our pride, our disobedience, our following after visible things, by our partaking of forbidden food, but it is imperative that we return to it by sorrow, obedience, contempt for visible things and by checking the desire of the flesh.

Thus by another way do we retrace our steps to our fatherland, because we, who have forsaken the joys of Paradise by our pleasure-seeking, are called back to them through lamentations. Wherefore, it is needful, dearest brethren, that constantly in fear and always with mistrust, we place before our heart's eyes, on the one hand, our sinful deeds, on the other, the judgment of extreme exactitude. Let us think how the severe Judge will come, who threatens judgment, yet keeps it hidden, who threatens sinners with terrible things, and yet until now keeps them back; He hesitates to come too quickly, in order that He may not find anything to condemn.

Let us blot out our faults with tears, and in the word of the Psalmist, "let us come before His presence with thanksgiving." So let no trickery of our desires deceive us, no foolish joy seduce us. For the Judge is near at hand, who declares: "Woe to you that now laugh, for you shall mourn and weep." By reason of this Solomon says: "Laughter shall be mingled with sorrow, and mourning taketh hold of the end of joy." For this reason he likewise says: "Laughter I counted error; and to mirth I said: "Why art thou vainly deceived?" Hence, again he says: "The heart of the wise is where there is mourning, and the heart of fools where there is mirth."

FIFTH DAY WITHIN THE OCTAVE OF THE EPIPHANY

The reading of the holy Gospel according to St. Matthew

When Jesus was born in Bethlehem of Judea, in the days of King Herod, behold, there came Magi from the East to Jerusalem, saying, "Where is the newly born king of the Jews?" And so forth.

Homily of St. Jerome, Priest

"For we have seen his star in the East." To the shame of the Jews, a star rises in the East so that they might learn of Christ's birth from the Gentiles. The Gentiles knew that Christ's birth was to take place from the prophecy of Balaam, whose descendants they were. (You can read this prophecy in the book of Numbers.) The Magi were brought to Judea by the appearance of the star in order that the priests, on being questioned by the Magi as to where Christ was to be born, might be inexcusable with regard to His coming.

"But they said to him: 'In Bethlehem of *Judea.*'" This is an error of the copyists. For we think that it was first written by the Evangelist as we read in the Hebrew, "Of Juda," not, "of *Judea.*" For what Bethlehem of other nations is there, that the phrase "of Judea" is placed here to distinguish it? Therefore, "of *Juda*" is to be written because there is another Bethlehem in Galilee. Read the book of Josue, son of Nun. And finally in the very testimony itself which is taken from the prophecy of Micheas we read the following: "And thou Bethlehem the land of Juda."

"And opening their treasures, they offered him gifts, gold, frankincense, and myrrh." Juvencus, the Priest, has expressed the mysteries of these gifts very beautifully in one little verse:

Incense, myrrh, and gold—they bring
   their gifts—to God, to Man, their King.

"And having received an answer in sleep that they should not return to Herod, they went back another way into their country." They who had offered gifts to the Lord in consequence receive an answer, not from an Angel, but from the Lord Himself, so that the privilege of Joseph's merits might be revealed. They return by another way because they were not to be joined to the infidelity of the Jews.

SIXTH DAY WITHIN THE OCTAVE OF THE EPIPHANY

The reading of the holy Gospel according to St. Matthew

When Jesus was born in Bethlehem of Judea in the days of King Herod, behold, there came Magi from the East to Jerusalem, saying, "Where is the newly born king of the Jews?" And so forth.

Homily of St. Ambrose, Bishop

What are these gifts of true faith? The gold is for Him as King; the frankincense for Him as God; the myrrh for Him when dead. The first is an ornament for the King; the next the sign of divine Power; the last a mark of reverence for the burial which does not corrupt the body of him who is dead, but preserves it. Let us, who hear and read these things, brethren, offer in like manner the same treasures from our hearts. For "we have treasure in earthen vessels." If, then, what you are in yourselves you must not think to be of yourselves, but of Christ, how much more should you value yourselves not as your own possession, but Christ's!

Thus the Magi offer gifts from their treasure. Do you want to know how fine a reward they receive? A star is seen by them; where Herod is, it is not seen; where Christ is, it is again beheld and points out the way. Thus this star is the way, and the way is Christ, because according to the mystery of Redemption Christ is the Star. For "a star shall rise out of Jacob and a man shall spring up from Israel." Finally, where Christ is, there the star is. He is "the bright and morning star." So by His own light He reveals Himself.

Take notice of another detail. The Magi came by one way; they returned by another. For they who had seen Christ had known Him to be Christ; they returned, better men surely than when they came. There are, of course, two paths: one which leads to ruin; the other which leads to the kingdom. The former is the way of sinners, which leads to Herod; the latter is Christ by which one is brought back to his homeland. For here is a temporal dwelling, as it is written: "My soul hath been long a sojourner."

SUNDAY WITHIN THE OCTAVE OF THE EPIPHANY

I Nocturn

From the First Epistle of St. Paul the Apostle to the Corinthians, c. 1, 1 - 13

II Nocturn

Sermon of St. Leo, Pope

Dearly beloved, it is a just and reasonable service of sincere piety on days which proclaim the works of divine mercy to rejoice with our whole heart and to celebrate with honor those things which have been performed for our salvation. To this devotion we are called by the seasons of the year which continually return, and especially by this present one, which, shortly after the day on which the Son of God, coeternal with the Father, was born, brings now the feast of the Epiphany, consecrated by the manifestation of our Lord.

On this day divine providence has formed a great bulwark for our Faith. For while we now call to mind in solemn worship how the childhood of the Savior was adored in its first infancy, we receive from the original Scriptures the doctrine that Christ was born with the true nature of man.

This is that which justifies wicked men; this is that which makes saints out of sinners—that in one and the same Lord, Jesus Christ, there is believed to be both true divinity and true humanity; the divinity by which He is before all ages equal to the Father in the form of God; the humanity by which in the last days He is united to man in the form of a servant.

Therefore, in order to strengthen this faith which was proclaimed against all errors, it was effected by the great love of divine counsel that the people dwelling in the vast region of the Orient, who excelled in the study of the stars, should receive sign of the begotten Child who was to reign over all Israel. For the new light of a very brilliant star appeared to the Magi, and it so filled with wonder the minds of those who saw its splendor, that they believed that what was announced by such a great sign should not in the least be ignored by themselves.

℟. Be enlightened, be enlightened, O Jerusalem, for thy light is come: * And the glory of the Lord is risen upon thee. ℣. And the nations shall walk in thy light and kings in the brightness of thy rising. And the glory. Glory. And the glory.

III Nocturn

The reading of the holy Gospel according to St. Luke

When Jesus was twelve years old they (his parents) went up to Jerusalem according to the custom of the feast. And after they had fulfilled the days, when they were returning, the boy Jesus remained in Jerusalem. And so forth.

Homily of St. Ambrose, Bishop

Our Lord's public discourses, as we read, began when He was twelve years old. This was to be the number of the apostles who were to preach the faith. Not without reason is He, who as man was filled with the wisdom and grace of God—unmindful of His parents in the flesh—found in the temple after three days. The reason was that it might be a sign that on the third day after His triumphant Passion He who had been thought dead would show Himself to our faith, restored to life, seated upon the heavenly throne and in His divine majesty.

"How is it that you sought me?" There are two generations in Christ: one paternal, the other maternal. His paternal generation is divine, but that from His mother renders Him subject to our hardships and necessities, and hence whatever happens surpassing the powers of His human nature or His age or the general practice must not be ascribed to human efforts but must be referred to divine powers.

Elsewhere, His mother urges Him to the ministry; but here the mother is gently reproved because she as yet considers what is human. But while here He is described as a boy of twelve years, there He is said to have disciples. You see that His mother, who had wondered at His miracles when a youth, had learned from her Son to call on the mightier nature for a work of power.

"And he came to Nazareth, and was subject to them." How would He be the Teacher of virtue unless He Himself would fulfill the duty of piety? And do we wonder if He who is subject to His mother shows deference to His Father? This subjection, it is true, is not one arising from infirmity but one of piety, yet one can expect a serpent (a heretic) coming out of his terrible hole to lift up his deceitful head and spit out poison from his serpentine breast. Since the Son says that He has been sent, the heretic calls the Father greater, thus ascribing an imperfection to the Son who could have a greater, asserting that He who is sent stands in need of another's help. Did He then need any human aid in order to obey His mother's command?

℞. The Holy Ghost appeared in the form of a dove and the voice of the Father was heard: * This is My beloved Son in whom I am well pleased. ℣. The heavens were opened above Him and the voice of the Father was heard. This is. Glory. This is.

✠ Continuation of the holy Gospel according to St. Luke.— When Jesus was twelve years old his parents went up to Jerusalem according to the custom of the feast. And after they had fulfilled the days, when they were returning, the boy Jesus remained in Jerusalem, and his parents did not know it. But thinking that he was in the caravan, they had come a day's journey before it occurred to them to look for him among their relatives and acquaintances. And not finding him, they returned to Jerusalem in search of him.

And it came to pass after three days, that they found him in the temple, sitting in the midst of the teachers, both listening to them and asking them questions. And all who were listening to him were amazed at his understanding and his answers. And when they saw him, they were astonished. And his mother said to him, "Son, why hast thou done so to us? Behold, thy father and I have been seeking thee sorrowing."

And he said to them, "How is it that you sought me? Did you not know that I must be about my Father's business?" And they did not understand the word that He spoke to them.

And he went down with them and came to Nazareth, and was subject to them; and his mother kept all these things carefully in her heart. And Jesus advanced in wisdom and age and grace before God and man.

Let Us Pray

Receive, we beseech Thee, O Lord, by Thy heavenly goodness, the prayers of Thy people who pray to Thee, that they may both see what must be done and have the strength to perform the same. Through our Lord.

January 13
OCTAVE DAY OF THE EPIPHANY

I Nocturn

From the First Epistle of St. Paul the Apostle to the Corinthians, c. 1, 1 - 13

II Nocturn

Sermon of St. Gregory Nazianzen

I cannot restrain my boundless joy, but in mind I am uplifted and moved; and, unmindful of my own meanness, I earnestly strive and desire to follow the great John in his office, or rather, in his service; and though I am not the precursor, yet I do come from the desert. Christ, therefore, is enlightened, or rather He enlightens us with His own effulgence; Christ is baptized, let us also descend at the same time, so that with Him we may likewise ascend.

John baptizes and Jesus approaches, sanctifying indeed him also who baptizes, but especially that He may bury the old Adam in the water, and above all that through these things the waters of the Jordan may be sanctified, so that, just as He was spirit and flesh, thus also to those who were to be baptized the heritage of sanctification in spirit and water might be passed on. The Baptist did not submit; Jesus contended. "I," he said, "have need to be baptized by thee." The lamp speaks to the Sun, and the voice addresses the Word.

Jesus came up out of the water, leading out and lifting up with Him the world, which was, in a certain sense, submerged. And he saw the heavens, which the first Adam had once closed to himself and to us after him, not divided, but opened, just as, by a fiery sword, Paradise had also been closed.

The Holy Spirit gives testimony; for similar things join themselves to one another. Testimony is given from heaven; for from thence came He who renders the testimony.

℟. All they from Saba shall come bringing gold and frankincense and showing forth praise to the Lord, * Alleluia, alleluia, allelluia. ℣. The kings of Tharsis and the islands shall offer presents, the kings of the Arabians and of Saba shall bring gifts. Alleluia. Glory. Alleluia.

III Nocturn

The reading of the holy Gospel according to St. John

At that time John saw Jesus coming to him, and he said, "Behold the lamb of God, who takes away the sin of the world!" And so forth.

Homily of St. Augustine, Bishop

Before the Lord came to be baptized by John in the Jordan, he knew Him, judging by his words where he said: "Comest thou to me to be baptized? Rather I ought to be baptized by thee." But behold, he had known the Lord; he had known the Son of God. How are we to prove that he already knew that He would baptize in the Holy Spirit? Before He came to the river, when many came to John to be baptized, he said to them: "I, indeed, baptize you with water; but He who shall come after me, He is greater than I, the latchet of whose shoe I am not worthy to loose; He shall baptize you with the Holy Ghost and with fire." This he already knew.

What, therefore, does he learn through the dove—lest he afterwards be found a liar (which God forbid that we should think)—except that there was to be some such prerogative in Christ, that, although many ministers would baptize, whether just or unjust, the holiness of the baptism would not be attributed except to Him upon whom the dove descended, of whom it was said: "He it is that baptizeth with the Holy Ghost"? When Peter baptizes, it is Christ who baptizes; when Paul baptizes, it is Christ who baptizes; when Judas baptizes, it is Christ who baptizes.

For if the holiness of the Baptism depended on the merits of the one baptizing, as these differ in merits, so also would the Baptisms differ, and one would be thought to receive a better Baptism if he received it from one having greater holiness. The saints themselves, that is, the good who are related to the dove, the good who are admitted to the lot of the city Jerusalem, the good men in the Church of whom the Apostle says, "The Lord knoweth who are his," these just men differ from one another by diversities of graces and are not all equally just.

There are some men holier than others, some better than others. Why, then, for example, if one is baptized by a just and holy man, and another is baptized by one of inferior merit with God—of lower rank, of lesser continence, of inferior life—is that baptism which they receive one, the same, and equal, unless because it is always Christ who baptizes?

℞. The star which the Magi had seen in the East went before them until they came to the place where the Child was: * And when they saw it, they rejoiced with great joy. ℣. And entering into the house, they found the Child with Mary His Mother, and falling down they adored Him. And. Glory. And.

☩ Continuation of the holy Gospel according to St. John.— At that time John saw Jesus coming to him, and he said, "Behold the lamb of God, who takes away the sin of the world! This is he of whom I said, 'After me there comes one who has been set above me, because he was before me.' And I did not know him. But that he may be known to Israel, for this reason have I come baptizing with water."
And John bore witness, saying, "I beheld the Spirit descending as a dove from heaven, and it abode upon him. And I did not know him. But he who sent me to baptize with water said to me, 'He upon whom thou wilt see the Spirit descending, and abiding upon him, he it is who baptizes with the Holy Spirit.' And I have seen and have borne witness that this is the Son of God."

Let Us Pray

O God, whose only-begotten Son appeared in the substance of our flesh, grant, we beseech Thee, that we may be inwardly reformed by Him whom we recognize to have been outwardly like unto ourselves, who liveth and reigneth with Thee.

II SUNDAY AFTER THE EPIPHANY

I Nocturn

From the second Epistle of St. Paul the Apostle to the Corinthians. c. 1, 1 - 14

II Nocturn

Sermon of St. John Chrysostom

When I pay diligent attention to the reading of the Epistles of St. Paul, often twice, or even three or four times during the separate weeks (whenever we celebrate the memory of the Martyrs), I rejoice in gladness, delighting in that spiritual trumpet,

II Sunday After The Epiphany

and I am stirred up and burn with desire, knowing it to be a friendly call to me, and I seem almost to behold him present and to hear him speaking. Yet, still I am sad and troubled that not all men know this man as he is; yes, some are so ignorant of him that they do not even know the number of his Epistles! Lack of intelligence, however, does not cause this, but the fact that they do not wish to keep the holy man's writings constantly in their hands.

For what we know, if anything, we do not know owing to any superlative talent or keenness of mind, but because, being strongly drawn towards this great man, we never cease from reading his works. For it is true that he who loves someone usually knows better than others what the one loved has done, for he makes greater effort to learn all about the beloved. St. Paul himself shows that this is true when he says to the Philippians: "I have the right to feel so about you all, because I have you in my heart, all of you, alike in my chains and in the defense and confirmation of the gospel."

Wherefore, if you also will desire to listen attentively to the reading, nothing else will be required of you. For true is the word of Christ who declares: "Seek, and you shall find; knock and it shall be opened to you."

Moreover, since very many among those who gather here with us have undertaken the education of their children, care for their wives, and management of their family, they are not able on that account to give themselves wholly to this work; but do you move yourselves to seize on those things, at least, which others have gathered; be as zealous in heeding those things which shall be spoken, as you are devoted to saving money. For although it may be a little thing to demand nothing from you but only zeal, it will nevertheless be a thing desired if you contribute at least that.

℞. Thou hast made known to me, O Lord, the ways of life: * Thou shalt fill me with joy with Thy countenance: at Thy right hand are delights forevermore. ℣. Thou art He that will restore my inheritance unto me. Thou shalt fill. Glory. Thou shalt fill.

III Nocturn

The reading of the holy Gospel according to St. John

At that time a wedding took place at Cana of Galilee, and the mother of Jesus was there. Now Jesus too was invited to the marriage, and also his disciples. And so forth.

II Sunday After the Epiphany

Homily of St. Augustine, Bishop

By the very fact that the Lord, having been invited, went to the marriage feast, He wished to show, even aside from the mystical signification, that He Himself instituted matrimony; for there were to come those of whom the Apostle spoke, prohibiting marriage and saying that matrimony is an evil instituted by the devil. The same Lord, when asked in the Gospel whether it were lawful for a man to put away his wife for any cause, said that it is not lawful, save on account of fornication. In which reply, if you recall, He said this: "What God hath joined together let no man put asunder."

Those, moreover, who are well instructed in the Catholic faith know that God instituted matrimony. Indeed, as the joining together is from God, so divorce is from the devil. One is permitted, however, on account of fornication, to put away his wife; for she first did not wish to be a wife who did not preserve conjugal fidelity to the marriage bond.

Neither are those without nuptials who vow their virginity to God, notwithstanding the fact that they enjoy a greater degree of honor and sanctity in the Church, for they together with the whole Church participate in those nuptials in which the Spouse is Christ.

And hence, when the Lord was invited, He came to the marriage for this reason, that conjugal chastity might be confirmed, and that the sacrament of matrimony might be manifested; for the spouse of that wedding, to whom it was said, "Thou hast kept the good wine until now," was also a figure of the Lord, for Christ has kept the good wine, that is, His Gospel even until now.

℟. The earth is the Lord's and the fullness thereof: * The world and all they that dwell therein. ℣. He hath founded it upon the sea and hath prepared it upon the rivers. The world. Glory. The world.

✠ Continuation of the holy Gospel according to St. John.— At that time a wedding took place at Cana of Galilee, and the mother of Jesus was there. Now Jesus too was invited to the marriage, and also his disciples. And the wine having run short, the mother of Jesus said to him, "They have no wine." And Jesus said to her, "What wouldst thou have me do, woman? My hour has not yet come." His mother said to the attendants, "Do whatever he tells you."

Now six stone water-jars were placed there, after the Jewish manner of purification, each holding two or three measures. Jesus said to them, "Fill the jars with water." And they filled them to the brim. And Jesus said to them, "Draw out now, and take to the chief steward." And they took it to him.

Now when the chief steward had tasted the water after it had become wine, not knowing whence it was (though the attendants who had drawn the water knew), the chief steward called the bridegroom, and said to him, "Every man at first sets forth the good wine, and when they have drunk freely, then that which is poorer. But thou hast kept the good wine until now.

LET US PRAY

O almighty and eternal God, who dost govern all things both in heaven and upon the earth, mercifully hear the prayers of Thy people and grant the gift of Thy peace in our times. Through our Lord.

III SUNDAY AFTER THE EPIPHANY

I Nocturn

From the Epistle of St. Paul the Apostle to the Galations, c. 1, 1 - 14

II Nocturn

From the Commentary of St. Augustine, Bishop, on the Epistle to the Galatians

The reason of the Apostle's writing to the Galatians was this: that they might understand that the grace of God had so worked in them that they were no longer under the law. For when the grace of the Gospel had been preached to them, there were some of those of the circumcision, although Christians in name, who had not yet understood that great benefit of grace, and desired still to be bound with the burdens of the law—burdens which the Lord God had laid, not upon such as serve righteousness, but upon such as serve sin, that is to say, laying upon the wicked a righteous law whereby their wickedness was made manifest, not taken away. For nothing takes away sin except the grace of faith which works through love.

These men of the circumcision would have the Galatians, who were under grace, to be under the burdens of the law, persuading them that the Gospel was of no profit to them unless they should also be circumcised and take upon themselves the other outward observances of the Jewish religion.

Whence the Galatians began to doubt concerning the Apostle Paul, by whom the Gospel had been preached to them, as though he did not hold the doctrine of the other Apostles, who compelled the Gentiles to submit to the law.

The same question is discussed in the Epistle to the Romans, with this difference, however, that in this latter the Apostle puts an end to the discussion and settles the difference that had arisen between the Jewish and the Gentile converts. For the Jews held that they had earned the knowledge of the Gospel as a reward for their observance of the law and begrudged the same knowledge to the Gentiles as not having merited it; whereas the Gentiles, on the other hand, maintained that they excelled the Jews because they were not murderers of the Lord. But in this Epistle to the Galatians he writes to those who were troubled by the authority claimed by certain Jewish converts who sought to force all to the observances of the old law.

℟. O Lord, rebuke me not in Thine anger nor chastise me in Thy wrath: * Have mercy upon me, O Lord, for I am weak. ℣. Fear and trembling are come upon me and darkness hath covered me. Have mercy. Glory. Have mercy.

III Nocturn

The reading of the holy Gospel according to St. Matthew

At that time when Jesus had come down from the mountain, great crowds followed him. And behold, a leper came and worshipped him. And so forth.

Homily of St. Jerome, Priest

Great multitudes met the Lord when He descended from the mountain, for they had not been able to follow Him as He went up. And first there came to Him a leper. This poor creature's disease had prevented him from hearing the Savior's long discourse on the Mount. It is to be noted that he is the first person specially named as being cured. The second one was the Centurion's servant; the third was Peter's mother-in-law, who was sick of a fever at Capharnaum; the fourth were they who, being troubled with evil spirits, were brought to Christ, from whom He, by His word, cast out the evil spirits, at the same time that He healed all that were sick.

"And behold, a leper came and adored Him, saying." Fittingly after preaching and instruction there was presented an occasion for a sign, so that by the persuasion of a miracle the instruction just given might be confirmed in the minds of the hearers. "Lord, if thou wilt, thou canst make me clean." He who beseeches the Lord to have the will, does not doubt that He has the power.

"And Jesus, stretching forth His hand, touched him, saying: 'I will; be thou made clean.'" As soon as the Lord put forth His hand the leprosy departed. Consider how humble and free from arrogance is His answer. The leper had said: "If thou wilt"; the Lord replied, "I will." The leper had affirmed: "Thou canst make me clean"; the Lord rejoined and said: "Be thou made clean." This latter sentence must not be joined, as some Latinists thought, to the former, and read: "I wish to make thee clean"; but must be taken separately, so that first He says: "I will"; then He commands: "Be thou made clean."

"And Jesus said to him: 'See thou tell no man.'" And indeed what need was there for him to express in words what he showed clearly in his body? "But go, show thyself to the priest." For various reasons did He send him to the priest. First, for humility's sake, that He might show reverence to the priests. For it was prescribed by law that whosoever was freed from leprosy should offer gifts to the priests. Moreover, that when the priests saw the leper cleansed, they might either believe in the Savior or refuse to believe; if they believed, that they might be saved; if they refused to believe, that they might have no excuse. Finally, that He might give no foundation for the charge that was so often brought against Him, that is, that He did not observe the law.

℞. Two Seraphim cried one to another: * Holy, holy, holy is the Lord God of hosts: All the earth is full of His glory. ℣. There are three who give testimony in heaven: the Father, the Word, and the Holy Spirit: and these three are one. Holy. Glory. Holy.

✚ Continuation of the holy Gospel according to St. Matthew.— At that time when Jesus had come down from the mountain, great crowds followed him. And behold, a leper came and worshipped him, saying, "Lord, if thou wilt, thou canst make me clean." And stretching forth his hand Jesus touched him, saying, "I will; be thou made clean." And immediately his leprosy was cleansed. And Jesus said to him, "See thou tell no one; but go, show thyself to the priest, and offer the gift that Moses commanded, for a witness to them."

Now when he had entered Capharnaum, there came to him a centurion who entreated him, saying, "Lord, my servant is lying sick in the house, paralyzed, and is grievously afflicted." Jesus said to him, "I will come and cure him." But in answer the centurion said, "Lord, I am not worthy that thou shouldst come under my roof; but only say the word, and my servant will be healed. For I, too, am a man subject to authority, and have soldiers subject to me; and I say to one, 'Go,' and he goes; and to another, 'Come,' and he comes; and to my servant, 'Do this,' and he does it."

And when Jesus heard this, he marvelled, and said to those who were following him, "Amen I say to you, I have not found so great a faith in Israel. And I tell you that many will come from the east and from the west, and will feast with Abraham and Isaac and Jacob in the kingdom of heaven, but the children of the kingdom will be put forth into the darkness outside; there will be the weeping, and the gnashing of teeth." Then Jesus said to the centurion, "Go thy way; as thou hast believed, so be it done to thee." And the servant was healed in that hour.

Let Us Pray

O almighty and eternal God, mercifully behold our weakness and extend the right hand of Thy Majesty to protect us. Through our Lord.

IV SUNDAY AFTER THE EPIPHANY

I Nocturn

*From the Epistle of St. Paul the Apostle
to the Philippians, c. 1, 1 - 18*

II Nocturn

From the Book of Morals of St. Gregory, Pope

We refresh the body with food lest it should become weak and fail us; we chasten it by abstinence lest it should grow heavy and become lord over us; we strengthen it by exercise lest it waste away through lack of use; but very soon we give it rest lest it faint with weariness; we protect it with clothing lest the cold should blight it; and we strip it of the same garments lest the heat should afflict it.

In all these many cares what do we do but serve the corruptible, at least that the multiplicity of cares spent on the body may sustain that which the anxiety of our changeable infirmity presses down? Thus it is well said by St. Paul: "For creation was made subject to vanity—not by its own will but by reason of him who made it subject—in hope, because creation itself also will be delivered from its slavery to corruption into the freedom of the glory of the sons of God."

"Creation was made subject to vanity—not by its own will." For when man of his own free will gave up his state of unchangeable happiness, the just sentence of death was passed upon him and, though not willing, he became subject to the state of change and corruption. But creation itself also will be delivered from its slavery to corruption when it shall rise again incorruptible and be made partaker of the glory of the children of God.

Here, then, the elect are still subject to sorrow, being yet bound by the sentence of corruption; but when we shall have put off this corruptible flesh, we shall be loosed from these bonds, as it were, of sorrow, by which we are bound. For though we already desire to appear before God, we are still hindered by the burden of this dying body. Rightly, then, are we called prisoners, since we are not yet free to go where we will, that is, to God. Well, therefore, did St. Paul, yearning after eternal things, but still weighed down with the burden of this corruptible body, cry out: "I desire to be loosed and to be with Christ." He would not have felt this desire to be loosed unless he saw that he was bound.

℞. O God, who sittest upon the throne and judgest justice, be Thou the refuge of the poor in tribulation: * For Thou alone considerest labor and sorrow. ℣. To Thee is the poor man left, Thou wilt be a helper to the orphan. For. Glory. For.

III Nocturn

The reading of the holy Gospel according to St. Matthew

At that time Jesus got into a boat, and his disciples followed him. And behold, there arose a great storm on the sea, so that the boat was covered by the waves; but he was asleep. And so forth.

Homily of St. Jerome, Priest

The fifth miracle that the Lord worked was when He entered the boat at Capharnaum and commanded the winds and the sea; the sixth, when in the country of the Gerasenes He suffered the devils to enter the swine; the seventh, when, as He came into His own city, He cured the man sick of the palsy lying on a bed. The first man sick of the palsy that He cured was the centurion's servant.

"But he was asleep. So they came and woke him, saying: 'Lord, save us.'" There is a type of this in the history of Jonas,

IV Sunday After The Epiphany

who, when the rest were in danger, was himself safe and lying fast asleep, and whom the sailors awakened to help them. Jonas then freed those who had awakened him by his command (to cast him into the sea) and by the mystery of his passion (for his being cast into the sea was a figure of Christ's passion).

"Then he arose and rebuked the wind and the sea." From this passage we understand that all creation knows its Creator. For those things He rebukes and those He commands give heed to Him who commands, not in accord with the error of heretics who think that all things have a soul, but because of the power of their Maker those things which are insensible to us are sensible to Him.

"And the men marveled, saying, 'What manner of man is this, that even the wind and the sea obey him?'" Not the disciples, but the sailors and the others who were in the boat, wondered. But if anyone wishes to interpret it otherwise and hold that they who wondered were the disciples, we reply that they were fittingly called simply men (and stripped of their title of disciples) who had not as yet known the power of the Savior.

℟. I will love Thee, O Lord, my strength: * The Lord is my support and my refuge. ℣. My deliverer, my God, my helper. The Lord. Glory. The Lord.

✠ Continuation of the holy Gospel according to St. Matthew.— At that time Jesus got into a boat, and his disciples followed him. And behold, there arose a great storm on the sea, so that the boat was covered by the waves; but he was asleep. So they came and woke him, saying, "Lord, save us! we are perishing!" But he said to them, "Why are you fearful, O you of little faith?" Then he arose and rebuked the wind and the sea, and there came a great calm. And the men marveled, saying, "What manner of man is this, that even the wind and sea obey him?"

Let Us Pray

O God, who dost know that we who live amid such great dangers are unable to stand firm because of our human frailty, grant us health of soul and body that, aided by Thy grace, we may overcome the things we suffer for our sins. Through our Lord.

V SUNDAY AFTER THE EPIPHANY

I Nocturn

From the first Epistle of St. Paul the Apostle to Timothy, c. 1, 1 - 16

II Nocturn

Sermon of St. Augustine, Bishop

This is a saying made for man, and worthy of all acceptation, that Christ Jesus came into this world to save sinners. Listen to the words of the Gospel: "The Son of man is come to seek and to save that which was lost." If man had not been lost, the Son of man would not have come. Therefore man had gone astray; God came, having become man, and man was found. Man had gone astray through his own free will; God-made-man came by grace which sets free.

Do you ask how free will avails to evil? Call to mind a sinner. Do you ask how the God-Man is able to help? Consider in Him the grace that liberates. Nowhere is it better and more plainly shown than in the first man how much the free will of man avails to evil when it is taken possession of by pride and used without God's help.

The first man went astray; and where would he be unless the second man had come? And because the former was a man, therefore the latter was also a man; hence this is a saying made for man. Nor is there any place where the benignity of grace and the liberality of the omnipotence of God so appears as in the Man that is Mediator between God and men, the Man, Christ Jesus,

For what do we say, my brethren? I speak to those who have been brought up in the Catholic Church or who have been gathered into the peace of that Church. We know and hold that the Mediator between God and men, the Man Christ Jesus, as regards His manhood is of the same nature as we. For our flesh is not of a different nature from His, nor is our soul. He took upon Himself that same nature which He had ordained to save.

℞. The Lord is at my right hand that I be not moved: * Therefore my heart hath been glad and my tongue hath rejoiced.
℣. The Lord is the portion of my inheritance and of my cup. Therefore. Glory. Therefore.

V Sunday After The Epiphany

III Nocturn

The reading of the holy Gospel according to St. Matthew

At that time Jesus spoke this parable to the multitudes: "The kingdom of heaven is like a man who sowed good seed in his field." And so forth.

Homily of St. Augustine, Bishop

When those placed at the head of the Church acted too negligently, or when the apostles fell into the sleep of death, the devil came and sowed those whom the Lord had termed "wicked children." But the question arises whether they are heretics or evil-living Catholics. The wicked children can be said to be the heretics, because, though procreated from the same seed of the Gospel and the name of Christ, they are turned away by depraved opinions to false teachings.

But, because He says they were planted in the midst of the wheat, they who are of one communion seem, as it were, to be signified. Yet, since the Lord interpreted the field not as the Church, but as this world, heretics are rightly understood; for not in the society of one Church or of one Faith, but only in that of the name of Christian, are they intermingled with the good.

Those, on the other hand, who are corrupted in their faith are to be considered as chaff rather than as cockle, for the chaff even has its very source and common root with the grain. Surely, though, bad Catholics are not wrongly understood to be in that net in which both bad and good fish are caught.

For the sea best typifies this world, while the fishing net appears to illustrate the communion of the one Faith or of the Church. Between heretics and bad Catholics there is this difference—that the heretics believe false things, while the latter, though believing true things, do not act as they believe.

℟. To Thee, O Lord, have I lifted up my soul: * In Thee, O my God, I put my trust, let me not be ashamed. ℣. Keep Thou my soul and deliver me. In Thee. Glory. In Thee.

✠ Continuation of the holy Gospel according to St. Matthew.— At that time Jesus spoke this parable to the multitudes: "The kingdom of heaven is like a man who sowed good seed in his field; but while men were asleep, his enemy came and sowed weeds among the wheat, and went away. And when the blade sprang up and brought forth fruit, then the weeds appeared as well. And the servants of the householder came and said to him,

'Sir, didst thou not sow good seed in thy field? How then does it have weeds?' He said to them, 'An enemy has done this.' And the servants said to him, 'Wilt thou have us go and gather them up?' 'No,' he said, 'lest in gathering the weeds you root up the wheat along with them. Let both grow together until the harvest; and at harvest time I will say to the reapers, Gather up first the weeds, and bind them in bundles to burn; but the wheat gather into my barn.'"

Let Us Pray

Protect Thy family, we beseech Thee, O Lord, by Thy constant goodness and care, that as it confides entirely in the hope of Thy heavenly grace, it may always be strengthened by Thy protection. Through our Lord.

VI SUNDAY AFTER THE EPIPHANY

I Nocturn

From the Epistle of St. Paul the Apostle to the Hebrews, c. 1, 1 - 14

II Nocturn

Sermon of St. Athanasius, Bishop

If the heretics had known the person, the matter, and the time of the words of the Apostle, they would never have spoken of the Godhead as if It were human, nor borne themselves so wickedly and foolishly towards Christ. You will be able to see this if you again consider the beginning of the lesson. For the Apostle says: "God, who at sundry times and in divers manners spoke in times past to the fathers by the prophets, last of all in these days has spoken to us by his Son."

And again, a little farther on: "When the Son had effected man's purgation from sin and taken his seat at the right hand of the Majesty on high, having become so much superior to the angels as he has inherited a more excellent name than they." The word of the Apostle makes mention of that time when God spoke to us through His Son, and when the same Son purged away our sins. For when did He speak to us through His Son, when did the Son purge away our sins, or when was He born as man, but after the prophets had spoken, that is, in these last days?

The Apostle, about to enter on the subject of the Word's human dispensation and the last days, naturally mentioned first that God had not been silent up to those days, but had spoken to the fathers by the prophets; and after the prophets had discharged their office and the law had been given through the ministry of the angels, that the Son came down to us to minister; then finally he necessarily added, "being made so much better than the angels," to show that as the Son differs from a servant, so much does the ministry of the Son excel the duty and office of servants.

The Apostle, seeing the difference between the new ministry and the old, uses great liberty of speech writing and speaking to the Jews. For this reason he does not compare the details of the two ministries, and then make the general conclusion that the new is better or more honorable than the old, (lest any should understand that the two ministries were of the same kind and that the conclusion that the new is better is arrived at by comparing the degrees in each of the things which they had in common), but he said "that the Son was made better" to distinguish at once and completely the nature of the Son from the nature of things created.

℟. Mercy and judgment I will sing unto Thee, O Lord: * I will sing and I will understand in the unspotted way when Thou shalt come unto me. ℣. I have walked in the innocence of my heart, in the midst of my house. I will sing. Glory. I will sing.

III Nocturn

The reading of the holy Gospel according to St. Matthew

At that time Jesus spoke to the multitudes this parable: "The kingdom of heaven is like to a grain of mustard seed, which a man took and sowed in his field." And so forth.

Homily of St. Jerome, Priest

The kingdom of heaven is the preaching of the Gospel and a knowledge of the Scriptures which lead to life, concerning which it was said to the Jews: "The kingdom of God shall be taken from you, and shall be given to a nation yielding the fruits thereof." Such a kingdom, therefore, is like to a grain of mustard seed which a man receiving, sowed in his field.

The man who sows the seed in his field is understood by many to be the Savior because He sows in the souls of the faithful; by others he is understood to be that man himself who sows in his own field, that is, in himself and in his own heart. Who is it that sows but our senses and our soul which, receiving the grain of preaching and nourishing it when sown, makes it by the mositure of faith to sprout forth in the field of the heart?

VI Sunday After The Epiphany

The preaching of the Gospel is the least of all exercises. Indeed for its very first doctrine the Gospel does not have even the semblance of truth, preaching as it does a man-God, Christ who died, and the proclamation of the stumbling block of the Cross. Compare such a doctrine with the tenets of philosophers, with their books and the brilliancy of their eloquence and the arrangement of their words, and you will see how much less than all these seeds is the seed of him who sows the seed of the Gospel.

Yet the former, when they have sprung up, show themselves without vigor, without spirit, without life; but altogether languid, degenerate, and soft, they develop into herbs and plants which quickly dry up and waste away. But this latter preaching (of the Gospel), which in the beginning seems small, when it is sown in the soul of the faithful or in the whole world, springs up not into a herb, but develops into a tree; so that the birds of the air (which we must understand to be the souls of the faithful or deeds of virtue performed in the service of God) come and dwell in its branches. I consider the branches of this tree of the Gospel, which sprang from the mustard seed, to be the various dogmas on which each of the above-mentioned birds rests.

℟. The Lord hath set my feet upon a rock and God hath directed my steps: * And He hath put a new song into my mouth. ℣. He hath heard my prayers: and hath brought me out of the pit of misery. And He hath. Glory. And He hath.

☩ Continuation of the holy Gospel according to St. Matthew.—
At that time Jesus spoke to the multitudes this parable: "The kingdom of heaven is like a grain of mustard seed, which a man took and sowed in his field. This indeed is the smallest of all the seeds; but when it grows up it is larger than any herb and becomes a tree, so that the birds of the air come and dwell in its branches."

He told them another parable: "The kingdom of heaven is like leaven, which a woman took and buried in three measures of flour, until all of it was leavened."

All these things Jesus spoke to the crowds in parables, and without parables he did not speak to them; in fulfillment of what was spoken through the prophet, who said, "I will open my mouth in parables, I will utter things hidden since the foundation of the world."

Let Us Pray

Grant, we beseech Thee, O almighty God, that always considering what is right, we may always please Thee by our words and actions. Through our Lord.

SEPTUAGESIMA SUNDAY

I Nocturn

From the Book of Genesis, c. 1, 1 - 26

II Nocturn

From the Enchiridion of St. Augustine, Bishop

The Lord had threatened man with the punishment of death if he would sin, giving to him free will, but in such a way that He might still rule him by His commandments, and cause him to fear by reason of his end; and He placed him in the joy of paradise as in the shadow of life, whence, having kept the commandments, he would ascend to a better life.

But Adam, having been exiled from Paradise after the sin, bound also by the punishment of death and damnation his posterity, which, by sinning, he infected in himself as in its root. Hence everyone that would be born of him and of his wife—also condemned—through whom he had sinned through carnal concupiscence and on whom a similar punishment of disobedience was inflicted, would contract original sin, by which he would be drawn through errors and various sorrows to that eternal punishment with the fallen angels and their fellow sinners and criminals.

"Thus through one man sin entered into the world and through sin death, and thus death has passed into all men because all have sinned." In this place the Apostle calls the whole human race the world. This, then, was the condition of the whole condemned mass of the human race. It lay prostrate in evil, or rather, was thrown about in evils, being cast from one evil to another, and, joined to that group of angels which had sinned, it was paying the punishment worthy of its wicked desertion.

To the just anger of God indeed pertains whatever the wicked freely do in their blind and unrestrained concupiscence and whatever they suffer unwillingly in their clear and apparent punishments; to the same it pertains—the goodness of the Creator not failing—to give life and the faculties of life to the bad angels (which ministration, if stopped, would cause them to cease to be), and to form the seed of men, even though born from a corrupt and condemned stock, and to animate them. Likewise He fits their limbs for the changing seasons of their life; He extends their knowledge in divers places, and gives them whereon to live. For He has judged it better to draw good from evil than not to permit the evil.

℞. Where is thy brother Abel? said the Lord to Cain. I know not, Lord, am I my brother's keeper? And He said to him: What hast thou done? * Behold the voice of thy brother Abel's blood crieth to Me from the earth. ℣. Cursed shalt thou be upon the earth which hath opened her mouth and received the blood of thy brother at thy hand. Behold. Glory. Behold.

III Nocturn

The reading of the holy Gospel according to St. Matthew

At that time Jesus spoke to his disciples this parable: "The kingdom of heaven is like a householder who went out early in the morning to hire laborers for his vineyard." And so forth.

Homily of St. Gregory, Pope

The kingdom of heaven is likened to a householder who hired laborers to tend his vineyard. Who has the likeness of this householder more than our Creator who governs those whom He has created, and possesses His chosen ones in this world as a master does the servants of his house? He it is who has the vineyard, namely, the universal Church, which, from the just Abel to the last of the elect who shall be born at the end of the world, has produced so many saints, as it were, as it has sent forth branches.

This householder, therefore, in order to cultivate his vineyard, hired laborers in the morning and at the third, sixth, ninth, and eleventh hours; for from the beginning of the world even to its end He does not cease to gather together preachers to instruct His faithful people. Now the early morning of the world was from Adam to Noe; and the third hour, from Noe to Abraham; the sixth hour, from Abraham to Moses; the ninth, from Moses to the coming of our Lord; the eleventh, from the coming of the Lord till the end of the world. In which last hour the holy Apostles have been sent as preachers, and albeit they came late, they have received a full reward.

For the instruction of His people, therefore,—as it were to cultivate His vineyard—the Lord never ceases to send out laborers. For, indeed, when He nurtured the moral uprightness of His people, in the beginning through the patriarchs, later on through the doctors of the law, and finally through the Apostles, He worked as it were through the instrumentality of laborers in the cultivation of His vineyard; on the other hand, each one who in any way or measure, with upright intention, has been a preacher by good example, is a laborer in that vineyard.

Therefore, the workman of the morning, be it of the third, sixth, or ninth hour, is a figure of that ancient and Hebraic people who from the beginning of the world—in their chosen ones—did not desist from laboring in the cultivation of the vineyard in so far as they ceased not to be zealous in worshipping God with the true faith. But at this eleventh hour the Gentiles are called to whom it is also said: "Why stand ye here all the day idle?"

℟. In the beginning God created heaven and earth, and the Spirit of God moved over the waters: * And God saw all things that He had made, and they were very good. ℣. So the heavens and the earth were finished and all the furniture of them. And God. Glory. And God.

✠ Continuation of the holy Gospel according to St. Matthew.—At that time Jesus spoke to his disciples this parable: "The kingdom of heaven is like a householder who went out early in the morning to hire laborers for his vineyard. And having agreed with the laborers for a denarius a day, he sent them into his vineyard. And about the third hour, he went out and saw others standing in the market place idle; and he said to them, 'Go you also into the vineyard, and I will give you whatever is just.' So they went. And again he went out about the sixth, and about the ninth hour, and did as before. But about the eleventh hour he went out and found others standing, and he said to them, 'Why do you stand here all day idle?' They said to him, 'Because no man has hired us.' He said to them, 'Go you also into the vineyard.' But when evening had come, the owner of the vineyard said to his steward, 'Call the laborers, and pay them their wages, beginning from the last even to the first.' Now when they of the eleventh hour came, they received each a denarius. And when the first in their turn came, they thought that they would receive more; but they also received each his denarius. And on receiving it, they began to murmur against the householder, saying, 'These last have worked a single hour, and thou hast put them on a level with us, who have borne the burden of the day's heat.' But answering one of them, he said, 'Friend, I do thee no injustice; didst thou not agree with me for a denarius? Take what is thine and go; I choose to give to this last even as to thee. Have I not a right to do what I choose? Or art thou envious because I am generous?' Even so the last shall be first, and the first last; for many are called, but few are chosen."

SEXAGESIMA SUNDAY

LET US PRAY

Graciously hear, we beseech Thee, O Lord, the prayers of Thy people, that we who justly suffer for our sins may be delivered for the glory of Thy name. Through our Lord.

SEXAGESIMA SUNDAY

I Nocturn

From the Book of Genesis, c. 5, 31; c. 6, 1 - 15

II Nocturn

From the Book of St. Ambrose, Bishop, on Noe and the Ark

We read that the Lord was angry. For although He thought, that is, He knew, that man, being placed on the earth and bearing a body, was not able to be without sin (because the earth is, as it were, a certain place of temptation, and the flesh a lure to corruption); still, even though men possessed a mind capable of reasoning and the power of the soul infused into the body, without any deliberation they rushed to their ruin, from which they did not wish to recall themselves.

God does not think as man—as if some new thought should come to Him—nor does He become angry, as if He were changeable;. rather these things are said in order that the awfulness of our sins might be demonstrated, which merit even the divine displeasure—as if our fault increases to such an extent that even God, who by nature is not moved by anger or hatred or any passion, would seem to be provoked to wrath.

He threatened, moreover, to destroy mankind. "From man," He says, "even to beast, and from the creeping things even to the fowls of the air I shall destroy them." What offense had the irrational things given? Yet, because they had been made for man, when he for whom they had been made was ruined, it had to follow that they also be destroyed, for there was no one to use them. But in a higher sense this is made manifest, that man is a being capable of reason. For man is defined as an animal—living, mortal, rational. Thus when the highest species of animal has been destroyed, why should the lower species remain? Why should anything be preserved alive when virtue, the basis of salvation, was no more.

However, with regard to the destruction of the rest of things (besides man) and to the manifestation of the divine love, Noe is said to have obtained a hearing before God. At the same time it is shown that the offense of other men does not overshadow the just man, since this latter alone is preserved for the propagation of the race. He is praised not for his nobility of birth, but for the merits of his justice and perfection. For the family of an upright man is a race of strength, because just as men are the offspring of men, so virtues are the offspring of minds. The families of men are ennobled by the splendor of their lineage, while the grace of souls is glorified by the splendor of their virtue.

℟. I will set My bow in the clouds, said the Lord to Noe: * And I will remember My covenant which I made with you. ℣. And when I shall cover the sky with clouds, My bow shall appear in the clouds. And I will. Glory. And I will.

III Nocturn

The reading of the holy Gospel according to St. Luke

At that time, when a very great crowd was gathering together and men from every town were resorting to Jesus, he said in a parable: "The sower went out to sow his seed." And so forth.

Homily of St. Gregory, Pope

The lesson from the holy Gospel which you, dearly beloved brethren, have just heard does not stand in need of explanation, but rather of a word of caution. For what Truth itself has expounded let no human frailty debate over. It is a duty, however, that we consider carefully what is contained in this exposition of our Lord. For if we should tell you that the seed signifies the word of God; the field signifies the world; the birds, the devil; and the thorns, riches; perhaps your mind would hesitate to believe us.

Whence, indeed, this same Lord Himself has deigned to explain what He spoke so that you might learn to seek also the meanings of those things He did not wish to explain Himself. By explaining, therefore, what He said, He showed that He spoke figuratively, in order that He might confirm us when our weakness would unveil to you the hidden meaning of His words.

For who would ever believe me if I should dare to call riches thorns? Most especially since the latter prick us while the former delight us. And yet riches are thorns for they torture the mind with the prickings of the thought of them. And when they entice one even to sin, they make one bleed as with an inflicted wound. By riches, in this place, according to the testimony of another Evangelist, the Lord evidently does not refer to riches, but to the deceitfulness of riches.

For deceitful is that which cannot remain with us for long; deceitful that which does not dispel the want of our mind. But those alone are true riches which make us rich in *virtues*. Therefore, dearly beloved brethren, if you desire to be rich, *love true riches*. If you are in quest of true honor, strive after a heavenly kingdom. If you prize the glory of high positions, hasten to be enlisted in that exalted court of the angels. Hold fast in your mind the words of the Lord perceived by the ear. For the food of the mind is the word of God. A word once heard and not retained in the interior of the mind is like food once eaten and thrown forth by a sick stomach. But we must indeed despair of the life of him who does not retain his food.

℟. When a very great multitude was gathered together to Jesus and had hastened out of the cities unto Him, He spoke by a similitude: * The sower went out to sow his seed. ℣. And as he sowed, some fell upon good ground and, being sprung up, yielded fruit a hundredfold. The sower. Glory. The sower.

✠ Continuation of the holy Gospel according to St. Luke.— At that time, when a very great crowd was gathering together and men from every town were resorting to Jesus, he said in a parable: "The sower went out to sow his seed. And as he sowed, some seed fell by the wayside and was trodden under foot, and the birds of the air ate it up. And other seed fell upon the rock, and as soon as it had sprung up it withered away, because it had no moisture. And other seed fell among thorns, and the thorns sprang up with it and choked it. And other seed fell upon good ground, and sprang up and yielded fruit a hundredfold." As he said these things he cried out, "He who has ears to hear, let him hear!"

But his disciples then began to ask him what this parable meant. He said to them, "To you it is given to know the mystery of the kingdom of God, but to the rest in parables, that 'Seeing they may not see, and hearing they may not understand.'

"Now the parable is this: the seed is the word of God. And those by the wayside are they who have heard; then the devil comes and takes away the word from their heart, that they may not believe and be saved. Now those upon the rock are they who, when they have heard, receive the word with joy; and these have no root, but believe for a while, and in time of temptation fall away. And that which fell among the thorns, these are they who have heard, and as they go their way are choked by the cares and riches and pleasures of life, and their fruit does not ripen. But that upon good ground, these are they who, with a right and good heart, having heard the word, hold it fast, and bear fruit in patience."

LET US PRAY

O God, Thou who dost see that we do not trust in the merit of our own actions, mercifully grant that we may be preserved from all adversities by the protection of the Teacher of the Gentiles. Through our Lord.

QUINQUAGESIMA SUNDAY

I Nocturn

From the Book of Genesis, c. 12, 1 - 19

II Nocturn

From the Book of St. Ambrose, Bishop, on the Patriarch Abraham

Abraham was an outstanding man, remarkable for his great and many virtues, of whom philosophy can find no equal among its votaries. What it pretends is less than what he did; and his simple belief of the truth is greater than the ambitious fiction of eloquence. Therefore, let us consider what sort of devotion was in this man.

That virtue, then, is first in order which is the foundation of the others. Rightly does God demand it of him, saying: "Go out from your land and your kindred and your father's house." It was sufficient to have said, "from your land," for that implied leaving kindred and home. But He therefore added the demands individually that He might try his devotion, lest by chance either he might seem to have set out imprudently or some fraud might be intended in the heavenly commands.

But just as numerous commandments have been laid before him lest anything remain hidden, so too rewards are placed before him lest perhaps he despair. He is tested in his fortitude; he is urged on in his fidelity; he is called upon in his justice; and rightly does he set out, as the Lord had told him. "And Lot went with him." To follow God—this is what is attributed to a great man among the seven sayings of the wise men. Abraham accomplished and anticipated by act the words of the wise, and, following God, he departed from his own land.

But because previously he had dwelt in another land, that is, the region of the Chaldeans, from which Thare, the father of

Abraham, had migrated, journeying into Haran, and because he to whom it had been said, "go out from thy kindred," took with him his nephew, let us consider whether to go out from one's own land may not, perhaps, be to depart from the dwelling of this earth, that is, of our body, from which Paul went out, who said: "Our conversation is in heaven."

℟. The Angel of the Lord called unto Abraham saying: * Lay not thy hand upon the boy, for thou fearest God. ℣. When he stretched forth his hand to slay his son, behold, the Angel of the Lord called unto him from heaven and said. Lay not. Glory. Lay not.

III Nocturn

The reading of the holy Gospel according to St. Luke

At that time Jesus, taking to himself the Twelve said to them, "Behold, we are going up to Jerusalem, and all things that have been written through the prophets concerning the Son of Man will be accomplished." And so forth.

Homily of St. Gregory, Pope

Our Redeemer, foreseeing that the minds of His disciples would be perturbed at His Passion, foretold to them long before both the ignominy of that same Passion and the glory of His Resurrection, so that when they would see Him dying, as He had foretold, they would not doubt that He would also rise again. But because the disciples, being as yet carnal, could not grasp the words of the mystery, He had recourse to a miracle. Before their very eyes the blind man received his sight, so that heavenly deeds might strengthen in the faith those who could not grasp the words of the heavenly mystery.

But the miracles of our Lord and Savior should so be understood, dearly beloved brethren, that on the one hand the deeds themselves are truly believed, and on the other, that they contain some mystic interpretation for our instruction. Indeed His works show forth one thing by their power and speak of another in symbol. For behold, who this blind man was historically we do not know, but yet we do know what he signifies mystically.

Truly blind is the human race which, once expelled from the joys of Paradise in the person of its first parent, now suffers the darkness of its own damnation, being ignorant of the brightness of divine light! It is, nevertheless, so illuminated by the presence of its Redeemer that it already sees by anticipation the joys of the internal light and makes strides on the way of a life of good works. It must be noted, however, that the blind man is illumined when Jesus is said to approach Jericho. Now the word Jericho means *the moon;* but the moon in sacred writing is used for carnal fickleness inasmuch as, while it decreases in its monthly phases, it signifies the changeableness of our mortality.

Therefore, whilst our Maker draws nigh to Jericho, the blind man returns to the light; for whilst divinity took on the weakness of our flesh, the human race received the light which it had lost. When God suffers human things, then man is lifted to divine things. And the blind man is rightly described as sitting by the wayside and as a beggar. For Truth Itself says: "I am the Way."

℟. A blind man sat by the wayside as the Lord passed by and cried out to Him: and the Lord said to him: * What wilt thou that I do for thee? Lord, that I may receive my sight. ℣. And Jesus standing, commanded him to be brought unto Him: and when he was come near, He asked him saying. What. Glory. What.

✢ Continuation of the holy Gospel according to St. Luke.— At that time Jesus, taking to himself the Twelve said to them, "Behold, we are going up to Jerusalem, and all things that have been written through the prophets concerning the Son of Man will be accomplished. For he will be delivered to the Gentiles, and will be mocked and scourged and spit upon; and after they have scourged him, they will put him to death; and on the third day he will rise again."

And they understood none of these things and this saying was hidden from them, neither did they get to know the things that were being said.

Now it came to pass as he drew near to Jericho, that a certain blind man was sitting by the wayside, begging; but hearing a crowd passing by, he inquired what this might be. And they told him that Jesus of Nazareth was passing by. And he cried out, saying, "Jesus, Son of David, have mercy on me!" And they who went in front angrily tried to silence him. But he cried out all the louder, "Son of David, have mercy on me!" Then Jesus stopped and commanded that he should be brought to him. And when he drew near, he asked him, saying, "What wouldst thou have me do for thee?" And he said, "Lord, that I may see." And Jesus said to him, "Receive thy sight, thy faith has saved thee." And at once he received his sight, and followed him, glorifying God. And all the people upon seeing it gave praise to God.

LET US PRAY

Graciously hear our prayers, we beseech Thee, O Lord, and having freed us from the bonds of our sins, protect us from all adversity. Through our Lord.

ASH WEDNESDAY

The reading of the holy Gospel according to St. Matthew

At that time Jesus said to his disciples: "When you fast, do not look gloomy like the hypocrites." And so forth.

Homily of St. Augustine, Bishop

From these precepts it is clearly shown that all our attention is to be directed to interior joys, lest, whilst seking a reward in exterior things, we conform ourselves to this world and lose the promise of that happiness (which is more genuine and lasting the more interior it is) in which God has chosen us to be made conformable to the image of His Son. We must, moreover, note in this chapter of the Gospel that pride can have a place not only in the splendor and pomp of earthly things, but even in unkempt mourning garments. And this latter is more full of dangers since it hides under the name of worship of God.

He who is conspicuous for immoderate care of his body, for his dress, or for the brilliance of other things is easily convicted of being a votary of the splendor of the world by these very traits, and misleads no one by deceitful imitation of sanctity. But, because our Lord commanded us to beware of wolves in sheep's clothing, saying, "By their fruits you shall know them," he who, professing Christianity, draws the eyes of men to himself by his unusual filth and soiled apparel (provided he is not constrained by necessity, but does this of his own accord) can be judged from the rest of his actions whether he acts thus from contempt of superfluous care or from a certain secret ambition.

For when, by a few tests, those very advantages which they have obtained or desire to obtain by that subterfuge begin to be taken away, then it is made manifest whether they are wolves in sheep's clothing or sheep in their own. Yet a Christian does not have to delight the gazes of men by undue superfluities because of the fact that very often hypocrites also don a very poor and needy garb in order to deceive the unwary; just as those sheep need not put off their own clothing if it happens at times that wolves hide themselves in them.

THURSDAY

The reading of the holy Gospel according to St. Matthew

At that time, when Jesus had entered Capharnaum, there came to him a centurion who entreated him, saying, "Lord, my servant is lying sick in the house, paralyzed, and is grievously afflicted." And so forth.

Homily of St. Augustine, Bishop

Let us see whether Matthew and Luke agree among themselves concerning this servant of the centurion. For Matthew says: "A centurion came to Him, asking and saying: My servant lieth at home sick of the palsy." This seems to be opposed to what Luke says: "And when he had heard about Jesus, he sent to him the ancients of the Jews asking him to come and heal his servant. And when they had come to Jesus, they earnestly asked him, saying to him: 'He is worthy that Thou shouldst do this for him. For he loves our nation, and he has built us a synagogue' And Jesus went with them. And when he was not far from the house, the centurion sent his friends to him, saying, 'Lord, trouble not Thyself, for I am not worthy that Thou shouldst enter under my roof.'"

For if this happened thus, how shall that be true which Matthew says, "A certain centurion came to him," when he did not come, but sent his friends, unless we, observing diligently, understand that Matthew has not entirely abandoned the customary manner of speaking? For not only are we accustomed to say that someone has come, even before he has reached the place to which he is said to have come,—and in this way also we say that one makes little or great progress towards that which he desires to attain—but we also often say that the interview itself, for the sake of which one goes, has already been had, even though he who seeks it does not actually see the one whom he is said to have interviewed, since he reaches him whose favor is necessary for him through the agency of a friend. The custom is such that even they are called *perventores* (ones who arrive), who, in their artful ambition, attain by the intervention of suitable persons to the nearly inaccessible favor of powerful men.

So then, though the centurion approached the Lord by other men, Matthew wished to put it briefly, saying: "The centurion came to him." Nevertheless, the profundity of the holy Evangelist's mystic speech ought not to be considered carelessly, as it is written in the psalm: "Come ye to him and be enlightened." Therefore, because the Lord praised the Centurion's faith (by which one truly comes to Jesus), saying, "I have not found such great faith in Israel," the Evangelist wisely chose to say that the Centurion himself had come to Christ rather than those by whom the message had been sent.

FRIDAY

The reading of the holy Gospel according to St. Matthew

At that time Jesus said to his disciples: "You have heard that it was said, 'Thou shalt love thy neighbor, and shalt hate thy enemy.'" And so forth.

Homily of St. Jerome, Priest

"But I say to you: Love your enemies, do good to them that hate you." Many men in their ignorance, not thinking of the virtues of holy persons, consider the commandments of God which have been prescribed to be impossible, and they say that it is virtuous enough not to hate one's enemies, but that to be commanded to love them is more than human nature can bear. It must, therefore, be understood that Christ did not command the impossible, but rather the perfect things. David performed these things towards Saul and towards Absalom; Stephen the Martyr also prayed for his enemies who stoned him, and Paul wished to be cursed in place of his persecutors. These things, too, Jesus taught and did, saying: "Father, forgive them, for they know not what they do."

"That you may be the children of your Father who is in heaven." If one is made a child of God by keeping the commandments, he is then not a child by nature, but through his free will. "Therefore when thou dost an alms-deed, sound not a trumpet before thee, as the hypocrites do in the synagogues and in the streets that they may be honored by men." He who sounds a trumpet in working charity is a hypocrite. He who saddens his face when fasting, in order to show the emptiness of his stomach by his countenance, is also a hypocrite. He who prays in the synagogue and on the corners of the streets in order to be seen by men, is likewise a hypocrite.

From all these examples it is gathered that they are hypocrites who do a thing in order to be honored by men. It seems to me that he also is a hypocrite who says to his brother: "Let me cast out the speck from thy eye"; for it appears that he does this for glory, so that he might seem to be a just man. Wherefore it is said to that man by the Lord: "Hypocrite, take out first the beam from thine own eye." For it is not the act of virtue that has value before God, but the reason for that act. And if you shall stray from the right path but a little, it does not matter whether you go to the right or to the left, since you have lost the true way.

SATURDAY

The reading of the holy Gospel according to St. Mark

At that time, when it was late, the ship was in the midst of the sea, and Jesus alone on the land. And so forth.

Homily of St. Bede the Venerable, Priest

The toil of the disciples in rowing and the winds contrary to them signify the many labors of holy Church, which, under the waves of the opposing world and the wind of the unclean spirits strives to come to the quiet of the heavenly fatherland as to her true haven. Thus it is well said that "the ship was in the midst of the sea, and he alone on the shore," because at times the Church of the Gentiles is not only afflicted by such great persecutions, but even disfigured, so that, if it were possible, the Redeemer would truly seem to have abandoned her for a time.

Whence is that voice of her who has been caught amidst the waves and storms of onrushing temptations and who cries for the help of His protection in mournful lament: "Why, O Lord, hast thou retired afar off? Why dost thou slight us in our wants, in trouble?" In like manner does she expose the voice of the persecuting fiend, adding in the following verses of that psalm: "For he hath said in his heart: God hath forgotten; he hath turned away his face not to see at all."

But He does not forget the prayer of the poor; neither does He turn His face from those who place their trust in Him. But He rather aids them who are struggling with their enemies to conquer, and He crowns them as victors forever. Wherefore it is also clearly stated that He saw them "laboring in rowing." Indeed the Lord beholds them laboring in the sea, although He is on the shore. For though He may seem to defer for a time in extending help to those who are troubled, nevertheless He strengthens them in respect to their love lest they faint in tribulations. And at times He even frees them by His manifest help, overwhelming their adversaries as the rolling waves were walked upon and made calm.

I SUNDAY IN LENT

I Nocturn

From the second Epistle of St. Paul the Apostle to the Corinthians, c. 6, 1 - 16; c. 7, 4 - 9

II Nocturn

Sermon of St. Leo, Pope

About to preach to you, dearly beloved, the holiest and greatest of fasts, what beginning could I more fittingly use than the words of the Apostle, through whom Christ Himself has spoken, saying: "Behold, now is the acceptable time, now is the day of salvation." For though there is no season which is not full of divine gifts and though free access to God's mercy is ever provided for us by His grace, yet now the minds of all should be moved with greater zeal to spiritual progress and be animated with fuller confidence—now when the return of that day on which we have all been redeemed invites us to every work of piety, so that, cleansed both in body and in mind, we may celebrate that mystery which surpasses all others—the Lord's Passion.

Such great mysteries justly lay claim to such a lasting devotion and abiding reverence that we should remain such in the sight of God as we ought to be found on the Paschal feast itself. But because such fervor is had but by few, and since the more severe discipline is relaxed because of the frailty of the flesh and our attention is divided among the many actions of this life, even the hearts of religious men must necessarily become soiled by the dust of worldly things. Hence it has been provided in the great wisdom of the divine plan that, in order to restore purity of mind, we should be chastened by the training of these forty days, during which pious works should redeem and chaste fasting melt away the faults of other times.

Therefore, dearly beloved, since we are about to enter upon these mystic days, instituted in a most sacred manner for the purifying of both soul and body, let us take care to obey the Apostolic precepts, cleansing ourselves from all defilement of flesh and spirit, so that, chastened by the struggles that go on between flesh and spirit, the soul, which under God's direction should be the established ruler of the body, may obtain the grace of self-control, that, giving no offense to any man, we may not be exposed to the reproaches of those who revile us.

For we shall justly be blamed by unbelievers, and the tongues of the wicked will arm themselves with our vices to the injury of religion, if the manners of those fasting do not show forth the purity of perfect continence. For the excellence of our fast does not consist merely in abstinence from food, nor is meat fruitfully denied to the body unless the mind be recalled from evil.

℟. The season of the fast opened to us the gates of heaven: let us enter therein with prayer and supplication: * That on the day of the Resurrection we may rejoice with the Lord. ℣. In all things let us approve ourselves as the ministers of God in much patience. That. Glory. That.

III Nocturn

The reading of the holy Gospel according to St. Matthew

At that time Jesus was led into the desert by the Spirit, to be tempted by the devil. And after fasting forty days and forty nights, he was hungry. And so forth.

Homily of St. Gregory, Pope

There are generally some who are not certain by what spirit Jesus was led into the desert because of this which is added: "The devil took him up into the holy city"; and again: "He took him up into a very high mountain." But in reality and beyond question, it is fittingly believed that He was led into the desert by the Holy Spirit—that His own Spirit led Him there where the evil spirit found Him in order to tempt Him.

But behold, when it is said that the God-man was taken by the devil upon a high mountain and into the holy city, the mind is loath to believe it; human ears tremble to hear it. Nevertheless, we know these facts are not incredible if we but consider the other things done to Him by the devil through his members.

Certainly the head of all evil is the devil, and all the wicked are the members of this head. For was not Pilate a member of the devil? Were not the Jews who persecuted Christ and the soldiers who crucified Him members of the devil? Why wonder, then, that He permitted Himself to be taken upon a high mountain by him by whose members He suffered Himself to be crucified? It is not, therefore, unworthy of our Redeemer, who had come to be put to death, that He willed to be tempted. On the contrary, it was fitting that thus by His own temptations He might vanquish ours, just as He had come to conquer our death by His own.

I Sunday In Lent

But we ought to know that a temptation develops in three stages: by suggestion, by pleasure, and by consent. And we, when we are tempted, are very often drawn into pleasure or even into consent, for, having been begotten in a sin of the flesh, we even carry about in ourselves that from which we suffer conflict. God, indeed, who, having taken flesh in the womb of the Virgin, came into this world without sin, permitted in Himself no contradiction. Consequently by suggestion He could be tempted; but no pleasure took hold of His mind. And for this reason that whole diabolic temptation was external, not internal.

℟. God hath given His Angels charge over Thee to keep Thee in all Thy ways: * In their hands they will bear Thee up, lest Thou dash Thy foot against a stone. ℣. Thou shalt walk upon the asp and the basilisk and Thou shalt trample under foot the lion and the dragon. In their hands. Glory. In their hands.

✠ Continuation of the holy Gospel according to St. Matthew.— At that time Jesus was led into the desert by the Spirit, to be tempted by the devil. And after fasting forty days and forty nights, he was hungry. And the tempter came and said to him, "If thou art the Son of God, command that these stones become loaves of bread." But he answered and said, "It is written, 'Not by bread alone does man live, but by every word that comes forth from the mouth of God.'"

Then the devil took him into the holy city and set him on the pinnacle of the temple, and said to him, "If thou art the Son of God, throw thyself down; for it is written, 'He will give his angels charge concerning thee; and upon their hands they shall bear thee up, lest thou dash thy foot against a stone.'" Jesus said to him, "It is written further, 'Thou shalt not tempt the Lord thy God.'"

Again, the devil took him to a very high mountain, and showed him all the kingdoms of the world and the glory of them. And he said to him, "All these things will I give thee, if thou wilt fall down and worship me." Then Jesus said to him, "Begone, Satan! for it is written, 'The Lord thy God shalt thou worship and him only shalt thou serve.'" Then the devil left him; and behold angels came and ministered to him.

Let Us Pray

O God, who dost purify Thy Church by the annual observance of Lent, grant to Thy family that what it seeks to obtain from Thee by fasting, it may secure by good works. Through our Lord.

MONDAY

The reading of the holy Gospel according to St. Matthew

At that time Jesus said to his disciples: "When the Son of Man shall come in his majesty, and all the angels with him, then he will sit on the throne of his glory; and before him will be gathered all the nations." And so forth.

Homily of St. Augustine, Bishop

If, without having observed the commandments, one is able to attain eternal life by faith alone—which without good works is dead—how will that be true which He will say to those whom He will place on His left: "Go ye into eternal fire which has been prepared for the devil and his angels"? not rebuking them for their unbelief but because they have not done good works. For lest anyone promise himself eternal life by reason of his faith—which without good works is dead—He went on to say that He would separate all nations, even those which, being mingled together, were using the same pastures, that it might be evident that it was those who had believed in Him but had not taken pains to do good works—as though they could attain unto eternal life by means of that same dead faith—that would say to Him: "Lord, when did we see thee suffering such and such afflictions and did not minister to thee?"

Shall they perhaps who have not performed works of mercy go into eternal fire, and they who have taken away the things of others not go? Or, shall those not go who by corrupting the temple of God within themselves have been unmerciful to themselves—as though works of mercy were of any profit without love when the Apostle says: "If I distribute all my goods to the poor, but have not charity, it availeth me nothing"? Or can anyone who does not love himself love his neighbor as himself? For "he that loveth iniquity hateth his own soul."

Nor can that be said here by which some deceive themselves: that the fire has been called eternal but not the burning itself. They think that those to whom they promise salvation through fire by reason of their dead faith, will pass through fire which is eternal, but, though the fire itself is eternal, their burning—that is, the action of the fire upon them—is not everlasting. Wherefore our Lord, foreseeing this, concluded His sentence with these words: "They will go into everlasting fire, but the just into eternal life." Therefore, the burning as well as the fire will be eternal. And Truth says that they will go into it whose good works, and not faith, He has declared wanting.

TUESDAY

The reading of the holy Gospel according to St. Matthew

At that time, when Jesus entered Jerusalem, all the city was thrown into commotion, saying, "Who is this?" And so forth.

Homily of St. Bede the Venerable, Priest

What the Lord signified by cursing the fig tree, this same He showed more clearly by casting the impious men from the temple. For the tree did nothing wrong in not having fruit when the Lord was hungry, since its season had not yet come. But the priests did sin who carried on worldly affairs in the house of the Lord, and who omitted to bear the fruit of love which they owed, and which the Lord hungered after in them. By cursing it the Lord dried up the tree, that men, seeing or hearing these things, might much better understand that they will be condemned by divine judgment if, without the fruit of works, they are flattered by applause for their religious speech alone, which resembles, as it were, the sound and appearance of green leaves.

But, because they did not understand, He consequently applied the severity of their merited punishment to them, and He threw the business transactions of mankind out of that house in which it was commanded that only divine things be done, sacrifices and prayers be offered, the Word of God be read, heard and sung. And indeed it must be believed that He found that those things only were sold and bought in the temple which were necessary to the ministry of the temple itself—according to that which we read elsewhere, when, entering the same temple, He found in it men selling and buying sheep, cattle, doves—because they who had come from afar were without doubt buying from the townsmen all these things only that they might be offered in the house of the Lord.

If therefore the Lord did not even wish those things to be sold in the temple which He wished to be offered in the temple because of avarice and fraud, which is the vice proper to business men, with what great punishment do you think he would afflict those whom He found idling there in laughter and vain chatter or giving themselves up to any other vice? For if those temporal transactions which they were able to carry on freely elsewhere were not permitted by the Lord to be done in His house, how much more do those things which are never permitted merit the wrath of heaven, if they are done in temples consecrated to God? But because the Holy Spirit appeared above the Lord as a dove, rightly are the gifts of the Holy Spirit signified by doves. But who are they who today sell doves in the temple of God but those who take pay for the imposition of hands, through which the Holy Spirit is given from heaven?

EMBER WEDNESDAY

The reading of the holy Gospel according to St. Matthew

At that time certain of the Scribes and Pharisees answered him, saying, "Master, we would see a sign from thee." And so forth.

Homily of St. Ambrose, Bishop

By the rejection of the Jewish nation is evidently expressed the mystery of the Church, which is gathered from all the ends of the earth—in the Ninivites through penance, and in the Queen of the South through the desire of obtaining wisdom—to hear the words of the peaceful Solomon. For the Church is truly a queen, whose kingdom is undivided, rising up out of various and distant nations into one body.

Thus that is an excellent figure of Christ and the Church; however, this is greater, because before it was only in figure, but now it is truly verified. In the former, Solomon is a type, but here Christ is present in His body. The Church consists of two classes of people: those who know not how to sin, and those who have ceased to sin. For penance wipes sin away and knowledge guards against it.

Moreover, the sign of Jonas, as a figure of the Lord's Passion, is also a testimony of the grave sins which the Jews committed. At the same time we may see in these words of our Lord a declaration of His power and a sign of His love. For by the example of the Ninivites both the punishment is foretold and a way of escape is pointed out. Hence even the Jews ought not to despair if they are willing to do penance.

THURSDAY

The reading of the holy Gospel according to St. Matthew

At that time Jesus went forth and retired into the coasts of Tyre and Sidon. And so forth.

Homily of St. Jerome, Priest

Upon leaving the calumniating Scribes and Pharisees, Christ proceeds into Tyre and Sidon in order to cure those inhabitants.

However, a woman of Canaan comes from these ancient lands, crying out in order to obtain health for her daughter. Observe that in the fifteenth place the daughter of the Canaanite is healed. "Have mercy on me, O Lord, thou Son of David." Thence she knew to call Him "Son of David," because she had already gone out of her land and had departed from the error of Tyre and Sidon by a change of place and faith.

"My daughter is grievously troubled by a devil." I think the daughter of the Canaanite is an image of the souls of unbelievers, who are grievously troubled by the devil, who recognize not their Creator and adore a stone. Christ answered her not a word, not because of Pharisaical pride, or arrogance such as that of the Scribes, but in order that He might not appear to contradict what He had commanded: "Go ye not into the way of the Gentiles, and into the city of the Samaritans enter ye not." For He did not wish to give an occasion to calumniators, and He reserved the perfect healing of the Gentiles until the time of His Passion and Resurrection.

And His disciples came and besought Him, saying: "Send her away, for she crieth after us." The disciples, being then still ignorant of the secret plans of the Lord, either moved by pity, or wishing to be rid of her importunity—for she was crying out repeatedly as though he were a harsh physician and not one full of mercy—pleaded for the woman of Canaan, whom the other Evangelist calls a Syro-Phoenician. And He answering, said: "I was not sent except to the sheep that are lost of the house of Israel." Not that He was not sent to the Gentiles, but that in the first place He was sent to the Israelites, in order that when they would not receive the Gospel, it would be just to change over to the Gentiles.

EMBER FRIDAY

The reading of the holy Gospel according to St. John

At that time there was a feast of the Jews, and Jesus went up to Jerusalem. And so forth.

Homily of St. Augustine, Bishop

Let us see what He wished to signify in that one whom He, keeping the mystery of unity, deigned to heal from among so many sick. He found in the years of this man's infirmity a number of infirmity. The man had been sick for thirty-eight years. How this number pertains more to infirmity than to health must be a little more diligently explained. I want you to be attentive; our Lord will help us, in order that I may speak appropriately and that you may hear with profit. The number forty is commended to us as being sacred by reason of a certain perfection; I think you already have a knowledge of this; the divine writings refer to it very frequently. You know well that fasting is made sacred by this number. Moses fasted for forty days, and Elias did the same; Jesus Christ, our Lord and Savior, Himself fulfilled this number in His own fasting. Through Moses is signified the Law; through Elias are signified the Prophets, and through our Lord is signified the Gospel. Therefore three appeared on the mount where Christ showed Himself to the disciples in the brilliancy of His countenance and His garments; for He appeared standing between Moses and Elias, as if the Gospel were receiving testimony from the Law and the Prophets.

Therefore, whether in the Law or in the Prophets or in the Gospel, this number is recommended to us in fasting. Now fasting, in its wide and general sense, is to abstain from iniquity and the illicit pleasures of the world—this is the perfect fast, that, as St. Paul says, "rejecting ungodliness and worldly lusts, we may live temperately and justly and piously in this world." What reward does the Apostle attach to this fast? Continuing, he says: "looking for the blessed hope and glorious coming of our great God and Savior." Therefore, in this world we practice, as it were, these forty days of abstinence when we live well and when we abstain from evil and illicit pleasures; and because this abstinence will not be without reward, we await that blessed hope and revelation of the glory of our great God and our Savior Jesus Christ. In that hope—since the fast is kept out of hope—we shall receive a denarius as a reward. For this reward is given to those workmen laboring in the vineyard according to the Gospel, which I trust you recall, for not all things must be recounted for you as for the rude and unlearned. Therefore, a denarius, which gets its name from the number ten, will be given, and ten added to forty makes fifty: wherefore, we spend Quadragesima—forty days—before the Pasch in penance, and Quinquagesima—fifty days—after the Pasch in joy, as though having received our reward.

Bear in mind that I am considering the number thirty-eight— the years of the sick man. I wish to expound why that number thirty-eight pertains rather to sickness than to health. Now charity fulfills the Law, and, as I said, in all works the number forty pertains to the fullness of the Law. In charity, moreover, two precepts are recommended to us: "Thou shalt love the Lord Thy God with Thy whole strength; and thou shalt love thy neighbor as thyself." Rightly, then, did the widow cast two mites—all her possessions—into the offerings of God; rightly did the innkeeper receive two coins for the injured man, wounded by the robbers, that he might be healed; rightly did Jesus remain two days with the Samaritans in order to strengthen them in charity. Thus, since good is signified by the number two, a twofold charity is especially recommended. If, then, the number forty has the perfection of the Law and the Law is not fulfilled except in the twofold precept of charity, why do you wonder that he who was two years less than forty was infirm?

EMBER SATURDAY

The reading of the holy Gospel according to St. Matthew

At that time Jesus took Peter, James and his brother John, and led them up a high mountain by themselves, and was transfigured before them. And so forth.

Homily of St. Leo, Pope

Dearly beloved, the Gospel reading which, entering in by our bodily ears, has knocked at the door of our inner mind, calls us to a consideration of a great mystery, which through the inspiration of God's grace we may more easily accomplish if we will turn our attention back to those things which have been narrated shortly before this. For the Savior of the human race, Jesus Christ, in instituting that faith which calls the wicked to justice and the dead to life, imbues His disciples with the instructions of His doctrine and the wonders of His works for the purpose that the same Christ should be believed to be both the only-begotten Son of God and the Son of man. For one of these without the other does not help towards salvation, and it is an equal loss that the Lord Jesus Christ should be believed to be either God only, without being man, or man only, without being God. Both must be acknowledged together, because as the true humanity was in God, so the true divinity was in the Man.

Therefore, in order to confirm the most salutary avowal of this faith, our Lord asked His disciples which among the diverse opinions of others concerning Him they themselves believed, or what they thought. Whereupon Peter the Apostle, through the revelation of the Almighty Father, passing beyond bodily things and transcending the human, beheld with the eyes of his mind the Son of the living God, and he gave praise to the glory of His divinity; for he did not look at the substance of flesh and blood alone, and he took such great delight in the sublimity of this faith, that, endowed with the happiness of eternal life, he received the sacred firmness of the inviolable rock, being founded upon which, the Church should prevail over the gates of hell and the laws of death; and neither in the loosing or binding of any cases whatsoever should anything else be ratified in heaven than what had rested in the judgment of Peter.

But, dearly beloved, the loftiness of Peter's admirable understanding had to be instructed in a mystery of lesser moment lest the faith of the Apostle, having been raised to the glory of confessing the divinity in Christ, should judge the taking on of our own lowliness as unworthy and unbefitting the immutable Deity, and thus should believe that the human nature had already been glorified in Christ, so that it could neither be affected by suffering, nor destroyed by death. And therefore—when our Lord said that it behoved Him to go to Jerusalem, and that He should suffer many things from the elders and the Scribes, and the chief priests, that He should be killed and should rise the third day—when Peter, who, being illumined by heavenly light, had burned in ardent praise of the Son of God, had—as he thought—with a pious and deliberate mind remonstrated against the ignominies of mockery and the opprobrium of a most cruel death, being corrected by the gentle word of Jesus, he was encouraged even to participate in that Passion with Him.

II SUNDAY IN LENT

I Nocturn

From the Book of Genesis, c. 27, 1 - 29

II Nocturn

From the Book of St. Augustine, Bishop, against Lying

What Jacob did by his mother's authorization, so that he seemed to deceive his father, if diligently and faithfully considered, is not a lie, but a mystery. If we called such things lies, then all parables and figures signifying any things whatsoever which are not to be taken literally, but in which one thing is to be understood in something else, are to be called lies, which God forbid.

For he who thinks this can impute the same calumny also to all the many figurative sayings; so that this very thing which is called a metaphor (in which a word is transferred from the meaning which is proper to it to some other), can for the same reason be called a lie. The things which are meant are really expressed, but they are considered as lies because the things which are truly meant are not understood as being uttered; instead those things which are false are believed to have been stated.

That this may be made clearer by examples, note well what Jacob did. Indeed, he covered his body with goat skins. If we seek the proximate cause, we shall consider it a lie; for he did this that he might be thought to be one who he was not. But if this deed is referred to that for the signifying of which it was really done, by the goat skins are signified sins; and by him who covered himself with them is signified He who bore not His own sins, but the sins of others.

Therefore, the true signification can in no way be rightly called a lie; moreover, as in deed, so also in word. For when the father had said to him, "Who art thou, son?" he answered, "I am Esau, thy first-born." If this is referred to those two twins, it will seem a lie; however, if it is referred to that, to signify which these doings and sayings have been written, He is understood here in that body of His which is His Church, who, speaking of this matter, says: "You shall see Abraham and Isaac and Jacob and all the prophets in the kingdom of God, but you yourselves cast forth outside." And "they shall come from the east and west, and from the north and south, and shall sit together in the kingdom of God." And "behold they who were first are last, and they who were last are first." Thus, then, in a certain way, the younger brother has taken away the primacy of the elder and has taken it unto himself.

℟. The Lord shall be my God and this stone which I have set up for a title shall be called God's house: and of all that Thou shalt give me, * I will offer tithes and peace-offerings to Thee. ℣. If I shall return prosperously to my father's house. I will offer. Glory. I will offer.

III Nocturn

The reading of the holy Gospel according to St. Matthew

At that time Jesus took Peter, James and his brother John, and led them up a high mountain by themselves, and was transfigured before them. And so forth.

From a Homily of St. Leo, Pope

Jesus took Peter, James, and the latter's brother John, and having ascended a high mountain with them, He showed them the brightness of His glory; for although they had realized the majesty of God in Him, they were not, however, aware of the potency of that body of His in which His divinity was enclosed. And therefore properly and significantly He had promised that some of the disciples who were standing about would not see death before they saw the Son of God coming in His kingly power, that is, in regal brightness, which, spiritually pertaining to the human nature He had assumed, He chose to make manifest to these three men.

For those as yet clothed in mortal flesh could in no way contemplate and see that ineffable and inaccessible vision of the Godhead Itself which is reserved unto eternal life for the clean of heart. When the Father said, "This is my beloved Son in whom I am well pleased; hear him," was not the evident sense, "This is My Son who has existence from Me and with Me from eternity"? For neither is the Father prior to the Son, nor the Son after the Father.

"This is My Son whom divinity does not separate from Me, nor power disunite, nor eternity distinguish. This is My Son, not adopted, but My very own; not created from another, but begotten of Me; not of another nature is He made like to Me, but of My very essence He is born equal to Me. This is My Son by whom all things were made and without whom nothing was made; Who likewise does all I do; and whatsoever I work, He worketh inseparably with Me and in the same manner.

"This is My Son who did not desire by robbery that equality He has with Me; neither did He assume it by usurpation. But, remaining in the form of My glory, He bowed down even to the form of a servant the unchangeable Godhead, so that He might execute our common counsel—to redeem the human race. This One, therefore, in whom I am in all things well pleased, by whose preaching I am made known, and by whose humility I am glorified, this One hear ye unhesitatingly, for He is Truth and Life; He is My Strength and My Wisdom."

℟. The Angel said to Jacob: * Let me go, for it is break of day. And he said: I will not let thee go except thou bless me. And he blessed him in the same place. ℣. And when Jacob arose, behold a man wrestled with him till morning, and when he saw that he could not overcome him, he said to him. Let me go. Glory. Let me go.

✠ Continuation of the holy Gospel according to St. Matthew.— At that time Jesus took Peter, James and his brother John, and led them up a high mountain by themselves, and was transfigured before them. And his face shone as the sun, and his garments became white as snow. And behold, there appeared to them Moses and Elias talking together with him. Then Peter addressed Jesus saying, "Lord, it is good for us to be here. If thou wilt, let us set up three tents here, one for thee, one for Moses, and one for Elias." As he was still speaking, behold, a bright cloud overshadowed them, and behold, a voice out of the cloud said, "This is my beloved Son, in whom I am well pleased; hear him." And on hearing it the disciples fell on their faces and were exceedingly afraid. And Jesus came near and touched them, and said to them, "Arise, and do not be afraid." But lifting up their eyes, they saw no one but Jesus only. And as they were coming down from the mountain, Jesus cautioned them, saying, "Tell the vision to no one till the Son of Man has risen from the dead."

Let Us Pray

O God, who seest that we are wholly without strength, protect us in both body and soul that our bodies may be defended from all dangers and our minds cleansed from evil thoughts. Through our Lord.

MONDAY

The reading of the holy Gospel according to St. John

At that time Jesus said to the Jews, "I go, and you will seek me, and in your sin you will die." And so forth.

Homily of St. Augustine, Bishop

The Lord spoke to the Jews, saying: "I go." To Christ our Lord death was a journeying to Him from whom He had come, yet from whom He had not departed. "I go," He said, "and you shall seek me," not with desire, but in hatred. After He had withdrawn from the eyes of men, there were those who hated Him and those who loved Him: the former persecuting Him, the latter desiring to possess Him. The Lord Himself has said in the psalms by the mouth of the prophet: "Means of escape have failed me, there is none that seeketh me"; and again in another place in the psalm He said: "May they be put to shame and confusion who seek to take my life."

He judges them guilty who sought Him not; He condemns those who did seek Him. Now it is good to seek Christ, but in that manner in which the disciples sought after Him; it is also an evil thing to seek after Christ, in the manner in which the Jews sought after Him. The disciples sought after Him that they might possess Him; the Jews, that they might destroy

Him. Finally what did He, continuing His words, say to these latter since they sought after Him in an evil way and with a perverse heart? "You shall seek me, and (lest you think that you seek me rightly), you shall die in your sin." This is to seek after Christ in an evil manner—to die in one's sin; this is to hate Him through whom alone one can be saved.

For although men whose hope is in God ought not render evil even for evil, these rendered evil for good. Therefore the Lord announced to these beforehand, and, foreknowing all things, He pronounced sentence that they should die in their sin. Then He added: "Whither I go, you cannot come." These same words He addressed to His disciples in another place. Yet to them He did not add: "You shall die in your sin." What then did He say? The same that He said to the Jews: "Whither I go, you cannot come." Christ did not take away hope, but only predicted a delay. For when He spoke thus to His disciples, they were unable at the time to come whither He was going, but they would come later. These Jews, however, to whom He had in prophecy said, "You shall die in your sin," would never be able to come.

TUESDAY

The reading of the holy Gospel according to St. Matthew

At that time Jesus spoke to the crowds and to his disciples, saying, "The Scribes and the Pharisees have sat on the chair of Moses. All things, therefore, that they command you, observe and do. But do not act according to their works." And so forth.

Homily of St. Jerome, Priest

Who is gentler, who more benignant than our Lord? He is tempted by the Pharisees; their snares are broken and according to the Psalmist: "The arrows of children are their wounds"; and yet, because of the dignity of the priesthood and of their title, He urges the people to be obedient to them, considering not their deeds, but their teaching. And when He says, "The Scribes and Pharisees have sat on the chair of Moses," He designates by *chair* the teaching of the Law. Thus that also which is spoken in the psalm, "He sat not in the chair of pestilence," and, "He overturned the chairs of those who were selling doves," we should understand as referring to teaching.

"For they bind heavy and insupportable burdens on men's shoulders; but with a finger of their own they will not move them."—This is generally understood in regard to all those teachers who demand very difficult things and themselves do not perform even the lesser ones. But it should be noted that "shoulders" and "fingers" and "burdens" and the chains by which they are bound are to be considered in a spiritual way. "And all their works they do to be seen by men."—Whoever, therefore, does something in order to be seen by men is a Scribe and a Pharisee.

"For they make their phylacteries broad, and enlarge their fringes. And they love the first places at feasts and the first chairs in the synagogues, and salutations in the marketplace, and to be called by men *Rabbi*."—Woe to us poor souls to whom the vices of the Pharisees have passed. When the Lord gave the commandments of the Law through Moses, He put at the end: "Thou shalt bind them as a sign on thy hand, and they shall be and shall move between thy eyes." And the meaning is this: Let My commands be in your hand that they be fulfilled by deed; let them be before your eyes that you may meditate upon them day and night. The Pharisees, interpreting this wrongly, wrote the decalogue of Moses—that is, the ten words of the Law—on skins, encircling them and binding them on their forehead, making, as it were, a crown for the head, so that they might be always moving before their eyes.

WEDNESDAY

The reading of the holy Gospel according to St. Matthew

At that time, as Jesus was going up to Jerusalem, he took the twelve disciples aside by themselves, and said to them, "Behold, we are going up to Jerusalem, and the Son of Man will be betrayed to the chief priests and the Scribes; and they will condemn him to death." And so forth.

Homily of St. Ambrose, Bishop

Consider what it is that the mother of the sons of Zebedee is asking, together with and on behalf of her sons. She is truly a mother, the extent of whose desires in her anxiety for the honor of her sons is indeed immoderate, but nevertheless pardonable, especially as she, a mother advanced in years, deeply religious, and deprived of consolation, suffered her sons to be absent from her at the very time when she needed their help and support, and preferred to her own pleasure the reward of followers of Christ for her sons. They, when called by the Lord, at His first word (as we read) leaving their nets and their father, followed Him.

Therefore this mother, so very generous in the duty of motherly solicitude, besought the Savior, saying: "Let these my two sons sit, one on thy right hand, and the other on thy left hand in thy kingdom." Although it be an error, still it is an error of love. For the maternal heart knew no patience. Although she is over-eager in her wish, nevertheless, it is hardly a desire which merits punishment, for it is a yearning not for money, but for grace. Nor is it a shameful petition which pleads not for herself, but for her children. Consider the mother; realize that she is a mother.

Christ considered the mother's love whose comfort in her old age was in the reward of her sons, and, though worn by maternal cares, suffered the absence of her dearest treasures. Do you also consider the woman, that is, the weaker sex which the Lord had not as yet strengthened by His own suffering. Consider, I say, the child of that first woman, Eve, whom the Lord had not yet redeemed by His blood, falling because of the heritage of unbridled desire which has been passed on to all men. Christ had not as yet purified by His own blood that desire for honor, immoderate beyond bounds, which had grown in the affections of all men. Therefore the woman was at fault, but it was a weakness inherited from Eve.

THURSDAY

The reading of the holy Gospel according to St. Luke

At that time Jesus said to the Pharisees: "There was a certain rich man who used to clothe himself in purple and fine linen, and who feasted every day in splendid fashion." And so forth.

Homily of St. Gregory, Pope

Whom, dearly beloved, does this rich man, who was clothed in purple and fine linen and feasted sumptuously every day, signify but the Jewish people, who outwardly clung to the worship of their life and who used the privileges of the Law they had received for their own glory, not for their profit? And whom does Lazarus, covered with sores, represent but the Gentile people? Inasmuch as they were not ashamed to turn to God and confess their sins, their wound was only on the skin. Indeed, by a wound of the skin the poison is drawn from within and is cast out.

What, therefore, is the confession of sins but the breaking open of wounds? Because in confession the poison of sin, which lies dangerously hidden in the mind, is opened up safely. For skin-wounds draw the pus to the surface. And in confessing our sins what else do we do but open up the evils that lie hidden within us? But Lazarus, covered with sores, desired to be filled with the crumbs that fell from the table of the rich man and no one gave them to him, because that proud nation refused to admit any Gentile to a knowledge of the Law.

Since they held to the doctrine of the Law, not for the sake of charity, but for their own glorification, they swelled up, as it were, from the riches they had received; and because words fell down to him from their knowledge, it was as though crumbs fell from the table. And moreover, the dogs licked the wounds of the poor man lying on the ground. Sometimes in Holy Scripture it is customary to understand by *dogs*, preachers. For when a dog's tongue licks a wound, it heals it; so also when the holy teachers instruct us in the confession of our sin, they, as it were, touch the wound of our mind with their tongue.

FRIDAY

The reading of the holy Gospel according to St. Matthew

At that time Jesus spoke this parable to the multitude of the Jews and to the chief priests: "There was a man, a householder, who planted a vineyard, and put a hedge about it." And so forth.

Homily of St. Ambrose, Bishop

Various ones give different meanings for the *vineyard*, but evidently Isaias made mention of the "vineyard of the Lord of hosts" as being the house of Israel. Who else but God planted this vineyard? He it is, therefore, who "let it out to husbandmen and went into a far country"; not that the Lord, who is always present everywhere, travels from place to place, but that He is closer to those who love Him and more distant from those who neglect Him. He was absent for a long time lest His demands seem overhasty. For the more indulgent the generosity, the more inexcusable is the stubbornness.

Thus it is well said by St. Matthew that He "made a hedge about it," that is, He fortified it by the protection of a divine watch, lest it should easily suffer from the attacks of spiritual wild beasts. "And he dug in it a press."—How do we understand what is meant here by *press*, unless perhaps because some psalms are inscribed *for the presses*—in which the mysteries of our Lord's Passion flow over in redundance in the manner of new wine warmed by the Holy Spirit? Thus they whom the Holy Spirit had imbued were thought to be inebriated. Therefore, too, "he dug a press" into which the interior fruit of the rational grape poured its spiritual richness.

"He built a tower," raising up, namely, the edifice of the Law; and so He let out this vineyard, fortified, built up, and beautified, to the Jews. "And in the time of the fruits he sent his servants." Well does he put "time of the fruits," and not "of the plentiful harvest." For no fruit of the Jewish people existed; there was no abundant harvest of that vineyard of which the Lord spoke: "I looked that it should bear grapes but it brought forth thorns." And so, not with the wine of joy, not with a spiritual nectar, but with the crimson blood of the prophets do their presses flow.

SATURDAY

The reading of the holy Gospel according to St. Luke

At that time Jesus spoke this parable to the Pharisees and the Scribes: "A certain man had two sons. And the younger of them said to his father, 'Father, give me the share of the property that falls to me.'" And so forth.

Homily of St. Ambrose, Bishop

You see that a divine patrimony is given to those who seek it. Think not that it was a fault of the father that he gave the portion of his inheritance to the youth. In the kingdom of God there is no weakness of age, neither is faith increased by years. He who asked certainly judged himself fit. Would that he had not departed from his father! Then he would not have experienced the drawback of his youth. But after leaving his paternal home and wandering about in a strange country, he "began to be in need." Rightly is he who has left the Church said to have squandered his patrimony.

"He went into a far-off land." What is a more distant journey than to go out of one's self, to be separated not by vast regions, but by morals; to be cut off not by earthly distance, but by the pursuits of the soul; and to be, as it were, divorced from the society of the saints by the burning chasm of earthly lust? He who has separated himself from Christ is indeed an exile from his fatherland; he is a citizen of this world. But we are not strangers nor pilgrims but fellow citizens of the saints and members of the household of God, since we who were once far away have been brought near by the blood of Christ. Let us not envy those wandering in the regions afar off, for we too were once in that territory as Isaias teaches. For there you read: "A light has risen to those who sat in the region of the shadow of death." Therefore this far-off region is the shadow of death.

But we, before the face of whose soul stands Christ the Lord, live in the shadow of Christ. And therefore the Church says: "I sat down under his shadow in great delight." The man who lives riotously wastes all the beauties of his nature. In like manner you, who have received the image of God, do not destroy it by irrational uncleanness. You are the work of God; say not then to a wooden idol, "Thou art my father," lest perhaps you become like it; for it is written, "Let those who make idols become like them."

III SUNDAY IN LENT

I Nocturn

From the Book of Genesis, c. 37, 2 - 28

II Nocturn

From the Book of St. Ambrose, Bishop, on holy Joseph

The life of holy men is for others a standard of living. Therefore we take up the whole list of the Scriptures more in detail, so that as by our reading we learn to know Abraham, Isaac, Jacob, and the other just men, we may, as it were, follow with imitative footsteps a certain path of innocence, opened up to us by their virtue. Since I have often treated of the above mentioned, today occurs the history of holy Joseph, in whom, although there were many kinds of virtues, the brilliance of chastity especially shone forth.

Therefore when in Abraham you have learned the untiring devotion of faith, in Isaac the purity of a sincere mind, in Jacob the remarkable patience of soul and endurance, it is fitting that, from their virtues in general, you should direct your mind to their characteristic examples of discipline. Therefore let holy Joseph be proposed to us as a mirror of chastity. For in his manners and in his actions purity is resplendent, and that certain, well-known companion of chastity—the splendor of grace— shines forth. For which reason also' he was more loved by his parents than the rest of their children.

But that became the reason of envy, which fact was not to be passed over in silence, for in this lies the whole argument of the story, by this we understand that the perfect man is neither moved by ill-will to avenge an injury, nor renders evil for evil. Whence David says: "I have not returned evil to those doing evil to me." Why should Joseph have merited to be placed before others if he had either injured those who injured him or loved those only who loved him? For many do this. But this is remarkable, if you love your enemy, as the Savior teaches.

Justly therefore should he be admired who did this before the preaching of the Gospel, who, being injured, was merciful; persecuted, he forgave; when sold, he did not return the injury, but paid kindness for contumely. After the preaching of the Gospel all of us have learned this, but are not able to observe it. Thus let us take note of the envy of the saints that we may imitate their patience; and let us realize that they have not been of a more excellent nature than we, but more alert; let us realize, not that they were ignorant of vices, but that they corrected them. And if envy fired even the saints, how much more care ought to be taken lest it inflame us sinners!

℟. When Jacob saw Joseph's coat, he rent his garments and wept, and said: * An evil wild beast hath devoured my son Joseph. ℣. And his brethren took his coat and sent it to his father. And he knew it and said. An evil wild beast. Glory. An evil wild beast.

III Nocturn

The reading of the holy Gospel according to St. Luke

At that time Jesus was casting out a devil, and the same was dumb; and when he had cast out the devil, the dumb man spoke. And the crowds marvelled. And so forth.

Homily of St. Bede the Venerable, Priest

This demoniac is narrated by Matthew as having been not only dumb, but also blind. Moreover, he is said to have been cured by our Lord, so that he spoke and saw. Therefore three signs were worked together in one man: the blind sees, the dumb speaks, he that was possessed is freed from the devil. This, it is true, happened then in the flesh, but now is daily wrought in the conversion of believers: first, after the devil has been driven out, they see the light of faith, and then their mouths, which before were silent, are loosed for the praises of God.

But some of them said: "He casteth out devils by Beelzebub, the prince of devils." It was not some of the multitude, but the Scribes and Pharisees who belittled these things, as the other Evangelists bear witness. For while the multitudes, seemingly less educated, were in admiration at the Lord's works, these on the contrary, either tried to deny them, or what they could not deny, they strove to pervert by a sinister interpretation—as if these had not been the works of the Divinity, but of an unclean spirit.

"And others tempting, sought of him a sign from heaven." They desired either that, after the manner of Elias, fire should come down from on high, or that, in imitation of Samuel, in the summer time the thunders should roll, the lightnings flash, and the rains pour down: as though they could not likewise belittle these signs and say that they happened on account of the hidden and divers tendencies of the atmosphere. But you who calumniate those very signs which you behold with your eyes, touch with your hands, and experience in use, what would you do about those things which should come down from heaven? Assuredly you will answer that even the wise men in Egypt produced many signs from heaven. But He, inasmuch as He beheld their thoughts, said to them: "Every kingdom divided against itself shall be brought to desolation, and house shall fall upon house." Not to their words, but to their thoughts, did He make reply; so that in this way they might be even compelled to believe in the power of Him who beheld the secrets of hearts.

Now if, on the one hand, every kingdom divided against itself shall be made desolate, the kingdom of the Father and of the Son and of the Holy Spirit, then, is not divided, because, being without any contradiction, it is not to be made desolate by any attack, but will remain in eternal security. On the other hand, if Satan is divided against himself, how shall his kingdom stand, for you say: "By Beelzebub I cast out devils"? Saying this, He wished it to be understood from their own confession that, in not believing in Him, they had chosen to be of the kingdom of the devil, which, being divided against itself, certainly cannot stand.

℞. We deserve to suffer these things because we have sinned against our brother: seeing the anguish of his soul when he besought us, and we would not hear him: * Therefore is this affliction come upon us. ℣. Ruben said to his brethren: Did I not say to you: Do not sin against the boy; and you would not hear me? Therefore. Glory. Therefore.

✠ Continuation of the holy Gospel according to St. Luke.— At that time Jesus was casting out a devil, and the same was dumb; and when he had cast out the devil, the dumb man spoke. And the crowds marvelled. But some of them said, "By Beelzebub, the prince of devils, he casts out devils." But others, to test him, demanded from him a sign from heaven.

But he, seeing their thoughts, said to them: "Every kingdom divided against itself is brought to desolation, and house will fall upon house. If, then, Satan also is divided against himself, how shall his kingdom stand? Because you say that I cast out devils by Beelzebub. Now if I cast out devils by Beelzebub, by whom do your children cast them out? Therefore they shall be your judges. But if I cast out devils by the finger of God, then the kingdom of God has come upon you. When the strong man, fully armed, guards his courtyard, his property is undisturbed. But if a stronger than he attacks and overcomes him, he will take away his whole armor on which he was depending, and will divide his spoils. He who is not with me is against me and he who does not gather with me scatters.

"When the unclean spirit has gone out of a man, he roams through waterless places in search of a resting place; and finding none, he says, 'I will return to my house which I left.' And when he has come, he finds the place swept. And then he goes and takes seven other spirits more evil than himself, and they enter in and dwell there; and the last state of that man becomes worse than the first."

Now it came to pass as he was saying these things, that a certain woman lifted up her voice from the crowd, and said to him, "Blessed is the womb that bore thee, and the breasts that nursed thee." But he said, "Rather, blessed are they who hear the word of God and keep it."

Let Us Pray

We beseech Thee, O almighty God, regard the desires of Thy humble servants and extend the right hand of Thy Majesty to defend us. Through our Lord.

MONDAY

The reading of the holy Gospel according to St. Luke

At that time Jesus said to the Pharisees: "You will surely quote me this proverb, 'Physician, cure thyself! Whatever things we have heard of as done in Capharnaum, do here also in thy own country!'" And so forth.

Homily of St. Ambrose, Bishop

There is here shown no mild form of envy, which, forgetful of civil charity, turns the reasons for love into bitter hate. Both by this example and by the divine response it is declared that in vain do you await the assistance of heavenly mercy if you envy the fruit of virtues in others. For the Lord despises the envious, and He turns away the wonders of His power from those who contemn the divine blessings in others. The acts of the Lord in the flesh are revelations of His divinity; and through those things which are visible, the secrets of His counsel are shown forth.

Not without reason, therefore, does the Savior excuse Himself because He has not wrought miracles in His own country, lest perchance anyone should think that he owes little affection for his own country. It was impossible for Him who loved all men not to love His own fellow countrymen, but they rejected this love because they were envious. "In truth, I say to you, there were many widows in the days of Elias." Not because they were the days of Elias, but because they were the days in which Elias labored, or because Elias brought day to those who saw the light of spiritual grace in his works and were converted to the Lord. Therefore heaven was opened to those seeing divine and eternal mysteries, but was closed, and there was hunger when divine knowledge was neglected. But of this we have spoken more fully when we wrote concerning widows.

"And many were the lepers in Judea in the times of Eliseus the prophet but none of them were cleansed, save Naaman, the Syrian." Evidently this word of the Lord teaches and encourages us to zeal for honoring the divine mysteries, because no one is shown to be cleansed, nor anyone washed from the disease of a stained body, except he who has been zealous for purity in religious worship. For the divine blessings are not bestowed on those sleeping, but on those watching. We have said in another book that that widow to whom Elias was sent was a prophetic type of the Church. The people that formed the Church, as it is clear, is that gathered from strange lands. That nation, struck with leprosy and plagued with disease before it was baptized in the mystic river, the same, after the sacrament of Baptism, cleansed from the stains of body and soul, is no longer leprous, but is now an immaculate virgin without spot.

TUESDAY

The reading of the holy Gospel according to St. Matthew

At that time Jesus said to his disciples: "If thy brother sin against thee, go and show him his fault, between thee and him alone." And so forth.

Homily of St. Augustine, Bishop

Why do you correct your brother? Because you are sorry that he has offended you? God forbid! If you do it out of love for yourself, you accomplish nothing; if you do it out of love for him, you are acting perfectly. Finally, notice in these same words for love of whom you are to do this—for yourself or for him. "If he shall hear thee," He says, "thou shalt gain thy brother." Accordingly, act for the sake of him that you may win him. By so doing you are the one who profits; he would have been lost unless you had corrected him. Why is it, then, that men contemn these sins, and say: "What serious thing have I done? I have sinned against a man." Do not contemn the fact that you have sinned against a man.

Do you want to know that in offending a man you perish? If the one against whom you have sinned will correct you between you and himself alone, and you hear him, he gains you back. What does this mean—He gains you—except that you would have perished had he not won you back? For if you were not lost, how could he gain you? So let no one think little of it when he has offended against his brother. For the Apostle says somewhere: "Now when you sin thus against your brother and wound his weak conscience, you sin against Christ, because we are all become members of Christ." How can you keep from sinning against Christ when you offend a member of Christ?

Therefore let no one declare: "I have not sinned against God, but against my brother. I have offended a man—it is a small sin, or no sin at all." Perhaps you say, "It is a small sin," because it is quickly passed over. You have offended your brother; make satisfaction and you will be healed. In a moment you have performed a fatal deed, and as quickly you have found a remedy for it. Which of you, my brethren, can expect the Kingdom of Heaven when the Gospel declares: "He who shall say to his brother, 'thou fool,' is guilty of hell-fire"? It is a very terrifying thing, but behold your means of reparation: "If you bring your gift to the altar, and there remember that your brother hath something against thee, leave there thy gift before the altar..." God is not angered because you postpone the offering of your gift; God seeks you yourself rather than your gift.

WEDNESDAY

The reading of the holy Gospel according to St. Matthew

At that time the Scribes and Pharisees from Jerusalem came to him, saying, "Why do thy disciples transgress the tradition of the ancients?" And so forth.

Homily of St. Jerome, Priest

Amazing stupidity of the Scribes and Pharisees! They reprove the Son of God because He does not keep the traditions and commands of men. "For they wash not their hands when they eat bread." It is the hands, that is, the works not indeed of the body, but of the soul, that must be washed so that the word of God may be fulfilled in them. "But he, answering, said to them:

'Why do you also transgress the commandments of God for your traditions?' " He refutes a wicked calumny with a true answer. "Since," He says, "you neglect the commandments of God for the traditions of men, why do you think that My disciples should be reproved because they make light of the injunctions of the elders in order to observe those of God?"

"For God said: 'Honor thy father and mother.' And: 'He that shall curse father or mother let him die the death.' But you say: 'Whoever shall say to his father or mother, "Any support thou mightest have had from me is dedicated to God," does not have to honor his father or his mother.' " Honor in the Scriptures is to be understood not so much in salutations and service rendered as in alms and in the bestowing of gifts. "Honor widows," says the Apostle, "who are truly widowed." Here honor is understood as a gift. And in another place: "Let priests be esteemed worthy of a double honor, especially those who labor in the word and doctrine of God." And by this command we are ordered not to muzzle the ox that treadeth out the corn. "The laborer is worthy of his hire."

Our Lord, bearing in mind either the weakness or the age or the infirmity of parents, had commanded children to honor their parents even to the point of providing for the necessities of life. But the Scribes and Pharisees, wishing to subvert this most providential law of God so that they might carry out their wrongdoing under the guise of piety, taught these wicked children that if one wished to vow to God, who is the true Father, what should be offered to the parents, he could make the offering to God instead of to his parents. Declining, of course, to accept what they saw was consecrated to God, lest they should fall into a crime of sacrilege, the parents were consumed with want. So then it came about that the offering of the children under pretext of being an offering to the temple and to God redounded to the gain of the priests.

THURSDAY

The reading of the holy Gospel according to St. Luke

At that time Jesus rose from the synagogue and entered Simon's house. Now Simon's mother-in-law was suffering from a great fever. And so forth.

Homily of St. Ambrose, Bishop

Behold the mildness of our Lord and Savior! He is not moved by indignation, nor offended by wickedness, nor, insulted by injury, does He depart from Judea, but on the contrary, forgetful of injury and mindful only of mercy, He softens the hearts of this faithless people, now by teaching, now by casting out devils, now by healing the sick. Rightly does St. Luke tell first of the man freed from an evil spirit and then of the cure of the woman. For the Lord had come to cure both sexes; but that one ought to have been healed first which had been created first, and yet the other sex should not have been neglected which had sinned more through fickleness of mind than from actual malice.

That the Lord began His works of healing on the Sabbath signifies that the new creation began where the old had stopped. It shows, moreover, that the Son of God was not subject to the Law but was above the Law in the very beginning, and that the Law was not destroyed by Him, but fulfilled. For the world was not made by the Law, but by the word, as we read: "By the word of the Lord the heavens were established." The Law was then not destroyed, but fulfilled, that the restoration of man, who was already falling, might be accomplished. Wherefore the Apostle says: "Stripping off the old man from yourselves, put on the new man who is created according to God."

Well did He begin on the Sabbath in order to show that He Himself was the Creator, who, following up the works of creation with works of healing, was continuing the work which He had already begun, just as a carpenter, arranging to renovate a house, does not begin to tear down the old one from the foundation but from the roof. And so He places His hand first there where He had before left off; then He begins with the smaller things that He may attain to those which are greater. Men also, by the power of God, are able to free those possessed by devils, but to command the resurrection of the dead pertains to divine power alone. In the type of that woman, the mother-in-law of Peter and Andrew, perhaps our flesh also languished with various fevers of crime and burned with the wanton promptings of various evil desires. Nor would I say that the fever of love is less than that of heat; the former inflames the soul, the latter inflames the body. Our fever is avarice; our fever is passion; our fever is lust; our fever is ambition; our fever is wrath.

FRIDAY

The reading of the holy Gospel according to St. John

At that time Jesus came to a town of Samaria called Sichar, near the field that Jacob gave to his son Joseph. And so forth.

III Week In Lent

Homily of St. Augustine, Bishop

Mysteries are already beginning. For Jesus is not tired without reason; the strength of God is not wearied without cause; He is not fatigued for nothing by whom the wearied are refreshed; nor is He exhausted to no purpose in whose absence we are wearied and in whose presence we are strengthened. Still, Jesus is tired and spent from His journey, and He sits down, and He sits beside the well, and He sat thus at the well, being wearied, about the sixth hour. All these things point to something; they indicate something; they bring us to attention; they excite us to action. Therefore may He who has deigned so to arouse us, saying, "Knock and it shall be opened to you," open to us and to you.

Jesus is exhausted by His travel for your sake. We have found Jesus strong; now we find Him weak. Strong and weak, —strong, because "in the beginning was the Word, and the Word was with God, and the Word was God. The same was in the beginning with God." Do you wish to see how powerful the Son of God is? "All things were made by Him and without Him was made nothing"; and without labor were they made. Therefore what is more mighty than He by whom were made all things without labor? Do you desire to know Him weak? "The Word was made flesh and dwelt amongst us." The strength of Christ has created you; the weakness of Christ has re-created you. The power of Christ has caused to exist that which was not; the weakness of Christ has kept from perishing that which was. In His power He has formed us; in His weakness He has sought us.

Thus does the weak nourish the weak as the hen doth her little chicks, for He has likened Himself to such a one. "How often have I willed," He says to Jerusalem, "to gather thy children under my wings as the hen doth her chicks, and thou wouldst not?" And you see, brethren, how the mother hen is bothered with her young. For no other fowl is recognized just because she is a mother. We notice some sparrows building a nest right before our eyes; the swallows, the storks, the doves we daily see building their nests, but we do not recognize them to be parent birds until we find them in the nests. But the hen is so worried with her young ones, that even if the chicks are not following her, even though you cannot see the little ones, you know that she is a mother nevertheless.

SATURDAY

The reading of the holy Gospel according to St. John

At that time Jesus went to the Mount of Olives. And at daybreak he came again into the temple. And so forth.

Homily of St. Augustine, Bishop

"Jesus went to Mount Olivet,"—to the mount of fruit, to the mount of ointment, to the mount of chrism. For where was it fitting that Christ should teach, except on Mount Olivet? For the name of "Christ" is derived from *chrism;* it is called *chrism* in the Greek, but in the Latin *unctio* (ointment). And therefore has He anointed us, because He has made us warriors against the devil. "And early in the morning he came again into the temple, and all the people came to him, and sitting down he taught them"; and He was not seized, because it was not yet the time for Him to suffer. Now, indeed, behold how the meekness of our Lord is tried by His enemies.

"And the Scribes and Pharisees bring unto him a woman taken in adultery, and they set her in the midst and said to him: 'Master, this woman was even now taken in adultery. Now Moses in the Law commanded us to stone such a one. But what sayest thou?' And this they said tempting him, that they might accuse him." Of what could they accuse Him? Had they caught Him in any crime, or was this woman said to have been concerned with Him in any way?

Let us recognize that the meekness of our Lord was admirable, brethren. They noticed that He was very meek, that He was exceedingly kind. Of Him, indeed, had it been said long before: "Gird thyself with thy sword about thy thigh, O most mighty one. With thy comeliness and thy beauty set out, proceed prosperously and reign: because of truth and meekness and justice." Thus He shows forth His truthfulness as a teacher, His meekness as a deliverer, His justice as a judge. On account of these things the prophet through the Holy Spirit had foretold that He should reign. When he spoke, His truthfulness was acknowledged; when He was not moved against His enemies, His meekness was lauded. And so, since His enemies had in their bitterness and envy been tormented over these two things, that is, His truthfulness and meekness, they tempted Him regarding the third, that is, His justice.

IV SUNDAY IN LENT

I Nocturn

From the Book of Exodus, c. 3, 1 - 15

II Nocturn

Sermon of St. Basil the Great

We know that by fasting Moses ascended the mountain. Nor would he have dared to mount the smoking summit or enter the darkness unless he had been fortified by fasting. By fasting he received the commandments written by the finger of God on the tablets. Likewise, upon the mountain fasting was the promoter of the law that had been given; but below, gluttony led the people to idolatry and contaminated them. "The people sat down," it says, "to eat and drink and they rose up to play." While the servant of God devoted himself to continual fast and prayer, one drunken revelry of the people rendered his labor and perseverance of forty days empty and void.

For the tablets, written by the finger of God, which fasting received, drunkenness shattered, since the most holy Prophet considered a wine-bibbing people unworthy to receive the Law from God. In one moment, on account of their gluttony, that people, though instructed in the worship of God by the greatest miracles, most shamefully fell into the idolatry of the Egyptians. From which, if we consider both at the same time, we may see that fasting leads to God, and delights destroy salvation.

What contaminated Esau and made him the servant of his brother? Was it not one meal, on account of which he sold his birthright? Did not prayer, accompanied with fasting, give Samuel to his mother? What made the brave Samson unconquerable? Was it not fasting, with which he was conceived in the womb of his mother? Fasting conceived, fasting nourished, and fasting made of him a man. The Angel wisely prescribed this for his mother, admonishing that whatever came from the vine she should not touch, neither wine nor any strong drink should she take. Fasting begot prophets, it confirmed and strengthened powerful men.

Fasting makes wise legislators; it is the best guardian of the soul, a sure friend of the body, strength and arms for the brave, training for athletes and contestants. Furthermore, fasting repels temptations, excites to piety, dwells with sobriety and is a promoter of temperance; it brings strength in time of war and teaches calmness in time of peace; it sanctifies the Nazarite; it perfects the priest; for it is not right to touch the sacrifice without fasting, not only now in the mystic and true adoration of God, but not even in that in which the sacrifice was offered in figure according to the Law. Fasting made Elias the spectator of a grand vision, for when he had cleansed his soul by a fast of forty days in the cave, he merited to see God, as far as this is permitted to man. Moses, receiving the Law again, had also a second time practiced fasting. The Ninivites, unless the very beasts fasted with them, would by no means have escaped the threats of ruin. Whose corpses fell in the desert? Were they not theirs who longed for flesh meats?

℟. Let us sing to the Lord: for He is gloriously magnified: the horse and the rider He hath thrown into the sea: * The Lord is my strength and my praise, and He is become salvation to me. ℣. The Lord is as a man of war, Almighty is His name. The Lord is my strength. Glory. The Lord is my strength.

III Nocturn

The reading of the holy Gospel according to St. John

At that time Jesus went away to the other side of the sea of Galilee, which is that of Tiberias. And there followed him a great crowd, because they were witnessing the signs he worked on those who were sick. And so forth.

Homily of St. Augustine, Bishop

The miracles which our Lord Jesus Christ wrought are in very deed divine works, and they admonish the human mind to understand God from visible things. For, after all, He is not such a substance as can be seen with the eyes. His miracles, by which He rules the whole world and ministers to every creature, have by their frequency become commonplace, so that scarcely anyone thinks it worth while to attend to the wonderful, yes, stupendous works of God in any grain of seed. In accordance with His mercy He has reserved to Himself certain miracles outside the ordinary course and order of nature, which He works at an opportune time, that they to whom the daily miracles have grown common might be astonished by witnessing not greater things, but uncommon ones.

For the governing of the whole world is a greater miracle than the feeding of five thousand men with five loaves of bread. Yet no one marvels at the one; but at the other, men are in admiration, not because it is greater, but because it is rare. For who is it that even now feeds the whole world but He who from a few grains creates the harvest?

He worked, therefore, as God. For, by the same power whereby He multiplies the harvests from a few grains, so also did He multiply in His hands the five loaves. The power, indeed, was in the hands of Christ. And those five loaves were as seeds, not indeed entrusted to the earth, but multiplied by Him who made the earth.

This prodigy, then, was brought under the realm of the senses, that thereby the mind might be uplifted; and it was displayed before the eyes, whereby the intellect might be exercised, that we might admire the invisible God through His visible works, and, raised aloft to faith and purified by faith, might yearn even to see that invisible Being whom, though invisible, we learned to know from visible things. And yet it does not suffice to view only these points in the miracles of Christ. Let us ask those very miracles what they tell us of Christ. Oh, yes, they have a tongue if they are only understood. For since Christ Himself is the Word of God, even a deed of the Word is a word for us.

℟. Give ear, O My people, unto My law: * Incline your ear unto the words of My mouth. ℣. I will open My mouth in parables: I will utter sayings from the beginning of the world. Incline. Glory. Incline.

✠ Continuation of the holy Gospel according to St. John.—At that time Jesus went away to the other side of the sea of Galilee, which is that of Tiberias. And there followed him a great crowd, because they were witnessing the signs he worked on those who were sick. Jesus therefore went up the mountain, and was sitting there with his disciples.

Now the Passover, the feast of the Jews, was near. When, therefore, Jesus had lifted up his eyes and seen that a very great crowd had come to him, he said to Philip: "Whence shall we buy bread that these may eat?" But he said this to try him, for he himself knew what he would do.

Philip answered him, "Two hundred denarii worth of bread is not enough for them, that each one may receive a little." One of his disciples, Andrew, the brother of Simon Peter, said to him, "There is a young boy here who has five barley loaves and two fishes; but what are these among so many?" Jesus then said, "Make the people recline."

Now there was much grass in the place. The men therefore reclined, in number about five thousand. Jesus then took the loaves, and when he had given thanks, distributed them to those reclining; and likewise the fishes, as much as they wished. But when they were filled, he said to his disciples, "Gather the fragments of the five barley loaves left over lest they be wasted." They therefore gathered them up; and they filled twelve baskets with the fragments of the five barley loaves left over by those who had eaten.

When the people, therefore, had seen the sign which Jesus had worked, they said, "This is indeed the Prophet who is to come into the world." So when Jesus perceived that they would come to take him by force and make him king, he fled again to the mountain, himself alone.

LET US PRAY

Grant, we beseech Thee, O almighty God, that we who justly suffer for our sins may obtain relief by the consolation of Thy grace. Through our Lord.

MONDAY

The reading of the holy Gospel according to St. John

At that time the Passover of the Jews was at hand, and Jesus went up to Jerusalem. And he found in the temple men selling oxen, sheep and doves. And so forth.

Homily of St. Augustine, Bishop

What have we heard, brethren? Behold that temple was yet a figure and the Lord cast out from there all who were seeking their own advantages and who had come to trade. And what were they selling there? The things men had need of for the sacrifices of those times. For you know that such sacrifices were given to those people on account of their carnality and their still stony heart, by which they were kept from falling into idolatry: and hence they were offering there in sacrifice oxen, sheep, and doves. You know this because you have read it.

Therefore it was not a great sin if they sold in the temple what was bought to be offered in the temple; but nevertheless He drove them thence. But if the Lord should have found them there given to drink, what would He have done, if indeed He expelled those who were selling things which were licit and not against justice (for things which are bought honestly are not sold illegally), and did not allow "the house of prayer to become a house of traffic"?

If the house of God ought not become a house of traffic, ought it become a house of drinking? For when we say these things men gnash their teeth at us; but the psalm you have heard consoles us: "They gnashed upon me with their teeth." We also know that we hear therein how we may be cured, although the scourges fall again and again upon Christ, because His word is scourged. "Scourges were gathered together against me," He says, "and they knew it not." He was scourged with the scourges of the Jews; He is scourged by the blasphemies of false Christians; they multiply scourges for the Lord their God and know it not. Let us do as much as He helps us to do. "But as for me, when they were troublesome to me, I was clothed with haircloth; I humbled my soul with fasting."

TUESDAY

The reading of the holy Gospel according to St. John

At that time when the feast was already half over, Jesus went up into the temple and was teaching. And the Jews marvelled. And so forth.

Homily of St. Augustine, Bishop

He who had been in hiding began to teach, and He spoke openly and was not seized. That fact that He should hide away was for the sake of example, but this act was a sign of power. But when He began to teach, the Jews wondered. So far as I can judge, all indeed were astonished, but not all were converted. And so why this admiration? Because many men knew where He was born, and how He had been brought up. They had never seen Him learning letters, but now they heard Him discussing the Law, bringing forth proofs from the Law which no man could have elicited unless he had read it; and no man could read who had not studied letters; and therefore they were astounded. But their surprise became the occasion for the Master to introduce a higher truth.

From their astonishment and from their remarks it appears that our Lord declares a thing worthy to be diligently looked into and discussed. What, then, does the Lord answer to them who wondered how He knew the letters which He had not learned? "My doctrine," He says, "is not mine, but his that sent me." This is a very profound remark, for in these few words He seems to have declared contrary things. He does not say, "This doctrine is not Mine," but, "My doctrine is not mine." If it is not Yours, how can it be Yours; if it is Yours, how can it not be Yours? For You say both: "It is my doctrine," and, "it is not mine."

If we consider a bit more deeply what the holy Evangelist says at the beginning, "In the beginning was the Word, and the Word was with God, and the Word was God," on that depends the solution to this question. What is the doctrine of the Father, except the Word of the Father? Christ is therefore Himself the doctrine of the Father if He is the Word of the Father. And because the Word cannot be of Itself, but must be of someone, so does He declare that His doctrine is Himself, and not His own, because He is the Word of the Father. For what is so much thine own as thyself? and what is so little thine own as thyself, if that which thou art is another's?

WEDNESDAY

The reading of the holy Gospel according to St. John

At that time, as Jesus was passing by, he saw a man blind from birth. And his disciples asked him, "Rabbi, who has sinned, this man or his parents, that he should be born blind?" And so forth.

Homily of St. Augustine, Bishop

The stupendous and wonderful things that our Lord Jesus Christ has done are both works and words. They are works because they have been done; they are words because they are signs. If therefore this deed signifies something, let us consider what it is. The blind man is the human race. This blindness befell the first man through his sin, from which we trace the origin not only of death, but also of evil. If infidelity is blindness and faith is sight, whom did Christ find faithful when He came? At one time the Apostle, born of the race of the prophets, said: "We were once by nature children of wrath, as also were the rest." If children of wrath, then also children of judgment, children of punishment, children of hell. If we are so by nature, how is this but that the first man by sinning brought this affliction on human nature? If he brought this penalty on human nature, then every man is born blind according to the spirit.

But then the Lord came. What did He do? He effected a great mystery. He spat on the ground and made clay of the spittle (for the Word was made flesh), and spread clay upon the eyes of the blind man. The man was therefore treated with the clay, but he did not as yet see. The Lord then sent him to the pool which is called Siloe. It was left for the Evangelist to give us the name of this pool which is, according to the interpretation, *Sent*. You all know who it is that is *sent*. Had this One not been sent, none of us would be free from our iniquity. The blind man therefore washed his eyes in that pool which according to the interpretation is called "(the One) Sent," that is, he was baptized in Christ. If Christ therefore gave sight to the man when He, so to speak, baptized him in Himself, then the rubbing of clay on his eyes perhaps signifies making him a catechumen.

You have heard a sublime mystery. Ask a man: "Are you a Christian?" He answers, "No." "Are you a pagan or a Jew?" If he should say, "No," then ask him if he is a catechumen or one of the faithful. If his answer is that he is a catechumen, then he has had clay spread on his eyes; but he has not yet been washed. But whence was it that the clay was spread on? Ask him and he will tell you that it was when he came to believe. Ask him in whom he believes. By the very fact that he is a catechumen he says, "In Christ." Behold now I speak both to the faithful and to catechumens. What is it that I have said about the spittle and the clay? I have said that the Word was made flesh. The Catechumens hear this, but it is not sufficient for them that their eyes have been covered with the clay (that is, that they believe); let them hasten to the font if they seek the Light.

THURSDAY

The reading of the holy Gospel according to St. Luke

At that time Jesus went to a town called Naim; and his disciples and a large crowd went with him. And so forth.

Homily of St. Ambrose, Bishop

This passage is filled with a twofold grace: namely, that we may believe that the divine mercy is quickly moved by the mourning of a widowed mother, especially of one who is broken by the suffering or death of an only son (and yet it was the crowd of mourners who obtained for this widow that work of power); and also that we may believe that this widow, surrounded by a crowd of people, should seem to be more than a simple woman who has deserved by her tears to obtain the resurrection of her only son, because holy Church also, who is restrained from weeping for those to whom resurrection is promised, also calls back to life by the sight of her own tears her younger people (the Gentiles) from the pomp of burial and the depths of the grave.

He who lay dead on the bier was being borne to the sepulchre by the four material elements, but he had hope of rising again because he was carried on wood. For, although wood had not been of value to us before, nevertheless, after Jesus had touched it, it began to profit unto life—showing that salvation was to be poured upon the people through the gibbet of the cross. Therefore, at the word of God, those gloomy pallbearers of the funeral, who were hastening with the mortal body to the fatal dissolution of material nature, stood still. What else is meant than that we lie lifeless as it were on a kind of funeral couch, that is, on our deathbed, whenever the fire of unrestrained lust burns, or cold sweat (resulting from the extinction of the flame of charity) pours forth, or the vigor of our mind grows dull from the listless disposition of our earthly body, or our spirit, devoid of pure light, feeds our mind with a mass of sinful thoughts? These are the pallbearers at our funeral.

Yet, though the final rites of death have driven away hope of any life and the bodies lie near to the grave, by the word of God the dead corpses arise—the voice returns; the son is given back to his mother; he is called back from the tomb, he is snatched out of the grave. What is your grave except your evil ways? Your grave is your infidelity; your throat your sepulchre. "For their throat is an open sepulchre from whence proceed deadly words." Christ frees you from this sepulchre; from this grave you shall rise again if you will listen to God's words. And if the sin is so grave that you cannot wash it away by tears of repentance, let mother Church weep for you, who, as the widowed mother, intervenes for each of us as for only sons. For she shares our sorrow by a connatural spiritual grief when she beholds her children forced on to their death by fatal vices.

FRIDAY

The reading of the holy Gospel according to St. John

At that time a certain man was sick, Lazarus of Bethany, the village of Mary and her sister Martha. And so forth.

Homily of St. Augustine, Bishop

In the former lesson you remember that the Lord escaped out of the hands of those who had wished to stone Him; then He went beyond the Jordan, where John was baptizing. While the Lord was there, Lazarus became sick in Bethany, a town near Jerusalem. Now Mary was she who anointed the Lord with oil and wiped His feet with her hair, "whose brother Lazarus was sick." "His sisters therefore sent to him." We already know where they sent—where Jesus was—because He was away, namely, across the Jordan. They sent to the Lord, saying that their brother was sick, so that, if He loved him, He might come and deliver him from his sickness. But He put off healing him in order to raise him from the dead.

What then did his sisters say? "Lord, behold, he whom thou lovest is sick." They did not say, "Come," for to Him who loved an announcement alone was necessary. They dared not say, "Come and heal"; they dared not say, "Command where you are, and Lazarus shall be made whole." But why could they not if the faith of the centurion was praised in a like event? For he said, "I am not worthy that thou shouldst enter under my roof; say but the word and my servant shall be healed." But these sisters said nothing of the kind, but only, "Lord, behold, he whom thou lovest is sick." It suffices that He know; for He does not love and desert the one He loves.

Someone may say, "How is the sinner signified by Lazarus, who was so loved by the Lord?" Let such a one listen to Christ who says, "I came not to call the just, but sinners." If God had not loved sinners, He would not have come down from heaven to earth. "Jesus, hearing it, said to them: 'This sickness is not unto death, but for the glory of God, that the Son of God may be glorified.'" Such a glorification of Him does not add anything to Him, but is to our benefit. This is, then, the meaning of that which He says, "the sickness is not unto death," because that death itself was not unto death, but rather for the sake of a miracle, by which, when performed, men would believe in Christ and avoid real death. Note well how, as it were indirectly, the Lord says that He is God—and this is for the benefit of some who denied that the Son of God was God.

SATURDAY

The reading of the holy Gospel according to St. John

At that time Jesus spoke to the multitude of the Jews, saying, "I am the light of the world. He who follows me does not walk in the darkness, but will have the light of life." And so forth.

Homily of St. Augustine, Bishop

I think that what the Lord says, "I am the Light of the world," is clear to those who have eyes whereby they may become partakers of this light; but those who do not have eyes except only in the flesh wonder at what is said by the Lord Jesus Christ: "I am the Light of the world." And perhaps there may not be wanting someone who will say to himself: "Is it that the Lord Christ is this sun which makes the day by its rising and setting?" For there have been heretics who thought this. The

Manicheans thought this sun which is visible to the eyes of the body, which is a public thing and visible to eyes not only of men but also of beasts, was Christ the Lord.

But the orthodox faith of the Catholic Church rejects such an idea and recognizes it as the teaching of the devil; and it does not only know it by believing it, but also in as far as it is possible proves it by reasoning. Let us, therefore, not accept such an error which holy Church has outlawed from the beginning. Let us not think that the Lord Jesus Christ is this sun which we see rising in the east and setting in the west; to whose course night succeeds; whose rays are overshadowed by the clouds; which goes from place to place in a fixed movement. This is not the Lord Christ. The Lord Christ is not the sun which has been made, but He through whom the sun has been made. For "all things were made by him, and without him was made nothing."

He is therefore the Light which has made this light. Let us love Him; let us desire to understand Him; let us crave Him that we may some day come to Him by His aid; and let us so live in Him that we may never altogether die. For He is the Light of which the Prophet long ago sang in the psalm: "Because with thee is the fount of life, and in thy light we shall see light." Notice what the ancient writings of the holy men of God said about such a Light. "Men and beasts thou wilt preserve, O Lord," they said, "O how hast thou multiplied thy mercy, O God!"

PASSION SUNDAY

I Nocturn

From the Book of Jeremias the Prophet, c. 1, 1 - 19

II Nocturn

Sermon of St. Leo, Pope

Among all the Christian solemnities, beloved, we are not unaware that the Paschal mystery is the principal one, for the worthy and fitting reception of which the arrangement of the whole cycle prepares us; but the present days, which we know to be close on that most sublime mystery of divine mercy, demand our devotion above all. During these days greater fasts were with reason ordained by the holy apostles through the teaching of the Holy Spirit, in order that through the common fellowship of the cross of Christ we also might do something in that which He did for us, as the Apostle says: "If we suffer with him, we shall also be glorified with him." Certain and secure is the hope of promised happiness where there is participation in the suffering of the Lord.

There is no one, beloved, to whom, through circumstance of time, the communication of this glory will be refused, as if the tranquility of peace is void of opportunity for virtue. For the Apostle foretells, saying, "All who wish to live piously in Christ will suffer persecution," and therefore never is there wanting the tribulation of persecution if the practice of piety be not lacking. And the Lord says in His exhortations: "Whoever does not take up his cross and follow me, is not worthy of me."

Nor should we doubt that this saying applies not only to the disciples of Christ, but also to all the faithful and to the entire Church which, in the person of those who were then present, heard for all time the way of her salvation. As therefore it is the duty of the whole body to live piously, so also is it the duty of all time to bear the cross. Rightly is each one persuaded to bear this cross, for it is borne by each one according to his proper disposition and capacity. There is only one name for persecution, but there is not just one type of struggle, and usually there is more danger in a hidden foe than in an open enemy.

Blessed Job, instructed in the fluctuating goods and evils of this world, piously and truly said: "Is not the life of man on earth a temptation?" For not by the mere pains and sufferings of the body is the faithful soul assailed, but when the health of his members is preserved, he is likewise oppressed by serious illness if he is weakened by the pleasure of the flesh. But when "the flesh lusteth against the spirit and the spirit against the flesh," the rational mind is strengthened by the protection of the cross of Christ, and, when enticed by evil desires, it does not consent, for it is transfixed by the piercing steel of continence and by the fear of God.

℞. O Lord, my trouble is very near and there is none to help me; before they pierce my hands and my feet, deliver me from the mouth of the lion, * That I may declare Thy name unto my brethren. ℣. O God, deliver my soul from the sword and my only one from the power of the dog. That I may.

III Nocturn

The reading of the holy Gospel according to St. John

At that time Jesus said to the multitude of the Jews: "Which of you can convict me of sin? If I speak the truth, why do you not believe me?" And so forth.

Homily of St. Gregory, Pope

Consider well, dearly beloved brethren, the benignity of God. He had come to loose sins and He said: "Which of you shall convict me of sin?" He who was able by the power of the Godhead to justify sinners did not disdain to show by argument that He Himself was not a sinner. But most terrible is that which is added: "He that is of God heareth the words of God. Therefore you hear them not because you are not of God." Now if he hears the words of God who is of God, and if whosoever is not of God cannot hear His words, let each one ask himself if he perceives the words of God in the ear of his heart and understands whence they come.

The Truth commands you to long for the heavenly homeland, to crush the desires of the flesh, to shun the glory of the world, not to covet the property of another, and to give generously of one's own. Let each one, therefore, weigh well within himself whether this voice of God has grown strong in the ear of his heart and whether he knows already that he is of God. For there are some who deem it not worth their while to listen to the precepts of God even with the ear of the body. And there are some who indeed hear these precepts with the ear of the body, but who do not embrace them with the affection of their mind. And there are some who willingly hear the words of God so that they are afflicted even unto tears, yet after they have wept they return to their iniquity.

They certainly do not hear the words of God who spurn to put them into practice. Hence, dearly beloved brethren, recall your life before the eyes of your mind, and in deep consideration fear greatly this which sounds from the mouth of Truth: "Therefore you hear them not because you are not of God." But this which the Truth speaks concerning reprobates, the reprobates show in themselves by their evil works, for the text continues: "The Jews therefore answered and said to him: 'Do we not say well that thou art a Samaritan and hast a devil?'"

Let us hear what the Lord answers after having suffered such an affront: "I have not a devil; but I honor my Father, and you have dishonored me." Now since the word *Samaritan* means a *guardian* and since He truthfully is the Guardian of whom the Psalmist speaks, "Unless the Lord guard the city, in vain do they keep watch who guard it," and since to Him it is said through Isaias, "O Guardian, what of the night? O Guardian, what of the night?" therefore the Lord did not wish to reply,

"I am not a Samaritan," but He said, "I have not a devil." Indeed concerning Him two things had been inferred: the one He denied; the other, by His silence, He acknowledged.

℟. Who will give water to my head and a fountain of tears to my eyes, and I will weep day and night? for my nearest brother hath supplanted me, * And every friend hath dealt deceitfully against me. ℣. Let their way become dark and slippery: and let the Angel of the Lord pursue them. And.

✠ Continuation of the holy Gospel according to St. John.— At that time Jesus said to the multitudes of the Jews: "Which of you can convict me of sin? If I speak the truth, why do you not believe me? He who is of God hears the words of God. The reason why you do not hear is that you are not of God."
The Jews therefore in answer said to him, "Are we not right in saying that thou art a Samaritan, and hast a devil?" Jesus answered, "I have not a devil, but I honor my Father, and you dishonor me. Yet I do not seek my own glory; there is one who seeks and who judges. Amen, amen, I say to you, if anyone keep my word, he will never see death."
The Jews therefore said, "Now we know that thou hast a devil. Abraham is dead, and the prophets, and thou sayest, 'If anyone keep my words he will never taste death.' Art thou greater than our father Abraham, who is dead? And the prophets are dead. Whom dost thou make thyself?"
Jesus answered, "If I glorify myself, my glory is nothing. It is my Father who glorifies me, of whom you say that he is your God. And you do not know him, but I know him. And if I say that I do not know him, I shall be like you, a liar. But I know him, and I keep his words. Abraham your father rejoiced that he was to see my day. He saw it and was glad." The Jews therefore said to him, "Thou art not yet fifty years old, and hast thou seen Abraham?" Jesus said to them, "Amen, amen, I say to you, before Abraham came to be, I am." They therefore took up stones to cast at him; but Jesus hid himself, and went out from the temple.

LET US PRAY

We beseech Thee, O almighty God, mercifully regard Thy family, that our bodies may be ruled by Thy goodness and our souls protected by Thy care. Through our Lord.

MONDAY

The reading of the holy Gospel according to St. John

At that time the rulers and Pharisees sent attendants to seize Jesus. And so forth.

Homily of St. Augustine, Bishop

How could they apprehend Him since He did not yet wish it? And so because they had not been able to lay hold on Him while He did not wish it, they were sent to listen while He taught. Taught what? "Jesus therefore said to them: 'Yet a little while I am with you. What you desire now to do, you will accomplish, but not just now, for I do not wish it right away. And why do I not desire it just yet? Because yet a little while I am with you, and then I go to him that sent me. I must complete my task, and thus come to my Passion.'"

"You shall seek me, and shall not find me; and where I am, thither you cannot come." In this He has already foretold His Resurrection, for they were not willing to acknowledge Him while He was present, but afterwards, when they saw the multitude who believed in Him, they sought for Him. For great miracles were wrought also after the Lord arose and ascended into heaven. At that time great things were performed by the disciples; but it was He, who had worked them by Himself, that worked through them. In truth He had told them: "Without me you can do nothing." When that lame man who sat at the gate arose at the word of Peter and walked by himself so that the people were astonished, Peter then told them that he did not do these things by his own power, but by the power of Him whom they had put to death. Many, being repentant, said: "What shall we do?"

For they beheld themselves bound by a terrible crime of hate, since they had killed Him whom they should have venerated and adored; and they thought that this was irreparable. For theirs was a heinous crime, the consideration of which caused them to despair. But they for whom our Lord prayed while hanging on the cross should not have despaired. For He had said: "Father, forgive them, for they know not what they do." Among the many strangers, He saw certain ones of His own. For them was He now seeking pardon from whom He was yet receiving injury. For He did not heed the fact that He was being put to death *by* them, but only that He was dying *for* them.

TUESDAY

The reading of the holy Gospel according to St. John

At that time Jesus went about in Galilee, for he did not wish to go about Judea because the Jews were seeking to put him to death. And so forth.

Homily of St. Augustine, Bishop

In this chapter of the Gospel, fellow Christians, our Lord Jesus Christ commends Himself to our faith, especially in regard to His humanity. For He has always striven by His actions and His words to the purpose that He should be believed to be God and man—as the God who made us and the man who sought for us; as God who is with the Father always, and as man who is with us in time. For He would not be seeking whom He had created unless He became that which He had made. But remember this, and do not put it out of your hearts: Christ became man in such a way that He did not cease to be God. Remaining God, He who had made man, took the form of man.

So when He as man hides away, it is not to be thought that He has lost His power, but that He has offered an example to our weakness. For when He wills it, He is imprisoned; when He desires, He is put to death. But because there were to be members of Him, that is, His faithful followers, who would not possess that power which our Lord Himself had, the fact that He hid away, that He concealed Himself, as it were, lest He should be killed—this fact indicates that His members, in whom He truly is, should so act.

For Christ is not in the Head only, nor is He in the body alone, but the whole Christ is in Head and body. Therefore, what His members are, He is; but it does not follow that what He is, His members are. For if they were not members of Him, He would not have said to Saul: "Why dost thou persecute me?" Saul was not persecuting Him, but His members, that is, His faithful ones on earth. Now He did not wish to say, "My saints," "My servants," or still more honorably, "My brethren," but "Me," that is, my members, of whom I am the Head.

WEDNESDAY

The reading of the holy Gospel according to St. John

At that time there took place at Jerusalem the feast of the Dedication; and it was winter. And Jesus was walking in the temple, in Solomon's porch. And so forth.

Homily of St. Augustine, Bishop

The *Encaenia* was the feast of the dedication of the temple. For the Greek word *kainon* means *new*. Whenever something new was dedicated, it was called the *Encaenia*. Even now common usage keeps this word. If anyone is clothed in a new tunic, this same word is used to express the fact. The Jews celebrated with solemnity that day on which the temple was dedicated. This feast day was being celebrated when the Lord spoke the things which have been read.

"It was winter and Jesus was walking in the temple, on the porch of Solomon. The Jews therefore gathered around him and said to him: 'How long dost thou keep us in suspense? If thou art the Christ, tell us openly.'" They did not desire the truth, but they were preparing calumny. "It was winter," and they were cold, for they were loath to approach to that divine fire. If approaching is believing, he who believes approaches; he who denies draws back. The soul moves not by feet, but by affections.

They had frozen as far as the charity of love was concerned, yet they burned with eagerness to harm Him. They had gone away, yet they were at hand. They had not drawn nigh to Him by believing, yet they pressed upon Him by persecuting Him. They sought to hear from the Lord, "I am the Christ"; and perhaps, as to the man, they had knowledge about the Christ. For the prophets foretold Him; but if heretics do not understand the divinity of Christ in the prophets, nor even in the Gospel itself, how much less the Jews, so long as a veil is over their hearts?

THURSDAY

The reading of the holy Gospel according to St. Luke

At that time one of the Pharisees asked Jesus to dine with him; so he went into the house of the Pharisee and reclined at table. And so forth.

Homily of St. Gregory, Pope

When I think of the penance of Mary Magdalene, it seems more fitting to weep than to speak. For what stony breast do not the tears of this sinner soften to repentance? She beheld what she had done, and she would not be moderate in what she must do in recompense. She made her way among the guests; she came under no compulsion; she brought her tears to the banquet. Learn with what sorrow she was inflamed who did not blush to exhibit her repentant tears among the diners.

This woman whom Luke names as a sinner, John calls Mary, that same Mary, we believe, whose deliverance from seven devils was recounted by Mark. What else is signified by seven devils but the very zenith of vice? Just as all time is expressed by seven days, so the number seven is understood as all-comprehensive. Therefore, since Mary had *seven* devils, she was full of every kind of wickedness.

But once having glimpsed the stains of her depravity, entirely unashamed before the guests, she hastened to the font of mercy to be cleansed. Because she was inwardly so heartily repentant, she considered external embarrassment to be as nothing. Brethren, which should we admire the more—Mary coming, or the Lord receiving? Receiving, shall I say, or drawing? Rather I should say both drawing and receiving, for He who received her outwardly in His meekness, drew her inwardly through His mercy.

FRIDAY

The reading of the holy Gospel according to St. John

At that time the chief priests and the Pharisees gathered together a council, and said, "What are we doing? for this man is working many signs." And so forth.

Homily of St. Augustine, Bishop

The chief priests and Pharisees took council among themselves and yet they said not: "Let us believe." For these wicked men considered how they could harm Christ and destroy Him rather than consult their own interests that they themselves might not be destroyed. And yet they feared, and held a sort of a council. For they said: "What do we, for this man doth many miracles? If we let him go thus, all men will believe in him and the Romans will come and will take away our place and our nation." They feared to lose temporal things while of eternal life they thought not, and so they lost both.

For after the suffering and glorification of our Lord, the Romans did take away from them both place and nation by conquering their city and carrying them away captive; and that is true of them which was said elsewhere: "but the children of the kingdom shall be cast out into the exterior darkness." What they feared, however, was this, that, if all should believe in Christ, there would remain no one to defend the city and temple of God against the Romans; for they felt the doctrine of Christ to be against that very temple and against their father's laws.

"But one of them, named Caiphas, being the high priest that year, said to them: 'You know nothing; neither do you consider that it is expedient for you that one man should die for the people and that the whole nation perish not.' And this he spoke not of himself, but being the high priest of that year, he prophesied that Jesus should die for the nation." Here we are taught that even wicked men can prophesy things to come by the spirit of prophecy; which, however, the Evangelist attributes to a divine mystery, "because he was the pontiff," that is, the high priest.

SATURDAY

The reading of the holy Gospel according to St. John

At that time the chief priests planned to put Lazarus to death also. For on his account many of the Jews were going away and believing in Jesus. And so forth.

Homily of St. Augustine, Bishop

When Lazarus was seen to have been raised from the dead (for such a great miracle of the Lord was substantiated by so much evidence and rendered undeniable by such openness that they could neither hide it nor deny that it was an actuality), look what the chief priests planned to do. "But the chief priests planned to put Lazarus to death also." What a stupid plot and what blind wickedness! Could not Christ the Lord, who could recall a dead man to life, also restore a murdered man? Would you, ye ancients, when you would do away with Lazarus, thereby also take away the Lord's power? Does it seem to you to be one thing to be dead and another to be murdered? But behold, the Lord accomplishes both, for He restored Lazarus, who had been dead, to life, and raised Himself, who had been killed, from the dead.

"On the next day a great crowd, which had come for the festival day, when they heard that Jesus had come also to Jerusalem, took branches of palm and accompanied him in procession, crying out: 'Hosanna, blessed is he that cometh in the name of the Lord, the King of Israel.'" The palm branches are praises signifying victory, because the Lord by dying was about to conquer death and by the trophy of the cross was soon to triumph over the devil, the prince of death. The cry of the crowd was "Hosanna," which—as some who knew Hebrew say—is indicative more of a strong sentiment than anything else; just as there are some words in our language which are called interjections, as, for instance, when we are sad, we say, "Alas!" and when joyful, "Hurrah."

These, then, were the praises the crowd rendered to Him: "Hosanna! blessed is he who comes in the name of the Lord, the King of Israel." What a mental agony the envy of the Jewish princes had to undergo when such a great multitude proclaimed Christ their King. But of what moment to the Lord was it to be King of Israel? Of what great merit was it for the King of ages to become King of man? For Christ was not the King of Israel to exact tribute, nor to equip an army, nor to overcome visible enemies, but King of Israel because He reigns over their minds, eternally provides for them, and leads to His kingdom in Heaven those who believe in Him, hope in Him, and love Him.

PALM SUNDAY

I Nocturn

From Jeremias the Prophet, c. 2, 12 - 22 and 29 - 32

II Nocturn

Sermon of St. Leo, Pope

Desired by us, dearly beloved, and desirable for the whole world, the feast of the Lord's Passion is at hand and suffers us not to remain silent amid the jubilation of spiritual joys. For even though it is difficult to treat of this solemnity with befitting dignity, a priest, nevertheless, is not at liberty in such a great mystery of divine mercy to withhold from the faithful people his office of preaching, for the very matter itself, inasmuch as it is ineffable, supplies occasion to speak. Nor can there be lack of what to say, so long as what is said can never be enough.

Let human infirmity, then, give way before the glory of God, and in explaining the works of His mercy, let it find itself ever unfit. Let us labor in thought, be at a loss for talent, fall short in eloquence; it is good that we are so little able to think rightly of the Lord's majesty. For as the Prophet says, "Seek ye the Lord and be strengthened, seek His face evermore," no one should presume that he has found the whole of what he seeks, lest, in ceasing to try, he leave off drawing near.

What deed among all the works of God—in which the attention of human admiration is exhausted—so delights and overwhelms the contemplation of the mind as does the Passion of the Savior? In order to free the human race from the bonds of fatal wickedness, He has both hidden the power of His majesty from the malicious devil, and has pitted against him the weakness of our lowliness. For, if the cruel and haughty enemy had been able to understand the design of God's mercy, he would rather have striven to temper the minds of the Jews with meekness than to enkindle them with unjust hatred, lest, while he pursued the liberty of One who owed him nothing, he should lose the servitude of all his captives.

Therefore his own evil design deceived him, for the suffering which he brought on the Son of God would be turned into joy for all the children of men. The just blood which he shed would be both ransom and drink for the world which was about to be reconciled. The Lord undertook what He had chosen according to the plan of His own will. He permitted the impious hands of the raging mob to be laid on Him, which, while they were intent on their own crime, were made to serve the Redeemer. The outpouring of His love towards His murderers was so great that, praying from the cross to His Father, He did not ask that He be revenged, but that they be forgiven.

℟. O Lord, be not Thou far from me: spare me in the day of evil: let them be confounded that persecute me, * But let not me be confounded. ℣. Let all mine enemies that seek after my soul be confounded. But let.

III Nocturn

The reading of the holy Gospel according to St. Matthew

At that-time, when they drew near to Jerusalem and came to Bethphage, on the Mount of Olives, then Jesus sent two disciples, saying to them. And so forth.

Homily of St. Ambrose, Bishop

Rightly does the Lord, when He had left the Jews and was about to take up His abode in the hearts of the Gentiles, go up into the temple. Now that temple is the true one wherein the Lord is adored not according to the letter, but in the spirit. That is the temple of God which has for its foundation not a structure of stone, but the truths of faith. Therefore those who hated Him are left; those who will love Him are chosen. And hence He comes to Mount Olivet that He might with sublime power plant those new olive sprouts whose mother is that Jerusalem which is above.

On this mount is the heavenly Husbandman; so that all those that have been planted in the house of God may each be able to say: "But I am as a fruitful olive tree in the house of the

Lord." And perchance the mountain itself is Christ. For who else could bring forth such fruits of new branches, bent down not with an abundance of olives, but spiritually fruitful with the fullness of the Gentiles? He it is by whom we ascend, and He also to whom we ascend. He is the gate; He is the way. He it is who is opened and He also who openeth; it is He at which those who wish to enter knock, and He also who is adored by those who are within.

Now the colt was in the village and was tied there with the ass; nor could it be loosed except at the Lord's bidding. It was the hand of an apostle that loosed it. He whose work and life are like theirs will have such a grace as they had. Be like the holy Apostles, and you too may be able to loose them that are bound. Now let us consider who those were who, discovered in their sin, were thrown out of Paradise and exiled to a village. Then you will see how Life recalled those whom death had expelled.

And therefore, according to Matthew, we read both of an ass and a colt, that as in two persons both sexes had been expelled, so in two animals, both are recalled. By the ass, then, He signified Eve, as it were, the mother of error; by the colt He signified the whole of the Gentile world, [who are, as it were, the children of error], and therefore He is seated on the colt of an ass. And rightly "on which no man has sat," because no one before Christ called the people of the Gentiles to the Church. To conclude, according to Mark you have it thus: "upon which no man *yet* hath sat."

℟. Liars have surrounded me: they have fallen upon me with scourges without cause: * But do Thou, O Lord, my defender, avenge me. ℣. For trouble is near and there is none to help. But do Thou.

✠ Continuation of the holy Gospel according to St. Matthew.— At that time, when they drew near to Jerusalem and came to Bethphage, on the Mount of Olives, then Jesus sent two disciples, saying to them, "Go into the village opposite you, and immediately you will find an ass tied, and a colt with her; loose them and bring them to me. And if anyone say anything to you, you shall say that the Lord has need of them, and immediately he will send them." Now this was done that thereby might be fulfilled what was spoken through the prophet, saying, "Tell the daughter of Sion: Behold, thy king comes to thee, meek and seated upon an ass, and upon a colt, the foal of a beast of burden."

So the disciples went and did as Jesus had directed them. And they brought the ass and the colt, laid their cloaks on them, and made him sit thereon. And most of the crowd spread their cloaks upon the road, while others were cutting branches from the trees, and strewing them on the road. And the crowds that went before him, and those that followed, kept crying out, saying, Hosanna to the Son of David! Blessed is he who comes in the name of the Lord!"

LET US PRAY

O almighty and eternal God, who, to give the human race an example of humility, didst decree that our Savior shouldst assume our nature and endure the sufferings of the Cross, mercifully grant that we may learn the lesson of His patience and share the blessings of His Resurrection. Through the same Jesus Christ.

MONDAY IN HOLY WEEK

The reading of the holy Gospel according to St. John

Jesus therefore, six days before the Passover, came to Bethany where Lazarus, whom Jesus had raised to life, had died. And so forth.

Homily of St. Augustine, Bishop

Lest men might think he had become a phantom because he had risen from the dead, Lazarus was one of them who were at table: he lived, conversed, ate; the truth was shown forth; the incredulity of the Jews was confounded. Now Jesus was at table with Lazarus and the others, and Martha—one of Lazarus' sisters—served. But Mary—Lazarus' other sister—"took a pound of ointment of right spikenard, of great price, and anointed the feet of Jesus, and wiped his feet with her hair, and the house was filled with the odor of the ointment." We have heard the fact; now let us seek out the mystery.

O soul, if you wish to be faithful, with Mary anoint the feet of our Lord with precious ointment. That ointment was justice; therefore, it was a pound; moreover, it was an ointment "of pure spikenard, of great price." The word *pistikes*, used by the Evangelist as the name of this ointment, we must understand to be the name of some place from which this costly perfume was imported; but this does not exhaust its meaning, and it agrees well with a mystic interpretation. For this Greek word, translated into our tongue, means *faith*. You were striving after justice. "The just man lives by faith." Therefore, anoint the feet of Jesus by living correctly; follow the footsteps of our

Lord. Dry them with your hair; if you have a superabundance, give to the poor, and then you have dried the feet of our Lord, for hair is considered among the superfluities of the body. You are considering what you are to do with your superfluities; they are superfluous to you, but they are necessary for the Lord's feet. Perhaps the feet of the Lord here on earth are in need.

For concerning whom—if not His members—will He speak at the end: "Because you did it to one of my least ones, you did it to me"? You have given of things superfluous to you, but you have satisfied My feet. "The house was filled with the odor"; the world is enriched with a good character, for a good reputation is as a good odor. Those who live in wickedness and are called Christians do harm to Christ, and concerning such it has been said that through them "the name of the Lord is blasphemed." If through such men the name of God is blasphemed, through good men the name of the Lord is praised. Hear the Apostle: "We are," he says, "the good odor of Christ in every place."

TUESDAY IN HOLY WEEK

From Jeremias the Prophet, c. 11, 15 - 20; c. 12, 1 - 4 and 7 - 11

WEDNESDAY IN HOLY WEEK

From Jeremias the Prophet, c. 17, 13 - 18; c. 18, 13 - 23

For the remaining days of Holy Week, see special Holy Week Manual

EASTER SUNDAY

I Nocturn

*From the Epistle of St. Paul the Apostle
to the Romans, c. 6, 2 - 13*

II Nocturn

Sermon of St. Gregory Nazianzen

The Pasch of the Lord, the Pasch, and again I say, the Pasch—in honor of the Trinity! This is for us the feast of feasts, and the celebration of celebrations, excelling all the other feasts—not only those of mankind and of things bound to the earth, but even those which are of Christ Himself, and are celebrated on account of Him—as much as the sun excels the stars. Yesterday the Lamb was slain and the doorposts smeared; Egypt mourned her first-born, and the exterminator (who was indeed a sign for the purpose of inspiring awe and terror) passed over us who have been protected by the precious blood.

Today we have wholly fled from Egypt and that cruel dominion of Pharao and the hostile overseers, and have been freed from the clay and the preparation of bricks; neither is there anyone who can keep us from celebrating the feast of the Exodus to the Lord our God; and indeed to celebrate, "not with the old leaven of malice and wickedness, but with the unleavened bread of sincerity and truth," carrying with us nothing of the Egyptian and impious leaven. Yesterday I suffered on the cross with Christ; today I am glorified together with Him! Yesterday I died with Him; today I am raised to life with Him! Yesterday I was buried with Him; today I rise together with Him!

But let us offer gifts to Him who suffered and rose for us. Do you perhaps think that I speak of gold or silver, or tapestries, or glittering stones of great price, the transient and perishable materials of the world which remain things of earth, and which, for the most part, the wicked and the slaves of earthly goods and the princes of the world usually possess? Rather, let us offer ourselves, that is, the dearest and most pleasing riches to God. Let us return the glory of our image to the One whose image we are; let us recognize our dignity; let us follow our Exemplar in honor; let us understand the power of this mystery, and for what Christ suffered death. Let us be as Christ, for Christ is also as we. Let us become gods for His sake, for He also was made man for us.

He took upon Himself what was poorer that He might give what was more glorious; He was made poor that we might be enriched by that poverty; He took the form of a servant that we might be set at liberty. He descended that we might be elevated; and that we might receive the power to overcome, He allowed Himself to be tempted. He was despised that glory might accrue to us; put to death, to bring salvation to us. He ascended into Heaven that He might draw to Himself those who had fallen into sin. Let everyone give all things; let him offer all things to Him, who gave Himself as the price of Redemption for us and as a recompense for our fault. But he can give nothing as great as when, rightly understanding this mystery, he offers himself and becomes for the sake of Him everything which He has become for our sake.

℞. I am the true vine, and you the branches: * He that abideth in Me, and I in him, the same beareth much fruit, alleluia, alleluia. ℣. As the Father hath loved Me, I also have loved you. He that. Glory. He that.

III Nocturn

The reading of the holy Gospel according to St. Mark

At that time Mary Magdalene, Mary the mother of James, and Salome, bought spices, that they might go and anoint him. And so forth.

Homily of St. Gregory, Pope

Dearly beloved brethren, you have just heard that the holy women who had followed the Lord came to the tomb with sweet spices; thus even in death they manifested the devotedness of their affection toward Him whom they had loved in life. But that which they did signifies something which must be done in holy Church. Hence it is expedient for us to hear what they have done that we may consider what we must do in imitation of them. And therefore if we, believing in Him who has died and filled with the odor of virtues, seek the Lord with the credit of good works, then do we in very truth come to His tomb with sweet spices.

The women who have come with sweet spices see angels, because those minds behold heavenly citizens who journey to the Lord by their holy desires. We should know, however, why the angel is seen sitting on the right side. For what is designated by the left side if not the present life? Wherefore it is written in the Canticle of Canticles: "His left hand is under my head and his right hand shall embrace me."

Therefore, since our Redeemer had already passed from the corruption of this present life, rightly did the angel, who had come to announce His eternal life, sit on the right side. He appeared clad in a white garment because he announced the joys of our festivity. For the whiteness of the garment denotes the splendor of our solemnity. *Ours*, shall we say or *his?* To speak more exactly we should say both *his* and *ours*. The Resurrection of our Redeemer was indeed our festivity because it led us back to immortality; it was at the same time the festival of the angels because by recalling us to heavenly things it filled up their number.

Therefore on his and our festival day the angel appeared clothed in white vesture, because when we, by the Resurrection of the Lord, are led back to the things of heaven, the losses to the heavenly fatherland are repaired. But let us hearken to what the angel speaks to the women who have just arrived: "Do not fear." As though he would plainly say: "Let them fear who love not the approach of celestial inhabitants; let them be very much afraid who, weighed down by carnal desires, despair of being able to belong to their society. But you, why do you fear who look upon your fellow citizens? Whence also Matthew, in describing the apparition of the angel, says: "His countenance was as lightning and his vesture as snow." As lightning, indeed, to express the terror of fear, but as snow to manifest the charm of his beauty.

℟. When the sabbath was passed, Mary Magdalene, and Mary, the mother of James and Salome, bought sweet spices, * That coming, they might anoint Jesus, alleluia, alleluia. ℣. And very early in the morning, the first day of the week, they came to the sepulchre, the sun being now risen. That. Glory. That.

✠ Continuation of the holy Gospel according to St. Mark.— At that time Mary Magdalene, Mary the mother of James, and Salome, bought spices, that they might go and anoint him. And very early on the first day of the week, they came to the tomb, when the sun had just risen. And they were saying to one another, "Who will roll the stone back from the doorway of the tomb for us?" And looking up they saw that the stone had been rolled back; for it was very large. But on entering the tomb, they saw a young man sitting at the right side, clothed in a white robe, and they were amazed. He said to them, "Do not be terrified. You are looking for Jesus of Nazareth, who was crucified. He has risen, he is not here. Behold the place where they laid him. But go, tell his disciples and Peter that he goes before you into Galilee; there you shall see him, as he told you."

EASTER MONDAY

LET US PRAY

O God, who through Thine only-begotten Son has on this day overcome death and opened to us the gates of everlasting life, grant that our holy desires, which already have been aroused within us by Thy grace, may by Thy further aid be happily fulfilled. Through the same Jesus Christ.

EASTER MONDAY

I Nocturn

From the first Epistle of St. Paul the Apostle to the Corinthians, c. 15, 1 - 22

II Nocturn

Sermon of St. Maximus, Bishop

Not without reason, brethren, is this psalm, in which the Prophet commands us to exult and rejoice, read today. Holy David invites all creatures to the festivity of this day. For on this day through the Resurrection of Christ limbo is opened; by the neophytes of the Church the earth is renewed; by the Holy Spirit heaven is unbolted.

For limbo, having been opened, gives up its dead; the earth, having ben renewed, buds forth those who are arising; heaven, having been unbolted, receives those who are ascending. Then, too, the thief ascends into paradise; the bodies of the Blessed enter into the Holy City; the dead are brought back to life; and by a certain dispensation in the Resurrection of Christ all the elements lift themselves to a higher level.

Limbo places in the regions above those whom it had retained; the earth sends to heaven those whom it had buried; heaven presents to the Lord those whom it receives. By one and the same act the Passion of the Savior raises men from the depths, lifts them up from the earth, and places them on high. For the Resurrection of Christ is life for the dead, pardon for the sinful, and glory for the saints. Therefore David invites every creature to the festivity of Christ's Resurrection. He says that we should "rejoice and be glad on this day which the Lord hath made!"

Therefore, brethren, all of us should rejoice on this holy day; let no one withdraw himself through consciousness of his sins from this common joy; let no one be kept away from public worship by the burden of his sins, for the sinner must not despair of forgiveness on this day, for this is its privilege that is by no means slight. If the thief merited paradise, why should not a Christian deserve pardon? And if our Lord showed mercy to the one when He was crucified, much more will He show mercy to the other when He arises. And if the humility of the Passion bestowed so great a thing on him who confessed, how great a thing shall the glory of the Resurrection confer on him who asks? For, as you yourselves know, a joyful victory is accustomed to be more generous in its giving than is condemned misery.

℟. With great power the Apostles gave * Testimony of the Resurrection of our Lord Jesus Christ, alleluia, alleluia. ℣. They were filled with the Holy Ghost, and they spoke the word of God with boldness. Testimony. Glory. Testimony.

III Nocturn

The reading of the holy Gospel according to St. Luke

At that time two of the disciples of Jesus were going that very day to a village named Emmaus, which is sixty stadia from Jerusalem. And so forth.

Homily of St. Gregory, Pope

You have heard, dearly beloved brethren, that whilst two of the Lord's disciples were walking along the road, indeed speaking of Him, but yet not believing, the Lord Himself appeared to them, but He did not show them the appearance which they would recognize. Hence, you see, the Lord produced outwardly in the eyes of their body what was going on inwardly in the eyes of their heart. Inwardly these disciples loved, yet doubted. Outwardly, the Lord was present to them, yet He did not show them who He was.

Because they were speaking of Him, He was present to them; but because they doubted, He hid from them the form they would recognize. Indeed, He spoke to them, He chided them for their hardness of heart, He opened to them the mysteries of holy Writ which concerned Him—and yet, because He was still a stranger to faith in their hearts, He made as though He would go farther. Now to say *He made as though* might seem to indicate deceit. But we must know that He who is perfect Truth did nothing through duplicity, for the word used here by the

Evangelist for *He made as though* means to *put together*—and that is what the Lord did—He put together His outward action with the inner state of mind of the disciples, that is, He showed Himself to them in His Body as He was to them in their minds.

They were as yet to be tried to see whether they, who still did not love Him as their God, would not at least be able to love Him as their fellow traveler. But because they with whom Truth Itself was journeying could not be strangers to charity, they invited Him to remain as their guest. But why do we say, "They invited Him," when it is written, "And they constrained Him"? From this example we may clearly gather that wayfarers are not merely to be given a passing invitation to our hospitality, but are to be pressed to accept it.

They therefore prepared a repast and set forth bread and other food; and then they recognized in the breaking of the bread the God whom they did not recognize in the exposition of the Scripture. They were not enlightened by hearing the precepts, but by the fulfillment of them, for it is written, "Not the hearers of the law are justified before God, but the doers of the law." Whosoever, therefore, desires to understand what he hears, let him be zealous to fulfill by deed those things which he has already been able to understand. Behold! the Lord was not recognized whilst He spoke, but He deigned to be recognized when He partakes of food.

℟. Mary Magdalene, and the other Mary went very early to the sepulchre. * Jesus whom you seek is not here, He is risen as He said, and goeth before you into Galilee: there you shall see Him, alleluia, alleluia. ℣. And very early in the morning, the first day of the week, they came to the sepulchre, the sun being now risen: and entering in, they saw a young man sitting on the right hand, who said to them. Jesus. Glory. Jesus.

✠ Continuation of the holy Gospel according to St. Luke.— At that time two of the disciples of Jesus were going that very day to a village named Emmaus, which is sixty stadia from Jerusalem. And they were talking to each other about all these things that had happened. And it came to pass, while they were conversing and arguing together, that Jesus himself also drew near and went along with them; but their eyes were held, that they should not recognize him. And he said to them, "What words are these that you are exchanging as you walk and are sad?"

But one of them, named Cleophas, answered and said to him, "Art thou the only stranger in Jerusalem who does not know the things that have happened there in these days?" And he said to them, "What things?"

And they said to him, "Concerning Jesus of Nazareth, who was a prophet, mighty in work and word before God and all the people; and how our chief priests and rulers delivered him up to be sentenced to death, and crucified him. But we were hoping that it was he who should redeem Israel. Yes, and besides all this today is the third day since these things came to pass. And moreover, certain women of our company, who were at the tomb before it was light, astounded us, and not finding his body, they came, saying that they had also seen a vision of angels, who said that he is alive. So some of our company went to the tomb, and found it even as the women had said, but him they did not see."

But he said to them, "O foolish ones and slow of heart to believe in all that the prophets have spoken! Did not the Christ have to suffer these things before entering into his glory?" And beginning then with Moses and with all the prophets, he interpreted to them in all the Scriptures the things referring to himself.

And they drew near to the village to which they were going, and he acted as though he were going on. And they urged him, saying, "Stay with us, for it is getting towards evening, and the day is now far spent." And he went in with them. And it came to pass when he reclined at table with them, that he took the bread and blessed and broke and began handing it to them. And their eyes were opened, and they recognized him; and he vanished from their sight. And they said to each other, "Was not our heart burning within us while he was speaking on the road and explaining to us the Scriptures?"

And rising up that very hour, they returned to Jerusalem, where they found the Eleven gathered together and those who were with them, saying, "The Lord has risen indeed, and has appeared to Simon." And they themselves began to relate what had happened on the journey, and how they recognized him in the breaking of the bread.

Let Us Pray

O God, who in the Paschal solemnity hast bestowed Thy saving remedies on the world, continue, we beseech Thee, to pour forth Thy heavenly gifts upon Thy people, that thereby they may deserve to obtain perfect liberty and arrive at life everlasting. Through our Lord.

EASTER TUESDAY

I Nocturn

From the Acts of the Apostles, c. 13, 25 - 37

II Nocturn

Sermon of St. John Chrysostom

Although all solemnities, dearly beloved, which are celebrated in the Church for the honor of God, are holy and venerable, nevertheless, this day of the Lord's Resurrection has a festivity all its own. For indeed, while all the other days hold in themselves gladness for the living, this day holds joy for the dead.

For this festivity is common alike to the lower regions as well as to those that are above, for the Lord, rising again from the dead, brought festivity there where He conquered death, and there too whither He has returned as the Victor over death. Well, therefore, does the Psalmist speak especially of this day saying: "This is the day the Lord has made; let us be glad and rejoice therein."

For, announcing the Lord's Resurrection, he indicated that it was a day of salubrious exsultation, not to the heavens alone, but also to the lower regions. When the Lord descended into the blackness of hell, even there, at the time when the Savior illumined it, it was without doubt a most bright day. Whence the Evangelist beautifully says: "And the light shone in the darkness, and the darkness did not comprehend it." Although the Lord descended into the darkness, He did not, however, feel its gloom.

He retained in that horror of night the inviolable splendor of His majesty; He shone in the splendor of His eternal nature, and so the Light was not overwhelmed by the night, but the night by the Light. Let us be glad, therefore, most dearly beloved, and let us rejoice in the Lord, for today is given to us by the Lord the Light of salvation, according to that which the same Psalmist says in one of the following verses: "The Lord is God, and he hath shone upon us."

℟. The Good Shepherd, who gave His life for His sheep and deigned to die for His flock, has risen: * Alleluia, alleluia, alleluia. ℣. For Christ our Pasch is sacrificed. Alleluia. Glory. Alleluia.

III Nocturn

The reading of the holy Gospel according to St. Luke

At that time Jesus stood in the midst of his disciples and said to them: "Peace to you! It is I, do not be afraid." And so forth.

Homily of St. Ambrose, Bishop

It is marvelous how Christ in bodily nature entered by a hidden way through an impenetrable body in the visible sight of all. He is easy to touch, but He is difficult to be understood. But the disciples, being troubled, "supposed that they saw a spirit." And therefore the Lord, in order to give us a tangible proof of His Resurrection, said: "Handle and see; for a spirit hath not flesh and bones, as you see me to have." Consequently, He penetrated things impervious and affording no passage, not by means of an incorporeal nature, but by a certain quality of His Resurrection. For what can be touched is a body; what can be handled is a body.

We also shall rise in the body. An animal body is sown, but a spiritual body arises—the latter more subtle, the former more dense, still marred, as it were, by a kind of earthly stain. For how could that not be a body in which remained the signs of wounds and the traces of scars, which our Lord offered to be touched? In which He not only strengthens our faith, but increases our devotion by the fact that He preferred to bear to heaven the wounds which He had received for our sake and did not wish to blot them out, that thus He might show the price of our liberty to God the Father. The Father has placed Him, just as He is, on His right hand, embracing Him, the trophy of our Redemption; He has shown us that the martyrs are there, just such as they were, with the crown of martyrdom.

And since our sermon has come this far, let us consider how it is that, according to St. John, the apostles believed and were glad, and, according to St. Luke, they were reproved for being incredulous. According to the former they received the Holy Spirit, but according to the latter they were commanded to remain there in the city until they were imbued with power from on high.

It seems to me that the one Apostle (St. John) has touched upon the greater and more important matters, and the other (St. Luke) upon things as they follow and which are related to things human; the latter makes use of the historic method, and the former offers a summary, because there can be no doubt about St. John who bears testimony of the things in which he took part, "and his testimony is true." Likewise it is right to reject any suspicion of negligence or deceit by the other who has merited to be an Evangelist. And therefore we think that each one has spoken the truth, and that they do not differ in a variety of opinions or a diversity of persons. For although St. Luke says that at first the Apostles did not believe, afterwards, however, he shows that they did believe. If we were to consider the first things alone, they would be contrary, but if we look to the following, it is certain that they will agree.

℟. With great power the Apostles gave * Testimony of the Resurrection of our Lord Jesus Christ, alleluia, alleluia. ℣. They were filled with the Holy Ghost, and they spoke the word of God with boldness. Testimony. Glory. Testimony.

✠ Continuation of the holy Gospel according to St. Luke.— At that time Jesus stood in the midst of his disciples and said to them: "Peace to you! It is I, do not be afraid." But they were startled and panic-stricken, and thought that they saw a spirit.

And he said to them, "Why are you disturbed and why do doubts arise in your hearts? See my hands and feet, that it is I myself. Feel me and see; for a spirit does not have flesh and bones, as you see I have." And having said this, he showed them his hands and his feet. But as they still disbelieved and marvelled for joy, he said, "Have you anything here to eat?" And they offered him a piece of broiled fish and a honeycomb. And when he had eaten in their presence, he took what remained and gave it to them.

And he said to them, "These are the words which I spoke to you while I was yet with you, that all things must be fulfilled that are written in the Law of Moses and the Prophets and the Psalms concerning me." Then he opened their minds, that they might understand the Scriptures. And he said to them, "Thus it is written; and thus the Christ should suffer, and should rise again from the dead on the third day; and that repentance and remission of sins should be preached in his name to all the nations."

Let Us Pray

O God, who dost ever multiply Thy Church by a new progeny, grant to Thy servants that they may retain in their lives the mystery which they have received by faith. Through our Lord.

WEDNESDAY IN EASTER WEEK

The reading of the holy Gospel according to St. John

At that time Jesus manifested himself again at the sea of Tiberias. Now he manifested himself in this way. There were together Simon Peter and Thomas, called the Twin. And so forth.

Homily of St. Gregory, Pope

Brethren, the lesson of the holy Gospel which has been spoken in our ears raises a question in the mind, but by its very disturbance it points to the need of sound judgment. For it can be asked why Peter, who had been a fisherman before his calling, afterwards returned to his fishing; and since the Truth Itself had declared, "No man putting his hand to the plough, and looking back, is fit for the kingdom of God," why did he seek what he had forsaken? But if the virtue of discretion is considered, the matter is quickly seen through, for surely it was no sin to return after his calling to that trade which he had practiced without sin before it.

We know that Peter was a fisherman, while Matthew was a tax-collector, and after their call Peter returned to fishing, but Matthew did not resume his business at the custom-house—for it is one thing to seek one's sustenance by fishing, and another to increase one's fortune by the gains of the custom-house. For there are many vocations which can scarcely or in no way at all be followed without incurring guilt. Thus it is demanded that the soul, after its conversion, do not run back to those things which implicate it in sin.

On this same matter it can likewise be questioned as to the reason why, while the disciples were laboring on the sea, our Lord, who before His Resurrection walked on the waves of the sea in the sight of the disciples, after His Resurrection stood on the shore. The reason for the fact is shortly perceived if the motive that is present behind it all is reflected upon. What else does the sea represent except the present world, which breaks upon itself in the tempests of destruction and the billows of corruptible life? What is pictured by the firmness of the shore but the perpetuity of eternal repose? And so, because the disciples were yet immersed in the surges of mortal life, "they labored on the sea." And because our Savior had passed beyond the corruption of the flesh, "after his resurrection he stood on the shore."

THURSDAY IN EASTER WEEK

The reading of the holy Gospel according to St. John

At that time Mary was standing outside weeping at the tomb. So, as she wept, she stooped down and looked into the tomb, and saw two angels in white sitting. And so forth.

Homily of St. Gregory, Pope

Mary Magdalene, who had been a sinner in the city, by loving the Truth washed away with her tears the stains of her crime, and the word of the Truth was fulfilled by whom it was said: "Many sins are forgiven her, because she has loved much." She who had remained cold in her sin, afterwards became fervent by her ardent love. For after she had come to the tomb and did not find our Lord's body there, she believed that it had been taken away and announced the fact to the disciples, who, coming, saw for themselves and believed it to be as the woman had told them. And it is written of them: "The disciples therefore departed again to their home." And then it is added: "But Mary stood at the sepulchre without, weeping."

Wherefore it must be considered how great a force of love enkindled the soul of the woman who did not depart from the tomb even though the disciples left. She was seeking One whom she had not found; in her search she wept, and, inflamed with the fire of her love, she burned in her yearning for Him whom she believed had been taken away. Thus did it happen that she alone then saw Him—she who had remained behind to look for Him; for truly, the virtue of a good work is perseverance, and it is declared by the voice of Truth: "He who shall persevere to the end, he shall be saved."

"Now as she was weeping, she stooped down and looked into the sepulchre." Certainly she had already seen that the tomb was empty; she had already announced that the Lord had been taken away—why is it that she bends down again, that she desires to look again? It does not satisfy one who loves to have looked but once, for the strength of love multiplies the reasons for the search. Therefore she sought before and did not find; she persevered in her search, and so it came about that she did find. This delay was made that her desires, by not being fulfilled at once, might increase, and, increasing, might meet with Him to whom they aspired.

FRIDAY IN EASTER WEEK

The reading of the holy Gospel according to St. Matthew

At that time the eleven disciples went into Galilee, to the mountain where Jesus had directed them to go. And so forth.

Homily of St. Jerome, Priest

After His Resurrection Jesus is seen on a mountain of Galilee and there is adored; although certain ones doubt, their doubt increases our faith. Then He is more plainly shown to Thomas, and He shows him the side pierced with the lance and the hands pierced by the nails. "Jesus coming spoke to them, saying: All power is given to me in heaven and on earth." Power has been given to Him who a little before was crucified, who was buried in the tomb, who lay dead, who afterwards rose again. Moreover, "in heaven and on earth" all power was given, that He who before reigned in heaven might also through the faith of the believers reign on earth.

"Going, therefore, teach ye all nations, baptizing them in the name of the Father, and of the Son, and of the Holy Ghost." First they teach all nations; then they wash with water those they have taught. For it cannot be that the body receive the sacrament of Baptism unless the soul has received the truth of faith before. Moreover, they are baptized "in the name of the Father, and of the Son, and of the Holy Ghost" that, since the name of the Trinity is the name of but one God, the giving of those whose divinity is one may also be one.

"Teaching them to observe all things whatsoever I have commanded you." A special order. He commanded the apostles that they should first teach all nations and then wash them in the sacrament of faith. And after faith and Baptism, they should command them the things that must be done. And lest we think the things commanded light and few, He added, "All things whatsoever I have commanded you," so that whoever believed and were baptized in the Trinity might do all things that were commanded. "And behold I am with you all days, even to the consummation of the world." He promises that He will be with the disciples even to the end of the world, and shows them that they will always conquer, and that He will never go away from them who believe.

SATURDAY IN EASTER WEEK

The reading of the holy Gospel according to St. John

At that time, on the first day of the week, Mary Magdalene came early to the tomb, while it was still dark. And so forth.

Homily of St. Gregory, Pope

The lesson of the holy Gospel which you, brethren, have just heard is very evident as to its historical sense, but there are mysteries there which we must briefly search out. "Mary Magdalene, when it was yet dark, came to the sepulchre." Following true history, the hour is noted; but according to a mystical understanding, the intelligence of the searcher is signified. Mary was seeking in the sepulchre the Author of all, whom she had seen dead in the flesh, and because she found Him not, she believed that the body was stolen away. It was still dark when she came to the sepulchre. She ran quickly and announced the fact to the disciples; but those ran before the rest who loved more than the rest, that is, Peter and John.

The two were running together, but John ran faster than Peter. He came first to the tomb, yet did not presume to enter. Then Peter came later and entered in. What, brethren, what does this running signify? Must we believe that this exact description of the Evangelist is devoid of mysteries? By no means! John would not say that he had gone before, yet had not entered, if he had believed that in his hesitation there was no mystery. What is signified by John but the synagogue, what by Peter but the Church?

It is not to be wondered at that the synagogue is signified by the younger, and the Church by the elder, because even if the synagogue precedes the Church of the Gentiles in the worship of God, yet the multitude of the Gentiles precedes the synagogue in the order of nature, as Paul testifies when he says: "That which is spiritual is not first, but that which is carnal." By the elder, then, that is, Peter, the Church of the Gentiles is prefigured; by the younger, that is, John, the synagogue of the Jews. Both ran together, because the Gentiles ran with the synagogue from the beginning to the end on a road similar and common to both, even though not with a like and common understanding. The synagogue came first to the tomb, but did not enter, because she perceived the commands of the law, heard the prophecies concerning the Lord's Incarnation and Passion, but would not believe in Him when dead.

LOW SUNDAY

I Nocturn

From the Epistle of St. Paul the Apostle to the Colossians, c. 3, 1 - 17

II Nocturn

Sermon of St. Augustine, Bishop

The paschal solemnity is concluded with today's feast, and therefore today the garment of the neophytes is changed—in such a manner, though, that the whiteness, which—as far as concerns the exterior garment—is laid aside, may always be retained in the heart. On which feast it is indeed our first duty to see to it that (because these are paschal days, that is, days of pardon and remission) the festivity of these holy days be so spent by us that purity may not be tarnished as a result of corporal relaxation; but rather, abstaining from all lust, drunkenness, and lasciviousness, we strive for a moderate relaxation and holy sincerity, in order that whatever we do not acquire by corporal abstinence, we may seek by purity of mind.

To all indeed whom our care embraces this admonition is directed; but today, when the solemnity of mysteries has been terminated, we address you as the new shoots of sanctity, regenerated from water and the Holy Spirit, a tender bud, a new creation, the flower of our honor and the fruit of our labor, my joy and my crown, all you who stand in the Lord.

I speak to you in the words of the Apostle: "Behold, the night is passed, and the day is at hand. Cast off the works of darkness, and put on the armor of light. Let us walk honestly, as in the day; not in rioting and drunkenness; not in chambering and impurity; not in contention and envy; but put ye on the Lord Jesus Christ." "We have," Peter says, "the more firm prophetical word, whereunto you do well to attend, as to a light that shineth in a dark place, until the day dawn and the daystar arise in your hearts."

"Let your loins be girt and lamps burning in your hands, and you yourselves like to men who wait for their lord, when he shall return from the wedding." Behold the days come in which the Lord says: "A little while, and you shall not see me, and again a little while and you shall see me." This is the hour of which He said, "You shall be sad and the world shall rejoice," that is, in this life, full of temptations, in which we travel without Him. But again He says, "I shall see you and your heart shall rejoice, and your joy no man shall take from you."

LOW SUNDAY

℟. With great power the Apostles gave * Testimony of the Resurrection of our Lord Jesus Christ, alleluia, alleluia. ℣. They were filled with the Holy Ghost, and they spoke the word of God with boldness. Testimony. Glory. Testimony.

III Nocturn

The reading of the holy Gospel according to St. John

At that time, when it was late that same day, the first of the week, though the doors where the disciples gathered had been closed for fear of the Jews, Jesus came and stood in the midst and said to them, "Peace be to you!" And so forth.

Homily of St. Gregory, Pope

Straightway upon reading this Gospel a question agitates the mind: How was it that the body of our risen Lord was a real one since it was able to pass through closed doors into the presence of His disciples? But we ought to know that the operation of God is not wonderful if it is comprehended by reason; neither has faith any merit in regard to that for which human reason offers demonstration. Nevertheless, those very works of our Redeemer, which can in themselves by no means be fully understood, must be considered in connection with another operation of His, so that to wonderful things even more wonderful facts might give credibility.

For it was that same body of the Lord that came in to the disciples through closed doors which had become known to human eyes by His birth from the closed womb of the Virgin. And what wonder is it if that body which, coming (into the world) to die, proceeded from the Virgin's womb without breaking the seal thereof, after the Resurrection and now destined to live forever, should have passed through closed doors? But because the faith of the onlookers wavered with regard to that body which could be seen, He immediately showed them His hands and side; the flesh which He had brought in through closed doors He submitted to be handled.

Wherefore He manifests two admirable and, according to our human reasoning, exceedingly opposite marks in as far as He showed His body after its Resurrection incorruptible, yet palpable. For what is palpable necessarily is also corruptible; and what is incorruptible cannot be palpable. But in a wonderful, nay, inestimable manner did our Redeemer after His Resurrection exhibit His body both incorruptible and palpable so that He might invite us to a reward by showing it as incorruptible, and that by showing it as palpable He might strengthen our faith. It was for this reason, then, that He manifested Himself both incorruptible and palpable: to show that His body after the Resurrection was truly of the same nature but of another glory.

He said to them: "Peace be to you. As the Father hath sent me, so I also send you," that is, "As God the Father hath sent me who am God, so I, as man, send you, who are men." The Father sent the Son and decreed that He should be made flesh for the Redemption of the human race. It is evident that He wished Him to come into the world to suffer; but nevertheless He loved the Son whom He sent to suffer. So also our Lord did not send the chosen apostles into the world to the joys of the world, but, as He Himself was sent, to sufferings. Therefore, just as the Son is beloved of the Father and nevertheless is sent to suffer, so also the disciples are beloved of the Lord, and, notwithstanding this, are sent into the world to suffer. Rightly, therefore, is it said: "As the Father hath sent me, so I also send you." That is, "When I send you among the scandals of persecutors, I love you with that same charity with which the Father loves me, whom He decreed should come to undergo sufferings.

℟. Purge out the old leaven that you may be a new paste: for Christ our Pasch is sacrificed. * Therefore, let us feast in the Lord, alleluia. ℣. He died for our offenses and rose again for our justification. Therefore. Glory. Therefore.

☩ Continuation of the holy Gospel according to St. John.—At that time, when it was late that same day, the first of the week, though the doors where the disciples gathered had been closed for fear of the Jews, Jesus came and stood in the midst and said to them, "Peace be to you!" And when he had said this, he showed them his hands and his side. The disciples therefore rejoiced at the sight of the Lord. He therefore said to them again, "Peace be to you! As the Father has sent me, I also send you." When he had said this, he breathed upon them, and said to them, "Receive the Holy Spirit; whose sins you shall forgive, they are forgiven them; and whose sins you shall retain, they are retained."

Now Thomas, one of the Twelve, called the Twin, was not with them when Jesus came. The other disciples therefore said to him, "We have seen the Lord." But he said to them, "Unless I see in his hands the print of the nails, and put my finger into the place of the nails, and put my hand into his side, I will not believe."

And after eight days, his disciples were again inside, and Thomas with them. Jesus came, the doors being closed, and stood in their midst, and said, "Peace be to you!" Then he said to Thomas, "Bring here thy finger, and see my hands; and bring here thy hand, and put it into my side; and be not unbelieving, but believing." Thomas answered and said to him, "My Lord and my God!" Jesus said to him, "Because thou hast seen me, thou hast believed. Blessed are they who have not seen, and yet have believed."

Many other signs also Jesus worked in the sight of his disciples, which are not written in this book. But these are written that you may believe that Jesus is the Christ, the Son of God, and that believing you may have life in his name.

LET US PRAY

Grant, we beseech Thee, O almighty God, that we who have celebrated the feasts of the Paschal solemnity may retain their fruits in our life and actions. Through our Lord.

II SUNDAY AFTER EASTER

I Nocturn

From the Acts of the Apostles, c. 1, 1 - 26

II Nocturn

Sermon of St. Leo, Pope

These days which passed between the Resurrection and Ascension of the Lord, dearly beloved, were not spent in an idle manner, but in them great sacraments were instituted, great mysteries were revealed. In these days, the fear of dread death is taken away, and not only is the immortality of the soul declared, but also that of the body. In them, through the breathing of the Lord, the Holy Spirit is poured upon all the apostles, and to the blessed Apostle Peter above all the rest is entrusted, after the keys of the kingdom, the care of the Lord's sheepfold.

In these days, our Lord joins Himself as a third companion to two of His disciples on a journey; and in order to clear away all the darkness of our doubt, the hesitation of these timorous and faltering souls is chided. Their enlightened hearts conceive the flame of faith, and those hearts, once cold, are made ardent when their Lord has explained the Scripture.

Also in the breaking of the bread the eyes of those who were eating together are opened; and far more blessed is the opening of the eyes of those to whom the glorification of their nature was manifested than was that of those first parents of our race upon whom was heaped the confusion of their prevarication.

But among these and other miracles, when the disciples were excited by fearful thoughts, and the Lord had appeared in their midst and said, "Peace be to you," He rebuked their thoughts, discordant with the truth, lest that which was revolving in their hearts remain their fixed opinion (for they thought they saw a spirit, not flesh). He presented to the eyes of the doubting the marks of the cross remaining in His hands and feet, and He invited them to examine Him more attentively. For the traces of the nails and of the lance were preserved for healing the wounds of unfaithful hearts, in order that not in doubtful faith, but by most steadfast knowledge it might be held that that nature would sit upon the throne of God the Father which had lain in the sepulchre.

℟. After our Lord Jesus was risen, standing in the midst of His disciples, He said: * Peace be to you, alleluia: the disciples rejoiced at the sight of the Lord, alleluia. ℣. On the first day of the week, when the doors were shut where the disciples were gathered together, Jesus came and stood in the midst of them and said to them. Peace. Glory. Peace.

III Nocturn

The reading of the holy Gospel according to St. John

At that time Jesus said to the Pharisees: "I am the good shepherd. The good shepherd lays down his life for his sheep." And so forth.

Homily of St. Gregory, Pope

Dearly beloved brethren, you have heard from the Gospel lesson your instruction; you have likewise become acquainted with the peril that is ours. For behold, He who is good, not by a chance gift, but in very essence, says: "I am the Good Shepherd." And He adds the nature of this same goodness which we are to imitate, saying: "The good shepherd giveth his life for his sheep." What He advised, He carried out in deed; what He commanded, He exemplified.

The Good Shepherd laid down His life for His sheep that He might change His body and blood into our Sacrament, and that He might satisfy with the nourishment of His own flesh the sheep which He had redeemed. The way of contempt for death which we ought to follow has been shown to us; the pattern has been prescribed; let us be moulded by it.

In the first place it is our duty that we in all mercy sacrifice for His sheep our extraneous things; but in the very end, if it be necessary, that we give up even our life for those same sheep. From the first very slight sacrifice we proceed, indeed, in the last instance to the greater one. But since the life by which we live is incomparably more precious than the earthly substance which we have extraneously, when will one who will not even give up his substance for his sheep, give up his life for them?

And some there are who, since they love earthly substance more than their sheep, deservedly lose the title of shepherd; concerning such it is immediately added: "But the hireling and he that is not the shepherd, whose own the sheep are not, seeth the wolf coming, and leaveth the sheep and flieth." He is not called a shepherd, but a hireling, who feeds the Lord's sheep not from heartfelt love, but for temporal gain. He verily is a hireling who holds the shepherd's place indeed, but seeks not the gain of souls. He longs after earthly comforts; he delights in the honor of preferment; he grows fat on temporal rewards; he is elated at the reverence men proffer him.

℟. The good shepherd who laid down His life for His sheep and deigned to die for His flock is risen again: * Alleluia, alleluia, alleluia. ℣. For Christ our Pasch is sacrificed. Alleluia. Glory. Alleluia.

✠ Continuation of the holy Gospel according to St. John.— At that time Jesus said to the Pharisees: "I am the good shepherd. The good shepherd lays down his life for his sheep. But the hireling, who is not a shepherd, whose own the sheep are not, sees the wolf coming and leaves the sheep and flees. And the wolf snatches and scatters the sheep; but the hireling flees because he is a hireling, and has no concern for the sheep.

"I am the good shepherd, and I know mine and mine know me, even as the Father knows me and I know the Father; and I lay down my life for my sheep. And other sheep I have that are not of this fold. Them also I must bring, and they shall hear my voice, and there shall be one fold and one shepherd."

LET US PRAY

O God, who hast raised up a fallen world in the humility of Thy Son, grant to Thy faithful servants eternal joy, that those whom Thou didst snatch from the dangers of eternal death may enjoy everlasting happiness. Through the same Jesus Christ.

III SUNDAY AFTER EASTER

I Nocturn

From the Apocalypse of St. John the Apostle, c. 1, 1 - 19

III Sunday After Easter

II Nocturn

Sermon of St. Augustine, Bishop

During these holy days dedicated to the Resurrection of the Lord, in as far as we are able with His help, let us treat of the resurrection of the flesh. For this is our faith; this gift was promised us in the flesh of our Lord Jesus Christ, and in Himself He has given us the example. For He willed not only to foretell what He promised us for the end of time, but also to demonstrate it to us. Those, indeed, who were then present, when they saw Him, and were frightened and thought they saw a spirit, grasped the solid substance of His body.

For He spoke to them not only with words for their ears, but likewise by a form for their eyes; indeed, it was of little avail to offer Himself to their sight had He not also offered Himself to be examined and touched. For He says: "Why are you perturbed, and why do doubts arise in your hearts?" For they thought they were looking at a spirit. "Why are you afraid," says He, "and why do doubts arise in your hearts? Sée my hands and my feet; touch them and see, because a spirit does not have bones and flesh, as you see me to have."

Men disputed against this evidence. But what else would men do, who think of things which are of men, than to dispute about God against God? For He is God; they are men. But God knows the thoughts of men that they are vain. In carnal man the one rule which determines what shall be understood is what can be seen. What they are accustomed to see they believe; what they are not accustomed to see they do not believe. But God works miracles beyond ordinary custom because He is God.

Greater, indeed, are the miracles that daily so many men are brought into life who were not, than that a few who had been living have arisen from the dead, and yet these miracles are not given much consideration, but have become ordinary because of their frequency. Christ has arisen; that is certain. He was body, and He was flesh; He hung on the cross, gave up the ghost, and His flesh was laid in the sepulchre. He who had lived in it showed that flesh to be living. Why do we wonder? Why do we not believe? It is God who has done these things.

℞. One of the seven Angels spoke with me saying: Come, and I will show thee the new bride, the spouse of the Lamb: * And I saw Jerusalem coming down from heaven, adorned with her jewels, alleluia, alleluia, alleluia. ℣. And he carried me away in spirit to a great and high mountain. And I saw. Glory. And I saw.

III Sunday After Easter

III Nocturn

The reading of the holy Gospel according to St. John

At that time Jesus said to his disciples: "A little while and you shall see me no longer; and again a little while and you shall see me, because I go to the Father." And so forth.

Homily of St. Augustine, Bishop

The "little while" is this whole space over which the present dispensation extends. And in this sense also this same Evangelist says in his epistle, "It is the last hour." For indeed, it was to show this that He added, "because I go to the Father," which is to be referred to the preceding clause wherein He says, "A little while and you shall not see me," and not to the subsequent clause wherein He says, "And again a little while and you shall see me," because it was by going to the Father that He would bring it about that they should not see Him.

And therefore by this it was not said that He was about to die, and, until He should rise again, He would withdraw from their sight, but, that He was about to go to the Father. And this He did after His Resurrection when, having conversed with them for forty days, He ascended into heaven. Therefore He said to them who saw Him then in bodily form, "A little while and you shall not see me," because He was about to go to the Father and never thereafter would they see Him in that mortal state in which, while He spoke these things, they beheld Him.

But that which He added, "And again a little while and you shall see me," He promised to the whole Church, just as to it also He promised: "Lo, I am with you even to the consummation of the world." The Lord delays not His promise. A little while and we shall see Him there where we shall neither have any requests to make nor questions to ask, because nothing will remain to be desired, nothing lie hid to be inquired about. This little while appears long to us because it is still continuing; when it shall have been completed, then shall we know that it was a little while.

Let not, then, our joy be such as the world delights in, whereof it is said: "But the world shall rejoice"; yet, on the other hand, let us not be sorrowful without any joy while bringing to fruition this desire of eternal life and happiness, but, as the Apostle says, let us be "rejoicing in hope, patient in tribulation," for even the woman in travail to whom we are compared is more joyful over the child that is soon to be than she is sorrowful over her present pains. But let this be the end of our present discourse, for the words that follow contain a very trying question and in order that they may the more fittingly be explained, if the Lord will, they must not be unduly curtailed.

℟. Your sorrow, alleluia, * Shall be turned into joy, alleluia, alleluia. ℣. And the world shall rejoice, yet you shall be made sorrowful, but your sorrow. Shall be turned. Glory. Shall be turned.

✠ Continuation of the holy Gospel according to St. John.— At that time Jesus said to his disciples: "A little while and you shall see me no longer; and again a little while and you shall see me, because I go to the Father."

Some of his disciples therefore said to one another, "What is this he says to us, 'A little while and you shall not see me, and again a little while and you shall see me'; and, 'I go to the Father'?" They kept saying therefore, "What is this 'little while' of which he speaks? We do not know what he is saying."

But Jesus knew that they wanted to ask him, and he said to them, "You inquire about this among yourselves because I said, 'A little while and you shall not see me, and again a little while and you shall see me.' Amen, amen, I say to you, that you shall weep and lament, but the world shall rejoice; and you shall be sorrowful, but your sorrow shall be turned into joy. A woman about to give birth has sorrow, because her hour has come. But when she has brought forth the child, she no longer remembers the anguish for her joy that a man is born into the world. And you therefore have sorrow now, but I will see you again, and your heart shall rejoice, and your joy no one shall take from you."

LET US PRAY

O God, who dost show forth the light of Thy truth that the erring may return to the path of justice, grant that all who profess they are Christians may reject whatever is opposed to that name and follow what is becoming to it. Through our Lord.

IV SUNDAY AFTER EASTER

I Nocturn

From the catholic Epistle of St. James the Apostle, c. 1, 1 - 16

II Nocturn

From the Treatise of St. Cyprian, Bishop and Martyr, on the Boon of Patience

When about to speak about patience, dearly beloved brethren, and to declare its utility and advantages, how shall I rather begin than by saying that right now I perceive that your patience is necessary to listen to me, since you cannot practice that which

IV Sunday After Easter

you hear and learn without patience? For a wholesome word and thought is only then effectually learned, if what is said be listened to in patience. Nor do I find, dearly beloved, among the other paths of heavenly discipline along which our life is divinely guided to the attainment of the rewards of our faith and hope, anything that is greater or more useful or more meritorious for glory than that we, who rely on God's commandments in our service of fear and devotion, should with every precaution especially safeguard the virtue of patience.

Philosophers also profess to follow this virtue, but their patience, in this case, is as false as their so-called wisdom. For how can anyone be either wise or patient who does not know the wisdom nor the patience of God. But let us, beloved brethren, who are philosophers, not in words, but in deeds, who are aware of a consciousness of virtues rather than a display of them, who do not speak great things, but live as servants and worshippers of God, let us forthwith show in our spiritual duties the patience we learn from heavenly masters!

For this virtue is common to us and God; from Him patience has its beginnings, from Him its glory and worth take their source. The rise and increase of patience begin from God who is its Author. The thing which is precious to God should be loved by man. The divine majesty commends the good which it loves. If God is Master and Father to us, let us consequently imitate the patience of our Master and Father, because it is behooving both that servants be obedient and that children be not dishonorable.

It is patience which commends us to, and keeps us for God; this it is which tempers wrath, which bridles the tongue, governs the mind, keeps peace, establishes discipline, breaks the attack of lust, suppresses the violence of passion, extinguishes the passion of deceit, checks the power of riches, refreshes the needy, protects the blessed integrity of virgins, the laborious chastity of widows, and the undivided love of the espoused and married; it makes us humble in prosperity, brave in adversity, and meek in the face of injuries and contumelies; it teaches us quickly to forgive offenders and to pray long and much if we ourselves sin; it conquers temptations, bears persecution, consummates sufferings and martyrdoms. This it is which firmly fortifies the foundations of our faith.

℟. With my whole heart, alleluia, have I sought after Thee, alleluia: * Let me not stray from Thy commandments, alleluia, alleluia. ℣. Blessed art Thou, O Lord, teach me Thy justifications. Let me not. Glory. Let me not.

IV Sunday After Easter

III Nocturn

The reading of the holy Gospel according to St. John

At that time Jesus said to his disciples: "I am going to him who sent me, and no one of you asks me, 'Where art thou going?'" And so forth.

Homily of St. Augustine, Bishop

After the Lord Jesus had foretold to His disciples the persecutions they would have to suffer after His departure, He went on to say: "But I told you not these things at the beginning because I was with you. But now I go to him that sent me." And here, first of all, we have to investigate whether He had not previously foretold to them the sufferings that were to come. Now the three other Evangelists make it sufficiently clear that He had uttered such predictions prior to the approach of the Supper, while, according to John, it was when the Supper was over that He added that passage where He says: "But I told you not these things at the beginning because I was with you."

Is, then perchance, the question settled because they too tell us that He was near His Passion when He spoke these words? Then it was not when He was with them at the beginning that He spoke thus, for He was now on the very eve of departing and going to the Father. And therefore, according to these Evangelists also, what is here said is true: "But I told you not these things from the beginning."

But are we to make of the credibility of the Gospel according to Matthew, who relates that such announcements were made to them by the Lord not only when He was about to eat the Pasch with His disciples, just before His Passion, but also at the beginning, when for the first time the twelve apostles are expressly named and sent forth on their divine mission?

What, then, is the meaning of what He says here, "But I told you not these things at the beginning because I was with you," except this, that it was those things which He says here of the Holy Spirit, namely, that He was to come to them and to bear witness when they would have to undergo those trials, that He did not tell them at the beginning because He was with them? At Christ's departure, then, that Comforter and Advocate (for both form the interpretation of the Greek word *Paraclete*) had become necessary. And for that reason He had not spoken of the Holy Spirit at the beginning when He was with them, because then they were comforted by His own presence.

℟. O God, to Thee I will sing a new canticle, alleluia: * On the psaltery of ten strings I will sing to Thee, alleluia, alleluia. ℣. Thou art my God, and I will praise Thee: Thou art my God, and I will exalt Thee. On. Glory. On.

✠ Continuation of the holy Gospel according to St. John.— At that time Jesus said to his disciples: "I am going to him who sent me, and no one of you asks me, 'Where art thou going?' But because I have spoken to you these things, sadness has filled your heart. But I speak the truth to you; it is expedient for you that I depart. For if I do not go, the Advocate will not come to you; but if I go I will send him to you. And when he has come he will convict the world of sin, and of justice, and of judgment: of sin, because they do not believe in me; of justice, because I go to the Father, and you will see me no more; and of judgment, because the prince of this world has already been judged.

"Many things yet I have to say to you, but you cannot bear them now. But when he, the Spirit of truth, has come, he will teach you all the truth. For he will not speak on his own authority, but whatever he will hear he will speak, and the things that are to come he will declare to you. He will glorify me, because he will receive of what is mine and declare it to you."

Let Us Pray

O God, who dost make the minds of the faithful to be of one accord, grant that Thy people may love what Thou dost command and desire what Thou dost promise, that amidst the changes of this life our hearts may ever remain fixed where the true joys are to be found. Through our Lord.

V SUNDAY AFTER EASTER

I Nocturn

*From the first Epistle of St. Peter the Apostle, c. 1, 1 - 12
and from his second Epistle, c. 1, 1 - 9*

II Nocturn

From the Book of St. Ambrose, Bishop,
on Faith in the Resurrection

Since the Wisdom of God could not die, and since that which had never died could not rise again, a body was assumed which would be able to die, so that when it had died, as was natural for it, it might also rise again. For there could be no resurrection except through man, "for as by a man came death, so also by a man the resurrection of the dead." Hence, as man He arose, because as man He had died, being raised up again as man, but raising Himself up as God. Then, according to the flesh, He was man; now in all things He is God. For now we no longer know Christ according to the flesh, but yet we retain the grace of His flesh, so that we know Him as "the first-fruits of them that sleep," "the first-born from the dead."

The first-fruits are of the same kind and nature as the remaining fruits, for the more abundant growth of which the first-fruits are offered as gifts to God—a sacred gift for all, and, as it were, a kind of sacrificial oblation of our redeemed nature. Christ is, therefore, the "first-fruits of them that sleep." But is He the first-fruits only of His own who sleep, who, as if freed from death, are held in a kind of sweet repose, or is He the first-fruits of all the dead? "And as in Adam *all* die, so also in Christ *all* shall be made alive."

Hence, as the first-fruits of death were in Adam, so likewise, all the first-fruits of the Resurrection shall arise in Christ. But let no one despair, nor let the just man be grieved at the common sharing in the resurrection, since he looks forward to the special reward of his virtue. All, indeed, shall arise, but, as the Apostle says, "everyone in his own order." For the fruit of the divine clemency is common, but the rank of merits is distinct.

We see how great a sacrilege it is not to believe in the resurrection. For if we shall not rise again, then Christ died for nothing, then Christ did not rise. For if He did not arise for our sakes, in truth He did not arise, since He had no reason why He should rise again for Himself. The world arose in Him; the heavens arose in Him; the earth arose in Him! "For there shall be a new heaven and a new earth." The Resurrection was not a necessity for Him whom the bonds of death did not hold. For although He died as man, nevertheless He was free in the lower regions. Do you wish to know how He was free? "I am become as a man without help, as one free among the dead." And He was truly free who could raise Himself up, according to that which is written: "Destroy this temple, and in three days I shall raise it up." He was truly free who went down to hell to redeem others.

℞. I will declare Thy name to my brethren, alleluia: * In the midst of the Church will I praise Thee, alleluia, alleluia. ℣. I will give praise to Thee, O Lord, among the people, and I will sing a psalm to Thee among the nations. In. Glory. In.

III Nocturn

The reading of the holy Gospel according to St. John

At that time Jesus said to His disciples: "Amen, Amen, I say to you, if you ask the Father anything in my name, he will give it to you." And so forth.

Homily of St. Augustine, Bishop

We have now to consider these words of the Lord: "Amen, amen, I say to you: If you ask the Father anything in my name, He will give it to you." It has already been said in the earlier portions of this discourse of our Lord (because of those who ask some things of the Father in Christ's name and receive them not) that whatsoever is asked contrary to the nature of salvation is not asked in the Savior's name. For not the sound of the letters and syllables, but what is rightly and truly to be understood by that sound, this must He be regarded as declaring when He says, "in my name."

Hence he who has such ideas of Christ as ought not to be entertained of the only Son of God does not ask in His name, even though he may not refrain from the mention of Christ in so many letters and syllables, since, when he asks, he asks in the name of him of whom he is (falsely) thinking (and hence he does not ask truly in the name of Christ). But he who has such ideas of Him as ought to be entertained asks in His name and receives what he asks, provided he asks nothing contrary to his eternal salvation. And he receives it when it is expedient for him to receive it. For certain things are not refused, but only deferred that they may be given at a suitable time.

In this way, surely, must be understood what He says, "He will give it to you," so that it may be known that by these words those benefits are signified which are properly applicable to those who ask. For all the saints are heard effectively in their own behalf, but are not so heard in behalf of everyone else, whether friends or enemies, or any others; for it is not said in a general way, "He will give," but, "He will give to *you*."

"Hitherto," He says, "you have not asked anything in my name. Ask and you shall receive, that your joy may be full." That which He calls a full joy is certainly not a carnal joy, but a spiritual one; and when it shall be so great that no more can be added to it, then without doubt will it be full. Therefore, if we understand divine grace and if we really seek a blessed life, whatsoever is asked that has reference to the acquisition of this joy, must be asked in the name of Christ. But if anything else is asked, nothing is asked; not that the thing itself is nothing at all, but that in comparison with what is so great anything else that is desired is nothing.

℟. If I forget Thee, alleluia, let my right hand be forgotten: * Let my tongue cling to my jaws if I do not remember Thee, alleluia, alleluia. ℣. By the waters of Babylon there we sat and wept when we remembered Thee, O Sion. Let my tongue. Glory. Let my tongue.

✠ Continuation of the holy Gospel according to St. John.— At that time Jesus said to his disciples: "Amen, amen, I say to you, if you ask the Father anything in my name, he will give it to you. Hitherto you have not asked anything in my name. Ask, and you shall receive, that your joy may be full.

"These things I have spoken to you in parables. The hour is coming when I will no longer speak to you in parables, but will speak to you plainly of the Father. In that day you shall ask in my name; and I do not say to you that I will ask the Father for you, for the Father himself loves you because you have loved me, and have believed that I came forth from God. I came forth from the Father and have come into the world. Again I leave the world and go to the Father."

His disciples said to him, "Behold now thou speakest plainly, and utterest no parable. Now we know that thou knowest all things, and dost not need that anyone should question thee. For this reason we believe that thou camest forth from God."

Let Us Pray

O God, from whom all good gifts come, grant to those who ask Thee that by Thy inspiration we may think what is right and by Thy guidance may also perform it. Through our Lord.

ROGATION MONDAY

The reading of the holy Gospel according to St. Luke

At that time Jesus said to his disciples: "Which of you shall have a friend and shall go to him in the middle of the night and shall say to him: 'Friend, lend me three loaves.'" And so forth.

Homily of St. Ambrose, Bishop

This is another passage of the precept, that in every moment, not only in the day, but even in the night, prayer should be offered. For you see that this man who went at midnight, asking three loaves of bread from his friend and persevering in the earnestness of his petition, was not deprived of the things he asked for. What are these three loaves of bread but the food of the divine mystery? But if you love the Lord your God, you shall be able to gain things not only for yourself, but for others as well. And who is more of a friend to us than He who delivered His own body for us?

At midnight David begged for bread and received it. For he begged when he said: "I rose at midnight to give praise to thee." In this way he merited those loaves of bread which he sets forth for us to eat. He asked this when he said: "I will wash my couch with tears." For he did not fear lest he should wake from sleep Him whom he knew to be always watching. And so, being mindful of these things which have been written, and constant in our prayer, day and night, let us beg pardon for our sins.

For if such a holy man, who was busied with the cares of his kingdom, gave praise to the Lord seven times a day, what is demanded of us who should ask for more because we have, through the frailty of our flesh and mind, fallen more frequently, so that, when worn out by the journey and greatly fatigued by the affairs of this world and the winding course of this life, there may not be lacking the food of refreshment, which strengthens the hearts of mankind? Nor does the Lord teach that He must be watched for at midnight only but, as far as possible, at every moment. For He comes in the vesper hour, in the second and third watch, and is accustomed then to knock. Therefore, "blessed are those servants, whom the Lord, when he cometh, shall find watching."

ROGATION WEDNESDAY

The reading of the holy Gospel according to St. John

At that time Jesus, raising up his eyes to heaven said: "Father, the hour is come; glorify thy Son." And so forth.

Homily of St. Augustine, Bishop

Our Lord, the only-begotten and co-eternal Son of the Father, in the form of a servant, and out of the form of a servant—if it had been necessary—could have prayed in silence; yet He thus wished to present Himself as a supplicant to the Father in order that He might remind us that He Himself is our Teacher. Hence, that prayer which He made for us He also made known to us. For not only the discourse of such a great Master to His disciples, but likewise His prayer to the Father for them is an instruction for them, and if for them who were present to hear the things said, it is certainly the same for us who read the things that were written.

Therefore, by that which He speaks, "Father, the hour is come; glorify thy Son," He makes it evident that all time and everything—whenever He would do it or permit it to be done—had been planned by Him who is not subject to time, because the things which are to happen at separate times have their efficient causes in God's wisdom in which there are no separate periods. Consequently it is not to be believed that "this hour" came through the inevitability of fate, but rather, through God's ordinance. Nor did the constant course of the stars determine the Passion of Christ, for God forbid that the stars should bind the Maker of the stars to their cycle.

Some men hold that the Son was glorified by the Father in the fact that He did not spare Him, but delivered Him up for all of us. But if He is declared to be glorified in His Passion, how much the more in His Resurrection? For in His suffering His humility is commended rather than His majesty, as the Apostle testifies, saying: "He humbled himself, becoming obedient unto death, even to the death of the cross." Immediately following he speaks of His glory: "For which cause God also hath exalted him, and hath given him a name which is above all names: that in the name of Jesus every knee should bow, of those that are in heaven, on earth, and under the earth. And that every tongue should confess that the Lord Jesus Christ is in the glory of God the Father." This is the glory of our Lord Jesus Christ which takes its beginning from His Resurrection!

THE ASCENSION OF THE LORD

I Nocturn

From the Acts of the Apostles, c. 1, 1 - 14

II Nocturn

Sermon of St. Leo, Pope

After the blessed and glorious Resurrection of our Lord Jesus Christ, wherein He raised up in three days that true temple of God which had been destroyed by the impiety of the Jews, there is this day fulfilled, dearly beloved, that number of forty holy days, which had been ordained by a most sacred dispensation and spent in giving us valuable instructions; so that, while the Lord permitted His bodily presence to tarry among us for this space of time, our faith in His Resurrection might be strengthened by necessary proofs.

For the death of Christ had greatly disturbed the hearts of the disciples, and a certain lethargy of disbelief had crept over their grief-laden minds at His torture on the cross, at His giving up the ghost, and at the burial of His lifeless body. Thus the most blessed apostles and all the disciples, who had been filled with fear at the final issue of the cross and uncertain in faith concerning the Resurrection, were so strengthened by the evident truth, that, when the Lord was going up into the heights of heaven, they were not troubled by any sadness, but rather were filled with great joy.

Greatly revered and ineffable was the cause of rejoicing when, in the sight of the holy multitude, the nature of the human race ascended above the dignity of all the celestial creatures to transcend the angelic orders and to be elevated above the heights of the archangels; nor will there be any limit to the extent of its advancement until, having received a seat with the Eternal Father, it shares with Him the throne of His glory to whose nature it is joined in the Son.

Since the Ascension of Christ is our own exaltation, and whither the glory of the Head has gone before, thither the hope of the body is also called, let us therefore rejoice, dearly beloved, with due gladness, and let us delight in loving thanksgiving. For today not only have we been confirmed as possessors of paradise, but in Christ have even penetrated the heights of heaven, having gained far more through the ineffable grace of Christ than we had lost through the malice of the devil. For those whom the virulent enemy cast down from the happiness of the first estate, these, the Son of God has placed as one body with Himself at the right hand of the Father, with whom He lives and reigns in the unity of the Holy Spirit, God, through all eternity. Amen.

℟. Let not your heart be troubled: I go to the Father: and when I am taken from you, I will send you, alleluia, * The Spirit of truth, and your heart shall rejoice, alleluia. ℣. I will ask the Father, and He will give you another Paraclete. The Spirit. Glory. The Spirit.

III Nocturn

The reading of the holy Gospel according to St. Mark

At that time Jesus appeared to the Eleven as they were at table; and he upbraided them for their lack of faith and hardness of heart, in that they had not believed those who had seen him after he had risen. And so forth.

Homily of St. Gregory, Pope

The fact that the disciples were slow to believe in the Resurrection of the Lord was not, as I shall point out, so much a weakness of theirs as it was our future strength. For as the Resurrection was made manifest to those who doubted by many proofs, what else can we do when, while reading, we come to know these proofs but be strengthened by their hesitancy? For Mary Magdalene, who believed so readily, proves less to me than Thomas, who doubted for a long time. He, because he doubted, touched the place of the wounds, and took away from our heart the wound of doubt.

To penetrate into the truth of the Lord's Resurrection we must take into consideration what Luke refers to, saying: "Eating together with them, he commanded them that they should not depart from Jerusalem"; and after a few words: "While they looked on, he was raised up and a cloud received him out of their sight." Note the words; mark the mysteries: "eating, he was raised up." He ate, and He ascended, evidently in order that as a result of the eating the reality of His flesh might become manifest.

But Mark relates that before the Lord ascended into heaven He upbraided the disciples for their infidelity and hardness of heart. What else must we consider here but that the Lord upbraided His disciples at that time when He left them corporally for this reason, that the words which He said while departing might remain the more deeply engraved on the hearts of His hearers.

Let us therefore hear what the Lord, after having rebuked their hardness of heart, commands them, saying: "Going into the whole world, preach the Gospel to every creature." Was the Gospel, brethren, ever to be preached to senseless things or to brute animals, that, concerning it, He should say to His disciples: "Preach to every creature"? But by the words *every creature* is signified *man*. Indeed man has something in common with every creature. For he has in common with stones, existence; with trees, life; with animals, sensation; and with angels, intelligence. If therefore man has something in common with every creature, in some respect man is every creature. Therefore the Gospel is preached to every creature when it is preached to man alone.

℟. I will ask the Father and He will give you another Paraclete, * That He, the Spirit of truth, may abide with you forever, alleluia. ℣. For if I go not, the Paraclete will not come to you: but if I go, I will send Him to you. That He. Glory. That He.

✠ Continuation of the holy Gospel according to St. Mark.— At that time Jesus appeared to the Eleven as they were at table; and he upbraided them for their lack of faith and hardness of heart, in that they had not believed those who had seen him after he had risen. And he said to them, "Go into the whole world and preach the gospel to every creature. He who believes and is baptized shall be saved, but he who does not believe shall be condemned. And these signs shall attend those who believe: in my name they shall cast out devils; they shall speak in new tongues; they shall take up serpents; and if they drink any deadly thing, it shall not hurt them; they shall lay hands upon the sick and they shall get well."

So then the Lord, after he had spoken to them, was taken up into heaven, and sits at the right hand of God. But they went forth and preached everywhere, while the Lord worked with them and confirmed the preaching by the signs that followed.

Let Us Pray

Grant, we beseech Thee, almighty God, that as we believe Thy only-begotten Son, our Redeemer, hath on this day ascended into heaven, we also in spirit may abide in the heavenly places. Through the same Jesus Christ.

FRIDAY

The reading of the holy Gospel according to St. Mark

At that time Jesus appeared to the Eleven as they were at table; and he upbraided them for their lack of faith and hardness of heart, in that they had not believed those who had seen him after he had risen. And so forth.

Homily of St. Gregory, Pope

"He who believes and is baptized, shall be saved; but he who believes not shall be condemned." Someone perhaps may say to himself: "I have already believed; I will be saved." He speaks truly if he holds to the faith in his actions. For that faith is true which does not contradict in deeds what it professes by words. Hence it is that St. Paul says of certain false believers: "They profess that they know God, but in their works they deny him." Therefore John says: "He who says that he knows God, and does not keep his commandments, is a liar."

Since this is the case, we ought to acknowledge in our lives the truth of our faith. For then are we truly faithful if we fulfill by our deeds what we promise by our words. Indeed, on the day of Baptism we promised to renounce all the works and all the pomps of the old enemy. Then let each of you draw the eyes of your mind to a self-examination; and if each keeps after Baptism what he promised before it, being now certain that he is faithful, let him rejoice.

Yet behold, if what he promised he has in no wise kept, if he has fallen away into doing evil deeds and desiring the pomps of this world, let us see if he knows how to bewail what he has done wrongly. For before the merciful Judge he who returns to the truth is not considered as a liar even after he lies; because Almighty God, while gladly receiving our repentance, in His judgment conceals that which we have done amiss.

SATURDAY

The reading of the holy Gospel according to St. Mark

At that time Jesus appeared to the Eleven as they were at table; and he upbraided them for their lack of faith and hardness of heart, in that they had not believed those who had seen him after he had risen. And so forth.

Homily of St. Gregory, Pope

"And these signs shall follow them that believe. In my name they shall cast out devils; they shall speak with new tongues; they shall take up serpents; and if they shall drink any deadly thing, it shall not hurt them; they shall lay their hands upon the sick, and they shall recover." My brethren, because you do not work these wonders, do you not believe? But these things were necessary in the beginning of the Church. For, in order that the multitude of believers might grow in their faith, they had to be supported by miracles; for we ourselves, when we set out plants, water them until the time when we see that they are rooted in the earth, but when once they have taken root, the watering ceases. Hence it is that Paul declares: "Tongues are for a sign not to believers, but to unbelievers."

There is something in these wonders and powers which we should consider more accurately. In truth, holy Church daily performs in a spiritual manner what she did at that time through the apostles. For when her priests, through the power of exorcism, impose their hands upon the faithful and forbid the malignant spirits to dwell in their minds, what else do they do but cast out devils? And all the faithful who now cast off the worldly language of their old life, and give praise to the holy mysteries of their Maker and, as far as they are able, tell of His power,—what else are they doing but speaking with new tongues? And when by their good exhortations they pluck out wickedness from the hearts of others, they take up serpents.

And when men hear the voice of temptation, but, nevertheless, are not in the least drawn to a shameful act, it is, indeed, a deadly thing which they drink, but it will not harm them. When they who, as often as they perceive their neighbors to weaken in their good work, assist them with all their power, and bolster by the example of their own deeds the life of those who waver in their duty—what else are they doing but laying their hands upon the sick that they may recover? What miracles, indeed, are as great as those of the spirit? They are so much the greater in that by them not bodies, but souls are raised to life!

SUNDAY WITHIN THE OCTAVE OF THE ASCENSION

I Nocturn

From the first Epistle of St. John the Apostle, c. 1, 1 - 10; c. 2, 1 - 6

II Nocturn

Sermon of St. Augustine, Bishop

Our Savior, beloved brethren, has ascended into heaven; let us not therefore be distraught upon the earth. There let our mind be, and here will be repose. Let us meanwhile ascend in heart with Christ; when His promised day will have come, we shall follow also in body. But we should know, brethren, that neither pride, nor avarice, nor dissipation ascend with Christ. No vice of ours ascends with our physician. Wherefore, if we desire to ascend after our physician, we should put aside vices and sin.

For all men press upon us, as it were, with bonds, and endeavor to bind us with the snares of sin. And therefore, with God's help, as the Psalmist says, "Let us break their bonds asunder," that in confidence we may say to the Lord, "Thou hast broken my bonds, and I will sacrifice to thee the sacrifice of praise." The Lord's Resurrection is our hope; the Lord's Ascension is our glorification.

Today we celebrate the solemn feast of the Ascension. If then rightly, if faithfully, if devotedly, if holily, if piously we celebrate the Lord's Ascension, let us ascend with Him and lift up our hearts. But as we go up, let us not be exalted, nor presume on our merits as though they were our own. We should lift up our hearts to the Lord. A heart lifted up, but not to the Lord, is called pride; while a heart lifted up to the Lord is called a place of safety. Behold, brethren, a great wonder! The Lord is high. You raise yourself, and He flees from you; you humble yourself, and He comes down to you. Why is this? Because He is exalted and regards lowly things, and the high things He knows from afar. The humble He regards from close at hand, to lift them up; the high, that is, the proud, He knows from afar, to bring them low.

Christ has risen to give us hope, for it is a mortal man that rises. He has made us sure lest we despair when we die, and think that our life is ended with death. We were anxious about our soul; He by rising has made us confident of the resurrection of the flesh. Believe, then, in order to be cleansed. You should first believe, that afterwards through faith you may merit to look upon God. Do you want to see God? Hear Him: "Blessed are the clean of heart, for they shall see God." Think first, then, of cleansing your heart; take away what you see there that displeases God.

℞. When Christ ascended on high, He led captivity captive, * He gave gifts to men, alleluia, alleluia, alleluia. ℣. God is ascended with jubilee, and the Lord with the sound of the trumpet. He gave. Glory. He gave.

III Nocturn

The reading of the holy Gospel according to St. John

At that time Jesus said to his disciples: "When the Advocate has come, whom I will send you from the Father, the Spirit of truth who proceeds from the Father, he will bear witness concerning me." And so forth.

Homily of St. Augustine, Bishop

In the sermon which the Lord Jesus spoke to His disciples after the Supper, at the time He was nearing His Passion and about to go away and take leave of them as regards His bodily presence (for with His spiritual presence He would be with all His members until the end of time), He exhorted them to endure the persecutions of the wicked whom He designated by the name of *the world*. And yet from this same world He said He had chosen these very disciples, so that they might know that it is by the grace of God that they are what they are, and, on the other hand, it was by their own vices that they were what they were.

Then He plainly told them that the Jews were both His persecutors and theirs, that it might become most plain that also those who persecute the saints are included in the epitaph of the accursed world. Now after He had said of these that they did not know Him from whom He was sent, and even more, that they had hated both the Son and the Father, that is, both Him who was sent and Him from whom He was sent (about which we have already treated in other sermons), we come to where He says: "That the word might be fulfilled which is written in their Law: 'They have hated me without cause.' "

Whereupon He added as a consequence (and this point we have now undertaken to examine), "But when the Paraclete cometh, whom I will send you from the Father, the Spirit of truth, who proceedeth from the Father, he shall give testimony of me: and you shall give testimony, because you are with me from the beginning."

How does this pertain to what He had said: "But now they have both seen and hated both me and my Father, but that the word may be fulfilled which is written in their Law: 'They have hated me without cause' "? Is it because when the Paraclete, the Spirit of truth, came, He convicted by a more unmistakable testimony those who saw and hated? Yea, more, by this manifestation of Himself He even converted to the faith which operates through love some of those who saw and had yet hated.

℟. The Lord hath set all His beauty above the stars: * His loveliness is in the clouds of heaven and His name endureth forever, alleluia. ℣. His going out is from the highest heaven, and His circuit even to the height thereof. His loveliness. Glory. His loveliness.

✠ Continuation of the holy Gospel according to St. John.— At that time Jesus said to his disciples: "When the Advocate has come, whom I will send you from the Father, the Spirit of truth who proceeds from the Father, he will bear witness concerning me. And you also will bear witness, because from the beginning you are with me."

"These things I have spoken to you that you may not be scandalized. They will expel you from the synagogues. Yes, the hour is coming for everyone who kills you to think that he is offering worship to God. And these things they will do because they have not known the Father nor me. But these things I have spoken to you, that when the time for them has come you may remember that I told you.

LET US PRAY

O almighty and eternal God, make us always to have a will that is devoted to Thee and to serve Thy Majesty with a sincere heart. Through our Lord.

MONDAY

The reading of the holy Gospel according to St. Mark

At that time Jesus appeared to the Eleven as they were at table; and he upbraided them for their lack of faith and hardness of heart, in that they had not believed those who had seen him after he had risen. And so forth.

Homily of St. Gregory, Pope

"And the Lord Jesus, after He had spoken to them, was taken up into heaven, and sitteth on the right hand of God."—In the old Testament we know that Elias was taken up into heaven. But the heaven of the air is one thing; the celestial heaven, another. The aerial heaven, of course, is that near to the earth; whence we say "the birds of heaven" because we see them flying in the air. Thus Elias was lifted up into the aerial heaven that he might be taken into a certain unknown region of the earth, where he is now living in great repose of body and soul, until he returns at the end of the world and pays the debt of death. For he has postponed death, but has not escaped it; whereas our Redeemer, in that He did not postpone His death, has overcome and conquered it by arising, and has declared the glory of His Resurrection by His Ascension.

It is likewise to be noted that Elias is said to have ascended in a chariot, so that it might thus be proved that he, being a mere man, needed an exterior help. This help was given to him by angels because it was impossible for one whom the weakness of his nature still weighed down to ascend even into the atmosphere. Our Redeemer, on the other hand, is not recounted to have been lifted up on a chariot, or by angels, because He who had made all things was surely borne up above all things by His own power. For He was returning thither where He had been; He was going back there where He had remained, for, while He ascended into heaven by His humanity, through His divinity He contained within Himself both earth and heaven.

Just as Joseph, sold by his brothers, prefigured the selling of our Redeemer, so Henoch being translated and Elias being lifted up unto the aerial heaven were both a type of our Lord's Ascension. Thus our Lord had heralds and witnesses of His Ascension—the one before the Law (Henoch), the other under the Law (Elias)—as if to show that at a later time He would come who could in truth penetrate the heavens. Hence, the very manner itself of their being lifted up is marked by a certain progress. For Henoch is recounted as having been translated, and Elias as having been lifted up, as if to show that He who would come afterwards, being neither translated nor lifted up, would penetrate the celestial heaven by His own power.

TUESDAY

The reading of the holy Gospel according to St. Mark

At that time Jesus appeared to the Eleven as they were at table; and he upbraided them for their lack of faith and hardness of heart, in that they had not believed those who had seen him after he had risen. And so forth.

Homily of St. Gregory, Pope

We must now consider why it is that Mark says, "He *sitteth* at the right hand of God," while Stephen says, "I see the heavens opened and the Son of Man *standing* at the right hand of God." Why is it that Mark avows Him to be sitting while Stephen affirms that he beheld Him standing? Surely you know, brethren, that it is characteristic of one judging to sit, but of one waging battle or giving aid to stand.

Therefore, since our Redeemer is taken up into heaven and now judges all creatures, and will come at the end of time as Judge of all, Mark here describes Him after His Ascension as sitting, because after the glory of His Ascension He will be seen at the end of time as Judge. On the other hand, Stephen, then in the struggle of his martyrdom, sees Him from whom he received aid standing because, in order that he might overcome the infidelity of the persecutors on earth, Christ fought for him from heaven by means of His grace.

It follows: "But they, going forth, preached everywhere, the Lord working withal and confirming the word with signs that followed."—In these happenings what should we consider, what should we commit to memory, if not the fact that the command resulted in obedience, and the obedience resulted in miracles.

Now that we have briefly touched upon, by the inspiration of God, the explanation of the Gospel reading, it remains that we should say something about the contemplation itself of so important a mystery.

WEDNESDAY

The reading of the holy Gospel according to St. Mark

At that time Jesus appeared to the Eleven as they were at table; and he upbraided them for their lack of faith and hardness of heart, in that they had not believed those who had seen him after he had risen. And so forth.

Homily of St. Gregory, Pope

But the first thing we have to consider is why, when the Lord was born, angels appeared, and yet we do not read that they were seen in white garments; but when the Lord ascended into heaven, we read that they were sent down and appeared robed in white. For so it is written: "While they looked on, he was raised up, and a cloud received him out of their sight. And while they were beholding him going up to heaven, behold two men stood beside them in white garments." Now white garments betoken festivity and joy of mind. Why is it, then, that the angels were not in white garments at the Lord's birth, while they did appear in white garments at His Ascension? Was it not because it was for the angels a day of great festivity when God, made man, entered heaven? For when the Lord was born, the divine nature seemed to be humiliated; but when the Lord ascended into heaven, human nature was exalted. Now white garments are better suited to exaltation than to humiliation.

And thus, at His Ascension, the angels were duly seen clad in white garments, because He, who at His birth appeared as God, yet in lowliness, at His Ascension was shown as man, but raised to loftiness. Yet, dearly beloved brethren, what we should consider above all things in this solemnity is this: that on this day the hand-writing of our condemnation is blotted out; the judgment by which we were sentenced to corruption is reversed. For that very nature to which it was said, "Dust thou art and into dust thou shalt return," has this day entered heaven. For indeed, it was on account of this exaltation of our flesh that blessed Job, speaking figuratively, called the Lord a bird. Because he saw that the Jews did not understand the mystery of the

Ascension, he passed judgment on their infidelity in this figure, saying: "He hath not known the path of the bird."

Now the Lord is rightly called a bird, for with His fleshly body He soared into the air. And whosoever does not believe in His Ascension has not known the path of this bird. Of this great feast it is said by the Psalmist: "Thy magnificence is elevated above the heavens." And again he says: "God is ascended with jubilee and the Lord with the sound of trumpet." And once more he says: "Ascending on high, he led captivity captive, he gave gifts to men." Verily, ascending on high, He led captivity captive; for He swallowed up our corruption. Of a truth He gave gifts to men, for having sent down the Spirit from on high, He gave to some the word of wisdom, to some the word of knowledge, to some the gift of power, to some the grace of healing, to some divers kinds of tongues, to some the interpretation of speeches.

OCTAVE DAY OF THE ASCENSION

I Nocturn

From the Epistle of St. Paul the Apostle to the Ephesians, c. 4, 1 - 21

II Nocturn

Sermon of St. Augustine, Bishop

Dearly beloved, all the miracles which our Lord Jesus Christ performed in this world, while in our frail form, are of profit to us. For in that He has lifted up our human condition to the stars, He has shown that the heavens can open to those who believe, and, in that He has lifted up the Conqueror of Death to things celestial, He has revealed to the conquerors whither they are to follow.

The Lord's Ascension was therefore a confirmation of Catholic belief, that thus we might confidently trust in our obtaining, in the life to come, a participation in that miracle, the effect of which we have already perceived in this present life, and that every faithful soul, since he has already received such great things, might learn, through these things which he knows have been granted, to hope for the things that have been promised, and hold the past and present goodness of his God as a forecast of things to come.

So, an earthly body is placed in the heights of heaven; the bones, a little while before confined within the narrow limits of the sepulchre, are borne to the choirs of angels; mortal nature is transported into the bosom of immortality; and thus the sacred account of the Evangelist testifies: "And when he had said these things, while they looked on, he was raised up." When you hear that "he was raised up," think of the service of the heavenly host; wherefore, today's festivity manifests to us the mysteries of Him as man and God. In one and the same Person, acknowledge the divine power in Him who lifts up, but the human substance in Him who is lifted up.

And hence in every way must be detested the poisons of that Eastern error which by an impious innovation presumes to assert that the Son of God and the Son of man are of one nature. For whichever side he takes, either he says that He was only man and thus denies the glory of the Creator, or he says that He was only God and so denies the mercy of the Redeemer. In this situation the Arian can not easily hold the truth of the Gospel, where we read now that the Son of God is equal to the Father, now that He is less. For he who will believe by this fatal argument that our Savior was of but one nature is forced to say either that man only, or God only was crucified. But this is not so. For God alone could not have experienced death, nor could man alone have conquered it.

℞. Let not your heart be troubled: I go to the Father; and when I am taken from you, I will send you, alleluia * The Spirit of truth, and your heart shall rejoice, alleluia. ℣. I will ask the Father, and He will give you another Paraclete. The Spirit. Glory. The Spirit.

III Nocturn

The reading of the holy Gospel according to St. Mark

At that time Jesus appeared to the Eleven as they were at table; and he upbraided them for their lack of faith and hardness of heart, in that they had not believed those who had seen him after he had risen. And so forth.

Homily of St. Gregory, Pope

The prophet Habacuc also speaks of the glory of His Ascension. "The sun was lifted up, and the moon stood in her place." Now who is designated by the moon but the Church, and who by the sun, but the Lord? Up to the time our Lord ascended into heaven, His holy Church greatly feared the attacks of the world; but after His Ascension she was strengthened, she preached openly what she had always secretly believed. Therefore "was the sun lifted up, and the moon stood in her place," for whilst the Lord pierced the heavens, His holy Church grew by the power of her preaching.

In the words of Solomon the Church says, "Behold he cometh, leaping upon the mountains, skipping over the hills." She ponders the exalted heights of His works, and says, "Behold he cometh, leaping upon the mountains." By coming to redeem us He made certain rapid leaps, if I may thus express it. Dearest brethren, do you wish to know what these leaps were? From heaven He came into a womb, from the womb into a crib, from the crib He leaped to the cross, from the cross to the tomb, from the tomb He returned to heaven.

Lo! that He might make us follow after Him, Truth Itself has appeared in the flesh and made certain bounds. "He hath exulted as a giant to run the way," that we might say to Him from our hearts, "Draw us; we will run after thee in the odor of thy ointments." Hence, dearly beloved brethren, it behooves us to follow Him in our hearts there where we believe Him to have ascended in the body.

Let us fly earthly desires; let nothing here below now please us, who have a Father in heaven. And certainly we must consider well the fact that He who was so mild on His ascent, on His return will be so terrible, and whatever He has commanded us with meekness He will require of us with severity. Let no one then disregard the allotted time for his repentance; let no one neglect the care of himself while he is able, because our Redeemer will then be all the more strict in judgment in proportion as He has shown greater patience before the judgment.

℟. When Christ ascended on high, He led captivity captive * He gave gifts to men, alleluia, alleluia. ℣. God is gone up in jubilation and the Lord with the sound of the trumpet. He gave. Glory. He gave.

✠ Continuation of the holy Gospel according to St. Mark.— At that time Jesus appeared to the Eleven as they were at table; and he upbraided them for their lack of faith and hardness of heart, in that they had not believed those who had seen him after he had risen. And he said to them, "Go into the whole world and preach the gospel to every creature. He who believes and is baptized shall be saved, but he who does not believe shall be condemned. And these signs shall attend those who believe: in my name they shall cast out devils; they shall speak in new tongues; they shall take up serpents; and if they drink any deadly thing, it shall not hurt them; they shall lay hands upon the sick and they shall get well."

So then the Lord, after he had spoken to them, was taken up into heaven, and sits at the right hand of God. But they went forth and preached everywhere, while the Lord worked with them and confirmed the preaching by the signs that followed.

Let Us Pray

Grant, we beseech Thee, O almighty God, that as we believe Thy only-begotten Son, our Redeemer, hath on this day ascended into heaven, we also in spirit may abide in the heavenly places. Through the same Jesus Christ.

VIGIL OF PENTECOST

The reading of the holy Gospel according to St. John

At that time Jesus said to his disciples: "If you love me, keep my commandments. And I will ask the Father and he will give you another Advocate." And so forth.

Homily of St. Augustine, Bishop

When the Lord says, "I will ask the Father, and he will give you another Paraclete," He shows that He is Himself a Paraclete. For in Latin, paraclete is called *advocatus* (advocate); and it is said of Christ: "We have an advocate with the Father, Jesus Christ the just." And even as He said that the world cannot receive the Holy Spirit, so it is said also: "The prudence of the flesh is an enemy of God; for it is not subject to the law of God, neither can it be"; just as if we were to say: "Injustice cannot be justice." For truly, in speaking here of the world, He signified the lovers of this world, which love is not of the Father. And therefore, opposed to the love of this world which we strive to diminish and extinguish in us, is the love of God which is poured forth in our hearts by the Holy Spirit, who is given to us.

The world, then, cannot receive Him because it does not see Him nor know Him. For worldly love has not those invisible eyes with which the Holy Spirit may be seen, for He cannot be seen save in an invisible manner. "But you," He says, "shall know him; because he shall abide with you, and shall be in you." He shall be in them, that He may abide; He shall not abide, that He may be in them; for, to abide in any place, it is necessary first to be there. Yet, lest they should suppose that these words, "Shall abide with you," were spoken in the same sense as that in which a guest usually abides with a man in a visible way, He explained what He said, "He shall abide with you," by adding, "And shall be in you."

Therefore He is seen in an invisible way. Nor can we have any knowledge of Him unless He be in us; for it is in a similar way that we come to see our conscience within us. For we see the face of another, but we cannot see our own; yet we do see our own conscience, but not that of another. Now our conscience is never anywhere save within ourselves; but the Holy Spirit can be also apart from us. In fact, He is given that He may also be in us; but He cannot be seen and known by us as He ought to be seen and known if He be not within us. After promising the Holy Spirit, lest any should think that the Lord was to give Him, as it were, in place of Himself, in such a way that He Himself would not likewise be with them, He added the words: "I will not leave you orphans; I will come to you." And therefore, although the Son of God has made us to be the adopted sons of His Father and willed that we should have by grace the same Father as He has by nature, yet even He Himself in some manner shows towards us a fatherly affection when He says: "I will not leave you orphans."

PENTECOST SUNDAY

I Nocturn

From the Acts of the Apostles, c, 2, 1 - 21

II Nocturn

Sermon of St. Leo, Pope

The hearts of all Catholics realize, dearly beloved, that today's solemnity must be ranked among the principal feasts, and there is no doubt that the greatest reverence is due to this day which the Holy Spirit has consecrated with the outstanding miracle of the gift of Himself.

For this day which has dawned upon us is the tenth from that on which the Lord ascended above every height of the heavens to sit at the right hand of the Father, and the fiftieth from His Resurrection, on which began the new dispensation of grace. This day holds within itself great mysteries of both ancient sacraments and new, whereby it is made most plain that grace has been foretold by the Law and the Law fulfilled by grace.

For as formerly, after the Hebrew people had been freed from the Egyptians, the Law was given on Mount Sinai on the fiftieth day after the sacrifice of the lamb, so now, after the Passion wherein the true Lamb of God was slain, on the fiftieth day from His Resurrection, the Holy Spirit has come down upon the apostles and upon the faithful. And thus with ease the observant Christian may recognize that the beginnings of the old Testament have ministered to the foundations of the Gospel, and that the second pact was established by the same Spirit as had been the first.

From this day, then, the trumpet of the preaching of the Gospel has sounded; from this day showers of spiritual gifts, rivers of blessings have watered every desert and all the dry land. For, to renew the face of the earth (with a spiritual progeny), the Spirit of God moved over the waters; and, to dispel the ancient darkness (of sin), flashes of the new light glittered when, in the splendor of sparkling tongues, alike the lightsome word of the Lord and the fiery speech was received, in which there was —for bringing about understanding and for destroying sin—the ability to enlighten and the power to burn.

℞. I will not now call you servants, but my friends; because you have known all that I have done among you, alleluia: * Receive ye the Holy Ghost, the Paraclete: He it is whom the Father will send you, alleluia. ℣. You are My friends if you do the things I command you. Receive ye. Glory. Receive ye.

Pentecost Sunday

III Nocturn

The reading of the holy Gospel according to St. John

At that time Jesus said to his disciples: "If anyone love me, he will keep my words, and my Father will love him, and we will come to him, and will make our abode with him." And so forth.

Homily of St. Gregory, Pope

It seems desirable, most dearly beloved, to pass briefly over the words of the Gospel lesson, that afterwards we may be able to rest for a longer time in contemplation of so grand a solemnity. For today, with a sudden sound, the Holy Spirit came down upon the disciples and transformed their love for carnal things into love for Him; while fiery tongues appeared without, within, their hearts were made to burn; while in the vision of fire they received God, they were sweetly aflame with love. For the Holy Spirit Himself is love; whence John says: "God is love."

Whoever, therefore, desires God with a pure mind truly already possesses Him whom he loves. For no one, indeed, could love God without possessing Him whom he loves. But behold, if any of you were asked whether he loves God, with a full faith and an unwavering affection he would answer: "I do love." Yet in the very beginning of the reading you heard what the Truth says: "If anyone loveth me, he will keep my words." The proof, therefore, of love is the demonstration of it in action. Wherefore in his Epistle the same John says: "He who saith, 'I love God,' and keepeth not his commandments, is a liar."

Truly, then, do we love God and keep His commandments, if we refrain from forbidden pleasures. For one who still gives himself up to illicit desires surely does not love God, for he contradicts Him in his own will. "And my Father will love him, and we will come to him and take up our abode with him." Ponder, dearest brethren, how great a dignity this is: to possess in the guest chamber of your heart the presence of God.

Certainly, if some wealthy or influential friend were to come to one's house, the whole dwelling would in all haste be cleansed lest perhaps there be something to offend the eyes of that guest upon his entrance. Let him, therefore, who prepares the house of his mind for God wash away the squalor of evil deeds. But see what the Truth says: "We shall come and take up our abode within him." For into the hearts of some He comes without *taking up His abode* there, because through compunction they indeed experience a reverence for God, but in the time of temptation they forget the very thing for which they had been sorry; and so they return to committing sins as though they had not felt the least compunction for them.

℟. When the days of Pentecost were accomplished, they were all together in one place, alleluia: and suddenly, there came a sound from heaven, alleluia, * As of a mighty wind, and it filled the whole house, alleluia, alleluia. ℣. When therefore the disciples were gathered together for fear of the Jews, suddenly a sound from heaven came upon them. As of. Glory. As of.

✠ Continuation of the holy Gospel according to St. John.— At that time Jesus said to his disciples: "If anyone love me, he will keep my words, and my Father will love him, and we will come to him and make our abode with him. He who does not love me does not keep my words. And the word that you have heard is not mine, but the Father's who sent me.

"These things I have spoken to you while yet dwelling with you. But the Advocate, the Holy Spirit, whom the Father will send in my name, he will teach you all things, and bring to your mind whatever I have said to you.

"Peace I leave with you, my peace I give to you; not as the world gives do I give to you. Do not let your heart be troubled, or be afraid. You have heard me say to you, 'I go away and I am coming to you.' If you loved me, you would indeed rejoice that I am going to the Father, for the Father is greater than I. And now I have told you before it comes to pass, that when it has come to pass you may believe. I will no longer speak much with you, for the prince of the world is coming, and in me he has nothing. But he comes that the world may know that I love the Father, and that I do as the Father has commanded me."

LET US PRAY

O God, who on this day didst instruct the hearts of the faithful by the light of the Holy Spirit, grant that by the same Spirit we may always be truly wise and ever rejoice in His consolation. Through our Lord Jesus Christ, Thy Son, who liveth and reigneth with Thee in the unity of the same Holy Spirit, one God world without end.

PENTECOST MONDAY

I Nocturn

From the Acts of the Apostles, c. 19, 1 - 12

II Nocturn

Sermon of St. Augustine, Bishop

Today's solemnity of the great Lord and God likewise marks a memorial of the great grace which was poured out upon us. For this solemnity is celebrated unto God lest what has once been accomplished might be erased from memory. The word *solemnity* is derived from the fact that it is wont to recur annually—in the same way as a river is said to be perennial if it does not dry up in the summer time, but flows throughout the year. Therefore, as *perennial* is derived from the Latin, *per annum*, so also *solemnity* is derived from *solet in anno*, because it is accustomed to be celebrated yearly.

We celebrate today the coming of the Holy Spirit. For the Lord sent from heaven the Spirit whom He had promised while on earth, and because He had promised that He was to be sent from heaven. "He cannot come," He said, "unless I go, but when I go, I will send him to you." He suffered, He died, He arose, He ascended: it remained that He do what He had promised. This His disciples were awaiting, as it is written, one hundred and twenty souls, which is ten times the number of the apostles; for He had chosen twelve, but He sent the Spirit to one hundred and twenty. Those who awaited this promise, therefore, were praying in one house, because they already desired with the same spiritual desire and with the same faith that for which with one mind they prayed; they were the new bottles; the new wine was looked for from heaven, and it came. For already the great Grape had been trodden upon and glorified. Thus we read in the Gospel: "The Spirit had not yet been given, because Jesus as yet had not been glorified."

You have already heard what took place—a great miracle! All who were present had learned but one tongue. The Holy Spirit came; they were filled; they began to speak with the various tongues of all the nations which they had neither known nor learned. But He who had come taught them. He entered; they were filled; He poured out grace upon them. And then this was the sign: not only those one hundred and twenty, but whosoever received the Holy Spirit, immediately being filled with the Spirit, spoke with the tongues of all.

℞. Go ye into the whole world and preach the Gospel, alleluia: * Whosoever will believe and be baptized shall be saved, alleluia, alleluia, alleluia. ℣. In My name they will cast out devils, they will speak with new tongues and will take up serpents. Whosoever. Glory. Whosoever.

III Nocturn

The reading of the holy Gospel according to St. John

At that time Jesus said to Nicodemus: "God so loved the world that he gave his only-begotten Son, that those who believe in him may not perish, but may have life everlasting." And so forth.

Homily of St. Augustine, Bishop

In so far as a physician is able, he comes to heal the sick. But the man who will not heed the physician's orders kills himself. Our Savior came into the world. Why is He called Savior of the world, if not that He is to save the world, not to judge it? If you do not wish to be saved by Him, you shall be judged by your own doing. And why should I say, "You shall be judged"? See what He says: "He that believeth in him is not judged; but he that doth not believe"—what are you expecting Him to say, but—"he is judged"?

He adds this, "He is already judged." The judgment hath not yet appeared, and judgment has already been made. For the Lord knew who were His; He knew who would persevere unto a crown, and who would continue unto the flame. He knew the wheat on His threshing-floor, and He knew the chaff; He knew the grain, and He knew the cockle. "He who believeth not is already judged." Why judged? "Because he has not believed in the name of the only-begotten Son of God."

"Now this is the judgment: The light has come into the world, yet men have loved the darkness rather than the light, for their works were evil."—My brethren, of what men does the Lord find good works? Of none! He finds all works evil. How, then, do some do the truth and come to the light? For this also follows: "But he that does the truth comes to the light."

"But men," He says, "loved the darkness rather than the light."—In this He places the deciding issue. For many have loved their own sins; yet many too have confessed them, because he who confesses his sins and accuses himself of them, even now works with God. God accuses you of your sins; if you also accuse yourself, you are united with God. There are, as it were, two creatures, the man and the sinner. The one of which you hear, *man*, God has made; the other, the *sinner*, man himself has made. Do away with that which you have made that God may save what He has made. It is required that you hate your own work within yourself, and love the work of God within you. When what you have made shall begin to displease, your good works then begin, because you accuse yourself of your evil works. The beginning of good deeds is the confession of evil works.

℟. I will not now call you servants, but My friends; because you have known all things whatsoever I have done among you, alleluia: * Receive ye the Holy Ghost, who is your Comforter within you: the same is He whom the Father will send unto you, alleluia. ℣. You are My friends if you do whatsoever I command you. Receive. Glory. Receive.

✠ Continuation of the holy Gospel according to St. John.— At that time Jesus said to Nicodemus: "God so loved the world that he gave his only-begotten Son, that those who believe in him may not perish, but may have life everlasting. For God did not send his Son into the world in order to judge the world, but that the world might be saved through him. He who believes in him is not judged; but he who does not believe is already judged, because he does not believe in the name of the only-begotten Son of God. Now this is the judgment: The light has come into the world, yet men have loved the darkness rather than the light, for their works were evil. For everyone who does evil hates the light, and does not come to the light, that his deeds may not be exposed. But he who does the truth comes to the light that his deeds may be made manifest, for they have been performed in God."

LET US PRAY

O God, who didst give the Holy Spirit to Thy Apostles, grant to Thy people the fruit of their pious prayers, that to those to whom Thou hast given faith Thou wouldst also grant peace Through our Lord ... in the unity of the same Holy Spirit.

PENTECOST TUESDAY

I Nocturn

From the Prophet Joel, c. 2, 23 - 32

II Nocturn

Sermon of St. John Chrysostom

Today the earth is made heaven for us, not by reason of the stars descending from heaven, but by the ascending of the apostles into heaven, because the bounteous grace of the Holy Spirit is poured out and forms heaven out of the whole earth, not by changing nature, but by correcting the will.

For it found a publican and made an Evangelist; it found a persecutor and made an Apostle; it found a thief, and brought him into Paradise; it found an adulteress and made her equal to the Virgins; it found wise men and made them Evangelists; it drove out wickedness and introduced kindness; it put an end to slavery and introduced liberty; it forgave the debt and bestowed the grace of God. Therefore the earth is made a heaven, and I shall not cease from declaring this.

"And suddenly there came a sound from heaven, as of a mighty wind coming, and it filled the whole house where they were sitting. And there appeared to them parted tongues as it were of fire." If it was fire, the Jew asks, how was it they did not burn? I shall also ask the Jew: If it was fire, how was it that the bush, an inflammable wood, did not burn? What is more devouring than fire? What is more combustible than a bush? Yet neither was the wood burned, nor was the fire extinguished.

And how was it that the fire did not burn the bodies of the three young men, but the furnace was turned into dew and the coals were thought to be as roses? It was a battle of fire and body, and the victory went to the body. What was more soluble than wax became firmer than iron. Interpret for me the things that have passed, for they came first that you might believe the truth. For the Holy Spirit appeared in a flame that minds might receive Him quickly. But not only for this reason, but also because as fire burns thorns, so the Holy Spirit does away with sins. He was sent to Daniel in the lions' den, and His divine power checked their terrible fury.

℞. The Lord has taught them discipline and wisdom, alleluia: He has confirmed the grace of His Spirit in them. * And He has filled their hearts with understanding, alleluia. ℣. Suddenly with a sound the Holy Spirit came upon them. And He has filled. Glory. And He has filled.

III Nocturn

The reading of the holy Gospel according to St. John

At that time Jesus said to the Pharisees: "Amen, amen I say to you, he who enters not by the door into the sheepfold, but climbs up another way, is a thief and a robber. But he who enters by the door is shepherd of the sheep. And so forth.

Homily of St. Augustine, Bishop

In today's discourse our Lord proposes a similitude concerning His flock and the door whereby one enters His fold. The pagans, therefore, may say, "We lead good lives," but if they enter not through the door, what advantage is that to them whereof they boast? For only to this end should it profit anyone to lead a good life, namely, that it be given him to live forever; for to him to whom it is not given to live forever, what profit is there in living a good life? Nor should they be said to live good lives who either from blindness know not the end of a good life, or from pride despise it.

And no one has a true and certain hope of life everlasting unless he know the Life, which is Christ, and enter through the door into the sheepfold. Now, there are many of such a nature that they seek even to persuade men to lead good lives, yet without being Christians. They wish to climb up another way, to rob and to kill—not, as the Good Shepherd, to protect and to save.

Accordingly, some philosophers have treated of many subtleties concerning the virtues and vices, making distinctions, defining, reasoning out the most ingenious conclusions, stuffing books with their ideas, advertising their wisdom with braying trumpets; and they even dared to say to men: "Follow us; embrace our way of life if you wish to live happily!" But they entered not through the door; they wished to corrupt, to plague, and to kill.

What shall I say of them? Behold, the Pharisees themselves read of Christ and talked of Christ; they looked for His coming. But when He was present, they knew Him not. They boasted that they themselves were among the Seers, that is, among the wise ones, but they denied Christ, and entered not through the door. Therefore if perhaps they seduced some, they seduced them only to afflict and to destroy—not to free. But let us pass these over, and let us see if perhaps they who glory in the name of Christ Himself (who pride themselves in the name of Christian) enter through the door. For there are countless numbers who not only boast that they are Seers, but who wish to be considered enlightened by Christ—but they are heretics.

℟. The Apostles spoke with divers tongues the wondrous works of God, * According as the Holy Ghost gave them to speak, alleluia. ℣. They were all filled with the Holy Ghost, and began to speak. According. Glory. According.

✠ Continuation of the holy Gospel according to St. John.— At that time Jesus said to the Pharisees: "Amen, amen, I say to you, he who enters not by the door into the sheepfold, but climbs up another way, is a thief and a robber. But he who enters by the door is shepherd of the sheep. To this man the gatekeeper opens, and the sheep hear his voice, and he calls his own sheep by name and leads them forth. And when he has let out his own sheep, he goes before them; and the sheep follow him because they know his voice. But a stranger they will not follow, but will flee from him, because they do not know the voice of strangers."

This parable Jesus spoke to them, but they did not understand what he was saying to them.

Again, therefore, Jesus said to them, "Amen, amen, I say to you, I am the door of the sheep. All whoever have come are thieves and robbers; but the sheep have not heard them. I am the door. If anyone enter by me he shall be safe, and shall go in and out, and shall find pastures. The thief comes only to steal, and slay, and destroy. I came that they may have life, and have it more abundantly."

LET US PRAY

May the power of the Holy Spirit be ever with us, we beseech Thee, O Lord, and may it both mercifully cleanse our hearts and keep them from all harm. Through our Lord... in the unity of the same Holy Spirit.

EMBER WEDNESDAY

The reading of the holy Gospel according to St. John

At that time Jesus said to the Jews: "No one can come to me unless the Father who sent me draw him." And so forth.

Homily of St. Augustine, Bishop

Do not think that you are drawn unwillingly; the soul indeed is drawn also by love. Nor should we be fearful lest we be accused concerning the Gospel word of the sacrèd Scripture by men who place emphasis on the words and are far removed from understanding matters wholly divine, and it be said to us: "How do I believe by my own will if I be drawn?" I declare: "It is of little consequence that you are drawn by the will, for you are drawn by desire also." What is it to be drawn by desire? It is to delight in the Lord, and He shall give to you the petitions of your heart. It is a certain desire of the heart whose sweet bread is that bread from heaven. Furthermore, if it is allowed the poet to say, One's own desire draws one; not necessity, but desire; not obligation, but delight; how much more vigorously should we declare that that man is drawn to Christ who is delighted with truth, who is delighted with happiness, who is delighted with justice, who is delighted with everlasting life—all of which Christ is! Or do the senses possess their desires, while the soul is deprived of its own? If the soul does not possess its desires, whence is it said: "But the children of men shall put their trust under the covert of thy wings. They shall be inebriated with the plenty of thy house; and thou shalt make them drink of the torrent of thy pleasure. For with thee is the fountain of life, and in thy light we shall see light"?

Propose this to one who loves, and he will sense what I am saying; propose it to one who desires; propose it to one who hungers; propose it to him who is journeying in this solitude and thirsts and sighs for the fountain of his eternal country; propose it to such a one, and he will sense what I am saying. But if I speak to one who is cold, he knows not whereof I speak. Such were those who murmured among themselves. He says: "He whom the Father draweth, cometh to me." What is this, "whom the Father draweth," when Christ Himself draws? Why did He wish to say, "whom the Father draweth"? If we are to be drawn, let us be drawn by Him to whom she who loves Him says: "We will run after the odor of thy ointments." But let us take note of what He wished to be understood, brethren, and grasp it in as far as we are able. The Father draws to the Son those who believe in the Son by reason of the fact that they believe He has God as His Father. For God the Father begot the Son equal to Himself, and whosoever thinks and feels in his faith and reflects that He in whom he believes is equal to the Father, him the Father draws to the Son.

Arius believed that the Son was a creature; the Father did not draw him, because he who does not believe the Son to be equal to the Father does not know the Father. What do you say, O Arius? What do you say, thou heretic? What are you talking about? What is Christ? "He is not," says he, "true God, but him whom the true God has made!" The Father has not drawn you, for you have not known the Father whose Son you deny. You think another thing—He is not His Son; you are neither drawn by the Father, nor are you drawn to the Son! "He is the Son" is one thing; what you say, another. Photinus states: "Christ is man alone; He is not also God." The Father has not drawn him who so believes. Whom has the Father drawn? Him who says: "Thou art the Christ, the Son of the living God." Show a green branch to a sheep, and you will draw it. Nuts are shown to a child, and it is drawn, and because it runs, it is drawn—drawn by love, drawn without harm to the body, drawn without binding the heart. If then those things which are among earthly delights and desires, when shown to those who love them, draw them—because it is true that the desires of a person draw him on—does not Christ, revealed by the Father, draw? For what does the soul more vehemently desire than the truth?

THURSDAY

The reading of the holy Gospel according to St. Luke

At that time Jesus, having summoned the twelve apostles, gave them power and authority over all the devils, and to cure diseases. And so forth.

Homily of St. Ambrose, Bishop

What kind of man he should be who is to preach the kingdom of God is described by the precepts of the Gospel: without staff, without scrip, without shoes, without bread, without money —that is, not requiring the supports of worldly aid, and sure in faith, he thinks that he can the better supply himself the less he requires. Those who wish may understand these things as meaning only our spiritual affection, which, not only having rejected power and despised riches, but also having given up the desires of the flesh, might seem to have taken off, as it were, a garment of the body. To them is given, first of all, the general commandment of peace and constancy, so that they are to bring peace, preserve constancy, and observe the customs of hospitable relations, implying that it is out of place for a preacher of the heavenly kingdom to pass from house to house, and to change the customs of sacred hospitality.

But, in order that the favor of hospitality be considered as something that should be tendered, it is also commanded them that, if they are not received, the dust should be shaken off their feet and they should leave the city. By this the reward of hospitality is declared to be of no small value, in that we not only bestow peace on our hosts, but likewise, if any stains of worldly wantonness should disfigure them, they are taken away when the bearers of the apostolic preaching are received. Nor, according to Matthew, is the house which the apostles enter to be carelessly selected, that there may be no reason for changing lodging or breaking obligations. However, the same precaution is not given to the harborer of the guest, lest, when a guest is chosen, the hospitality itself be lessened.

But just as this heavenly teaching, according to the letter, is an admirable form of precept with regard to the duty of hospitality, so does it also attract us with its mystery. For when a house is being selected, a worthy host is sought for. Let us see, then, whether the Church and Christ are not designated as the ones to be preferred. For what house is more worthy of the entrance of apostolic preaching than the holy Church? Or who seems to be more preferred above all than Christ, who was accustomed to wash the feet of His guests, and who would not allow any whom He received in His house to dwell there with soiled feet, but, although they were stained in early life, He nevertheless deigned to cleanse their steps for the remainder of their lives? Therefore He alone is the One whom no one should forsake, whom no one should exchange. To Him it is well said: "Lord, to whom shall we go? Thou hast the words of eternal life"; and we believe them.

EMBER FRIDAY

The reading of the holy Gospel according to St. Luke

At that time it came to pass on one of the days, that Jesus sat teaching. And there were Pharisees and teachers of the Law sitting by, who had come out of every village of Galilee and Judea and out of Jerusalem. And the power of the Lord was present to heal them. And so forth.

Homily of St. Ambrose, Bishop

It is not a useless or insignificant remedy for this paralytic when the Lord is first said to have prayed, not, indeed, by way of supplication, but for the sake of example. For He was offering a model to be imitated; He was not making a display of His prayer. And the fact that the Doctors of the Law from all Galilee, Judea, and Jerusalem were gathered together is mentioned when, among all the cures of the rest of the infirm the healing of this paralytic is described. First of all—as we have said before—because everyone who is ill should make use of men to pray for the health that he seeks, through whom the enervated frame of our life and the halting steps of our actions may be strengthened by the healing effect of the heavenly word.

Consequently, let there be some counsellors of the mind who can lift up man's soul to higher things—even though it is dulled by the weakness of the exterior body—by whose hands it may again be easily lifted up and set down before Jesus, worthy to be beheld by the Lord's countenance. For the Lord does have regard for humility, since "He hath regarded the humility of his handmaid." As soon as He beholds their faith, He says: "Man, thy sins are forgiven thee." The Lord is great in that by the merits of some He forgives others, and while He tries some, He forgives the faults of others. Why does thy comrade not have influence with thee, O man, when before God a servant has both the privilege of intervening and the right of obtaining what he asks?

You who pass judgment, learn to forgive; you who are sick, learn to pray. If you despair of pardon for serious sins, make use of men of prayer; make use of the Church who will pray for you, at the sight of which the Lord will forgive what He was able to withhold from you. And while we should not omit the historical truth of the account so that we may truly believe that the body of this paralytic was healed, nevertheless, let us understand the healing of the interior man whose sins are forgiven. When the Jews assert that sins can be remitted by God alone, they confess that Christ is God; they betray their infidelity by their own decision when they (in saying that sins can be forgiven by God alone) place emphasis on the act in order to deny the person.

EMBER SATURDAY

The reading of the holy Gospel according to St. Luke

At that time Jesus rose from the synagogue and entered Simon's house. Now Simon's mother-in-law was suffering from a great fever. And so forth.

Homily of St. Ambrose, Bishop

Behold the mildness of our Lord and Savior! He is not moved by indignation, nor offended by wickedness, nor, insulted by injury, does He depart from Judea, but on the contrary, forgetful of injury and mindful only of mercy, He softens the hearts of this faithless people, now by teaching, now by casting out devils, now by healing the sick. Rightly does St. Luke tell first of the man freed from an evil spirit and then of the cure of the woman. For the Lord had come to cure both sexes; but that one ought to have been healed first which had been created first, and yet the other sex should not have been neglected which had sinned more through fickleness of mind than from actual malice.

That the Lord began His works of healing on the Sabbath signifies that the new creation began where the old had stopped. It shows, moreover, that the Son of God was not subject to the Law but was above the Law in the very beginning, and that the Law was not destroyed by Him, but fulfilled. For the world was not made by the Law, but by the word, as we read: "By the word of the Lord the heavens were established." The Law was then not destroyed, but fulfilled, that the restoration of man, who was already falling, might be accomplished. Wherefore the Apostle says: "Stripping off the old man from yourselves, put on the new man who is created according to God."

Well did He begin on the Sabbath in order to show that He Himself was the Creator, who, following up the works of creation with works of healing, was continuing the work which He had already begun, just as a carpenter, arranging to renovate a house, does not begin to tear down the old one from the foundation but from the roof. And so He places His hand first there where He had before left off; then He begins with the smaller things that He may attain to those which are greater. Men also, by the power of God, are able to free those possessed by devils, but to command the resurrection of the dead pertains to divine power alone. In the type of that woman, the mother-in-law of Peter and Andrew, perhaps our flesh also languished with various fevers of crime and burned with the wanton promptings of various evil desires. Nor would I say that the fever of love is less than that of heat; the former inflames the soul, the latter inflames the body. Our fever is avarice; our fever is passion; our fever is lust; our fever is ambition; our fever is wrath.

TRINITY SUNDAY

I Nocturn

From Isaias the Prophet, c. 6, 1 - 12

II Nocturn

From the book of St. Fulgentius, Bishop, on Faith, addressed to Peter

The faith which the holy patriarchs and prophets received from heaven before the Incarnation of the Son of God, which also the holy Apostles heard from the incarnate Lord Himself, and which, under the direction of the Holy Spirit, they not only preached by word but also left in writing for the wholesome instruction of posterity—that faith preaches one single God, the Trinity: that is, Father, Son, and Holy Spirit.

But it would not be a true Trinity if one and the same person were called Father, Son, and Holy Spirit. For if there would be one person, as there is one substance, of the Father, Son, and Holy Spirit, there would be nothing at all which could truly be called a Trinity. Again, there would indeed be a true Trinity, but this same Trinity would not be one God if, as the Father, Son and Holy Spirit are distinguished from each other by what is proper to their persons, they were separate also by diversity of nature.

But because in that one, true, triune God it is essentially true not only that there is but one God, but also that He is triune, it follows that in this same true God there is Trinity in persons and unity in nature. By this natural unity the Father is wholly in the Son and Holy Spirit, the Son wholly in the Father and Holy Spirit, and the Holy Spirit wholly in the Father and the Son.

None of these is outside any of the others; for no one either precedes another in eternity or exceeds in magnitude or is superior in power. For the Father is neither before nor greater than the Son and Holy Spirit, as far as the divine nature is concerned. Nor can the eternity and immensity of the Son either precede or exceed the immensity and eternity of the Holy Spirit.

℟. Great is the Lord, and greatly to be praised: * And of His wisdom there is no end. ℣. The Lord is great, and great is His power: and there is no limit to His wisdom. And. Glory. And.

III Nocturn

The reading of the holy Gospel according to St. Matthew

At that time Jesus said to his disciples: "All power in heaven and on earth has been given to me. Go, therefore, and make disciples of all nations, baptizing them in the name of the Father, and of the Son, and of the Holy Spirit. And so forth.

Homily of St. Gregory Nazianzen

What Catholic does not know that the Father is truly Father, that the Son is truly Son, and that the Holy Spirit is truly the Holy Spirit? In such wise the Lord Himself spoke to the Apostles: "Going, baptize all nations in the name of the Father and of the Son and of the Holy Spirit." This is the perfect Trinity, consisting in that unity which we profess to be a unity of substance.

For we make no division in God according to the flesh; but according to the power of the divine nature, which does not consist in matter, we believe that the respective persons truly exist and we testify also to the unity of the Godhead. Nor do we hold, as some have thought, that the Son of God is the extension of one part from the other; neither do we say that He is a word without substance, as the mere sound of a voice, but we believe that the three persons are of one essence, and of one majesty and power.

And consequently we confess that there is but one God, because the unity of His majesty forbids His being named by a word signifying plurality, that is Gods. In fine, we, as all Catholics, speak of a Father and of a Son, but we cannot and must not say there are two Gods. Not that the Son of God is not God, for He is indeed true God of true God; but because we know that the Son of God is from no other source than the one Father Himself; hence we say there is one God. This the prophets, this the Apostles have handed down; this the Lord Himself taught, saying: "I and the Father are one." The *one* (unum) refers to the unity of the Godhead, as I have mentioned; the *are* (sumus) designates the Persons.

℞. O blessed Trinity, we praise Thee, we bless Thee, we adore Thee: increase within us faith, hope, and love, * O Blessed Trinity. ℣. To Thee be praise, glory, and thanksgiving forever and ever. O blessed Trinity.

The reading of the holy Gospel according to St. Luke

At that time Jesus said to his disciples: "Be merciful, therefore, even as your Father is merciful." And so forth.

Homily of St. Augustine, Bishop

Two are the works of mercy which set us free; these the Lord Himself in a few words puts forth in the Gospel: "Forgive, and it shall be forgiven you. Give, and it shall be given you." "Forgive, and it shall be forgiven you" pertains to pardoning; "give, and it shall be given you" pertains to bestowing favors. In reference to what He says concerning pardoning: you wish to be pardoned for your sin, and, on the other hand, you also have another whom you can pardon. Again, in reference to what He says concerning bestowing favors: a beggar asks of you, and you also are a beggar of God. For all of us, when we pray, are God's beggars; we stand before the door of the great Father; yea, we even prostrate ourselves and suppliantly groan, desiring to receive something; and that something is God Himself. What does the beggar seek from you? Bread? And you, what do you seek from God but Christ, who says: "I am the living bread which came down from heaven"? Do you wish to be pardoned? Pardon others. "Forgive and it shall be forgiven you." Do you wish to receive? "Give and it shall be given you."

℟. Let us bless the Father and the Son and the Holy Ghost: * Let us praise and exalt Him above all forever. ℣. Blessed art Thou, O Lord, in the height of heaven: worthy of praise and glorious forever. Let us. Glory. Let us.

✠ Continuation of the holy Gospel according to St. Matthew.— At that time Jesus said to his disciples: "All power in heaven and on earth has been given to me. Go, therefore, and make disciples of all nations, baptizing them in the name of the Father, and of the Son, and of the Holy Spirit, teaching them to observe all that I have commanded you; and behold, I am with you all days, even unto the consummation of the world."

LET US PRAY

O almighty and eternal God, who hast given Thy servants to know the glory of the eternal Trinity in the profession of the true faith and to adore the unity in the power of majesty, we beseech Thee, that by the firmness of the same faith, we may always be preserved from all adversity. Through our Lord.

Thursday after Trinity Sunday

THE FEAST OF CORPUS CHRISTI

I Nocturn

From the first Epistle of St. Paul the Apostle to the Corinthians; c. 11, 20 - 32

II Nocturn

Sermon of St. Thomas Aquinas

The boundless favors of the divine goodness shown to the Christian people confer an inestimable dignity upon it. For there is not, nor has there been at any time, so wonderful a nation having its gods so near to it as our God is to us. For indeed, the only-begotten Son of God, willing that we should be partakers of His Divinity, has assumed our nature, so that, having been made man, He might make men gods. And still more, that which He has assumed from us He has offered in its entirety for our salvation. For He offered on the altar of the cross His own body as an oblation for our reconciliation; He shed His own blood both as a ransom and as a purifying laver, so that we, being bought back from wretched slavery, might be cleansed from all sin. And in order that the remembrance of such a great gift should remain constantly with us, He left His own body for food and His own blood for drink to be partaken of by the faithful under the species of bread and wine.

O precious and admirable banquet! Life-giving and filled with every sweetness! For what can be more treasured than this banquet? This banquet in which, not the flesh of bullocks and goats —as was formerly in the Law—but Christ, true God, is served to us to be partaken of! What is more marvelous than this Sacrament? For in it bread and wine are converted substantially into the body and blood of Christ; and He, perfect God and man, is contained under the species of a little bread and wine.

He is, consequently, eaten by the faithful, but He is by no means broken into parts; what is more, when the Sacrament is divided, He remains entirely in each particle. Moreover, in the Sacrament the accidents remain without their subject that faith may play its part when the visible is taken invisibly, hidden under a different exterior form (that is, when the body and blood of Christ, which of themselves are visible, are received in the Eucharist under the appearances of bread and wine), and the senses, which judge of accidents known to them, may be rendered free from deception.

Likewise, there is no sacrament more salutary than this by which sins are purged away, virtues increased, and the mind enriched with an abundance of all spiritual charismata. It is offered in the Church for the living and the dead, that what has been instituted for the salvation of all may be of profit to all. Finally, no one is able to describe the sweetness of this Sacrament by which spiritual sweetness is tasted at its very source, and there is recalled the memory of that supreme charity which Christ displayed during His Passion. Wherefore, in order that the immensity of this charity might be more deeply fixed in the hearts of the faithful, Christ, when about to pass from this world to the Father, having celebrated the Pasch with His disciples, instituted this Sacrament at the Last Supper as an everlasting remembrance of His Passion, the fulfillment of the ancient types, and the greatest of the miracles worked by Him; and He left it as a special comfort for those who are saddened by His absence.

℟. I am the bread of life; your fathers did eat manna in the desert, and are dead: * This is the bread which cometh down from heaven, that if any man eat of it, he may not die. ℣. I am the living bread, which came down from heaven: If any man eat of this bread, he shall live forever. This. Glory. This.

III Nocturn

The reading of the holy Gospel according to St. John

At that time Jesus said to the multitudes of the Jews: "My flesh is food indeed, and my blood is drink indeed." And so forth.

Homily of St. Augustine, Bishop

Although men seek to satisfy hunger and thirst by means of food and drink, these are indeed of no avail to them unless they render them immortal and incorruptible, that is, partakers of the society of the saints, where peace and perfect unity are had. Therefore, indeed, as men of God even before us understood it, our Lord Jesus Christ entrusted His own body and blood in the likeness of those things, which were reduced into one thing from many. For the one is made from many grains of wheat; the other is made from the juice of many grapes flowing together into one wine.

Now finally He shows in what manner this about which He is speaking is to take place, and how it is that we are to eat His body and drink His blood. "He who eats my flesh and drinks my blood abides in me and I in him." Therefore to eat of that food and to drink of that drink is to abide in Christ and to have Him abiding in us.

And therefore he who does not abide in Christ, and in whom Christ does not abide, without a doubt neither spiritually eats His flesh nor drinks His blood, although carnally and visibly he consumes the Sacrament of the body and blood of Christ; nay, on the contrary, he eats and drinks the Sacrament unto judgment for himself, because, as one unclean, he dares to approach the Sacraments of Christ, which no one receives worthily except he who is pure, of whom it is said: "Blessed are the pure of heart, for they shall see God."

"As the living Father," He says, "has sent me, and I live because of the Father, so he who eats me, he also shall live because of me." Just as if He were to say: "That I live because of the Father, that is, that I refer My life to Him as to a greater, My emptying out of Myself has effected; but that anyone lives because of Me, it is that participation of Me in which he eats Me that effects it. Therefore I, having been sent down to earth, live because of the *Father*, while he (who eats me), having been lifted up, lives because of *Me*." But if it is thus said, "I live because of the Father," for the reason that the Son is from the Father, not the Father from the Son, it is said without detriment to their equality. Yet by saying, "He who eats me, he also shall live because of me," He did not mean that there is an equality between Him and us, but He showed the grace of His mediatorship.

℟. He that eateth My flesh and drinketh My blood, * Abideth in Me and I in him. ℣. There is no other nation so great, that hath gods so near to them, as our God is present to us. Abideth. Glory. Abideth.

☩ Continuation of the holy Gospel according to St. John.—
At that time Jesus said to the multitudes of the Jews: "My flesh is food indeed, and my blood is drink indeed. He who eats my flesh, and drinks my blood, abides in me and I in him. As the living Father has sent me, and as I live because of the Father, so he who eats me, he also shall live because of me. This is the bread that has come down from heaven; not as your fathers ate the manna, and died. He who eats this bread shall live forever."

LET US PRAY

O God, who hast left us a memorial of Thy Passion in this wonderful Sacrament, grant us, we beseech Thee, so to reverence the sacred mystery of Thy Body and Blood that we may always enjoy within our souls the fruit of Thy Passion, who livest and reignest with God the Father.

FRIDAY

The reading of the holy Gospel according to St. John

At that time Jesus said to the multitudes of the Jews: "My flesh is food indeed, and my blood is drink indeed." And so forth.

Homily of St. Augustine, Bishop

We have heard from the Gospel the Lord's words which follow His previous sermon. Hence a sermon is due for your ears and minds, and it is not out of place today, for it is in reference to our Lord's body, which He said that He gave to be eaten for the sake of eternal life. And He has explained the manner of this bestowal of His gift, how He would give His flesh to eat, saying: "He who eats my flesh, and drinks my blood, abides in me and I in him." The sign that one has eaten and drunk is this: if he abides in Christ and Christ in him; if he dwells in Christ and Christ in him; if he clings to Christ so that he is not forsaken.

This, then, he has taught and advised us by His mystical words, that we may be in His body, among His members subject to Him, the Head, partaking of His flesh and not breaking away from unity with Him. But of those who were present, many, not understanding, were scandalized, for on hearing these words they did not think of anything but that flesh which they themselves were. So the Apostle says, and says truly: "The wisdom of the flesh is death." Our Lord gives His flesh to us to eat; and to know His flesh according to the flesh is death. When He declares of His flesh that in it is eternal life, we must not understand His flesh according to the flesh, as was the case of which we read: "Many, therefore, (not of his enemies, but) of his disciples, hearing it, said: 'This saying is hard, and who can hear it?'"

If the disciples held this saying as hard, how did His enemies consider it? And still, it was necessary that that be declared which would not be believed by all. The mystery of God should make us attentive, not contrary; these, however, quickly fell away when our Lord Jesus Christ spoke of such things. They did not believe that He was declaring something great and enveloping a certain grace in those words; rather, as they willed, so they understood (and that in the way of men) that Jesus was able or was planning to distribute the flesh with which the Word was clothed, as it were, in little parts to those who believed in Him. "This saying is hard," they say, "who can hear it?"

SATURDAY

The reading of the holy Gospel according to St. John

At that time Jesus said to the multitudes of the Jews: "My flesh is food indeed, and my blood is drink indeed." And so forth.

From a Homily of St. Augustine, Bishop

We have said, brethren, that the Lord recommended in the eating of His flesh and the drinking of His blood that we should remain in Him, and He in us. But we remain in Him when we are His members, and He remains in us if we are His temple. And in order that we may be His members, unity binds us to Him. What, but charity, causes that unity to bind us? And whence the charity of God? Inquire of the Apostle. "The charity of God," he says, "is poured forth in our hearts by the Holy Spirit who is given to us."

Hence it is the spirit which quickeneth, for the spirit gives the members life, but it does not make any members to live except those which it finds in the body to which it giveth life. For does the spirit which is in you, O man, by reason of which you are a man, give life to a member which it finds separated from your body? I call your soul your spirit. Your soul does not quicken any but the members which are in your flesh; if you take one away, it is no longer made to live by your soul because it is not joined to the unity of your body.

These things are stated so that we may love unity and be fearful of separation. For a Christian should dread nothing so much as to be separated from Christ's body. Because, if he is separated from Christ's body, he is not a member of Him; if he is not a member of Him, he is not given life by His Spirit. "Now if any man," says the Apostle, "have not the Spirit of Christ, he is none of his." Therefore, "it is the spirit that quickeneth; the flesh profiteth nothing. The words that I have spoken to you, are spirit and life." What is this, "are Spirit and life"? They must be understood in a spiritual sense. Have you understood them in a spiritual sense? "They are spirit and life." Have you understood them in a carnal way? Even so, they are spirit and life, but not to you!

SUNDAY WITHIN THE OCTAVE OF CORPUS CHRISTI

I Nocturn

From the first Book of Kings, c. 1, 1 - 11

II Nocturn

Sermon of St. John Chrysostom

Because the Word has said, "This is my body," let us acknowledge it, believe it, and perceive it with the eyes of our understanding. For Christ has not given us something that the senses can perceive, but something that can, nevertheless, be entirely understood by means of sensible things. Thus in Baptism through a sensible sign, namely, water, the gift is conferred; but what is effected, that is, regeneration and renewal, can be understood. If you were incorporeal, He would confer simple and incorporeal blessings upon you; but because the soul is in the body, He makes these things intelligible to you by sensible manifestations. How often do men now say: "I want to see His form, His figure, His garments, and His shoes"? Behold, you see Him; you touch Him; you consume Him. And do you wish to see His garments? He has allowed you not only to see Him, but even to truly consume and touch Him, and to receive Him within yourself.

Wherefore let no one approach Him with disgust, nor carelessly, but let all be enkindled, ardent and fervent. For if the Jews stood with feet shod, and, carrying staves in their hands, ate the lamb with haste, it behooves you the more to be prepared. For they indeed were about to go to Palestine and therefore had the appearance of travelers; but you are to pass to heaven.

Therefore it is fitting that you be on your guard in all things, for the punishment that is imposed on those receiving unworthily is not small. Consider how greatly indignant you are against the traitor (Judas) and against those who crucified Him, and then look to yourself, lest you also should be guilty of the body and of the blood of Christ. They put to death that most sacred body; but you receive with a polluted soul, and after so many benefits! For it was not enough for Him to become man, to be felled by blows and to be crucified, but He must even make Himself one with us, and not only by faith, but in very deed He makes us His own body.

Who ought therefore to be more spotless than the one partaking of such a sacrifice? And ought not the hand which distributes this flesh, the mouth which is filled with spiritual fire, the tongue reddened by the blood, awful beyond compare, be purer than the sunbeam? Consider what a distinctive honor is yours, what a banquet you enjoy! That whereon angels fear to look, nor dare to gaze at freely because of the splendor shining from it, upon that we feed; to that we are joined and are made one body and one flesh with Christ. Who shall declare the powers of the Lord and make known all His praises? What shepherd feeds his flock with his own blood? And why do I say a shepherd? There are many mothers who, after the pains of birth, give their children to other nurses. This, however, He does not suffer, but He feeds us by His own blood, and through all things He binds us to Himself.

℞. Whilst they were at supper, Jesus took bread, and blessed, and broke, and gave to His disciples, and said: * Take ye and eat: this is My Body. ℣. The men of my tabernacle said: Who will give us of his flesh, that we may be filled. Take. Glory. Take.

III Nocturn

The reading of the holy Gospel according to St. Luke

At that time Jesus spoke to the Pharisees this parable: "A certain man gave a great supper and he invited many." And so forth.

Homily of St. Gregory, Pope

Dearly beloved brethren, one is wont to observe this difference between the delights of the flesh and those of the heart, namely, that carnal delights, when they are not had, set one on fire with the desire of them; but when they are greedily devoured, by their very satisfaction they beget a loathing in him who eats them.

But spiritual delights, on the contrary, when they are not had, are disdained; but when they are had, they are yet more desired; and the more they are eaten by him who is hungry, so much the more are they hungered for by him who eats.

With carnal delights the desire of them pleases, their actual enjoyment displeases; while with spiritual delights the desire is of little worth but their enjoyment pleases more. With the first, appetite begets satiety, and satiety, disgust; with the latter, the appetite indeed begets fullness, but the fullness, on its part, generates a greater appetite. Spiritual delights intensify the desire of the mind even while they satisfy; for the more a relish for spiritual things is felt, so much the more is it understood how ardently they should be loved; if this relish is not perceived, they cannot be loved, for their sweetness is unknown. For who can love what he knows not?

On this account the Psalmist admonishes us, saying: "Taste and see that the Lord is sweet." As though he would clearly say: "His sweetness you do not know if you have in no way tasted thereof; but touch the food of life with the palate of your heart, that, experiencing its sweetness, you may be able to love it." These spiritual delights man then lost when he sinned in Paradise; he went forth from Paradise when he closed his mouth to the food of everlasting sweetness.

Wherefore we also, who have been born in the misery of this earthly sojourn, begin our existence already afflicted with ennui; we know not what we ought to desire. This affliction of ours becomes so much the greater the more the soul separates itself from the desire of this sweetness. And because for an exceedingly long time it neglected to nourish itself with internal delights, it now does not desire them. For this reason we languish under a spiritual laziness and are fatigued by the long-continued ravages of fasting. And because we will not taste the sweetness prepared for us within, we miserably love our own starvation in outward things.

℞. A certain man made a great supper, and he sent his servants at the hour of supper to say to them that were invited that they should come, * Because all things were ready. ℣. Come, eat my bread, and drink the wine which I have mixed for you. Because. Glory. Because.

✠ Continuation of the holy Gospel according to St. Luke.—At that time Jesus spoke to the Pharisees this parable: "A certain man gave a great supper, and he invited many. And he sent his servant at supper time to tell those invited to come, for everything is now ready. And they all with one accord began to excuse themselves. The first said to him, 'I have bought a farm, and I must go out and see it; I pray thee hold me excused.' And another said, 'I have bought five yoke of oxen, and I am on my way to try them; I pray thee hold me excused.' And another said, 'I have married a wife, and therefore I cannot come.'

"And the servant returned, and reported these things to his master. Then the master of the house was angry and said to his servant, 'Go out quickly into the streets and lanes of the city, and bring in here the poor, and the crippled, and the blind, and the lame.' And the servant said, 'Sir, thy order has been carried out, and still there is room.' Then the master said to the servant, 'Go out into the highways and hedges, and make them come in, so that my house may be filled. For I tell you that none of those who were invited shall taste of my supper.'"

LET US PRAY

Grant us, O Lord, a constant love and reverence for Thy holy name, for Thou dost never forsake in Thy care those whom Thou dost choose in Thy unchanging love. Through our Lord.

MONDAY

The reading of the holy Gospel according to St. John

At that time Jesus said to the multitudes of the Jews: "My flesh is food indeed, and my blood is drink indeed." And so forth.

From a Homily of St. Augustine, Bishop

"This is the bread that came down from heaven." Manna was a type of this bread; the altar of God signified this bread. These were mysteries; they were different in their types, but they are the same in that which they signify. Listen to the Apostle: "For I would not have you ignorant, brethren," he says, "that our fathers were all under the cloud, and all passed through the sea. And all in Moses were baptized in the cloud, and in the sea, and did all eat the same spiritual food." The same *spiritual* food indeed; for they ate a different material food, since *they* ate manna, *we* something else. They truly ate the spiritual food which we eat; but our fathers ate it, not their (the Jews') fathers, that is, the fathers to whom we are like, not to whom the Jews were like. And he adds, "and all drank the same spiritual drink." They drank one thing; we, another; but only in its visible form, since it signifies the same thing in its spiritual virtue. For how did they drink the same spiritual drink? He says: "They drank of the spiritual rock that followed them; and the rock was

Christ." Thence the bread; thence the drink. The rock was Christ in type; the true Christ is in the Word and in the flesh. And how did they drink? The rock was smitten twice with a rod; the double smiting signifies the two wooden beams of the cross.

The faithful know the body of Christ if they do not neglect to be the body of Christ. Let them become the body of Christ if they wish to live by the Spirit of Christ. One does not live by the Spirit of Christ except through the body of Christ. Understand, my brethren, what I have to say. You are man, and you have a spirit, and you have a body. I name that spirit which is called the soul, by reason of which you are a man; for you consist of body and soul. You have an invisible spirit and a visible body. Tell me, how does it live? Does your spirit receive life from your body, or your body from your spirit? All who live can answer this; he who cannot respond to this—I am not sure if he is living. What will everyone who lives respond? "My body, indeed, lives by my spirit." Therefore do you wish to live by the Spirit of Christ? Be in the body of Christ.

For can my body live by your spirit? My body lives by my spirit, and your body lives by your spirit. The body of Christ cannot live except by the Spirit of Christ. Whence it is that the Apostle Paul, explaining to us this bread, says: "For we, being many, are one bread, one body." O mystery of love! O token of unity! O bond of charity! He who desires to live has wherein he may live, and has whereon he may live. Let him approach, believe, be incorporated, that he may be made to live. He should not shrink from the union of the members; let him not be a putrefying member, which deserves to be cut off; let him not be a deformed member, by which the body is disgraced. Let him be a beautiful member; fit, healthy, he should cleave to the body; he should live to God through God. Let him now labor on earth so that afterwards he may reign in heaven.

TUESDAY

The reading of the holy Gospel according to St. John

At that time Jesus said to the multitudes of the Jews: "My flesh is food indeed, and my blood is drink indeed." And so forth.

From a Homily of St. Augustine, Bishop

"Not as your fathers did eat manna and are dead." Why have they eaten and died? Because they believed that which they saw; what they did not see, they did not understand. Therefore were they *your* fathers, because you are similar to them. For as far, my brethren, as relates to this visible and corporeal death, do we not also die who eat the bread that comes down from heaven? They died just as we shall die, so far, as I said, as relates to the visible and carnal death of this body.

But as to what pertains to that death concerning which the Lord terrifies us, and which their fathers died: Moses ate manna, Aaron ate manna also, Phinees too and many others there who were pleasing to God ate manna, and they did not die. Why? Because they understood the visible food spiritually, hungered for it spiritually, tasted it spiritually, in order that they might be filled spiritually. For we also at the present day receive a visible food: but the sacrament is one thing, the virtue of the sacrament another.

How many receive from the altar and die—die indeed by receiving! Whence the Apostle says: "Eateth and drinketh judgment to himself." Was not the morsel given by the Lord poison to Judas? And yet he took it! And when he took it, the enemy entered into him, not because he received an evil thing, but because as an evil man he received a good thing in an evil way. Therefore, brethren, see that you eat the heavenly bread in a spiritual manner; bring innocence to the altar. Although your sins are venial and not deadly, before you approach the altar, consider diligently what you are to say: "Forgive us our debts, even as we forgive our debtors." If you forgive, it shall be forgiven you; approach untroubled; it is bread, not poison.

WEDNESDAY

The reading of the holy Gospel according to St. John

At that time Jesus said to the multitudes of the Jews: "My flesh is food indeed, and my blood is drink indeed." And so forth.

Homily of St. Hilary, Bishop

In discussing the things of God we must not speak in a human or worldly sense. Let us read what is written, and let us understand what we have read, and then we shall fulfill the duty of perfect faith. For what we say about the real truth of Christ in us, unless we learn from Him, we speak foolishly and irreverently. For He Himself says: "My flesh is meat indeed, and my blood is drink indeed. He that eateth my flesh and drinketh my blood abideth in me, and I in him." Concerning the truth of the flesh and blood, no room is left for doubt.

For now both by the testimony of the Lord Himself and by our faith it is truly flesh and truly blood. And these, when received and consumed, effect that we are in Christ and Christ is in us. Is not this the truth? It certainly is not true to those who deny that Jesus Christ is true God. Therefore He Himself is in us by His flesh, and we are in Him since that which we are is with Him in God. But that we are in Him through the Sacrament of His communicated flesh and blood, He Himself testifies, saying: "And this world seeth me now no more; but you shall see me, because I live, and you shall live; because I am in my Father and you in me, and I in you."

That this union is real in us He Himself thus testified: "He that eateth my flesh and drinketh my blood abideth in me, and I in him." For no one will be in Christ except him in whom Christ has been first, who, having so marvelously assumed to Himself our flesh, has bestowed upon us His own. He had already previously taught that it is a Sacrament of perfect unity, saying: "As the living Father hath sent me and I live because of the Father, so he that eateth my flesh, he shall also live because of me." Christ therefore lives because of the Father; and in that manner in which He lives because of the Father, in the same manner we shall live because of His flesh.

OCTAVE DAY OF CORPUS CHRISTI

I Nocturn

From the first Epistle of St. Paul the Apostle to the Corinthians, c. 11, 20 - 32

II Nocturn

Sermon of St. Cyril, Bishop of Jerusalem

The doctrine itself of blessed Paul seems fully to suffice to make certain for you the faith in the divine mysteries, by which, having been rendered worthy by them, you have, so to say, been made the one body and the one blood of Christ. For Paul was just proclaiming that on the night in which He was betrayed, our Lord Jesus Christ, taking bread and giving thanks, broke and gave to His disciples, saying: "Take ye and eat, this is my body." And taking the chalice and giving thanks, said: "Take ye and drink, this is my blood." Therefore, when He has pronounced over the bread and said, "This is my body," who will dare henceforth to doubt? And when He has likewise so positively stated, "This is my blood," who will ever doubt and say that it is not His blood?

Once at Cana of Galilee He changed water into wine, which has a certain relationship with blood; and shall we esteem Him less worthy of belief when He has changed wine into blood? Invited to those nuptials in which bodies are joined, He performed this miracle beyond the understanding of everyone; and should we not be much more firmly convinced that He has thus given His body and blood to be enjoyed by us that we may receive them with all certainty as His very body and blood?

For under the appearance of bread He gives us His body and under the appearance of wine He gives us His blood, that, when you receive, you may taste of the body and blood of Christ, having been made a partaker of that same body and blood. Thus, indeed, we are made Christ-bearers—that is, bearing Christ in our bodies when we receive His body and blood into our own members; thus, according to St. Peter, we are become "partakers of the divine nature."

Once Christ, speaking with the Jews, said: "Unless you eat my flesh and drink my blood, you shall not have life in you." But because they did not take these words spiritually, they went away offended; for they thought that He was exhorting them to eat flesh. There were even in the old Testament loaves of proposition, but, since they were of the old Testament, they have already reached their end. In th new Testament, however, the bread is heavenly and the wine saving, which sanctify both body and soul. Wherefore I do not wish you to look upon these elements as if they were plain and simple bread, plain and simple wine; for they are the body and blood of Christ. And, even if sense denies it to you, yet let faith confirm you. Do not judge this mystery from taste; rather let faith render you certain beyond all doubt that you may be made worthy to become a partaker of Christ's body and blood.

III Nocturn

The reading of the holy Gospel according to St. John

At that time Jesus said to the multitudes of the Jews: "My flesh is food indeed, and my blood is drink indeed." And so forth.

Homily of St. Cyril, Bishop of Alexandria

"He that eateth my flesh," He says, "and drinketh my blood, abideth in me, and I in him." For just as, when one pours other wax upon melted wax, it is inevitable that the one mix completely with the other, thus also he who receives the flesh and blood of the Lord is so joined with Him that Christ is found in him and he in Christ.

You will find the same doctrine expressed in a similar way in the Gospel of St. Matthew. He says: "The kingdom of heaven is like to leaven, which a woman took and hid in three measures of meal." Just as a little bit of leaven—as St. Paul declares—causes fermentation in the whole lump, so the blessed Particle (that is, the Host), draws man to Itself and fills him with Its grace, and in this way Christ abides in us, and we in Christ.

But if we wish to obtain eternal life, if we desire to have the Giver of immortality within us, let us run gladly to receive the blessed Particle and let us beware lest the devil propose to us by way of a snare a false piety. "Rightly do you say," reminds the devil, " 'I know that it is written that he who eats of the bread and drinks of the chalice unworthily, eats and drinks judgment to himself. Therefore I examine myself and find myself unworthy.' " When will you be worthy then—whoever you are who say these things? When will you offer yourself to Christ? For if you are unworthy because of sin, and if you do not cease to sin (for as the Psalmist says, "who can understand sins?"), you will be deprived forever of this life-giving means of holiness.

Wherefore, I. pray, may you foster loving thoughts; may you live circumspectly and holily and partake of the Sacrament which, believe me, not only drives off death, but likewise every disease. For Christ, when He dwells within us, assuages the fierce law of our members; He confirms our love; He suppresses the disturbances of the mind; He cures the sick; He makes the broken whole again; and like a good shepherd who has laid down his life for his sheep, He delivers us from every mishap.

Friday after the Octave of Corpus Christi

FEAST OF THE MOST SACRED HEART OF JESUS

I Nocturn

*From Jeremias the Prophet, c. 24, 5 - 7;
c. 30, 18 - 24; c. 31, 1 - 3 and 31 - 33*

II Nocturn

Among the wonderful developments of sacred teaching and piety by which the plans of divine wisdom are daily made clearer to the Church, hardly any is more manifest than the triumphant progress made by the devotion to the most Sacred Heart of Jesus. Very often indeed, during the course of the past ages, Fathers, Doctors, and Saints have celebrated our Redeemer's love, and have said that the wound opened in the side of Christ was the hidden fountain of all graces. Moreover, from the middle ages onward, when the faithful began to show a certain more tender piety towards the most sacred humanity of the Savior, contemplative souls became accustomed to penetrate through that wound almost to the very Heart itself, wounded for the love of men. And from that time, this form of contemplation became so familiar to all persons of saintly life that there was no country or religious order in which during this period witnesses to it were not to be found.

To none, indeed, did the monastic order yield in propagating this devotion; and outstanding at that period are the nuns of Helfta, Gertrude and Mechtilde, from whose lives and writings it is very plain with what great love they burned for the divine Heart. For now they magnify it as a treasure in which all the riches of heaven are placed; again, as a font from which flow torrents of grace, or as a harp plucked by the Holy Spirit and resounding with ineffable harmony, or a censer, emitting most sweet perfume in the presence of God the Father, in another manner also as an altar upon which the supreme and eternal Priest, Jesus Christ, immolates Himself. Finally, during the recent centuries, and especially at that period when heretics, in the name of a false piety, strove to discourage Christians from receiving the most holy Eucharist, the veneration of the most Sacred Heart began to be openly practised, principally through the exertions of St. John Eudes, who is by no means unworthily called the founder of the liturgical worship of the Sacred Hearts of Jesus and Mary.

But in order to establish fully and entirely the worship of the most Sacred Heart of Jesus, and to spread the same throughout the whole world, God Himself chose as His instrument a humble virgin from the order of the Visitation, St. Margaret Mary Alacoque, who even in her earliest years already had a burning love for the Sacrament of the Eucharist. Christ the Lord appeared many times to her and was pleased to make known the riches and desires of His divine Heart. The most famous of these appearances was that in which Jesus appeared to her while she prayed before the blessed Sacrament, showed her His most Sacred Heart, and, complaining that in return for His unbounded love, He met with nothing save outrages and ingratitude from mankind, He ordered her to be solicitous for the establishment of a new feast on the Friday after the octave of Corpus Christi, on which His Heart should be venerated with due honor, and the insults offered Him by sinners in the Sacrament of love should be expiated by worthy satisfaction. But there is no one who does not know how many and how great were the obstacles which the handmaid of God experienced in carrying out the commands of Christ; but, endowed with strength by the Lord Himself, and actively aided by pious spiritual directors, who exerted themselves with an almost unbelievable zeal, she never ceased till the time of her death to carry out faithfully the duty entrusted to her by heaven.

At length, in the year 1765, the Supreme Pontiff, Clement XIII, approved of the Mass and Office in honor of the most Sacred Heart of Jesus, and Pius IX extended the feast to the universal Church. Thenceforward, the worship of the most Sacred Heart, like an overflowing river, washing away all obstacles, has poured itself over the whole earth, and at the dawn of the new century, Leo XIII, having proclaimed a Jubilee, willed to dedicate the whole human race to the most Sacred Heart. This consecration was actually carried out with solemn rites in all the churches of the Catholic world, and brought about a great increase of this devotion, leading not only nations, but also private families to it, who in countless numbers dedicated themselves to the divine Heart and submitted themselves to Its royal sway. Finally the Sovereign Pontiff, Pius XI, in order that by its solemnity the feast might answer more fully to the so greatly widespread devotion of the Christian people, raised the feast of the most Sacred Heart of Jesus to the rite of a double of the first class with an octave; and moreover, that the violated rights of Christ, the supreme King and most loving Lord, might be repaired, and that the sins of the nations might be bewailed, he ordered that annually, on this same day, there should be recited an expiatory prayer in all the churches of the Christian world.

℟. All the nations whatsoever Thou hast made shall come * And shall adore before Thee, O Lord. ℣. And they shall glorify Thy name, for Thou art great, and dost wonderful things. And shall. Glory. And shall.

III Nocturn

The reading of the holy Gospel according to St. John

At that time the Jews, since it was the Preparation Day, in order that the bodies might not remain upon the cross on the Sabbath (for that Sabbath was a solemn day), besought Pilate that their legs might be broken, and that they might be taken away. And so forth.

Homily of St. Bonaventure, Bishop

In order that the Church might be formed from the side of Christ, sleeping on the cross, and that the Scripture might be fulfilled which says, "They shall look upon him whom they have pierced," it was permitted by divine providence that one of the soldiers should open His sacred side by piercing it with a lance, so that, by the blood flowing forth with water, the price of our redemption would be shed, which, once poured out from the fountain, that is, from the secret recesses of His Heart, would give to the Sacraments of the Church the power to confer the life of grace, and would be to those already living in Christ a draught of the living fountain, springing forth unto life eternal. Arise, then, O soul, well-pleasing to Christ; cease not to watch; place your mouth at His wounded side that you may draw waters from the fountains of the Savior.

For once we have come to the Heart of the most sweet Lord Jesus (and it is good for us to be here), we are not easily torn away from it. Behold how good and how pleasant it is to dwell in this Heart. Your heart, O dearest Jesus, is a goodly treasure, a precious pearl, which we have found in the torn field of Your body. Who will snatch away this pearl? Yea, I will rather give up all other pearls; I will change all my thoughts and affections, and I will buy for myself that one pearl, casting my every thought into the Heart of my good Jesus which will nourish me without fail.

Hence, O sweetest Jesus, having found this Heart, both Yours and mine, I will pray to Thee, my God: "Admit my prayers into the sanctuary of Thy hearing; yea, more, draw me entirely into Thy Heart. For this purpose was Thy side wounded, that we, being removed from exterior disturbances, could dwell therein. Over and above this it was also wounded to show us by means of a visible wound the invisible wound of love." How could the ardor of this love be better manifested than by His permitting not only His body, but His very Heart also to be wounded with a lance? The bodily wound makes known the spiritual wound.

Who will not love that Heart so wounded? Who would not return love to such a lover? Who would not embrace such purity? In so far as we can, therefore, let us while still in the flesh love in our turn this Lover; let us embrace our wounded One whose hands and feet, whose side and Heart wicked husbandmen have dug; and let us pray that He may deign to wound with the dart of His love and to bind up with the bond of that same love our heart, still so hard and impenitent.

℟. If I be lifted up from the earth, * I will draw all things to Myself. ℣. Now this He said, signifying what death He should die. I will draw. Glory. I will draw.

☩ Continuation of the holy Gospel according to St. John.—At that time: The Jews therefore, since it was the Preparation Day, in order that the bodies might not remain upon the cross on the Sabbath (for that Sabbath was a solemn day), besought Pilate that their legs might be broken, and that they might be taken away. The soldiers therefore came and broke the legs of the first, and of the other, who had been, crucified with him. But when they came to Jesus, and saw that he was already dead, they did not break his legs; but one of the soldiers opened his side with a lance, and immediately there came out blood and water.

And he who saw it has borne witness, and his witness is true; and he knows that he tells the truth, that you also may believe. For these things came to pass that the Scripture might be fulfilled, "Not a bone of him shall you break." And again another Scripture says, "They shall look upon him whom they have pierced."

LET US PRAY

O God, who hast mercifully placed for us the infinite treasures of Thy love in the Heart of Thy Son, wounded by our sins, grant, we beseech Thee, that as we offer It the devoted reverence of our love, we may also fulfill the duty of a worthy atonement. Through the same Jesus Christ.

SATURDAY

The reading of the holy Gospel according to St. John

At that time the Jews, since it was the Preparation Day, in order that the bodies might not remain upon the cross on the Sabbath (for that Sabbath was a solemn day), besought Pilate that their legs might be broken, and that they might be taken away. And so forth.

Homily of St. John Chrysostom

Do you see how strong the truth is? Through the striving of the Jews a prophecy is fulfilled. Another prediction also receives its fulfillment. For the soldiers came and broke the legs of the others, but not so of Christ. Yet they, as a favor to the Jews, pierce His side with a lance, and inflict contumely on the dead body. O wicked and cursed crime! But be not troubled nor cast down, beloved. For the evil which they maliciously did to Him advanced the truth. For indeed the prophecy was: "They shall look upon him whom they have pierced." Not only this, but the crime was also to be a proof to those who would be unbelieving, as Thomas and those like him. For these reasons, too, was the ineffable mystery consummated. For blood and water issued forth. Not without cause, not by chance did these fountains flow, but because out of both was the Church established.

This the initiated know—they who are regenerated by water and nourished by blood and flesh. Thence the Sacraments take their origin; so that when you approach the awe-inspiring cup, you should come as if you were about to drink from this side. "And he that saw it hath given testimony and his testimony is true." That is to say: "Not from others have I heard it, but, being present, I saw it myself, and the testimony is true." Deservedly indeed. He speaks of contumely, not of something great and admirable of which you might be suspicious. But he, shutting the mouths of heretics and announcing future mysteries, and considering the treasure contained in these very things, enumerates one by one the events that have taken place. Yet that prophecy was fulfilled: "You shall not break a bone of him." For though this was said of the lamb of the Jews, yet for the sake of the truth, the figure has gone before, and in Him it was more completely fulfilled. For this reason he brings the prophecy to the fore.

Inasmuch as he who bears witness to himself might not in every case be held credible, he quotes Moses in order to intimate that this did not happen by chance, but long ago was already foretold in writing. It was he who said: "You shall not break a bone of him." And again he establishes the Prophet's veracity by his own word. "I have said these things," he says, "that you may learn the great resemblance there is between the figure and the reality." Do you see what great care he takes in order that that which seems disgraceful and ignominious may be believed. Now for the body to be treated with contumely by the soldier was far worse than for it to be crucified. "However, I have both said these things," he says, "and said them with great diligence that you may believe." Therefore let no one refuse his belief, nor for shame damage ours. For whatever things seem most worthy of scorn, these are in fact our greatest pride.

SUNDAY WITHIN THE OCTAVE OF THE FEAST OF THE SACRED HEART

III SUNDAY AFTER PENTECOST

I Nocturn

From the first book of Kings, c. 9, 18 - 27; c. 10, 1

II Nocturn

From the Encyclical Letter of Pope Pius XI

Among all the other proofs of the infinite goodness of our Savior none stands out more prominently than the fact that, as the love of the faithful grew cold, the very love of God was proposed to us to be honored by a very special devotion, and the rich treasures of His goodness were thrown wide open by means of that devotion by which we honor the most Sacred Heart of Jesus "in whom are hid all the treasures of wisdom and knowledge." For as formerly the divine goodness wished to show to the human race, as it came from the Ark of Noe, a sign of the renewed covenant between them, "a bow appearing in the clouds," so in our own most troubled times, when that heresy was creeping in which was known as Jansenism, the most insidious of all heresies, the enemy of the love of God and of filial affection for Him (for this heresy preached that God was not so much to be loved by us as a Father as to be feared as an unrelenting Judge), the most kind Jesus manifested to the nations His Sacred Heart, as it were, our banner of peace and love, an augury of certain victory in the battle before us.

Are we not to see in that happy sign, and in the devotion which flows from it, a compendium of the whole of our religion and the rules to guide us to a more perfect form of life, since the Sacred Heart is the way which will most surely lead us to know intimately Jesus Christ and will cause our hearts to love Him more tenderly and to imitate Him more generously than we have heretofore done? Since this is so, it is no wonder then that our Predecessors have always defended this most praiseworthy devotion to the Sacred Heart from the objections launched by calumniators, that they have praised it most highly and have always promoted it with the greatest possible zeal in so far as the conditions of time and place seemed to demand. Surely it is by the inspiration of God that the childlike love of the faithful for the Sacred Heart increases day by day.

Among the different practices which directly accompany devotion to the most Sacred Heart assuredly the foremost is the act of consecration by which we offer to the Heart of Jesus both ourselves and all that belongs to us, recognizing that all we have comes to us from the infinite charity of God. Moreover, it is expedient that another practice be added. We refer to the act of expiation, or of reparation, as it is called, to be made to the Sacred Heart of Jesus. For if in the act of consecration the intention to repay, as it were, the love of the Creator with the love of the creature stands out most prominently, there follows almost naturally from this another fact, namely, that if this same uncreated Love has either been passed over through forgetfulness or offended by our sins, then we should repair such outrages, no matter in what manner they have occurred. Ordinarily, we call this duty *reparation*.

Although we are held to both these duties for the same reasons, yet we are held to the duty of making reparation by the even more powerful motives of justice and of love: of justice, in order to expiate the injury done to God by our sins and to establish by means of penance the divine order which has been violated; and of love, in order to suffer with Christ, patient and covered with opprobrium, so that we may bring to Him, in so far as our human weakness permits, some comfort in His sufferings. Since we are all sinners, burdened with many offenses, we should honor God not only by means of that cult by which we adore, in the veneration due Him from us, His infinite Majesty, or by means of prayer when we recognize His supreme dominion over us, or by acts of thanksgiving when we praise His infinite generosity towards us. It is necessary to do more than all this. We must also satisfy the just anger of God because of the "numberless sins, offenses, and negligences" which we have committed. Therefore we must add to the act of consecration (by which we vow ourselves to God and become holy and sacred with that holiness and stability which, as the Angelic doctor teaches, is the essence of consecration) an act of expiation, by means of which all our faults are blotted out, lest perchance the sanctity of infinite Justice spurn our arrogant unworthiness and look upon our gift as something to be rejected rather than to be accepted.

℟. Let us therefore be followers of God, * And walk in love.
℣. As Christ also hath loved us and hath delivered Himself for us. And walk. Glory. And walk.

III Nocturn

The reading of the holy Gospel according to St. Luke

At that time the publicans and sinners were drawing near to him to listen to him. And so forth.

Homily of St. Gregory, Pope

You have heard, my brethren, in the Gospel lesson that sinners and publicans approached our Redeemer; they were received, moreover, not only to converse but also to dine with Him. When the Pharisees saw this, they were indignant. Gather from this fact that true justice has compassion, but false justice feeleth scorn.

Although even good men rightly make it a point to be angry at sinners, still it is one thing when done as a mark of pride, quite another when done out of zeal for discipline. Good men become angry indeed, but they are not scornful; they have little hope, but they do not despair; they inflict punishments, but lovingly; for even if exteriorly in their punishment they overdo corrections, still interiorly they preserve sweetness through charity.

They place before themselves in their own mind those whom they are wont to correct; even those whom they judge they consider better than themselves. By so doing they keep a guard over their subjects by correction, and a guard over themselves by humility. On the other hand, those who are wont to make a show of false justice despise everyone else; being without mercy, they are most uncondescending towards the weak; and the more they believe themselves not to be sinners, so much the worse sinners do they become.

Of the number of these were certainly the Pharisees, who, upbraiding the Lord because He received sinners, closed up by their own barren heart the very font of mercy. But because they were so sick that they knew not their own malady, and in order to appraise them of their condition, the heavenly Physician cared for them with soothing remedies; He offered them His own benign example; and in their heart He assuaged the swelling of their wound.

℟. The Lord is nigh to all that call upon Him, * To all that call upon Him in truth. ℣. The Lord is gracious and merciful, patient and plenteous in mercy. To all. Glory. To all.

☩ Continuation of the holy Gospel according to St. Luke.— At that time the publicans and sinners were drawing near to him to listen to him. And the Pharisees and the Scribes murmured, saying, "This man welcomes sinners and eats with them."

But he spoke to them this parable, saying, "What man of you having a hundred sheep, and losing one of them, does not leave the ninety-nine in the desert, and go after that which is lost, until he finds it? And when he has found it, he lays it upon his shoulders rejoicing. And on coming home he calls together his friends and neighbors, saying to them, 'Rejoice with me, because I have found my sheep that was lost.' I say to you that, even so, there will be joy in heaven over one sinner who repents, more than over ninety-nine just who have no need of repentance.

"Or what woman, having ten drachmas, if she loses one drachma, does not light a lamp and sweep the house and search carefully until she finds it? And when she has found it, she calls together her friends and neighbors, saying, 'Rejoice with me, for I have found the drachma that I had lost.' Even so, I say to you, there will be joy among the angels of God over one sinner who repents."

Let Us Pray

O God, the protector of all who trust in Thee, without whom there is nothing good or holy, increase Thy mercy towards us, that by Thy guidance and assistance we may so use the temporal goods of this world that we lose not the eternal. Through our Lord.

MONDAY

The reading of the holy Gospel according to St. John

At that time the Jews, since it was the Preparation Day, in order that the bodies might not remain upon the cross on the Sabbath (for that Sabbath was a solemn day), besought Pilate that their legs might be broken, and that they might be taken away. And so forth.

Homily of St. Lawrence Justinian, Bishop

"When they came therefore to Jesus and saw that he was already dead, they did not break his legs, but one of those who stood by, thrusting his lance, opened his side, and immediately there came out blood and water." A tremendous and unheard of prodigy—that blood and water should come from a dead body. Yet in this deed God's wisdom wished to commend to us a great mystery, namely, the unity of Himself and the Church. Now a figure of this spiritual union had gone before, when from the sleeping Adam's side one of his ribs is said to have been taken, and from it Eve, the mother of all, who was the type of the Church, was formed. The Holy Spirit then indicated that there would come a true and spiritual Adam, formed by the power of the Comforter; and that while He slept on the cross and water and blood flowed from His side, a bride—the Church—beautiful, without wrinkle and without spot, should be formed.

These are indeed the sacraments of the Church by which the whole body of the Church is washed and made holy. In the laver of regenerating water, consecrated by Christ's death, she is indeed cleansed from the taint of original sin. But not only is she purged of every fault in the Redeemer's blood, but also access to the heavenly kingdom is opened for her. Both these together produce a single result; for one without the other avails nothing for salvation. Apart from the sacrament of Baptism and the remission of sins no one can receive the heritage of future bliss. This everywhere in the world holy Mother Church acknowledges; it is confirmed by numerous proofs from Holy Scripture. Moreover, he who saw water and blood come out from Christ has borne witness, and his witness is true. For this is that John, Apostle and Evangelist, who was loved by the Lord with a special love.

Surely these things were done that the Scripture might be fulfilled which says: "You shall not break a bone of him." To be sure, Moses was commanded that in the sacrifice of the passover, when the lamb was immolated, no bone should be broken. But in the Lord Jesus, the most innocent of lambs, the truth of the figure is realized. Never were His legs broken as were those of the two wicked men hanging with Him; but only His side was opened so that another Scripture might be fulfilled which says: "They shall look upon him whom they have pierced." Furthermore, the Lord wanted to keep the scars from His wounds upon His body that as to the elect they would be an incentive to devotedness, so for the reprobate they would become an irrefutable witness to their damnation. Thus all things that were fulfilled in Christ had long before been announced by the oracles of the prophets to the end that the Catholic Faith should be made secure not alone to her own profit but likewise against the errors of heretics.

TUESDAY

The reading of the holy Gospel according to St. John

At that time the Jews, since it was the Preparation Day, in order that the bodies might not remain upon the cross on the Sabbath (for that Sabbath was a solemn day), besought Pilate that their legs might be broken, and that they might be taken away. And so forth.

Homily of St. Bernardine of Siena

John adds: "One of the soldiers opened his side with a lance, and immediately there came out blood and water." O love that melts all things! How is it that for our redemption you have abandoned our Lover? For in order that the deluge of love might flood all things, great abysses have burst over us, namely, the innermost depths of the Heart of Jesus, which the cruel lance, penetrating to the limit, did not spare. Blood and water flowed out: the blood unto redemption, but also water came forth for cleansing. From these the Church was formed out of the side of Christ, so that she might learn that she was one eternally with Christ and loved by Him, and that she might recognize how displeased He was with that guilt for which the divine blood so flowed forth from the Man-God, alive and dead. For we are of no small account if the divine blood was poured out for us.

Literally the water did not flow out indistinguishable from the blood. For it could not have been ascertained by the unwise if it flowed forth mixed with the blood. And perhaps all the blood ran out from that divine body as a sign of the love completely expended, after which the water followed. And indeed in this a deep mystery has occurred: that first the redeeming price should come out of that body, then the water, in which is signified the multitude of the redeemed peoples. For many waters are many peoples; yet those who belong to the Christian Faith are one faithful people, so that there are not waters, but water which emanated from the side of Christ as the Apostle says in the tenth chapter of the first letter to the Corinthians: "We being many are all one bread and one body, who partake of one bread and one chalice." And again in the letter to the Ephesians in the fourth chapter, he says, "One God, one faith, one baptsim."

It should be carefully noted, however, that the side of Christ is said to have been opened, not wounded; because a wound properly speaking is only associated with a living body. For John the Evangelist says, "One of the soldiers opened his side with a lance," so that we could learn by the opened side the love of His Heart even unto death, and that we could enter into that ineffable love through that side whence it came to us. Let us therefore draw near to His Heart, that deep heart, that secret heart, that heart knowing all things, that heart thinking all things, that heart loving, yea, rather burning with love. And let us understand that opened gate at least in the greatness of its love; and, made like that heart, let us penetrate that secret hidden from all eternity, but now revealed in death, so to speak, by that opened side. For the opening of the side declares the opening of the eternal temple wherein is consummated the eternal happiness of all men.

WEDNESDAY

The reading of the holy Gospel according to St. John

At that time the Jews, since it was the Preparation Day, in order that the bodies might not remain upon the cross on the Sabbath (for that Sabbath was a solemn day), besought Pilate that their legs might be broken, and that they might be taken away. And so forth.

Homily of St. Peter Canisius, Priest

Ponder carefully how unspeakable was that love by which the most high God, with great torment to His Heart and with the whole world's scorn, underwent for you, vile worm, the cruelest of deaths on the cross. Note that Christ the Savior showed the greatest generosity to all His own. At one time, standing in the midst of the people, He cried out: "If any man thirst, let him come to me and drink." He showed himself ready to come to the help of all in all their needs. Consider that He freely gave up His Heart's precious blood when His sacred side was opened and He poured out whatever blood remained in His body.

Therefore, that I be not wholly ungrateful, I often place before my eyes these perennial fountains of gifts and every good, since there is concerning them that sweetest of promises: "You shall draw water with joy out of the Savior's fountains, and you shall say in that day, 'Praise ye the Lord.'" To those thrice-blessed clefts in the rock that is not to be rent will I fly; in them will I put my nest secure, having no other wish than that in my trials and troubles I take heart in recalling the Lord's wounds.

And do you in every temptation take care to flee to Christ's lovable Heart; put before your mind His goodness and love, and compare with it your own worthlessness, malice, infidelity, arrogance. How great is the love of that Christ who gathers all to Himself: "Come to me all you that labor and are burdened, and I will refresh you." He presents Himself all ready and desirous, for love of us, to bear the burdens of each and every one. Wherefore with great confidence throw your sins into the abyss of His love, and straightway you will find yourself relieved of your burden.

THURSDAY

The reading of the holy Gospel according to St. John

At that time the Jews, since it was the Preparation Day, in order that the bodies might not remain upon the cross on the Sabbath (for that Sabbath was a solemn day), besought Pilate that their legs might be broken, and that they might be taken away. And so forth.

Homily of St. Cyril, Bishop of Alexandria

The blessed Evangelist does not say these things as though admitting any godliness in the savage and cruel Jews, but rather that he may show how foolishly and ignorantly they strained out a gnat and swallowed a camel, as Christ Himself had said. For they are found to make light of most grievous and awful crimes while they observe very carefully and anxiously the least trivialities, in both ways displaying their ignorance. This can readily be shown. For behold, having put Christ to death, they give honor to the great Sabbath; and, with incredible insolence, they make a show of reverence for that Law whose Author they have dishonored.

And they who have put to death the Lord of that great day pretend to show a special reverence for that great Sabbath day; and they earnestly solicit a favor worthy of them alone, namely, that the legs of the crucified ones be broken, inflicting an intolerable pain, a more bitter misfortune than death itself, on those already almost dead. "The soldiers, therefore, came, and they broke the legs of the first, and of the other that was crucified with him." The soldiers, sent at the request of the Jews, were laboring under a like rage of cruelty, so they break the legs of the two thieves, who were indeed found to be still alive. But when they found that Jesus had bowed His head, and concluded that He had already expired, they thought it useless to break His legs; but still, not quite certain that He was dead, they pierced His side with a spear, whence blood mixed with water flowed out, a figure and also the first-fruit of the mystical banquet and of holy Baptism.

And from these things which came to pass, the most wise Evangelist proves to his hearers that this is the Christ who was long ago foretold in Holy Scripture; for all that happened agrees with what was divinely prophesied concerning Him. Thus, according to the Scriptures, not a bone of Him was broken, and He was pierced with the soldier's spear. The Evangelist does certainly say that the one who saw this thing was the same disciple who gave testimony concerning these things, and that he knew that his testimony was true: by this expression meaning not another, but himself.

OCTAVE DAY OF THE FEAST OF THE MOST SACRED HEART

I Nocturn

*From Jeremias the Prophet, c. 24, 5 - 7;
c. 30, 18 - 24; c. 31, 1 - 3 and 31 - 33*

II Nocturn

From the Encyclical Letter of Pope Pius XI

As the act of consecration proclaims and confirms our union with Christ, so the act of expiation, by purifying us from sins, is the beginning of this union; our participation in the sufferings of Christ perfects it; the offering we make to Him of our sacrifices for the welfare of our brethren brings it to its final consummation. This was precisely the design of the mercy of Jesus when He unveiled to our gaze His Sacred Heart, surrounded by the emblems of His Passion, and aflame with the fire of love, that we, on the one hand, perceiving the malice of sin, and on the other, filled with a knowledge of the infinite love of our Redeemer, might more heartily detest sin and substitute for it an ardent love of Him. As a matter of fact, on the occasion when He revealed Himself to St. Margaret Mary, though He insisted on the immensity of His love, at the same time, with sorrowful mien, He grieved over the great number of horrible outrages heaped upon Him by the ingratitude of mankind. These words which He used should be engraved on the hearts of all pious souls so as never to be forgotten by them: "Behold this Heart which has loved men so much, which has heaped upon them so many benefits. In exchange for this infinite love, It finds ingratitude; It is confronted with forgetfulness, indifference, outrages—and all this at times even from souls closely bound to It by the bonds of a very special love."

Now, anyone who uses his eyes and mind, if he but think of this world "seated in darkness," can see, as we stated above, how urgent, especially in our own times, is the need of expiation and of reparation. There comes to our ears from every side the cries of nations whose rulers or governments have actually risen up and have conspired together against the Lord and against His Church. Nor is that other spectacle less sad, that even among the faithful, washed as they have been by Baptism in the blood of the innocent Lamb and enriched by His grace, we encounter so many of every station of life who, ignorant of things divine, are poisoned by false doctrines and live a sinful life far from their Father's house, without the light of the true Faith, without the joy of hope in a future life, deprived of the strength and comfort which come with the spirit of love. Of them one may say quite truthfully that they are immersed in darkness and in the shadow of death.

There must be added to this accumulation of evils the sloth and laziness of those who, like the sleeping or fleeing disciples, because they are not firmly rooted in the faith, have shamefully abandoned Christ, burdened with sorrows and attacked by the satellites of Satan, as well as the perfidy of those others, who, following in the footsteps of Judas the traitor, either approach Holy Communion with sacrilegious temerity, or go over to the camp of the enemy. There thus comes to mind, almost involuntarily, the thought that we have arrived at the hour prophesied by our Lord when He said: "And because iniquity has abounded, the charity of many shall grow cold." If the faithful, burning with love for the suffering Christ, would meditate on all these considerations, it is unthinkable that they would not expiate with greater zeal both their own faults and those of others, that they would not repair the honor of Christ, and be filled with zeal for the eternal salvation of souls.

Assuredly we may apply to our own age what the Apostle wrote, "When sin abounded, grace did more abound," for even though the sinfulness of man has greatly increased, by the grace of the Holy Spirit, there has also increased the number of the faithful who most gladly try to make satisfaction to the divine Heart of Jesus for the numerous injuries heaped upon Him. What is more, they joyfully offer themselves to Christ as victims for sin. Anyone who has been considering in a spirit of love all that has been recalled to his mind thus far, if he has impressed these thoughts, as it were, upon the fleshly tablets of his heart, such a one assuredly cannot but abhor and flee all sins as the greatest of evils. He will also offer himself whole and entire to the will of God and will strive to repair the injured majesty of God by constant prayer, by voluntary penances, by patient suffering of all those ills which may befall him; in a word, he will so organize his life that in all things it will be inspired by the spirit of reparation.

III Nocturn

The reading of the holy Gospel according to St. John

At that time the Jews, since it was the Preparation Day, in order that the bodies might not remain upon the cross on the Sabbath (for that Sabbath was a solemn day), besought Pilate that their legs might be broken, and that they might be taken away. And so forth.

Homily of St. Augustine, Bishop

"But after they were come to Jesus, when they saw that he was already dead, they did not break his legs. But one of the soldiers with a spear opened his side and immediately there came out blood and water." The Evangelist, as one who is attentive perceives, does not say, "he struck His side," or, "he wounded it," but, "he opened it," that in Him, in a certain manner, the portal of life might be opened whence flowed the Sacraments of the Church, without which no one enters into that life which is the true life. The blood was poured forth for the remission of sins. The water tempers the cup of salvation; it offers us wherein to wash as well as to drink.

All this was prefigured when Noe was ordered to make a doorway in the side of the Ark, by which the animals which were not to perish in the flood might enter in. By these the Church was prefigured. For this reason, the first woman was made from the side of the man as he lay sleeping, and she was called *life* and *the mother of the living*. A great good was signified before the evil of the fall. The second Adam, bowing His head, slept on the cross that thereby the Spouse might be formed who was to come from His side as He slept.

O death, whence the dead are vivified! What is more cleansing than this blood? What more beneficial than this wound? "And he who saw it," the Gospel says, "has borne witness; and his witness is true. And he knows that he tells the truth, that you also may believe." He did not say, "that you also may know," but, "that you may believe." For he who sees, knows, while he who does not see may believe the testimony of him who sees. To believe is more in accord with faith than to see.

The Evangelist has cited two testimonies from the Scriptures about the events which he has narrated as having taken place. Because he had said, "But after they were come to Jesus, when they saw that he was already dead, they did not break his legs," he cites this testimony, "You shall not break a bone of him." This command was given to those in the old Law who had to celebrate the Pasch by the immolation of the lamb, a figure foreshadowing the Passion of our Lord. "Christ our Passover is immolated." It was of Him that Isaias prophesied: "He was led as a lamb to the slaughter." Secondly, because the Evangelist had added, "But one of the soldiers opened his side with a spear," he recalls a testimony which refers to the incident, namely, "They shall look upon him whom they have pierced." By this statement it is promised that Christ will come in the very same flesh which suffered crucifixion.

IV SUNDAY AFTER PENTECOST

I Nocturn

From the first Book of Kings, c. 17, 1 - 16

II Nocturn

Sermon of St. Augustine, Bishop

The children of Israel stood against their adversaries for forty days. The forty days, because of their relation to the four seasons and to the four parts of earth, typify the present life in which the Christian people does not cease to battle against Goliath and his army, that is, against the devil and his angels. However, it would not be able to conquer him unless Christ, the true David, had come down with His staff, that is with the mystery of the cross.

For prior to Christ's advent, dearest brethren, the devil had full power; when Christ came, He acted according to that which is declared in the Gospel: "No one can enter into the house of the strong and rifle his goods unless he first bind the strong." So Christ came and placed the devil in bonds. But someone will remark: "If he is in bonds, why does he still prevail so much?" It is true, dearest brethren, that he still prevails to a great extent, but he rules only over the lukewarm and indifferent, and the ones who do not fear God in truth.

For he is bound as a dog tied up with chains, and he can bite no one but him who comes near to him in a fatal boldness. Just consider, brethren, what a fool that man is whom a dog placed in chains, bites. Do not go near to him in the desires and lusts of the world, and he will not presume to come near to you. He can bark; he can make noise; but he cannot in any way set his teeth in anyone but in him who wishes it. For he injures no one by force, but by persuasion; he does not wring consent from us, but begs for it.

Thus David came and found the Jewish people at war with the devil; and, since there was no one who would dare to enter into a single-handed conflict, he who bore the figure of Christ entered into the fight, took up his staff in his hand and went out against Goliath. And in him, indeed, was typified what was to be accomplished in our Lord Jesus Christ. For Christ, the true David, when about to fight against the spiritual Goliath, that is against the devil, came, bearing His own cross. See, my brethren, where David strikes Goliath: on the forehead, of course, where he did not have the sign of the cross. For as the staff was a type of the cross, so also the stone with which he was struck prefigured Christ the Lord.

℞. I took thee from the house of thy father, saith the Lord, and set thee to feed the flock of My people: * And I have been with thee wheresoever thou hast walked, establishing thy kingdom forever. ℣. And I have made thy name great, like unto the name of the great ones that are on the earth: and I have given thee rest from all thy enemies. And I have been. Glory. And I have been.

V SUNDAY AFTER PENTECOST

I Nocturn

From the second Book of Kings, c. 1, 1 - 15

II Nocturn

From the Book of Morals of St. Gregory, Pope

Why is it that David, who did no wrong to those who did evil to him, cursed the mountains of Gelboe when Saul and Jonathan fell in battle, saying: "Ye mountains of Gelboe, let neither dew nor rain come upon you; neither be they fields of first-fruits; for there was cast away the shield of the valiant, the shield of Saul, as though he had not been anointed with oil"?

Why is it that Jeremias, when he perceived that his preaching was impeded by the stubbornness of his hearers, cursed them, saying: "Cursed be the man that brought the tidings to my father, saying: 'A man child is born to thee' "? What wrong, then, did the mountains of Gelboe do at Saul's death, that neither dew nor rain should fall on them and the word of that utterance should dry them of every slip of green?

But since Gelboe is interpreted *descent*, by the anointing and death of Saul is signified the death of our Mediator. Not undeservedly are the proud hearts of the Jews represented by the mountains of Gelboe. For while they pour themselves out in the desires of this world, they participate in the killing of Christ, that is, the Anointed, and because their anointed King dies in their midst, they are dried of every dew of grace.

Of them it is well said that they cannot "be the fields of first-fruits." The proud minds of the Hebrews, indeed, bore no first-fruits, because at the Redeemer's coming, remaining for the most part in their infidelity, they did not wish to follow the beginnings of faith. And so holy Church, abounding with first-fruits among the multitudes of the Gentiles, at the end of the world will with difficulty take up the Jews whom She shall find, and, collecting these last, will harvest them as the left-over fruit.

℟. Ye mountains of Gelboe, let neither dew nor rain come upon you, * For upon you have fallen the valiant ones of Israel. ℣. O all ye mountains that are in His circle, may the Lord visit you: but let Him pass over Gelboe. For. Glory. For.

VI SUNDAY AFTER PENTECOST

I Nocturn

From the second Book of Kings, c. 12, 1 - 16

II Nocturn

From the Book of St. Ambrose, Bishop, on the Defense of David

How many times in every hour does each one of us commit faults? Yet not every one thinks that his sin should be confessed. This great and mighty king did not for the slightest moment even permit the consciousness of his sin to remain with him, but by an unhesitating confession and in deepest grief laid bare his sin to the Lord.

What esteemed and wealthy person can you find for me now, who, if accused of some fault, will not become angry? But this man, glorious in his kingly command, deemed worthy of so many divine graces, when chided by a private citizen because he had sinned grievously, did not rage as one indignant; rather, having acknowledged it, he wept in sorrow for his wrong. And consequently his grief moved the Lord, so that Nathan declared: "Because you have repented, the Lord has taken away your sin." The readiness of the pardon showed the genuine character of the king's repentance, which took away the guilt of so great a wrong.

Some men, when reproved by the priests, increase their sins by wanting to deny or defend them, and their fall becomes worse there where their amendment is hoped for. But if the saints of the Lord, who are trying to carry on a loyal fight and to run salvation's course, perchance fall at any time, more through nature's weakness than through the pleasure of sinning, they rise again to run with more spirit, entering into greater battles under the spur of their shame, so that their fall is reckoned not only to have produced no impediment, but even to have added incentives to swift action.

David sinned as kings are wont, but he performed penance, he wept, he lamented in a way that kings are not wont to do. He confessed his fault; he begged for forgiveness; he deplored the misery of depraved flesh; he fasted, prayed, and handed down for all ages to come a testimony of his confession in his well known lamentation. What private citizens are ashamed to do, the king did not blush to confess publicly. They who are bound by laws dare to deny their sin; they disdain to plead for the pardon for which he asked who was bound by no human laws. That he sinned was due to his condition; that he made supplication was a sign of his amendment. His fall is common, but his confession is outstanding. That he fell into sin was due to his nature; that he cleansed himself of it was a mark of his virtue.

℟. Who is a great God like our God? * Thou art the God that dost wonders. ℣. Thou hast made known Thy power among the nations: with Thine arm Thou hast redeemed Thy people. Thou art. Glory. Thou art.

VII SUNDAY AFTER PENTECOST

I Nocturn

From the third Book of Kings, c. 1, 1 - 8 and 11 - 15

II Nocturn

From a letter of St. Jerome, Priest, to Nepotianus

When seventy years old, David, once a man of war, now chilled by old age, was unable to keep warm. As a result, a young maid was sought out from all the regions of Israel, Abisag the Sunamitess, to sleep with the king and to warm his aged body. Who is this Sunamitess, this wife and virgin, so fervent that she could warm the cold old man, so holy that she did not provoke to lust him whom she warmed?

Let Solomon, as the wisest of men, explain his father's delights and let him, as the peacemaker, tell of the attachments of the man of war. "Get wisdom; get prudence; forget not, neither decline from the words of my mouth. Forsake her not, and she shall keep thee; love her, and she shall preserve thee. The beginning of wisdom, get wisdom; and with all thy possessions purchase prudence. Take hold on her, and she shall exalt thee; honor her, and she shall embrace thee, so that she shall give to thy head a crown of graces. With a crown of delights she shall protect thee."

In old men almost all the powers of the body are changed, and, while wisdom alone increases, the rest wane; the fastings, vigils, mortifications, that is, sleeping on the ground, pilgrimages hither and thither, the reception of travellers, the sheltering of the poor, constancy and perseverance in prayer, the visitation of the sick, the toil with one's hands from which alms may be given, and, lest I draw out my sermon any longer, all the things which are performed by the body become more difficult when the body is broken.

But I do not say that wisdom, which is decreased by age in many old men, is lessened in youths and those of a more robust age, who have acquired knowledge by labor and ardent study, by sanctity of life and frequent prayer to the Lord Jesus; but, because adolescence must sustain much bodily warfare, it is smothered, amidst incentives to vice and nervous reactions of the flesh, as fire in green wood, so that it cannot unfold its beauty. But again, the old age of those who have developed upright habits during youth and have meditated day and night on the Law of the Lord becomes more learned with years, more expert by practice, wiser with the passing of time, and reaps most delicious fruits from its earnest endeavors of old.

℟. God heareth all things: He hath sent His angel and taken me from guarding my father's sheep: * And He hath anointed me with the oil of His mercy. ℣. The Lord, who delivered me out of the mouth of the lion, and freed me from the paw of the wild beast. And. Glory. And.

VIII SUNDAY AFTER PENTECOST

I Nocturn

From the third Book of Kings, c. 9, 1 - 14

II Nocturn

From the book of St. Augustine, Bishop, on the City of God

In Solomon also there was a type of the future reality, in that he built the temple and enjoyed peace according to his name (the name Solomon denotes *the peaceful one*), and in the beginning of his reign was exceedingly praiseworthy. But though in his own person, by a foreshadowing of the future, he prophesied Christ, our Lord, he did not give us the reality.

There are some things written of Solomon which are, as it were, written concerning Christ. Holy Scripture in this way, by giving the history of things past, prophesied at the same time things to come. For besides the books of divine history wherein his reign is recorded, the seventy-first psalm is likewise inscribed with his name.

In this psalm many things are said which cannot apply to Solomon at all, whereas they fit Christ the Lord very exactly. Hence it is clearly apparent that in Solomon is foreshadowed a type of that which was later revealed in truth in the Person of Christ.

For it is known by what boundaries the kingdom of Solomon was inclosed, and yet we read in that psalm: "He shall rule from sea to sea, and from the river to the ends of the earth." This we see fulfilled in Christ, whose dominion took its beginning from the river where, after His Baptism by John—who also pointed

IX Sunday After Pentecost

Him out—He began to be recognized by His disciples, who called Him not only *Master* but also *Lord*.

℟. I took thee from the house of thy father, saith the Lord, and set thee to feed the flock of My people: * And I have been with thee wheresoever thou hast walked, establishing thy kingdom forever. ℣. And I have made thy name great, like unto the name of the great ones that are on the earth: And I have given thee rest from all thy enemies. And I have. Glory. And I have.

IX SUNDAY AFTER PENTECOST

I Nocturn

From the fourth Book of Kings, c. 1, 1 - 10

II Nocturn

Sermon of St. Augustine, Bishop

With reference to the lessons which are being read to us during these days, dearly beloved brethren, I have frequently admonished that we ought not follow the letter which killeth and forsake the spirit which giveth life. For so the Apostle declares: "For the letter killeth, but the spirit quickeneth." If we want to understand only that which is in the letter, we shall grasp little or almost no useful material from the divine readings.

Now all those things which are recounted were types and figures of things to be. For, the things which among the Jews were prefigured, among us, through the gift of God's grace, have been accomplished. The blessed Elias, for instance, stood as a type of the Lord, our Savior. Because just as Elias suffered persecution at the hands of the Jews, so also the true Elias, our Lord, was made reprobate and contemned by the same Jews.

Elias forsook his own nation, and Christ abandoned the Synagogue. Elias withdrew into a desert, and Christ came into the world. In the desert Elias was fed by ministering ravens, and in the desert of this world Christ is refreshed by the faith of the Gentiles.

For those ravens which at the Lord's bidding ministered to blessed Elias in truth prefigured the people of the Gentiles, and therefore it is said of the Church of the Gentiles: "I am black but beautiful, O ye daughters of Jerusalem." How is the Church black, yet beautiful? She is black by nature, beautiful by grace. Whence black? "Behold, I was conceived in iniquities; and in sins did my mother conceive me." Whence beautiful? "Thou shalt sprinkle me with hyssop, and I shall be cleansed; thou shalt wash me, and I shall be made whiter than snow."

℟. Ye mountains of Gelboe, let neither dew nor rain come upon you, * For upon you have fallen the valiant ones of Israel. ℣. O all ye mountains that are in His circle, may the Lord visit you; but let Him pass over Gelboe. For. Glory. For.

X SUNDAY AFTER PENTECOST
I Nocturn
From the fourth Book of Kings, c. 9, 29 - 37; c. 10, 1 - 7

II Nocturn
Sermon of St. John Chrysostom

Let us not think that we shall have an excuse if at times we find associates in our sins, for this will rather increase the guilt. While it is true, indeed, that the serpent was punished more than the woman, so also was the woman punished more than her husband. Jezabel also suffered greater punishment than Achab, who seized the vineyard. She, in fact, contrived this whole affair and was the occasion of the king's falls. Therefore you also, if you are the cause of the ruin of others, will pay more severely than they who have been seduced by you. For to sin personally does not imply as much evil as to lead others to sin.

Consequently, whenever we see men sin, not only are we not to encourage them, but we should even draw them out of that trap of their evil-doing, lest we should receive punishment for another's downfall. Let us likewise be constantly mindful of that terrible judgment-seat, of the river of fire, of the unbreakable chains, of the profound darkness, of the gnashing of teeth, and of the poisonous worm. "But," you will say, "God is lenient." Are these things then all talk, and is not the rich man, the scorner of Lazarus, punished, nor the foolish virgins rejected by their spouse? Will they, then, who have not feared Christ, not go into the fire prepared for the devil? Will he who wears soiled raiment not perish, bound hand and foot? Will he who exacted the hundred denarii from his fellow-servant not be delivered to the torturers? Will that which is said of adulterers—especially that their worm will not die and their fire will not be extinguished—not be true?

Is God but threatening these things? You answer, "Yes." And how, I pray, do you dare to speak such a thing in public and to proffer this opinion on your own initiative? I, to be sure, shall be able to prove the contrary, both from those things which God has spoken, and from those things which He has done. But if you do not believe on account of future things, then at least believe on account of those things which have already happened.

For those things which have happened and have come into very act surely are not only threats and words.

Who, then, deluged the whole world by causing the flood, and effected that awful storm and the complete destruction of our race? Who cast those lightning-bolts and fiery darts upon the land of the Sodomites? Who drowned all the army of Egypt in the sea? Who burned the synagogue of Abiròn? Who slew those seventy thousand men in one moment of time because of David's sin? Has not God brought about all these things and more?

℟. And it came to pass that when the Lord would take Elias by a whirlwind into heaven, * Eliseus cried, saying: My father, my father, the chariot of Israel, and the driver thereof. ℣. And as they went on walking and talking together, behold a fiery chariot and fiery horses parted them both asunder and Elias went up by a whirlwind into heaven. Eliseus. Glory. Eliseus.

XI SUNDAY AFTER PENTECOST

I Nocturn

From the fourth Book of Kings, c. 20, 1 - 11

II Nocturn

From the Exposition of St. Jerome, Priest, on the Prophet Isaias

Lest the heart of Ezechias be elated after his unbelievable triumphs and his deliverance from the midst of captivity, he is visited with sickness in his own body, and he hears that he will die, so that, being converted to the Lord, he may ward off his condemnation. Of the very same thing we read both in the Prophet Jonas and in the threats against David; these things are spoken as if about to come, yet they are not accomplished, although God does not commute His decision, but rouses the human race to a knowledge of itself. For God is impatient with evil-doing.

And Ezechias "turned his face to the wall," because he was unable to go to the Temple. He turned to the wall of the Temple, beside which Solomon had built the palace; or simply, he turned towards the wall of the room, in order that he would not seem to show his tears to those around him. And on hearing that he was to die, he did not plead for life and many years; rather he left it in the judgment of God what He should will to grant.

For he knew that Solomon had been pleasing to God in that he had not requested a greater number of years of life; and now, about to go to God, he speaks of his deeds, how he walked before Him in truth and with a perfect heart. Happy the conscience that, at the time of affliction, is mindful of its good works! "Blessed are the clean of heart, for they shall see God." But how, then, is it elsewhere written: "Who will boast that he has a pure heart?" This is explained in the following way: perfection of heart is said to be in him now because he destroyed the idols, he opened the doors of the temple, crushed the brazen serpent, and did other things which Holy Scripture narrates.

Now Ezechias wept many tears because of the Lord's promise to David, which he saw would fail with his death. For at that time Ezechias had no sons—because, after his death, Manasses began to reign in Judea at the age of twelve years, from which it follows that he was born after the third year of the fifteen-year prolongation of life granted to Ezechias. Therefore all this weeping was because he despaired of Christ being born of his posterity. Others say that even holy men are frightened by death on account of the uncertainty of judgment and their ignorance of God's decision concerning their lot in the next life.

℟. The number of my sins is greater than that of the sands of the seashore, and my sins are multiplied: and I am not worthy to look up to the height of heaven because of the multitude of my iniquities: for I have provoked Thy wrath, * And done evil in Thy sight. ℣. For I acknowledge my iniquity, and my sin is continually before me, for against Thee only have I sinned. And done. Glory. And done.

I SUNDAY OF AUGUST

I Nocturn

From the Proverbs of Solomon, c. 1, 1 - 22

II Nocturn

From a Treatise of St. Ambrose, Bishop, on Psalm 118

"The fear of the Lord is the beginning of wisdom," says the Prophet. Now what is the beginning of wisdom but to renounce the world? For to be wise in worldly things is folly. In fine, the Apostle declares that "the wisdom of this world is foolishness with God." But even the fear of the Lord itself, unless it be according to knowledge, is of no profit; rather it is the greatest hindrance.

The Jews really have zeal for the things of God, but since they do not have it according to knowledge, in their very zeal and fear they incur the greater displeasure of God. Since they circumcise their infants and keep the Sabbaths, it is evident that they have the fear of God; but because they do not know that the Law is spiritual, they circumcise their body, not their heart.

But why do I speak of the Jews? There are even among us those who have the fear of God, but nŏt according to knowledge, making severe precepts which our human condition is not able to observe. Their fear lies in this: that they seem to educate themselves in discipline, and exact the performance of virtue; but their ignorance lies in this: that they do not sympathize with nature, nor reckon on its capability. Therefore fear should not be beyond reason. For true wisdom starts with fear of God; nor is wisdom spiritual without the fear of God; consequently, our fear should not be without wisdom.

Holy fear is a kind of pedestal for the word of God. For just as any image placed on a pedestal assumes a more elegant appearance and acquires a firmness of position, so the word of God is the better based on holy fear, and is the more strongly rooted in the breast of him who fears the Lord, so that it does not fall from the heart of the man, nor do the birds of the air come and pluck it out of the affections of an indifferent and dissimulating soul.

℟. Give me, O Lord, wisdom that sitteth by Thy throne, and cast me not off from among Thy children: * For I am Thy servant, and the son of Thy handmaid. ℣. Send her from the throne of Thy greatness, that she may be with me, and may labor with me. For I am. Glory. For I am.

II SUNDAY OF AUGUST

I Nocturn

From the Book of Ecclesiastes, c. 1, 1 - 17

II Nocturn

Sermon of St. John Chrysostom

When Solomon was held captivated by the concupiscence of worldly things, he reckoned them great and wonderful and spent much labor and care upon them—building magnificent houses, heaping up plenty of gold, gathering choirs of singers and divers kinds of servers for the table and feasts, seeking pleasure for his soul in the beauties of gardens and handsome bodies, and, if I may say so, pursuing every way of delight and refreshment.

But when he had come to himself, and was able, as it were, from a shadowy abyss, to look again on the light of true wisdom, then he uttered that sublime word, worthy of heaven: "Vanity of vanities," he said, "and all is vanity." This maxim, and one more sublime, you too will utter concerning this untimely pleasure if you cut yourself off for a little while from evil habits.

Although in the times before Solomon so great a love of wisdom was not demanded—for the old Law neither forbade pleasures nor considered as vain the enjoyment of superfluities—nevertheless, though this be the case, it is still possible to see how worthless and vain are the things of earth.

But we are called to a worthier life. We ascend to a higher summit and are trained in worthier arenas. And what else are we commanded but to live like those supernal, incorporeal, and intellectual powers?

℟. The fear of the Lord is the beginning of wisdom: * A good understanding have all they that do it: His praise endureth forever and ever. ℣. Love is the keeping of His laws: for the fear of the Lord is the whole of wisdom. A good. Glory. A good.

III SUNDAY OF AUGUST

I Nocturn

From the Book of Wisdom, c. 1, 1 - 13

II Nocturn

From the Book of Offices of St. Ambrose, Bishop

Great is the splendor of justice which, being made for others rather than for herself, strengthens our bond of union and our intercourse with each other; she holds the highest place in order to hold all things subject to her judgment, be of assistance to others, bestow riches, refuse not obligations, and take upon herself the perils of others. Who would not desire to possess this citadel of virtue, unless, perhaps, previous covetousness had weakened and distorted the strength of so great a virtue? For while we wish to increase our possessions, amass money, occupy lands, and excel in riches, we put off the form of justice and lose ordinary kindness.

The excellence of justice can be grasped from this, that it makes an exception neither of places, persons, nor times, and is even reserved for enemies; so that if either a place or day of battle has been decided upon with the enemy, it would be considered contrary to justice to anticipate either the place or time; for it makes a difference whether one is overcome in some battle or difficult encounter by superior strength, or by some chance event.

If therefore justice prevails in war, how much more ought it to be observed in peace? Therefore, the foundation of justice is faith. For the hearts of the just meditate on faith; and the just one who accuses himself bases his justice upon faith. For then does his justice appear if he manifest those things which are true.

And finally the Lord says through Isaias: "Behold, I lay a stone in the foundation of Sion"; that is, Christ in the foundation of the Church. For the faith of all is Christ, while the Church is in a certain sense a pattern of justice, the common law for all: she prays in common, works in common, and is tried in common. Finally, he who (through faith) denies himself is indeed just, is indeed worthy of Christ. And therefore did Paul make Christ the foundation, in order that we might place our works of justice upon Him, because faith is the foundation.

℟. Remove far from me the wicked and deceitful word, O Lord: * Give me neither riches nor beggary, but give me only the necessaries of life. ℣. Two things I have asked of Thee, deny them not to me before I die. Give. Glory. Give.

IV SUNDAY OF AUGUST

I Nocturn

From the Book of Ecclesiasticus, c. 1, 1 - 16

II Nocturn

From the Book of Morals of St. Gregory, Pope

There are some men who have no regard for their own life, and since they are in quest of things transitory, either because they do not understand eternal things, or contemn them if understood, they have no sense of sorrow, nor do they know how to take counsel, and because they do not dwell upon the heavenly things which they have lost, they, miserable wretches, think they are fortunate in their blessings. They do not in the least raise the eyes of their mind to the light of the truth to which they have been directed; not in the least do they turn the keenness of their desire to the contemplation of their eternal homeland; rather, forsaking themselves in the things for which they have been destined, in place of their fatherland they fall in love with the exile that they are undergoing, and take joy in the blindness they are suffering as in the brilliance of light.

On the other hand, the minds of the elect, since they perceive that all things transitory are nothing, go in search of the things for which they have been created, and since nothing outside of

God satisfies them, their thinking mind, fatigued by the very toil of their search, finds rest in the hope and contemplation of their Creator and longs to be numbered among heaven's citizens; each one of them, too, while yet held in the world in body, nevertheless, rises in mind beyond the world; each one laments the bitterness of the exile he is undergoing and rouses himself with ceaseless incitements of love for his sublime homeland.

Therefore, when a man in sorrow beholds how everlasting that is which he has lost, he finds the wholesome counsel to despise these temporal things that pass quickly on; and the more he grows in the understanding of the counsel to abandon the things that will perish, the more his sorrow is increased, because he cannot yet arrive at the things that will endure. It is to be noticed likewise that there is no sorrow of mind in a rash and hasty action. For they who live without advice, who recklessly abandon themselves to the tide of affairs, are not, in the meanwhile, burdened by any sorrow from thinking.

But he who wisely fixes his mind on the counsel of life cautiously watches over himself by due deliberation in every act, and lest in something that comes about a sudden and contrary end overtake him, he calmly works against this beforehand, his foundation being set in measured thought; he is on the watch so that fear may not hinder him from the things that must be done, and that rashness may not drive him on to the things that should be put off; so that things perverse may not conquer him through concupiscence in open war, nor righteous things through vainglory supplant him in ambush.

℟. Leave me not, O Lord, father and ruler of my life, lest I fall before my adversaries: * Lest my enemy rejoice over me. ℣. Take hold of arms and shield and rise up to help me. Lest my enemy. Glory. Lest my enemy.

V SUNDAY OF AUGUST

I Nocturn

From the Book of Ecclesiasticus, c. 5, 1 - 16.

II Nocturn

Sermon of St. John Chrysostom

Do not be slow in turning to the Lord, and do not put it off from day to day, for you do not know what the coming day will bring. There is, in fact, danger and fear in postponement, while salvation is certain and assured if there be no delay. Hence, cultivate virtue; because thus, even if you die as a youth, you will take your leave with confidence, and if you arrive at an old age, you will depart from this life with great ease and no worry; you will possess a double happiness in that you have refrained from wickedness in life, and have cultivated virtue. Do not say, "There will be a time when it will be suitable to convert," for these words greatly exasperate God.

For why, when He Himself has promised time eternal to you, do you not want to labor in this present life that is short and of a moment's duration? You act so lazily and indolently as if you were looking for a life shorter than this. Do not these daily revelries, do not these banquets, these impure persons, the theatres, the riches pay witness to your unspeakable desire for evildoing? Consider well that, as often as you have sinned against purity, so often have you condemned yourself, for sin is such that, as soon as it has been perpetrated, the Judge passes sentence on it.

Have you been drunk? Have you glutted your stomach? Have you stolen? Stop at once on the down-grade, and turn yourself in the opposite direction. Give thanks to God that He has not snatched you away in the midst of your sins; do not seek to gain a little more time in order to do evil. Many people, while they were living evil and vicious lives, have perished and have passed to their evident damnation. Be fearful lest the same thing happen to you!

"But to many," you will say, "God has given time for them to confess their fault in extreme old age." What then? Will it be given to you? "Perhaps He will grant it," you say. Why do you say, "Perhaps"? Does it happen often? Mark that you are concerned with your soul; then also consider the other possibility, and say: "But what if He does not grant it?"—"But what if He does," do you say? All right! Then He grants it, but the first consideration is surer and more advantageous than this other.

℞. O Lord, Father and God of my life, do not abandon me to evil thoughts; give me not haughtiness of my eyes, and turn away from me all evil desires, O Lord; remove concupiscence from me, * And give me not over to a shameless and foolish mind, O Lord. ℣. O Lord, leave me not, lest my ignorances increase, and my offenses be multiplied. And give. Glory. And give.

I SUNDAY OF SEPTEMBER

I Nocturn

From the Book of Job, c. 1, 1 - 11

II Nocturn

From the Book of Morals of St. Gregory, Pope

Sacred Scripture is placed as a kind of mirror before the eyes of the mind so that our internal appearance may be beheld therein. For there we recognize the ugly things, there the beautiful things in ourselves; there we realize how far we have advanced, or how far we are from progress. It tells of the deeds of holy men, and encourages the hearts of the weak to imitate them; by making mention of their victorious works, it strengthens our weakness against the onslaughts of vices, and through its accounts it is effected that our minds become less afraid in their conflicts the more we view the triumphs of so many brave men set before us.

Sometimes, too, Holy Scripture not only declares these men's virtues to us, but also makes note of their falls, in order that in the victory of the strong we may see what we are to seize upon to imitate, and likewise, in their falls, what we are to fear. For example, Job is pictured as being made great in temptation, while David in his trial is prostrated; accordingly the virtue of great men nourishes our hope, and the mishaps of great men serve us as a guard of humility, so that while the former (their virtues) bolster us up in our joy, the latter (their falls) weigh upon us in our fear. Thus the soul of him who listens to Scripture, being grounded by the one in the confidence of hope and by the other in the lowliness of fear, neither grows proud in overconfidence because it is laden with fear, nor, when burdened with anxiety, does it despair, because it is strengthened in the assurance of its hope through the example of virtue.

"There was a man in the land of Hus, whose name was Job." Where the holy man dwelt is told that the merit of his virtue might be revealed. For indeed, who does not know that Hus is in the land of the Gentiles? Now the Gentile people live in subjection to vices because of the fact that they had no knowledge of their Creator.

Hence it was told where Job dwelt that this might add to his praise, that he was good among evil men. For it is nothing especially praiseworthy to be good among the good, but to be good among evil men is worthy of praise. Just as it is a greater fault not to live as a good man among the good, so it is of the greatest credit to have lived as a good man even among the evil.

℟. My flesh is clothed with rottenness and the filth of dust, my skin is withered and drawn together; * Remember me, O Lord, for my life is but wind. ℣. My days have passed more swiftly than the web is cut by the weaver, and are consumed without any hope. Remember. Glory. Remember.

II SUNDAY OF SEPTEMBER

I Nocturn

From the Book of Job, c. 9, 1 - 17

II Nocturn

From the Book of Morals of St. Gregory, Pope

"Indeed I know it is so, and that man cannot be justified compared with God." If God is not taken into consideration, a man may be said to be just, but when placed alongside of God, he no longer appears so, because whoever compares himself with the Author of all good things deprives himself of the good which he has received. He who appropriates to himself the good things he has received, fights against God with His own gifts. It is therefore fitting that the grounds on which he ought to have been humbled, but upon which he exalted himself, should be used to destroy his vainglory.

A holy man, however, because he sees that all the merit of our virtue is deficient if it is judged strictly by Him who sees our interior, rightly adds: "If he will contend with him, he cannot answer him one for a thousand."

In Holy Scripture the number *one thousand* usually denotes totality. Hence the Psalmist says, "Of the word which he commanded unto a thousand generations," whereas it is clearly evident that from the beginning of the world until the coming of the Redeemer not more than seventy-seven generations are named by the Evangelist. What is then to be understood here by *one thousand* except the perfect totality of the foreseen generation for the bringing forth of a new offspring? Hence also it is said by John, "And they will reign with him a thousand years," because the kingdom of holy Church is made firm by the perfection of totality.

For ten times one is ten, and ten times ten is a hundred, and ten times a hundred is a thousand. Since we begin with one in order to attain a thousand, what is signified by *one* (in the text from Job cited above) except the beginning of a good life? what is designated by a *thousand* except the perfection of the same good life? Moreover, *to contend with God* (as mentioned in the text) is *to give the glory of one's virtue not to Him, but to appropriate it to oneself.* But a holy man sees that even he who has already received the greatest gifts—if he becomes proud because of them—loses all that he has received.

℟. The fewness of my days shall be ended shortly; suffer me, Lord, that I may lament my sorrow a little, * Before I go to a land that is dark and covered with the mist of death. ℣. Thy hands have made me, O Lord, and fashioned me wholly round about; and dost Thou cast me down headlong of a sudden? Before. Glory. Before.

III SUNDAY OF SEPTEMBER

I Nocturn

From the Book of Tobias, c. 1, 1 - 15

II Nocturn

Sermon of St. Leo, Pope

I know well enough, dearly beloved, that many among you are so careful in those things which pertain to the observance of the Christian Faith that they do not have to be encouraged by our exhortations. This fact tradition has for a long time upheld and custom has established; neither is our zeal unaware of it, nor does our love overlook it. Yet, because it is the duty of the priestly office to have a common concern for all the children of the Church, we arouse one and all to that which is of profit both to the ignorant and to the learned, whom we love equally, so that, by chastisement of soul and body, we may celebrate with a lively faith the fast which the return of this seventh month points out to us.

Now, then, this observance of continence is assigned to the four seasons in order that in the passing course of the whole year we might realize that we are constantly in need of purification and must be always taking care, since we are cast about in the changing ways of this life, that the sin which is contracted through the weakness of our flesh and the corruption of our desires may be blotted out by fasts and alms-giving.

Let us go hungry for a while, dearly beloved, and take from our usual fare some small thing that may be of service to the poor who are in need of help. Let the conscience of the benevolent be delighted with the fruits of their own generosity, and in spreading joy you will receive that by which you yourself will be gladdened. The love of neighbor is the love of God, which, in the unity of this double charity, constitutes the fullness of the Law and of the Prophets, so that no one is to doubt that he has offered to God that which he has bestowed on his neighbor, since the

Lord, our Savior, declared when He was speaking of feeding and aiding the poor: "That which you did to one of these, you did unto me."

So let us fast on Wednesday and Friday; then on Saturday let us celebrate the Vigil at the tomb of the blessed Apostle Peter, by whose merits and prayers we believe we shall be helped to please our merciful God through our fast and devotion.

℟. It is time that I return to Him that sent Me, * But bless ye God and publish all His wonderful works. ℣. Give glory to Him in the sight of all that live, because He hath shown His mercy to you. But. Glory. But.

EMBER WEDNESDAY

The reading of the holy Gospel according to St. Mark

At that time one of the crowd answering, said, "Master, I have brought to thee my son, who has a dumb spirit." And so forth.

Homily of St. Bede the Venerable, Priest

This possessed person whom the Lord healed when He came down from the mountain Mark mentions as being deaf and dumb, while Matthew says that he was a lunatic. At any rate he represents those of whom it is written: "A fool is changed as the moon." Such men, never remaining in the same state, are turned now to these, now to those evil deeds, and thus increase and decrease as the moon. They are dumb, since they do not confess their faith; they are deaf, because they do not hear the word of truth. They foam at the mouth as they pine away in their folly. For it is usual for fools and morons to discharge saliva from their mouths. They gnash their teeth when they grow hot with the fury of their anger; they wither away when they grow enfeebled through the dulling effect of pleasure, and, not strengthened by the exercise of their faculties, they live a listless life.

Now when the man says, "And I spoke to thy disciples to cast him out and they could not," he indirectly makes a charge against the apostles, whereas the impossibility of a cure sometimes is to be imparted not to the incapability of those who offer the cure, but to the faith of those who are to be cured, as appears from the words of the Lord: "May it be done to thee according to thy faith." "Who answering, said: 'O incredulous generation, how long shall I be with you? How long shall I suffer you?'" Not that He, gentle and meek as he was, who as a lamb before the shearer did not open His mouth, was overcome with disgust, nor did He break out in words of anger; but as a physician who sees a sick person acting contrary to his prescriptions,

He says: "How much longer shall I be coming to your home? How much longer shall I waste the labor of my practice, since I order one thing, and you do the other?"

"And he said to them: 'This kind can go out by nothing, but by prayer and fasting.'" While He teaches the apostles how the most wicked of the demons is to be cast out, He is preparing all men for life, so that we might realize that all the worst temptations of impure spirits or of men are to be conquered by fasting and prayer; that the wrath of God too, when it has been enkindled to wreak vengeance on our crimes, can be placated by this singular remedy. Now fasting, in a wide sense, is not only to abstain from food, but also from all allurements of the flesh, and more, to restrain oneself from all the disorders of vice. So again, in a general sense, prayer consists not only in the words by which we call upon the divine clemency, but likewise in all the things which we, inspired by the devotion of our faith, do in the service of our Creator.

EMBER FRIDAY

The reading of the holy Gospel according to St. Luke

At that time one of the Pharisees asked Jesus to dine with him; so he went into the house of the Pharisee and reclined at table. And so forth.

Homily of St. Gregory, Pope

Whom does the Pharisee, presuming concerning his false sense of justice, exemplify but the Jewish nation? Whom does the sinful woman, coming and weeping at the feet of our Lord, represent but the converted Gentiles? She came with an alabaster box, poured out the ointment, stood behind at the feet of the Lord, washed His feet with her tears, dried them with her hair, and did not cease to kiss those feet which she had anointed and washed. And so that woman represents us, if with our whole heart we return to our Lord after sinning, if we imitate her penitent grief. For what is expressed by the ointment except the odor of good repute? Wherefore Paul declares: "We are the good odor of Christ in every place."

If then we perform righteous acts by which we fill the Church with the odor of good fame, what do we pour on the body of our Lord but ointment? And the woman stood behind at the feet of Jesus; for we stood against our Lord's feet when, given up to sin, we resisted Him in His ways. But if after sin we are converted to honest repentance, we too "stand behind at his feet," because we follow the paths of Him against whom we had been fighting. The woman washes His feet with her tears; this we also truly do if we are inclined to every least member of the Lord through a sense of compassion; if we sympathize with His saints in their suffering; if we consider their sorrow as our own.

We dry the feet of the Lord with our hair, when from those things that are superfluous to us we minister to His saints, whom we compassionate out of charity, in so far as our mind so grieves through compassion that it even displays the feeling of our sorrow by our generous gift. For he truly washes the feet of the Redeemer, but does not dry them with his hair, who, although he is compassionate in his neighbors' pain, nevertheless does not show mercy to them with those things that are superfluous to him. He weeps and does not dry them, who indeed offers words of sorrow, but does not in the least relieve the force of pain by ministering the things that are lacking. The woman kisses the feet which she dries; this we also perform if we constantly love those whom we sustain out of charity lest our neighbor's need become burdensome to us; or lest his very want which is relieved be irksome to us; and though our hands bestow what is necessary, our soul weakens in its love.

EMBER SATURDAY

The reading of the holy Gospel according to St. Luke

At that time Jesus spoke to the multitude this parable: "A certain man had a fig tree planted in his vineyard; and he came seeking fruit thereon, and found none." And so forth.

Homily of St. Gregory, Pope

Our Lord and Redeemer through His Gospel sometimes speaks in figures, sometimes by examples; sometimes He says one thing in figure, and another thing by example; and sometimes He says in figure what He says also by example. For, brethren, you have heard of two things in this Gospel: the barren fig tree and the woman who was afflicted, and a due consideration must be given to both. The first He speaks of through a simile; the other He treats of by example. Now the barren fig tree signifies what the woman was when she was bent over; likewise does the fig tree, when it was preserved, denote the same thing as the woman when she was straightened.

What does the fig tree represent but our human nature? What does the woman who was bent over typify except the same nature? Human nature was also planted well—as was the fig tree—and created well—as was the woman—but, having fallen into sin of its own will, it neither bore the fruit of its work, nor kept its figure of uprightness. Yes, falling by its own will into sin, because it did not wish to bring forth the fruit of obedience, it lost its figure of stateliness. It had been formed according to the image of God, but when it did not persevere in that honorable condition, it refused to remain as it had been planted or created. For three years did the Lord of the vineyard visit His fig tree, for He sought after the nature of the human race before the Law, under the Law, and at the time of Grace, by watching over her, by teaching her, by coming to her.

He came before the Law, because be indicated through the natural intelligence how, by the knowledge of himself, everyone should act towards his neighbor. He came in the Law, because He taught by giving commandment. He came after the Law by grace because He showed the presence of His love by showing Himself. But within those three years He complained that He found no fruit, for the inborn voice of the natural law could not correct the minds of certain wicked men, nor could the commandments instruct them, nor could the miracles of His Incarnation convert them. But what is designated by the dresser of the vineyard except the order of the hierarchy? These, when they rule over the Church, take exceedingly great care of the Lord's vineyard.

IV SUNDAY OF SEPTEMBER

I Nocturn

From the Book of Judith, c. 1, 1 - 12; c. 2, 1 - 3

II Nocturn

From the Book of St. Ambrose, Bishop, on Elias and Fasting

Men of power are forbidden to drink wine lest, when they have drunk, they forget their wisdom. In fine, the mighty men who were willing to surrender themselves to Holofernes, chief of the army of the Assyrian king, drank wine till they were drunk, but the woman, Judith, did not drink, abstaining all the days of her widowhood, except for the solemn occasions of the feast-days. Fortified with these weapons, she went out and overcame the entire force of the Assyrians. Through the strength of her sober wisdom she cut off the head of Holofernes, preserved her purity, and brought back the victory.

Now she, girded with fasting, set out for the camp of the enemy. He lay, buried in wine, so that he could not feel the fatal stroke of the sword. In this way one woman's fast overcame the innumerable Assyrian troops. Esther too was made more beautiful by her fasting, for the Lord increased the grace of her sober mind. She freed all her kindred, that is, the whole Jewish people, from the hardships of persecution, and she made even the king subject to her.

Thus did the other woman (Judith), who had fasted for three consecutive days and had bathed her body with water only, become more pleasing and achieve her people's deliverance. Aman, on the other hand, while he boasted at the royal banquet, paid the punishment for his drunkenness amid the wine itself. Fasting, consequently, is a sacrifice of reconciliation and effects an increase of virtue, for it has made even women stronger by means of an increase of grace.

Fasting knows no debtor, nor is it aware of the burden of debt. The table of men who fast is not savored with borrowed money. In fact, fasting adds pleasure to the festal meals. After hunger, the dishes' which are repulsive because of their frequency and grow disgusting in their daily repetition, become more tasty. Fasting is a condiment to food. The sharper the appetite, the more agreeable is the food.

℟. We know no other God but the Lord, in whom we hope: * He despiseth us not, neither doth He put away His salvation from our nation. ℣. Let us seek His mercy with tears, and humble our souls before Him. He. Glory. He.

V SUNDAY OF SEPTEMBER

I Nocturn

From the Book of Esther, c. 1, 1 - 9

II Nocturn

From the Book of Offices of St. Ambrose, Bishop

What did Queen Esther do? Did she not, in order to save her people from danger, expose herself to death and bravely face the anger of the cruel king? The king of the Persians, cruel and exceedingly violent as he was, thought it fitting to show favor to him who had told him of the plot that had been made against him, to free the people from slavery, and to deliver them from death, but not to spare him who had persuaded such iniquity.

Finally, he sentenced to die on a gibbet him whom he had held second only to himself and foremost among all his friends, because he found himself dishonored through his wicked advice. For that proven friendship which safeguards righteousness is certainly to be preferred to riches, honor, and power; it is not accustomed, however, to be preferred to uprightness, but rather to follow it.

Such was the friendship of Jonathan, who, out of love for David, willingly risked the anger of his father and his own safety. Such was the friendship of Achimelech, who, for the sake of the duties of hospitality, chose rather to die himself than to betray his fugitive friend.

Nothing, therefore, is to be preferred to righteousness; and Holy Scripture admonishes us that not even for the sake of friendship is virtue to be set aside. The philosophers had raised various questions on this matter: whether or not one should, for the sake of his friend, oppose his country?—whether or not it is right for a man to serve his friend even at the cost of a breach of faith?

Holy Scripture indeed says: "As a club and a sword and an iron-pointed arrow, so is he who bears false witness against his friend." But note what is here condemned is not bearing witness against a friend, but bearing false witness. For what if the cause of God or of one's country compels one to testify against a friend? Is friendship to be placed above religion? is vice to outweigh charity?

℟. Remember me for good, O Lord God: * And set not aside the works of mercy which I wrought in the house of my God and in His sacred rites. ℣. Be mindful of me, O Lord my God. And. Glory. And.

I SUNDAY OF OCTOBER

I Nocturn

From the first Book of Machabees, c. 1, 1 - 16

II Nocturn

From the Book of Offices of St. Ambrose, Bishop

There may perhaps be some who are so infatuated with the glory of war that they think there is no valor but that of war, and that I have avoided this subject because among us there is no bravery on which to discourse. How valiant was Josue, son of Nun, who in one battle overcame five kings with their armies! Again, when he was fighting against the Gabanites and feared lest the night would impede his victory, in the greatness of his soul and of his faith he cried, "Let the sun stand still," and it stood until the victory was one. How valiant was Gedeon, who with three hundred men gained the victory over a vast people and a savage enemy! How valiant was the youth, Jonathan, who showed great bravery in battle!

What shall I say of the Machabees? But first let me speak of their fathers, who, although they were ready to fight for the temple of God and for their own rights, when attacked by a trick of their enemies on the Sabbath, preferred to offer their unprotected bodies to the blows of the enemy than to fight back lest they violate the Sabbath. And thus they joyfully gave themselves up to death. But the Machabees, considering that by this example the whole nation would perish, when they were provoked to battle, even on the Sabbath avenged the innocent blood of their brethren. Afterwards, when the enraged king Antiochus waged war through his leaders, Lysias, Nicanor, and Gorgias, they, together with his Eastern and Assyrian forces, were completely crushed, and forty-eight thousand were struck down on the field by only three thousand of the Jews.

Of the valor of Judas Machabeus judge from just one of his soldiers. When Eleazar saw an elephant bigger than the rest and adorned with the king's harness, he thought that the king was riding thereon, and rushing forward he dashed into the midst of the legion, and having thrown away his shield, he slew the enemy on either hand until he reached the beast. He then went under the elephant, and stabbing upward, he killed it with his sword. The falling beast crushed Eleazar and thus he died.

How great was the valor of that soul! first, that he did not fear death; then, that, being surrounded by the legions of the enemy, he cast himself into the midst of their ranks, penetrated their line, and, becoming all the fiercer by his contempt of death, having thrown away his shield that fighting with both hands he might attain the huge bulk of the beast, he went under it that he might there strike a more effective blow. Included in the ruin of the elephant, it should rather be said that he was buried in his own triumph than that he was crushed by the fall of the beast.

℟. Thine is power; Thine is the kingdom, O Lord: Thou art above all nations; * Give peace in our days, O Lord. ℣. O God, Creator of all things, dreadful and strong, just and merciful. Give. Glory. Give.

II SUNDAY OF OCTOBER

I Nocturn

From the first Book of Machabees, c. 4, 36 - 51

II Nocturn

From the Book of St. Augustine, Bishop, on the City of God

When the Jewish nation ceased to have prophets—at that period, namely, when the Jews thought that, after the captivity of Babylon, when the temple had been restored, their nation would become better—it undoubtedly became worse. For thus did that carnal people understand what had been foretold by the Prophet Aggeus when he said: "Great shall be the glory of this last house, more than that of the first." That this was said of the new Testament, he proved shortly before when he clearly stated: "And I will move all nations; and the Desired of all nations shall come."

For the benefit of those chosen from the Gentiles, the house of God is erected through the new Covenant, of living stones, a house far more glorious than was that temple which had been built by King Solomon and restored after the captivity. For this reason, then, the nation had no prophets from that time on, but was afflicted with many disasters by kings of other countries, and by the Romans themselves, lest it be thought that this prophecy of Aggeus had been fulfilled by that restoration of the temple.

Not long after, at Alexander's coming, the people were enslaved, and though at the time no pillage was made—since they did not dare resist him, and consequently, being so easily subdued, received his favorable consideration—nevertheless, the glory of the temple was not as great as it was under the free rule of their own kings. Next, Ptolemy, the son of Lagus, following Alexander's death, carried them off captive into Egypt; his successor, Ptolemy Philadelphus, very kindly sent them back from there. (It is due to this latter that we possess the Scriptures of the seventy interpreters—the Septuagint.)

Thereupon they were crushed in the wars which are narrated in the books of the Machabees. They were made captive after this by Ptolomy, the king of Alexandria, who was called Epiphanes, and then compelled by Antiochus, the king of Syria, by many grievous evils to worship idols. The temple itself was filled with sacrilegious superstitions of the Gentiles, but the Jews' mighty leader, Judas, who is likewise called Machabeus, having overwhelmed the generals of Antiochus, cleansed it from all that idolatrous filth.

℞. The nations are come together against us to destroy us, and we know not what we should do: * O Lord God, our eyes look to Thee that we may not perish. ℣. Thou knowest what they intend against us. How shall we be able to stand before their face unless Thou help us? O Lord God. Glory. O Lord God.

III SUNDAY OF OCTOBER

I Nocturn

From the first Book of Machabees, c. 9, 1 - 20

II Nocturn

From the Book of Offices of St. Ambrose, Bishop

Because courage is proved not only by favorable, but also by adverse things, let us observe the death of Judas Machabeus. For after Nicanor, King Demetrius's captain, had been overcome, Judas, waging battle very confidently with his eight hundred men against the twenty thousand troops of the king's army, urged on to a glorious death rather than a shameful flight those who wanted to withdraw lest they be overwhelmed by the great number of the enemy. "Let us not stain our glory," he said.

So as the battle was waged, when they had been fighting from the dawn of day to evening, attacking the right wing where he had noted the most powerful forces of the enemy to be, he easily overcame it. But when he pursued those who fled, he exposed himself to attack from the rear, and thus found a death more glorious than triumph. What shall I add of his brother, Jonathan, who, fighting with a small force against the royal armies, deserted by his men and left with only two, renewed the battle, turned back the foe, and called back his fleeing soldiers to a share in the triumph.

Here you see warlike courage in which is no mediocre form of uprightness and beauty of character, because it prefers death to slavery and disgrace. But what shall I say of the sufferings of the martyrs. To be brief—the sons of the Machabees did not gain a lesser triumph over the proud king Antiochus than did their parents; if indeed the latter, being armed, conquered, the former triumphed without weapons.

The troop of the seven sons stood unflinching, encircled by the royal legions; the tortures had failed, the persecutors had given up, but the martyrs did not give way. One, stripped of the skin of his head, had changed his countenance, but he increased in virtue. Another, on being ordered to stick out his tongue so that it might be cut off answered: "The Lord who heard Moses when he was silent does not hear only those who speak. He hears the silent thoughts of his own people more than the words of all. You fear a tongue's scourging; are you not afraid of a scourging of blood? Blood, too, has its own voice with which it cries unto God as it cried in Abel."

℟. Thine is power; Thine is the kingdom, O Lord: Thou art above all nations: * Give peace in our days, O Lord. ℣. O God, Creator of all things, dreadful and strong, just and merciful. Give. Glory. Give.

IV SUNDAY OF OCTOBER

I Nocturn

From the second Book of Machabees, c. 1, 1 - 6

II Nocturn

From the Treatise of St. John Chrysostom on Psalm 43

"We have heard, O God, with our ears; our fathers have declared to us the work thou hast wrought in their days." A prophet indeed speaks this psalm, though he speaks not in his own person, but in the person of the Machabees, narrating and predicting events which at that time were yet to take place. For the prophets are such as transcend all times, the present, past, and future.

It is necessary first to say who these Machabees were, what they suffered, and what they did, so that those things which are said in the discussion may be clear. For when Antiochus, who was called Epiphanes, had laid waste to everything and had forced many who were there to depart from the laws of their fathers, these men remained untouched by these temptations. And when, indeed, serious war broke out, and they could not do anything which would be of any help, they hid themselves; for this the apostles also did. For they did not always rush openly into the midst of danger; but sometimes they withdrew, fleeing and hiding.

But after they had rested a little, like eager animals leaping out of their caves and coming forth from their lairs, they swore that henceforth they would no longer save only themselves, but others also, whomsoever they could. And going into the city and the whole country, they gathered together as many as they found who were still healthy and strong, and even many who were weak and had been led away they persuaded to return to the Law of their fathers.

For they said that God is kind and merciful, and that He never withholds salvation which flows from penitence. And saying these things, they held an election of the ablest men. For they were fighting not for their wives, children, and servants, or because of the ruin and captivity of their fatherland, but for the Law and state of their fathers. And their leader was God. When they arrayed their battle-line, therefore, and threw their whole souls into the conflict, trusting not in arms, but in place of all armor considering the cause of the conflict as sufficient, they confounded their adversaries. Moreover, going forth to battle, they did not call forth lamentations, nor sing battle songs, as some do; nor did they admit flute players, as was done in other camps, but they invoked the aid of the most high God, that He might be with them, and help them, and strengthen their hand, because that war which they waged was fought for His glory.

℟. Open Thine eyes, O Lord, and behold our affliction; for the Gentiles have come round about us to punish us. * But do Thou, O Lord, stretch forth Thine arm and deliver our souls. ℣. Punish them that afflict us and with pride do us wrong, and keep Thy portion. But. Glory. But.

I SUNDAY OF NOVEMBER

I Nocturn

From the Book of Ezechiel the Prophet, c. 1, 1 - 12

II Nocturn

From the Exposition of St. Gregory, Pope, on Ezechiel the Prophet

It is the Prophet's manner of speaking that he first describes the person, the time, and the place, and afterwards begins to deliver the mystery of the prophecy. In order that the truth be more solidly established, he first sets its root in history, and then by symbols and allegories brings forth the fruit of the Spirit. Thus Ezechiel makes mention of his age, saying: "Now it came to pass in the thirtieth year, in the fourth month, on the fifth day of the month." Pointing out, also, the place, he adds: "When I was in the midst of the captives by the river Chobar, the heavens were opened, and I saw the visions of God." He then indicates the time, continuing: "On the fifth day of the month, the same was the fifth year of the captivity of king Joachim." In order that he might accurately point out the person, he even speaks of his lineage when he subjoins: "The word of the Lord came to Ezechiel the priest, the son of Buzi."

But the problem arises for us why he, who had said nothing yet, begins speaking in this way: "And it came to pass in the thirtieth year." *And* is, in fact, a conjunctive word, and we know that a sentence following it is not joined to any other but the preceding sentence. Why, therefore, does he, who as yet had said nothing, say, "And it came to pass," when there is no sentence to which he may join what he is about to say? In this regard it must be observed that as we in our thought take note of bodily things, so the Prophets take note of spiritual things, and those things are really present to them which seem absent to our ignorance.

Wherefore it happens that in the minds of the prophets the interior things are joined to the exterior in such a way that they see both things at one time, and the word which they hear inwardly and that which they speak outwardly are made one and the same within them. Hence, the reason is apparent why he, who had said nothing, began by saying, "And it came to pass in the thirtieth year"; namely, because this word which he uttered outwardly he subjoined to that word he had heard inwardly.

Thus he joined the words which he spoke aloud to those of the inward vision, and thereupon he began, saying, "And it came to pass." For he subjoined that which he began to speak outwardly as if that which he saw interiorly was also visible exteriorly. However, what is here stated—that he received the spirit of prophecy in his thirtieth year—indicates that something else is to be considered by us, that is, that according to the mode of our reasoning, our speech is not fit for teaching until a perfect age. For this very reason, our Lord Himself, in His twelfth year, willed to be found sitting in the temple in the midst of the doctors, not teaching them, but asking them questions.

℟. Upon thy walls, O Jerusalem, I have appointed watchmen: * All the day and the night they shall not hold their peace to praise the name of the Lord. ℣. They shall proclaim My might unto the nations, and declare My glory unto the Gentiles. All the day. Glory. All the day.

II SUNDAY OF NOVEMBER

I Nocturn

From the Book of Ezechiel the Prophet, c. 21, 1 - 15

II Nocturn

From the Exposition of St. Jerome, Priest,
on Ezechiel the Prophet

Because Ezechiel had said above, "They say to me: 'Does not this man speak by parables?'" and because the people had demanded a clear meaning, therefore the Lord now speaks more plainly that which He spoke by metaphor or parable, or, as others translate, by proverb. He says that the forest of Nageb and Darom and Thamen are figures of Jerusalem and its temple, the

Holy of Holies, and all the land of Judea, and that flame which shall consume the forest is to be understood as the devouring sword which has been drawn from its sheath to cut off the just and the wicked. The green wood and the dry are figures of the just and the wicked. Wherefore the Lord also says:. "For if in the green wood they do these things, what shall be done in the dry?"

At first He had said: "Set thy face against the way of the south, and drop towards the south, and prophesy against the forest of the south field." Because this seemed obscure and the people did not understand the words of the Prophet, it is on the second occasion stated that the south forest is Jerusalem, and all the fruitful trees, to whose roots the ax will be laid, are to be understood as its inhabitants, and the fire is to be interpreted as the sword.

In the third place the Prophet is commanded that, when they are silent, not asking why he has prophesied these things, he should do things because of which he may be questioned, and should answer the things which the Lord has spoken. "Sigh," said the Lord, "cry aloud, not with a weak voice nor with restricted grief, but with the breaking of thy loins that thy groaning may come from thine innermost being and from the bitterness of thy soul."

"And you shall do this before them, that when they shall ask you why you are shaken with such great sorrow, and what evil has befallen you that you mourn in such a manner, you may answer them in my words: 'For this reason do I weep, and cannot hide the sorrow of my heart, because the warning which is continuously resounding in my ears shall be fulfilled in deed and is now coming, namely, the approaching army of the fierce Babylonian. Then, when he shall have come and surrounded Jerusalem, every heart shall melt and all hands shall be made feeble, so that the minds of men being filled with terror, no one will dare fight back.' "

℞. We looked for peace and it came not; we sought good and behold trouble; we acknowledge, O Lord, our wickedness: * Forget us not forever. ℣. We have sinned, we have done wickedly, we have acted unjustly, O Lord, against all Thy justices. Forget. Glory. Forget.

III SUNDAY OF NOVEMBER

I Nocturn

From the Book of Daniel the Prophet, c. 1, 1 - 15

III Sunday Of November

II Nocturn

From the Book of St. Athanasius, Bishop, to Virgins

Should some come up to you and say, "Do not fast often lest you become weak," do not believe them nor give ear to them. For by them the enemy suggests these things. Be mindful of that which is written—how, when the three young men and Daniel and other youths were taken captive by Nabuchodonosor, king of Babylon, and it was ordered that they should eat of the king's own table and drink of his wine, Daniel and the three young men were unwilling to be defiled with the king's table, but spoke to the eunuch who had received them in his care: "Give us some vegetables, and we shall eat." To whom the eunuch answered: "I fear the king, who hath appointed you meat and drink, lest your faces appear leaner than the other youths' who are fed from the royal table, and he punish me."

They said to him: "Try thy servants for ten days, and give us vegetables." So he gave them vegetables to eat and water to drink; and he brought them before the king, and their faces appeared fairer than the other youths' who were fed from the royal table. Do you see what fasting does? It heals sickness; it dries the humors of the body, puts demons to flight, drives out lewd thoughts, makes the mind cleaner, makes the heart pure, sanctifies the body, and finally, presents man before God's throne.

Think not that these things are said rashly; you have witness of this very matter given by the Savior in the Gospels. For when the disciples asked how unclean spirits might be cast out, the Lord replied: "This kind is not cast out but by prayer and fasting." Whoever, therefore, is troubled by an unclean spirit, if he recognizes it and uses this remedy—fasting—I declare the oppressed evil spirit will straightway depart, fearful of the strength of fasting. For the demons mightily delight in surfeit, drunkenness, and bodily luxuries.

There is great strength in fasting, and great and notable things are done by it. By what other way would men accomplish such marvelous things, would miracles be performed by them, would God grant through them health to the sick, except, to be sure, through spiritual exercises and humility of mind and a good life? For fasting is the food of angels, and whoever employs it is to be reckoned of angelic rank.

℟. The Lord hath sent His angel and hath shut up the mouth of the lions, * And they have not hurt me, forasmuch as before Him injustice hath not been found in me. ℣. God hath sent His mercy and His truth: He hath delivered my soul from the midst of the young lions. And they. Glory. And they.

IV SUNDAY OF NOVEMBER

I Nocturn

From the Book of Osee the Prophet, c. 1, 1 - 11

II Nocturn

From the Book of St. Augustine, Bishop, on the City of God

The Prophet Osee, in that he speaks the more profoundly, is understood with so much the more difficulty. But something must be selected from him, and set down here according to our promise. "And it shall come to pass," he says, "that in the place where it was said to them, 'you are not my people,' they shall be called the very sons of the living God." The apostles also understood that this was a prophetic testimony concerning the calling of the Gentiles, who did not belong to God before.

And because this people of the Gentiles also is spiritually among the sons of Abraham, it is by this fact rightly named Israel; consequently he continues and declares: "And the children of Juda, and the children of Israel shall be gathered together: and they shall appoint themselves one head, and shall come up out of the land."

If we wish to explain this further, the eloquence of the prophetic word will suffer. But let the reader recall the cornerstone, and those two walls, one of the Jews, the other of the Gentiles, and they will be recognized, the one by the name of the sons of Juda, the other by the name of the sons of Israel, leaning on their one Head, and coming up out of the land.

Moreover, that these carnal Israelites who now do not wish to believe in Christ afterwards will believe, that is, their children will believe (for these indeed will by death pass to their proper place), the same Prophet is witness to, saying: "For the children of Israel shall sit many days without king, and without prince, and without sacrifice, and without altar, and without priesthood, and without revelation." Who does not see that so the Jews are now?

℟. Before the face of Thine anger, O God, the whole earth is troubled: * But Thou, O Lord, have mercy, and make not an end utterly. ℣. O Lord, our Lord, how admirable is Thy name! But Thou. Glory. But Thou.

V SUNDAY OF NOVEMBER

I Nocturn

From the Book of Micheas the Prophet, c. 1, 1 - 9

II Nocturn

Sermon of St. Basil the Great on Psalm 33

Whenever the desire to sin comes upon you, I wish you would consider that dreadful and awful tribunal of Christ where the judge will sit upon a high and elevated throne, and every creature will stand before Him, trembling at His glorious appearance. Every single one of us must be led before Him to give an account of whatever we have done in this life.

Near to those who have perpetrated many evils in this life certain terrifying and ugly angels will take their stand, bearing fiery countenances and breathing fire, by which they show their animosity of will and intention, and in mien like to the night, because of their grief and hatred towards the human race.

On this point consider the deep abyss, the impenetrable darkness, the fire lacking brilliance, having indeed the power to burn, yet without light; then consider a kind of worm giving forth poison, feasting on the flesh, eating insatiably, never feeling any satiety, inflicting unbearable torture by its gnawing. And besides all this, think also of that hate and eternal pandemonium which is the gravest of all torments. Fear these things, and, chastened by this fear, curb your soul from the desire of sin as with a bridle.

The Prophet promised that he would teach this fear of the Lord, but he did not promise simply that he would teach, but he promised to teach those alone who wished to hear him; not those who have wandered afar off, but those who run to him desiring salvation; not strangers to the promises, but those who were reconciled and united to the Word Himself by the Baptism of the adoption of sons. Wherefore he says, "Come," that is, "Through good works approach me, O my sons, who indeed by regeneration have been made worthy to become sons of light. Hear, you who have the ears of your heart open; I shall teach you the fear of the Lord"—of Him, namely, whom we described a little before in our discourse.

℟. Leave me not, O Lord, father and ruler of my life, lest I fall before my adversaries: * Lest my enemy rejoice over me. ℣. Take hold of arms and shield and rise up to help me. Lest. Glory. Lest.

HOMILIES AND GOSPELS
FOR THE SUNDAYS AFTER PENTECOST
✠

IV SUNDAY AFTER PENTECOST
III Nocturn
The reading of the holy Gospel according to St. Luke

At that time, while the crowds were pressing upon Jesus to hear the word of God, he was standing by Lake Genesareth. And so forth.

Homily of St. Ambrose, Bishop

When the Lord imparted to so many such a variety of cures, the people could be restrained neither by time nor place from their quest for health. Evening came, still they followed Him; He went down to the lake, they pressed upon Him; and therefore He entered into Peter's boat. This is that boat which, according to St. Matthew, still weathers the storms of this life, and, according to St. Luke, is filled with fishes; this is said that you may understand that the beginnings of the Church are troubled, but afterwards she is fruitful.

Now the fish are those Christians who yet travail in this life. At times Christ seems to sleep, at times He commands, but He is always with His disciples; to the tepid He seems to sleep, to the perfect He keeps watch. His ship (the Church) is never troubled; in it, prudence holds the helm; treachery has no place; and faith fills the sails. Indeed, how could it be troubled since over it He presides in whom the Church has her firm foundation? Hence there is anxiety where faith is weak, while security reigns where love is perfect.

Although to others it is commanded that they let down their nets, to Peter alone is it said, "Launch out into the deep," that is, into the depths of disputed questions. For what is so deep as to gaze upon the depth of all riches, to know the Son of God, and to take on oneself to profess the divine generation? This is that which the mind cannot fully comprehend by the investigation of reason alone, but which the fullness of faith embraces.

For albeit it is not given me to know how He was born, nevertheless, concerning the fact that He was born, I must not be ignorant. I know not the exact order of His generation; but the Author of that generation I do know. We were not present when the Son of God was born of the Father, but we were present when He was called the Son of God by the Father. If we do not believe God, whom shall we believe? For whatsoever we believe, we believe either because we have seen it or have heard it. Sight is often deceived; hearing is based on faith.

℟. God heareth all things: He hath sent His angel, and taken me from guarding my father's sheep: * And He hath anointed me with the oil of His mercy. ℣. The Lord, who delivered me out of the mouth of the lion, and freed me from the paw of the wild beast. And. Glory. And.

☩ Continuation of the holy Gospel according to St. Luke.— At that time, while the crowds were pressing upon Jesus to hear the word of God, he was standing by Lake Genesareth. And he saw two boats moored by the lake, but the fishermen had gotten out of them and were washing their nets. And getting into one of the boats, the one that was Simon's, he asked him to put out a little from the land. And sitting down, he began to teach the crowds from the boat. And when he had ceased speaking, he said to Simon, "Put out into the deep, and lower your nets for a catch."

And Simon answered and said to him, "Master, the whole night through we have toiled and have taken nothing; but at thy word I will lower the net." And when they had done so, they enclosed a great number of fishes, but their net was breaking. And they beckoned to their comrades in the other boat to come and help them. And they came and filled both the boats, so that they began to sink.

But when Simon Peter saw this, he fell down at Jesus' knees, saying: "Depart from me, for I am a sinful man, O Lord." For he and all who were with him were amazed at the catch of fish they had made; and so were also James and John, the sons of Zebedee, who were partners with Simon. And Jesus said to Simon, "Do not be afraid; henceforth thou shalt catch men." And when they had brought their boats to land, they left all and followed him.

Let Us Pray

Grant, we beseech Thee, O Lord, that for us the affairs of the world may be peacefully directed according to Thy plan and Thy Church may be made joyful by a peaceful devotion. Through our Lord.

V SUNDAY AFTER PENTECOST

III Nocturn

The reading of the holy Gospel according to St. Matthew

At that time Jesus said to his disciples: "Unless your justice exceeds that of the Scribes and Pharisees, you shall not enter the kingdom of heaven." And so forth.

Homily of St. Augustine, Bishop

The righteousness of the Pharisees consists in this, that they do not kill; the righteousness of those who are to enter the kingdom of Heaven requires that they be not angry without cause. The least, therefore, is not to kill, and whosoever will have broken that commandment will be called the least in the kingdom of heaven. But he who shall have kept this commandment not to kill, will not immediately be perfect and fit for the kingdom of heaven, although he has made some progress; he will be perfected, however, if he does not become angry without cause; if he keep this, he will be the farther off from murder.

Therefore He who teaches that we should not become angry does not destroy the law which forbids killing, but rather fulfills it. Let us then keep ourselves innocent externally by not killing, and inwardly in our hearts by not becoming angry. There are indeed various degrees in these sins, the first of which is that, while being angry, one nevertheless retains the motion of passion hidden in his heart. Now if the motion of anger should extort a cry from the indignant one—not meaning anything definite, but betraying the inner state of his soul—it is more serious than if the arising anger were repressed in silence.

If, however, not only a general exclamation of indignation is heard, but also a word designating a definite censure against him at whom it is directed, who will doubt that this is more than if merely a general expletive of anger had been uttered? Behold now the three degrees of guilt, that of judgment, of the council, and of the fire of Gehenna. For in judgment there is still room for defense.

In the council, however, although there is also generally a judgment, yet because the very distinction demands that some difference be admitted here, it seems that the pronouncement of the sentence pertains to the council. Here it is no longer a question whether the guilty one is to be condemned, but those who judge confer among themselves as to what punishment should be inflicted on him who is evidently to be condemned. In the fire of Gehenna there is no doubt concerning the guilt as in the judgment, nor concerning the punishment as in the council, but here the condemnation is certain as well as the punishment of the one condemned.

℟. Prepare your hearts for the Lord and serve Him only: * And He will deliver you out of the hands of your enemies. ℣. Turn to the Lord with all your hearts, and put away the strange gods from among you. And. Glory. And.

VI Sunday After Pentecost

✠ Continuation of the holy Gospel according to St. Matthew.— At that time Jesus said to his disciples: Unless your justice exceeds that of the Scribes and Pharisees, you shall not enter the kingdom of heaven.

"You have heard that it was said to the ancients, 'Thou shalt not kill'; and that whoever shall murder shall be liable to judgment. But I say to you that everyone who is angry with his brother, shall be liable to judgment; and whoever says to his brother, 'Raca,' shall be liable to the Sanhedrin; and whoever says, 'Thou fool!' shall be liable to the fire of Gehenna. Therefore, if thou art offering thy gift at the altar, and there rememberest that thy brother has anything against thee, leave thy gift before the altar and go first to be reconciled to thy brother, and then come and offer thy gift."

Let Us Pray

O God, who hast prepared unseen blessings for those who love Thee, pour forth into our hearts a love for Thee, that loving Thee in all things and above all things, we may obtain Thy promises, which surpass all our desires. Through our Lord.

VI SUNDAY AFTER PENTECOST

III Nocturn

The reading of the holy Gospel according to St. Mark

At that time, when again there was a great crowd, and they had nothing to eat, Jesus called his disciples together and said to them, "I have compassion on the crowd, for behold, they have now been with me three days, and have nothing to eat." And so forth.

Homily of St. Ambrose, Bishop

After she who was a type of the Church had been healed from the flow of blood and the apostles had been appointed to preach the Kingdom of God, the food of heavenly grace was given. But notice to whom it was given—not to the idle, not in the city, as, for instance, in the synagogue or to those residing in worldly splendor—but in a desert place to those seeking Christ.

For those who are not fastidious are received by Christ, and with these the Word of God speaks, not of worldly things, but of the Kingdom of God. And if any bear with them the ulcers of carnal passions, He freely gives to them His medicine. It was therefore as a consequence that He relieved by a spiritual food the fasting of those whom He had cured of the affliction of wounds.

Hence, no man receives the food of Christ unless he first be healed; moreover, those who are called to the supper are first healed by the invitation. If one was lame, he received the power to walk that he might come; if deprived of the light of his eyes, he could certainly not enter into the house of the Lord unless his sight were restored.

Everywhere, therefore, is preserved the order of the sacraments, so that first medicine is applied to the wounds by the remission of sins, and then one abounds with the food of the heavenly table; for truly this multitude may not yet feed upon the stronger meats nor pasture their hearts, as yet devoid of a more solid faith, upon the body and blood of Christ. "I gave you milk to drink," says St. Paul, "and not meat; for hitherto you were not able to bear it, but neither indeed are ye now able." The five loaves are, in a certain manner, your milk; the stronger meat is the body of Christ; the stronger drink is the blood of the Lord.

℟. The number of my sins is greater than the sands on the seashore, and my sins are multiplied: and I am not worthy to look up to the height of heaven because of the multitude of my iniquities: for I have provoked Thy wrath, * And done evil in Thy sight. ℣. For I acknowledge my iniquity: and my sin is continually before me, for against Thee only have I sinned. And done. Glory. And done.

✠ Continuation of the holy Gospel according to St. Mark.— At that time, when again there was a great crowd, and they had nothing to eat, Jesus called his disciples together and said to them, "I have compassion on the crowd, for behold, they have now been with me three days, and have nothing to eat; and if I send them away to their homes fasting, they will faint on the way, for some of them have come from a distance." And his disciples answered him, "How will anyone be able to satisfy these with bread, here in a desert?" And he asked them, "How many loaves have you?" And they said, "Seven."

And he bade the crowd recline on the ground. Then taking the seven loaves, he gave thanks, broke them and gave them to his disciples to distribute; and they set them before the crowd. And they had a few little fishes; and he blessed them, and ordered them to be distributed. And they ate and were satisfied; and they took up what was left of the fragments, seven baskets. Now those who had eaten were about four thousand. And he dismissed them.

Let Us Pray

O God all powerful, who art all good, implant in our hearts a love of Thy name and increase within us the spirit of piety; and as Thou dost foster and care for the good that is within us, so mayest Thou also protect what Thou dost foster. Through our Lord.

VII SUNDAY AFTER PENTECOST

III Nocturn

The reading of the holy Gospel according to St. Matthew

At that time Jesus said to his disciples: "Beware of false prophets, who come to you in sheep's clothing, but inwardly are ravenous wolves." And so forth.

Homily of St. Hilary, Bishop

Our Lord here warns us that we must weigh the worth of flattering words and a seeming meekness by the fruits which they that manifest such things bring forth in their deeds, and that, to see what a man is, we should look not at his words, but at his deeds. For in many there is concealed the fierceness of a wolf under sheep's clothing. But as thorns do not produce grapes, nor thistles, figs, and as evil trees do not bring forth good fruit, so neither in these men, the Lord teaches, is there found the fruit of good works, and therefore all are to be judged by their fruits.

For lip-service alone will not procure for us the Kingdom of Heaven, nor will he who will say, "Lord, Lord," be an heir thereof. What recompense is there in saying to the Lord, "Lord"? Will He not be the Lord unless He be called so by us? And what is the holiness of this service, this calling of a name, when obedience rather to God's Will, not the invocation of a name, will discover for us the way to the heavenly kingdom?

"Many will say to me in that day: 'Lord, Lord, have we not prophesied in thy name?'" Here the Lord condemns the deceit of false prophets and the shams of hypocrites, who take to themselves glory by reason of the power of their words, their prophesying in teaching, their casting out of devils, and such like mighty works. Because of these things they promise themselves the Kingdom of Heaven, as though what they speak or do were anything of their own and not rather the power of God which, when invoked, brings all things to a successful end; for it is reading that brings knowledge and the name of Christ that agitates the devils.

That blessed eternity must be merited by us; we must give something of our own by willing what is good, by shunning every evil, by obeying the heavenly precepts with our whole heart, that by such acts we may be friends of God. Let us therefore do what

God wills rather than boast of what He can do. And we must repudiate and thrust away those who have turned from the knowledge of Him to works of iniquity.

℟. Saul slew his thousands, and David his ten thousands: * For the hand of the Lord was with him; he struck the Philistine and took away the reproach from Israel. ℣. Is not this David of whom they sang in chorus, saying: Saul slew his thousands and David his ten thousands. For. Glory. For.

✠ Continuation of the holy Gospel according to St. Matthew.— At that time Jesus said to his disciples: "Beware of false prophets, who come to you in sheep's clothing, but inwardly are ravenous wolves. By their fruits you will know them. Do men gather grapes from thorns, or figs from thistles? Even so, every good tree bears good fruit, nor can a bad tree bear good fruit. Every tree that does not bear good fruit is cut down and thrown into the fire. Therefore, by their fruits you will know them.

"Not everyone who says to me, 'Lord, Lord,' shall enter the kingdom of heaven; but he who does the will of my Father in heaven shall enter the kingdom of heaven."

Let Us Pray

O God, whose Providence doth not fail in its plans, we humbly beseech Thee to take away from us whatever is harmful and grant unto us whatever it good for us. Through our Lord.

VIII SUNDAY AFTER PENTECOST

III Nocturn

The reading of the holy Gospel according to St. Luke

At that time Jesus spoke to his disciples this parable: "There was a certain rich man who had a steward, who was reported to him as squandering his possessions." And so forth.

Homily of St. Jerome, Priest

If the dispenser of the mammon of iniquity is praised by his master because he provided justice for himself by an evil action, and if the master, suffering the loss of what was spent, praises the prudence of the steward because he acted prudently for himself—though deceitfully with his master—how much more will Christ, who can sustain no loss, and is so prone to clemency, praise His disciples if they have been merciful to those who were to believe in Him?

Then, after the parable, He said: "And I say to you: Make to yourselves friends of the mammon of iniquity." Riches which are collected unjustly are called *mammon*, not in the Hebrew, but in the Syrian tongue. If therefore iniquity well dispensed is turned to justice, how much more will the divine word, in which there is no iniquity, and which was entrusted to the apostles, if it be well dispensed, lift its dispensers up to heaven?

Hence it follows, "He that is faithful in that which is least," that is, in carnal things, "is faithful also in that which is greater," that is in spiritual things. But he who is malicious in a small thing, so that he would not even give to his brother to use what has been created by God for all men, the same would also be malicious in distributing spiritual coin, and would not distribute the teaching of the Lord according to necessity, but in respect of persons.

"But if," He said, "you do not care well for worldly riches which pass away, who will entrust to you the true and eternal riches of the doctrine of God? And if in those things which are foreign (and everything which is of the world is foreign to us) you have been unfaithful, who will entrust to you those things which are yours and properly given over to man?"

℞. Remember, O Lord, Thy covenant, and say to the destroying Angel: Hold now thy hand, * That the land be not laid waste, and that Thou destroy not every living soul. ℣. I am he who has sinned; I have done wickedly: these that are sheep, what have they done? I beseech Thee, O Lord, let Thine anger be turned from Thy people. That. Glory. That.

✠ Continuation of the holy Gospel according to St. Luke.— At that time Jesus spoke to his disciples this parable: "There was a certain rich man who had a steward, who was reported to him as squandering his possessions. And he called him and said to him, 'What is this that I hear of thee? Make an accounting of thy stewardship, for thou canst be steward no longer.'

"And the steward said within himself, 'What shall I do, seeing that my master is taking away the stewardship from me? To dig I am not able; to beg I am ashamed. I know what I shall do, that when I am removed from my stewardship they may receive me into their houses.' And he summoned each of his master's debtors and said to the first, 'How much dost thou owe my master?' And he said, 'A hundred jars of oil.' He said to him, 'Take thy bond and sit down at once and write fifty.' Then he said to another, 'How much dost thou owe?' He said, 'A hundred kors of wheat.' He said to him, 'Take thy bond and write eighty.'

"And the master commended the unjust steward, in that he had acted prudently; for the children of this world are in relation to their own generation more prudent than are the children of the light. And I say to you, make friends for yourselves with the mammon of wickedness, so that when you fail they may receive you into the everlasting dwellings."

LET US PRAY

Grant to us, we beseech Thee, O Lord, the spirit of always thinking and of doing what is right, that we, who cannot live without Thee, by Thy help may live according to Thy Will. Through our Lord.

IX SUNDAY AFTER PENTECOST
III Nocturn

The reading of the holy Gospel according to St. Luke

At that time when Jesus drew near to Jerusalem and saw the city, he wept over it, saying, "If thou hadst known, in this thy day, even thou, the things that are for thy peace! But now they are hidden from thy eyes." And so forth.

Homily of St. Gregory, Pope

No one who has read the history of the destruction of Jerusalem effected by the Roman princes, Vespasian and Titus, can be ignorant that it is that destruction which is described by our Lord with tears. These Roman princes are indicated when it is said: "For the days shall come upon thee, and thy enemies shall enclose thee with a wall."

The very destruction of that same city even now testifies to the prophecy in which is added: "And they shall not leave in thee a stone upon a stone." For, while the walls have now been reconstructed outside the gate in that place where the Lord was crucified, the old Jerusalem, as history relates, has been totally destroyed.

To this prophecy is added the crime for which this punishment of her destruction was inflicted: "Because thou hast not known the time of thy visitation." Behold, the Creator of men deigned through the mystery of His incarnation to visit this city, but she was unmindful of His love and solicitude. On account of this the very birds of the air are brought forward by the Prophet in his rebuke of the human heart where he says: "The kite in the air hath known her time; the turtle and the swallow and the stork have observed the time of their coming; but my people have not known the judgment of the Lord."

For the Redeemer wept, even before it came to pass, over that destruction of the faithless city which she herself knew not would befall her. To her aptly does the weeping Lord speak: "If thou hadst known, even thou." Supply: "Thou wouldst weep, you who now rejoice, knowing not your impending fate." Whence also it is added: "At least in this thy day, the things that are to thy peace." For while she gave herself up to the pleasures of the flesh and would not foresee coming evils, still in her own day she had those things which could have been for her peace.

℟. O Lord, Thou hast heard the prayer of Thy servant, that I might build a temple unto Thy name: * Bless and sanctify this house forever, O God of Israel. ℣. O Lord, who keepest covenant with Thy servants that walk before Thee with all their heart. Bless. Glory. Bless.

☩ Continuation of the holy Gospel according to St. Luke.— At that time, when Jesus drew near to Jerusalem and saw the city, he wept over it, saying, "If thou hadst known, in this thy day, even thou, the things that are for thy peace! But now they are hidden from thy eyes. For days will come upon thee when thy enemies will throw up a rampart about thee, and surround thee and shut thee in on every side, and will dash thee to the ground and thy children within thee, and will not leave in thee one stone upon another, because thou hast not known the time of thy visitation."

And he entered the temple, and began to cast out those who were selling and buying in it, saying to them, "It is written, 'My house is a house of prayer,' but you have made it a den of thieves."

And he was teaching daily in the temple.

Let Us Pray

In Thy mercy, O Lord, mayest Thou be ready to hear the prayers of Thy servants; and that Thou mayest grant unto us what we ask, make us ask for those things which are pleasing to thee. Through our Lord.

X SUNDAY AFTER PENTECOST

III Nocturn

The reading of the holy Gospel according to St. Luke

At that time Jesus spoke this parable also to some who trusted in themselves as being just and despised others. "Two men went up to the temple to pray, the one a Pharisee and the other a publican." And so forth.

X Sunday After Pentecost

Homily of St. Augustine, Bishop

The Pharisee might at least have said: "I am not like *many* men." Who are the "rest of men" save all but himself? "I," he says, "am just; the rest are sinners. I am not like the rest of men, unjust, robbers, adulterers." And notice for yourself how from the publican nearby there arose the occasion for greater arrogance. "Such as," he says, "that publican." "I," he adds, "stand alone; he is of the rest of men. I am not such a one as he because of my good works, by reason of which I am not a sinner."

"I fast twice a week; I give tithes of all I possess." Seek in his words what he asked of God; you will find nothing. He came up to pray; he does not wish to beg for aught of God but rather to praise himself. It is not enough for him to ask nothing of God, and instead, to praise himself; yea, more, he even insults him who is praying.

The publican stood afar off, yet he was near to God. The consciousness of his own sinful heart held him back; piety drew him forward. The publican indeed stood afar off, but the Lord heard him from very near. For the Lord is high and regardeth the lowly, but the exalted, as was this Pharisee, He knoweth from afar. The exalted He knoweth indeed from a distance, but He does not overlook them.

Hear further of the humility of the publican. That he stood at a distance is not all; he did not even raise his eyes to heaven. That he might be looked upon, he did not look up; he dared not raise his eyes. His conscience oppressed him, but hope raised him up. Hear further: He struck his breast. Of himself he sought punishment; therefore was the Lord indulgent to him who was so penitent. He struck his breast, saying: "Lord, be merciful to me, a sinner." Behold what sort of man it was who asked! What wonder that God forgives sins when they are so acknowledged by the sinner.

℟. Hearken, O Lord, to the hymn and the prayer which Thy servant prayeth before Thee this day, that Thy eyes may be opened, and Thy ears attentive, * Upon this house day and night. ℣. Look down, O Lord, from Thy holy place, and from Thy dwelling in the height of heaven. Upon. Glory. Upon.

☩ Continuation of the holy Gospel according to St. Luke.—At that time, Jesus spoke this parable also to some who trusted in themselves as being just and despised others. "Two men went up to the temple to pray, the one a Pharisee and the other a publican. The Pharisee stood and began to pray thus within himself: 'O God, I thank thee that I am not like the rest of men, robbers, dishonest, adulterers, or even like this publican. I fast twice a week; I pay tithes of all that I possess.' But the publican, standing afar off, would not so much as lift up his eyes to heaven, but kept striking his breast, saying, 'O God, be merciful to me the sinner!'

"I tell you, this man went back to his home justified rather than the other; for everyone who exalts himself shall be humbled, and he who humbles himself shall be exalted."

Let Us Pray

O God, who dost manifest Thy great power by sparing and by having mercy on us, increase Thy mercy towards us and make those who hasten forward to Thy promises to be sharers in Thy heavenly blessings. Through our Lord.

XI SUNDAY AFTER PENTECOST
III Nocturn

The reading of the holy Gospel according to St. Mark

At that time, Jesus, departing again from the district of Tyre, came by way of Sidon to the sea of Galilee, through the midst of the district of Decapolis. And so forth.

Homily of St. Gregory, Pope

Why is it that God, the Creator of all things, wishing to heal the deaf and dumb man, put His fingers into his ears and, spitting, touched his tongue? What are signified by the fingers of the Redeemer if not the gifts of the Holy Spirit? With reference to this He spoke on another occasion when He had cast out a devil: "If I by the finger of God cast out devils, doubtless the kingdom of God is come upon you." Moreover, by another Evangelist He is described as saying: "If by the Spirit of God I cast out devils, then is the kingdom of God come upon you." By comparing both of these texts, we must conclude that the Spirit is called the finger.

To place His fingers, then, into the ears is to open, by means of the gifts of the Holy Spirit, the deaf man's mind to obedience. But why is it that He touched his tongue with spittle? Saliva from the mouth of the Redeemer represents the wisdom that comes to us in the divine discourse. For saliva flows from the head into the mouth. That wisdom, therefore, which He Himself is, when touched to our tongue, is soon formed into words of preaching.

"And looking up to heaven, he sighed"; not that it was necessary for Him, who Himself gave what He prayed for, to sigh, but He taught us to send up our sighs to Him who presides in heaven in order that our ears also might be opened by the gifts of the Holy Spirit and our tongue loosed for the preaching of the word by the saliva of His mouth, that is, by the knowledge of the divine word.

Now to him it is presently said, "Ephpheta," that is, "Be thou opened." And straightway his ears were opened and the bond of his tongue was loosed. Here it is to be noted that it was because of the closed ears that it was said, "Be thou opened." But to him, the ears of whose heart have been opened to obedience, without doubt the bond of his tongue is also loosed, so that the good which he himself does he might exhort others to do also. Whence it is appropriately added: "And he spoke right." For he speaks rightly who first does himself by obedience what he afterwards, by his preaching, admonishes to be done.

℟. Remember, O Lord, Thy covenant and say to the destroying angel: Hold now thy hand, * That the land be not laid waste, and that Thou destroy not every living soul. ℣. I am he who has sinned, I have done wickedly: these that are sheep, 'what have they done? I beseech Thee, O Lord, let Thine anger be turned away from Thy people. That. Glory. That.

☩ Continuation of the holy Gospel according to St. Mark.— At that time, Jesus, departing again from the district of Tyre, came by way of Sidon to the sea of Galilee, through the midst of the district of Decapolis. And they brought to him one deaf and dumb, and entreated him to lay his hand upon him. And taking him aside from the crowd, he put his fingers into the man's ears, and spitting, he touched his tongue. And looking up to heaven, he sighed, and said to him, "Ephpheta," that is, "Be thou opened." And his ears were at once opened, and the bond of his tongue was loosed, and he began to speak correctly. And he charged them to tell no one. But the more he charged them, so much the more did they continue to publish it. And so much the more did they wonder, saying, "He has done all things well. He has made both the deaf to hear and the dumb to speak."

Let Us Pray

O almighty and eternal God, who in the greatness of Thy love dost exceed our merit and our desires, pour forth Thy mercy upon us, we beseech Thee, and pardon the sins which trouble our conscience and grant those petitions for which our prayers do not presume to ask. Through our Lord.

XII SUNDAY AFTER PENTECOST
III Nocturn

The reading of the holy Gospel according to St. Luke

At that time Jesus said to his disciples: "Blessed are the eyes that see what you see! For I say to you, many prophets and kings have desired to see what you see, and they have not seen it; and to hear what you hear, and they have not heard it." And so forth.

Homily of St. Bede the Venerable, Priest

"Blessed are the eyes"—not those of the Scribes and Pharisees, which saw only the body of the Lord, but those which can know His mysteries, whereof it is said: "And thou hast revealed them to little ones." Blessed are the eyes of the little ones to whom the Son deigned to reveal both Himself and the Father. Abraham rejoiced to see Christ's day: and he saw it and was glad.

Isaias, also, and Micheas and many other prophets saw the glory of the Lord; for that very reason they were called Seers; but perceiving and greeting only from afar, they saw Him, as it were, through a glass and in a dark manner. The apostles, however, having the Lord present with them, and learning by asking whatsoever they wished, had not the slightest need to be taught by angels or by divers kinds of visions.

Those whom Luke speaks of as "many prophets and kings," Matthew more plainly calls "prophets and upright men." For they were great kings in that they knew how to dominate the lurings of temptations by ruling them and not to fall by consenting to them. "And behold, a certain lawyer rose, tempting Him and saying: 'Master, what must I do to possess eternal life?'"

The lawyer who, tempting the Lord, asks about eternal life takes occasion for his question, I suppose, from the words of the Lord: "But you, rejoice that your names are written in heaven." By his very question he manifests how true is that saying of the Lord which He spoke to His Father: "Thou hast hidden these things from the wise and prudent and hast revealed them to little ones."

℟. Before the face of Thine anger, O God, the whole earth is troubled: * But Thou, O Lord, have mercy, and make not an end utterly. ℣. O Lord, our Lord, how admirable is Thy name. But Thou. Glory. But Thou.

☩ Continuation of the holy Gospel according to St. Luke.— At that time Jesus said to his disciples: "Blessed are the eyes that see what you see! For I say to you, many prophets and kings have desired to see what you see, and they have not seen it; and to hear what you hear, and they have not heard it."

And behold, a certain lawyer got up to test him, saying, "Master, what must I do to gain eternal life?" But he said to him, "What is written in the Law? How dost thou read?" He answered and said, "Thou shalt love the Lord thy God with thy whole heart, and with thy whole soul, and with thy whole strength, and with thy whole mind; and thy neighbor as thyself." And he said to him, "Thou hast answered rightly; do this and thou shalt live." But he, wishing to justify himself, said to Jesus, "And who is my neighbor?"

Jesus took him up and said, "A certain man was going down from Jerusalem to Jericho, and he fell in with robbers, who after both stripping him and beating him went their way, leaving him half-dead. But, as it happened, a certain priest was going down the same way; and when he saw him, he passed by. And likewise a Levite also, when he was near the place and saw him, passed by. But a certain Samaritan as he journeyed came upon him, and seeing him, was moved with compassion. And he went up to him and bound up his wounds, pouring on oil and wine. And setting him on his own beast, he brought him to an inn and took care of him. And the next day he took out two denarii and gave them to the innkeeper and said, 'Take care of him; and whatever more thou spendest, I, on my way back, will repay thee.'

"Which of these three, in thy opinion, proved himself neighbor to him who fell among the robbers?" And he said, "He who took pity on him." And Jesus said to him, "Go and do thou also in like manner."

LET US PRAY

O almighty and merciful God, by whose grace Thy people are able to serve Thee in a true and praiseworthy manner, grant unto us, we beseech Thee, that without sin we may hasten to the rewards Thou hast promised. Through our Lord.

XIII SUNDAY AFTER PENTECOST

III Nocturn

The reading of the holy Gospel according to St. Luke

At that time, as Jesus was going to Jerusalem, he was passing between Samaria and Galilee. And as he was entering a certain village, there met him ten lepers. And so forth.

XIII Sunday After Pentecost

Homily of St. Augustine, Bishop

Concerning the ten lepers whom the Lord cleansed when He said, "Go, show yourselves to the priests," it can be asked why He sent them to the priests, that, as they went, they might be made clean. For none of them upon whom He had conferred corporal blessings did He send to the priests except the lepers. For it was from leprosy also that He had cleansed him to whom He said: "Go, show thyself to the priests, and offer for thyself as a testimony to them the sacrifice which Moses commanded."

It is to be sought, therefore, what leprosy signifies, for those who are cured of it are not said to be *healed* but to be *cleansed*. It is indeed a sickness which affects the color (of the skin), not of the health or integrity of the senses or members of the body. Not without reason, therefore, may lepers be understood to signify those who, not having the knowledge of the true Faith, profess various erroneous doctrines. They do not hide their ignorance, but spread it abroad as the highest knowledge, and make it known by the boastfulness of their speech.

Verily there is no false doctrine that does not contain some admixture of truth. Therefore truths mingled haphazard with falsehoods in a single controversy or discussion of a man, as though appearing in the color of one body, signify leprosy, which discolors and soils human bodies by true and false spots of color.

These men must be so shunned by the Church that, being removed far away, they may, if it be possible, cry out to Christ with a loud voice, just as the ten lepers stood afar off and raised their voices, saying: "Jesus, master, have mercy on us." Now even the fact that they styled Him *master* (by which name I know not whether anyone else asked the Lord for a bodily cure), I think is sufficient to show that the leprosy signifies false doctrine, which a good master rectifies.

℞. Blessed is the people * Whom the Lord God hath blessed, saying: Thou art the work of My hands, O Israel, thou art My inheritance. ℣. Blessed is the nation whose God is the Lord, the people whom He hath chosen for His own inheritance. Whom. Glory. Whom.

✠ Continuation of the holy Gospel according to St. Luke.—At that time, as Jesus was going to Jerusalem, he was passing between Samaria and Galilee. And as he was entering a certain village, there met him ten lepers, who stood afar off and lifted up their voice, crying, "Jesus, master, have pity on us." And when he saw them he said, "Go show yourselves to the priests." And it came to pass as they were on their way, that they were

XIV Sunday After Pentecost

made clean. But one of them, seeing that he was made clean, returned, with a loud voice glorifying God, and he fell on his face at his feet, giving thanks; and he was a Samaritan.

But Jesus answered and said, "Were not the ten made clean? But where are the nine? Has no one been found to return and give glory to God except this foreigner?" And he said to him, "Arise, go thy way, for thy faith has saved thee."

Let Us Pray

O almighty and eternal God, grant unto us an increase of faith, hope, and charity; and that we may merit to obtain what Thou dost promise, make us love what Thou dost command. Through our Lord.

XIV SUNDAY AFTER PENTECOST

III Nocturn

The reading of the holy Gospel according to St. Matthew

At that time Jesus said to His disciples: "No man can serve two masters." And so forth.

Homily of St. Augustine, Bishop

"No man can serve two masters." To this point must be added what our Lord subsequently expounds, saying, "For he will either hate the one and love the other; or he will sustain the one and despise the other." These words we must carefully consider, because in the next sentence He points out to us who these two masters are, saying: "You cannot serve God and mammon."

Riches among the Hebrews are said to be called *mammona*. A Punic word corresponds to this, for *mammon* in the language of the Carthaginians means *lucre*. But he who serves mammon serves him indeed who, by reason of his wickedness, is rightly termed by our Lord the ruler of earthly things and "the prince of this world."

"For a man will either hate the one and love the other," that is, God; "or he will sustain the one and despise the other." But whosoever serves mammon serves a hard and evil master. Such a one, involved in crime by his own evil desires, is subject to the devil—though he loves him not. For who is there who loves the devil? And yet he sustains him!

"Therefore," our Lord says, "I say to you, be not solicitous for your life, what you shall eat, nor for your body, what you shall put on," lest perhaps, although superfluities are not sought after, our heart becomes divided because of the necessities themselves, and in the acquisition of these necessities our intention be distorted while we labor seemingly out of mercy, wishing to appear as working for another's welfare, whereas in reality we are looking to our own advantage rather than to his gain. And hence it is that to ourselves we do not seem to be guilty of sin, because we are striving to acquire not superfluities but only the necessities of life.

℟. Give me, O Lord, wisdom that sitteth by Thy throne, and cast me not off from among Thy children: * For I am Thy servant and the son of Thy handmaid. ℣. Send her from the throne of thy greatness, that she may be with me and may labor with me. For. Glory. For.

✠ Continuation of the holy Gospel according to St. Matthew.— At that time Jesus said to his disciples: "No man can serve two masters; for either he will hate the one and love the other, or else he will stand by the one and despise the other. You cannot serve God and mammon.

"Therefore I say to you, do not be anxious for your life, what you shall eat; nor yet for your body, what you shall put on. Is not the life a greater thing than the food, and the body than the clothing? Look at the birds of the air: they do not sow, or reap, or gather into barns; yet your heavenly Father feeds them. Are not you of much more value than they? But which of you by being anxious about it can add to his stature a single cubit?

"And as for clothing, why are you anxious? See how the lilies of the field grow; they neither toil nor spin, yet I say to you that not even Solomon in all his glory was arrayed like one of these. But if God so clothes the grass of the field, which today is alive and tomorrow is thrown into the oven, how much more you, O you of little faith!

"Therefore do not be anxious, saying, 'What shall we eat?' or 'What shall we drink?', or, 'What are we to put on?' (for after all these things the Gentiles seek); for your Father knows that you need all these things. But seek first the kingdom of God and his justice, and all these things shall be given you besides."

LET US PRAY

Protect Thy Church, we beseech Thee, O Lord, with Thy constant care, and since our human weakness doth fail without Thy help, may Thy assisting grace restrain us from evil and guide us in the way of salvation. Through our Lord.

XV SUNDAY AFTER PENTECOST
III Nocturn

The reading of the holy Gospel according to St. Luke

At that time Jesus went to a town called Naim; and his disciples and a large crowd went with him. And so forth.

Homily of St. Augustine, Bishop

The widowed mother rejoiced over her son who had been brought to life again; holy Mother the Church rejoices over those men who, as happens daily, are quickened in the spirit. The former was dead, it is true, in the body, but these latter in the soul. His visible death was bewailed visibly; the invisible death of these latter is neither looked for nor seen. He alone sought them who knew them to be dead. He alone knew them to be dead who could enliven them. For had He not come to quicken the dead the Apostle would never have said: "Arise, you who sleep, and rise up from the dead, and Christ shall enlighten thee."

Only three men do we find who were raised from the dead visibly by the Lord, but we find thousands raised invisibly. But who knows how many dead men He raised visibly to life? For not all things which He did are recorded. "There are also many other things which Jesus did, which, if they were written everyone, the world itself, I think, would not be able to contain the books that should be written." Therefore, beyond question, many others were raised to life; but not without a special reason have these three been recorded.

For our Lord Jesus Christ wished those things to be understood spiritually which He did in the flesh. And neither did He work miracles for the miracles' sake alone, but in order that what He did might inspire wonder in those who see and convey the truth to those who understand. Even as he who sees a book very well written, but knows not how to read, praises indeed the hand of the ancient copyist, admiring the beauty of the characters; but what they mean, what these characters signify, he does not know; with his eyes he praises, but his mind is without understanding.

And as, on the other hand, another both praises the calligraphic skill and grasps its meaning (he, namely, who can not only see, as can all men, but can also read—that which he who has not learned cannot do), even so those who saw the miracles of Christ and knew not what they meant, nor what they hinted at in some way to those who did understand, marvelled only concerning the fact that they were done; others, however, both marvelled at the facts and grasped them with their mind. Such must we all be in the school of Christ.

℟. Prepare your hearts for the Lord and serve Him only: * And He will deliver you out of the hands of your enemies. ℣. Turn to the Lord with all your hearts, and put away the strange gods from among you. And. Glory. And.

✠ Continuation of the holy Gospel according to St. Luke.—
At that time Jesus went to a town called Naim; and his disciples and a large crowd went with him. And as he drew near the gate of the town, behold, a dead man was being carried out, the only son of his mother, and she was a widow; and a large gathering from the town was with her. And the Lord, seeing her, had compassion on her, and said to her, "Do not weep." And he went up and touched the stretcher; and the bearers stood still. And he said, "Young man, I say to thee, arise." And he who was dead, sat up, and began to speak. And he gave him to his mother.

But fear seized upon all, and they began to glorify God, saying, "A great prophet has risen among us," and "God has visited his people."

Let Us Pray

May Thy constant mercy, O Lord, cleanse and strengthen Thy Church, and since without Thy help she cannot be safe, may Thy grace rule and guide her always. Through our Lord.

XVI SUNDAY AFTER PENTECOST

III Nocturn

The reading of the holy Gospel according to St. Luke

At that time, when Jesus entered the house of one of the rulers of the Pharisees on the Sabbath to take food, they were watching him. And behold, there was a certain man before him who had the dropsy. And so forth.

Homily of St. Ambrose, Bishop

First there is cured the man with dropsy, in whom the excess swelling of the flesh rendered the duties of the soul burdensome and extinguished the ardor of the spirit. After that, humility is taught, when at the wedding banquet, desire for a better place is curbed. Mercifully, nevertheless, in order that kindly persuasion might exclude bitterness of coercion, that reason might bring about the effect of persuasion, and correction amend the will.

To this humility, as to its next-door neighbor, kindness is joined. And by the Lord's own saying it may thus be recognized if it be shown to the poor and the weak; for to be hospitable to those able to return your hospitality is to be moved by avarice. And finally, just as a salary is prescribed to a soldier only as a recompense, as it were, for the riches that must be contemned, so also he who, intent on lower desires, has procured for himself earthly possessions, cannot attain to the Kingdom of Heaven, for the Lord said: "Sell all that thou hast and follow me."

Nor yet he who bought the oxen; for Eliseus killed what oxen he had and divided them amongst the people. And he who has taken a wife will think on the things of the world, and not of God. Not because marriage is disapproved, but because virginal chastity is called the greater honor; for the unmarried woman and the widow think on those things that are the Lord's—how they may be holy in body and soul.

But that we may again be in favor, as above with widows, so now with married people—we do not exclude that opinion, held by many, namely, that we reckon only three kinds of men to be excluded from fellowship in that great banquet: pagans, Jews, and heretics. And therefore it is that the Apostle tells us that we must flee avarice, lest, weighed down in pagan fashion with iniquity, malice, lewdness, and avarice, we be unable to come to Christ's kingdom. For "no unclean person, or covetous one (which is idolatry) has any inheritance in the kingdom of Christ and God."

℞. Why have you detracted the words of truth? You dress up speeches only to rebuke, and you endeavor to overthrow your friend: * However, finish what you have in mind. ℣. Judge what is just and you shall not find iniquity in my tongue. However. Glory. However.

☩ Continuation of the holy Gospel according to St. Luke.— At that time, when Jesus entered the house of one of the rulers of the Pharisees on the Sabbath to take food, they were watching him. And behold, there was a certain man before him who had the dropsy. And Jesus asked the lawyers and Pharisees, saying, "Is it lawful to cure on the Sabbath?"

But they remained silent. And he took and healed him and let him go. Then addressing them, he said, "Which of you shall have an ass or an ox fall into a pit, and will not immediately draw him up on the Sabbath?" And they could give him no answer to these things.

But he also spoke a parable to those invited, observing how they were choosing the first places at table, and he said to them, "When thou art invited to a wedding feast, do not recline in the first place, lest perhaps one more distinguished than thou have been invited by him, and he who invited thee and him come and say to thee, 'Make room for this man'; and then thou begin with shame to take the last place. But when thou art invited, go and recline in the last place; that when he who invited thee comes in, he may say to thee, 'Friend, go up higher!' Then thou wilt be honored in the presence of all who are at table with thee. For everyone who exalts himself shall be humbled, and he who humbles himself shall be exalted."

Let Us Pray

May Thy grace, we beseech Thee, O Lord, always precede and follow our actions, and may it make us always faithful in performing good works. Through our Lord.

XVII SUNDAY AFTER PENTECOST

III Nocturn

The reading of the holy Gospel according to St. Matthew

At that time the Pharisees came to Jesus, and one of them, a doctor of the Law, putting him to the test, asked him, "Master, which is the great commandment in the Law?" And so forth.

Homily of St. John Chrysostom

After the Sadducees had been put to confusion, the Pharisees once again came forward. When it behooved them to forbear, they desired to dispute; and wishing not to learn, but to tempt the Lord, they sent one to the fore who professed a knowledge of the Law. Thus they ask what is the first commandment in the Law. Now since the first is this, "Love the Lord thy God," they question Him in this manner thinking that He would take occasion to correct this precept by adding something to it, because He made Himself God.

What then did Christ say? In order to show that they had brought up these questions because they themselves possessed no charity, but instead were languishing under an envious ill-will, He said: "Thou shalt love the Lord thy God. This is the first and great commandment. The second is like to this: Thou shalt love thy neighbor as thyself."

How is the second like to the first? Because the first leads to the second, and on its part is strengthened by the second. "For whosoever dealeth perversely, hateth the light and cometh not to the light." And again: "The fool said in his heart: 'There is no God.'" Then this follows: "They are corrupt and become

XVII Sunday After Pentecost

abominable in their ways." And again: "The root of all evils is avarice; and those addicted to it have strayed from the faith." And, "He who loveth me keepeth my commandments," of which the head and root is, "Thou shalt love the Lord thy God and thy neighbor as thyself."

If then to love God is to love one's neighbor ("for if you love me, Peter," He said, "feed my sheep"), if, too, the love of your neighbor makes you observe the commandments, then He rightly says that upon these two commandments depend the whole Law and the Prophets. And as before, when He was asked about the Resurrection, He taught them more than they, tempting Him, had asked, so also here, being asked concerning the first commandment, He of His own accord declares the second to be not far inferior to the first, "for the second is like to the first." And thus He tactfully insinuated that in their queries they were goaded on by hate. "For charity," St. Paul tells us, "envieth not."

℟. Bless ye the God of heaven, give glory to Him in the sight of all that live, * Because He hath shown His mercy to you. ℣. Bless ye Him and sing praises to Him: and publish all His wonderful works. Because. Glory. Because.

✠ Continuation of the holy Gospel according to St. Matthew.— At that time the Pharisees came to Jesus, and one of them, a doctor of the Law, putting him to the test, asked him, "Master, which is the great commandment in the Law?" Jesus said to him, " 'Thou shalt love the Lord thy God with thy whole heart, and with thy whole soul, and with thy whole mind.' This is the greatest and the first commandment. And the second is like it, 'Thou shalt love thy neighbor as thyself.' On these two commandments depend the whole Law and the Prophets."

Now while the Pharisees were gathered together, Jesus questioned them, saying, "What do you think of the Christ? Whose son is he?" They said to him, "David's." He said to them, "How then does David in the Spirit call him Lord, saying, 'The Lord said to my Lord: Sit thou at my right hand, till I make thy enemies the footstool of thy feet'? If David, therefore, calls him 'Lord,' how is he his son?" And no one could answer him a word; neither did anyone dare from that day forth to ask him any more questions.

Let Us Pray

Grant Thy people, we beseech Thee, O Lord, to avoid all the sinful influences of the devil and with a pure mind to serve Thee, the only true God. Through our Lord.

XVIII SUNDAY AFTER PENTECOST
III Nocturn

The reading of the holy Gospel according to St. Matthew

At that time, getting into a boat, Jesus crossed over and came to his own town. And so forth.

Homily of St. Peter Chrysologus

Today's Gospel shows that Christ by human actions effected divine mysteries, and with visible things carried out invisible activities. "He entered into a boat," it tells us, "and passed over the water, and came into his own city." Is this not He who, having driven back the waves, laid bare the depths of the sea that the people of Israel might pass dry-shod between the stilled waters as through the hollows of the mountains?

Is this not He who inclined the crests of the sea to the feet of Peter so that the watery way might present to his feet a solid footing? Then how does it happen that He here refuses for Himself this service of the sea in order to make the crossing of such a small lake by the hire of a ship? "He went up," it says, "into a boat, and crossed over the sea."

But why do you wonder, brethren? Christ came to take on Himself our infirmities and to confer on us His strength; to seek that which is human, to give what is divine; to receive injuries, to bestow honors; to take away all troubles, to restore what is healthful. For a physician who will not bear infirmities will not know how to heal, and he who will not make himself infirm with the infirm man cannot give him health.

Christ therefore, had He held fast to His own glorious prerogatives, would have had nothing in common with men; and had He not taken on Himself the weaknesses of flesh, His taking on of flesh alone would have been of no avail. "He went up into a boat," it says, "and crossed over the water and came into his own city." The Creator of all things, the Lord of the world, after He had for our sakes clothed Himself with our flesh, began to have an earthly fatherland, to be a citizen of the Jewish commonwealth; He, the Parent of all parents, began to have parents, so that love might invite us, charity draw us on, affection conquer us, and affability win us whom despotism had driven away, fear had scattered, and the civil power had made exiles.

℟. O Lord, Ruler of the heavens and the earth, Creator of the waters, King of all creatures: * Hear the prayer of Thy servants. ℣. For the prayer of the humble and the meek hath always pleased Thee. Hear. Glory. Hear.

XIX Sunday After Pentecost

☩ Continuation of the holy Gospel according to St. Matthew.— At that time, getting into a boat, Jesus crossed over and came to his own town. And behold, they brought to him a paralytic lying on a pallet. And Jesus, seeing their faith, said to the paralytic. "Take courage, son; thy sins are forgiven thee." And behold, some of the Scribes said within themselves, "This man blasphemes." And Jesus, knowing their thoughts, said, "Why do you harbor evil thoughts in your hearts? For which is easier, to say, 'Thy sins are forgiven thee,' or to say, 'Arise, and walk'? But that you may know that the Son of Man has power on earth to forgive sins," then he said to the paralytic, "Arise, take up thy pallet and go to thy house." And he arose, and went away to his house. But when the crowds saw it, they were struck with fear, and glorified God who had given such power to men.

Let Us Pray

We beseech Thee, O Lord, let our hearts be guided by Thy merciful grace, for without Thy help, we cannot please Thee. Through our Lord.

XIX SUNDAY AFTER PENTECOST
III Nocturn

The reading of the holy Gospel according to St. Matthew

At that time Jesus spoke to the chief priests in parables, saying, "The kingdom of heaven is like a king who made a marriage feast for his son." And so forth.

Homily of St. Gregory, Pope

You remember that I have often said that in the holy Gospel the Church on this earth is generally called the Kingdom of Heaven. The congregation of the just is indeed called the Kingdom of Heaven. For since the Lord says by the Prophet, "Heaven is my throne," and Solomon declares, "The soul of the just man is the seat of wisdom," and Paul says that Christ is the power of God and the wisdom of God, evidently we should conclude that if God is wisdom and the soul of the just is the seat of wisdom, then, since heaven is called the throne of God, the soul of the just man is therefore *heaven*. Hence by the Psalmist it is said of holy preachers: "The heavens show forth the glory of God."

Therefore the Kingdom of Heaven is the Church of the just: for by the fact that, as their hearts seek to gain nothing on earth, they aspire to heavenly things, the Lord already reigns in them as in heaven. Hence it may be said, "The kingdom of heaven is likened to a king who made a marriage for his son."

Your charity already knows who this King is, the Father of a Son, also a King: He, of course, to whom the Psalmist addresses the words: "Give to the king thy judgment, O God, and to the king's son thy justice."

"Who made a marriage for his son." For God the Father made a marriage for His Son at the time when He joined Him in the Virgin's womb to human nature, when He willed that, being God before all ages, He should become a man in the end of time. But because this nuptial union is as a rule a union of two persons, let us by no means conclude that we believe the Person of God and man, our Redeemer, Jesus Christ, to be a union of two persons.

Through these two and in these two natures we declare that He exists, but that He be believed to be composed of two persons, we shun as erroneous. Hence it can be very plainly and correctly stated that the Father made a marriage for His royal Son in this, that He (the Father) united to Christ His holy Church through the mystery of the Incarnation. And the womb of the Virgin Mother was the wedding chamber of this Spouse. Whence the Psalmist says: "He hath set his tabernacle in the sun: and he is as a bridegroom coming out of his chamber."

℟. Lord, Almighty King, all things are in Thy power and there is none that can resist Thy will * Deliver us for Thy name's sake. ℣. Hear our prayer and turn our mourning into joy. Deliver. Glory. Deliver.

✠ Continuation of the holy Gospel according to St. Matthew.— At that time Jesus spoke to the chief priests and Pharisees in parables, saying: "The kingdom of heaven is like a king who made a marriage feast for his son. And he sent his servants to call in those invited to the marriage feast, but they would not come. Again he sent out other servants, saying, 'Tell those who are invited, behold, I have prepared my dinner; my oxen and fatlings are killed, and everything is ready; come to the marriage feast.' But they made light of it, and went off, one to his farm, and another to his business; and the rest laid hold of his servants, treated them shamefully, and killed them.

"But when the king heard of it, he was angry; and he sent his armies and destroyed those murderers, and burnt their city. Then he said to his servants, 'The marriage feast indeed is ready, but those who were invited were not worthy; go therefore to the crossroads, and invite to the marriage feast whomsoever you shall find.' And his servants went out into the roads, and gathered all whom they found, both good and bad; and the marriage feast was filled with guests.

XX Sunday After Pentecost

"Now the king went in to see the guests, and he saw there a man who had not on a wedding garment. And he said to him, 'Friend, why didst thou come in here without a wedding garment?' But he was speechless. Then the king said to the attendants, 'Bind his hands and feet and cast him forth into the darkness outside, where there will be the weeping, and the gnashing of teeth.' For many are called, but few are chosen."

Let Us Pray

O almighty and merciful God, graciously protect us from all danger, that, ready in both body and soul, we may with a free spirit seek to do Thy will. Through our Lord.

XX SUNDAY AFTER PENTECOST
III Nocturn

The reading of the holy Gospel according to St. John

At that time there was a certain royal official whose son was lying sick at Capharnaum. And so forth.

Homily of St. Gregory, Pope

The reading of the holy Gospel, which you have just heard, brethren, needs no explanation; however, lest we seem to pass over it in silence, let us say something rather by way of exhortation than of explanation. I see only this to be investigated, why he who had come to seek health for his son heard the words: "Unless you see signs and wonders you believe not." For he who asked health for his son undoubtedly believed; because he would not seek health from Him whom he did not believe to be the Savior.

Therefore, why is he, who believed before he saw signs, told, "Unless you see signs and wonders, you believe not"? But remember what he petitioned and straightway you will know that he was lacking in faith. He asked that Christ come down and heal his son. Hence, he sought the bodily presence of the Lord, who in spirit was nowhere absent.

Thus, he did not believe perfectly in Him whom he did not think able to give health unless He were also present in the body. If he had believed perfectly, he would have known without doubt that there is no place where God is not. Therefore, to a great extent he who attributed power not to His majesty, but to His bodily presence, did lack faith.

So he petitioned health for his son, and yet he was doubtful in his faith, because he thought that He to whom he had come, and whom he believed able to cure, was nevertheless absent from his dying son. But the Lord, who is begged to come, indicates that He is not absent from the place to which He is invited; by a mere command He, who by His will created all things, restored health.

℟. Be ye not afraid of the assault of the enemy. Remember in what manner our fathers were saved, * And now let us cry to heaven and our God will have mercy on us. ℣. Remember His marvelous works which He hath done to Pharao and his host in the Red Sea. And. Glory. And.

✠ Continuation of the holy Gospel according to St. John.— At that time there was a certain royal official whose son was lying sick at Capharnaum. When he heard that Jesus had come from Judea into Galilee, he went to him and besought him to come down and heal his son, for he was at the point of death.

Jesus therefore said to him, "Unless you see signs and wonders, you do not believe." The royal official said to him, "Sir, come down before my child dies." Jesus said to him, "Go thy way, thy son lives."

The man believed the word that Jesus spoke to him, and departed. But even as he was now going down, his servants met him and brought word saying that his son lived. He asked of them therefore the hour in which he had got better. And they told him, "Yesterday, at the seventh hour, the fever left him." The father knew then that it was at that very hour in which Jesus had said to him, "Thy son lives." And he himself believed, and his whole household.

Let Us Pray

Grant, we beseech Thee, O Lord, pardon and peace to Thy faithful people, that, cleansed from every sin, they may serve Thee with a peaceful mind. Through our Lord.

XXI SUNDAY AFTER PENTECOST

III Nocturn

The reading of the holy Gospel according to St. Matthew

At that time Jesus spoke to his disciples this parable: "The kingdom of heaven is likened to a king who desired to settle accounts with his servants." And so forth.

Homily of St. Jerome, Priest

It is an ordinary thing with the Syrians, and especially the Palestinians, to join parables to every discourse, so that what cannot be grasped by the hearers through simple injunction, may be understood by means of a similitude and example. Therefore under the comparison of the king and lord and the servant who, owing a debt of ten thousand talents, had obtained indulgence from his master upon asking, the Lord commanded Peter that he also should forgive his fellow-servants when they erred in lesser things.

For if that king and lord so easily forgave his servant who owed him ten thousand talents, how much more ought servants forgive their fellow-servants lesser debts? In order that this be made clearer, let us speak by way of example. If anyone of us should commit adultery, murder, or sacrilege, these greater crimes—signified by the ten thousand talents—are forgiven to those who ask if they themselves forgive others who commit lesser crimes.

But if, on the other hand, we are irreconcilable because of an insult, and because of a bitter word we have perpetual strifes, would it not seem to us that we are rightly cast into prison, and thus through our own example bring it about that forgiveness of our greater transgressions be not granted to us?

"So also my heavenly Father will do to you, if you do not each forgive your brother from your hearts." This is an ominous declaration, if the decision of God is bent and formed according to our own mind—if we do not forgive our brethren little things, the great things shall not be forgiven us by God. And because everyone can say, "I have nothing against him; he (the brother) knows it; he has God as his judge; I do not care what he wants to do; I have forgiven him," God strengthens His word and rejects all simulation of a feigned peace, saying: "If you do not each forgive your brother *from your hearts.*"

℞ They blessed the Lord with hymns and thanksgiving: * The Lord Almighty who had done great things in Israel and given them the victory. ℣. They adorned the front of the temple with crowns of gold and dedicated the altar to the Lord. The Lord. Glory. The Lord.

✠ Continuation of the holy Gospel according to St. Matthew.— At that time Jesus spoke to his disciples this parable: "The kingdom of heaven is likened to a king who desired to settle accounts with his servants. And when he had begun the settlement, one was brought to him who owed him ten thousand talents. And as he had no means of paying, his master ordered him to be sold, with his wife and children and all that he had, and payment to be made. But the servant fell down and besought him, saying, 'Have patience with me and I will pay thee all!' And moved with compassion, the master of that servant released him, and forgave him the debt.

"But as that servant went out, he met one of his fellow-servants who owed him a hundred denarii, and he laid hold of him and throttled him, saying, 'Pay what thou owest.' His fellow-servant therefore fell down and began to entreat him, saying, 'Have patience with me and I will pay thee all.' But he would not; but went away and cast him into prison until he should pay what was due.

"His fellow-servants therefore, seeing what had happened, were very much saddened, and they went and informed their master of all that had happened. Then his master called him, and said to him, 'Wicked servant! I forgave thee all the debt, because thou didst entreat me. Shouldst not thou also have had pity on thy fellow-servant, even as I had pity on thee?' And his master, being angry, handed him over to the torturers until he should pay what was due to him. So also my heavenly Father will do to you, if you do not each forgive your brother from your hearts."

Let Us Pray

O Lord, we beseech Thee, in Thy constant goodness protect Thy family, that under Thy protection it may be free from all danger and devoted to Thy name in performing good works. Through our Lord.

XXII SUNDAY AFTER PENTECOST

III Nocturn

The reading of the holy Gospel according to St. Matthew

At that time the Pharisees went and took counsel how they might entrap Jesus in his talk. And so forth.

Homily of St. Hilary, Bishop

Frequently the Pharisees are embittered against Him, but can gain no occasion from past events with which to prosecute Him. In fact, vice could not intrude itself upon His deeds and words; yet because of their disposition to evil-doing, they exerted themselves to the most careful search in order to find a charge. Now He had been calling all men from the crimes of the world and from the superstitions of man-made religions to the hope of the Heavenly Kingdom.

Thereupon they tried to catch Him through the dilemma of their proposed question as to whether one might violate secular authority, or whether he was obliged to pay tribute to Caesar. He, aware of the interior secret of their thoughts (for God does not have to search for any of the things which are hidden within man), commanded that a denarius be brought to Him, and He asked them whose inscription and image was on it.

The Pharisees replied that it was that of Caesar. He told them that the things which were Caesar's should be rendered to Caesar, but that the things which were God's should be rendered to God. O answer filled with miraculous power! O perfect solution of this heavenly reply! He so moderated all things between a contempt of the world and the disrespect that would have been offered to Caesar that He freed the minds devoted to God from all worry and human obligations when He decided that only the things which were Caesar's must be rendered to him. For if nothing of Caesar's lies in our possession, we will not be held by the obligation of rendering to him what is his.

Hence if we depend on his power, if we make use of his authority, and as hirelings subject ourselves to a dependence on another's estate, it is beyond the complaint of injustice that we pay to Caesar that which is his. On the other hand, we are obliged to render to God the things that are His: our body, our soul, our will. For we have these things in their perfection and growth from God. Consequently it is just that they give themselves back completely to Him to whom they consider themselves due. both in their origin and in their perfection.

℟. The sun shone upon the shields of gold and the mountains glittered therewith: * And the strength of the nations is scattered. ℣. For the army was exceedingly great and strong. And Judas and his army drew near for battle. And. Glory. And.

☩ Continuation of the holy Gospel according to St. Matthew.— At that time the Pharisees went and took counsel how they might entrap Jesus in his talk. And they sent to him their disciples with the Herodians, saying: "Master, we know that thou art truthful, and that thou teachest the way of God in truth and that thou carest naught for any man; for thou dost not regard the person of men. Tell us, therefore, what dost thou think: Is it lawful to give tribute to Caesar, or not?" But Jesus, knowing their wickedness, said, "Why do you test me, you hypocrites? Show me the coin of the tribute." So they offered him a denarius. Then Jesus said to them, "Whose are this image and the inscription?" They said to him, "Caesar's." Then He said to them, "Render, therefore, to Caesar the things that are Caesar's, and to God the things that are God's."

Let Us Pray

O God, our refuge and our strength, hear the devout prayers of Thy Church, Thou who art the Author of goodness, and grant that what we ask in faith we may surely obtain. Through our Lord.

XXIII SUNDAY AFTER PENTECOST

III Nocturn

The reading of the holy Gospel according to St. Matthew

At that time, as Jesus was speaking to the multitudes, behold, a ruler came up and worshipped him, saying, "My daughter has just now died." And so forth.

Homily of St. Jerome, Priest

The eighth sign is that in which the ruler, not wishing to be excluded from the true circumcision, asks that his daughter be raised to life. But the woman with the issue of blood steps in and is healed in the eighth place; as a result the daughter of the ruler, being excluded from this number, takes the ninth place, according to that saying contained in the psalms, "Ethiopia will stretch forth her hand to God," and, "When all the Gentiles shall have entered in, then all Israel will be saved."

"And behold, a woman who was troubled with an issue of blood for twelve years came from behind and touched the hem of his garment." In the Gospel according to Luke it is written that the daughter of the ruler was twelve years old. Take notice, therefore, that this woman, that is, the Gentile people, had been sick for the same time that the Jewish nation, of which the ruler's daughter was the figure, had been living in faith.

But this woman who was suffering from an issue of blood did not approach the Lord in a house nor in the city—because by the Law she was excluded from the cities—but while the Lord was walking along the highway; and thus it happened that while He was going to one, another was healed. Whence the Apostles also say: "To you it behooved us first to preach, but because you have judged yourselves unworthy of salvation, we have gone over to the Gentiles."

"For she said within herself: If I shall touch the hem of his garment, I shall be healed." According to the Law anyone who touched a woman having an issue of blood became unclean; this woman therefore touched the Lord that she might be cured of her issue of blood. "Be of good heart, daughter, thy faith hath made thee whole." For this reason, daughter, because thy faith hath made thee whole. He did not say, "Thy faith shall make thee whole," but rather, "Thy faith hath made thee whole." For, because you believed in Him, you were already whole.

℟. The nations are come together against us to destroy us, and we know not what we should do: * O Lord God, our eyes look to Thee that we may not perish. Thou knowest what they

XXIV Sunday After Pentecost

intend against us. ℣. How shall we be able to stand before their face unless Thou help us? O Lord. Glory. O Lord.

✠ Continuation of the holy Gospel according to St. Matthew.— At that time, as Jesus was speaking to the multitudes, behold, a ruler came up and worshipped him, saying, "My daughter has just now died; but come and lay thy hand upon her, and she will return to life." And Jesus arose and followed him, and so did his disciples.

Now a woman who for twelve years had been suffering from hemorrhage, came up behind him and touched the tassel of his cloak, saying to herself, "If I touch but his cloak I shall be saved." But Jesus, turning and seeing her, said, "Take courage, daughter; thy faith has saved thee." And the woman was restored to health from that moment.

And when Jesus came to the ruler's house, and saw the flute players and the crowd making a din, he said, "Begone, the girl is asleep, not dead." And they laughed him to scorn. But when the crowd had been put out, he went in and took her by the hand; and the girl arose. And the report of this spread throughout all that district.

Let Us Pray

O Lord, we beseech Thee, forgive the sins of Thy people, and in Thy goodness deliver us from the bonds of those sins we have committed by our weakness. Through our Lord.

XXIV SUNDAY AFTER PENTECOST

III Nocturn

The reading of the holy Gospel according to St. Matthew

At that time Jesus said to his disciples: "When you see the abomination of desolation, which was spoken of by Daniel the prophet, standing in the holy place—let him who reads understand—." And so forth.

Homily of St. Jerome, Priest

The exhortation to the reader to understand this passage of the Gospel shows that it contains a mystical signification. In Daniel the text is as follows: "and in the half of the week the victim and the sacrifice shall fail: and there shall be in the temple the abomination of desolation: even until the consummation of the time; and a consummation shall be given to the desolation."

The Apostle also, in this regard, declares that the man of iniquity and the adversary is to be raised up in opposition to all that is called and worshipped as God, so that he will even dare to stand in the temple of God and to give evidence that he himself is God; whose coming will, according to the working of the devil, destroy and drive away from God those who shall receive him.

This can be simply taken in reference to the Anti-Christ, or to the statue of Caesar which Pilate placed in the temple, or to the equestrian statue of Hadrian which has stood in the very Holy of Holies even to the present day. Likewise, according to the ancient Scriptures an idol is called an abomination, and because the idol was placed in the desolate and ruined temple, it is therefore added *of desolation,* that is, *abomination of desolation.*

The *abomination of desolation* can be understood also as every perverse dogma, and, when we shall see it standing in the Holy Place, that is, in the Church, and showing itself as God, we must flee from Judea to the mountains, that is, we must abandon the letter which kills, and Jewish impiety, and approach the eternal mountains from which God in a wonderful way sheds His light. We must be on the roof and on the housetops, where the fiery darts of the devil are not able to reach, and must not descend to carry anything from the home of our old way of living, nor seek those things which are behind, but rather sow in the field of spiritual writings, so that we may reap the fruits thereof; neither must we take an extra cloak, which the apostles were forbidden to have.

℟. O Lord God, * Have mercy on the sinful nation, upon a people laden with iniquity. ℣. Be appeased concerning the transgression of Thy people. Have mercy. Glory. Have mercy.

✚ Continuation of the holy Gospel according to St. Matthew.—At that time Jesus said to his disciples: "When you see the abomination of desolation, which was spoken of by Daniel the prophet, standing in the holy place—let him who reads understand—then let those who are in Judea flee to the mountains; and let him who is on the housetop not go down to take anything from his house; and let him who is in the field not turn back to take his cloak. But woe to those who are with child, or have infants at the breast in those days! But pray that your flight may not be in the winter, or on the Sabbath. For then there will be great tribulation, such as has not been from the beginning of the world until now, nor will be. And unless those days had been shortened, no living creature would have been saved. But for the sake of the elect those days will be shortened.

"Then if anyone say to you, 'Behold, here is the Christ,' or 'There he is,' do not believe it. For false christs and false proph-

XXIV Sunday After Pentecost

ets will arise, and will show great signs and wonders, so as to lead astray, if possible, even the elect. Behold, I have told it to you beforehand. If therefore they say to you, 'Behold, he is in the desert,' do not go forth; 'Behold, he is in the inner chambers,' do not believe it. For as the lightning comes forth from the east and shines even to the west, so also will the coming of the Son of Man be. Wherever the body is, there will the eagles be gathered together.

"But immediately after the tribulation of those days, the sun will be darkened, and the moon will not give her light, and the stars will fall from heaven, and the powers of heaven will be shaken. And then will appear the sign of the Son of Man in heaven; and then will all tribes of the earth mourn, and they will see the Son of Man coming upon the clouds of heaven with great power and majesty. And he will send forth his angels with a trumpet and a great sound, and they will gather his elect from the four winds, from end to end of the heavens.

"Now from the fig tree learn this parable. When its branch is now tender, and the leaves break forth, you know that summer is near. Even so, when you see all these things, know that it is near, even at the door. Amen I say to you, this generation will not pass away till all these things have been accomplished. Heaven and earth will pass away, but my words will not pass away."

Let Us Pray

Arouse, we beseech Thee, O Lord, the wills of Thy faithful people, that more zealously seeking the fruit of the divine grace, they may receive greater helps from Thy goodness. Through our Lord.

THE SANCTORAL CYCLE

November 30
ST. ANDREW, APOSTLE

I Nocturn

*From the Epistle of St. Paul the Apostle
to the Romans, c. 10, 4 - 21*

II Nocturn

Andrew the Apostle, the brother of Peter, was born at Bethsaida, a town of Galilee. He was one of the disciples of John the Baptist and heard him say of Christ, "Behold the Lamb of God." Immediately he followed Jesus, bringing his brother also with him. Some time later, when he was fishing in the Sea of Galilee together with his brother, they were both called, before any of the other apostles, by Christ the Lord, as He was going by, with the words, "Follow me, and I will make you fishers of men." They delayed not, but leaving their nets they followed Him at once. After Christ's death and Resurrection the province of Scythia was allotted to Andrew as the place of his preaching. After working there, he went through Epirus and Thrace and converted multitudes to Christ by his teaching and miracles.

Finally he went to Patras in Achaia, and there likewise he converted many to the knowledge of the Gospel. He fearlessly rebuked Aegeas, the Proconsul, who opposed the preaching of the Gospel, because he, who wished to be considered as a judge of his fellow-men, was himself so deceived by the devil as not to know the Judge of all, Christ the Lord. Filled with anger, Aegeas answered him: "Boast no more of thy Christ. He spoke as you do, but His words did not help Him, for He was crucified by the Jews." Andrew boldly answered that Christ had delivered Himself for the salvation of mankind, but he was insultingly interrupted by the Proconsul and told to look out for himself and to sacrifice to the gods. Andrew then replied: "We have an altar, on which I offer up to God every day, not the flesh of bulls not the blood of goats, but a spotless Lamb; and when all the faithful have eaten the flesh thereof, this Lamb that was slain still remains whole and lives."

Aegeas was then filled with anger and he sent the Apostle, bound, to prison. The people would have set him free, but he calmed them and begged of them not to take away from him the palm of martyrdom, which he so much desired and which was now within his reach. Shortly thereafter he was brought before the judgment seat where he extolled the mystery of the cross and rebuked Aegeas for his impiety. Aegeas, not being able to bear with him any longer, commanded him to be crucified as was Christ.

Andrew was then led to the place of martyrdom, and as soon as he saw the cross he cried out, "O precious cross, which the members of my Lord have made so honorable, how long I have desired thee! How fervently have I loved thee! How constantly have I sought thee! And now that thou art come to me, how my soul is attracted to thee. Take me from among men and unite me to my Master, that as by thee He redeemed me, so by thee also He may take me unto Himself." Then he was fastened to the cross, where he continued to live for two days, not ceasing to preach the faith of Christ. Finally he passed into the presence of Him, the likeness of whose death he had loved so well. The above particulars of his martyrdom were written by the priests and deacons of Achaia, who had personal knowledge of them. Under the reign of Constantine the bones of Andrew were taken first to Constantinople and afterwards to Amalfi. During the pontificate of Pope Pius II his head was carried to Rome and kept in the Basilica of St. Peter.

℞. The Lord, walking by the sea of Galilee, saw Peter and Andrew casting their nets into the sea, and He called them, saying: * Follow Me and I will make you fishers of men. ℣. For they were fishermen and He saith unto them. Follow Me. Glory. Follow Me.

III Nocturn

The reading of the holy Gospel according to St. Matthew

At that time, as Jesus was walking by the sea of Galilee, he saw two brothers, Simon, who is called Peter, and his brother Andrew, casting a net into the sea, for they were fishermen. And so forth.

Homily of St. Gregory, Pope

Dearest brethren, you have heard that at a single command Peter and Andrew, leaving their nets, followed the Redeemer. Up to that time they had not seen Him perform any miracles; they had heard nothing from Him concerning a reward of eternal joy, and still, at a single bidding of our Lord, they forgot about that which they seemed to possess. What great miracles of His have we seen, with how many scourges are we afflicted, by what great anxieties of threatening things are we disheartened, and nevertheless we contemn Him who calls us to follow!

He who counsels us in our manner of life already sits enthroned in heaven; already has He bowed the necks of the Gentiles to the yoke of the Faith; already He has laid low the glory of the world; already, with the world's disasters increasing more and more, does He announce the approaching day of His severe judgment, and yet our proud mind still does not wish to abandon of its own accord that which it is daily losing unwillingly.

What, then, dearly beloved brethren, what shall we say in His judgment, we who are not turned from the love of this present world by His counsels, nor corrected by His chastisements? But perhaps someone will say in his silent ruminations: "What or how much did either of these fishermen, who possessed almost nothing, forfeit at the call of the Lord?

In this matter, dearest brethren, we must consider the disposition rather than the personal wealth. He forsakes much who keeps nothing for himself; he forsakes much who gives up every little thing, his all. But we, on the other hand, hold with love the things we have, and even out of desire seek those things which we do not have. Therefore, Peter and Andrew forsook much when both forfeited even their desire to possess.

℟. Holy Andrew prayed, looking up to heaven, and cried out with a loud voice, saying: Thou art my God whom I have seen; suffer me not to be taken down from hence by the impious judge: *. For I know the virtue of the holy cross. ℣. Thou art Christ, my Master, whom I have known and loved, whom I have confessed; hear me now in this prayer. For I know. Glory. For I know.

✠ Continuation of the holy Gospel according to St. Matthew.—At that time, as Jesus was walking by the sea of Galilee, he saw two brothers, Simon, who is called Peter, and his brother Andrew, casting a net into the sea (for they were fishermen). And he said to them, "Come, follow me, and I will make you fishers of men." And at once they left the nets, and followed him. And going farther on, he saw two other brothers, James the son of Zebedee, and his brother John, in a boat with Zebedee their father, mending their nets; and he called them. And immediately they left their nets and their father, and followed him.

Let Us Pray

We humbly beseech Thy Majesty, O Lord, that as blessed Andrew was both a preacher and ruler for Thy Church, so may he also be for us a constant intercessor with Thee. Through our Lord.

December 8
THE IMMACULATE CONCEPTION OF THE BLESSED VIRGIN MARY

I Nocturn

From the Book of Genesis, c. 3, 1 - 15

II Nocturn

Sermon of St. Jerome, Priest

Of what nature and how great was the blessed and glorious Mary, ever a Virgin, is divinely declared by the Angel when he says: "Hail, full of grace, the Lord is with thee, blessed art thou among women." For it was truly fitting that the Virgin, who gave glory to the heavens, the Lord to the earth, peace and faith to the nations, an end to sin, order to life, and discipline to morals, should, as a pledge of such gifts, be full of grace. And truly full of grace, because to others grace is given in measure, but upon Mary the whole plenitude of grace was poured. Truly full, for although grace was believed to have been in the patriarchs and prophets, however, not to such a degree: for the fullness of all the grace which was in Christ came into Mary, although in another manner than it was in Him. And therefore the Angel says, "Blessed art thou among women," that is, more blessed than all women. And through this fact whatever evil was incurred by Eve was entirely removed by Mary's blessedness. Concerning her, Solomon in the Canticles says, as if in her praise: "Come, my dove, my immaculate one; for winter is now passed, the rain is over and gone, come from Libanus, come, thou shalt be crowned."

Not unreasonably, therefore, was she ordered to come from Libanus, because Libanus is interpreted *whiteness*. For she was white by the many virtues of her merits, and made whiter than snow by the gifts of the Holy Spirit. She represents the simplicity of a dove in all things, because whatever was accomplished in her was entirely purity and simplicity, entirely truth and grace, entirely mercy and justice, which looks down from heaven; and therefore she is immaculate, because she is corrupted in no way. For she encompassed a man in her womb, as holy Jeremias testifies, and she did not receive Him from another. "The Lord has created," he says, "something new upon the earth, a woman shall encompass a man."

It was a wholly new thing and of all wonders the most stupendous when God—whom the world cannot contain nor anyone behold and live—so entered into the chamber of the womb that He was not subject to the limitation of her body, and was so borne about that the whole Godhead was within her, and departed thence in such a way that the entrance remained sealed— as Ezechiel prophesied. Wherefore is it sung in the same Canticle: "A garden enclosed, a fountain sealed up. Thy plants are a paradise." She is truly a garden of delights in which are placed all kinds of flowers and the perfumes of virtues; she is so enclosed that she knows neither violation nor corruption by any deceitful frauds. Thus she is the fountain sealed with the sign of the whole Trinity.

From the Acts of Pope Pius IX

Pope Pius IX, assenting to the wishes of the whole Church, decided by his infallible and supreme word to proclaim solemnly the victory of the Virgin Mother of God over the terrible enemy of the human race in her conception, which divine revelation, venerable tradition, the constant sentiment of the Church, the unanimous opinion of the bishops and faithful, and the extraordinary acts and constitutions of the supreme pontiffs have already wonderfully manifested. Thus, on the 8th of December, 1854, in the Vatican Basilica, a great crowd of Cardinals and bishops of the Roman Church, even from distant regions, being present, and with the whole world applauding, he solemnly pronounced and defined: That the doctrine which holds that the Blessed Virgin Mary in the first instant of her conception, by a special privilege of God, was preserved untouched by the stain of original sin, was revealed by God and henceforth must be firmly and constantly believed by all the faithful.

℟. By one man in whom all have sinned, sin entered into this world. * Fear not, Mary, for thou hast found grace with God. ℣. The Lord hath delivered my soul from death and hath become my protector against the enemy. Fear not. Glory. Fear not.

III Nocturn

The reading of the holy Gospel according to St. Luke

Now in the sixth month the angel Gabriel was sent from God to a town of Galilee called Nazareth, to a virgin betrothed to a man named Joseph, of the house of David, and the virgin's name was Mary. And so forth.

Homily of St. Germanus, Bishop

Hail, Mary, full of grace, holier than the saints, more exalted than the heavens, more glorious than the Cherubim, more honorable than the Seraphim, and venerable above every creature. Hail

O dove, bringing to us the olive twig, preserving us from a spiritual deluge, and announcing to us the haven of salvation; thou whose silvered wings and whose pinions in green shimmering gold are radiant with the brightness of the most holy and illuminating Spirit. Hail, most delightful and rational paradise of God, planted this day in the East by His most benevolent and omnipotent right hand, sending forth for Him the sweet fragrance of the lily, and producing the ever-fresh rose for the cure of those who have drunk the destructive and fatal bitterness of death in the West; thou paradise in which the life-giving tree blossoms forth unto the knowledge of truth, from which those who have tasted obtain immortality.

Hail, O divinely built, immaculate, and most pure palace of God, the most high King, adorned round about with the magnificence of this same divine King, hospitably receiving and refreshing all with mystical delights, in which, shining with manifold beauty, is the nuptial chamber, not made with hands, of the spiritual Spouse; in which the Word, desirous of recalling the erring human race, took to Himself flesh that He might reconcile to the Father those who by their own free will had become estranged from Him. Hail, most fertile and secluded mountain of God on which the rational Lamb, who bore our infirmities and sins, was fed; O mountain from which the Rock, uncut by any hand, rolled down, broke the altars of the idols and became the cornerstone, wonderful in our eyes. Hail, holy throne of God, divine shrine, house of glory, ornament of exceeding beauty, elect treasure, propitiatory of the whole world, the heaven which speaketh forth the glory of God. Hail, vessel of pure gold, containing the most sweet delight of our souls, namely, Christ, who is our manna.

O Virgin most pure, most worthy of all praise and homage, consecrated temple of God, excelling in estate all creatures, land unbroken, meadow unplowed, most flourishing vine, fountain gushing forth waters, Virgin with Child, Mother who knew not man, hidden treasury of innocence, perfection of sanctity, by thy most acceptable and, because of thy maternal authority, thy most powerful prayers to our Lord and God, Creator of all things, thy Son, begotten by thee without a father, deign to guide the helm of the Church and to bring it to a tranquil port.

Gloriously clothe our priests with justice and with the joy of an approved, pure, and sincere faith. Direct in tranquility and prosperity the scepters of orthodox princes, who, in preference to purple and the splendor of gold and in preference to pearls and precious stones, have chosen thee to be the diadem, the royal cloak, and the most steadfast adornment of their kingdom. Overthrow those unfaithful nations which blaspheme thee and the God born of thee; give strength to the submissive people that they may persevere in the sweet yoke of obedience according to the precept of God. With the triumphs of victory crown this thy city which considers thee its watch tower and foundation; protect the habitation of God by surrounding it with strength; preserve always the beauty of the temple. Free those who sing thy praises from all danger and distress of soul, grant redemption to the captives, show thyself the solace of pilgrims destitute of home or any protection. Stretch forth thy helping hand to the whole world that with joy and gladness we may in the most splendid manner conclude thy solemnities, together with that feast which we have recently celebrated in Christ Jesus, the King of all and our true God, to whom is, glory and strength, together with the Father, the holy Principle of life, and the coeternal, consubstantial, and co-reigning Spirit now and always, unto all ages. Amen.

℞. Magnify the Lord with me: * Because the mercy of the Lord is great towards me. ℣. The prince of this world has nothing in common with me. Because. Glory. Because.

✠ Continuation of the holy Gospel according to St. Luke.—At that time the angel Gabriel was sent from God to a town of Galilee called Nazareth, to a virgin betrothed to a man named Joseph, of the house of David, and the virgin's name was Mary. And when the angel had come to her, he said, "Hail, full of grace, the Lord is with thee. Blessed art thou among women."

Let Us Pray

O God, who by the Immaculate Conception of the Virgin didst prepare a worthy dwelling for Thy Son, we beseech Thee, that as Thou didst preserve her from every stain through the foreseen merits of that same Son, Thou, by her intercession, wouldst grant us, cleansed from sin, to come to Thee. Through the same Jesus Christ.

December 9

SECOND DAY WITHIN THE OCTAVE OF THE IMMACULATE CONCEPTION

From the Dogmatic Bull of Pope Pius IX

Since the ineffable God, whose ways are mercy and truth, whose will omnipotence, and whose wisdom reaches from end to end mightily and orders all things sweetly, from eternity foresaw that the most lamentable ruin of the whole human race was to flow from the transgression of Adam, and, in the mystery hidden for ages, decreed to complete through the Incarnation of the Word the first work of His goodness by a more hidden mystery lest man, led into sin by the cunning of diabolical iniquity, should perish, contrary to His merciful decree, and in order that what was to fall in the first Adam might be more happily elevated in the second, from the beginning and before all ages He chose and ordained for His only-begotten Son a Mother, of whom, having been made flesh in the blessed fullness of time, He would be born. And with such great love did God pursue her beyond all creatures that He took pleasure in her most earnest love of Him.

Wherefore, far above all the angelic spirits and all the saints, He has so marvelously ladened her with an abundance of all heavenly graces drawn from the treasure of the Divinity, that, always free from every stain of sin, and all beautiful and perfect, she might show forth that fullness of innocence and holiness greater than which, under God, can in no wise be conceived, and which no one, save God, can attain to in thought. And by all means was it truly befitting that so venerable a mother, to whom God the Father chose to give His only Son in such a way that He whom, begotten equal to Himself from His own bosom, He loved as Himself, should be by nature one and the same common Son of God the Father and of the Virgin, should shine forth, ever adorned with the splendors of most perfect holiness, and especially that, entirely free from the stain of original sin, she should achieve the fullest triumph over the old serpent.

This original innocence of the august Virgin, wholly consonant with the admirable holiness and sublime dignity of the same Mother of God, the Catholic Church, which, being ever guided by the Holy Spirit, is the pillar and ground of truth, has never ceased, by deeds more glorious each day, to explain, declare, and cherish, holding it as a doctrine divinely received and contained fundamentally in the deposit of heavenly revelation. This teaching, flourishing from the earliest times and firmly imbedded in the minds of the faithful, and, by the care and efforts of holy bishops, wonderfully propagated through the Catholic world, the Church itself expressed when she did not hesitate to propose the Conception of the same Virgin for the public worship and veneration of the faithful. By which illustrious act she has, indeed, showed this Virgin's Conception to be singular, wonderful, and entirely set apart from that of the rest of mankind, and a thing wholly worthy of veneration, since the Church otherwise celebrates only the festal days of the saints.

December 10
THIRD DAY WITHIN THE OCTAVE OF THE IMMACULATE CONCEPTION
From the Dogmatic Bull of Pope Pius IX

The Church has been accustomed, both in ecclesiastical offices and in the most sacred liturgy, to apply and transfer to the origin of the Virgin, which was indeed decreed at one and the same time with the Incarnation of the Divine Wisdom, the very words in which the divine Scriptures speak of uncreated Wisdom and set forth His eternal origin. And although the acceptance of all these passages by almost all the faithful shows with what care the Roman Church herself, the mother and mistress of all the churches, cultivated the doctrine of the Immaculate Conception of the Virgin, yet her illustrious deeds in this respect are worthy of individual mention. For the dignity and authority of that Church are such as are due to her who is the center of Catholic truth and unity, in whom alone religion has been kept inviolate, and from whom it behooves all other churches to receive the tradition of faith. That Roman Church, therefore, had nothing so much at heart as that the Immaculate Conception of the Virgin, both as to doctrine and cult, should in the most eloquent manner be asserted, defended, promoted, and vindicated.

Wherefore our predecessors greatly rejoiced to institute in the Roman Church the feast of the Conception with the proper Office and Mass, in which should be plainly asserted the prerogative of immunity from the hereditary stain. They rejoiced, moreover, to increase, enrich, honor, and promote by every means in their power the cult so instituted by the grant of indulgences as well as of faculties bestowed on cities, provinces, and kingdoms to choose as their patron the Mother of God under the title of the Immaculate Conception, by privileges granted to approved sodalities, congregations, and religious families founded in honor of the Immaculate Conception, by praising the piety of those who build monasteries, hospitals, altars or temples, under the title of the Immaculate Conception, or again, who promise by vow to defend the doctrine of the Immaculate Conception of the Mother of God.

Moreover, they rejoiced above all things to decree that the feast of the Conception should be considered by the whole Church as a feast of the same rank and class as that of the Nativity; that that feast of the Conception should be celebrated by the universal Church with an octave; that it should be piously observed by all as a feast of obligation; and that Mass should be solemnly celebrated every year on the day of the Virgin's Conception in the pontifical chapel of our patriarchal basilica of St.

Mary Major. Furthermore, since it was their earnest desire to foster in the souls of the faithful an ever-increasing devotion to the doctrine of the Immaculate Conception of the Mother of God and to arouse within them piety and veneration for the Virgin conceived without the stain of original sin, they willingly and gladly granted permission to proclaim the Immaculate Conception of that Virgin in the Litany of Loretto, and even in the very Preface of the Mass, that thus the law of faith might be confirmed by the law of prayer.

December 11

FOURTH DAY WITHIN THE OCTAVE OF THE IMMACULATE CONCEPTION

From the Dogmatic Bull of Pope Pius IX

Because those things which pertain to worship are joined with the object of worship by a very close bond, and cannot remain stable and fixed if that object stand as uncertain and doubtful, therefore our predecessors, the Roman Pontiffs, furthering the cultus of the Conception with all solicitude, have striven most earnestly to declare and inculcate its object and dogma. For they have clearly and openly taught that a feast of the Virgin's Conception should be kept, and they have outlawed as false and wholly alien to the mind of the Church the doctrine of those men who judge and affirm that not the Conception, but her sanctification, should be honored by the Church.

Neither have they thought that those men should be gently treated, who, in order to impugn the teaching concerning the Immaculate Conception of the Virgin, made an imaginary distinction between a first and second instant and moment of the Conception, and then asserted that the Conception should, indeed, be celebrated, but not that of the first instant and moment. For these our predecessors have deemed it their duty to guard and uphold by every effort both the feast of the Conception of the most blessed Virgin, and the Conception in the first instant as the true object of worship. Hence the words are clearly decisive by which our predecessor, Alexander VII, expressed the sincere mind of the Church, saying: "Verily of long standing is the veneration for Christ's most blessed Mother, the Virgin Mary, by His faithful, who hold that her soul, at the first instant of its creation and infusion into the body, was through a special grace and privilege of God preserved free from the stain of original sin by anticipation of the merits of Jesus Christ, her Son, the Redeemer of the human race; and in this sense is understood the veneration of those who honor and celebrate the feast of her Conception with solemn rite."

Now this was an especially important duty for our predecessors—to keep the doctrine of the Immaculate Conception of the Mother of God safe and sound with every care, effort and endeavor. For they would not only in no way permit this teaching to be censured or ridiculed in any way, but going even further, they proclaimed in very clear statements and time after time that: The doctrine by which all acknowledge the Virgin's Immaculate Conception is, and is held by its own merit, completely in harmony with ecclesiastical worship, and that it is long-lived and well nigh universal and of the kind which the Roman Church takes upon herself to foster and protect, and that it is in every way worthy to be celebrated in the Sacred Liturgy itself and in the more solemn devotions. And not content with these acts, in order that this teaching concerning the Virgin's Immaculate Conception should stand unimpaired, they most strictly forbade that any opinion in opposition to this holy teaching be defended, either publicly or privately, and they desired that any such opinion be killed, as it were, by many wounds.

December 12

FIFTH DAY WITHIN THE OCTAVE OF THE IMMACULATE CONCEPTION

From the Dogmatic Bull of Pope Pius IX

All know with what great zeal the doctrine of the Immaculate Conception of the Virgin Mother of God has been handed down, avowed, and defended by the most illustrious religious communities and the more celebrated theological schools, as well as by the most eminent doctors in the science of things divine. Likewise do all know how solicitous the bishops have been for things sacred, especially to profess openly and publicly in ecclesiastical assemblies that the most holy Virgin Mary, Mother of God, was, through the foreseen merits of Christ, our Lord and Redeemer, never under the bond of original sin, but was completely preserved from the original stain, and therefore redeemed in a more sublime manner. To these declarations is immediately joined that most important and greatest of all, that of the Council of Trent itself, when it issued the dogmatic decree concerning original sin; by which decree, in accordance with the testimonies of the Sacred Scriptures, of the holy Fathers, and the most approved Councils, it declared and defined that all men are born stained with original sin. However, it solemnly declared that in this decree and in such a great scope of the definition it did not embrace the blessed and immaculate Virgin Mary, Mother of God. By this declaration the Fathers of Trent sufficiently indicated for the contemporary circumstances and times that the most blessed Virgin was free from original sin, and they made it correspondingly evident that nothing from the divine writings, nothing from tradition and the authority of the Fathers can be justly cited that might gainsay such a prerogative of the Virgin.

And truly indeed this doctrine of the Immaculate Conception of the most blessed Virgin, daily more and more explained, proclaimed and confirmed so splendidly by the weightiest opinion, teaching, care, wisdom and knowledge of the Church, spread, likewise, in a manner to be marvelled at among all the peoples and nations of the Catholic world. That this doctrine has always so existed in the Church, being accepted by the majority and marked with the character of a revealed dogma, the illustrious documents from the venerated antiquity of the Eastern and Western Church most forcibly give witness. Moreover, the Fathers and ecclesiastical writers, instructed by divine words, have nothing more ancient in their books on the explanation of the Scriptures, the defense of dogmas, and instruction of the faithful at the nightly vigils, than the Virgin's supreme sanctity, her dignity, and her freedom from all stain of sin, and they confidently preach and proclaim in many wonderful ways her glorious victory over the most terrible enemy of mankind.

Wherefore repeating the words with which God—foretelling the remedy of His loving kindness prepared for the restoration of us mortals—at the beginning of the world crushed the boldness of the deceitful serpent and bolstered the hope of our race, saying, "I will put enmities between thee and the woman, and thy seed and her seed," the Fathers have taught that by this divine utterance plainly and clearly the merciful Redeemer of the human race has been pointed out—namely, the only-begotten Son of God, Christ Jesus—and also that His most blessed Mother, the Virgin Mary, has been designated, and, at the same time, the individual enmities of each against the devil have been remarkably expressed. Thus, as Christ, the Mediator between God and men, having assumed our human nature, by blotting out the handwriting of the decree which was against us, affixed it, as Victor, to the cross, so the most holy Virgin, joined to Him by the strictest and indissoluble bond, together with Him and by Him, carrying on everlasting strifes against the venomous serpent, crushed his head beneath her own spotless foot.

December 14

SEVENTH DAY WITHIN THE OCTAVE OF THE IMMACULATE CONCEPTION

From the Dogmatic Bull of Pope Pius IX

This exceptional and singular triumph of the Virgin, her surpassing innocence, purity, holiness, her integrity free of any spot, and the ineffable plenitude and extent of all heavenly graces, virtues and privileges: all these the same Fathers saw not alone in that ark of Noe which, divinely established, escaped quite safe and unharmed the common shipwreck of the whole world, but also in that ladder which Jacob saw reaching from earth even to heaven, whose rungs the angels of God were ascending and at whose top the Lord Himself was resting; likewise in that bush which Moses saw in the holy place entirely aflame, and yet amidst the crackling tongues of fire not burnt nor suffering even the least damage, rather he beheld it thrive and blossom beautifully; in that impregnable tower from the face of the enemy, from which a thousand shields hang and all the armor of the strong; in that enclosed garden, which knows not violation or corruption by any deceitful trickery; as likewise in that radiant city of God whose foundations are in the holy mounts; and in that awesome temple of God which, bright with divine splendor, is full of the glory of God; and in several other instances quite of the same kind in which the Fathers tell us that the exalted dignity of the Mother of God, her unstained innocence and sanctity, never marred by a birthmark, were foretold.

To describe this same totality, as it were, of divine gifts and the original integrity of which Jesus was born, the same Fathers, using the writings of the Prophets, have honored this august Virgin not otherwise than as a pure dove, as the holy Jerusalem, as the exalted throne of God, as the ark and home of sanctification which eternal Wisdom built for itself, as that Queen, flowing with delights and leaning upon her Beloved, who came forth from the mouth of the Most High, entirely perfect, beautiful and exceedingly precious in God's sight, and in no way ever stained by the birthmark of the fall.

Inasmuch, then, as the same Fathers and writers of the Church are wont wholeheartedly to reckon that the ever-blessed Virgin was called full of grace in the name of, and at the command of God Himself, by the Angel Gabriel when he announced to her that sublimest dignity of being God's Mother, they teach that by this singular and solemn greeting, never elsewhere heard, it is shown that the Mother of God was the seat of all divine graces, adorned with all the charismata of the divine Spirit, an almost infinite treasure and inexhaustible abyss of these same charismata; so that, never subject to the cursed one, together with her Son a sharer of endless blessing, she merited to hear from Elizabeth, moved by the divine Spirit: "Blessed art thou amongst women and blessed is the fruit of thy womb." To this add these same writers' opinion, not less splendid than concordant, that the ever glorious Virgin, to whom "He that is mighty hath done great things," has shone with such an abundance of all heavenly gifts, with such fullness of grace, with such innocence, that, as it were, by an ineffable miracle of God—rather, the crown of all miracles—she has been established the worthy Mother of God, approaching God Himself, as much as is possible in consideration of her created nature, and become more sublime than the eulogies of both men and angels alike.

December 15

OCTAVE DAY OF THE IMMACULATE CONCEPTION

I Nocturn

Lessons from the occurring Scripture

II Nocturn

From the Dogmatic Bull of Pope Pius IX

From ancient times the bishops, ecclesiastics, regular orders, and even Emperors and Kings have earnestly requested of this Apostolic See that the Immaculate Conception of the most holy Mother of God might be defined as a dogma of the Catholic Faith. Which requests have been repeated likewise in this, our age, and have been presented especially to our predecessor of happy memory, Gregory XVI, and to us, by bishops, by both the secular clergy and religious communities, and also by the sovereign rulers and the faithful.

We therefore with singular joy of soul, knowing well all these things and seriously considering them, as soon as we were, though unworthy, elevated to this exalted throne of Peter by some hidden purpose of divine Providence and had undertaken the government of the whole Church, we certainly considered nothing a more revered duty than, in accord with our most intense love and affection from our tenderest years towards the most holy Virgin Mother of God, to do all those things that could yet be in the wishes of the Church that the most Blessed Virgin's honor might be increased and that her prerogatives might shine with a more abundant light.

Therefore, greatly assured in the Lord that the opportune time has come for defining the Immaculate Conception of the most holy Virgin Mary, Mother of God, which divine revelation, venerable tradition, the constant mind of the Church, the joint agreement of the Bishops and the faithful, and the noteworthy acts and decretals of our predecessors, wonderfully illustrate and declare, after having diligently weighed all things and pouring forth to God our assiduous and fervent prayers, we have decided that we should not delay to sanction and define by our supreme judgment the Immaculate Conception of the same Virgin, and thereby to satisfy the loving desires of the Catholic world and our own filial love towards this most holy Virgin; and at the same time to honor in her more and more the only-begotten Son of God, Jesus Christ, our Lord, since whatever honor and praise is given to His Mother redounds to the Son.

Wherefore, after we have not neglected to offer, in humility and fasting, our private prayers and those of the Church to God the Father through His Son that He might deign to direct and confirm our mind by the power of the Holy Spirit, having sought the help of the whole heavenly court, having invoked with sighs the comforting Spirit, and thus by His inspiration—for the honor of the holy and undivided Trinity, for the glory and ornament of the Virgin Mother of God, for the exaltation of the Catholic Faith and the increase of the Christian Religion—by the authority of our Lord Jesus Christ, of the blessed Apostles Peter and Paul, and of our own, we hereby declare, proclaim, and define: The doctrine which holds that the most Blessed Virgin Mary, in the first instant of her conception, was by a singular grace and privilege of the omnipotent God, in view of the merits of Jesus Christ, Savior of mankind, preserved immune from all stain of original sin, was revealed by God, and therefore must firmly and constantly be believed by all the faithful. Wherefore, if any have presumed to think in their heart otherwise than has been defined by us (which God forbid), let them know and indeed realize that they are condemned by their own judgment, that they have suffered shipwreck in a matter of Faith, and have lapsed from the Unity of the Church.

℟. Magnify the Lord with me: * Because the mercy of the Lord is great towards me. ℣. The prince of this world has nothing in common with me. Because. Glory. Because.

III Nocturn

The reading of the holy Gospel according to St. Luke

At that time the angel Gabriel was sent from God into a city of Galilee, called Nazareth, to a Virgin espoused to a man whose name was Joseph, of the house of David, and the virgin's name was Mary. And so forth.

Homily of St. Epiphanius, Bishop

What shall I say, or what shall I declare concerning the excellent and holy Virgin? For with the exception of God alone, she stands far above all; she is more grand by nature than the Cherubim and Seraphim themselves and all the angelic army; no heavenly or earthly tongue is in the least able to praise her, nay, not even the tongue of angels. O blessed Virgin, pure dove and heavenly spouse, Mary, heaven, temple, and throne of the Divinity, who possesses Christ—the Sun shining in heaven and on earth! Bright cloud, who drew Christ as most brilliant lightning from heaven that He might illumine the world.

Hail, full of grace, gate of the heavens, concerning whom the Prophet in the course of prayer in the Canticle plainly and clearly speaks, exclaiming: "My sister, my spouse, is a garden enclosed, a fountain sealed up." The Virgin is an immaculate lily, who begot an undying rose—Christ. O thou holy Mother of God, spotless ewe, who has brought forth Christ the Lamb, the Word who has taken His flesh from you! O thou most holy Virgin, who hast brought the army of angels to wonder!

Marvelous is the miracle in the heavens, a woman clothed with the sun, carrying the light in her arms; marvelous is the miracle in the heavens, the bridal chamber of a Virgin bearing the Son of God; marvelous is the miracle in the heavens, the Lord of angels has become the Infant of a Virgin. The angels condemned Eve; now, however, in glory they follow Mary who raised up the fallen Eve and who sent into heaven Adam who had been cast out of paradise. For she herself is the mediatrix between heaven and earth, who effected their union by nature.

The grace of the holy Virgin is immeasurable. Hence Gabriel first salutes the Virgin by saying: Hail, full of grace, you are a glorious heaven. Hail, full of grace, a Virgin adorned with many virtues. Hail, full of grace, you are a golden vessel containing the heavenly manna. Hail, full of grace, you satisfy the thirsty by the sweetness of an everlasting fountain. Hail, most holy Mother Immaculate, you have given birth to Christ, who existed before you. Hail, royal purple, you have clothed the King of heaven and earth. Hail, unfathomable book, you show forth the Son of the Father and the Word to be read by the world.

℟. My soul doth magnify the Lord; * Because He that is mighty hath done great things to me, and holy is His name. ℣. For behold from henceforth all generations shall call me blessed. Because. Glory. Because.

✠ Continuation of the holy Gospel according to St. Luke.— At that time the angel Gabriel was sent from God to a town of Galilee called Nazareth, to a virgin betrothed to a man named Joseph, of the house of David, and the virgin's name was Mary. And when the angel had come to her, he said, "Hail, full of grace, the Lord is with thee. Blessed art thou among women."

LET US PRAY

O God, who by the Immaculate Conception of the Virgin Mary didst prepare a worthy dwelling for Thy Son, we beseech Thee, that as Thou didst preserve her from every stain through the foreseen merits of that same Son, Thou, by her intercession wouldst grant us, cleansed from sin, to come to Thee. Through our Lord.

December 21

ST. THOMAS, APOSTLE

I Nocturn

From the first Epistle of St. Paul the Apostle to the Corinthians, c. 4, 1 - 15

II Nocturn

Thomas the Apostle, also named the Twin, was a Galilean. After he had received the Holy Spirit, he travelled through many provinces, preaching the Gospel of Christ. He transmitted the precepts of the Christian Faith and life to the Parthians, Medes, Persians, Hyrcanians, and Bactrians. He finally went to the Indies, and instructed the inhabitants in the Christian religion. Up to the last, by the holiness of his life and teaching, and by the greatness of the miracles which he wrought, he excited the admiration of all men and led them to the love of Jesus Christ. The king of that nation, a worshipper of idols, was furiously angry, and gave orders that Thomas should be pierced with javelins, and thus, at Calamina, the crown of martyrdom adorned the glory of his apostolate.

Sermon of St. Gregory, Pope

It is written, "The spirit of the Lord adorned the heavens." For the ornaments of the heavens are the virtues of its preachers, which adornments Paul enumerates saying: "To one indeed, by the Spirit, is given the word of wisdom; and to another the word of knowledge, according to the same Spirit; to another, faith in the same Spirit; to another, the grace of healing in one Spirit; to another, the working of miracles; to another, prophecy; to another, the discerning of spirits; to another, diverse kinds of tongues; to another, interpretation of speeches. But all these things one and the same Spirit worketh, dividing to every one according as he will."

Therefore as many as are the virtues of the preachers, so many are the ornaments of the heavens. Hence it is again written, "By the word of the Lord the heavens were established." Now the Word of the Lord is the Son of the Father. But in order that at the same time the complete Holy Trinity be shown to have formed these heavens, that is, the holy apostles, it is immediately added in reference to the divinity of the Holy Spirit: "And all the power of them by the Spirit of his mouth." Therefore the power of the heavens is drawn from the Spirit; because they would not have dared to withstand the powers of this world unless the fortitude of the Holy Spirit had confirmed them.

And it must be considered that He whom, when bound on earth, Peter denied, when suspended from the cross, the thief confessed. But let us hear what kind of person this man of such great timidity became after the coming of the Holy Spirit. There was a gathering of the magistrates and seniors and it was commanded the apostles, with blows, that they cease preaching in the name of Jesus. With great authority Peter answered: "It behooveth us to obey God rather than men."

℟. I saw men standing together, clad in shining garments; and the Angel of the Lord spoke to me, saying: * These holy men became the friends of God. ℣. I saw a mighty Angel of God, flying through the midst of heaven, crying out with a loud voice and saying. These. Glory. These.

III Nocturn

The reading of the holy Gospel according to St. John

At that time Thomas, one of the Twelve, called the Twin, was not with them when Jesus came. And so forth.

Homily of St. Gregory, Pope

Dearest brethren, what do you notice among these words? Do you suppose that it happened by chance that the chosen disciple was absent at the time, but on arriving afterwards, heard, and hearing, doubted, and doubting, touched with his hand and on touching believed? No, this was not by chance, but was brought about by divine dispensation. For the Divine Goodness acted so that the doubting disciple, when he had touched the wounds of the flesh in his Master, might heal the wounds of infidelity in us.

For the faithlessness of Thomas aids us in our belief more than does the faith of the disciples who believed, because when he is brought to believe by feeling with his own hand, every doubt having been removed, our own mind is confirmed in faith. Thus the Lord indeed permits His disciple to be in doubt after His Resurrection, but He does not forsake him in his doubt; just as before His birth He wished that Mary should have a spouse who, however, did not come to wed her. For the disciple who doubted and touched was made a witness of the truth of the Resurrection, just as the spouse of His mother had been the guardian of her unspotted virginity.

He touched Him and exclaimed: "My Lord and my God." Jesus said to him: "Because you have seen me, you have believed." Since the Apostle Paul declares, "Faith is the substance of the things hoped for and the argument of those things not apparent," certainly it is evident that faith is the support of the things which cannot be apparent. For as to the things which are apparent, we do not have faith, but knowledge.

When, therefore, Thomas has seen and felt, why is it said to him: "Because thou hast seen me, thou hast believed"? For he has seen one thing, but believed another. The Divinity cannot, indeed, be seen by any mortal man. Therefore, he saw man and confessed Him to be God, saying: "My Lord and my God." On seeing, then, he believed, who, on beholding a true man, proclaimed the same to be God whom he could not see. That which follows gives much joy: "Blessed are they who have not seen and yet have believed." Undoubtedly we are especially signified by this sentence who hold in our mind Him whom we have not seen in the flesh. But we are signified only if we follow up our faith by works. For he really believes who carries out in deed what he believes.

℟. These are the conquerors and the friends of God, who, despising the orders of princes, merited an eternal reward: * Now they are crowned, and they receive the palm. ℣. These are they who have come out of great tribulation, and have washed their robes in the blood of the Lamb. Now. Glory. Now.

✠ Continuation of the holy Gospel according to St. John.—At that time Thomas, one of the Twelve, called the Twin, was not with them when Jesus came. The other disciples therefore said to him, "We have seen the Lord." But he said to them, "Unless I see in his hands the print of the nails, and put my finger into the place of the nails, and put my hand into his side, I will not believe."

And after eight days, his disciples were again inside, and Thomas with them. Jesus came, the doors being closed, and stood in their midst, and said, "Peace be to you!" Then he said to Thomas, "Bring here thy finger, and see my hands; and bring here thy hand, and put it into my side; and be not unbelieving, but believing." Thomas answered and said to him, "My Lord and my God!" Jesus said to him, "Because thou hast seen me, thou hast believed. Blessed are they who have not seen, and yet have believed."

Let Us Pray

Grant us, we beseech Thee, O Lord, to rejoice in the solemn feast of blessed Thomas, Thy Apostle, that we may be always assisted by his help and imitate his faith with sincere devotion. Through our Lord.

January 15

ST. MAURUS, ABBOT

I Nocturn

From the Book of Ecclesiasticus, c. 44, 1 - 15

II Nocturn

From the second book of the Dialogues of St. Gregory, Pope

The holy man, St. Benedict, having returned to Subiaco, long continued to shine by his virtue and miracles, and assembled a great number of solitaries who consecrated themselves to the service of God, so that, with the aid of our Lord Jesus Christ, he built twelve monasteries, placing in each twelve Religious with an Abbot to govern them. He retained with himself only a few of his disciples who, he thought, still needed his presence to be better formed to perfection. It was at this time that many persons in Rome, conspicuous for their nobility and virtue, began to visit him and offer their children that he might mould them to piety, and teach them to live for God alone. Aequitius and Tertullus, who had the honor of being Roman Patricians, came to see the saint and confided to his care their two children; the former offered his son Maurus, and the latter, his son Placidus. Maurus was distinguished for spotless innocence of life, and merited, though young, to be chosen by his master to assist him in his functions. As to Placidus, being only a boy, he was subject to the weaknesses inseparable from tender age.

On another occasion, a certain Goth, a man of much simplicity, presented himself to Saint Benedict to become a monk, and the man of God most gladly received him among his disciples. One day the saint ordered a hook to be given him to cut some bush and thorns occupying the place intended for a garden. The place given him to clear was situated on the border of a lake, and as he worked with might and main, the iron slipped off the handle and flew into the lake which was so deep that there could be no hope of recovering the lost blade. The Goth, seeing his iron lost, went, trembling with fear, to the monk, Maurus, and told him the loss the monastery sustained and underwent penance. Maurus made the matter known at once to Benedict, the servant of God, who, as soon as he had heard it, went to the shore. He took the handle from the Goth and immersed it a little in the water. Immediately the blade returned from the bottom of the lake and adjusted itself to the handle. The hook having been thus restored, Benedict returned it to the Goth, saying: "Take thy hook, go to work, and trouble thyself no further."

The venerable Benedict being one day in his cell, the boy Placidus, one of his religious, went out to fetch water from the lake, but, when dipping his pitcher into the water, not taking sufficient heed, his body followed the vessel and he fell into the lake. The waves immediately bore him out from the land as far as the usual flight of an arrow. The saint, who was in his cell, knew of the sad accident at that very instant, and at once calling Maurus, his disciple, said to him: "Brother Maurus, run with all speed; the boy who went to fetch water fell into the lake and has been already carried off a long distance."

A thing wonderful and unheard of since that instance of the Apostle Peter! Maurus having asked and received the blessing, ran to the lake to execute the order of his Abbot. Thinking he was treading upon dry land, he advanced to the very place whither the waves had carried off the child, and laying hold of him by the hair, brought him back with great haste to the shore. Having reached the land, he began to reflect on what he did, and casting a look behind, saw that he had been running over the waves. He was astonished thereat and very much afraid, seeing that he had performed what he would not have dared to undertake if he had been aware of what he was doing. Having returned to the monastery, he narrated the whole occurrence to the Abbot. The venerable Benedict did not attribute this miracle to his own merit, but to the obedience of the disciple. Maurus, on the other hand, said he was only fulfilling a command, and could have no share in a miracle which he unconsciously performed.

During this pious dispute arising from the humility of the holy Abbot and his disciple, the boy rescued from peril presented himself as arbitrator, and put an end to the contest thus: "When I was being drawn out of the waves, I saw the Abbot's robe above my head, and it seemed to me that it was he who delivered me from the water." This is narrated by Pope St. Gregory. An ancient tradition says that the monk Maurus was sent into Gaul by the same holy Father. There, according to the same tradition, he founded a monastery at Glannofol; after having governed it for a long time, he died in the Lord in a good old age, renowned for his sanctity and miracles.

℟. This man knew righteousness and saw great wonders, and made his prayer to the Most High: * And he is numbered among the Saints. ℣. This is he who despised the life of the world, and hath attained to the heavenly kingdom. And. Glory. And.

III Nocturn

The reading of the holy Gospel according to St. Matthew

At that time Peter answered Jesus and said, "Lord, if it is thou, bid me come to thee over the water." And he said, "Come." And so forth.

Homily of St. Jerome, Priest

In all places Peter is found to be a man of a most ardent faith. When the apostles were asked whom men said Jesus was, Peter confessed Him to be the Son of God. He restrained Him in His desire to push on to His Passion; and although by not wishing Him to die whom he had just before confessed to be the Son of God, he errs in perception, yet he does not err in affection. As the first among the first, he ascends the mountain with the Savior, and at the Passion he followed alone. The sin of denial which had come upon him from a sudden fear, he quickly washed away with bitter tears. After the Passion when they were on Lake Genesareth fishing and Jesus was standing on the shore, while the others slowly advanced, Peter brooked no delay, but, girt with his coat, instantly cast himself into the waves.

While the rest remain silent, he now believes, with the same burning faith with which he always believed, that he can do, by the will of his Master, that which the Master could do by His very nature. "Bid me come to thee upon the waters." Do Thou command, and on the spot the waves will become firm; let the body which of itself is heavy become light. "And Peter, going down out of the boat, walked upon the waters to come to Jesus." Let those who think that the body of the Lord is not a real body because, not being weighty, it easily passed over the unresisting waters, explain how Peter, whom they will certainly not deny was a true man, walked upon the waves.

"But seeing the wind strong, he was afraid, and when he began to sink he cried out, saying, 'Lord, save me!'" The faith of his soul was ardent; nevertheless, human frailty was drawing him into the deep. He was therefore abandoned to the temptation for a time that his faith might be increased and that he might know that he was saved not by merely asking, but by the power of the Lord. "And Jesus, immediately stretching forth his hand, took hold of him and said to him, 'O thou of little faith, why didst thou doubt?'" If these words are addressed to the Apostle Peter, concerning whose faith and ardor we have spoken above, who confidently besought the Savior, saying to Him, "Lord, if it be thou, bid me come to thee upon the waters," what is to be said to us who have not even the smallest portion of his little faith?

"And they that were in the boat came and adored him, saying, 'Indeed thou art the Son of God.'" At this one event when the tranquility of the sea was restored, which after fierce storms usually happens gradually and by natural order, sailors and fishermen confess that the Lord is indeed the Son of God, and does Arius preach in the church that He is a creature?

℟. The Lord hath loved him and hath adorned him: * He hath clothed him with a robe of glory. ℣. And hath crowned him at the gates of Paradise. He. Glory. He.

✠ Continuation of the holy Gospel according to St. Matthew.—At that time Peter answered Jesus and said, "Lord, if it is thou, bid me come to thee over the water." And he said, "Come." Then Peter got out of the boat and walked on the water to come to Jesus. But when he saw the strong wind, he was afraid; and as he began to sink he cried out, saying, "Lord, save me!" And Jesus at once stretched forth his hand and took hold of him, saying to him, "O thou of little faith, why didst thou doubt?" And when they got into the boat, the wind fell. But they who were in the boat came and worshipped him, saying, "Truly thou art the Son of God."

Let Us Pray

O God, who, to teach us obedience, didst make St. Maurus walk dry-shod upon the waters, grant that we may merit to follow the example of his virtues and share in his reward. Through our Lord.

January 21
ST, MEINRAD, MARTYR, AND PATRON OF THE ABBEY

I Nocturn

*From the Epistle of St. Paul the Apostle
to the Romans, c. 8, 12 - 19 and 28 - 39*

II Nocturn

Meinrad, born of noble parentage in Alemannia, while yet a boy was sent by his father Bertholde, count of Sulgovia, to the holy monastery at Auga, and was entrusted to his relative Erlebald, a monk of remarkable holiness. From that time on Meinrad held him as his model, so that when he was twenty-five years old, as a priest—afterwards becoming a monk also—he was far in advance of those seeking the more perfect life. And after his perfection in Christian virtues had been publicly approved, especially those of chastity, humility, and obedience, he became spiritual director of the school at Bollingen; in this place he soon began to long for a life of solitude.

And so in time, when the possibilities of a nearby wood had been explored and the permission of the Abbot obtained, taking along with him a Missal, a Breviary, the Rule of our holy father Benedict, and a small edition of Cassian, he retired to Mt. Etzel, rising above the Lake of Zurich; here, although he was severe in his fasts, vigils, and discipline of the body, he nevertheless spent seven delightful years in prayer and contemplation of things divine. And when the frequent concourse of men who were attracted by his holiness became overly burdensome, in order to forestall it and at the same time to enjoy seclusion, he betook himself to the vast solitude of a hidden glen and lived the rest of his life in admirable sanctity.

Although at other times also the devil tried him by recurring onslaughts, on one day, however, while he was praying very recollectedly, he attacked him with a fury more violent than usual; besides the terrifying screams and uproar, he was enveloped by so great a number of srecters about him that the princes of darkness even cut out the very light of day. Meinrad, in the midst of the horrors of the night and of the onrushing phantoms, sought help from heaven, and received it. For immediately an angel of the Lord, vested in a most brilliant light, so forcefully dispersed the evil spirits that from that time on they never again dared to approach him. Another consolation from heaven also followed. A little boy of seven years of very noble mien seemed to come to him from the chapel and pray with him, and to relate to him mysteries of which it is not given man to speak.

After twenty-six years had been passed by the holy man in this great wilderness, two evil men who had plotted against him ventured into the solitude, and, although received by him in a most hospitable manner and told of their purpose by him (for he had, indeed, during the Sacrifice which he had just offered shortly before in the presence of the Most High, been admonished of the design of the assassins), they nevertheless wickedly and miserably strangled him after he had been brutally beaten, on the twenty-first of January, in the year of Redemption, 861. How pleasing this victim was to God, several miracles soon after proved. For the candle placed at the head of the Martyr was divinely lighted; the whole hermitage was pervaded with the sweetest odor; and the wicked men, betrayed by the nipping and pecking of ravens which the Saint had formerly fed, were burned alive head downward. Some years after, a great monastery was erected over the place of his martyrdom, which today is venerated over the whole world in memory of this martyr, and especially because the chapel of the Virgin Mother of God has been divinely consecrated, and, moreover, because of the graces and frequent miracles from this same Virgin.

℟. The Saints of God feared not the stripes of the tormentors, dying for Christ's name: * That they might be heirs in the house of the Lord. ℣. They gave their bodies to torments for God. That. Glory. That.

III Nocturn

The reading of the holy Gospel according to St. Matthew

At that time Jesus said to his disciples: "Do not think that I came to send peace upon the earth; I have come to bring a sword, not peace." And so forth.

Homily of St. Peter Chrysologus

"Think ye that I came to send peace on the earth? Not so, I tell you, but separation." But what of that saying, "Behold the Lamb of God"? What of this other, "As a sheep that is led to the slaughter and as a lamb that is dumb in the presence of its shearer, so he did not open his mouth"? And of this one, "Say to the daughter of Sion: 'Behold, thy King cometh to thee in meekness'"? Why is it that this Lamb strikes so harshly in His preaching? Why does He grow so violent in word who in His passion holds His peace with such patience and who in death submits in all humility?

And indeed, brethren, Christ entered into the world in all things meek and gentle: for He is sweetly born into our race; in the cradle He allows Himself to be fondled lovingly, being Himself even more affectionate. He shows Himself as a little boy and even relaxes on a human lap; being caressed on the neck of His Mother, He returns the caress with a whole-hearted embrace of love. He always acts like a poor man; He always goes about as a solitary, because the poor man is always approachable; the solitary is accessible to all.

And how is it that He by His words spreads about such a great fire which inflames so greatly and so much, and spreads abroad so widely? Water begets fire—thus one must think—a union of things so contrary! Water begets flame, and the flame increases the water. What is this? How reconcile such discord? Herein is made known the action of the divine Husbandman; for absolutely everything springs forth by His heat, and by His moisture is nourished.

Whence God, the origin of all, by the mingling together of fire and water begets us and nourishes us, for whom He longs, wishes, seeks, and desires with such ardent affection. "Think you," He says, "that I came to send peace on earth?" No! Why? Because heavenly union is in this earthly separation. No one can be attached to the earth and joined to heaven. Precious, therefore, and dear is this earthly separation which so separates us from earthly things that it makes us participate in those that are divine.

℞. Thou hast crowned him * With glory and honor, O Lord. ℣. And hast set him over the works of Thy hands. With. Glory. With.

✠ Continuation of the holy Gospel according to St. Matthew.— At that time Jesus said to his disciples: "Do not think that I came to send peace upon the earth; I have come to bring a sword, not peace. For I have come to set a man at variance with his father, and a daughter with her mother, and a daughter-in-law with her mother-in-law; and a man's enemies will be those of his own household. He who loves father or mother more than me is not worthy of me; and he who loves son or daughter more than me is not worthy of me. And he who does not take up his cross and follow me, is not worthy of me. He who finds his life will lose it, and he who loses his life for my sake, will find it.

"He who receives you, receives me; and he who receives me, receives him who sent me. He who receives a prophet because he is a prophet, shall receive a prophet's reward; and he who receives a just man because he is a just man, shall receive a just man's reward. And whoever gives to one of these little ones but a cup of cold water to drink because he is a disciple, amen I say to you, he shall not lose his reward."

Let Us Pray

O almighty and eternal God, who art ever wonderful in the merits of St. Meinrad, Thy Martyr, we beseech Thee that as Thou hast granted him the eminent glory of martyrdom, thus also wouldst Thou grant us Thy mercy through his prayers. Through our Lord.

January 22

II DAY IN THE OCTAVE OF ST. MEINRAD

Sermon of St. Ambrose, Bishop

Although such a great witness of Christ, rich in his praise, richer in his blood, in his cruel wound, and more resplendent in his stained robe, may be thought to be withdrawn from us by the honor of his burial place, yet he belongs to us all through the communion of prayer. What is poured out in merits is not confined within bounds! You have, in every place, invoked the martyr; in every place has He heard you who is honored in the martyr. According to the determination of Him who examines your prayers and distributes His blessings, the presence of the powerful advocate is made so much the more intimate as the faith of you who call upon him shall be devoted. For the prayer which is enhanced by acts of chastity, justice, and charity passes beyond the world, penetrates into Paradise, soars up even into the very sight of the Supreme Majesty, borne by an angel.

Since these things are so, let us honor the blessed martyrs, the princes of our Faith, the mediators for the world, the heralds of the Kingdom, co-heirs of God. Perhaps you will say to me: "Why do you honor the things of the flesh already dissolved and consumed, for which God has now no care?" But whence is that, dearly beloved, which Truth Itself speaks by the Prophet? He says: "Precious in the sight of the Lord is the death of his saints." And again: "But to me thy friends, O God, are made exceedingly honorable." We are to honor the servants of God; how much more God's saints! Of them it is declared in another passage: "The Lord keepeth all their bones, not one of them shall be broken."

And so I honor in the flesh of the martyr the wounds received in the name of Christ; I honor the memory of him living through the enduring of his virtue. I honor the ashes made sacred by praise for their Lord; I honor in these ashes the seed of eternity; I honor the body which has shown me how to love my Lord, which has taught me not to fear death for my Lord's sake. Why should not the faithful honor that body which even the demons reverence? That body which the demons have tormented with suffering they now glorify in its sepulchre! Therefore do I honor the body which Christ has glorified by the sword, and which shall reign with Christ in heaven.

January 23
III DAY IN THE OCTAVE OF ST. MEINRAD
Sermon of St. Augustine, Bishop

May the Holy Spirit teach us at this time what we should say, for we are about to speak the praises of Saint Meinrad, the ever-glorious martyr, whose birthday, as you know, we keep today. And these, that is, the birthdays, the Church celebrates in such wise that she calls the precious death of the martyrs birthdays. What is this, brethren? When he was born we know not; but because today he suffered, today we keep his birthday. Yet that former day, even though we knew it, we would not keep. For on that day he contracted original sin; but on this he overcame every sin.

For us the suffering of the most blessed martyr Meinrad has made this day a feast; the fame of his victory has brought us, his devoted clients, to this place. But the celebration of the martyrs' solemnities should be an imitation of their virtues. It is easy to celebrate a martyr's honor; it is a great thing to imitate the faith and patience of a martyr. Let us so do the latter that we may desire the former; let us so celebrate the latter that we may the more prize the former. Why do we praise the faith of a martyr? Because even to death he battled for the truth and therefore he conquered. The alluring world he spurned; to the raging world he yielded not; therefore, a victor, he approaches God. Errors and terrors abound in this world. Our blessed martyr overcame the errors with wisdom, the terrors with suffering.

Spurn the world therefore, Christians, spurn, spurn the world. The martyrs spurned it, the Apostles spurned it. Blessed Meinrad, whose memory we keep today, spurned it. Do you wish to be rich? honored? healthy? All these he spurned in whose memory you have come together. Why, I beg, do you love so much what he whom you so honor spurned? Surely, if he had not spurned these things, you would not so honor him. Why do I find you a lover of those things whose scorner you venerate? Without doubt if he had loved them you would not venerate him. Do not love them; for he has not entered and closed the door against you. Do you spurn them too and enter after him.

January 24
IV DAY IN THE OCTAVE OF ST. MEINRAD
Sermon of St. Peter Chrysologus

Because today we gather with God on the birthday of the martyr St. Meinrad, when he triumphed in glorious battle over the devil, leaving us the wonderful example of his virtues, it is therefore fitting that we rejoice and be glad. So when you hear the word *birthday*, dearly beloved, do not think that that day is spoken of when men are born on earth in the flesh; but the day when they are born from the earth into heaven, from toil to rest, from trials to peace, from hardships to delights, not passing, but constant, stable and eternal—from the vanities of the world to a crown and glory. Such birthdays of the martyrs are worthily celebrated.

Thus, dearly beloved, when a feast of this kind is held, do not reckon that martyrs' birthdays are to be celebrated solely with luncheons and more lavish banquets; rather, what you honor on the commemoration of a martyr is proposed to you for imitation. Hence consider, dearly beloved, the spirit of the people standing about, for once on this day a mob of wicked men looked on while St. Meinrad, by the tyrant's command, was being flogged; they were crowds of evil men, groups of spectators; now, a multitude of the faithful, set on praising him, has gathered together; then there was a mob of savages, now a crowd of rejoicers; then a mob of despairing men, now a crowd of men who hope.

For this reason, then, the birthdays of the martyrs are celebrated with joy each year, so that what happened but once might forever remain in the memory of the faithful. The act was performed, dearly beloved, that you might not say you did not know; it is celebrated yearly lest you should say, "I forgot." So spur yourselves on to imitate these things, dearly beloved; yearn for the grace of generous love; beg that that might be granted to you which he merited to obtain!

January 25

CONVERSION OF ST. PAUL

I Nocturn

From the Acts of the Apostles, c. 9, 1 - 16

II Nocturn

Sermon of St. Augustine, Bishop

We have heard today from the Acts of the Apostles how the Apostle Paul was changed from a persecutor of the Christians to a preacher of Christ. Christ struck down the persecutor that He might raise him up a teacher of His Church. He struck him and healed him; He slew him and re-enlivened him. For Christ is the Lamb that was slain by the wolves and that now changes the wolves into lambs. In Paul was fulfilled that which was clearly prophesied by the Patriarch Jacob at the time when he blessed his sons, laying hands on those who were then present, but looking forward to the happenings of the future.

Paul tells us himself that he was of the tribe of Benjamin. When Jacob, blessing his sons, came to Benjamin, he said, "Benjamin, a ravenous wolf." What then? Shall Benjamin always be a ravenous wolf? God forbid! "In the morning he shall devour the prey, and at night he shall divide the spoil." This is exactly what was fulfilled in Paul.

Now, if it please you, we will consider how he devoured the prey in the morning, and how he divided the spoil at night. Here morning and evening signify beginning and end. So we may read, "In the beginning he shall devour the prey, and in the end he shall divide the spoil." First, then, in the beginning he devoured the prey, as we read that he, having received letters from the chief priests, went forth in order that, if he should find any Christians, he might bring them to the priests for punishment.

He went breathing out threatenings and slaughter; indeed he was devouring the prey. When the first martyr, Stephen, was stoned for confessing the name of Christ, Saul gave his consent to the crime, and, as though it were not enough for him to cast stones, he kept the garments of all those who did it, thus venting his rage more than if he had cast stones with his own hands. Thus in the morning he devoured the prey. How did he divide the spoil in the evening? Struck down by the voice of Christ from heaven, and receiving from above a prohibition to further raging, he fell upon his face, first to be prostrated, then to be raised up; first to be wounded, then to be healed.

℟. Thou art a vessel of election, O holy Apostle Paul, a preacher of the truth to the whole world: * Through whom all nations have known the grace of God. ℣. Intercede for us with God, who chose thee. Through. Glory. Through.

III Nocturn

The reading of the holy Gospel according to St. Matthew

At that time Peter said to Jesus: "Behold, we have left all and followed thee; what then shall we have?" And so forth.

Homily of St. Bede the Venerable, Priest

He is a perfect man who, going, sells all that he has and gives to the poor, and coming, follows Christ, for he shall have a never-ending treasure in heaven. And hence at Peter's well-chosen question Jesus says to men of this kind, "Amen I say to you, that you who have followed me, in the regeneration, when the Son of man shall sit on the seat of his majesty, you also shall sit on twelve seats judging the twelve tribes of Israel."

He taught those who labor for His name's sake in this life to hope for a reward in the next; that is, in the regeneration, when they who were born as men into this frail life shall have been regenerated into life eternal by rising again. And truly it is a just reward that they, who here disregard the glory of human greatness for the sake of Christ, who could not be drawn away from following His footsteps by any motive, should there sit with Him as glorified judges.

But let no one think that only the twelve apostles (for Matthias was chosen in the place of the apostate Judas) will be judges; just as not only are the twelve tribes of Israel to be judged. Otherwise the tribe of Levi, which is the thirteenth, would escape judgment. And Paul, who is the thirteenth Apostle, would be deprived of his privilege of judging, although he himself says, "Know ye not that we shall judge angels? how much more the things of this world?"

For you should know that all who, after the example of the apostles, have left all things and followed Christ, are going to sit in judgment with Him, just as every race of mortal men is to be judged. For since universality is often denoted in Scripture by the number twelve, the great number of all those who are to judge is shown by the twelve seats of the Apostles, just as by the twelve tribes of Israel the universality of all those to be judged is designated.

℟. O holy Apostle Paul, preacher of the truth and teacher of the Gentiles, * Intercede for us to God who chose thee, that we may be made worthy of the grace of God. ℣. Thou art a vessel of election, O holy Apostle Paul, a preacher of the truth. Intercede. Glory. ` Intercede.

✠ Continuation of the holy Gospel according to St. Matthew.— At that time Peter said to Jesus: "Behold, we have left all and followed thee; what then shall we have?" And Jesus said to them, "Amen I say to you that you who have followed me, in the regeneration when the Son of Man shall sit on the throne of his glory, shall also sit on twelve thrones, judging the twelve tribes of Israel. And everyone who has left house, or brothers, or sisters, or father, or mother, or wife, or children, or lands, for my name's sake, shall receive a hundredfold, and shall possess life everlasting."

LET US PRAY

O God, who hast instructed the whole world by the preaching of blessed Paul the Apostle, grant us, we beseech Thee, that we who honor the memory of his conversion may come to Thee through his example. Through our Lord.

January 26
VI DAY IN THE OCTAVE OF ST. MEINRAD
Sermon of St. Bernard

"Precious in the sight of the Lord is the death of his saints." Let the sinner "hear and be angry," let him "gnash his teeth and pine away." He has been caught in his own craftiness, he has fallen into the pit he has made, he has entangled himself in the snare which he hath set for us. For it was by the envy of the devil that death came into the world, and now behold, "precious in the sight of the Lord is the death of his saints." For it was not otherwise than by this bodily death that the holy martyr whose festival we are keeping today triumphed over Satan. He made a virtue out of necessity; he changed what was the penalty of sin into a title to eternal glory; he proved himself faithful in a little thing in order that he might be found worthy to be placed over many things.

Therefore he proved himself faithful to the Benefactor to whom he owed everything by despising everything for His love, and by "counting all things to be but loss and esteeming them as dung that he might gain Christ." But perhaps the enemy is not satisfied even yet, and begins to murmur: "Skin for skin and all that a man hath he will give for his life." What then? Deemest thou that when there is question of sacrificing his bodily life he will be found unfaithful to the Lord from whom he received it, so as even to prefer that life to his God? "Behold, he is in thy hand." Command thy satellites to rush upon him and to reduce him to such straits that he shall be under the necessity of either renouncing his allegiance to the Lord or of losing his corporal life. Devise various and cruel kinds of torture, but remember that thou art only fashioning crowns for our martyr.

He shall be crowned, consequently, because he has "lawfully striven," because he has faithfully conquered, because neither the pleasures of this world nor the fear of death could separate him from the charity of Christ. What do we say to this, brethren? We felicitate the martyr on his triumph, but the thought of his glory ought to cover us with confusion. For the blessed Meinrad "was a man passible like unto us," "encompassed with infirmity," and like unto us attached to his body by the bonds of natural affection. Therefore if he thus glorified Christ in his body and took the chalice of salvation, what have we rendered to the Lord for all the things that He hath rendered to us?

January 28

OCTAVE DAY OF THE FEAST OF ST. MEINRAD

Sermon of St. Augustine, Bishop

Men who are ill patiently allow themselves to be cut by the surgeons, to be cauterized, and to be annoyed by different compounds of bitters, so that they may be restored finally to temporal health; how much better has this blessed man perseveringly suffered all the bitterness of temporal torments that he might be crowned with mercy and compassion, and that his desire might be satiated with riches? In the wine-press, therefore, he wished to be trodden upon so that as a ripened grape he might change into wine and give the wine of pomegranates to his Beloved to drink—which inebriated religious minds know is to tread manfully and to pant with unflinching eyes for things eternal.

Therefore he, who in the beginning of his life has despised worldly riches, who has likewise tamed the lusts of the body, who in the carrying on of his warfare has suffered many injuries, by keeping nothing back for himself in the consummation of the sacrifice, has offered himself as a holocaust, drinking of that precious chalice which he had seen first placed before him by his Host while sitting at the great table of sacred reading. His death, however much it may appear despicable in the sight of reprobates, is nevertheless precious in the eyes of Him who "is wonderful in his saints."

For He, in the first place, has called His soldier; He has Himself justified him; He has made him great; He has granted him to fight; He has granted him to conquer. Far different is this warfare from warfare in the world, in which they are reckoned as victors who achieve what they wrongly desire, who are made glad when they have committed evil and exult in their most infamous acts.

In a Christian's martyrdom, then, the penalty is manifest, the victory hidden, according to which the Psalmist cries out in the person of the martyrs, "Grant us help from trouble, for vain is the help of man. Through God we shall do mightily," as if they would declare, "Our victory, our glory is within; it is not without. On the outside we are despised; within, beloved."

February 2

PURIFICATION OF THE BLESSED VIRGIN

I Nocturn

From the Book of Exodus, c. 13, 1 - 3, 11 - 13, and from the Book of Leviticus, c. 12, 1 - 8

II Nocturn

Sermon of St. Augustine, Bishop

It was once thus prophesied: Mother Sion says, "And a man was made man in her, and the Highest Himself hath founded her." O the all-powerfulness of Him who is born! O the majesty of Him who comes down from heaven to earth! He was yet carried within the womb, and was greeted by John the Baptist who was also in his mother's womb. He was presented in the temple, and was recognized by Simeon, a famous old man, full of years, upright and venerable.

First he recognized Him; next he adored Him; then he declared: "Now thou dost dismiss thy servant, O Lord, in peace; because my eyes have seen thy salvation." He had delayed to leave the world so that he might see Him born by whom the world was made. The old man recognized the Infant; through the Child he became a child. He who was filled with filial love was renewed in age. Simeon the old man held the Infant Christ, but Christ ruled over Simeon's old age.

It had been told him by the Lord that he should not taste death until he had seen the Anointed of the Lord born. Christ was born, and the old man's desire was fulfilled in the old age of the world itself. He who found the world grown old comes to the aged man. Indeed he was not desirous to remain long in this world, yet he desired to see Christ in this world, chanting with the Prophet and saying: "Show us, O Lord, thy mercy; and grant us thy salvation."

Finally, in order that you might know that such was his joy, he ended by saying: "Now thou dost dismiss thy servant, O Lord, in peace, because my eyes have seen thy salvation." The Prophets had sung of the Creator of heaven and earth who was to be on earth with men; the Angel announced that the Maker of flesh and spirit was coming in the flesh; from the womb John greeted the Savior within the womb; Simeon, as an old man, recognized the Infant as God.

℟. Simeon received an answer from the Holy Ghost that he should not see death before he had seen the Christ of the Lord: * And he blessed God and said: Now Thou dost dismiss Thy servant, O Lord, in peace, because my eyes have seen Thy salvation. ℣. When His parents brought in the Child Jesus to do for Him according to the custom of the law, he took Him into his arms. And. Glory. And.

III Nocturn

The reading of the holy Gospel according to St. Luke

At that time, when the days of Mary's purification were fulfilled according to the Law of Moses, they took Jesus up to Jerusalem to present him to the Lord—as it is written in the Law of the Lord. And so forth.

Homily of St. Ambrose, Bishop

"And behold there was a man in Jerusalem whose name was Simeon, a just and devout man, waiting for the consolation of Israel." The birth of the Lord is testified to not only by the angels, prophets, and shepherds, but also by the elders and the just. Every age and both sexes, as well as the miraculous course of events, confirm the belief.

A virgin conceives, the sterile woman gives birth to a child, the dumb man speaks, Elizabeth prophesies, the wise man adores, the infant in the womb leaps for joy, the widow praises, and the just man is in expectation. And he is indeed just who seeks not his own gain but that of the people, desiring himself to be freed from the bonds of this bodily frailty, yet waiting for the promised One; for he knew that those eyes that should see Him would be blessed.

"He also took Him into his arms, and blessed God, and said: 'Now dismiss thy servant, O Lord, according to thy word, in peace.'" Behold a just man confined, as it were, in the prison of a bodily substance, wishing to be dissolved that he might begin to be with Christ. For to be dissolved and to be with Christ is much more desirable. But let him who wished to be dissolved come to the temple, let him come to Jerusalem, let him wait for the Anointed of the Lord, let him take into his hands the Word of God, let him embrace Him with good works, the arms, as it were, of his faith; then let him be dismissed, for he who has seen the Life shall not see death.

You see the grace, diffused by the Lord's birth, abounding in all; you see, too, that prophesying was denied to the unbelievers, but not to the just. Behold, now Simeon also prophesies that the Lord Jesus Christ has come for the fall and resurrection of many, to discern the merits both of the just and the wicked, and as a true and just judge to mete out either punishment or reward according to the quality of our actions.

℟. The old man bore the Child, but the Child was the old man's King: * Whom a Virgin conceived, a Virgin brought forth, a Virgin she remained, and adored Him whom she had brought forth. ℣. Simeon, taking the Child into his arms, gave thanks and blessed the Lord. Whom. Glory. Whom.

☩ Continuation of the holy Gospel according to St. Luke.— At that time when the days of Mary's purification wer fulfilled according to the Law of Moses, they took Jesus up to Jerusalem to present him to the Lord—as it is written in the Law of the Lord, "Every male that opens the womb shall be called holy to the Lord"—and to offer a sacrifice according to what is said in the Law of the Lord, "a pair of turtledoves or two young pigeons."

And behold, there was in Jerusalem a man named Simeon, and this man was just and devout, looking for the consolation of Israel, and the Holy Spirit was upon him. And it had been revealed to him by the Holy Spirit that he should not see death before he had seen the Christ of the Lord. And he came by inspiration of the Spirit into the temple. And when his parents brought in the child Jesus, to do for him according to the custom of the Law, he also received him into his arms and blessed God, saying, "Now thou dost dismiss thy servant, O Lord, according to thy word, in peace; because my eyes have seen thy salvation, which thou hast prepared before the face of all peoples: a light of revelation to the Gentiles, and a glory for thy people Israel."

Let Us Pray

O almighty and eternal God, we suppliantly beseech Thy Majesty that as Thy only-begotten Son was on this day in the substance of our flesh offered in the temple, Thou wouldst grant us to be offered to Thee with purified souls. Through the same Jesus Christ.

February 10
ST. SCHOLASTICA, VIRGIN

I Nocturn

From the Canticle of Canticles, c. 2, 1 - 5; c. 8, 1 - 7

II Nocturn

From the second book of the Dialogues
of St. Gregory, Pope

Scholastica was the sister of the venerable father Benedict. She had been consecrated to almighty God from her very infancy, and was accustomed to visit her brother once a year. The man of God came down to meet her at a house belonging to the monastery, not far from the gate. It was the day for the usual visit, and her venerable brother came down to her with some of his brethren. The whole day was spent in the praises of God and holy conversation; and at nightfall they took their repast together. Whilst they were at table and it grew late, as they conferred with each other on sacred things, the holy woman thus spoke to her brother: "I beseech thee, stay the night with me, and let us talk till morning on the joys of heaven." He replied: "What is this thou sayest, O sister? On no account may I remain out of the monastery." The evening was so fair that not a cloud could be seen in the sky.

Therefore, when the holy woman heard her brother's refusal, she clasped her hands together, and, resting them on the table, she hid her face in them and prayed to the almighty God. As soon as she raised her head from the table, there came down so great a storm of thunder and lightning and torrents of rain that neither the venerable Benedict nor the brethren who were with him could set foot outside the place where they were sitting. Indeed, the holy woman, bowing her head in her hands, had shed a torrent of tears on the table; and as she wept, the clear sky produced rain. The rain fell in torrents immediately after the prayer, and such was the accord between the prayer and the storm that, when she raised her head from the table, the thunder came, since it was in one and the same instant that she raised her head and that the rain fell.

Then the man of God, seeing it was impossible to reach the monastery in lightning and thunder and torrential rain, was sad, and said complainingly, "Almighty God forgive thee, sister; what hast thou done?" But she replied: "I asked thee a favor, and thou wouldst not hear me; I asked it of my God, and He heard me. Go now if thou canst; send me away and go back to the monastery." But it was not in his power to leave the shelter; so that he who would not have stayed willingly had to stay unwillingly. And so it came about that they passed the whole night without sleep, entertaining each other with discussions about the mysteries of the spiritual life.

On the morrow the holy woman returned to her own cell and the man of God to the monastery. When lo! three days after, as he was in his cell, raising his eyes, he saw the soul of his sister going up to heaven in the shape of a dove. Full of joy at her being thus glorified, he thanked almighty God in hymns of praise, and told the brethren of her death. He straightway bade them go and bring the body to the monastery, and he had it buried in the tomb he had prepared for himself. Thus it was that as they had ever been one soul in God, their bodies were united in the same grave.

℟. After her shall virgins be brought to the King; her neighbors * Shall be brought to thee with gladness and rejoicing. ℣. With thy comeliness and thy beauty set out, proceed prosperously and reign. Shall. Glory. Shall.

III Nocturn

The reading of the holy Gospel according to St. Matthew

At that time Jesus spoke to his disciples this parable: "Then will the kingdom of heaven be like ten virgins who took their lamps and went forth to meet the bridegroom and the bride." And so forth.

Homily of St. Hilary, Bishop

Our Lord and God in the body is the bridegroom and the bride. For as the spirit is the bridegroom of the flesh, so the flesh is the bride of the spirit. At length at the sounding of the trumpet the virgins went forth to meet the bridegroom alone; for now the two were one, because the lowliness of the body had been drawn beyond itself into spiritual glory. By our first progress, by the duties of this life, we are prepared to hasten to the resurrection from the dead. The lamps are the light of shining souls, made brilliant by the Sacrament of Baptism. The oil is the fruit of good works. The vessels are the human bodies, in the interior of which the treasure of a good conscience lies hidden. The sellers are those who are in need of the mercy of the faithful, yet of themselves give ample return for the help which they seek, namely, the relief of their necessity, by selling, as it were, their knowledge of our good works. For these are the plentiful fuel for the unfailing light which must be purchased with the fruits of mercy and stored up.

The wedding itself is the assumption of immortality and the union in a new state between corruption and incorruption. The delay of the bridegroom is the repose of those who believe; and in the time of penance this sleep is the temporary death of all. The cry in the middle of the night, when all are unaware, is the voice of the trumpet preceding the coming of the Lord and rousing all to go forth to meet the bridegroom. The taking up of the lamps signifies the return of the soul into the bodies, and the light of the lamps, which is contained in the vessels of the bodies, is the consciousness of good works shining forth.

Those who, while in the body, have taken advantage of the opportune time for working and have prepared to go forth immediately at the coming of the bridegroom are the prudent virgins. The foolish ones are they who, careless and negligent, cared only for the things of the present, and, unmindful of the Lord's promises, have not concerned themselves with any hope of the resurrection. And now, because they could not go out to meet the bridegroom with unlighted lamps, they besought those who were prudent to lend them oil. But these answered that they could not give any, lest perhaps there would not be enough for all. By this is signified that no one can be helped by the works and merits of others, since it is necessary that each one buy oil for his own lamp. The wise exhorted the foolish to return and buy oil, in order that, although late in observing the precepts of God, they might, with lamps lighted, perhaps be made worthy for the coming of the bridegroom.

Whilst the foolish were thus delayed, the bridegroom came; and the wise ones, who were encircled by the carefully prepared light of their lamps, entered with him to the wedding feast; that is, they at once entered into heavenly glory at the coming of the majesty of the Lord. And because there is now no time for penance, the foolish hasten and ask that the door be opened to them. To whom the bridegroom makes answer that he does not know them. These were not at the ceremony of the Lord's coming, neither had they hastened at the sound of the trumpet warning them, neither had they joined the company of those entering with the bridegroom, but, by delaying, had wasted their time and so were unworthy of entering into the wedding feast.

℟. This is a wise virgin whom the Lord found watching, who, when she took her lamp, brought oil with her: * And when the Lord came, she went in with Him to the marriage. ℣. At midnight there was a cry made: Behold the Bridegroom cometh, go ye forth to meet Him. And. Glory. And.

✠ Continuation of the holy Gospel according to St. Matthew.—
At that time Jesus spoke to his disciples this parable: "Then will the kingdom of heaven be like ten virgins who took their lamps and went forth to meet the bridegroom and the bride. Five of them were foolish and five wise. But the five foolish, when they took their lamps, did not take oil with them; but the wise took oil in their vessels with the lamps. Then as the bridegroom was long in coming, they all became drowsy and slept. And at midnight a cry arose, 'Behold, the bridegroom is coming, go forth to meet him!' Then all those virgins arose and trimmed their lamps. And the foolish said to the wise, 'Give us some of your oil, for our lamps are going out.' The wise answered, saying, 'Lest there may not be enough for us and for you, go rather to those who sell, and buy for yourselves.'

"Now while they were away buying, the bridegroom came; and those who were ready went in with him to the marriage feast, and the door was shut. Finally there came also the other virgins, and said, 'Sir, sir, open the door for us!' But he answered and said, 'Amen I say to you, I do not know you.' Watch therefore, for you know neither the day nor the hour."

LET US PRAY

O God, who to show us the path of innocence didst cause the soul of Thy blessed virgin Scholastica to enter heaven in the likeness of a dove, grant us by her merits and prayers to live so innocently that we may merit to attain the eternal joys. Through our Lord.

February 22

ST. PETER'S CHAIR

I Nocturn

From the first Epistle of St. Peter the Apostle, c. 1, 1 - 21

II Nocturn

Sermon of St. Leo, Pope

When the twelve apostles, after having received the gift of all tongues through the Holy Spirit, began to imbue the world with the Gospel (according to the different sections of the land assigned to them), the most blessed Peter, prince of the apostolic order, was appointed to the citadel of Roman power, in order that the Light of Truth which was revealed for the salvation of all nations might shed itself more efficaciously from the head upon the whole body of the world.

Now what nation of men was not present in this city at that time? Or what tribes were ignorant of what Rome was teaching? Here the systems of philosophy had to be stamped out; here the follies of worldly wisdom had to be exterminated; here had to be repressed the worship of demons; here had to be wiped out the malice of every sacrilegious act—here where there had been collected with the strictest superstitious observance whatever had been inaugurated up to that time by foolish errors.

To this City, therefore, most blessed Apostle Peter, thou didst not fear to come, and while the Apostle Paul, companion of thy glory, was yet busied with the founding of other Churches, thou didst enter this forest of raging beasts and ocean of terribly troubled depths, far more courageous than when thou didst walk upon the sea!

Already thou hadst instructed those of the circumcision who had believed; thou hadst already established the church of Antioch where the name "Christian" had first arisen; already thou hadst confirmed Pontus, Galatia, Cappadocia, Asia, and Bithynia by the laws of the evangelical teaching; and neither doubting the outcome of thy work, nor unaware of the length of thy life, thou didst bear the trophy of the cross to the palaces of Rome, whither by Divine orders the honor of thy authority and the glory of thy martyrdom had preceded thee.

℞. Peter, lovest thou Me? Lord, Thou knowest that I love Thee. * Feed My sheep. ℣. Simon, son of John, lovest thou Me more than these? Lord, Thou knowest that I love Thee. Feed. Glory. Feed.

III Nocturn

The reading of the holy Gospel according to St. Matthew

At that time Jesus, having come into the district of Caesarea Philippi, began to ask his disciples, saying, "Who do men say the Son of Man is?" And so forth.

Homily of St. Hilary, Bishop

The Lord asked the disciples whom men were saying that He was, and He added, "Son of Man." For this manner of testimony must be retained, in order that, as we are mindful of the Son of God, so we also may be mindful of the Son of Man, for one without the other grants no hope for salvation. And so, after the opinions of men had been expressed, which differed concerning Him, He asked what they themselves thought of Him. Peter replied: "Thou art Christ, the Son of the living God!"

But Peter had been considering the terms of the proposition. For our Lord had said: "Whom do men say I, the Son of Man, am?" And surely the sight of His body gave evidence that He was the Son of Man. But by adding, "Whom do they say *I* am," He indicated that, besides what was to be seen in Him, something else must be considered, for He was indeed the Son of Man. What decision, then, did He want concerning Himself? We do not think it was that which He Himself had declared of Himself; rather, that which He was asking for, which the faith of those who believe must itself bring out, was something hidden.

A fully just reward did Peter's testimony receive, because he saw in the man the Son of God. Blessed is he who was praised because he strained his eyes to see beyond the human, and, not viewing that which was of flesh and blood, but beholding, through the revelation of the heavenly Father, the Son of God, was judged worthy to be the first to recognize what was in the Anointed of God.

O happy foundation of the Church in the declaration of your new name! O rock, worthy of that edifice, which would destroy the infernal laws, the gates of hell, and all the bonds of death! O blessed keeper of the heaven's gate, to whose judgment the keys of the heavenly portals are entrusted; whose earthly decision is a preconceived decree in heaven, so that what is bound or loosed on earth obtains the same status in heaven!

℟. Jesus said to His disciples: Whom do men say that the Son of Man is? Peter answered and said: Thou art Christ, the Son of the living God. * And I say to thee that thou art Peter, and upon this rock I will build My Church. ℣. Blessed art thou, Simon Bar-Jona, because flesh and blood hath not revealed it to thee, but My Father who is in heaven. And. Glory. And.

✠ Continuation of the holy Gospel according to St. Matthew.—
At that time Jesus, having come into the district of Caesarea Philippi, began to ask his disciples, saying, "Who do men say the Son of Man is?" But they said, "Some say, John the Baptist; and others, Elias; and others, Jeremias, or one of the prophets." He said to them, "But who do you say that I am?" Simon Peter answered and said, "Thou art the Christ, the Son of the living God." Then Jesus answered and said, "Blessed art thou, Simon Bar-Jona, for flesh and blood has not revealed this to thee,

but my Father in heaven. And I say to thee, thou art Peter, and upon this rock I will build my Church, and the gates of hell shall not prevail against it. And I will give thee the keys of the kingdom of heaven; and whatever thou shalt bind on earth shall be bound in heaven, and whatever thou shalt loose on earth shall be loosed in heaven."

LET US PRAY

O God, who didst give the keys of the heavenly kingdom and the priestly power of binding and loosing to blessed Peter, Thy Apostle, grant by the power of his intercession that we may be freed from the bonds of our sins, who livest and reignest with God the Father.

February 24
(In Leap Year, February 25)
ST. MATTHIAS, APOSTLE

I Nocturn

From the Acts of the Apostles, c. 1, 15 - 26

II Nocturn

From the Commentary of St. Augustine, Bishop, on Psalm 86

"The foundations thereof are in the holy mountains; the Lord loveth the gates of Sion." How are the apostles and prophets the *foundations?* Because their authority supports our weakness. Why are they *gates?* Because through them we enter the kingdom of God. For they preach to us, and when we enter through them, we enter through Christ. For He is the *door.* And although they are called the twelve gates of Jerusalem, yet Christ is the one gate, and Christ is likewise the twelve gates, because Christ is in the twelve gates, and therefore the number of the apostles was twelve.

A great mystery is signified by this number of twelve. "You shall sit," He said, "upon twelve thrones, judging the twelve tribes of Israel." If there are but twelve seats, there is no place for the thirteenth Apostle—Paul—to sit, and there will be no way for him to judge; yet he himself said that he will judge not only men, but even angels. What angels, but the apostate angels? "Do you not know," he says, "that we shall judge angels?" Therefore the people might answer: "Why do you boast that you will judge? Where will you sit? The Lord spoke of twelve thrones for the twelve Apostles; one fell—Judas—in whose place Matthias was ordained; the number of twelve seats is completed. First find the place where you will sit and then threaten to judge."

Therefore let us see what the twelve seats mean. It is a sign of a certain universality, for the Church was to be spread throughout the whole world, from whence, then, this edifice is called to union with Christ. And therefore, because they shall come from everywhere to judge, there are twelve thrones; just as, because they enter that city from all sides, there are twelve gates.

Therefore not only those twelve and the Apostle Paul, but as many as shall judge, shall sit on the twelve seats, because they symbolize the whole; just as howsoever many shall enter, shall enter through the twelve gates. For there are four divisions in the world—East, West, North, and South. These four parts are constantly mentioned in the Scriptures. From these four winds— for our Lord says in the Gospel that He will gather His elect from the four winds—the Church is called. How is she called? From every side she is called in the Trinity. She is not called except by Baptism in the name of the Father and of the Son and of the Holy Spirit. Thus—three times four equals twelve!

℟. These are they who, living in the flesh, planted the Church in their blood: * They drank the chalice of the Lord, and became the friends of God. ℣. Their sound hath gone forth into all the earth, and their words unto the ends of the world. They drank. Glory. They drank.

III Nocturn

The reading of the holy Gospel according to St. Matthew

At that time Jesus spoke and said, "I praise thee, Father, Lord of heaven and earth, that thou didst hide these things from the wise and prudent and didst reveal them to little ones." And so forth.

Homily of St. Augustine, Bishop

"Come to me all you that labor." Now why do we all labor, if not because we are mortal men, frail, weak, carrying about vessels of clay that are continually causing difficulties for one another? But if the vessels of the flesh do cause distress, let the avenue of charity be broadened. Why then does He say, "Come to me all you that labor," unless that you might not labor? In this case His promise is clear, for since He has called for laborers, perhaps they will ask about the reward to which they are called. "And I," He says, "will refresh you."

"Take up my yoke upon you and learn of me," not how to make a world, not how to create all things, visible and invisible, not how to work wonders in the world and to raise the dead, but—

"for I am meek and humble of heart." Dost thou wish to be great? Begin from the very least. Art thou planning on constructing a great and lofty edifice? Then first of all give thy thought to the foundation of humility.

Now when one wishes and determines to construct a building, the higher the building is to be, the deeper does one dig the foundation. As the building is under construction, it rises in the heights, but he who digs the foundation is forced down into the depths. And therefore the edifice is lowly before it is majestic; the pinnacle is reached only after humiliation.

What is this pinnacle of the edifice which we are striving to erect? To what height is the summit to reach? Without delay I answer, "Even to the sight of God." You see how exalted it is, how great a thing to behold God. He who desires, understands both what I say and what he hears. There is promised to us the sight of God, of the true God, of the most high God. This in very truth is something good—to see Him who sees. Those who worship false gods easily see these gods, but they see gods who have eyes and see not. But to us is promised the vision of the God who lives and sees.

℟. Blessed are ye when men shall revile and persecute you, and speak all that is evil against you, untruly, for My sake: * Be glad and rejoice, for your reward is very great in heaven. ℣. When men shall hate you, and when they shall separate you and shall reproach you, and cast out your name as evil, for the Son of Man's sake. Be glad. Glory. Be glad.

✠ Continuation of the holy Gospel according to St. Matthew.—At that time Jesus spoke and said, "I praise thee, Father, Lord of heaven and earth, that thou didst hide these things from the wise and prudent, and didst reveal them to little ones. Yes, Father, for such was thy good pleasure. All things have been delivered to me by my Father; and no one knows the Son except the Father; nor does anyone know the Father except the Son, and him to whom the Son chooses to reveal him.

"Come to me, all you who labor and are burdened, and I will give you rest. Take my yoke upon you, and learn from me, for I am meek and humble of heart; and you will find rest for your souls. For my yoke is easy, and my burden light."

Let Us Pray

O God, who didst join blessed Matthias to the company of Thy Apostles, grant, we beseech Thee, that by his intercession we may always experience Thy loving kindness towards us. Through our Lord.

March 12
ST. GREGORY THE GREAT
I Nocturn
From the Book of Ecclesiasticus, c. 39, 1 - 14
II Nocturn

Gregory the Great was a Roman, the son of a Senator named Gordian. In his youth he studied philosophy and later held the office of Prætor. His father having died, he built six monasteries in Sicily and a seventh one in his own house at Rome, near the church of SS. John and Paul, at the ascent of the hill called Scaurus. In this monastery, which he called after St. Andrew, he and his masters, Hilarion and Maximian, made profession as monks, and after some time Gregory was made Abbot. Later he was made Cardinal Deacon and sent as a legate to Constantinople. There he was the envoy of Pope Pelagius to the Emperor Tiberius Constantine. He disputed so successfully against the Patriarch Eutychius, who had denied that our bodies will truly rise again, that the Emperor, who was present, ordered the book of Eutychius to be thrown into the fire. Soon after this Eutychius fell sick, and when he saw death approaching he seized the skin of his own hand and said in the hearing of those present: "I acknowledge that we shall all rise again in this flesh."

Pelagius having died in a plague, Gregory, on his return to Rome, was unanimously chosen Pope. He refused the honor of this office as long as he was able to do so. Disguised, he hid in a cave, but a fiery pillar betrayed him. Having been discovered, his objections were overruled and he was consecrated at the tomb of St. Peter. To those who have succeeded him as Pope he left much to be imitated as regards doctrine and holiness. He brought pilgrims to his table daily and among them he entertained not merely an angel, but also the Lord of angels, who came in the guise of a pilgrim. He charitably provided for the poor, of whom he kept a list, both within and without the city. In many places where the Catholic Faith had been weakened Gregory restored it, successfully opposing the Donatists in Africa and the Arians in Spain. Alexandria was cleared of the Agnoites through his efforts. He refused to give the pallium to Syagrius, the Bishop of Autun, unless he would expel the Neophyte heretics from Gaul, and he induced the Goths to abandon the Arian heresy.

Pope Gregory sent Augustine and other holy and learned monks into England, who converted the inhabitants of that country to

Christ. Hence he is justly called by the Venerable Bede, the *Apostle of England*. He rebuked the presumption of John, Patriarch of Constantinople, who had assumed the title of Bishop of the Universal Church, and he persuaded the Emperor Maurice to revoke the decree by which he had forbidden soldiers to become monks. Gregory enriched the Church with holy customs and laws. He called a Synod at St. Peter's and in it decreed many things, including the repetition of the *Kyrie Eleison* nine times in the Mass, the use of *Alleluia* in the Church service except between Septuagesima and Easter, and the addition to the Canon of the Mass of the words, *And mayest thou dispose our days in thy peace*. He augmented the Litanies, the Stations, and the ecclesiastical office.

Gregory desired that the decrees of the four Councils of Nice, Constantinople, Ephesus and Chalcedon should be honored like the four Gospels. He dispensed the Sicilian Bishops from visiting Rome every three years, and allowed them to come every five years instead. He wrote many books, and Peter the Deacon declared that he often saw the Holy Spirit on the head of Gregory in the form of a dove when the holy Pope was dictating his books. It is a matter of great wonder that he spoke, did, wrote, and legislated so much, being all the time weak and sickly. He also worked many miracles. Finally God called him to a lasting happiness in heaven on March 12, the thirteenth year, the sixth month and the tenth day of his pontificate. This day is kept by the Greeks as well as by us as a festival, because of the great wisdom and holiness of this pope. His body was buried in the Basilica of St. Peter, near the Secretarium.

℟. This is he who worked great wonders before God, and all the earth is filled with his teaching: * May he intercede for the sins of all peoples. ℣. This is he who despised the life of the world and attained to the heavenly kingdom. May. Glory. May.

III Nocturn

The reading of the holy Gospel according to St. Matthew

At that time Jesus said to his disciples: "You are the salt of the earth; but if the salt loses its strength, what shall it be salted with?" And so forth.

Homily of St. Gregory, Pope

We must reflect that if a pastor cannot admonish all by one and the same exhortation, he should strive to instruct and build up each one by private conferences, in as far as this is possible. For we ought unceasingly to weigh well what is said to the holy apostles, and through them to us, "You are the salt of the earth." If then we are salt, we should season the minds of the faithful.

You, therefore, who are pastors, earnestly consider the fact that you feed the flocks of God, concerning which it is indeed said to God by the Psalmist, "Thy animals shall dwell in her" (the Church). Moreover, we often see that a rock of salt is placed before brute animals that they may lick this same rock and so be improved. What the rock of salt is among brute animals, that the priest should be amongst his people. For the priest must be very careful to adopt himself to the qualities of each one, so that whosoever comes in contact with him is thereby seasoned with the savor of eternal life, as from the touch of salt.

Now we are not the salt of the earth if we do not season the hearts of our listeners. He certainly uses this condiment who does not refrain from preaching the word of God. But only then do we truly preach the truth to others if we demonstrate our teaching with deeds. My dearly beloved brethren, God, so I think, suffers no greater injury than that caused by priests when He sees those whom He has appointed for the correction of others give themselves up to wickedness,—when we priests, who ought to crush sins, sin ourselves. We do not seek after the welfare of souls when we daily devote ourselves to our own pursuits, when we unlawfully desire earthly things, when we eagerly receive the glory of men. And because we are placed over others we have the greater opportunity to do what we please. We turn the sacred ministry which we have taken upon ourselves into a means of furthering our ambition. We give up the cause of God and devote ourselves to worldly affairs. Indeed we receive a position in sacred matters, but we are involved in earthly entanglements.

℟. The Lord hath sworn and He will not repent: * Thou art a priest forever according to the order of Melchisedech. ℣. The Lord said to my Lord, sit Thou at My right hand. Thou art. Glory. Thou art.

✠ Continuation of the holy Gospel according to St. Matthew.— At that time Jesus said to his disciples: "You are the salt of the earth; but if the salt loses its strength, what shall it be salted with? It is no longer of any use but to be thrown out and trodden underfoot by men.

"You are the light of the world. A city set on a mountain cannot be hidden. Neither do men light a lamp and put it under the measure, but upon the lamp-stand, so as to give light to all in the house. Even so let your light shine before men, in order that they may see your good works and give glory to your Father in heaven.

"Do not think that I have come to destroy the Law or the Prophets. I have not come to destroy, but to fulfill. For amen I say to you, till heaven and earth pass away, not one jot or one tittle shall be lost from the Law till all things have been accomplished. Therefore whoever does away with one of these least commandments, and so teaches men, shall be called least in the kingdom of heaven; but whoever carries them out and teaches them, he shall be called great in the kingdom of heaven."

Let Us Pray

O God, who didst give the reward of eternal happiness to the soul of Thy servant Gregory, mercifully grant that we, who are burdened by the weight of our sins, may be raised up by his prayers. Through our Lord.

March 19

ST. JOSEPH, SPOUSE OF THE BLESSED VIRGIN MARY, CONFESSOR

I Nocturn

From the Book of Genesis, c. 39, 1 - 5; c. 41, 37 - 44

II Nocturn

Sermon of St. Bernard, Abbot

Who and what sort of man St. Joseph was, conjecture from the title with which he so merited to be honored, that, although but guardian, he was called and believed to be the father of God. Consider, too, his very name, which, no doubt, is interpreted *increase.* Likewise remember that former exalted patriarch, sold into Egypt, and realize that this Joseph not only inherited his name, but moreover has attained to his chastity, and arrived at his innocence and grace.

While that Joseph, sold through his brothers' envy and led into Egypt, prefigured the selling of Christ, this Joseph, fleeing from the envy of Herod, carried Christ into Egypt. That one, keeping faith with his lord, did not wish to be defiled with his mistress; this one, knowing his wife, the Mother of his Lord, to be a virgin, and himself being a continent man, faithfully guarded her.

An understanding of the mysteries of dreams was given to the former; to the latter it was granted to be made aware of and to be partaker in heavenly mysteries. The former stored up provisions, not for himself, but for his people; the other received the living bread from heaven to guard it for himself and for the whole world.

There is no doubt that this Joseph, to whom the Mother of our Savior was espoused, was a good and faithful man. A faithful servant, I say, and prudent, whom the Lord appointed as guardian of His Mother, provider of the necessities of life for His own body, and finally, the only trustworthy aid on earth to His great design.

℟. Arise, and take the Child and His Mother, and fly into Egypt; * And be there until I shall tell thee. ℣. That it might be fulfilled which the Lord spoke by the prophet saying: Out of Egypt have I called My Son. And. Glory. And.

III Nocturn

The reading of the holy Gospel according to St. Matthew

When Mary, the mother of Jesus, had been betrothed to Joseph, she was found, before they came together, to be with child by the Holy Spirit. And so forth.

Homily of St. Jerome, Priest

Why is He conceived not by a simple virgin, but by an espoused woman? In the first place, that the origin of Mary might be manifested by means of the genealogy of Joseph. Secondly, that Mary might not be stoned by the Jews as an adulteress. Thirdly, that she might have a guardian during the flight into Egypt. Ignatius the Martyr adds a fourth reason why He was conceived by an espoused woman: namely, that His birth might be concealed from the devil, who thought Him to have been born of a wife, not of a virgin.

"Before they came together, she was found with child of the Holy Ghost." Not by another was she discovered, but by Joseph, who by marital privilege knew almost all things concerning his future wife. But because it is said, "before they came together," it does not follow that afterwards they did come together. Scripture, indeed, shows that this did not happen.

"Whereupon Joseph, her husband, being a just man and not willing publicly to expose her, was minded to put her away privately." If one be joined to an adulteress, they are made, as it were, one body, and in the Law there is a precept whereby not only the accused, but those who are accomplices in the crime as well are guilty of sin. How, then, is Joseph represented as a just man while concealing the crime of his wife? But this is a testimony in Mary's favor, that Joseph, aware of her chastity and filled with awe at what had come to pass, cloaked in silence the mystery of that which he did not understand.

"Joseph, son of David, fear not to take unto thee Mary thy wife." Above we stated that spouses are called wives; which fact the Book against Helvidius explains more fully. Now, by way of approval the Angel speaks to him during sleep, to sanction the appropriateness of his silence. It is likewise to be noted that Joseph is called the son of David in order that Mary also might be shown to be of the offspring of David.

℞. Joseph went up from Galilee out of the city of Nazareth into Judea, to the city of David, which is called Bethlehem: * Because he was of the house and family of David. ℣. To be enrolled with Mary, his espoused wife. Because. Glory. Because.

✠ Continuation of the holy Gospel according to St. Matthew.— When Mary, the mother of Jesus, had been betrothed to Joseph, she was found, before they came together, to be with child by the Holy Spirit. But Joseph her husband, being a just man, and not wishing to expose her to reproach, was minded to put her away privately. But while he thought on these things, behold, an angel of the Lord appeared to him in a dream, saying, "Do not be afraid, Joseph, son of David, to take to thee Mary thy wife, for that which is begotten in her is of the Holy Spirit. And she shall bring forth a son, and thou shalt call his name Jesus; for he shall save his people from their sins."

Let Us Pray

May we be assisted by the merits of the Spouse of Thy most holy Mother, we beseech Thee, O Lord, that we may obtain by his intercession what we could not obtain by ourselves alone, who livest and reignest with God the Father.

March 21

OUR MOST HOLY FATHER ST. BENEDICT

I Nocturn

From the Book of Ecclesiasticus, c. 44, 1 - 15

II Nocturn

Benedict was born of noble parentage at Nursia. He received a liberal education at Rome, after which, in order that he might give himself entirely to Jesus Christ, he withdrew to a place called Subiaco and there hid himself in a deep cave. There he passed three years, unknown to anyone except a monk named Roman, who brought him the necessities of life. One day, subjected to violent temptations against holy purity by the devil, he rolled himself amongst thorny bushes until, his body being completely lacerated, he extinguished the desire of carnal pleasure by the pain.

The fame of Benedict's sanctity now began to spread and certain monks came to put themselves under his guidance. The laxity of their lives, however, was such that they could not endure his reproofs and they resolved to put poison into his drink. But when they offered him the poisoned drink, he broke the vessel by making the sign of the cross over it, and, leaving this monastery, he retired again into solitude. But since many disciples daily came to him, he built twelve monasteries and established them with most holy laws.

Afterwards he went to Cassino where he destroyed a statue of Apollo, who was still worshipped there, overturned the altar, and burnt the groves. There he built a chapel which he named in honor of St. Martin, and also one which he called after St. John the Baptist, and he taught the inhabitants of the surrounding region the elements of Christianity. Daily Benedict advanced in divine grace, so that he was able to foretell things that were to come. When Totila, King of the Goths, determined to investigate the truth of this fact, sending his sword-bearer with the royal insignia and attendants, he instructed him to pretend that he was the king. When Benedict saw him, he said: "Put off, my son, put off this dress, for it is not thine." Concerning Totila, he predicted that he would reach Rome, cross the sea, and that his death would occur after nine years.

Some months before he departed from this life he told his disciples on what day he would die. He ordered the sepulchre in which he wished his body to be buried to be opened six days before he was carried to it. On the final day of his life he desired to be carried to the church, and there, having received the Holy Eucharist, with his eyes raised in prayer towards heaven, and supported by his disciples, he breathed forth his soul, which two monks saw ascending into heaven, adorned with a most precious garment and surrounded by shining lamps. They also heard a man of noble and venerable appearance, standing above his head, speak thus: "This is the way whereby Benedict, the beloved of the Lord, ascends into heaven."

℟. This is he who wrought great things before God, and praised the Lord with his whole heart: * May he intercede for the sins of all men. ℣. Behold a man without reproach, a true worshipper of God, keeping himself from every evil deed, and ever abiding in innocence. May. Glory. May.

III Nocturn

The reading of the holy Gospel according to St. Matthew

At that time Peter said to Jesus: "Behold, we have left all and followed thee; what then shall we have?" And so forth.

Homily of St. Peter Damian, Bishop

"Behold, we have left all things, and have followed thee." A solemn word, a great promise, a holy deed worthy of blessing—to leave all things and to follow Christ! These are the words exhorting voluntary poverty that have given birth to monasteries, that have filled cloisters with monks, that have peopled the forests with anchorites. It is of them the Church sings: "For the sake of the words of thy lips I have kept hard ways"—words promising rest for labor, riches for poverty, reward for tribulation. Indeed, it is a great thing to leave all things, but it is greater to follow Christ. This is the work, this is the labor, yea this is the very summit of man's sanctification. Unless we abandon all, it is impossible for us to follow Christ, for He "rejoices as a giant to run the way," and one who is weighed down cannot follow Him.

"Behold," he says, "we have left all things," not only the goods of this world, but also the desires of our souls; for that man has not abandoned all things who retains himself; yea, it profits him nothing to have left all things if he has not left himself, since no burden weighs more heavily on a man than the man himself. What tyrant is more cruel, what power more violent to a man than his own will? Then he continues: "What, therefore, shall we have?" Peter has already left all, and not only does he follow Christ now, but he has done so for a long time; yet now for the first time does he ask what he will receive. What does this mean, Peter? Have you not promised obedience at the hearing of the ear, not in the form of a contract? Yet, hearken to what the Lord God speaks, and consider the hope we ought to have amidst this world's vicissitudes. "You shall be seated," says the Lord, who is the Truth. O august session, delightful rest, consummate bliss!

But lest long expectation distort the sweetness of this great promise, He soothes the perturbation of our mind with a sweeter word. For He knows our frame—that our littleness would brook no delays; therefore in His benignity He brushes aside also this thought and accedes to us even in this regard, saying: "And everyone that hath left house or father or mother or brother or wife or fields or children for my name's sake shall receive a hundredfold and shall possess life everlasting." Indeed "the mouth of them that speak wicked things is stopped." And now "let all them be confounded that do unjust things without cause." We have a promise both for this present, life and for that which is to come, the former being evidently that of the hundredfold, as may be deduced from that which follows: "and he shall possess eternal life."

Therefore they who have not yet received the hundredfold should scrutinize their hearts and carefully examine all the works of their hands; without a doubt, they will find some nook and corner strange to the Savior. But what is this hundredfold except the visitations, the consolations, the first-fruits of the Spirit who is sweeter than honey? What is it but the testimony of our conscience? what but the joyous and most delightful expectation of the just, the remembrance of the abundance of God's sweetness, yea, the superabundance of His sweetness, concerning which it is not necessary to speak to those who have experienced it; and as for those who have not experienced it, who can describe such things in words? Now to whom can this whole passage of the Gospel lesson be so fittingly applied as to our father and guide, Saint Benedict? From early youth he abandoned the world with its allurements and pursued Christ with the most rapid strides, never faltering in his course until he had reached Him.

℟. The Lord hath loved him and hath adorned him; He hath clothed him with a robe of glory, * And hath crowned him at the gates of paradise. ℣. The Lord hath put on him the breastplate of faith, and hath adorned him. And. Glory. And.

✠ Continuation of the holy Gospel according to St. Matthew.—
At that time Peter said to Jesus: "Behold, we have left all and followed thee; what then shall we have?" And Jesus said to them, "Amen I say to you that you who have followed me, in the regeneration when the Son of Man shall sit on the throne of his glory, shall also sit on twelve thrones, judging the twelve tribes of Israel. And everyone who has left house, or brothers, or sisters, or father, or mother, or wife, or children, or lands, for my name's sake, shall receive a hundredfold, and shall possess life everlasting."

LET US PRAY

O almighty and eternal God, who on this day, having freed Thy most holy confessor Benedict from the prison of the body, didst raise him up to heaven, grant, we beseech Thee, to Thy servants celebrating this feast, the remission of all their sins, that they who with joyful hearts rejoice at his glory may, by his intercession with Thee, share also in his merits. Through our Lord.

March 25
ANNUNCIATION OF THE BLESSED VIRGIN MARY

I Nocturn

From Isaias the Prophet, c. 7, 10 - 15; c. 11, 1 - 5; c. 35, 1 - 7

II Nocturn

Sermon of St. Leo, Pope

The omnipotent and tender God, whose nature is goodness, whose will is power, whose work is mercy, at the very beginning of the world—as soon as the devil's malice had destroyed us with the poison of his envy—preordained the remedies of His love which were intended to restore mortals, announcing to the serpent the future seed of a woman which would crush down by its strength the pride of his venomous head—that is, that Christ would come in the flesh; marking as God and man Him who, born of a Virgin, would condemn by His stainless birth the violater of the human race.

For the devil boasted that man, having been deceived by his trickery, was without the divine favors, and, stripped of the endowment of immortality, had been subjected to the hard sentence of death, and that he (the devil) had in his evils found a kind of solace in the comradeship of the prevaricator. He boasted also that, because of the need of just severity, God had changed His original design towards man, whom He had created in such great honor. And so, beloved, in the dispensation of His secret plan it was necessary that the unchangeable God, whose will cannot be deprived of its tenderness, should fulfill the first disposition of His love by a more hidden mystery; and that man, forced into sin by the cunning of diabolical iniquity, should not, contrary to God's plan, perish.

As the time approached, beloved, which had been ordained for the redemption of men, our Lord Jesus Christ entered these depths, coming down from His heavenly throne, yet not departing from the Father's glory, born in a new order, begotten by a new birth; in a new order, for invisible in His own, He has become visible in ours; incomprehensible, He willed to be understood; abiding before time, He began to exist in time; Lord of all, the dignity of His majesty having been overshadowed, He took on the form of a servant; as God unable to suffer, He did not disdain to be man subject to suffering; and immortal, He did not disdain to submit to the law of death.

For, while many things might wondrously be of service to Him in restoring mankind, the true and efficacious mercy of God chose above all this way of helping, by which, to destroy the devil's work, He would use not the might of dominion, but the reckoning of justice. For not without reason was the pride of the old enemy asserting a tyrannical rule over all men; nor was he oppressing with an undue sway those whom of their own choice he had enticed from God's command to the service of his own will. Therefore he would not justly lose the original slavery of the surrendered race unless he should be overcome by the race he had subdued.

R̸. Behold a Virgin shall conceive and bear a Son, saith the Lord: * And His name shall be called Wonderful, God, the Mighty. V̸. He shall sit upon the throne of David, and upon his kingdom forever. And His name. Glory. And His name.

III Nocturn

The reading of the holy Gospel according to St. Luke

At that time the angel Gabriel was sent from God to a town of Galilee called Nazareth, to a virgin betrothed to a man named Joseph, of the house of David, and the virgin's name was Mary. And so forth.

Homily of St. Ambrose, Bishop

Divine mysteries are indeed hidden, and, according to the saying of the prophets, it is not easy for any man to know the counsel of God. Nevertheless, from the other deeds and precepts of our Lord and Savior we are able to understand that this was also more in keeping with the divine plan, that she who was espoused to a husband should be chosen to give birth to the Lord. But why did she not become pregnant before her espousal? Perhaps lest it be said that she had conceived in adultery.

And the Scripture clearly demonstrates that she would be both espoused and a virgin: a virgin, that it might be clear that she was free from intercourse with man; espoused, lest she be seared by the infamy of violated virginity, to which desecration the pregnant womb would plainly seem to point. For the Lord preferred that some should be in doubt rather about the manner of His birth than about the purity of His mother. For He knew the delicate reserve of the Virgin and the elusive fame of modesty, and He did not think that faith in His birth should be built up by injuries to His mother.

"And when the angel had come to her." Study the Virgin in her actions; study her in her modesty; study her in her conversation; study her in the mystery. It is the nature of virgins to tremble at and to fear the approach of man, to dread all conversation with man. Let women learn to imitate this example of modesty. Alone in her room, she, whom no man ever gazed at, and whom an angel alone discovered; alone—without companion or witness by whose discourse she might be distracted—she was saluted by an angel.

For the mystery of so great a message must be proposed not by the mouth of man, but by that of an angel. Today for the first time is heard: "The Holy Spirit will overshadow thee." And it is heard and believed. Finally, "Behold," she says, "the handmaid of the Lord; be it done unto me according to thy word." See the humility, behold the devotion! She who is chosen to be the Mother of the Lord calls herself His handmaid; nor is she suddenly elated by the promise.

℟. Rejoice, O Virgin Mary, thou alone hast trampled down all heresies because thou didst believe the Archangel Gabriel's words: * When thou, a virgin, didst give birth to God and man, and after childbirth didst remain ever a virgin. ℣. Blessed art thou who didst believe: for those things have come to pass which were told thee by the Lord. When. Glory. When.

☩ Continuation of the holy Gospel according to St. Luke.—At that time the angel Gabriel was sent from God to a town of Galilee called Nazareth, to a virgin betrothed to a man named Joseph, of the house of David, and the virgin's name was Mary. And when the angel had come to her, he said, "Hail, full of grace, the Lord is with thee. Blessed art thou among women." When she had seen him she was troubled at his word, and kept pondering what manner of greeting this might be.

And the angel said to her, "Do not be afraid, Mary, for thou hast found grace with God. And behold, thou shalt conceive in thy womb and shalt bring forth a son; and thou shalt call his name Jesus. He shall be great, and shall be called the Son of the Most High; and the Lord God will give him the throne of David his father, and he shall be king over the house of Jacob forever; and of his kingdom there shall be no end."

But Mary said to the angel, "How shall this happen, since I do not know man?"

And the angel answered and said to her, "The Holy Spirit shall come upon thee and the power of the Most High shall overshadow thee; and therefore the Holy One to be born shall be called the Son of God. And behold, Elizabeth thy kinswoman also has conceived a son in her old age, and she who was called barren is now in her sixth month; for nothing shall be impossible with God."

But Mary said, "Behold the handmaid of the Lord; be it done to me according to thy word."

LET US PRAY

O God, who hast willed that Thy Word should become Man in the womb of the Virgin Mary at the message of an Angel, grant to us Thy servants that we, who believe she is truly the Mother of God, may be assisted by her intercession with Thee. Through the same Jesus Christ.

April 25

ST. MARK THE EVANGELIST

I Nocturn

From the Book of Ezechiel the Prophet, c. 1, 1 - 13

II Nocturn

From the Book of St. Jerome, Priest, on Ecclesiastical Writers

Mark, the disciple and *mouthpiece* of Peter, when requested by the brethren at Rome, wrote a short Gospel according as he had heard Peter relating. When Peter heard this, he approved of it and by his own authority appointed that it should be read to the Church. Then, taking the Gospel which he had composed, Mark made his way to Egypt. At Alexandria, where he first preached Christ, he organized the Church with such wonderful instruction and purity of life that he drew all of Christ's followers to his own example.

To conclude—Philo, one of the most learned Jews, seeing the Church at Alexandria while it was at first still Jewish in its way, wrote a book on their manner of life, as it were in praise of his own nation. And as Luke tells that at Jerusalem the faithful had all things in common, so also did Philo relate what was done at Alexandria under the teaching of Mark. Mark died in the eighth year of the reign of Nero and was buried at Alexandria, being succeeded by Anianus.

From the Commentary of St. Gregory, Pope, on the Prophet Ezechiel

The four sacred animals which were foreseen through the spirit of prophecy are described in a subtle account when it is declared: "Every one had four faces, and every one had four wings." What is expressed by "face" except knowledge, and what by "wings" except the power of flight? Every one, of course, is known by his face, and by their wings the bodies of the birds are lifted on high. The face, then, refers to faith; the wings to contemplation. For through faith indeed we are known to God, as He Himself says of His sheep: "I am the good shepherd; and I know my sheep, and mine know me." Elsewhere He says: "I know whom I have chosen."

And through contemplation, by which we are raised above ourselves, we are, as it were, lifted into the air. Thus, "Every one had four faces," because, if you search into what Matthew thinks of our Lord's Incarnation, he thinks precisely the same as Mark, Luke, and John. If you search into what John thinks, beyond a doubt he thinks the same as Luke, Mark, and Matthew. If you search into what Mark thinks, it is the same as Matthew, John, and Luke. If you search into what Luke thinks, it is the same as John, Matthew, and Mark.

℟. With great power the Apostles gave * Testimony of the Resurrection of Jesus Christ our Lord, alleluia, alleluia. ℣. They were indeed filled with the Holy Spirit, and they spoke the word of God with boldness. Testimony. Glory. Testimony.

III Nocturn

The reading of the holy Gospel according to St. Luke

At that time the Lord appointed seventy-two others, and sent them forth two by two before him into every town and place where he himself was about to come. And so forth.

Homily of St. Gregory, Pope

Our Lord and Savior, dearly beloved brethren, admonishes us sometimes by words and sometimes by works. For His very deeds are precepts; for even when He does anything without speaking, He lets us know what we ought to do. Behold, He sends His disciples two by two to preach, because two are the commandments of charity—namely, the love of God and the love of neighbor—and because between less than two charity cannot be had.

No one properly speaking is said to have charity towards himself, but, that it may be charity, love tends towards another. For look, the Lord sent the disciples by two's to preach, in order to show us without sound of words that he who does not have charity towards his neighbor ought by no means to take up the office of preaching.

But it is well said that He sent them before His face into every city and place whither He Himself was to come, for the Lord follows His preachers; the preaching comes first; and then, when the words of exhortation have gone before, the Lord comes to the dwelling-place of our mind; and by this means truth is received into the soul.

Hence Isaias says to these same preachers: "Prepare ye the way of the Lord; make straight the paths of our God." Hence also the Psalmist says to the people of God: "Make a way for him who ascendeth upon the west." Indeed the Lord hath risen upon the west; for as He set, as it were, in His Passion, He rose in greater glory in His Resurrection. To be sure, He rose upon the west, for by rising again He trampled under foot that death which He had suffered. For Him, therefore, who rose upon the west do we prepare the way when we preach His glory to your minds, so that He Himself, coming afterwards, may enlighten them by the presence of His love.

℟. I am the true vine, and you the branches: * He that abideth in Me and I in him, the same beareth much fruit, alleluia, alleluia. ℣. As the Father hath loved Me, I also have loved you. He. Glory. He.

✠ Continuation of the holy Gospel according to St. Luke.— At that time the Lord appointed seventy-two others, and sent them forth two by two before him into every town and place where he himself was about to come. And he said to them, "The harvest indeed is abundant, but the laborers are few. Pray therefore the Lord of the harvest to send forth laborers into his harvest.

"Go. Behold, I send you forth as lambs in the midst of wolves. Carry neither purse, nor wallet, nor sandals, and greet no one on the way. Whatever house you enter, first say, 'Peace to this house!' And if a son of peace be there, your peace will rest upon him; but if not, it will return to you. And remain in the same house, eating and drinking what they have; for the laborer deserves his wages. Do not go from house to house. And whatever town you enter, and they receive you, eat what is set before you, and cure the sick who are there, and say to them, 'The kingdom of God is at hand to you.'"

Let Us Pray

O God, who didst elevate blessed Mark Thy Evangelist to the dignity of a preacher of the Gospel, grant, we beseech Thee, that we may always profit by his knowledge and be protected by his prayers. Through our Lord.

Wednesday of the III Week after Easter

SOLEMNITY OF ST. JOSEPH
SPOUSE OF THE BLESSED VIRGIN MARY
CONFESSOR AND PATRON OF THE UNIVERSAL CHURCH

I Nocturn

From the Book of Genesis, c. 39, 1 - 6; c. 41, 37 - 49

II Nocturn

Sermon of St. Bernardine of Siena

For all special graces granted to any rational creature it is a general rule that whenever divine Grace selects someone for some singular office or some very high state, it grants all the favors which are necessary for that person so chosen and for his mission, and adorns him in a lavish way. This was especially true in the case of the foster father of our Lord Jesus Christ and the true spouse of the Queen of the world and of the angels, St. Joseph, who was chosen by the Eternal Father as support and guardian of His chief treasures, namely, His own Son and his (St. Joseph's) Spouse—which task he most faithfully performed. On that account the Lord said to him: "Thou good and faithful servant, enter into the joy of thy Lord."

If you compare him to the whole Church of Christ, does not he become that chosen and particular man by whom and under whom Christ was properly and in a becoming manner brought into the world? Thus, if the whole Church is indebted to the Virgin Mother because through her she has been made worthy to receive Christ, likewise, after Mary, special gratitude and reverence are due to Joseph. For he is the key of the old Covenant in which the worthiness of the patriarchs and prophets obtains the promised Fruit. Still more, he alone it is who in body possesses what the Divine Majesty had promised to them. Fittingly, therefore, is he prefigured by that patriarch Joseph who stored up food for the nations. But he even excels that Joseph, for he brings not only the bread of corporal life to the Egyptians, but with great solicitude he nourishes all chosen souls with the bread from heaven which bestows eternal life.

Indeed it should not be doubted that Christ certainly did not in heaven deny the intimacy, reverence, and most exalted honor which He showed to Joseph, as a son towards his father, while on earth; nay, rather He perfected and consummated it. Wherefore in the word set forth by our Lord, not undeservedly is it said: "Enter into the joy of thy Lord." Although the joy of eternal happiness enters into the heart of man, nevertheless, our Lord preferred to say to him, "Enter into joy," in order to show mystically that that joy would not only be within him, but would encompass and engulf him on all sides and overwhelm him as an infinite abyss.

Remember us, therefore, O blessed Joseph, and by the help of thy prayers intercede with thy foster Son; and do thou also render propitious to us thy spouse, the most Blessed Virgin, Mother of Him, who with the Father and the Holy Spirit liveth and reigneth world without end. Amen.

℟. Thou hast given me the protection of thy salvation, and thy right hand hath held me up: * Thou art my protection, the horn of my salvation and my support, alleluia. ℣. I am thy protector, and thy reward exceedingly great. Thou. Glory. Thou.

III Nocturn

The reading of the holy Gospel according to St. Luke

At that time it came to pass when all the people had been baptized, Jesus also having been baptized and being in prayer, that heaven was opened. And so forth.

Homily of St. Augustine, Bishop

It is evident that what the Evangelist said, "Being—*as was supposed*—the son of Joseph," he said on account of those who believed Him to have been born of Joseph as other men are born. Still it troubles some that Matthew enumerates certain ancestors, descending from David to Joseph, whereas Luke, going from Joseph back to David, enumerates different ones. It is easy to see that Joseph could have had two fathers, one by whom he was begotten, the other by whom he was adopted. For it is an ancient custom, even among that people of God, to adopt children with the view of making sons for themselves of those whom they themselves had not begotten. Whence it is understood that Luke in his Gospel has taken as the father of Joseph not him by whom he was begotten, but him by whom he was adopted, whose progenitors he records backwards through the years to David.

Since it was necessary, therefore, that one of them have the lineage of the father who begot him, the other of the father who adopted him (because both Luke and Matthew speak the truth), whom should we more probably believe to have set down the ancestry of the father who adopted him than he who did not wish to state that Joseph was begotten by him whose son he declared him to be? But Matthew, in saying, "Abraham begot Isaac, Isaac begot Jacob," and continuing thus with this word "begot," until at last he says, "Jacob begot Joseph," has clearly shown that he had traced the line of ancestors to that father by whom Joseph was not adopted but begotten.

On the other hand, even if Luke had said that Joseph was begotten by Heli, this assertion should not influence us to believe anything else but that the father who begot him is referred to by one Evangelist, and the father who adopted him by the other.

For it is not absurd to say that one who has adopted a son has begotten him, not indeed in the flesh, but in charity. For us also, whom He has given power to be His sons, God has not begotten of His nature and substance, as He begot His only Son, but He has adopted us out of love.

℟. Arise, and take the Child and His Mother, and fly into Egypt: * And be there until I shall tell thee, alleluia. ℣. That it might be fulfilled which the Lord spoke by the prophet, saying: Out of Egypt have I called My Son. And be. Glory. And be.

✠ Continuation of the holy Gospel according to St. Luke.—At that time it came to pass when all the people had been baptized, Jesus also having been baptized and being in prayer, that heaven was opened, and the Holy Spirit descended upon him in bodily form as a dove, and a voice came from heaven, "Thou art my beloved Son, in thee I am well pleased."

Let Us Pray

O God, who in Thy wonderful providence didst choose blessed Joseph to be the spouse of Thy most holy Mother, grant, we beseech Thee, that we may merit to have him as our intercessor in heaven, whom we venerate as our protector on earth, who livest and reignest with God the Father.

THURSDAY

Sermon of St. Bernardine of Siena

Since between Mary and Joseph a true marriage was contracted under divine inspiration, and since in matrimony the union of souls becomes such that husband and wife are together called one person so that this union may be said to be the most intimate, how can any discerning mind think that the Holy Spirit would join to such a virgin any soul but that most like to her in virtue? Therefore I believe that this holy man, Joseph, was most chaste in his virginity, most profound in his humility, most burning in his charity and love of God, most lofty in his contemplation. And because the Virgin knew that he was given to her by the Holy Spirit as her spouse, as a faithful guardian of her own virginity, and as one taking part in the charitable love and devoted care of the divine Offspring of God, therefore do I believe that she loved this holy Joseph most sincerely with the affection of her whole heart.

Joseph had a most ardent love for Christ. Who, I pray, will deny that when he held Christ in his arms or when he talked to Him, Christ, whether as an Infant or adult, gave expression to ineffable thoughts and beautiful ideas concerning Himself, and that, by His speech and caresses, the charm of the divine Child added exteriorly to His filial reverence? O how sweet the kisses he received from Him! O with what great delight did he hear the lisping Child call him, "Father," and with what great sweetness did he feel himself embraced by Him! Do you also consider with what great tenderness he made the little lad Jesus, tired out from the toil on the trips they took when He was grown a bit, rest on his bosom, for he was carried away by an all-transforming love for Him, as for a dearest Son, given to him by his virgin wife through the Holy Spirit.

Therefore this wisest of mothers, who had experienced His affections, said to her child Jesus when He was found again in the temple: "Son, why hast thou done so to us? behold thy father and I have sought thee sorrowing." To understand these words it must be noted that Christ holds two kinds of savor within Himself: one of sweetness, one of sorrow; and because the most holy Joseph was partaker of these two savors in a wonderful way, the Blessed Virgin on that account calls him, with special meaning, the father of Christ. Here alone is it said that the Virgin called Joseph the father of Jesus, for the sense of sorrow which he had over Jesus being lost showed a true fatherly affection towards Him. For if according to human laws, divinely approved, one can exteriorly adopt someone for his son, much more should the Son of God, given to this Joseph through his most holy spouse in the wonderful sacrament of virginal matrimony, be called his son and likewise be believed to be such, because in him there was a fatherly sense of love and sorrow in regard for his beloved Jesus.

FRIDAY

Sermon of St. John Chrysostom

Antiquity generally kept the custom that the espoused should dwell in the home of the spouse. Thus, Mary also lived with her spouse, and what was the reason, I pray, that she did not conceive as a virgin before she was espoused? In order, perhaps, that the mystery might for the time being remain, as it were, secret, and that the Virgin might avoid entirely every chance for evil suspicion. For when it is recognized that he, who had the right to be inflamed with righteous jealousy, not only did not put away his spouse nor reveal her in shame to the public, but even received her into his companionship, and served her after she had conceived, it is assuredly manifest that unless he had clearly known that this conception existed through the work of the Holy Spirit, he never would have kept her with himself or have served her in all her necessities.

"Whereupon Joseph, being a just man, and not willing publicly to expose her, was minded to put her away privately." After the Evangelist had said that this conception was of the Holy Spirit and free from carnal intercourse, he likewise confirmed his word through another person. For lest one should say: "And how can this be proven? Who witnessed it? Who ever heard of such a thing happening?" and lest you should think that the Evangelist had invented these things, as it were, to please his Master, he introduces Joseph, who in all the things he suffered, through all kept his trust in the things which were told him. Thus, the Evangelist plainly seems to say: "If you do not believe me, and if you doubt my testimony, believe at least Mary's husband."

"For Joseph, her husband, being a just man..." The just man he here declares to be perfect in every virtue. Since, then, he was a just man, that is, virtuous and good, "he was minded to put her away privately." On that account does the Evangelist tell what happened to this just man before his understanding of the matter, so that you might not doubt in the least about the things which were done after his knowledge of the affair. And surely, if Mary had been such as his suspicion depicted her, she would have deserved not only to have been exposed, but also to have been punished by the authority of the Law. Yet Joseph not only did not wish to condemn her, but he did not wish even to expose her. Here you see a man sublimely philosophizing, and free from the tyrranical passion of suspicion. And yet in this case, would this indeed be said to be suspicion when the very enlargement of the womb seemed to prove the fact? But nevertheless this man was so pure and free from passion of this sort that he did not wish even in the slightest way to inflict grief on the Virgin; and while still living under the Law, he reasons above the Law. Indeed, since Grace was already approaching, it was fitting that examples of a far more sublime doctrine should shine forth.

SATURDAY

Sermon of St. John Chrysostom

"Joseph, son of David, fear not to take unto thee Mary thy wife." What is it, then, "to take"? Undoubtedly to keep at his home, for in his mind he had already expelled her; "but," the Angel says, "bring back her whom you have dismissed, whom God, not her parents, joins to you. He joins you, however, not for the sacred union of marriage, but for the company of a common dwelling, and He joins you through the medium of my word." For as Christ Himself afterwards commends her to His disciple, so also now the Angel commends her to her spouse—but only in order that she may have him for her solace, free from the bond of marriage. Consequently, when the reason for her bringing forth had been very honestly and nobly explained, Joseph forthwith put away his suspicion. "Not only," said the angel, "is she not defiled by an unlawful embrace, but she has even become pregnant in a manner above nature and custom. Do not, then, draw sorrow from so happy a child-bearing of your spouse; yea, rather break forth in great gladness, for that which is born in her is of the Holy Spirit."

"And she shall bring forth a Son, and *thou* shalt call his name Jesus"—for because He is of the Holy Spirit, you are not for that reason to consider yourself as separated from the ministry of such a great plan. Even though you have nothing in common with this birth (the Virgin, truly, has remained undefiled), nevertheless, that which is the right of the father and which in no way stains the dignity of the Virgin, I readily grant to you, namely, that you give the name to Him who is born, for you shall be the first to call Him. While He who is born will not be your Son, still you are to show to Him the care and the devotion of a parent, and on that account I unite you to Him in a positive way immediately from the giving of His name. Then, lest someone conjecture from this that he was His father, the angel says: "*She* shall bring forth a Son"; he does not say, "She shall bring forth a son to you," but simply states an indefinite and unqualified fact. For she was to bring forth Christ not to him, but directly to the whole world.

On that account, too, the Evangelist has noted that the Angel brought His name from heaven, so that in this way also—by which he informs us that His name was sent to Joseph both through an angel and from God—he might show that it was indeed a marvelous birth. For even the word itself, which certainly contains thousands of treasures, was not proposed without reason. Therefore the Angel also interprets it, encouraging him who was sorrowful with blessed hopes, and in this manner he invites him to believe what he says. For we are more solicitous for prosperous things, and we more quickly accommodate our faith to favorable things. "For," he says, "he shall save his people from their sins." Hence there is likewise indicated the strangeness of the gift. Not from a visible war, not from the sword of barbarians, but what is by far greater than these things, he announces that the nation is to be freed from its sin—a thing which was never possible for any man to grant.

MONDAY

Sermon of St. Bernard, Abbot

Mary was espoused to Joseph, or rather, as the Evangelist expresses it, "to a man whose name was Joseph." He calls Joseph a man (vir), not because he was Mary's husband, but to indicate that he was a man of virtue (homo virtutis). Since he is called her husband by another Evangelist, it may be said that, as he necessarily seemed to stand in that relation to her, he was justly entitled to the name. It was therefore right to speak of him as if he really were what people could not help supposing him; just as he also merited, not indeed to be, but to be called and reputed the father of the Savior, as we read in St. Luke, "And Jesus himself, when he began his work, was about thirty years of age, being—as was supposed—the son of Joseph."

There can be no manner of doubt that this Joseph, to whom was espoused the Savior's Mother, was singularly good and faithful. He was, I say, the good and faithful servant whom the Lord appointed to be the consolation of His Mother, the support of His humanity, and His one most faithful coadjutor on earth in the execution of His mighty purpose. To this must be added that he is declared to have been of the house of David. Truly this Joseph was descended from David, truly he came of a royal stock, yet, though noble by his ancestry, he was nobler still by his virtues and character. He was indeed the son of David, and well worthy to have David for his father. He was, I say, the son of David, and that, not only according to the flesh, but also by his faith, by his sanctity, and by his devotion. The Lord found him, like another David, to be a man according to His own heart, and one to whom He might safely entrust the most hidden and the most holy secret of His mind. To him, therefore, as to his father David, He "made known the uncertain and hidden things of His wisdom," and He admitted him to the knowledge of the mystery "which none of the princes of this world knew."

Finally, to him was given what many kings and prophets, though they desired to see, did not see, and to hear, but did not hear; to him it was given not only to see and hear Him, but even to carry in his arms, to lead by the hand, to embrace, to kiss, to support, and to protect Him. But we must also believe that Mary as well as Joseph was descended from David. For unless she also belonged to the house of David, she could not have been espoused to one of that royal stock. Therefore both Mary and Joseph were of David's lineage; but in Mary was fulfilled the promise which the Lord gave under oath to David, while it was Joseph's office to be cognizant of, and to bear witness to, the promise that had been fulfilled.

TUESDAY

Sermon of St. Bernard, Abbot

It is written, "Whereupon Joseph, her husband, being a just man and not willing publicly to expose her, was minded to put her away privately." Rightfully, since he was a just man, did he not wish to expose her publicly, because, as he would by no means be just if he had sympathized with one known to be guilty, so neither would he be just if he had condemned her who had been proved innocent. Therefore, "being a just man and not willing publicly to expose her, he was minded to put her away privately." Why did he want to put her away? Hear in this matter not mine, but the opinion of the Fathers. Joseph wished to put her away for the same reason for which Peter repelled our Lord from himself, saying: "Depart from me, O Lord, for I am a sinful man"; for the same reason that the centurion also kept Him out of his house when he declared: "Lord, I am not worthy that thou shouldst enter under my roof."

Thus Joseph too, esteeming himself unworthy and a sinner, said within himself that such intimate familiarity should not be granted to him by such and so great a person, whose dignity, high above him, he feared. He beheld and was afraid of her who bore an unmistakable sign of the divine presence, and, because he was unable to fathom the mystery, he was minded to put her away. Peter feared the immensity of His power; the centurion was in awe at the majesty of His presence; and Joseph was frightened exceedingly, as a man, at the strangeness of this great wonder. Do you wonder that Joseph reckoned himself unworthy of the company of the pregnant Virgin when you hear that the holy Elisabeth could not bear her presence, except, indeed, with trembling and reverence? For she said: "And how have I deserved that the mother of my Lord should come to me?"

Therefore Joseph was minded to put her away. But why privately and not openly? For this reason—lest the cause of the divorce be searched into, the reason for the divorce demanded. For what would the just man answer to a stiff-necked people, to a people unbelieving and obstinate? If he should declare what he thought, what he had proved of her purity, would not the incredulous and cruel Jews immediately have put him to scorn and stoned her? For how, indeed, should they have believed in the Truth, silent within her womb, whom they afterwards contemned when He cried out in the temple? What would they have done to Him who had not yet appeared, on whom afterwards, even when He shone bright with miracles, they laid their wicked hands? Rightly, then, lest he be forced either to lie or to slander her who was innocent, was the just man "minded to put her away privately."

OCTAVE DAY OF THE SOLEMNITY OF ST. JOSEPH

I Nocturn

From the Book of Genesis, c. 39, 1 - 6; c. 41, 37 - 49

II Nocturn

Sermon of St. Augustine, Bishop

The Angel did not in deceit say to Joseph: "Fear not to take unto thee Mary thy wife." She, whom he had not known nor would know by any union, is called *wife* from the first promise of marriage; the name of wife was not lost, nor did it remain as a lying term, where there had not been nor ever was to be any union of flesh. She was, indeed, a Virgin, and therefore was she more holily and more wonderfully pleasing to her husband, for she had become pregnant without man; as to her Child, she had no intercourse with him, but in her fidelity, she was truly his consort. Because of this faithful union both merited to be called the parents of Christ—not only she, the Mother, but also he, the father, as spouse of His Mother—united in mind, but not in body. Yet, whether he as father in mind alone, or she as Mother in body as well, both were the parents of His lowliness, not of His majesty; of His infirmity, not of His Divinity.

The Gospel does not lie when it says: "And his father and mother were wondering at those things which were spoken concerning him." And in another passage: "And his parents went every year to Jerusalem." Likewise, just shortly after this: "And his mother said to him: 'Son, why hast thou done so to us? Behold thy father and I have sought thee sorrowing.'" And He, in order to show that, besides them, He had a Father who, as well as His Mother, begot Him, answered them: "How is it that you sought me? Did you not know that I must be about my Father's business."

And, on the other hand, lest He be thought to have, by this statement, denied that they were His parents, the Evangelist, continuing, adds: "And they understood not the word that he spoke unto them. And he went down with them, and came to Nazareth, and was subject to them." To whom was He subject, but to His parents? And who was subject, but Jesus Christ, "Who, being in the form of God, thought it not robbery to be equal to God."

Why, then, was He subject to them who were far below the form of God, except that He "emptied himself, taking the form of a servant," of which form they were the parents. Yet surely both would not have been the parents of this same form of a servant unless they had been united—of course without carnal intercourse—to each other. Whence the series of generations was rather to be traced down to Joseph (as was done) when the parents of Christ were described in connection with their ancestry, so that, in that marriage, disrespect should not be paid to the male sex—indeed the more noble—while nothing should be lost to the truth, because both Joseph and Mary were of the seed of David, from whom it was foretold Christ would come. Every blessing of marriage was thus fulfilled in Christ's parents—a Child, the promise, the sacrament. We recognize the Lord Jesus Himself as the Child; the promise, because there was no adultery; the sacrament, because there was no divorce.

III Nocturn

The reading of the holy Gospel according to St. Luke

At that time it came to pass when all the people had been baptized, Jesus also having been baptized and being in prayer, that heaven was opened. And so forth.

Homily of St. Augustine, Bishop

Today is, in a certain sense, another birthday of the Savior. By means of the same wonderful signs and miracles we recognize

Him as when He was begotten, but now, when baptized, we recognize Him by a yet greater mystery. For God says: "This is my beloved Son in whom I am well pleased." This second birthday is distinctly more remarkable than the first. For that first day saw Christ begotten in silence, without a witness; on this second the Lord is baptized accompanied by a declaration of His Divinity. From that first birthday Joseph, who was thought to be His father, excused himself; on this, the Father, who was not believed to be such, announces Himself. At that time His Mother suffered from false suspicions, because no father was professedly known; but here the Mother is honored, because God protests that Christ is His Son.

The second birthday, I say, is more filled with honors than the first. On this day His Father is recorded as the God of majesty; on that, Joseph, an artisan, is considered His father. And although on both days our Lord was born and also baptized by the Holy Spirit, still He who cries from heaven is more worthy of honor than he who labors on earth.

Now on earth, Joseph the carpenter was thought to be the father of the Lord, our Savior; yet neither is God, who is truly the Father of our Lord, Jesus Christ, excluded from such type of work, for He too is an artisan. He is the Artist who designed the entire arrangement of the universe, not only with a wonderful, but with an ineffable power.

As a wise architect He hung the heavens in their heights; He established the earth on its foundation; He enclosed the seas with their shores; He is the Artist who casts down the exaltation of pride to its proper level and exalts the lowliness of humility. He is the Artist who, in our daily acts, cuts off all superfluous works and preserves only the useful ones. He is the Artist whose axe, as St. John the Baptist warns us, is laid to the root, in order that every tree which exceeds the norm of due discretion, after being cut out by the roots, may be cast into the fire, and that every tree which has the proper measure of truth may be consigned to the heavenly building.

May 1

SS. PHILIP AND JAMES, APOSTLES

I Nocturn

From the Catholic Epistle of St. James the Apostle, c. 1, 1 - 16

II Nocturn

Philip was born in the town of Bethsaida and was one of the first of the twelve apostles to be called by our Lord. It was from

Philip that Nathanael learned that the Messias, who was promised in the Law, had come, and by him he was brought to the Lord. That Philip was very close to Christ is shown from the fact that certain Gentiles, wishing to see Christ, came first to Philip; also when the Lord was in the wilderness and was about to feed the multitude, He said to Philip: "Whence shall we buy bread that these may eat?" Philip, after he had received the Holy Spirit and had been sent to preach the Gospel in Scythia, converted almost the entire population there to the Christian Faith. Finally, when he reached Hierapolis, a city of Phrygia, he was crucified for the name of Christ and stones were cast at him, and thus he died on the first of May. His body was buried by the Christians in that same place but it was afterwards taken to Rome and placed in the Basilica of the twelve apostles together with the body of St. James the Apostle.

James, surnamed the Just, was the brother of the Lord. From his childhood he never drank wine or strong drink; he never ate meat, nor cut his hair, nor used ointments or the bath. He alone was permitted to enter the Holy of Holies. His garments were of linen. He was so much given to prayer that the skin of his knees became hardened, resembling the hide of a camel in toughness. After the Ascension of Christ he was made bishop of Jerusalem, and it was to him that St. Peter sent the news of his deliverance from prison by an angel.

When a dispute had arisen in the council of Jerusalem regarding the Law and circumcision, James followed the opinion of Peter, and in a discourse which he made before the brethren, he approved the reception of the Gentiles and said that those absent were to be informed by letter that they were not to impose the yoke of the Mosaic Law on the Gentiles. It is of him that St. Paul speaks in his letter to the Galatians: "But other of the apostles I saw none, saving James, the brother of the Lord."

Such was James' holy life that people used to strive with each other in their desire to touch the hem of his garment. At the age of ninety-six years—thirty of which he had spent governing the Church of Jerusalem in a most saintly manner—while he was one day preaching Christ, the Son of God, with great courage, he was attacked with stones, and was then taken to the highest part of the Temple and cast headlong down. His legs were broken by the fall, and, as he was lying half dead upon the ground, he raised his hands to heaven and prayed to God for their salvation in these words: "Forgive them, O Lord, for they know not what they do." Whilst thus praying, he received a heavy blow on the head from a fuller's club, and gave up his soul to God, in the seventh year of Nero's reign. He was buried near the Temple, from which he had been thrown down. He wrote one of the seven Catholic epistles.

℟. Your sorrow, alleluia, * Shall be turned into joy, alleluia, alleluia. ℣. The world shall rejoice, but you shall be made sorrowful, but your sorrow. Shall. Glory. Shall.

III Nocturn

The reading of the holy Gospel according to St. John

At that time Jesus said to his disciples: "Let not your heart be troubled. You believe in God, believe also in me. In my Father's house there are many mansions." And so forth.

Homily of St. Augustine, Bishop

We must pay greater attention to God, brethren, that we may be able in some manner to comprehend with our minds the words of the holy Gospel which have just now resounded in our ears. For our Lord Jesus says: "Let not your heart be troubled; you believe in God, believe also in me." And lest as men they should be fearful of death, and thus be troubled, He consoles them, testifying that He Himself is God.

"You believe," He says, "in God; believe also in me." For it follows that if you believe in God, you must also believe in me. But this would not follow if Christ were not God. You believe in God; believe also in Him who by nature, not by robbery is equal to God, for He has emptied Himself, not losing the form of God, but taking on the form of a servant. Do you fear death for this form of a servant? "Let not your heart be troubled"; the form of God will raise it up.

But why that which follows, "In my Father's house there are many mansions," unless because the apostles were afraid even for themselves? Therefore it was also necessary that they hear, "Let not your heart be troubled." For who of them would not fear when it was said to Peter, overconfident and more impetuous than they, "The cock shall not crow till thou deny me thrice"?

Therefore, being about to be separated from Him, they are deservedly troubled; but when they hear, "In my Father's house there are many mansions; if not, I would have told you, for I go to prepare a place for you," they are refreshed in their troubles, and they become certain and confident that, even after the perils of temptations, they will remain near to God with Christ; because, although one is braver than another, one wiser than another, one more just than another, one holier than another, nevertheless, "In my Father's house there are many mansions." None of them will be excluded from this house, where each one will receive a mansion according to his deserts.

℟. I am the true Vine, and you the branches: * He that abideth in Me, and I in him, the same beareth much fruit, alleluia, alleluia. ℣. As the Father hath loved Me, I also have loved you. He that abideth. Glory. He that abideth.

☩ Continuation of the holy Gospel according to St. John.—At that time Jesus said to his disciples: "Let not your heart be troubled. You believe in God, believe also in me. In my Father's house there are many mansions. Were it not so, I should have told you, because I go to prepare a place for you. And if I go and prepare a place for you, I am coming again, and I will take you to myself; that where I am, there you also may be. And where I go you know, and the way you know."

Thomas said to him, "Lord, we do not know where thou art going, and how can we know the way?" Jesus said to him, "I am the way, and the truth, and the life. No one comes to the Father but through me. If you had known me, you would also have known my Father. And henceforth you do know him, and you have seen him."

Philip said to him, "Lord, show us the Father and it is enough for us." Jesus said to him, "Have I been so long a time with you, and you have not known me? Philip, he who sees me sees also the Father. How canst thou say, 'Show us the Father'? Dost thou not believe that I am in the Father and the Father in me? The words that I speak to you I speak not on my own authority. But the Father dwelling in me, it is he who does the works. Do you believe that I am in the Father and the Father in me? Otherwise believe because of the works themselves. Amen, amen, I say to you, he who believes in me, the works that I do he also shall do, and greater than these he shall do, because I am going to the Father. And whatever you ask in my name, that I will do, in order that the Father may be glorified in the Son. If you ask me anything in my name, I will do it."

Let Us Pray

O God, who dost gladden us by the annual celebration of the feast of Thy Apostles Philip and James, grant, we beseech Thee, that as we rejoice in their merits, we may be instructed by their example. Through our Lord.

May 3

FINDING OF THE HOLY CROSS

I Nocturn

*From the Epistle of St. Paul the Apostle to the Galatians,
c. 3, 10 - 14; to the Philippians, c. 2, 5 - 11;
to the Colossians, c. 2, 9 - 15*

II Nocturn

After that famous victory which the Emperor Constantine gained over Maxentius, on the eve of which the banner of the cross of the Lord had been given to him from heaven, Helena, the mother of Constantine, admonished in a dream, came to Jerusalem, eagerly searching for the cross. There she brought about the destruction of the marble statue of Venus, which had been set up by the Gentiles in place of the cross of Christ about a hundred and eighty years before in an attempt to wipe out the memory of the Passion of Christ the Lord. She did likewise at the crib of the Savior and at the place of the Resurrection, removing from the former an image of Adonis and from the latter, an idol of Jupiter.

Having thus cleansed the place where the cross had stood, Helena caused deep excavations to be made, as a result of which three crosses were found, as well as the inscription which had been nailed on that of our Lord. It was not known which of these crosses was that of the Lord until it was made manifest by a miracle. The Bishop of Jerusalem, Macarius, having offered solemn supplications to God, touched with each of the three crosses a woman who was afflicted with a serious sickness. At the touch of the first two there was no result, but when the third one touched her she was immediately cured.

Having thus found the true cross, Helena built on the site of the Lord's Passion a church of very great splendor, in which she deposited a part of the cross inclosed in a silver case. She also gave a part to her son Constantine, which was placed in the church of the Holy-Cross-in-Jerusalem, which he built at Rome on the site of the Sessorian palace.

She gave also to her son the nails with which the most holy body of Jesus Christ had been fixed to the cross. Constantine issued a decree that from that time forward the cross should not be used as an instrument of punishment; and thus that which heretofore had been an object of reproach and contempt among men, became now an object of veneration and glory.

℟. It behooveth us to glory in the Cross of our Lord Jesus Christ, in whom is our salvation, life and resurrection: * By whom we have been saved and delivered, alleluia. ℣. We adore Thy Cross, O Lord, and we remember Thy glorious Passion. By whom. Glory. By whom.

III Nocturn

The reading of the holy Gospel according to St. John

At that time there was a certain man among the Pharisees, Nicodemus by name, a ruler of the Jews. This man came to Jesus at night, and said to him, "Rabbi, we know that thou hast come a teacher from God, for no one can work these signs that thou workest unless God be with him." And so forth.

Homily of St. Augustine, Bishop

Nicodemus was one of those who had believed in the name of Jesus, seeing the signs and wonders which He did. For it is said above: "Now, when he was at Jerusalem at the Pasch, upon the festival day, many believed in his name." Why did they believe in His name? Holy Scripture goes on to say: "Seeing the signs which he did."

And what does it say of Nicodemus? "There was a ruler of the Jews named Nicodemus. This man came to him by night and said to him: 'Rabbi, we know that thou art come a teacher from God.'" He also, then, had believed in His name. And why had he believed? It continues: "For no man can do these things which thou dost unless God be with him."

If therefore Nicodemus was one of those who had believed in His name, let us now consider in the person of this Nicodemus why Jesus did not trust Himself to them. "Jesus answered and said to him: 'Amen, amen, I say to thee, unless a man be born again, he cannot see the kingdom of God.'" Hence, to them who have been born again does Jesus trust Himself. Behold, those men had believed in Him, and yet Jesus did not trust Himself to them. Such are all the catechumens—they already believe in the name of Christ, yet Jesus does not trust Himself to them.

Let your charity give ear and understand. If we say to a catechumen, "Dost thou believe in Christ?" he answers, "I believe," and signs himself with the cross of Christ; he bears it on his forehead, and is not ashamed of the cross of his Lord. Observe, he believes in His name. Let us ask him: "Dost thou eat of the flesh of the Son of Man, and drink the blood of the Son of Man?" He knows not what we say, because Jesus has not trusted Himself to him.

℟. O sweet the wood, sweet the nails, sweet the burden they sustain: * That wood alone was worthy to bear the ransom of this world, alleluia. ℣. This sign of the Cross will be in the heavens when the Lord shall come to judge. That wood. Glory. That wood.

✠ Continuation of the holy Gospel according to St. John.— At that time there was a certain man among the Pharisees, Nicodemus by name, a ruler of the Jews. This man came to Jesus at night, and said to him, "Rabbi, we know that thou hast come a teacher from God, for no one can work these signs that thou workest unless God be with him." Jesus answered and said to him, "Amen, amen, I say to thee, unless a man be born again, he cannot see the kingdom of God." Nicodemus said to him, "How can a man be born when he is old? Can he enter a second time into his mother's womb and be born again?"

Jesus answered, "Amen, amen, I say to thee, unless a man be born again of water and the Spirit, he cannot enter into the kingdom of God. That which is born of the flesh is flesh; and that which is born of the Spirit is spirit. Do not wonder that I said to thee, 'You must be born again.' The wind blows where it will, and thou hearest its sound but dost not know where it comes from or where it goes. So is everyone who is born of the Spirit."

Nicodemus answered and said to him, "How can these things be?"

Answering him, Jesus said, "Thou art a teacher in Israel and dost not know these things? Amen, amen, I say to thee, we speak of what we know, and we bear witness to what we have seen; and our witness you do not receive. If I have spoken of earthly things to you, and you do not believe, how will you believe if I speak to you of heavenly things? And no one has ascended into heaven except him who has descended from heaven: the Son of Man who is in heaven.

"And as Moses lifted up the serpent in the desert, even so must the Son of Man be lifted up, that those who believe in him may not perish, but may have life everlasting."

Let Us Pray

O God, who in the wonderful finding of Thy saving Cross hast renewed the miracles of Thy Passion, grant that by the price of this life-giving wood we may obtain the right to eternal life: Who livest and reignest with God the Father.

May 6
ST. JOHN, APOSTLE, BEFORE THE LATIN GATE
I Nocturn

*From the first Epistle of St. John the Apostle,
c. 1, 1 - 10; c. 2, 1 - 6*

II Nocturn

From the Book of St. Jerome, Priest, against Jovinian

The Apostle John, one of the Lord's disciples who in age is said to have been the youngest among the apostles and whom the holiness of Christ found a virgin, remained a virgin, and on that account he was the more loved by the Lord, and reclined upon Jesus' bosom. What Peter, who had a wife, did not dare himself to ask, he besought John to ask. Likewise after the Resurrection, when Mary Magdalene brought the news that our Lord had arisen, both ran to the sepulchre, but John arrived first. Again, when they were in the boat and were fishing on Lake Genesareth, and Jesus stood on the shore, the apostles did not recognize whom they saw; only the virgin knew the Virgin, and he said to Peter: "It is the Lord."

John was an Apostle and an Evangelist and a Prophet: an Apostle because he wrote to the churches as their teacher; an Evangelist since he composed a book of the Gospel, which, excepting Matthew, none of the other twelve apostles had done; a Prophet, for, on the island of Patmos where he had been exiled by the prince Domitian for bearing witness to his Lord, he received the revelation which contained many mysteries concerning things to come.

Tertullian relates that at Rome, when cast into a cauldron of boiling oil, John came out from it purer and stronger than he had entered. His Gospel, however, differs greatly from the others. Matthew begins to write of a man, as it were: "The book of the generation of Jesus Christ, the son of David, the son of Abraham..." Luke starts with the priesthood of Zachary. Mark begins with the prophecy of Malachias and of Isaias.

The first has the face of a man, because of his list of Christ's lineage; the second, the face of an ox, because of his reference to the priesthood; the third, the face of a lion, because of the words, "A voice of one crying in the desert: 'prepare ye the way of the Lord, make straight his paths.'" But our John soars as an eagle to the heights, and comes to the Father Himself, declaring: "In the beginning was the Word, and the Word was with God, and the Word was God."

℟. You have not chosen Me: but I have chosen you, and have appointed you * That you should go and should bring forth fruit, and your fruit should remain, alleluia, alleluia. ℣. As the Father hath sent Me, I also send you. That you. Glory. That you.

III Nocturn

The reading of the holy Gospel according to St. Matthew

At that time the mother of the sons of Zebedee came to Jesus with her sons: and worshipping, she made a request of him. And so forth.

Homily of St. Jerome, Priest

Whence does the mother of the sons of Zebedee get this idea of His Kingdom, that she should beg for the glory of Him triumphant, when our Lord had said, "The Son of man shall be betrayed to the chief priests and scribes, and they shall condemn him to death, and shall deliver him to the Gentiles to be mocked, and scourged, and crucified," and so announced to His frightened disciples the ignominy of His Passion? It was, I believe, from this fact, that after all these things the Lord declared, "And the third day he shall rise again." The woman thought that after His Resurrection He was to rule then and there, and that which He promised in His second coming was to be fulfilled in the first, and with a woman's eagerness she desired the present things, being unmindful of those to come.

The question, "What wilt thou?" which the Lord made in answer to her, when she petitioned Him, does not come from ignorance, but is rather spoken from His human person, which would be beaten and crucified. The same is true in the case of the woman with the issue of blood: "Who is it that touched me?" And with regard to Lazarus: "Where have they laid him?" Also in the old Testament: "Adam, where art thou?" Again: "I will go down and see whether they have done according to the cry that is come to me; or whether it be not so, that I may know." But the mother of the sons of Zebedee makes her petition through a woman's weakness and the affection of her motherly love, not knowing what she asked. Nor is it strange that she is accused of ignorance when it is said even of Peter, when he wished to build the three tents, that he knew not what he said.

St. John Before the Latin Gate

The mother makes the request, but our Lord replies to the disciples, knowing that her pleas came from the desires of her sons. "Can you drink the chalice that I shall drink?" In the divine Writings we understand *chalice* as suffering, in accord with that word: "Father, if it be possible, let this chalice pass from me." Also in the psalm: "What shall I render to the Lord, for all the things that he hath rendered to me? I will take the chalice of salvation, and I will call upon the name of the Lord." And immediately he intimates what this chalice is: "Precious in the sight of the Lord is the death of his saints."

The question arises as to how the sons of Zebedee, namely, James and John, drank the chalice of martyrdom, since the Scriptures narrate that only the Apostle James was decapitated by Herod, while John died a natural death. However, if we peruse the Church histories in which it is told that the latter was cast into a cauldron of boiling oil to be martyred, and in that way advanced as Christ's champion, to receive the crown, and was forthwith exiled to the isle of Patmos, we shall perceive that John had the soul of a martyr, and that he drank of the chalice of praise, of which the three young men in the fiery furnace also drank, even though the persecutor did not shed their blood.

℟. When ye stand before kings and governors, take no thought how or what you shall speak: * For it shall be given you in that hour what ye shall speak. ℣. For it is not you that speak; but the Spirit of your Father that speaketh in you. For. Glory. For.

✠ Continuation of the holy Gospel according to St. Matthew.—At that time the mother of the sons of Zebedee came to Jesus with her sons; and worshipping, she made a request of him. He said to her, "What dost thou want?" She said to him, "Command that these my two sons may sit, one at thy right hand and one at thy left hand, in thy kingdom." But Jesus answered and said, "You do not know what you are asking for. Can you drink of the cup of which I am about to drink?" They said to him, "We can." He said to them, "Of my cup you shall indeed drink; but as for sitting at my right hand and at my left, that is not mine to give you, but it belongs to those for whom it has been prepared by my Father."

Let Us Pray

O God, who dost behold that we are everywhere troubled by all our sins, grant, we beseech Thee, that the glorious intercession of blessed John, Thy Apostle and Evangelist, may protect us Through our Lord.

May 13
FEAST OF THE HOLY RELICS

I Nocturn
From the Apocalypse of St. John the Apostle, c. 6, 9 - 11; c. 7, 14 - 17; c. 12, 9 - 12; c. 14, 9 - 12

II Nocturn
Sermon of St. Bernard, Abbot

Since the saints do not need our honor, nor is anything excellent given them by it, it is clearly for our own interest more than for their benefit that we venerate their memory. Do you wish to know how it is for our benefit? Remembering them I find myself inflamed most vehemently by a three-fold desire. The first desire that the memory of the saints either arouses or increases in us is to enjoy their most desirable companionship, to merit brotherhood with them, to live in common with those blessed spirits, and finally to enjoy the communion of the saints.

The remembrance of the individual saints enkindles the minds of the devout as single sparks, or rather as brightly burning torches, making them thirst for the sight and embrace of those blessed ones, so much so that many consider themselves as already numbered among them, vehemently longing, with hearts all afire, now for all the saints together, again for these or those certain ones. We ought to long not only for the society of the saints, but also for their happiness. Let us seek, too, their glory with a most fervent desire. This second desire which burns in us from the commemoration of the saints is that Christ may so appear to us during our life as He does to them, and that we also may dwell with Him in glory.

Indeed, if we are allowed to hope for such glory and aspire to such happiness, we should also desire the intercession of the saints, so that what is impossible for us may be obtained through their intercession. "Have mercy on me, have mercy on me, at least you, my friends." You, O saints, know our dangers, ignorance, the attacks of the enemy, our violent impulses, our frailty. I speak to you who fought the same temptations, who overcame in the same conflicts, who evaded the same snares, who have learned compassion from those things which you yourselves have suffered. With greater confidence I take refuge in you. I have you as possessors of the same human nature; so it behooves you to show a special and more familiar mercy to bone of your bone and flesh of your flesh.

Passing from this world to the Father, the saints have left us a pledge. Their bodies are indeed buried in peace amongst us, but their names shall live forever; that is, their glory is never buried. Far be from us, O holy souls, far be from us that cruelty of the chief butler of Pharao, who, when restored to his former position in Egypt, presently forgot holy Joseph, who lay bound in prison. For the Egyptians were not members of one head, nor had the unfaithful part with the faithful, that is, Egypt with Israel, any more than does darkness with light. For Egypt means darkness; Israel means the living God; and therefore where Israel was, there was light. But our union with the saints is such that while we rejoice with them, they suffer with us; while we, by devout meditation, reign with them, they, by their devoted intercession, fight with us and for us.

℟. Let the just rejoice in the Lord and let them hope in Him, and they shall be praised. * All ye right of heart rejoice in the Lord and exult. ℣. And ye shall be glorified, alleluia, alleluia. All. Glory. All.

III Nocturn

The reading of the holy Gospel according to St. Luke

At that time Jesus, coming down from the mountain, took his stand on a level stretch, with a crowd of his disciples, and a great multitude of people from all Judea and Jerusalem, and the sea coast of Tyre and Sidon, who came to listen to him and to be healed of their diseases. And so forth.

Homily of St. Ambrose, Bishop

Observe the right order of things. It is fitting that you become poor in spirit; for humility of spirit is the richness of virtue. Unless you be poor, you cannot be meek. He who is meek can mourn over present things, and he who mourns over inferior things can desire better things. He who seeks higher things avoids inferior things that he may be aided by the higher things. He who shows mercy cleanses his own heart. For what is it to cleanse the mind except to wipe away the filth of death? For alms free from death. Next, patience is truly the perfection of charity. And finally, he who, when placed in the final combat, suffers persecution, is tried by contrary things that, when he has fought manfully, he may receive the crown.

Certain ones hold that these are the degrees of virtue by which we may ascend from the lowest to the highest. In short, as the growth in virtue, so also the growth in recompense; for to be a child of God is more than to possess the earth and to merit consolation. But because the kingdom of heaven is both the first as well as the last recompense, shall the reward for those who are just beginning be equal to that of the perfect?

The first kingdom has place when the saints are snatched up in the clouds to meet Christ. For those sleeping will rise, some unto life everlasting, others to perdition. The first kingdom of heaven is set before the Saints after the dissolution of the body; the second kingdom is to be with Christ after the Resurrection. When you have entered into the kingdom of heaven, your reward is permanently fixed. And although the kingdom is only one, the rewards there are different.

After the resurrection, being freed from death, you will begin to possess your land. For that (corruptible flesh) to which it is said, "Dust thou art, and into dust thou shalt return," shall not possess its land; for that which does not receive the fruit cannot be the possessor (that is, if that corruptible flesh again returns to earth, it cannot possess the earth). Therefore, having been freed from death by the cross of the Lord (but only, however, if you have been found under the yoke of the Lord), you shall reap consolation in that possession. Delight follows consolation, divine mercy follows delight. And him upon whom the Lord has mercy, He also calls; he who is called sees Him who calls; he who sees God, is assumed into the right of divine generation; then, finally, as a son of God, he will be delighted by the celestial riches of the Kingdom.

℞. Rejoice, ye just, in the Lord, alleluia. * Jubilation is becoming for the just, alleluia. ℣. Sing to Him a new canticle, sing to Him psalms in a loud voice. Jubilation. Glory. Jubilation.

✠ Continuation of the holy Gospel according to St. Luke.—At that time, Jesus, coming down from the mountain, took his stand on a level stretch, with a crowd of his disciples, and a great multitude of people from all Judea and Jerusalem, and the sea coast of Tyre and Sidon, who came to listen to him and to be healed of their diseases. And those who were troubled with unclean spirits were cured. And all the crowd were trying to touch him, for power went forth from him and healed all.

And he lifted up his eyes to his disciples, and said, "Blessed are you poor, for yours is the kingdom of God. Blessed are you who hunger now, for you shall be satisfied. Blessed are you who weep now, for you shall laugh. Blessed shall you be when men hate you, and when they shut you out, and reproach you, and reject your name as evil, because of the Son of Man. Rejoice on that day and exult, for behold your reward is great in heaven."

Let Us Pray

O God, who hast willed to enrich this most holy Church with so many Relics of the Saints, increase our faith in the resurrection, and make us to be partakers of that immortal glory whose pledge we honor in these holy Relics. Through our Lord.

June 11

ST. BARNABAS, APOSTLE

I Nocturn

From the Acts of the Apostles, c. 13, 43 - 52; c. 14, 1 - 3

II Nocturn

Barnabas, who was also called Joseph, was a Levite and of the country of Cyprus, and was appointed with Paul, the Apostle of the Gentiles, to preach the Gospel of Jesus Christ. He sold the land he possessed and bringing the money, laid it at the feet of the apostles. Having been sent to preach at Antioch, he rejoiced greatly when he had ascertained that many people there had already been converted to the Faith of Christ, our Lord, and he exhorted them to continue in this Faith. This exhortation did much good, for he was held by them all to be a good man and full of the Holy Spirit.

Barnabas then departed to Tarsus to look for Paul, and when he had found him, they both went back to Antioch where they remained for a year, giving to the people there the commandments of the Christian Faith. It was here at Antioch that the followers of Christ were first called Christians. The newly made disciples of Paul and Barnabas supported the Christians who were in Judea, sending their alms through Paul and Barnabas. After they had accomplished this work of charity, they took with them John, surnamed Mark, and went back again to Antioch.

And while Paul and Barnabas, together with the other prophets and doctors, ministered to the Lord in the Church of Antioch in fasting and prayer, the Holy Spirit said: "Set apart for me Saul and Barnabas unto the work to which I have called them." The others then, fasting and praying, laid their hands upon Paul and Barnabas and sent them away. They went first to Seleucia and then to Cyprus, and passing through many cities and towns they preached the Gospel with the greatest benefit to their hearers.

Finally Barnabas separated from Paul and sailed to Cyprus together with John, surnamed Mark. There, about the seventh year of the reign of Nero, on the eleventh of June, he added the martyr's crown to the dignity of the apostolic office. During the rule of the Emperor Zeno the body of Barnabas was discovered on the island of Cyprus. On his breast lay the Gospel according to St. Matthew, which he had copied with his own hand.

℟. Take up My yoke upon you, saith the Lord, and learn of Me, because I am meek and humble of heart: * For My yoke is sweet and My burden light. ℣. And you shall find rest for your souls. For my yoke. Glory. For My yoke.

III Nocturn

The reading of the holy Gospel according to St. Matthew

At that time Jesus said to his disciples: "Behold, I am sending you forth like sheep in the midst of wolves." And so forth.

Homily of St. John Chrysostom

When the Lord had banished all anxiety from the disciples' hearts, and had confirmed them by the performance of wonderful deeds, and had made them, now estranged from all worldly affairs and freed from all the care of temporal matters, of a firm and unbending nature—then, finally, He foretold the adversities that were to befall them.

For many benefits were to follow from this prediction of future things. First, the fact that they learned the power of His foreknowledge. Next, that no one might suspect that such serious evils resulted from the Master's weakness. Again, so that they who were to suffer these things might not be shaken by a sudden and unlooked for turn of affairs. And lastly, that they might not be too greatly moved at hearing of these things at the very time of His Passion.

However, in order that they might realize that this was a new method of war and an unusual manner of battle, when He sent them out stripped, clothed with but one tunic, without shoes, without staff, and without girdle and wallet, and commanded that they be fed by those who received them, He did not then cease speaking, but, exhibiting His own ineffable virtue, He said: "And so going forth, display, nevertheless, the gentleness of sheep, even though you are going out to wolves, and not simply *to* the wolves, but even *in the midst* of wolves (and yet He does not order that they possess only the gentleness of sheep, but the simplicity of a dove as well), for so shall I the better demonstrate My power when the wolves will be conquered by sheep, and while the latter may be in the midst of wolves and torn by innumerable bites, they will not in the least be devoured, but will transform the wolves into their very own nature."

It is assuredly a greater and more wonderful thing to change the mind of enemies and transform their spirit into a different one than it is to kill them, especially since the sheep were but twelve in number, and the wolves filled the entire world. Let us on this account blush with shame, who, acting very differently, run as wolves upon our foes. For as long as we are sheep, we shall conquer; even if a thousand wolves surround us, we shall overcome them and be the victors; but should we be like wolves, we shall be defeated. For then the help of the Shepherd, who feeds not wolves, but His sheep, will be withdrawn from us.

℟. These are they who, living in the flesh, planted the Church in their blood: * They drank the chalice of the Lord, and became the friends of God. ℣. Their voice hath gone forth into all the earth, and their words unto the ends of the world. They drank. Glory. They drank.

✠ Continuation of the holy Gospel according to St. Matthew.— At that time Jesus said to his disciples: "Behold, I am sending you forth like sheep in the midst of wolves. Be therefore wise as serpents, and guileless as doves. But beware of men; for they will deliver you up to councils, and scourge you in their synagogues, and you will be brought before governors and kings for my sake, for a witness to them and to the Gentiles. But when they deliver you up, do not be anxious how or what you are to speak; for what you are to speak will be given you in that hour. For it is not you who are speaking, but the Spirit of your Father who speaks through you. And brother will hand over brother to death, and the father his child; children will rise up against parents, and put them to death. And you will be hated by all for my name's sake; but he who has persevered to the end will be saved."

LET US PRAY

O God, who dost make us glad by the merits and intercession of blessed Barnabas, Thy Apostle, mercifully grant that we who ask Thy favors through his intercession may receive them by the gift of Thy grace. Through our Lord.

June 23

VIGIL OF ST. JOHN THE BAPTIST

The reading of the holy Gospel according to St. Luke

In the days of Herod, king of Judea, there was a certain priest named Zachary, of the course of Abia; and his wife was of the daughters of Aaron, and her name was Elizabeth. And so forth.

Homily of St. Ambrose, Bishop

Holy Scripture instructs us that it is fitting that not only the characters of those who are worthy of praise should be extolled, but their parents also, so that, as it were, the heritage of an unstained purity which has been passed on may stand out in those whom we wish to laud. What else is the holy Evangelist's aim in this passage but that John the Baptist be ennobled through his parents, his miracles, his character, his mission, his martyrdom? In this way also Anna, the mother of holy Samuel, is praised; thus does Isaac receive that noble godliness which he in turn passed on to his children. And so the priest Zachary is not only a priest, but likewise of the course of Abia, that is, renowned among the more honorable families.

"And his wife," it says, "was of the daughters of Aaron." Therefore, not only from his parents, but also from his ancestors is the noble rank of St. John traced, sublime not in worldly power, but venerable in the inheritance of religious devotion. For the herald of Christ had to have such ancestry lest he should appear to preach the faith in our Lord's coming as if it were conceived of a sudden, rather than received from his forefathers and infused into him by the law of nature. It continues: "They were both just before God, walking in all the commandments and justifications of the Lord without blame." What do they say to this, who, seeking to console themselves in their own sins, think that man cannot be without frequent sins, and make use of the brief word written in Job: "No one is free of stain, not even if his life on earth be of one day."

To these it is to be replied, first, that they should explain what it is for man to be without sin: whether it implies that he has never sinned at all, or that he has ceased to sin. For if they think that to be without sin is to have never sinned at all, then I myself agree with them. "For all men have sinned and have need of the glory of God." But if they deny that he can abstain from sin who has mended his old error and has changed his life so that he now refrains from evil, I cannot conform to their opinion, since we read that our Lord has so loved the Church "that he may present it to himself as the glorious Church not having spot or wrinkle, or any such thing; but that it should be holy, and without blemish."

June 24

NATIVITY OF ST. JOHN THE BAPTIST

I Nocturn

From the Book of Jeremias the Prophet, c. 1, 1 - 10 and 17 - 19

II Nocturn

Sermon of St. Maximus, Bishop

The natural birth of the venerable John the Baptist, dearest brethren, has made sacred the festival of this day. On this account, he was sent into this world by heavenly dispensation not only that he himself might be honored by the office of Prophet, but also that the praises due all the prophets might be confirmed in him. Not undeservedly do we venerate with special honor him who by a certain, singular favor was the last to foretell the Savior of the world that he might be the first to point Him out to us.

For it was he alone of the prophets who merited to see with his own eyes our Lord Jesus Christ, whom the rest foreknew would come after a long time, and to announce Him as being at hand. He is the one whom, through the inspiration of God, Isaias foretold, saying: "The voice of one crying in the desert: 'Prepare ye the way of the Lord.'" How fittingly, dearly beloved brethren, was John announced beforehand as a voice, since he was to be sent as herald and witness of the celestial Word.

He is the one whose birth and name and merit were foretold by the Angel Gabriel. He is the one who in the judgment of a heavenly declaration is placed before all mortal men, according to the saying of our Lord, "There hath not risen among them that are born of women a greater than John the Baptist." How beautifully is it said, "Among them that are born of *women* there is none greater," for He who was born of the Virgin was in every way greater than John!

Having reflected on these things, consider what great respect, what great devotion we should tender this man, who, in order that he might be honored, was foretold by the Holy Spirit, promised by an angel, praised by God, and sanctified by the undying glory of a holy death! For it was fitting that a wonderful life should follow his extraordinary birth, and that a death consecrated to God should close his holy and perfect life. Consequently, brethren, does Christ's Church over the whole world most correctly celebrate today with the greatest joy the first moments of the life of him who, as a most faithful witness, revealed to the awestruck world that eternal joys were come to mortal men.

℟. The Angel of the Lord came down to Zachary, saying: Thou shalt receive a son in thine old age: * And his name shall be John the Baptist. ℣. This child is great before the Lord: for His hand is with him. And his name. Glory. And his name.

III Nocturn

The reading of the holy Gospel according to St. Luke

Elizabeth's time was fulfilled that she should be delivered, and she brought forth a son. And her neighbors and kinsfolk heard that the Lord had magnified his mercy towards her, and they rejoiced with her. And so forth.

Homily of St. Ambrose, Bishop

Elizabeth brought forth a son, and her neighbors congratulated her. The birth of saints holds a joy for many since it is a common blessing, for justice is a common virtue. And hence in the birth of this just man a pledge of his future life is given beforehand, and the grace of the virtue that is to follow is betokened through the rejoicing of his neighbors. Very properly indeed is the time while the Prophet was in the womb described lest Mary's presence go unmentioned, but the time of his infancy is not mentioned because he knew not the restrictions of infancy.

And so in the Gospel we read nothing about him except his birth and the prophecy, his leaping in the womb, and his voice in the desert. For he did not experience any period of infancy, who, beyond his nature, beyond his age, when still placed in his mother's womb began to be of the measure of the age of the fullness of Christ. The holy Evangelist thought it should be premised that many people thought John should be called by his father's name, Zachary, so that you might take note that that name which had been revealed by the Holy Spirit and foretold by an angel to Zachary did not displease the mother.

Indeed Zachary, unable to speak, could not intimate the name of their child to his wife; but Elizabeth learned through a prophecy what she had not learned from her husband. "John," she says, "is his name"—that is, "we are not going to give a name to him who has already received a name from God; he has his name which we have recognized but which we have not chosen."

The merits of the saints have this reward, that they receive their name from God. So Jacob is called Israel because he saw God. So our Lord, to whom not an angel, but His Father gave the name, was called Jesus before He was born. You see that the angels announce the things which they have heard, not the things which they have invented. Nor should you marvel that the woman insisted on a name which she had not heard, since the Holy Spirit, who had given the command to the Angel, revealed it to her.

℞. The Angel Gabriel appeared to Zachary, saying: A son shall be born to thee, and his name shall be called John: * And many shall rejoice on his birthday. ℣. For he shall be great before the Lord, and he shall drink no wine nor strong drink. And many. Glory. And many.

☩ Continuation of the holy Gospel according to St. Luke.— Elizabeth's time was fulfilled that she should be delivered, and she brought forth a son. And her neighbors and kinsfolk heard that the Lord had magnified his mercy towards her, and they rejoiced with her. And it came to pass on the eighth day, that they came to circumcise the child, and they were going to call him by his father's name, Zachary. And his mother answered and said, "Not so, but he shall be called John."

And they said to her, "There is none of thy kindred that is called by this name." And they kept making signs to his father what he would have him called. And asking for a writing-tablet he wrote the words, "John is his name." And they all marvelled. And immediately his mouth was opened and his tongue loosed, and he began to speak, blessing God. And fear came on all their neighbors; and all these things were spoken abroad in all the hill country of Judea. And all who heard them laid them up in their heart, saying, "What then will this child be?" For the hand of the Lord was with him. And Zachary his father was filled with the Holy Spirit, and prophesied, saying, "Blessed be the Lord, the God of Israel, because he has visited and wrought redemption for his people."

LET US PRAY

O God, who hast made this present day glorious for us by the birth of blessed John, grant to thy people the grace of spiritual joys and guide the minds of all the faithful in the way of eternal salvation. Through our Lord.

June 25

SECOND DAY WITHIN THE OCTAVE OF ST. JOHN THE BAPTIST

Sermon of St. Maximus, Bishop

The memory of all the prophets, dearest brethren, should be venerated. The blessed John the Baptist, whose natural birthday is honored today, has so far superseded the glory of all the others that he revealed in the truth of his personal testimony not only that the Lord Jesus, our Savior, was to come, but that He had already come and was dwelling among men. When he beheld Him among the common crowds approaching to be baptized by himself, pointing, as it were, with his finger, he declared: "Behold the Lamb of God, behold him who taketh away the sin of the world." How innocent is the life of this man! And how can we compensate by our devotion the merits of him who first recognized the coming of the heavenly Lamb and alone pointed Him out! How wonderful before all is his praise, from whose mouth the world for the first time heard its absolution!

This is he, dearest brethren, of whom it was foretold in the pronouncement of the Prophet: "The voice of one crying in the desert: Prepare ye the way of the Lord: make straight the paths of our God." For he was to cry out—as indeed he did cry out—in order that, by his shouting the message of salvation, his heavenly preaching might open the long deafened ears of mortal men. Who then would not consider with great admiration a prophet of this sort, whom one recognizes to have been so great as to have obtained from God that his merits should be lauded ere his birth had taken place.

So the most just high priest, Zachary, when he had come to an old age and despaired of the issue of a cherished offspring because of the barrenness of his aged wife, this John is promised by the providence of almighty God through an angel. And rightly to these elderly parents is given a young child who was to point out to an aging and tottering world the only-begotten Son of God as a pledge of its future youthfulness. How greatly is it to be wondered at that Zachary himself, when he was a little slow to believe that the precursor of the saving Word would be conceived in the womb of his aged wife, was suddenly struck dumb and did not regain the use of his speech until the child's name, by which he was to be called, loosed the bonds of his tongue? And so it happened that the merit of the newborn child opened the mouth of the priest, which his doubting hesitation had closed, and the restored speech of the father gave witness to the glory of the infant.

June 26

THIRD DAY WITHIN THE OCTAVE OF ST. JOHN THE BAPTIST

Sermon of St. Augustine, Bishop

What feast we are celebrating today need not be told you, dearly beloved, since you all have heard, as the Gospel was read. Today we acclaim holy John, the Lord's precursor, the son of a barren woman announcing the Son of a Virgin, and a servant proclaiming his Lord. For because the God-man was about to come through a Virgin, a remarkable man born of a barren woman preceded Him, so that the God-man might be recognized when the remarkable man declares that he is unworthy to loose His shoestring. Admire John as much as you can; the fact that you admire redounds to Christ's glory. It redounds to Christ's glory; I say, not that you bestow anything on Christ, but that you may make progress in Christ.

Admire John, therefore, as much as you can. You have heard what you should admire. By the Angel it was announced to the priest and father; the Angel took away the speech of the unbelieving father; he was left dumb, awaiting the use of his tongue at his son's nativity. A barren woman conceived; more, an aged woman conceived in spite of this double impediment, barrenness and old age. By the Angel it is told what sort of man John would be; there is fulfilled in him what is said of him; and, what is most marvelous, he is filled with the Holy Spirit from his mother's womb. Then, when Blessed Mary comes, he leaps within the womb, and he greets by his actions Him whom he could not salute with words. He is born; he gives speech to his father; the father in speaking gives his son a name; all admire so great a grace. For what else is this but grace? For when did this John gain the favor of God? When did he gain God's favor before he even existed to merit? O grace freely given!

All admire; all are awed; all speak with the movement of the heart, so that what was said would be written for us: "What an one, think ye, shall this child be? For the hand of the Lord was with him." What do you think this child shall be? He surpasses the limits of human nature. Children we have known, but what do you think this child will be? Why do you say, "What an one, think ye, shall this child be? For the hand of the Lord is with him"? We already know that the Lord's hand is with him; but what he will be, we do not know. He will indeed be great who began so great. What will he be, who as a little child is so great? What will he be? Human infirmity grows weak, the hearts of all tremble at the thought: What do you think this boy will become? He will be great; but what will He be who is greater than John? This one indeed is great; but what will He be who is greater than this great man? If he who just began to exist will be so great, what will He be, who *was?*

June 27
FOURTH DAY WITHIN THE OCTAVE OF ST. JOHN THE BAPTIST

Sermon of St. Bede the Venerable, Priest

The birth of the Lord's forerunner, as the sacred story of the Gospel lesson sets forth, shines with a great display of miracles; for it was most fitting that he, than whom amongst those born of women none greater has arisen, should be in his very birth, by reason of the bright display of wonders, more glorious than other saints. His parents, old, and long childless, exult in the gift of a noble offspring. Incredulity had made the father dumb; now his mouth and tongue are opened to greet the preacher of new grace. Not alone is the ability to bless God restored, but the power to prophesy is increased. Roused by report of the event, all the neighbors are overcome with fear and wonder; all round about that have heard are prepared in their hearts for the coming of the new prophet.

Rightly, therefore, is holy Church, which throughout the world keeps those victories of so many blessed martyrs by which they merited their entrance into the heavenly Kingdom, accustomed to celebrate, after that of the Lord, the birthday of this Saint alone. That this custom arose without Gospel authority is not at all to be believed; rather, we should ponder more carefully that just as, when the Lord was born, the Angel that appeared to the shepherds said: "Behold I bring you good tidings of great joy that shall be to all the people; for this day is born to you a Savior, who is Christ the Lord"; so also the Angel, telling Zachary of John's approaching birth, says: "Thou shalt have joy and gladness, and many shall rejoice in his nativity. For he shall be great before the Lord."

Justly, then, the birthday of each is kept with festive devotion. Yet in the former's birth glad tidings are brought to all the people, for Christ the Lord, the Savior of the world, the Son of God almighty, the Sun of Justice, is born; but in the latter's birth it is said many will rejoice, for there has arisen the Lord's forerunner, an exceptional servant of God, a burning and a shining light. Of this man it is related that he will be great before the Lord; but of the former the Prophet bears witness, "that the Lord is great and exceedingly to be praised and of his greatness there is no end." This man avoided the company of sinners and abstained from everything that might intoxicate; while the former associates with sinners and remains free from every sin. The latter from his mother's very womb was filled with the Holy Spirit; but in the former the entire fullness of the Godhead dwells bodily, and by the gift of His Own Spirit He sanctified for Himself the throne of that virginal womb in which He took our flesh.

June 28

FIFTH DAY WITHIN THE OCTAVE OF ST. JOHN THE BAPTIST

Sermon of St. Augustine, Bishop

The holy John the Baptist was sent before the face of Christ to prepare His way. Christ's testimony concerning John is: "There hath not risen among them that are born of women a greater than John the Baptist." John's testimony concerning Christ is: "He that shall come after me is mightier than I, whose shoe I am not worthy to loose." Let us consider both testimonies: the one which the Lord offered concerning His servant, and the one which the servant offered concerning his Lord. What is the Lord's testimony concerning His servant? "There hath not arisen among them that are born of women a greater than John the Baptist." What is the servant's testimony concerning the Lord? "He that shall come after me is mightier than I." If, then, "there hath not arisen among them that are born of women a greater than John the Baptist," what is He who is greater than he? John is a great man, but a man; Christ is greater than John, because He is God and man.

Both were born in a marvelous manner—the herald and the Judge; the light and the Day; the voice and the Word; the servant and the Lord! The Lord formed the servant for Himself within a sterile womb, of an old father and an aged mother; the the same Lord, who formed the first man without father or mother, formed a body for Himself within the womb of a Virgin, without a man as His father. No one has arisen among them that are born of women greater than John the Baptist. John seemed so great that he was thought by some even to be the Christ. But he did not follow the error of another in his pride, nor did he dare to declare: "I am that which you think me"; but, because it was a blessing for him, he recognized himself, so that he was humbled as a servant at the feet of his Lord and at His shoelace, lest as a light he be blown out by the wind of pride.

VIGIL OF SS. PETER AND PAUL

The reading of the holy Gospel according to St. John

At that time, Jesus said to Simon Peter: "Simon, son of John, dost thou love me more than these do?" And so forth.

Homily of St. Augustine, Bishop

A triple confession is made in return for Peter's triple denial, lest the tongue should serve love less than fear, and imminent death seem to have provoked his words more than the Life which was present. Let it be a service of love to feed the Lord's flock, since it was a sign of fear to deny the Shepherd. They who feed Christ's sheep in such a spirit that they desire the sheep to be their own—either in their desire for glory, or power, or possessions, not out of love for obeying, serving, and pleasing God—are shown to love themselves, not Christ.

June 29

SS. PETER AND PAUL, APOSTLES

I Nocturn

From the Acts of the Apostles, c. 3, 1 - 16

II Nocturn

Sermon of St. Leo, Pope

The whole world, indeed, dearly beloved, is partaker of all holy solemnities, and the sense of union of our Faith demands that whatever is honored as having been done for the salvation of all should be everywhere celebrated with mutual joy. Yet today's festival, beyond that reverence which it deserves from the whole world, ought to be venerated with a special and singular gladness in our own city (Rome), and there, where the departure of the chief Apostles is glorified, ought to be on the day of their martyrdom the chief center of joy. For these are the men through whom Christ's Gospel shone upon thee, O Rome, and thou, who hadst been the mistress of error, art made a disciple of truth!

These are thy fathers and true pastors who, to implant thee in the heavenly realms, founded thee in a better and happier manner than did they by whose zeal the first foundations of thy walls were laid, from among whom the very one who has given thee thy name dishonored thee by the murder of his brother. These are they who have lifted thee up to this glory, that as "a holy nation," "a chosen people," "a priestly and royal city," being made the head of the world by the holy throne of blessed Peter, thou shouldst rule more widely by a divine religion than by an earthly domination.

For while, being enlarged by many victories, thou hast extended the rule of thy empire over land and sea, still, that is a lesser thing which the labor of war has subjected to thee than is

SS. PETER AND PAUL, APOSTLES 387

that which Christian peace has placed at thy feet. It was, indeed, most fitting for the work which had been divinely ordered, that many kingdoms should be united in one empire, and that the widespread teaching should quickly spread among those people whom the rule of one city bound together.

This city, not knowing the author of her own advancement, while she ruled almost every nation, was subservient to the errors of all the nations, and she seemed to have accepted an immense religion to herself since she rejected no false teaching. Wherefore, in as much as she was the more firmly shackled by the devil, so much the more marvelously was she freed by Christ!

℟. Thou art the shepherd of the sheep, O Prince of the Apostles; to thee did God entrust all the kingdoms of the world: * And therefore to thee were given the keys of the kingdom of heaven. ℣. Whatsoever thou shalt bind on earth, it shall be bound also in heaven; and whatsoever thou shalt loose on earth, it shall be loosed also in heaven. And. Glory. And.

III Nocturn

The reading of the holy Gospel according to St. Matthew

At that time Jesus, having come into the district of Caesarea Philippi, began to ask his disciples, saying, "Who do men say the Son of Man is?" And so forth.

Homily of St. Jerome, Priest

Our Lord beautifully asks: "Whom do men say that the Son of Man is?" He speaks thus, for those who speak of the Son of Man are men; on the contrary, those who understand His Divinity are not called men, but gods. "But they said: 'Some, John the Baptist, and other some, Elias.'" I marvel at the fact that certain interpreters inquire into the causes of each of these errors and weave a lengthy disputation on why some thought our Lord Jesus Christ to be John, others Elias, and other some Jeremias or one of the prophets, since they could err just as easily in considering Him as Elias or Jeremias as Herod erred in mistaking Him for John when he said: "John whom I have beheaded has risen from the dead and therefore mighty works show forth themselves in him."

"But whom do you say that I am?" Prudent reader, note well that from the following text of His speech the apostles are not called men but gods. For when He said, "Whom do *men* say that I am?" He added, "But whom do *you* say that I am?" "Since others, being men, have thoughts only for the things of men, whom do you, being gods, consider Me?"

Peter, in the name of all the apostles, professes: "Thou art Christ, the Son of the living God." He says "living God" to distinguish Him from those false gods who are considered as gods, but are really dead. "And Jesus answering said to him: 'Blessed art thou, Simon Bar-Jona.'" He gave a reward for the Apostle's testimony concerning Himself. Peter had said, "Thou art the Christ, the Son of the living God." This true confession received its reward: "Blessed art thou, Simon Bar-Jona." And why blessed? "Because flesh and blood have not revealed it to thee, but the Father has revealed it."

What flesh and blood could not reveal has been revealed by the grace of the Holy Spirit. Therefore on account of his confession the announcement comes to him that he has the revelation from the Holy Spirit, whose son he must even be called, because in our language "Bar-Jona" is rendered, "Son of the Dove."

℟. I have prayed for thee, Peter, that thy faith fail not: * And thou, being once converted, confirm thy brethren. ℣. Flesh and blood hath not revealed it to thee, but My Father, who is in heaven. And. Glory. And.

✠ Continuation of the holy Gospel according to St. Matthew.—At that time Jesus, having come into the district of Caesarea Philippi, began to ask his disciples, saying, "Who do men say the Son of Man is?" But they said, "Some say, John the Baptist; and others, Elias; and others, Jeremias, or one of the prophets." He said to them, "But who do you say that I am?" Simon Peter answered and said, "Thou art the Christ, the Son of the living God." Then Jesus answered and said, "Blessed art thou, Simon Bar-Jona, for flesh and blood has not revealed this to thee, but my Father in heaven. And I say to thee, thou art Peter and upon this rock I will build my Church, and the gates of hell shall not prevail against it. And I will give thee the keys of the kingdom of heaven; and whatever thou shalt bind on earth shall be bound in heaven, and whatever thou shalt loose on earth shall be loosed in heaven."

Let Us Pray

O God, who hast consecrated this day by the martyrdom of Thine Apostles Peter and Paul, grant to Thy Church to follow their commands in all things through whom She received the beginning of her religion. Through our Lord.

June 30
COMMEMORATION OF ST. PAUL, APOSTLE
I Nocturn

From the Acts of the Apostles, c. 13, 1 - 13

II Nocturn

From the Book of St. Augustine, Bishop,
on Grace and Free Will

Let us see what the Apostle Paul—whom we have for a certainty found to be without any good merits, yea, rather with many demerits—on having attained to the grace of God, who returns blessings for evils, says as the moment of his martyrdom nears. Writing to Timothy, he states: "I am even now ready to be sacrificed, and the time of my dissolution is at hand. I have fought a good fight, I have finished my course, I have kept the faith." These things he mentions, indeed, as his own good merits, so that, following upon his good merits, he might obtain a crown, who after his demerits had obtained grace.

Now take note of what follows. "For the rest, there is laid up for me a crown of justice, which the Lord, the just judge, will render to me in that day." To whom would the just Judge award a crown had not the merciful Father bestowed grace on him? And how would it be a crown of justice had not grace which justifies the wicked gone before? How could this crown which was due be awarded had not that grace been bestowed first?

Hence let us consider these merits of the Apostle Paul for which he said the just Judge was to offer him a crown, and let us see whether his merits were his own, as of himself, that is, acquired for him by his own efforts, or whether they were God's gifts. He says: "I have fought a good fight, I have finished my course, I have kept the faith." First of all, the good works would themselves never exist if good thoughts had not preceded them Therefore observe what he says about these thoughts. He declared in writing to the Corinthians: "Not that we are sufficient of ourselves to think anything, as from ourselves, but our sufficiency is from God." Now we shall study these things separately.

"I have fought the good fight," he says. I ask, by what power did he fight? was it his as from himself, or was it given to him from above? But God forbid that such a great teacher be ignorant of God's Law, as it is written in Deuteronomy: "Lest thou shouldst say in thy heart: 'My own might and the strength of my own hand have achieved all these things for me.' But remember the Lord thy God, that he hath given thee strength to do virtue.'" Of what profit is a good fight unless victory follows? And who will give the victory but He of whom Paul himself declares: "Thanks be to God, who gives us the victory through our Lord Jesus Christ."

℟. By the grace of God I am what I am: * And His grace in me hath not been void, but remaineth always with me. ℣. He who wrought in Peter to the Apostleship wrought in me also among the Gentiles. And His grace. Glory. And His grace.

III Nocturn

The reading of the holy Gospel according to St. Matthew

At that time Jesus said to his disciples: "Behold, I am sending you forth like sheep in the midst of wolves." And so forth.

Homily of St. John Chrysostom

Christ seems to speak thus: "Be not troubled if I command you to be as sheep and doves when I send you among wolves. For though I can command the contrary and not permit you to suffer any hurt, nor be as sheep subject to wolves, but can make you more terrible than lions, yet I will have it as I said. Thereby you become more glorious, and My power is made manifest." It was thus that Christ afterwards spoke to Paul, "My grace is sufficient for thee, for virtue is made strong in infirmity. I myself have made you to be in the condition in which you are."

But let us see what prudence Christ demands—assuredly that of the serpent. Just as the serpent glides along with its whole self and cares little if it be necessary for its body to be struck, provided its head is not harmed, so do you also bother not about the loss of things other than faith, be they monies, the flesh, or even the giving up of life itself. Faith is the head and at the same time the root, and if you keep your faith intact, even if you lose all else, yet you will recover everything again unto your greater glory.

He did not command them to be simple alone, nor prudent alone, but to unite both these qualities into one, so that they may cooperate as powerful allies. If you desire to see how this was done, read the Acts of the Apostles. There you will certainly see that when the Jewish people rose up against the apostles and gnashed their teeth against them, the apostles, by imitating the simplicity of the dove and answering with becoming modesty, repressed the ire of the Jews, soothed their fury, and warded off a vicious attack.

For when the Jews said to them: "Did we not command you most emphatically not to teach in his name?" the apostles, although they could have worked miracles without number, neither said nor did anything harsh, but answering with the greatest meekness, said, "If it be just in the sight of God to hear you rather than God, judge ye." You have perceived the simplicity of the dove; observe now the prudence of the serpent. "For we cannot but speak," they say, "the things which we have seen and heard."

℟. Thou art a vessel of election, O holy Apostle Paul, a preacher of truth to the whole world, * Through whom the Gentiles have known the grace of God. ℣. Intercede for us with God, who chose thee. Through whom. Glory. Through whom.

✠ Continuation of the holy Gospel according to St. Matthew.— At that time Jesus said to his disciples: "Behold, I am sending you forth like sheep in the midst of wolves. Be therefore wise as serpents, and guileless as doves. But beware of men; for they will deliver you up to councils, and scourge you in their synagogues, and you will be brought before governors and kings for my sake, for a witness to them and to the Gentiles. But when they deliver you up, do not be anxious how or what you are to speak; for what you are to speak will be given you in that hour. For it is not you who are speaking, but the Spirit of your Father who speaks through you. And brother will hand over brother to death, and the father his child; children will rise up against parents, and put them to death. And you will be hated by all for my name's sake; but he who has persevered to the end will be saved."

Let Us Pray

O God, who hast instructed the whole world by the preaching of blessed Paul the Apostle, grant us, we beseech Thee, that we, who honor his heavenly birthday, may experience the effects of his intercession with Thee. Through our Lord.

July 1

FEAST OF THE MOST PRECIOUS BLOOD

I Nocturn

From the Epistle of St. Paul the Apostle to the Hebrews,
c. 9, 11 - 22; c. 10, 19 - 24

II Nocturn

Sermon of St. John Chrysostom

Do you wish to hear of the power of the Blood of Christ? Let us go back to its type; let us recall its foreshadowing; let us talk about the early Sacred Scripture. In Egypt, at midnight, God threatened the Egyptians with a tenth plague, that their first-born would perish because they were detaining His first-born people. But, lest the beloved Jewish people be struck together with them (for the one region held them all), a means to distinguish them was found. Here is an admirable example whereby you may learn of the power in the reality. The wrath of divine indignation was roused, and the bearer of death was passing through every home. What then did Moses do? "Slay a lamb," he says, "that is one year old, and smear your doors with its blood." What are you saying, Moses? Is the blood of a sheep wont to deliver rational man? "Indeed so!" he says, "not because it is blood, but because the Blood of the Lord is represented by this figure."

For just as the statues of rulers, which are without reason and speech, sometimes give strength to men, possessing mind and reason, who fly to them for refuge, not because they are made of bronze, but because they set forth the image of a prince; so also that blood, which was irrational, set at liberty men who were rational, not because it was blood, but because it pointed to the appearance of this Blood. And at that time the destroying Angel, seeing the marked posts and entrance, continued on and did not dare to enter. Therefore if the enemy shall now behold not the typical blood sprinkled on posts, but the true Blood of Christ, consecrated on the posts (that is, the altar) of the temple, shining in the mouth of the faithful, all the more will he withdraw himself. For if the Angel halted at the figure, how much more shall the enemy be terrified if he shall perceive the reality itself.

Do you wish to inquire further concerning the power of this Blood? I wish you to see whence it first ran and from what font it flowed. It proceeded first from the cross itself; the Lord's side was its source. The soldier opened His side and laid open the wall of the temple, and thus I have discovered a wonderful treasure and congratulate myself on finding the shining riches. So did it happen with that lamb also: the Jews killed the sheep, and (in that it preserved them from death by the sword of the angel) I have recognized the fruit of the sacrament. From the side came blood and water. I would not want you, O listener, to pass over the secrets of such a great mystery, for there rests with me a mystical and secret prayer. I have said that that water and blood are a symbol of Baptism and of the Mysteries. From these Holy Church was established through her rebirth at the font and her renewal by the Holy Spirit. Through Baptism, I say, and the Mysteries which are seen to have been produced from His side.

So, from His own side Christ built up His Church, just as Eve was produced from the side of Adam. Regarding this, Paul likewise testifies, saying, "We are members of His body, and of his bones," signifying, of course, that side. For as God made woman to be produced from the side of Adam, so Christ gave to us from His own side the water and blood by which the Church was renewed.—On the occasion of the nineteenth centenary of the Redemption of the human race, the Supreme Pontiff, Pius XI, in order to honor such an ineffable benefit, desired a sacred Jubilee to be celebrated, so that more abundant fruits of the Precious Blood of Christ, the immaculate Lamb, by which we were redeemed, might flow down upon mankind, and His memory be commended more vividly to the faithful. The same Supreme Pontiff elevated the Feast of the Most Precious Blood of our Lord Jesus Christ, which is to be celebrated yearly by the universal Church, to the rite of a double of the first class.

℟. God commendeth His charity towards us: * Because, when as yet we were sinners, in due time Christ died for us. ℣. Much more, therefore, being now justified by His Blood, shall we be saved from wrath through Him. Because. Glory. Because.

III Nocturn

The reading of the holy Gospel according to St. John

At that time, when Jesus had taken the wine, he said, "It is consummated!" And bowing his head, he gave up his spirit. And so forth.

Homily of St. Augustine, Bishop

The Evangelist used careful wording, not saying, "the soldier struck his side," or "he wounded it," or anything else, but "he opened his side," in order that, in a certain way, the gate of life might there be revealed whence the sacraments of the Church, without which that life which is true cannot be entered upon, have flown out. That Blood which was shed, was shed unto the remission of sins. That water tempers the saving cup; it serves both as a laver and as a drink. All this was prefigured when Noe was ordered to make a door in the side of the ark, by which the animals which were not to perish in the deluge might enter. By these animals the Church was prefigured. For this reason the first woman was made from the side of the man while he slept, and she was called *life* and *mother of the living.* Indeed, she was a type of a great blessing before the great evil of her fall. This second Adam, with His head bowed, slept on the cross, that in this way there might be created for Him a spouse who came out from His side while He slept. O death through which the dead live again! What is more purifying than this Blood? What more salutary than this wound?

Men were held as captives of the devil and served the demons, but they have been bought back from captivity. For they could sell themselves, but they were unable to redeem themselves. The Redeemer came and paid the price; He shed His own Blood, and He purchased the whole world. Do you ask what He has bought? Look to what He paid, and you will find out what He purchased. The Blood of Christ is the price. What is it worth? What, but the whole world! What, but all the nations of men! They are very ungrateful for the price paid, or they are exceedingly proud who declare either that the price was so small that it purchased the Africans only, or that they themselves are so great that it was paid for them alone. Let them not, therefore, rejoice or grow haughty. As much as He gave, He gave for all.

He possessed the Blood by which He was to redeem us, and for this purpose He had received that blood, that He might have it to pour out for our redemption. The Blood of your Lord was given for you if you wish it; if you do not want it to be so, it was not given for you. For perchance you will say: "My God did possess the Blood by which He could redeem me, but when He suffered, He shed it all; what remains for Him to give for me?"

This is a great thing that He gave it once and gave it for everyone. Christ's Blood is the salvation of him who wills it, the condemnation of him who wills it not. Why then do you hesitate, you who do not wish to die, to be freed from a second death? In this you are freed if you desire to take up your cross and follow the Lord, because He has taken up His own and has gone in search of His servant.

℟. God hath predestined us unto the adoption of sons through Jesus Christ, * In whom we have redemption through His Blood. ℣. The remission of sins according to the riches of His grace, which hath superabounded in us. In whom. Glory. In whom.

☩ Continuation of the holy Gospel according to St. John.—
'At that time, when Jesus had taken the wine, he said, "It is consummated!" And bowing his head, he gave up his spirit.

The Jews therefore, since it was the Preparation Day, in order that the bodies might not remain upon the cross on the Sabbath (for that Sabbath was a solemn day), besought Pilate that their legs might be broken, and that they might be taken away. The soldiers therefore came and broke the legs of the first, and of the other, who had been crucified with him. But when they came to Jesus, and saw that he was already dead, they did not break his legs; but one of the soldiers opened his side with a lance, and immediately there came out blood and water.

And he who saw it has borne witness, and his witness is true.

LET US PRAY

O almighty and eternal God, who hast appointed Thy only begotten Son to be the Redeemer of the world and wast willing to be appeased by His Blood, grant us, we beseech Thee, so to reverence with solemn devotion the price of our salvation, and by its power to be preserved from the evils of the present life, that we may rejoice in its eternal fruit in heaven. Through the same Jesus Christ.

July 2

VISITATION OF THE BLESSED VIRGIN

I Nocturn

From the Canticle of Canticles, c. 2, 1 - 17

II Nocturn

Sermon of St. John Chrysostom

When the Redeemer of our race had come to us, straightway He went to His friend John, while He was yet in His mother's womb. And when John from the womb beheld Him in the womb, rending the bounds of nature, he cried out: "I see the Lord who gave bounds to nature; I await not the time of birth; for me there is no need of nine months' time, for He that is eternal is in me; I will come forth from this darksome habitation; I will declare briefly wondrous things. I am a sign; I will signify Christ's advent. I am a trumpet; I will sound forth the dispensation of the Son of God in the flesh. With the trumpet will I sing; I will bless Him with my father's tongue, and I will loose it that it may speak. With the trumpet will I sing, and I will enliven my mother's womb."

See, beloved, how new and wondrous the mystery! Not yet is he born and he talks in leaps; not yet is he seen and he sounds warning; not yet is he allowed to cry out, and by deeds is he heard; not yet does he live and he preaches God; not yet does he behold the light and he points out the Sun; not yet is he born and he hastens to run before; in the presence of the Lord, he does not suffer himself to be restrained; he cannot bear to await the time of nature, but strives to break the prison of the womb and is eager to herald the coming Savior. "He that loosens bonds," he says, "has arrived. And why do I sit bound? Why am I forced to remain? The Word has come that He may establish all things, and am I still held back? I will go forth; I will run before; I will preach to all: 'Behold the Lamb of God that taketh away the sins of the world!'"

But tell us, John, while you are still shut up in the darksome womb of your mother, how do you look about and hear? How do you contemplate divine things? How do you leap and rejoice? "It is a great mystery," says he, "that is done, a deed beyond human understanding. Rightly do I do things new in nature on account of Him who is to do new things that are above nature."

"I see, though I am still in the womb, for I see the Sun of Justice carried in the womb. Through my ears I receive understanding, for I am born the voice of the great Word. I cry out, for I look upon the Only-Begotten of the Father clothed in flesh. I exult, for I see the Maker of all take on the form of man. I leap, for I think on the Redeemer of the world in His body. I run before His coming, and, in a way, go before you in praise."

℟. Blessed art thou because thou hast believed, for those things shall be fulfilled in thee which were spoken to thee by the Lord. And Mary said: * My soul doth magnify the Lord. ℣. Come, and listen, and I will relate what things God hath done for my soul. My soul. Glory. My soul.

III Nocturn

The reading of the holy Gospel according to St. Luke

At that time Mary arose and went with haste into the hill country, to a town of Juda. And she entered the house of Zachary and saluted Elizabeth. And so forth.

Homily of St. Ambrose, Bishop

It must be noted that the greater comes to the inferior that the inferior may receive aid: Mary to Elizabeth; Christ to John. Just as afterwards also, the Lord, that He might sanctify the baptism of John, came to be baptized. At the same moment both the coming of Mary and the benefits of the divine presence are made manifest. See the difference; see also the appropriateness of every word. Elizabeth was the first to hear the voice, but John the first to feel the grace.

She heard in the order of nature; he exulted by reason of the mystery, that is, the secret workings of grace. She perceived the coming of Mary; he, that of the Lord. The women speak of grace; the infants (Jesus and John) work within, and from their very beginnings in their mothers' wombs, they commence a mystery of godliness (their godly lives); thus by twin miracles the mothers prophesy by the spirit of their little ones. The infant leaped for joy; the mother was filled with the Holy Spirit. The mother is not filled before the son; but when the son had been filled with the Holy Spirit, he in turn also filled his mother.

"And whence is this to me that the mother of my Lord should come to me?" In other words, whence does so great a good befall me that the Mother of my Lord should come to me? I perceive a miracle; I recognize a mystery; the Mother of the Lord pregnant with the Word is full with God. "But Mary remained with her three months and returned to her own home." Well is holy Mary shown to have fulfilled this office, and to have observed the mystic number.

For friendship was not the only reason why she remained so long, but she remained also for the benefit of so great a prophet. Because if at the first meeting there was so great a benefit conferred that at the salutation of Mary the infant in the womb leaped for joy and the mother was filled with the Holy Spirit, how much more do we suppose the presence of the Blessed Mary added during the lapse of so long a time? And thus the prophet was anointed and like a good athlete was exercised in the womb of his mother, for his strength was being prepared for a very great struggle.

℞. Truly happy art thou, O holy Virgin Mary, and worthy of all praise: * For from thee hath dawned the Sun of justice, Christ our God. ℣. Pray for the people, plead for the clergy, intercede for all devout women; may all feel thy aid who celebrate thy holy Visitation. For. Glory. For.

☩ Continuation of the holy Gospel according to St. Luke.—At that time Mary arose and went with haste into the hill country, to a town of Juda. And she entered the house of Zachary and saluted Elizabeth. And it came to pass, when Elizabeth heard the greeting of Mary, that the babe in her womb leapt. And Elizabeth was filled with the Holy Spirit, and cried out with a loud voice, saying, "Blessed art thou among women and blessed is the fruit of thy womb! And how have I deserved that the mother of my Lord should come to me? For behold, the moment that the sound of thy greeting came to my ears, the babe in my womb leapt for joy. And blessed is she who has believed, because the things promised her by the Lord shall be accomplished."

And Mary said, "My soul magnifies the Lord, and my spirit rejoices in God my Savior."

Let Us Pray

Grant to Thy servants, we beseech Thee, O Lord, the gift of heavenly grace, that as the birth of the Blessed Virgin was the beginning of our salvation, so the solemn feast of her Visitation may give us an increase of peace. Through our Lord.

July 3

V DAY WITHIN THE OCTAVE OF SS. PETER AND PAUL

From a Sermon of St. Leo, Pope

"Precious in the sight of the Lord is the death of his saints." The religion, established through the mystery of Christ's cross, cannot be destroyed by any form of cruelty. The Church is not diminished by persecutions; rather, it is increased, and the Lord's field is always clothed with a richer harvest when the grains which die singly spring forth in multiple number. Wherefore, thousands of blessed martyrs proclaim into what a great plant these two wonderful shoots have grown—the martyrs, who, emulous of the triumphs of the apostles, have encompassed our city with people clothed in purple and shining far and wide, and have crowned her with one diadem, as it were, from the glory of many gems fashioned together.

In the commemoration of all saints, dearly beloved, we should indeed be gladdened by their protection, divinely arranged for us as an example to our patience and as a confirmation of our faith, but we ought to glory in a more special manner in the excellence of our Fathers (Peter and Paul) whom God's grace has raised up to such a great height among all the Church's members, that it has set them as the light of twin eyes in the body whose head is Christ. With regard to their merits and virtues, which surpass all possibility of speech, we ought to admit no difference, no separation, because their election places them on a par, their labor makes them similar, and their end makes them equal.

But as we ourselves have experienced and our elders have proved, we believe and trust that among all the toils of this life we are always to be helped by the mercy of God through the prayers of special patrons, so that the more we are weighed down by our own sins, the more are we lifted up through the merits of the apostles—through our Lord Jesus Christ, to whom there is, together with the Father and the Holy Spirit, the one divinity, the same power for ever and ever. Amen!

July 4

VI DAY WITHIN THE OCTAVE OF SS. PETER AND PAUL

From the Commentary of St. John Chrysostom on the Epistle to the Romans

Since the Apostle Paul begs for us the grace of our Lord Jesus Christ—the source of all blessings—it remains for us to show ourselves worthy of such great solicitude, so that we may not only hear Paul's voice here, but also, after we have gone thence, may merit to see Christ's athlete. Yes, more, if we shall have heard him here, we shall by all means see him there; although not standing close to him, we shall, nevertheless, see him, resplendent near the royal throne where the Cherubim glorify God, where the Seraphim hover. There we shall see Paul with Peter, prince and leader of the choir of saints, and enjoy his affectionate love.

For if, while he was here, he loved men so much that, although he desired "to be dissolved and to be with Christ," he nevertheless, chose to be here, much more will he reveal a more ardent charity there. For this reason I do, indeed, love Rome, even though I might be able to praise her from other points of view—her great realm, her antiquity, her beauty, her great population, her power, riches, and mighty deeds wrought in war. But passing over these things, I proclaim her blessed because, while he was living, Paul was so kind to, and loved the Romans so much, and discoursed before them, and finally ended his life among them. His holy body they possess, and so on this account that city has been made famous more than by all other things, and as a great and strong body she possesses two brilliant eyes, namely, the bodies of these saints, Peter and Paul.

The sky, when the sun sends down its rays, is not as resplendent as the city of the Romans sending forth over the whole earth these two flashes of lightning. From there shall Paul be borne away; from there, Peter. Consider and tremble at the spectacle which Rome shall see: Paul suddenly rising from the tomb with Peter to be carried to the Lord above. What kind of rose shall Rome send to Christ! With what two crowns is this city adorned! With what golden chains has she been girt! What fountains she possesses! So I admire this city, not for the abundance of its gold, not for its columns, nor for any other such thing, but because of those pillars of the Church. Who shall grant me to be bound to the body of Paul, to be affixed to his sepulchre, to behold the dust of the body of him who fills up the things which are lacking in Christ, who bears His stigmata and who sows everywhere the preaching of the Gospel!

July 5

VII DAY WITHIN THE OCTAVE OF SS. PETER AND PAUL

Sermon of St. Maximus, Bishop

Since all the most blessed apostles obtain a like reward of sanctity with the Lord, I do not know by what consideration Peter and Paul, nevertheless, appear to excel in a certain virtue of faith; which fact, in truth, we can prove from the judgment of our Lord Himself. For to Peter, as to a good steward, He gave the key to the heavenly Kingdom; on Paul, as an apt teacher, He enjoins the teaching office of the Church, so that those whom the latter instructs unto salvation, the former receives into their reward, and to the souls of those whose hearts Paul enlightens by the word of teaching, Peter opens the realm of heaven. In a way Paul, too, received the key of knowledge from Christ. For that must be called a key by which the hard hearts of sinners are unbolted to belief, the secrets of minds are revealed, and whatever is kept inclosed within is brought forth plainly by a reasonable manifestation. That is a key, I say, which, on the one hand, opens the conscience to the confession of its sin, and, on the other, makes fast unto eternity the grace of the saving mystery.

Consequently, both men received keys from their Lord: the latter (Paul) the key of knowledge, the former (Peter) the key of power; the former bestows the riches of an immortal life; the latter grants the treasures of knowledge. For there are treasures of knowledge, as it is written: "In whom are hidden all the treasures of wisdom and knowledge." Hence, the blessed Peter and Paul stand out above all the apostles and supersede them by a certain, peculiar prerogative. But between these two it is uncertain who is to be placed first. I think they are equal in merits, for they were equal in their suffering; and I think they, whom we see to have come together to the glory of martyrdom, have both lived in a like devotion to their faith, because we are not of the opinion that it came about without cause that on the same day, in the same place, they suffered the condemnation of the same tyrant.

They suffered on the same day in order that they might go to Christ together; in the same place, lest Rome be deprived of one of them; under the same persecutor, so that an equal torture should afflict them both. Accordingly, I believe, the day was decreed for their merit; the place, for their glory; the persecutor, for their virtue. Yet where did they finally suffer martyrdom? In the city of Rome which stands as the prince and head of nations, so that there, where the source of superstition was, the source of sanctity should repose; and where the rulers of the nations were dwelling, there the princes of the Church should stay. Of what merit the Blessed Peter and Paul might be, we can comprehend from this, that while our Lord glorified the region of the Orient by His own Passion, He deigned to make bright the land of the Occident (lest it should be of lesser account) in its turn by the blood of the Apostles, and, while His own Passion served us for salvation, He held forth their martyrdom as an example.

July 6

OCTAVE OF SS. PETER AND PAUL

From the first Epistle of St. Paul the Apostle to the Corinthians, c. 4, 1 - 15

II Nocturn

Sermon of St. John Chrysostom

What thanks shall we pay back to you, O blessed Apostles, who have labored so much for us? I remember thee, Peter, and I am dumbfounded; I call thee to mind, Paul, and, going beyond myself in mind, I am overcome by tears. For what I should say or what I should speak, in contemplating your afflictions, I know not. How many prisons have you sanctified? How many binding chains have you embellished? How many torments have you endured? How many curses have you borne? How have you carried Christ? How have you rejoiced the churches by your preaching. Your tongues are blessed instruments; your members are sprinkled with blood for the Church's sake.

In all things you have imitated Christ. "Your sound hath gone forth into all the earth, and your words unto the ends of the world." Do thou rejoice, O Peter, to whom it has been granted to share in the wood of the cross of Christ! And, after the likeness of your Master, thou hast indeed willed to be crucified, not, indeed, in the exact position, but with thy head turned toward the earth, as if thou wouldst journey from earth to heaven.

Blessed are the nails which pierced those holy limbs. Thou, the most faithful of all the Apostles, who hast loved the Lord with a burning spirit, who hast zealously served Him and His spouse, the Church, hast in complete confidence placed thy soul in the hands of the Lord. And do thou also rejoice, O blessed Paul, whose head was severed by a sword, whose virtues can be described by no words!

What sword, pray, was passed through thy throat, which, being the instrument of the Lord, is held in admiration by heaven and revered on earth? What place has received thy blood, appearing under the form of milk on the tunic of him who struck thee? The blood which, rendering the soul of that barbarian (the executioner) sweet above measure, made him a believer together with his comrades! May that sword be as a crown for me! And may the nails of Peter be as gems set in a diadem!

III Nocturn

The reading of the holy Gospel according to St. Matthew

At that time Jesus made his disciples get into the boat and cross the sea ahead of him, while he dismissed the crowd. And so forth.

Homily of St. Jerome, Priest

The Lord ordered the disciples to go over the water, and He compelled them to go up into the boat. By these words it is shown that they were unwilling to withdraw from the Lord, for, because of their love of Him, they did not wish to be separated from Him even for a moment of time. And, the crowd having been dismissed, He goes up into a mountain alone to pray. If there had been with Him the disciples Peter, James, and John, who had seen the glory of the transfigured Lord, perhaps they would have gone up into the mountain with Him; but the crowd could not follow to the heights, until He taught them beside the seashore and fed them in the desert.

Now the fact that He went up alone to pray, you should not ascribe to Him who with five loaves filled five thousand men, besides women and children; but to Him who, having heard of the death of John, withdrew into solitude: not that we may separate the *person* of the Lord, but because His *works* are divided between God and men.

"But the boat in the midst of the sea was tossed about by the waves." Rightly were the apostles unwilling and hesitant about withdrawing from the Lord lest, in His absence, they might suffer shipwreck. Then suddenly, as the Lord remained in prayer on the mountain top, a contrary wind arises and disturbs the sea, and the apostles are imperiled; and shipwreck remains imminent until Jesus comes.

"And in the fourth watch of the night He came to them, walking upon the sea." Military guards and watches are divided into three hour periods. When therefore it says that in the fourth watch of the night the Lord came to them, it shows that they were in danger all night long; and at the end of the night, as at the consummation of the world, aid is given them.

July 11

SOLEMNITY OF OUR HOLY FATHER ST. BENEDICT

I Nocturn

From the Book of Ecclesiasticus, c. 45, 1 - 6; c. 47, 9 - 12; c. 48, 1, 5 - 7, 10, and 13 -15

II Nocturn

Sermon of St. Bernard, Abbot

The most-sweet name of our glorious Father, Benedict, ought to be embraced and honored by you with every sign of joy because he is your Leader, your Master, and your Lawgiver. Let his sanctity, his piety, his justice refresh you. The blessed Benedict was a great and fruitful tree, like a tree which is planted near the running waters. He was so planted near the running waters that he brought forth his fruit in due season. To his fruit belong the three things whereof I have made mention above: his sanctity, his justice, his piety. Miracles prove his sanctity; his teaching, his piety; his life, his justice.

But why am I to propose his miracles to you? In order that you may want to perform miracles? By no means! But that you may lean on his miracles for support. In other words, that you may be confident and glad because you have merited such a great Protector. For most certainly he who was so great and powerful on earth is very powerful in heaven, being exalted to a greatness of glory corresponding to the magnitude of his grace. For the branches are known to shoot forth according to the size of the roots, and with as many roots as the tree is supported, with so many branches, as they say, is it adorned. Thus, then, though we may not have the power to perform miracles, the miracles of our Patron should be a great consolation to us.

His teaching, too, instructs us and guides our steps to the path of peace. Further, the justice of his life in every way strengthens and vivifies us, so that we are so much the more enkindled to do the things he has taught us as we are assured that he has not taught us otherwise than he acted. The example of his work is, indeed, a living and effective sermon, making what is said very pleasing to hear in that it shows that what is urged can be done. Consequently, in this manner his sanctity consoles us; his piety enlightens us; his justice strengthens us. Of what great piety was he that he not only benefited those present to him, but was also solicitous for those to come? Not only for those who lived then did this tree produce its fruit, but even today its fruit multiplies and remains.

Surely beloved of God *and men* is he whose presence was not only in benediction (for there are many who are beloved of God alone because they are now known to God alone), but his memory also is even now in benediction. For even until this day, as a three-fold confession of his love for his Lord, he feeds the flock of the Lord with this threefold fruit. He feeds it by his life; he feeds it by his teaching; he feeds it through his intercession. Being unceasingly aided by him, do you also, dearest brethren, bear fruit, because for this have you been appointed, "that you should go and bring forth fruit."

℟. This is he who wrought great things before God, and praised the Lord with his whole heart: * May he intercede for the sins of all men. ℣. Behold a man without reproach, a true worshipper of God, keeping himself from every evil deed and ever abiding in innocence. May he. Glory. May he.

III Nocturn

The reading of the holy Gospel according to St. Matthew

At that time Peter addressed Jesus, saying, "Behold, we have left all and followed thee; what then shall we have?" And so forth.

Homily of St. Bede the Venerable, Priest

In the final judgment there will be two classes of the elect: the one judging with the Lord, of which He speaks in this place, who have left all things and followed Him; the other to be judged by the Lord, who indeed have not wholly left all things, but who, nevertheless, took care to bestow alms daily on Christ's poor ones out of the goods which they possessed. Wherefore these will hear in the judgment: "Come, ye blessed of My Father, possess you the kingdom prepared for you from the foundation of the world. For I was hungry and you gave me to eat; I was thirsty and you gave me to drink," and the other things which the Lord enumerates in the preceding lines of this lesson when a certain leader had asked what good he must do in order to possess life everlasting. "If thou wilt enter into life," He said, "keep the commandments." Therefore he who keeps the commandments of the Lord enters into life everlasting; but he who also follows the counsels of the Lord shall not only attain life himself, but shall also judge with the Lord the life of others.

Moreover, as the Lord testifies, we find that there will be two classes of the reprobate also: the first of these will comprise those who, having been initiated into the mysteries of the faith, spurn to do the works of faith. Of these it is said in the judgment: "Depart from me, ye cursed, into everlasting fire, which was prepared for the devil and his angels. For I was hungry and you gave me not to eat." The other class will comprise those who either never receive the faith and the mysteries of Christ or who, having once received them, wholly forsake them by apostasy, concerning whom He says: "But he that doth not believe is already judged, because he believeth not in the name of the only-begotten Son of God."

But now, after having for a brief moment recounted these things with fear and trembling, let us turn our attention rather to the more joyful promises of our Lord and Savior. Let us see what is the recompense of such great piety. To His followers He promises not only the reward of eternal life, but also extraordinary gifts in this present life. "And everyone," He says, "that hath left house, or brethren, or sisters, or father, or mother, or wife, or children, or lands, for my name's sake, shall receive a hundredfold, and shall possess life everlasting."

The more one who shall have renounced earthly desires or possessions to become a disciple of Christ shall advance in His love, the more will he find who rejoice to receive him with heartfelt affection as one of their own and to sustain him with their own goods. Being companions in his profession and life, they delight to receive him who has made himself poor for Christ's sake into their homes and lands, and to cherish him with a more devoted love than ever did a wife, a parent, a brother, or son according to the flesh.

℟. This man did all things which God hath told him, and He said to him: Enter thou into My rest: * For thee I have seen righteous before Me among all nations. ℣. This is he who despised the life of the world and attained to the kingdom of heaven. For. Glory. For.

✠ Continuation of the holy Gospel according to St. Matthew.— At that time Peter said to Jesus: "Behold, we have left all and followed thee; what then shall we have?" And Jesus said to them, "Amen I say to you that you who have followed me, in the regeneration when the Son of Man shall sit on the throne of his glory, shall also sit on twelve thrones, judging the twelve tribes of Israel. And everyone who has left house, or brothers, or sisters, or father, or mother, or wife, or children, or lands, for my name's sake, shall receive a hundredfold, and shall possess life everlasting."

LET US PRAY

O God, who hast deigned to fill Thy blessed Confessor Benedict with the spirit of all the just, grant to us his children who celebrate his feast, that, being filled with his spirit, we may faithfully fulfill what by Thy inspiration we have promised. Through our Lord.

July 13

III DAY WITHIN THE OCTAVE OF THE SOLEMNITY OF ST. BENEDICT

From the second book of the Dialogues of St. Gregory, Pope

There was a man most venerable for the holiness of his life, named Benedict, who from his earliest youth possessed the heart and wisdom of old age. For even then, more sedate in his manners than is usual at that period of life, he did not give way to pleasure, but even while yet in this land of exile, he despised the world with all its empty show and deceitful riches, although he had every opportunity of enjoying them freely in his life, and he viewed them as a withered and barren tree. Being of a very respectable family in the vicinity of Nursia, his parents sent him to Rome to receive a liberal education. But seeing that many of those who studied there allowed themselves to be swept down by the flood of vice, and although it was his first entrance into the world, he resolved to fly from it, lest, becoming infected with its false maxims, he might be cast headlong into the abyss of sin. Taking no pains, then, to acquire learning, he left his father's house and estate, and, aspiring only to please God, he proceeded to seek one who had the power to invest him with the religious habit. He withdrew, therefore, *knowingly ignorant, and wisely unlearned.*

Having given up his studies, Benedict retired into a desert. He was accompanied only by his nurse who loved him tenderly. When he reached a place called Enfide, he met many respectable persons who, through charity, engaged him to converse with them a while and stop in the church of St. Peter. His nurse, in the meantime, borrowed a sieve from some women of the neighborhood to clean wheat, and, when finished, carelessly laid it on a table where it was accidently broken, completely split in two. The woman, having come back to the table, was grieved to find the sieve, which was only lent to her, broken, and in her sorrow shed abundant tears. The pious and tender-hearted Benedict, beholding her thus weeping, was moved to compassion, and to console her took the two pieces of the sieve aside. There he prayed to God with fervent tears, and his petition was granted; for no sooner had he risen from the ground than he found the sieve so perfectly sound that there remained not the slightest trace of its having been broken. He came immediately to his nurse, and, restoring the article which he had taken away broken, gently soothed her pain.

This fact became known to all the inhabitants and filled them with surprise. They hung up the sieve at the entrance of their church to make known to those then living and to posterity the progress the youthful Benedict had made in grace and virtue when he commenced to walk the narrow path of perfection. This sieve was thus exhibited to the eyes of all for many years, and remained above the entrance of the church until the invasion of the Lombards.

July 15

V DAY WITHIN THE OCTAVE OF THE SOLEMNITY OF ST. BENEDICT

From the second book of the Dialogues of St. Gregory, Pope

The province of Campania (where Monte Cassino is situated) was afflicted with famine, and all the inhabitants found themselves reduced to a great scarcity of provisions. Consequently, flour failed in Benedict's monastery. Most of the loaves had been consumed, and the monks had only five remaining for the next repast. The venerable father, seeing them sad and grieved, reproved them gently for their weakness and want of confidence in God, and at the same time consoled them, saying: "Why are you saddened because you are in want of bread? There is but little of it today, but tomorrow you shall have it in abundance." In fact, they found on the following day before the gate of the monastery two hundred bushels of wheat in sacks, and up to the present no one has known by whose agency Almighty God sent them to the holy Abbot. The monks, seeing themselves relieved in so wonderful a manner, gave thanks to God, and learned thereby to have more confidence in His bounty and to expect plenty even in the time of the greatest scarcity.

At another time when Campania was afflicted with a great famine, the man of God distributed all the provisions of the monastery to the poor. There remained almost nothing in the cellar but a little oil in a small glass bottle. There came, however, a deacon, named Agapitus, who earnestly asked for a little oil. The saint, who had resolved to give all he had on earth to receive it again in heaven, ordered the little that remained to be given to him. The religious who was then procurator heard the order, but delayed to execute it. And when the saint inquired shortly after if he had done what was told him, the procurator replied that he had not, for if he gave the oil none would remain for his brethren. Then the saint, greatly displeased, commanded other disciples to go and take the vessel containing the oil and throw it out the window, so that no one might be able to say that disobedience had preserved anything to the monastery. And so was it done. Now there was beneath the window a very steep precipice, at the bottom of which were pointed fragments of rocks.

Nevertheless, the glass vessel, falling on these rough stones, remained as safe and sound as if it had not been cast forth, and as if it could not be broken, nor the oil spilled. When this was told the saint, he gave orders to go and pick up the vessel and give it as it was to the person who had requested the oil. Then, having assembled the brethren, he reproved the disobedient monk for his pride and want of faith. The saint, having thus reprimanded the procurator, betook himself to prayer with the brethren. In the very place in which he was praying with his disciples there was a barrel in which there was no more oil, but which, nevertheless, had the lid on. Benedict persevering in prayer, the lid began to rise, forced upwards by the abundance of oil in the barrel, and finally was displaced altogether. The oil overflowed the brim, innundating the pavement. The servant of God, seeing it spreading, ended the prayer, and the oil ceased to overflow on the pavement.

July 16
FEAST OF THE BLESSED VIRGIN MARY OF EINSIEDELN

I Nocturn

From the Canticle of Canticles, c. 1, 1 - 16

II Nocturn

Sermon of St. Bernard, Abbot

The Lord has effected something new on the earth that a woman should encompass a Man, who is no other than Christ, of whom it is said: "Behold the Man, the Orient is his name." God has accomplished also a new thing in heaven that a woman should appear clothed with the sun. She both crowned Him and merited to be crowned in turn by Him. "Go forth, daughters of Sion, and see King Solomon in the diadem with which his mother hath crowned him." But of this elsewhere. Meanwhile, rather go in and see the Queen in the diadem with which her Son has crowned her. "And on her head," it says, "a crown of twelve stars."

Indeed worthy to be crowned by stars is that head which, shining far more brilliantly than they, rather enhances them than is adorned by them. For why do the stars crown her whom the sun clothes? As on a day of spring the roses and the lilies of the valley surrounded her. Yea, more! the left hand of the Spouse is under her head and His right hand already embraces her. Who can appreciate those gems? Who can name the stars of which the royal diadem of Mary is composed?

What, then, shines as a star in the generation of Mary? Surely the fact that she is begotten of royal ancestors, of the seed of Abraham, of the root of David. If this seems insignificant, add that which was divinely given to her at her birth on account of the singular privilege of her sanctity; that long before she had been promised from heaven to these same Fathers; that she was prefigured by mystical miracles and foretold by prophetic declarations. For the priestly rod, when it flourished without a root, the fleece of Gedeon, when it was moist in the midst of the dry ground, the eastern gate in the vision of Ezechiel, which was never opened to anyone, all prefigured her. Finally, she was promised especially by Isaias, now as the rod that was to spring up from the root of Jesse, again more evidently as the Virgin who was to bear a Child.

Rightly is it written that this great sign appeared in the sky, since it is known to have been promised from heaven so long before. The Lord said: "He himself will give you a sign. Behold a Virgin shall conceive." Indeed He gave a great sign because He also who gave it is great. Whose eyes, then, does not the brightness of this prerogative vehemently dazzle? Already in the fact that she was greeted so reverently and respectfully by the Archangel that he seemed to see her already exalted on a royal throne above all the regions of the heavenly spirits, and in the fact that he, who was heretofore accustomed to be venerated by all men alike, was now, being a little less than she, about to venerate the woman, the most excellent merit and singular grace of our Virgin is commended to us.

℟. Who is she that cometh forth as the sun and as beautiful as Jerusalem? * The daughters of Sion saw her and declared her blessed, and the queens praised her. ℣. And round about her, as in spring time, were flowers of roses and lilies of the valley. The daughters. Glory. The daughters.

III Nocturn

The reading of the holy Gospel according to St. Luke

At that time, as Jesus spoke these things to the multitude, a certain woman lifted up her voice from the crowd, and said to him, "Blessed is the womb that bore thee, and the breasts that nursed thee." And so forth.

Homily of St. Irenæus, Bishop and Martyr

Just as the first-formed man, Adam, received his substance from untilled and as yet virgin soil (for God had not yet sent rain nor had man yet tilled the land) and was formed by the hand of God, that is, by the Word of God (for all things were made by Him; and again, the Lord took slime of the earth and formed man), so did this same Word, recapitulating Adam in Himself and taking His own existence from Mary, who was still a virgin, becomingly receive a birth like unto Adam's. Now if the first man was indeed taken from the earth and formed by the Word of God, it was proper that this same Word, making a recapitulation of Adam in Himself, should have an analogous generation. Why, then, did not God again take the slime of the earth rather than effect this formation from Mary? It was that no new formation should come into being, nor any other than that which was to be saved, but that the very same formation (which had already been created) should be recapitulated, thus preserving the analogy.

They err, therefore, who say that He received nothing from the Virgin, since, in order to reject the inheritance of the flesh, they reject also the analogy (between Christ and Adam). But this is to say both that He appeared putatively as man while He was not man, and also that He was made man though taking nothing from man. For if He did not take the substance of flesh from man, then He was not made man, nor was He the Son of Man. But the Apostle Paul in his epistle to the Galatians unmistakably asserts: "God sent his Son, made of a woman."

And again in his letter to the Romans he says: "Concerning his Son, who was made to him of the seed of David, according to the flesh, who was predestined the Son of God in power, according to the Spirit of sanctification, by the Resurrection of our Lord Jesus Christ from the dead."

Otherwise His descent into Mary has been in vain. For why did He descend into her if He were to take nothing from her? But if He had taken nothing from Mary, He would never have received that food by which the body is nourished, nor would His body have hungered forty days seeking nourishment.

℟. All generations shall call me blessed, * Because the Lord who is mighty hath done great things to me, and holy is His name. ℣. And His mercy is from generation unto generations to them that fear Him. Because. Glory. Because.

✠ Continuation of the holy Gospel according to St. Luke.— At that time, as Jesus spoke these things to the multitude, a certain woman lifted up her voice from the crowd, and said to him, "Blessed is the womb that bore thee, and the breasts that nursed thee." But he said, "Rather, blessed are they who hear the word of God and keep it."

Let Us Pray

Grant us Thy servants, we beseech Thee, O Lord, to enjoy continual health of both soul and body, and, by the glorious intercession of the Blessed Mary ever Virgin, to be delivered from the sorrows of this present life and to enjoy eternal happiness. Through our Lord.

July 17

II DAY WITHIN THE OCTAVE OF OUR LADY OF EINSIEDELN

Sermon of St. Augustine, Bishop

Mary exults and joyfully wonders at the fact that she is a mother and rejoices that she has given birth through the Holy Spirit. Nor is she terrified because she, though unwedded, gives birth, but she wonders with joy that she should have begotten a Child. O woman blessed among women! who has certainly not known man and yet has enclosed a Man within her womb! Mary encloses a Man by giving faith to the angel because Eve destroyed man by consenting to the serpent. O happy obedience! O wonderful grace! whereby, when she humbly believed, she incorporated within herself the Maker of heaven. Through this did she merit the glory which she afterwards increased: "Behold," she says, "from henceforth all generations shall call me blessed."

O Blessed Mary, who can worthily render thanks and praise to you who, by your singular assent, sustained the fallen world? What praises can the frailty of the human race, which has found the way to its recovery in your action alone, render to you? Accept, then, our thanks, however poor, however unequal to thy merits; and when you have received our supplications, excuse our faults by your prayers. Admit our prayers into the sanctuary of your hearing, and obtain for us the means of our reconciliation!

Through you, may that be without blame which, through you, we have undertaken; may we easily obtain that which we plead for with a confident mind. Accept what we offer; give what we ask; pardon what we fear, because you are the only hope of sinners. Through you we hope for forgiveness of sins, and in you, O most blessed one, is the expectation of our rewards. Holy Mary, help the unfortunate, aid the pusillanimous, cherish the weak, pray for the people, plead for the clergy, intercede for the women vowed to God! May all experience your aid who celebrate your holy feast.

THE SAME DAY

VII DAY WITHIN THE OCTAVE OF THE SOLEMNITY OF ST. BENEDICT

From the second book of the Dialogues of St. Gregory, Pope

On one occasion, the saint having gone to the fields to work with his brethren, a peasant whose son had been carried off by death came to the monastery, holding in his arms the body of his son and manifesting extreme grief at his loss. Inquiring for Father Benedict, and having been told he was in the field with the brethren, he laid down the body of his son before the gate of the monastery and, altogether discomposed and overcome with grief, ran with great speed to find the venerable father. Just at that moment the man of God was coming home from work in the company of his monks. As soon as the bereaved peasant saw him, he began to cry out: "Restore my son, restore my son!"

At these words Benedict stopped short and said: "Have I

taken away your son?" "He is dead," replied the peasant, "come and restore him to life." The servant of God, listening to this demand, was greatly troubled and said: "Retire, brethren; it is not for us, but for the holy Apostles, to work miracles. Why do you lay upon us burdens which we are unable to bear?" But the man, overcome by the violence of grief, persisted in his demand, and swore that he would not leave him until he had restored his son.

"Where is your son?" asked the saint. "His body lies near the monastery gate," replied the peasant. The man of God, having arrived there with his brethren, went on his knees, stooped down over the body of the child, and, raising himself again, extended his hands towards heaven and said: "O Lord, look not on my sins, but on this man's faith, who implores that his son be restored to life. Replace in this little body the soul Thou hast thence withdrawn!" His prayer was hardly ended when the boy's whole body trembled as the soul returned, a thing noticed by all present, for they clearly saw the boy throb with life in an extraordinary and wonderful manner. Then the saint took him by the hand and, presenting him to his father, restored him full of life and health.

July 18

OCTAVE DAY OF THE SOLEMNITY OF OUR HOLY FATHER, ST. BENEDICT

I Nocturn

From the third Book of Kings, c. 17, 2 - 24

II Nocturn

Sermon of St. Odo, Abbot

Wherever Holy Church is spread, through tribes, through nations, through tongues, the praise of Benedict is popular. For if in the multitude of people is the dignity of the king, as Solomon says, how great do we suppose is the dignity of this king whom such a numerous host of monks follow? What king or emperor ever ruled in so many parts of the world, or drew out from such differing nations such great legions as this king has indeed enlisted as voluntarily sworn members of either sex and every age in Christ's militia?

Looking upon him as present, and marching after the banner of his corps, they crush the battalions of the devil. For these, that saying of the prophet is appropriated, "Thy eyes shall see thy teacher." There is a strong opinion that each of the saints shall arise at the regeneration in the company of those whom he has gained for the Lord. Therefore, when all the followers of his rule are brought together in a body, what a token of his apostolic work shall that numerous army then render to Benedict? And with what joy shall he who shall be able to join himself to these cohorts then dance about!

At this time let all men, whether associated by place or by affection, direct the vision of their hearts to him, for he is become all things to all men. Children first have in him, as a boy, a model which they may follow in order that, since they have been offered to God after the example of Isaac, they may take care to fill their early life with zeal. And so continuing, let their every advance in age be perfected in understanding so that they do not fall away from the paternal love of their guardian; lest perhaps, if they should fall from a higher rank, they be the more seriously injured. But even we who have sinned should by no means fail in our hope for mercy, because he (Benedict), both while living and after his death, raised the dead to life, mended that which was broken, and healed that which was despaired of.

And although we have not done His Will, let us, nevertheless, invoke the Lord; and let our eyes be upon His hands until He lift them above us and have mercy on us. May Benedict ever be with us in our heart, on our lips, and in our actions, so that, if we desire virtue, if we desire the praise of discipline, imitating that admonition of the Apostle, we may attain to what we have seen in him, what we have heard from him, and what we have heard of him, in order that the God of peace may be with us through him forever and ever. Amen!

III Nocturn

The reading of the holy Gospel according to St. Matthew

Then Peter addressed him, saying, "Behold, we have left all and followed thee; what then shall we have?" And so forth.

Homily of St. Bernard, Abbot

I think that the words of this lesson are those with which the Church cries from the ends of the earth to her Immortal Spouse: "For the sake of the words of thy lips I have kept hard ways." These are indeed the words which urge a contempt of the world on the whole world and voluntary poverty on men. These are the words which fill the cloisters with monks and the deserts with anchorites. These, I say, are the words which despoil Egypt and snatch away all her choicest vessels. This is a living and efficacious word, converting souls by the happy desire for sanctity and the faithful promise of truth.

For both the world and its concupiscence pass away, and so it is more profitable to leave these things than to be left by them. "Behold," he says, "we have left all things and have followed thee"; surely, because he hath rejoiced as a giant to run his course. Nor could you, being overburdened, overtake him as he ran. Yet it is not a useless exchange to have left all things for Him who is above all things; for, to be sure, all things are given together with Him, and when you shall have taken hold of Him, He Himself shall be all things to all men who have left all for Him. Truly do I say all things; not possessions only, but desires also, and these especially.

Peter, casting his care upon the Lord and placing his own worry on Him, confident that He would care for him, left all things and followed the Lord, not even asking about a reward until, because the Savior was talking about the danger of riches, he took the occasion of inquiring: "What therefore shall we have?" And Jesus said to him: "Amen, I say to you." A word of avowal is prefaced; you will recognize that it is a great thing which follows. "In the regeneration you also shall sit." "You shall go with Him," He declares, "whom you follow, so that when He shall sit (in judgment), you too shall sit with Him." O what an enthronement! Who will give me to express in fitting words what I conceive in the affection of my heart concerning this enthronement? Yes, more, who will give me to share the undisturbed repose of this sitting which I desire, for which I long, after which I seek?

For behold, as I have declared, nothing is at rest within me, but all things are in motion; everything is unsettled; all things are disturbed. In short, where the flesh still lusts against the spirit, and the spirit against the flesh, what should indeed appear to be at rest in man? Already, to be sure, the Son of Man sits on His throne of majesty; for now that He has ascended into heaven, He sits at the right hand of God. But it was said, "when he shall sit," that is, when He shall appear sitting, in the same way as the Apostle says, "When Christ, who is your life, shall appear, then you also shall appear with him in glory." What could be more glorious? Let the sons of pride judge now and pass sentence beforehand; let them sit with their king who has chosen the sides of the North for himself. We shall pass beyond, and lo! they shall not be there.

July 19

IV DAY WITHIN THE OCTAVE OF OUR LADY OF EINSIEDELN

Sermon of St. John Chrysostom

The Son of God did not choose for His Mother a rich or wealthy woman, but that blessed Virgin, whose soul was adorned with virtues. For it was because the blessed Mary had observed chastity in a way that was above all human nature that she conceived Christ the Lord in her womb. Let us then fly to this most holy Virgin and Mother of God and avail ourselves of her patronage. Therefore let all of you who are virgins flee to the Mother of the Lord; for she, by her patronage, will guard in you that beautiful, precious, and incorruptible possession.

The blessed Mary, ever a Virgin, dearest brethren, was in truth a great wonder. For what greater or more wonderful one has ever at any time been discovered or can at any time be discovered? She alone is far greater than heaven and earth. Who is holier than she? Not the Prophets, not the Apostles, not the Martyrs, not the Patriarchs, not the Angels, not the Thrones, not the Dominations, not the Seraphim, not the Cherubim; in truth, no creature whatever, whether visible or invisible, is to be found greater or more excellent than she. She is at once the handmaid of God and His Mother; at once a Virgin and a parent.

She is the Mother of Him who was begotten of the Father before the beginning of all things, and whom Angels and men acknowledge to be the Lord of all things. Would you know how much greater is this Virgin than any of the heavenly Powers? They stand in His presence with fear and trembling and veiled faces; she offers human nature to Him whom she brought forth. Through her we obtain the forgiveness of our sins. Hail, then, O Mother, heaven, maiden, virgin, throne, ornament, glory, and foundation of our Church; pray without ceasing for us to Jesus, thy Son and our Lord, that through you we may find mercy in the day of judgment and may be able to obtain those good things which are prepared for those who love God, through the grace and loving-kindness of Jesus Christ our Lord, to whom, with the Father and the Holy Spirit, be glory and honor and dominion, now and forever, world without end. Amen.

July 20
V DAY WITHIN THE OCTAVE OF OUR LADY OF EINSIEDELN
From the Book of St. Epiphanius, Bishop, against Heresies

The blessed Mother of God, Mary, was prefigured by Eve, who in a mysterious way was given to be called the mother of the living. For she (Eve) was called the mother of the living even when, after her transgression, she had heard: "Thou art earth, and unto earth thou shalt return." It is truly an odd thing that after her transgression she kept this great title. And, as to what pertains to sensible matter, the birth of all mankind on earth was indeed brought about through Eve; but here He who was the Life was truly born into the world through Mary, so that Mary gave birth to one already living and so became the Mother of the living. In a mystical way, then, Mary was named the Mother of the living.

To Eve it was given to clothe the sensible body, because of the sensible nakedness; while to Mary it was given by God to bring forth for us the Lamb and His sheep (the Church), and that by the glory of this Lamb and His sheep there might be made for us, as it were, from His fleece, in His wisdom and by His power, a garment of incorruptibility. Eve, in truth, became the cause of death for men, for by her, death came into the world. But Mary, through whom the Life was born to us, was made the cause of life; through her the Son of God came into the world, and where sin abounded, grace did more abound; and whence death was brought in, thence life also proceeded, so that death might be converted into life, and He who became Life for us through a woman might exclude the death brought in through a woman. And because Eve, in the one instance, transgressed by her disobedience while still a virgin, so in the other, when His coming in the flesh was announced from heaven, obedience to grace and life eternal was brought about through a Virgin also.

Through Mary is achieved, if I may so speak, what was written concerning the Church: "A man shall leave father and mother and shall cleave to his wife; and they shall be two in one flesh." The Holy Apostle declares: "This is a great sacrament; but I speak in Christ and in the Church." And note the Scripture's accurate term of expression, in that, on the one hand, it says with regard to Adam, "He *formed* him," while it does not say that Eve was formed, but that she was *built*. It states: "He took one of his ribs, and built it for him into a woman." By which it may be shown that the Lord, too, formed a body for Himself from Mary, while from His own rib was built the **Church, in that His side was pierced** and opened, and the mysteries of the blood and water were made the price of redemption.

July 21

VI DAY WITHIN THE OCTAVE OF OUR LADY OF EINSIEDELN

Sermon of St. Cyril, Bishop of Alexandria

I see a joyful congregation of all the saints who have come together with ready hearts, called by the holy Mother of God, Mary ever a Virgin. Praise and glory be to Thee, O Holy Trinity, which has called all of us to this celebration. Praise also to you, O holy Mother of God. For you are the precious pearl of the whole earth; you are an inextinguishable lamp, the crown of virginity, the scepter of the true faith, the indestructible temple containing Him who can be nowhere contained; Mother and Virgin; through whom He who comes in the name of the Lord is called blessed in the holy Gospels.

Through you the Trinity is sanctified, through you the holy Cross is celebrated and venerated in the whole world. Through you heaven rejoices, the angels and archangels exult, the demons flee, and man himself is called back to heaven. Through you every creature held in the error of idolatry has been turned to the knowledge of the truth, faithful men have come to holy Baptism, and throughout the whole earth churches have been built.

Helped by you, the nations come to penance. What more? Through you the only begotten Son of God, the true Light, has shone upon those sitting in darkness and in the shadow of death. Through you the prophets prophesied; through you the apostles preached salvation to the Gentiles. Who is able to celebrate your praises, O Mary, Mother and Virgin? Let us honor her, dearly beloved, adoring her Son, the Immaculate Spouse of the Church, to whom be honor and glory forever and ever. Amen.

July 23

OCTAVE DAY OF THE BLESSED VIRGIN MARY OF EINSIEDELN

I Nocturn

From the Canticle of Canticles, c. 1, 1 - 16

II Nocturn

From the Exposition of St. Gregory, Pope, on the Books of Kings

"There was a certain man of Ramathaimsophim, of Mount Ephraim." The most blessed and ever Virgin Mary, Mother of God, can be signified by the name of this mountain. For she was truly a mountain, transcending by the dignity of her calling all the perfection of every other chosen creature.

Is not this mountain—Mary—sublime who, in order to attain to the conception of the Eternal Word, elevated the height of her good actions above all the choirs of angels, even to the throne of the Godhead? Isaias, speaking in prophecy of the exceedingly excellent dignity of this mountain, said: "And in the last days the mountain of the house of the Lord shall be prepared on the top of mountains." Truly the mountain was on the top of mountains, for the loftiness of Mary showed forth above all the saints.

From the Epistle of St. Leo, Pope, to Pulcheria Augusta

None of the types (of the Old Testament) paid the price of our reconciliation, determined before all ages, because the Holy Spirit had not as yet come upon the Virgin, nor had the power of the Most High overshadowed her, in order that within her inviolate womb, as Wisdom building a house for Himself, the Word might be made flesh, and, the form of God and the form of the servant uniting in one Person, the Creator of time might be born in time, and He by whom all things were made might Himself be begotten in the midst of all things. For unless the new Man, made unto the likeness of our flesh of sin, had taken on Himself our old nature, and, being consubstantial with the Father, had deigned to be consubstantial with His Mother, and, as the only man free from sin, had united our nature to Himself, human bondage would have wholly been kept beneath the yoke of the devil.

From the Exposition of St. Basil, Bishop, on Isaias the Prophet

He (Isaias) says: "I went to the prophetess, and she conceived, and bore a Son." That Mary was the Prophetess to whom Isaias went by the inspiration of the Spirit, no one who is mindful of the words which Mary, inspired by a prophetic spirit, spoke, will deny. And what did she speak? "My soul doth magnify the Lord: And my spirit hath rejoiced in God my Savior. Because he hath regarded the humility of his handmaid: for behold, from henceforth all generations shall call me blessed."

Now if you will but apply your mind to all these, her words, you will certainly not through ill-will deny that she was a prophetess, that the Spirit of the Lord came upon her, and that the power of the Most High overshadowed her.

III Nocturn

Homily on the Gospel as on the day of the Feast, page 410

July 24
VIGIL OF ST. JAMES, APOSTLE

The reading of the holy Gospel according to St. John

At that time Jesus said to his disciples: "This is my commandment, that you love one another as I have loved you." And so forth.

Homily of St. Gregory, Pope

Since all the sacred words of the Lord are full of His precepts, why is it that He speaks of love as of a special commandment—"This is my commandment, that you love one another,"—except that every mandate is from love alone, and all are but one precept? For whatever is ordered is established solely in charity. Now just as the many branches of a tree shoot forth from one root, so are the many virtues generated from charity alone. Nor does the branch of a good deed have any verdure if it does not remain in union with the root of charity.

Hence the commands of our Lord are both many and one: many by reason of the diversity of the work; one in the root of love. After what manner this love should be held He Himself intimates, when in the many sentences of His Writings He commands, first, that friends should be loved in Him, and enemies for Him. That man, indeed, truly possesses charity who loves both his friend in God, and his enemy for God's sake. For there are some men who love their neighbors, but by attachment through relationship or the flesh; these, however, the sacred words do not condemn in their love; yet what is willingly conceded to nature is one thing; that which is due the commands of the Lord through love of obedience, another.

These men undoubtedly love their neighbor, and still, they do not achieve those sublime rewards of love, because they proffer their love not in a spiritual way, but in a carnal manner. Consequently, when the Lord declared, "This is my commandment, that you love one another," He immediately added, "As I have loved you!" As if He would manifestly say: "Do you love after that manner according to which I have loved you." Wherefore, my dearest brethren, it must be wisely observed that the old enemy, while he is drawing our mind to a love for temporal things, is urging a more dishonest neighbor on against us to endeavor to take away those very things we love.

July 25

ST. JAMES, APOSTLE

I Nocturn

From the first Epistle of St. Paul the Apostle to the Corinthians, c. 4, 1 - 15

II Nocturn

James, the son of Zebedee and brother of John, the Apostle, was a Galilean and with John was among the first called by the Lord to be apostles. Leaving his father and his fishing-nets, he followed Jesus. Christ called these two brothers *Boanerges,* which means *sons of thunder.* James was one of the three apostles whom the Lord loved best, and whom He permitted to witness His Transfiguration and to be present when He raised from the dead the daughter of the ruler of the synagogue, and also when He retired to the Mount of Olives to pray to His Father before He was taken captive by the Jews.

After Christ's Ascension James preached His divinity in Judea and in Samaria, and converted many to the Christian Faith. He afterwards set out for Spain, where he led many more to Christ, including seven who were later made bishops by St. Peter and sent as the first bishops into Spain.

From Spain James returned to Jerusalem where he taught the Faith to various persons, including the magician Hermogenes. Thereupon Herod Agrippa, who had been made king under the Emperor Claudius, in order to gain the favor of the Jews, condemned James to death for his firm confession that Jesus Christ is God. The officer who led James to the judgment seat, seeing the courage with which he went to his death for Christ, declared that he too was a Christian.

As they were being hastened to execution this man asked pardon of James. The Apostle kissed him, saying, "Peace be to you." Then, shortly after James had healed a paralytic, the Apostle and his newly-made convert were beheaded. The body of James was taken to Compostella in Spain, where his tomb is very famous. Many pilgrims from all parts of the earth come there to pray out of devotion and to fulfill their vows. The commemoration of his feast is kept by the Church today, which is that of the bringing of his body to Compostella, though it was at Jerusalem, around the Feast of Easter, that he, the first of the apostles thus to die, bore witness to Jesus Christ with his blood.

℟. I saw men standing together, clad in shining garments; and the Angel of the Lord spoke to me, saying: * These holy men became the friends of God. ℣. I saw a mighty Angel of God, flying through the midst of heaven, crying out with a loud voice and saying. These. Glory. These.

III Nocturn

The reading of the holy Gospel according to St. Matthew

At that time the mother of the sons of Zebedee came to Jesus with her sons; and worshipping, she made a request of him. And so forth.

Homily of St. John Chrysostom

Let no one take scandal if we say now that the apostles were not perfect, for the mystery of the cross had as yet not been consummated; the grace of the Holy Spirit had not yet been infused into their hearts. If you are desirous of knowing their virtue, consider what kind of men they were after the grace of the Spirit had been given, and you will see that they overcame every perverse inclination in them. For this very purpose their imperfection is now revealed that you might clearly see what they suddenly became through the operation of grace.

That they once sought nothing spiritual, nor thought about the Kingdom of Heaven, is very clear. But still let us consider how they approached our Lord and what they said. "We desire," they said, "that whatsoever we ask of thee, thou wilt grant us." To which Christ replied, "What do you desire?"—certainly not because He did not know, but that He might compel them to answer and thereby might lay open the wound and thus apply the remedy. But they, blushing and held back by shame because they had come to Him motivated by human aspirations, took Christ apart from the rest and questioned Him. They moved aside lest perhaps they be heard by the rest. And so at last they said what they wished.

I conjecture that they had heard that the disciples were to be seated on twelve thrones and they wished to ask for the place of honor in this assembly; they knew that at other times they were given precedence over the rest, but fearing that Peter might be put before them, thy were bold enough to request, "Say that one may sit on thy right hand, the other on thy left." And they pressed Him saying, "Speak thus." And what did He say? That He might show that they sought nothing spiritual, and did not even realize what they were asking—for had they known they would not have asked it—Jesus said to them, "You know not what you ask; you know not how great, how admirable a thing this is, far surpassing even the higher Powers."

And He added further: "Can you drink the chalice which I shall drink, and be baptized with the baptism wherewith I am baptized?" Notice how He moves them from their present state of mind by bringing to their attention things entirely contrary. "For," He says, "you ask me for crowns and honors, but I speak to you of struggle and perspiration. This is not a time for rewards, nor will my glory appear at this time, but the present is the time of death and dangers." But observe how by His very manner of questioning He exhorts and consoles. He did not say, "Can you undergo suffering? Can you shed your blood?" But He said, "Can you drink the chalice?" Then by way of consolation He adds, "which I am to drink." So that by their very union with Him they might become more eager for hardships.

℟. Behold I send you as sheep in the midst of wolves, saith the Lord: * Be ye therefore wise as serpents and simple as doves. ℣. Whilst you have the light, believe in the light, that you may be the children of light. Be ye. Glory. Be ye.

✠ Continuation of the holy Gospel according to St. Matthew.— At that time the mother of the sons of Zebedee came to him with her sons; and worshipping, she made a request of him. He said to her, "What dost thou want?" She said to him, "Command that these my two sons may sit, one at thy right hand and one at thy left hand, in thy kingdom." But Jesus answered and said, "You do not know what you are asking for. Can you drink of the cup of which I am about to drink?" They said to him, "We can." He said to them, "Of my cup you shall indeed drink; but as for sitting at my right hand and at my left, that is not mine to give you, but it belongs to those for whom it has been prepared by my Father."

LET US PRAY

Be Thou, O Lord, the sanctifier and guardian of Thy people that, strengthened by the protection of Thy Apostle James, they may please Thee by their manner of life and serve Thee with a peaceful soul. Through our Lord.

July 26
SS. JOACHIM AND ANNE, PARENTS OF THE BLESSED VIRGIN MARY

I Nocturn

From Jeremias the Prophet, c. 33, 12 - 17 and 19 - 26

II Nocturn

Sermon of St. John Damascene

Joachim and Anne were the parents of the most blessed Virgin. While Joachim was being led by the Lord God as a sheep, he was in need of none of those things which are the best. But let no one think that I call those things the best which are pleasing to most men, and for which the mind of greedier men is accustomed to yearn, yet which are neither lasting in their nature, nor know how to make a better man of him by whom they are held, even though they are possessed by him abundantly. Such are the pleasures of this world found to be, which truly cannot be firm and stable, but rapidly pass away, and, as a rule, almost in the same hour in which they are gained, they are taken away.

May these things be far from us! It is in no way proper that we be moved by them, nor is such the lot of those who fear the Lord. On the other hand, those things are really blessings that are sought after and greatly loved by men of sound judgment; which last forever, and, at the same time, please the Divine Majesty and produce a seasonable fruit for their possessors. Blessings of this type, I say, are the virtues which will bring forth their fruit in due time, that is, will, in the world to come, bestow eternal life on all who cultivate them here, and direct their labors to them to the best of their ability. Toil, of course, comes first; eternal happiness will follow.

Joachim was accustomed to nourish his thoughts interiorly, as "in a place of pasture," that is, he dwelt in contemplation on the sacred words. He revived his soul "on the water of refreshment" of divine grace, and through this norm of comporting himself, wholly turning his mind away from things unlawful, he directed it "on the paths of virtue." And Anne was united with him as consort, no less by the bond of character than by marriage.

Joachim, then, by marriage had joined to himself this venerable woman, Anne, who was worthy of the highest praise. Just as the Anne of olden times, though she suffered from the affliction of sterility, having made a vow, begot Samuel by promise, so this Anne in a similar manner, by her prayer and by divine promise, received the Mother of God. Wherefore, enduring no loss of dignity in the honor of motherhood, she will not appear unequal to any illustrious woman. Accordingly, grace (for this is what the word *Anne* expresses) gave birth to the Queen (for so the name of *Mary* is interpreted), and most assuredly was she (Mary) made Queen of all created things, since she was the Mother of their Creator.

℟. O happy Joachim, who didst beget the child who was to bear the Redeemer of the world: * Rejoice, and intercede for us to the Queen of heaven. ℣. O happy father of a happier daughter, who brought forth the only-begotten Son of God, made incarnate of her own flesh. Rejoice. Glory. Rejoice.

III Nocturn

The reading of the holy Gospel according to St. Matthew

The book of the origin of Jesus Christ, the Son of David, the son of Abraham. Abraham begot Isaac, Isaac begot Jacob, Jacob begot Judas and his brethren. And so forth.

Homily of St. Leo, Pope

Most dearly beloved, the divine Goodness has always cared for the human race in divers ways and in many measures, and has benignly imparted to all past ages the very numerous gifts of His providence; but He has surpassed all the abundance of His wonted kindness in these recent times, when in Christ Mercy itself came down to sinners, the very Truth to the erring, and Life itself to the dead. For as that Word, coequal and coeternal with the Father in the unity of His Godhead, took on Himself the nature of our lowliness, so was that same God, born of God, born also as man from man.

Indeed this was promised from the foundation of the world and had been repeatedly foretold by many typifying signs and words; but how many men would these figures and hidden mysteries have saved had Christ not fulfilled their long-foretold and mysterious predictions! Moreover, what was then profitable for a few believers as something that was to come to pass, has now, having been fulfilled, benefited countless faithful souls. Hence we are now brought to faith not by signs and representations, but, having been strengthened by the Gospel narrative, we adore what we believe has certainly happened; having attained to our knowledge of the reality by means of these prophetic instruments (the prophecies and types), we can in no wise consider doubtful what we know was foretold by such great prophecies.

From this follows what our Lord said to Abraham: "In thy seed shall all the nations be blessed." Therefore also David in prophetic vision sings of the promise of God with the words: "The Lord has sworn to David the truth and he will not bring it to naught: 'Of the fruit of thy womb I will set one upon thy throne.'" So also the Lord said through Isaias, "Behold a virgin shall conceive in her womb and bear a Son, and his name shall be called Emmanuel," which is interpreted, *God with us*. And again: "There will come forth a rod out of the root of Jesse and a flower shall rise up from his root." In this rod without any doubt the Blessed Virgin Mary is foretold, who was born from the family of Jesse and David, and was made a mother by the Holy Spirit; she brought forth the new flower of human flesh, in a maternal womb, it is true, but by a virginal birth.

Let the just therefore rejoice in the Lord, and their hearts in the praise of God, and let the sons of men praise His wonderful works; for especially in this work of God (the Incarnation) does our lowliness begin to understand how much its Creator has prized it. God gave much with the origin of mankind in that He made us according to His own image, but far more has He given for our restoration, since the very Lord of all adapted Himself to the form of a slave. Although whatever the Creator has given to the creature comes from one and the same mercy, yet it is less wonderful for man to ascend to God than for God to descend to man.

℟. To the righteous a light is risen up in darkness; * The Lord is merciful and compassionate and just. ℣. He hath made straight the way of the just and hath prepared the path of the Saints. The Lord. Glory. The Lord.

✠ Beginning of the holy Gospel according to St. Matthew.— The book of the origin of Jesus Christ, the Son of David, the son of Abraham. Abraham begot Isaac, Isaac begot Jacob, Jacob begot Judas and his brethren. Judas begot Phares and Zara of Thamar, Phares begot Esron, Esron begot Aram. And Aram begot Aminadab, Aminadab begot Naasson, Naasson begot Salmon. Salmon begot Booz of Rahab. Booz begot Obed of Ruth, Obed begot Jesse, Jesse begot David the king.

And David the king begot Solomon of the former wife of Urias. Solomon begot Roboam, Roboam begot Abia, Abia begot Asa. And Asa begot Josaphat, Josaphat begot Joram, Joram begot Ozias. And Ozias begot Joatham, Joatham begot Achaz, Achaz begot Ezechias. And Ezechias begot Manasses, Manasses begot Amon, Amon begot Josias. And Josias begot Jechonias and his brethren at the time of the carrying away to Babylon.

And after the carrying away to Babylon Jechonias begot Salathiel, Salathiel begot Zorobabel. And Zorobabel begot Abiud,

Abiud begot Eliachim, Eliachim begot Azor. And Azor begot Sadoc, Sadoc begot Achim, Achim begot Eliud. And Eliud begot Eleazar, Eleazar begot Matthan, Matthan begot Jacob. And Jacob begot Joseph, the husband of Mary, and of her was born Jesus who is called Christ.

Let Us Pray

O God, who didst choose holy Joachim and Anne as the parents of the glorious Mother of Thy only-begotten Son; grant that by their prayers we may ever praise thy loving kindness in the company of Thy elect. Through the same Jesus Christ.

August 1

ST. PETER'S CHAINS

I Nocturn

From the Acts of the Apostles, c. 12, 1 - 11

II Nocturn

During the reign of the Emperor Theodosius the younger, his wife Eudocia went to Jerusalem to fulfill a vow. There many presents were given to her, among which was an iron chain, adorned with gold and precious stones, which they declared was the one with which the Apostle Peter had been bound by King Herod.

With pious reverence Eudocia sent this chain to her daughter Eudoxia at Rome. She in turn brought it to the Pope, who brought forth another chain which had been used to bind the same Apostle during the persecution of the Emperor Nero. When the Pope put the Roman chain and the one which had been brought from Jerusalem together, they became so united with one another that they semed no longer to be two chains, but only one, made by the same workman.

As a result of this miracle these holy chains began to be so venerated that Eudoxia's church of St. Peter on the Esquiline hill was dedicated under the name of St. Peter-in-chains; and in memory of the miracle a feast was instituted to be celebrated on the first day of August. Henceforth the honor which before had been given on this day to the profane festivities of the heathens, began now to be given to the chains of St. Peter. The mere touch of these chains was sufficient to cure the sick and to put the demons to flight.

Among other such cases there happened in the year 969, that of a certain Count, a servant of the Emperor Otto, who was possessed by an unclean spirit, so that he even tore himself with his own teeth. The Emperor ordered this man to be taken to Pope John, and as soon as he had touched the Count's neck with the sacred chains, the wicked spirit went out of him and left him free. From that time on reverence for these holy chains greatly increased in the city of Rome.

℞. Arise, Peter, and cast thy garment about thee, and receive strength for the salvation of the Gentiles: * For the chains have fallen off from thy hands. ℣. An Angel of the Lord stood by him, and a light shone in the prison cell, and he, striking Peter on the side, raised him up, saying: Arise quickly. For. Glory. For.

III Nocturn

The reading of the holy Gospel according to St. Matthew

At that time Jesus, having come into the district of Caesarea Philippi, began to ask his disciples, saying, "Who do men say the Son of Man is?" And so forth.

Homily of St. Augustine, Bishop

Peter alone, among the Apostles, merited to hear, "Amen I say to thee, that thou art Peter, and upon this rock I will build my Church." Truly worthy was he who was to be the foundation stone for the people that were to be built into the house of God, the column of support, the key to the Kingdom.

Of him the Divine Word says: "And they brought forth the sick ... that, when Peter came, his shadow at least might overshadow them." If at that time the shadow of his body was able to produce aid, how much more now the fullness of his power? If the mere breath of him as he passed along was then of value to those who begged of him, how much more the grace of him who now remaineth forever?

Deservedly is the iron of his prison chains considered by all the churches of Christ more precious than gold. If the shadow of him as he passed along was so beneficial, how much more the chain of him in his victory? If such an idle image of an empty form could hold within itself the power of cure, how much greater healing power have the chains of his suffering, pressed on his sacred members with their iron weight, merited to draw from his body?

If before his martyrdom he was so powerful in helping those who implored his favor, how much more effective must he be after his triumph? Blessed are those bonds which were to be changed from manacles and shackles into a crown; which by fettering the Apostle made him a martyr! Blessed are the chains which bound their victim even to the cross of Christ, not to condemn him, but to consecrate him!

℟. Thou art Peter, and upon this rock I will build My Church, and the gates of hell shall not prevail against it: * And to thee I will give the keys of the kingdom of heaven. ℣. Whatsoever thou shalt bind on earth, it shall be bound also in heaven; and whatsoever thou shalt loose on earth, it shall be loosed also in heaven. And to thee. Glory. And to thee.

✠ Continuation of the holy Gospel according to St. Matthew.— At that time Jesus, having come into the district of Caesarea Philippi, began to ask his disciples, saying, "Who do men say the Son of Man is?" But they said, "Some say, John the Baptist; and others, Elias; and others, Jeremias, or one of the prophets." He said to them, "But who do you say that I am?" Simon Peter answered and said, "Thou art the Christ, the Son of the living God." Then Jesus answered and said, "Blessed art thou, Simon Bar-Jona, for flesh and blood has not revealed this to thee, but my Father in heaven. And I say to thee, thou art Peter, and upon this rock I will build my Church, and the gates of hell shall not prevail against it. And I will give thee the keys of the kingdom of heaven; and whatever thou shalt bind on earth shall be bound in heaven, and whatever thou shalt loose on earth shall be loosed in heaven."

LET US PRAY

O God, who didst free St. Peter from his chains and bring him forth from the prison unharmed, we beseech Thee, break the bonds of our sins and mercifully protect us from all evil. Through our Lord.

August 5

DEDICATION OF ST. MARY MAJOR

I Nocturn

From the Proverbs of Solomon, c. 8, 12 - 25 and 34 - 36; c. 9, 1 - 5

II Nocturn

During the pontificate of Liberius a Roman patrician named John, and his wife, of equal nobility, not having any children to whom they might leave their estate, resolved to use their wealth to honor the most holy Virgin Mother of God. They assiduously begged of her to make known to them in what particular way she desired them to use the money. The Blessed Virgin Mary graciously heard their heartfelt prayers and wishes, and acknowledged them by a miracle.

Dedication of St. Mary Major

On the 5th of August, when the city of Rome usually experiences the most intense heat, snow covered a part of the Esquiline hill during the night. During the same night the Mother of God informed separately John and his wife, while asleep, that on the spot which would be found covered with snow they should build a church, which was to be dedicated in the name of the Virgin Mary; thus it was that she wished to be their heiress. John brought this news to Pope Liberius, who declared that the same thing had happened to him in a dream.

He went therefore in solemn procession to the snow-covered hill, accompanied by the clergy and the people. There he marked out the plan of a church, which was constructed with the money of John and his wife. It was later restored by Sixtus III, and was called by various names: the *Liberian Basilica*, and *St. Mary at the Crib*.

But since there were already many churches in Rome named in honor of the Blessed Virgin, in order that the name of this one might indicate the preeminence acquired by the greatness of the miracle and its dignity, it was called *St. Mary Major*. A commemoration of this dedication is kept by an annual feast, called after the snow which fell so miraculously on this day.

℞. O holy and spotless virginity, how to proclaim thy praises, I know not: * For thou hast borne in thy bosom Him whom the heavens cannot contain. ℣. Blessed art thou among women, and blessed is the fruit of thy womb. For. Glory. For.

III Nocturn

The reading of the holy Gospel according to St. Luke

At that time, as Jesus spoke these things to the multitude, a certain woman lifted up her voice from the crowd, and said to him, "Blessed is the womb that bore thee, and the breasts that nursed thee." And so forth.

Homily of St. Bede the Venerable, Priest

This woman is shown to be of great devotion and faith, who, while the Scribes and Pharisees are trying our Lord and at the same time blaspheming Him, better than anybody else, understands the Incarnation so well and proclaims it with such confidence, that she puts to shame the slanderous attack of the leaders there present, as well as the faithlessness of future heretics. For as the Jews then, by blaspheming the works of the Holy Spirit, denied that the Son of God was the true Son of, and consubstantial with, the Father, so afterwards have heretics, by denying that Mary ever a Virgin, through the operation of the power of the Holy Spirit, furnished the matter for His flesh when the Only-Begotten of God was to be born with human members, declared that the Son of man must not be acknowledged the true Son of, and consubstantial with, His mother.

But, if the flesh of the Word of God is pronounced independent of the flesh of the Virgin Mother, the womb which bore it and the breast which nourished it are called blessed without a reason. Moreover, the Apostle says: "God sent his Son, *made* of a woman, made under the Law." And they are not to be listened to who conjecture that it should be read: "*born* of a woman, made under the Law," but it is "*made* of a woman," because, when conceived in the virginal womb, Christ did not draw His flesh out of nothing, nor from any other place, but from the body of His Mother; otherwise, He who would not have His origin from man should not be truly called the Son of Man.

And so, having directed these facts against Eutychius, let us raise our voice with the Catholic Church, whose type this woman was; let us raise our mind also from the midst of the multitudes, and let us declare: "Blessed is the womb that bore thee, and the breasts which nourished thee." For truly is that Mother blessed "who," as someone has said, "didst bring forth the King who ruleth heaven and earth forever and ever."

"Yea, rather, blessed are they who hear the word of God, and keep it." In a beautiful manner the Savior assents to the woman's avowal, asserting that not only she who had merited to give birth to the Word of God in body was blessed, but that all, too, who strive to conceive the same Word in a spiritual way through the preaching of the Faith, and to bring it forth and, as it were, to foster it, whether in their own, or in the heart of their neighbors, are also blessed, because the Mother of God herself was, on the one hand, indeed blessed by the fact that she was made the temporal minister of the Incarnation of the Word; but, on the other, she is far more blessed by the fact that she remained the everlasting protectress of the same Word who must be loved always.

℟. Rejoice with me all ye that love the Lord: for while I was a little one, I pleased the Most High, * And from my womb I have brought forth God and man. ℣. All generations shall call me blessed, because God hath regarded His lowly handmaid And from. Glory. And from.

✠ Continuation of the holy Gospel according to St. Luke.—At that time, as Jesus spoke these things to the multitude, a certain woman lifted up her voice from the crowd, and said to him, "Blessed is the womb that bore thee, and the breasts that nursed thee." But he said, "Rather, blessed are they who hear the word of God and keep it."

Let Us Pray

Grant us Thy servants, we beseech Thee, O Lord, to enjoy continual health of both soul and body, and by the glorious intercession of the Blessed Mary ever Virgin to be delivered from the sorrows of this present life and to enjoy eternal happiness. Through our Lord.

August 6

THE TRANSFIGURATION OF OUR LORD

I Nocturn

From the second Epistle of St. Peter the Apostle, c. 1, 10 - 21

II Nocturn

Sermon of St. Leo, Pope

The Lord reveals His glory before His chosen witnesses, and glorifies that bodily form which He has in common with others, so that His face was like to the brilliance of the sun and His garments equal to the whiteness of snow. In this transfiguration it was, indeed, intended principally to take away from the disciples' hearts the scandal of the cross, lest the voluntary abjectness of His Passion should shake the faith of those men to whom had been revealed the excellence of His hidden Majesty.

But neither by a lesser providence was the hope of Holy Church established, in that the whole Body of Christ would recognize by what kind of recompense it was to be blessed, so that its members might promise to themselves a participation in that honor which had shone in their Head. Yet, while the apostles were being strengthened and raised up to the summit of learning, another lesson also was given in that wonderful act. For Moses and Elias, that is, the Law and the Prophets, appeared talking with the Lord, so that most assuredly in the presence of these five men was effected what had been declared: "In the mouth of two or three witnesses every word shall stand."

What is more lasting, more firm than the Word, in the proclamation of which the trumpet of both the old and the new Testaments blares forth, since the forecasts of the ancient testimonies agree also with the teaching of the Gospel? For the pages of both Covenants corroborate one another, and Him whom the signs that went before had promised under the veil of mysteries, the splendor of His present glory reveals manifest and within sight.

So, being aroused by the revelations of these mysteries, the Apostle Peter, spurning the things of the world and loathing all earthly things, in a kind of ecstasy of mind was ravished with a desire for things eternal, and overflowing with joy at the whole vision, he was desirous of dwelling there with Jesus, where he was gladdened by His manifested glory. And therefore he said: "Lord, it is good for us to be here: if thou wilt, let us set up three tents here, one for thee, and one for Moses, and one for Elias." But to this suggestion the Lord gave no answer, showing that what he desired was not indeed unrighteous, but out of order, since the world could not be saved except through Christ's death; indeed, by our Lord's example the faith of believers should be made to note that, while it is behooving that the promises of final happiness should not be questioned, we should, nevertheless, realize that in the midst of the trials of this life patience should be asked for by us rather than glory.

℞. Behold what manner of charity God the Father hath bestowed upon us, * That we should be called and should be the sons of God. ℣. For we know that, when He shall appear, we shall be like to Him, because we shall see Him as He is. That we. Glory. That we.

III Nocturn

The reading of the holy Gospel according to St. Matthew

At that time Jesus took Peter, James and his brother John, and led them up a high mountain by themselves, and was transfigured before them. And so forth.

Homily of St. John Chrysostom

Though the Lord has spoken much about dangers, much about His Passion, much about His death and the martyrdom of His disciples, and has enjoined upon them very many grievous and hard things, and although these were to be of the present life and were even then impending, good things, however, were to be hoped for and expected, as, for example, if they should lose their life they should find it. Moreover, He would come in the glory of His Father to render to them their rewards. Now in order to assure them even by sight, and to show them, in as far as they were able to grasp it in this present life, what this glory would be when He would come, He showed and unveiled it to them, lest they, and especially Peter, should either grieve over their own death or that of their Lord.

Now see how He proceeds when He discourses about heaven and hell. For by that which he spoke, "Whosoever will save his life shall lose it, and whosoever shall lose his life for my sake shall find it," and again when He said, "He shall reward every man according to his works," He designated heaven and hell.

But although He treated of both, He allows heaven alone to be glimpsed with the eyes, but hell not at all, as would have really been necessary with the more uncultured and dull; but since these (His apostles) were upright and keen men, it was enough that they be confirmed by the better things. This truly was much more becoming to Him; and yet He did not omit mention of hell altogether, but at times He also places, as it were, its severity before our eyes, as when He narrated the parable of Lazarus, and when He mentioned the man who demanded back the hundred pieces of money.

But consider the wisdom of Matthew who hid not the names of those who were placed at the head. John also does this very often when he most truly and diligently describes the extraordinary praises of Peter. For ill-will or empty glory had no place in the society of the apostles. As I was saying, then, He took aside by themselves the chief ones of the apostles. Why did He take them only? Because they were in truth more excellent than the rest. But why did He not do this on the spot instead of six days later? Lest the rest, namely, His disciples or followers, might be moved by jealousy. For this reason He did not call by name those whom He was about to take with Him.

℞. God hath called us by His holy calling, according to His own grace which is now made manifest * By the illumination of our Savior Jesus Christ. ℣. Who destroyed death and brought to light life in incorruption. By the illumination. Glory. By the illumination.

✠ Continuation of the holy Gospel according to St. Matthew.— Now after six days Jesus took Peter, James and his brother John, and led them up a high mountain by themselves, and was transfigured before them. And his face shone as the sun, and his garments became white as snow. Anb behold, there appeared to them Moses and Elias talking together with them. Then Peter addressed Jesus, saying, "Lord, it is good for us to be here. If thou wilt, let us set up three tents here, one for thee, one for Moses, and one for Elias." As he was still speaking, behold, a bright cloud overshadowed them, and behold, a voice out of the cloud said, "This is my beloved Son, in whom I am well pleased; hear him." And on hearing it the disciples fell on their faces and were exceedingly afraid. And Jesus came near and touched them, and said to them, "Arise, and do not be afraid." But lifting up their eyes, they saw no one but Jesus only.

And as they were coming down from the mountain, Jesus cautioned them, saying, "Tell the vision to one, till the Son of Man has risen from the dead."

LET US PRAY

O God, who in the glorious Transfiguration of Thy only-begotten Son hast confirmed the mysteries of our faith by the testimony of the fathers, and by the voice coming from the bright cloud has wonderfully foreshown the perfect adoption of sons, mercifully grant us to be made co-heirs of this same King of glory and partakers of the same glory. Through the same Jesus Christ.

August 9

VIGIL OF ST. LAWRENCE

The reading of the holy Gospel according to St. Matthew

At that time Jesus said to his disciples, "If anyone wishes to come after me, let him deny himself, and take up his cross, and follow me." And so forth.

Homily of St. Gregory, Pope

Because our Lord and Redeemer came into the world as a "new man," He gave new commandments to the world. For to our old life, nurtured with its vices, He set the contrary of His new life. What, in fine, did the old man, the carnal man, think of, except to hold on to things that were his own, to seize the things of others, if he could; or to covet them, if he was not able to seize them? But the heavenly Physician applies a thwarting remedy to each individual vice.

Thus, just as in the practice of medicine fevers are cured by cold applications, chills by hot applications, so our Lord has set out opposing remedies for our sins, so that He prescribes continency for the intemperate, generosity for the avaricious, meekness for the angry, humility for the proud. When He proposed His new commandments to those who followed Him, He definitely declared: "Unless one renounce everything he possesses, he cannot be my disciple." As if He openly says: "You who in your old life coveted the things of others, now in your pursuit of a new mode of living give away what is yours."

Let us hear, then, what He says in this lesson: "If any man will come after me, let him deny himself..." In the one place it is stated that we should sacrifice what is ours; here it is declared that we are to deny ourselves. Perchance indeed, it is not hard for a man to forsake what he has, yet it is very hard to forsake himself. In truth, it is a rather small thing to sacrifice what one possesses, while it is a very great thing to sacrifice what one is.

ST. LAWRENCE, MARTYR

I Nocturn

From the Book of Ecclesiasticus, c. 51, 1 - 17

II Nocturn

Sermon of St. Leo, Pope

While the fury of the heathen powers was raging against all the most renowned members of Christ, and was principally seeking out those who were of priestly rank, the wicked persecutor poured out his hatred upon the Levite Lawrence, who was in charge not only of the administration of the Sacraments, but likewise of the distribution of the Church's treasury, promising to himself a double booty in taking the one man; for if he would make him a betrayer of the sacred money, he would also make him an apostate from the true religion.

So the man, a seeker of wealth and an enemy to the truth, is armed with a double incentive: avarice, in that he would steal the gold, and impiety, in that he would do away with Christ. He demands that there be brought to him by the irreproachable guardian of the treasury the ecclesiastical treasures for which he was craving. To him, the Levite, revealing where he kept these treasures, brought countless groups of saintly poor people, in whose food and clothing he had invested the resources which now could not be lost since the more piously they were spent, the better were they preserved.

The despoiler, being thus thwarted, is in a tantrum, and fuming in hatred for the religion which had instituted such a use for riches, he undertakes the seizure of the more worthy treasure from him on whom he had found not the makings of a penny, so that he would take away from him that deposit (his religion) by which he was the more sacredly rich. He commands Lawrence to deny Christ, and attempts to force the invincible fortitude of that priestly soul by horrible sufferings. When the first of these achieve nothing, more terrible ones follow. He orders his limbs, torn and cut by the great lashing with stripes, to be roasted on a fire, so that through the alternate turning of his members on the gridiron, which by its constant heat had the power to burn, his agony was made the more terrible and his punishment was drawn out.

You achieve nothing! Your savage cruelty is of no avail! His mortal frame is done away with by your tortures, but while Lawrence goes up into heaven, you perish in your own flames. The charity of Christ could not be extinguished by a flame; indeed, the fire which burned him exteriorly was not as hot as that which burned within him. As a persecutor you have raged against the martyr; you have raged and have enlarged his crown when you increased his suffering. For why should not your temper redound to the glory of the conqueror, when even the instruments of torture have had part in the glory of his triumph? Let us then rejoice, most dearly beloved, with a spiritual joy, and through the very happy end of this wonderful man let us glory in the Lord, who is wonderful in His saints, in whom He has established for us our help and example, and has rendered His own glory so illustrious over the whole world, that as, "from the rising of the sun even to the going down thereof," through the brightness of His sacerdotal lights, Jerusalem is glorified by Stephen, so Rome becomes illustrious through Lawrence.

℟. Blessed Lawrence cried out and said: I worship my God and Him only do I serve: * And therefore I am not afraid of your torments. ℣. Night hath no darkness for me, but all things become visible in the light. And therefore. Glory. And therefore.

III Nocturn

The reading of the holy Gospel according to St. John

At that time Jesus said to his disciples: "Amen, amen, I say to you, unless the grain of wheat fall into the ground and die, it remains alone." And so forth.

Homily of St. Augustine, Bishop

The Lord Jesus Himself was that grain which had to die and to be multiplied: to die by the infidelity of the Jews; to be multiplied by the faith of all peoples. He it is who now, truly exhorting us to follow in the footsteps of His Passion, says, "He who loveth his life shall lose it." This can be understood in two ways. "Whoever loves his life will lose it"; that is, if you love your life you will die. Therefore, if you desire to hold fast to life in Christ, do not fear death for the sake of Christ.

Again, it may mean: "He who loves his life shall lose it; do not love lest you lose; do not love this life lest you lose eternal life." This second interpretation seems to express better the sense of the Evangelist. For there follows: "And he who hateth his life in this world keepeth it unto life eternal." Therefore, that which has been said above, that he who loves his life—*in this world*, which is understood—he indeed will lose it; he, however, who hates his life—in this world, of course—will keep it unto eternity.

A great and wonderful saying, that a man must love his life to lose it, and hate his life to save it! If thou hast loved amiss, thou hast hated; if thou hast hated well, thou hast loved. O blessed are they who by keeping watch have hated their lives, lest by loving they should lose them. But take care lest the thought that you should wish to kill yourself take hold of you, thus understanding falsely that you must hate your life in this world.

Because of this false notion certain badly-disposed and perverse men, more cruel and more wicked toward themselves than murderers, would consign themselves to the flames, would drown themselves, or would cast themselves headlong from a precipice and thus perish. This Christ did not teach; He even responded to the devil suggesting that He cast Himself from a cliff, saying, "Begone, Satan! it is written: 'Thou shalt not tempt the Lord, thy God.'" Moreover, to Peter He said, signifying by what death he was to glorify God, "When thou wast younger thou didst gird thyself, and didst walk where thou wouldst. But when thou shalt be old, thou shalt stretch forth thy hands, and another shall gird thee, and lead thee whither thou wouldst not." Here it is plainly shown that he who follows Christ's footsteps must be killed not by his own hand, but by another.

℟. Leave me not, O holy father, for I have already distributed thy treasures. * I do not leave thee, my son, nor forsake thee: but sterner struggles for Christ's faith await thee. ℣. We, as old men, are given an easier race to run, but for those in youth there is kept a more glorious triumph over the tyrant; in three days' time thou, the levite, wilt follow after me, the priest. I do not. Glory. I do not.

✠ Continuation of the holy Gospel according to St. John.— At that time Jesus said to his disciples: "Amen, amen, I say to you, unless the grain of wheat fall into the ground and die, it remains alone. But if it die, it brings forth much fruit. He who loves his life, loses it; and he who hates his life in this world, keeps it unto life everlasting. If anyone serve me, let him follow me; and where I am there also shall my servant be. If anyone serve me, my Father will honor him."

Let Us Pray

Grant us, we beseech Thee, almighty God, to extinguish the flames of our vices, Thou who didst grant blessed Lawrence the grace to conquer the fire of his executioners. Through our Lord.

August 14
VIGIL OF THE ASSUMPTION OF THE BLESSED VIRGIN MARY

The reading of the holy Gospel according to St. Luke

At that time, as Jesus spoke these things to the multitude, a certain woman lifted up her voice from the crowd, and said to him, "Blessed is the womb that bore thee, and the breasts that nursed thee." And so forth.

Homily of St. John Chrysostom

Because you have heard the woman saying, "Blessed is the womb that bore thee, and the breasts that nursed thee," and our Lord replying, "Rather, blessed are they who hear the word of God, and keep it," do not think from this utterance that He was neglectful of His Mother. He was showing merely that the name of mother would contribute nothing of profit to her unless she excelled in goodness and in faith. Now if Mary's love without womanly virtue would have been of no benefit, far less will the goodness of a father, a brother, a mother, a son, be of advantage to us, unless we bring forth some good of our own.

For not in anyone else, but in one's own virtues alone, following divine grace, is salvation to be hoped for. Indeed, if the divine motherhood had been profitable to Mary (abstracting from her virtues), the Jews, to whom Christ was a blood relation according to the flesh, would also have been benefited; the city in which He was born would have profited, and it would have been of advantage to His relatives. Instead, while His brethren took care of their own affairs, the name which made them His relatives brought nothing to them; rather, they were condemned with the rest of the world.

For the time being they were in admiration while they shone with His singular glory; but their country, having gained nothing from this, fell and was consumed with fire; its citizens, wretchedly slain, perished; men, related to Him by the flesh, gained nothing towards their salvation, since they lacked the support of His power. The apostles, on the other hand, glorified before all men, escaped, because they had gained for themselves by their obedience a true and desirable friendship with Him. From this we conclude that we are always in need of faith and of a life that glows with virtue; only this can save us.

August 15
ASSUMPTION OF THE BLESSED VIRGIN MARY
I Nocturn
From the Canticle of Canticles, c. 1, 1 - 16
II Nocturn
Sermon of St. John Damascene

Today the sacred and animated ark of the living God, who conceived her Creator within her womb, rests in the temple of the Lord which has not been built with hands. And David as her forefather rejoices and leads the choirs of the angels on with him; the archangels celebrate; the virtues glorify her; the principalities are in joy; the powers are gladdened; the dominations rejoice; the Thrones keep the festal day; the Cherubim sing her praise; the Seraphim proclaim her glory.

Today Eden receives the Paradise of the new Adam, where condemnation is rescinded; where the tree of life is planted; where our nakedness is clothed. Today the immaculate Virgin, who was sullied by no earthly attachments, but nourished with heavenly thought, has not returned to dust; rather, since she was a living heaven, she is placed within the celestial tabernacles.

For how should she, from whom the true Life flowed out to all men, taste death? Yet she accedes to the Law enacted by Him whom she begot. As the daughter of the old Adam she suffered the primal punishment—for even her Son, who is Life Itself, did not refuse it—and as the Mother of the living God she is rightly taken up to Him. Eve, who gave assent to the serpent's suggestion, is condemned to pain in giving birth and to the punishment of death, and is set within the chambers of the lower regions.

But how was death to consume this blessed one, who gave heed to God's word and was filled with the operation of the Holy Spirit, and, at the spiritual greeting of the Archangel, conceived the Son of God, without any voluptuous desire or the cooperation of man, and brought Him forth without pain, and consecrated her whole self to God? How could the regions below admit her? How was corruption to attack that body in which Life took Its beginning? For her there was prepared a straight, smooth, and easy path to heaven. For if Christ, the Life and Truth, said, "Where I am, there also shall my minister be," how shall not His Mother with greater reason be with Him?

℟. Who is she that cometh forth as the sun, and as beautiful as Jerusalem? * The daughters of Sion saw her and declared her blessed, and the queens praised her. ℣. And round about her, as in spring time, were flowers of roses and lilies of the valley. The daughters. Glory. The daughters.

III Nocturn

The reading of the holy Gospel according to St. Luke

At that time Jesus entered a certain village; and a woman named Martha welcomed him to her house. And so forth.

Homily of St. Augustine, Bishop

In the reading of the holy Gospel we heard that the Lord was hospitably received by a religious woman who was called Martha. Now, while she was busy in the care of serving, her sister Mary sat at the feet of the Lord and listened to His word. The former was busily occupied, the latter unoccupied; the first ministered, the second was filled.

Martha, however, being much occupied in the task and business of serving, appealed to the Lord and complained about her sister who would not help her with the work. But the Lord answered Martha on behalf of Mary, and He who had been called upon to be her judge became her advocate. "Martha," He says, "thou art busy about many things when only one thing is necessary. Mary has chosen the better part which shall not be taken from her."

We have heard the appeal of the plaintiff and the sentence of the Judge. This sentence answered the plaintiff and defended her whom the Lord had taken under His protection, for Mary was absorbed with the charm of the Lord's word. Martha was intent upon how she should feed the Lord; Mary was intent upon how to be fed by the Lord. Martha was preparing a banquet for the Lord, at whose banquet Mary was even then being made joyful.

While Mary, then, listened with delight to His most gracious words and with a heart most ardent was being nourished, how could we think that she feared that the Lord, to whom her sister had appealed, would say to her, "Arise, and help thy sister"? For she was gripped by a wonderful charm which assuredly is perceived more by the mind than by the bodily appetite. She has been vindicated; she reclines more at ease. But how has she been vindicated? Let us attend to this point, and closely examine and scrutinize it in so far as we can, that we too may be fed.

℟. Truly happy art thou, O holy Virgin Mary, and worthy of all praise: * For from thee hath dawned the Sun of justice, Christ, our God. ℣. Pray for the people, plead for the clergy, intercede for all women vowed to God: may all experience thy help who celebrate thy holy festival. For from thee. Glory. For from thee.

✠ Continuation of the holy Gospel according to St. Luke.— At that time Jesus entered a certain village; and a woman named Martha welcomed him to her house. And she had a sister called Mary, who also seated herself at the Lord's feet, and listened to his word. But Martha was worried about much serving. And she came up and said, "Lord, is it no concern of thine that my sister has left me to serve alone? Tell her therefore to help me."

But the Lord answered and said to her, "Martha, Martha, thou art anxious and troubled about many things; and yet only one thing is needful. Mary has chosen the best part, and it will not be taken away from her."

Let Us Pray

Forgive, O Lord, we beseech Thee, the sins of Thy people, that we who are unable to please Thee by our own actions may be saved by the prayers of the Mother of Thy Son, our Lord, who liveth and reigneth with Thee.

August 16

SECOND DAY WITHIN THE OCTAVE OF THE ASSUMPTION

From a Sermon of St. John Damascene

We, who worship God, God, I say, not created out of nothingness, but an Eternal Being from an Eternal Being and superior to every cause, reason, and consideration both of time and of nature, honor and venerate the Mother of God. Not that we hold that His Divinity took its origin from her (for indeed the generation of God is independent of time and is equally eternal with the Father), but we profess a second nativity, through a voluntary assumption of flesh, the cause of which we both know and praise. For because of us and for the sake of our salvation, He, who has been incorporeal from all eternity, is made flesh that He might bring salvation to a like creature through a like nature; and having assumed flesh without the cooperation of man, He is born of this holy Virgin, yet remaining wholly God and made wholly man: wholly God together with His flesh and wholly man with His Divinity. In this way we recognize that Virgin as the Mother of God and thus do we celebrate her falling asleep.

Let us who have been enriched by the Incarnate God praise today with holy canticles this, His Mother, and let us honor her by our nightly vigils, that we may be and may be called the people of Christ. We delight her by purity of soul and body; her, I say, who is truly pure and surpassing all, after God, in purity. Similar people are accustomed to rejoice over similar things. Let us then venerate and imitate her by mercy and sympathy towards the needy. For if God is honored by nothing so much as by mercy, who will deny that His Mother also rejoices over this same virtue?

She has appropriated for our use an ineffable abyss of divine love. Through her, that long war which was waged with our Creator has been brought to an end; through her, reconciliation with Him has been established for us, and peace and favor have been given us; wherefore the angels sing praises together with men, and we, who before were despised, have been made sons of God. We have gathered a grape from that vine: from her we have extracted the germ of immortality. She has acquired all good things for us. In her, God has been made man, and man, God. And what is more admirable than this? What more blessed?

August 17

THIRD DAY WITHIN THE OCTAVE OF THE ASSUMPTION

From a Sermon of St. John Damascene

Let us rejoice over the ark of the Lord with our whole heart and the walls of Jericho, namely, the hostile fortifications of the powers opposing us, will fall. Let us rejoice in spirit with David, for the ark of the Lord today has rested. Let us cry with Gabriel, who holds the first place among the angels: "Hail, full of grace, the Lord is with thee." Hail, inexhaustible sea of joy; hail, remedy of all the sorrows of the heart. Hail, holy Virgin, through whom death has indeed been cast out and life brought in!

But, O thou holiest of holy sepulchres—except the sepulchre of the Lord which gave the beginning of life, which was the fount of the Resurrection—(for I speak to thee as to an animate being), where is the gold which the hands of the apostles placed in thee? Where are the riches which cannot be consumed? Where is that precious treasure which has received life? Where is the new volume in which the Word of God has been ineffably inscribed without a hand? Where is the abyss of grace? Where, the sea of cures? Where is that desirable body of the Virgin Mother of God?

Why do you seek in the tomb her who has been translated to the heavenly tabernacles? Why do you demand of me the reason of her custody? I am not able to resist the divine commands. That most holy body, which has imparted holiness to me also and has filled me with the fragrance of a most precious ointment and made me a divine temple, leaving behind its linen coverings, has been snatched up on high, accompanied by the angels, archangels, and all the heavenly powers. Now the angels surround me; now divine grace dwells in me. I have become medicine to those who are ill; a perennial fount of cures; a remedy against the demons; a city of refuge to all who flee to me.

August 18

FOURTH DAY WITHIN THE OCTAVE OF THE ASSUMPTION

From a Sermon of St. John Damascene

An ancient tradition has been handed down to us, that at the time of the glorious falling-asleep of the blessed Virgin, all the holy apostles, who were wandering throughout the world preaching salvation to the Gentiles, were caught up aloft in the twinkling of an eye and met together in Jerusalem. And when they were all there, a vision of angels appeared to them and the chant of the heavenly powers was heard; and so with divine glory she gave up her holy soul into the hands of God. But her body, which bore God in so ineffable a manner, was buried amid the hymns of angels and apostles, being laid in a tomb in Gethsemane. There for three whole days the angelic song was heard.

But after three days the chant of the angels ceased, and the apostles who were present opened the tomb (for Thomas, the only one who had been absent, came after the third day and wished to venerate the body that had borne God); but they could by no means find her sacred body in any part of it. But when they found only those garments in which she had been buried and were filled with the indescribable fragrance which emanated from them, they closed the tomb. Amazed at this wonderful mystery, they could only think that He, who had been pleased to take flesh from the Virgin Mary, to be made man, and to be born, though He was God the Word and Lord of glory, who had preserved her virginity without stain after childbirth, should also have been pleased to honor her pure body after her death, keeping it incorrupt, and translating it to heaven before the general resurrection.

At this time there were present with the apostles the most holy Timothy, first bishop of Ephesus, and Dionysius the Areopagite, as he himself declares in the letters he wrote to the aforesaid Timothy about the blessed Hierotheus, who was also present. He speaks thus: "For even when we also, as you know, and many of our holy brethren among those divinely inspired rulers of the Church had assembled for the purpose of viewing the body which gave the beginning of life and conceived God (and there were present both James, the brother of the Lord, and Peter, the first and most celebrated chief of theologians), and having beheld the sacred body, it pleased us all, according as each one was able, to celebrate with hymns the infinite goodness of the divine power.

August 19

FIFTH DAY WITHIN THE OCTAVE OF THE ASSUMPTION

Sermon of St. Bernard, Abbot

No doubt the glorious virgin, ascending today above the heavens, added an immense increase to the joys of the heavenly citizens. For this is she whose word of salutation makes even those whom the maternal womb still incloses exult in joy. But if the soul of a child not yet born was melted when Mary spoke, what do we think was that rejoicing of the heavenly citizens when they merited not only to hear her voice, but to see her face, and to enjoy her blessed presence?

But who can imagine how much the glorious Queen of heaven advanced today and by how great affection of devotion the whole multitude of the heavenly legions, by whose chants she was led to the throne of glory, profited by her coming; by how placid a countenance, by how serene a face, by what divine embraces she was received by her Son and raised above every creature with that honor of which such a Mother was worthy, with that glory which so well befitted her Son?

Happy indeed the kisses impressed by the lips of the infant whom the Mother embraced on her virginal bosom. But shall we not think those yet happier which she received today in joyful salutation from the mouth of Him sitting on the right hand of the Father, when she ascended to the throne of glory, singing the nuptial song and saying: "Let him kiss me with the kiss of his mouth"? Who will describe the generation of Christ and the assumption of Mary? For the more she has received grace above others on earth, so much the more singular glory does she obtain in heaven.

August 21

SEVENTH DAY WITHIN THE OCTAVE OF THE ASSUMPTION

Sermon of St. Bernard, Abbot

It is the time for all flesh to speak when the Mother of the Incarnate Word is taken up into heaven, nor ought human mortality cease to give praise when the nature of man is in the Virgin exalted above the immortal spirits. But neither does our devotion allow us to be silent, nor can our sterile thought conceive, nor our unlearned speech give forth, anything worthy concerning her glory. Hence it is that those princes of the heavenly court in the consideration of such an unheard-of thing cry out with admiration: "Who is she who ascends from the desert abounding with delights?"

As though they said more manifestly: "How great is she, or whence is she, ascending indeed from the desert, so abounding in delights?" For delights are not found equal in us whom the impetus of the river rejoices in the City of the Lord, who are given to drink by the countenance of Thy glory from the torrent of pleasure. Who is she who ascends from under the sun, where there is nothing but suffering and sadness and affliction of spirit, abounding in spiritual delights? Why should I not call delights the glory of virginity with the gift of fecundity, the ensign of humility distilling the honeycomb of charity, the bowels of mercy, the plenitude of grace, the prerogative of a singular glory?

Ascending, therefore, from the desert, the Queen of the world, as the Church sings, was made beautiful even to the holy angels and sweet in her delights. But let them cease to wonder at the delights of this desert, for the Lord hath given goodness and our earth hath yielded its fruit. Why do they wonder that Mary ascends from the desert of the earth abounding with delights? Let them wonder rather at Christ, being poor, descending from the plenitude of the heavenly Kingdom, for it seems by far a greater miracle that the Son of God deigned to be made a little less than the angels than that the Mother of God should be exalted above the angels. Indeed, His humiliation has been made our exaltation; His miseries are the delights of the world. Finally, being rich, He was made poor on account of us, that He might enrich us by His poverty.

August 22

OCTAVE OF THE ASSUMPTION OF THE BLESSED VIRGIN MARY

I Nocturn

From the Canticle of Canticles, c. 8, 5 - 14

II Nocturn

Sermon of St. Bernard, Abbot

To tell the truth, there is not anything that gives me more delight, but neither is there anything that frightens me more, than to speak of the glory of the Virgin Mary. For behold! If I shall praise virginity in her, to me there seem to be offered many virgins after her. If I preach on her humility, there will be found, perhaps, at least a few who, as her Son teaches, are meek and humble of heart. If I wish to magnify the greatness of her mercy, there will be some men of mercy, and also some women.

There is one thing in which she seems to have no rival, neither before nor after her: the possession of a mother's joy together with the honor of virginity. It is Mary's prerogative; it shall not be given to another; it is a singular thing, but on that very account it is found indescribable. Still, if you study with diligence, you will find that in Mary all the rest of the virtues which seemed to be common to all are wholly unparalleled. What purity, however angelic, could be compared with that virginity which was worthy of being made the temple of the Holy Spirit and the dwelling place of the Son of God!

How truly great and how precious her virtue of humility, together with such great purity, with such great innocence, with her conscience absolutely without sin, yea, together with the fullness of such great grace! Whence is your humility, and such great humility, O blessed one! O humility wholly worthy to be regarded by the Lord, whose beauty the King desired, by whose most sweet odor He was drawn from the eternal repose in the bosom of His Father!

Behold, we have accompanied thee by the avowals of which we are capable, as thou hast ascended to the Son, and we have followed thee at least from afar, O blessed Virgin. May it be a mark of thy love to make known to the world the grace which thou hast found with God by obtaining through thy holy prayers pardon for the guilty, remedy for the sick, strength for the weak of heart, consolation for the afflicted, help and deliverance for those in danger. Through thee also, O gracious Queen, on this day of solemnity and gladness, may Jesus Christ thy Son, our

Lord, who is God above all things, blessed forever, grant to thy servants who invoke thy sweetest name with praise the gifts of His grace. Amen!

℞. Like a cedar of Libanus I was exalted, and as a cypress tree on Mount Sion: like the best myrrh * I yielded a sweet odor. ℣. And like cinnamon and aromatical balm. I yielded. Glory. I yielded.

III Nocturn

The reading of the holy Gospel according to St. Luke

At that time Jesus entered a certain village; and a woman named Martha welcomed him to her house. And so forth.

Homily of St. Bernard, Abbot

Why do we say that He entered into the town? He likewise entered the very confined lodging place of the womb of the Virgin. To continue, "and a certain woman ... received him into her house." Happy the woman whose house was found clean when the Savior was received in it, but not, indeed, empty! For who will say that she was empty whom the Angel greeted as "full of grace"?

And not only this, but he further asserts that the Holy Spirit will come upon her. For what reason, do you reckon, but that He might also fill her with abundance? For what reason, but that she, who at the coming of the Spirit had already been filled for herself, might by the same coming be made full above measure for us too, and overflowing. Let the Savior then enter, and frequently visit that house which the penitent Lazarus purifies, Martha adorns, and Mary, devoted to interior contemplation, makes full.

Perhaps, then, some curious person will ask why, in the present Gospel reading, no mention is made directly of Lazarus. For my part I think that the reason for it is that it should in no way detract from the proposed simile. For the Spirit, wishing that the house of a Virgin be understood, kept silence, not inappropriately, about repentance, which, of a truth, is a companion of evil. For God forbid that this house be said to have had at any time any personal stain whatsoever, so that the broom of Lazarus should be looked for in it.

It should disturb no one that the woman who receives our Lord is called not Mary, but Martha, when in this one and greatest Mary both the industry of a Martha and the leisure, but by no means idleness, of a Mary, are found. True, "all the glory of the king's daughter is within," but she is nevertheless "within golden borders, clothed round about with varieties." She is not of the number of the foolish virgins; she is a prudent virgin; she possesses a lamp, but she carries oil in her vessel.

℟. Thou art blessed, O Virgin Mary, who didst bear the Lord, the Creator of the world: * Thou didst bring forth Him who made thee, and thou remainest a Virgin forever. ℣. Hail, Mary, full of grace; the Lord is with thee. Thou didst. Glory. Thou didst.

✠ Continuation of the holy Gospel according to St. Luke.— At that time Jesus entered a certain village; and a woman named Martha welcomed him to her house. And she had a sister called Mary, who also seated herself at the Lord's feet, and listened to his word. But Martha was worried about much serving. And she came up and said, "Lord, is it no concern of thine that my sister has left me to serve alone? Tell her therefore to help me."

But the Lord answered and said to her, "Martha, Martha, thou art anxious and troubled about many things; and yet only one thing is needful. Mary has chosen the best part, and it will not be taken away from her."

LET US PRAY

Forgive, O Lord, we beseech Thee, the sins of Thy people, that we who are unable to please Thee by our own actions may be saved by the prayers of the Mother of Thy Son, our Lord, who liveth and reigneth with Thee.

August 23

VIGIL OF ST. BARTHOLOMEW, APOSTLE

Lessons from the Homily on the Gospel as on the vigil of St. James, page 420

August 24

ST. BARTHOLOMEW, APOSTLE

I Nocturn

From the first Epistle of St. Paul the Apostle to the Corinthians, c. 4, 1 - 15

II Nocturn

The Apostle Bartholomew was a Galilean. When he had arrived in India, which was apportioned to him for the preaching of the Gospel of Jesus Christ, he preached to the various peoples there concerning the coming of the Lord Jesus, according to the Gospel of St. Matthew.

When he had converted many in that province to Jesus Christ and had undergone many sufferings and hardships, he went into greater Armenia. There he converted to the Christian Faith the king Polymius, together with his wife and the inhabitants of twelve cities.

This brought upon him the great envy of the priests of that nation, and they so incited Astyages, the brother of the king, against the Apostle, that he ordered Bartholomew to be flayed alive and then to be beheaded. In this martyrdom the Apostle gave his soul back to God.

His body was buried at Albanopolis, a city in greater Armenia, where he had suffered. Afterwards it was taken to the island of Lipari and thence to Benevento. Finally it was brought to Rome by the emperor Otto III, and was placed in the church dedicated to God in the Saint's name on the island in the Tiber.

℟. When ye stand before kings and governors take no thought how or what ye shall speak: * For it shall be given you in that hour what ye shall speak. ℣. For it is not you that speak but the Spirit of your Father that speaketh in you. For it shall. Glory. For it shall.

III Nocturn

The reading of the holy Gospel according to St. Luke

At that time Jesus went out to the mountain to pray, and continued all night in prayer to God. And when day broke, he summoned his disciples. And so forth.

Homily of St. Ambrose, Bishop

All great men, all men of lofty aims, ascend a mountain. It was not to everyone that the Prophet said, "Thou who bringest good tidings to Sion, go up into a high mountain; thou who bringest good tidings to Jerusalem, cry out with a loud voice." Ascend this mountain, not by the footsteps of the body, but by your noble deeds, and follow Christ that you too may be able to become a mountain. "Mountains were all around him." This is the reason why you will find in the Gospel that only the disciples went up with our Lord into the mountain.

There our Lord prays not for Himself, but He intercedes for me. Although the Father has placed all things in the power of the Son, yet the Son, that He might fulfill His role as Man, deems it necessary, as our Advocate, to intercede for us with the Father. "And he remained," says the Gospel narrative, "all that night in prayer to God." O Christian, an example is given to you, a model is proposed to you, which you ought to imitate.

Now what ought you to do for your own salvation if Christ spent the night for you in prayer? What, I say, ought you to do, since you wish to flatter yourself with some semblance of piety, if Christ first prayed before He sent out His disciples—yes, and prayed alone? And if I am not mistaken, nowhere is Christ found praying with His disciples—everywhere He prayed alone. Human desires do not fathom the thought of God; no one can be a participant of the interior thoughts of Christ.

He called His disciples, says the Gospel, and chose from amongst them twelve, whom He sent forth as sowers of the faith to give to men throughout the world those helps necessary for their eternal salvation. Notice at the same time the heavenly plan. He did not choose any wise, nor rich, nor noble men, but fishermen and publicans to use as His instruments. This He did lest He should seem to have led men on by wisdom, or redeemed them by riches, or drawn them to His grace by the weight of His power or nobility. He chose fishermen and publicans that truth might prevail of itself, and not by virtue of subtle disputations.

℞. Take up My yoke upon you, saith the Lord, and learn of Me, because I am meek and humble of heart: * For My yoke is sweet and My burden light. ℣. And you shall find rest for your souls. For My yoke. Glory. For My yoke.

✠ Continuation of the holy Gospel according to St. Luke.—
At that time Jesus went out to the mountain to pray, and continued all night in prayer to God. And when day broke, he summoned his disciples; and from these he chose twelve (whom he also named apostles): Simon, whom he named Peter, and his brother Andrew; James and John; Philip and Bartholomew; Matthew and Thomas; James the son of Alpheus, and Simon, called the Zealot; Jude the brother of James, and Judas Iscariot, who turned traitor.

And coming down with them he took his stand on a level stretch, with a crowd of his disciples, and a great multitude of people from all Judea and Jerusalem, and the sea coast of Tyre and Sidon, who came to listen to him and to be healed of their diseases. And those who were troubled with unclean spirits were cured. And all the crowd were trying to touch him, for power went forth from him and healed all.

LET US PRAY

O almighty and eternal God, who hast given us the holy and spiritual joy of this day on the feast of Thy blessed Apostle Bartholomew, grant, we beseech Thee, that Thy Church may love what he believed and preach what he taught. Through our Lord.

September 8

NATIVITY OF THE BLESSED VIRGIN MARY

I Nocturn

From the Canticle of Canticles, c. 1, 1 - 16

II Nocturn

Sermon of St. Augustine, Bishop

There is present to us, dearly beloved, the longed-for day of the blessed and venerable Mary, ever Virgin, and therefore our whole earth rejoices because it is so honored by the birth of such a Virgin. For she is the flower of the field from whom sprang the precious lily of the valley; by whose birth the stained nature that we have from our first parents is changed, and sin is blotted out.

That sad curse of Eve, in which it was said, "in sorrow shalt thou bring forth children," is, as regards Mary, taken away, because she brought forth the Lord in joy. For Eve mourned, but Mary rejoiced; Eve bore tears in her womb, Mary bore joy, for the former begot a sinner, the latter begot Him who was perfect Innocence. The mother of our race brought punishment into the world; the Mother of our Lord brought salvation.

Eve was the author of sin; Mary, the author of merit. Eve by killing harmed all; Mary by enlivening profits all. The former struck; the latter has healed. Obedience is exchanged for disobedience; fidelity atones for infidelity. Let Mary play now upon instruments, and let the timbrels resound between the active fingers of the young mother. Let the choirs sing together joyfully, and let their sweet songs be mingled with alternating strains.

Hear then how our timbrel-player sang, for she says: "My soul doth magnify the Lord, and my spirit hath rejoiced in God my Savior. Because he hath regarded the humility of his handmaid; for behold, from henceforth all generations shall call me blessed. Because he that is mighty hath done great things to me." Therefore the miracle of the new birth overcame the prevailing error, and the song of Mary put an end to the lamentation of Eve.

℟. Thy birth, O Virgin Mother of God, brought tidings of joy to the whole world: * For from thee rose the Sun of Justice, Christ our God: who has taken away the curse and given a blessing: and confounding death, has given us everlasting life. ℣. Blessed art thou amongst women, and blessed is the fruit of thy womb. For from thee. Glory. For from thee.

III Nocturn

The reading of the holy Gospel according to St. Matthew

The book of the origin of Jesus Christ, the Son of David, the son of Abraham. Abraham begot Isaac, Isaac begot Jacob, Jacob begot Judas and his brethren. And so forth.

Homily of St. Jerome, Priest

In Isaias we read: "Who shall declare his generation?" Let us not think that there is any contradiction between the Prophet and the Evangelist, because what the Prophet had said could not be done, the Evangelist begins to narrate; for the one speaks of the generation of the Divinity, the other of the Incarnation. Matthew begins with carnal things, that by learning of His manhood we may go on to learn of His Godhead.

"The Son of David, the Son of Abraham." The reversal of the order in these clauses is necessary. If Abraham had been put first and David afterwards, Abraham would have had to be named again in order that the genealogy might be properly arranged.

For this reason therefore, without mentioning the others, he calls Him the son of these, for to these only was the promise of Christ made. To Abraham it was said: "In thy seed (which is Christ) shall all nations be blessed." To David: "Of the fruit of thy womb shall I set upon thy throne."

"And Judas begot Phares and Zara of Thamar." It is to be noted that in the genealogy of the Savior no holy women are named, but rather those whom the Scriptures reprehend; so that He who came for the sake of sinners, being born of sinners, would destroy the sins of all. Whence also in that which follows Ruth is called a Moabitess and Bethsabee the wife of Urias.

℟. Truly happy art thou, O holy Virgin Mary, and worthy of all praise, * For from thee hath dawned the Sun of Justice, Christ our God. ℣. Pray for the people, plead for the clergy, intercede for all devout women; may all feel thy aid who celebrate thy holy Birthday. For from thee. Glory. For from thee.

✠ Beginning of the holy Gospel according to St. Matthew.— The book of the origin of Jesus Christ, the Son of David, the son of Abraham. Abraham begot Isaac, Isaac begot Jacob, Jacob begot Judas and his brethren. Judas begot Phares and Zara of Thamar, Phares begot Esron, Esron begot Aram. And Aram begot Aminadab, Aminadab begot Naasson, Naasson begot Salmon. Salmon begot Booz of Rahab. Booz begot Obed of Ruth, Obed begot Jesse, Jesse begot David the king.

And David the king begot Solomon of the former wife of Urias. Solomon begot Roboam, Roboam begot Abia, Abia begot Asa. And Asa begot Josaphat, Josaphat begot Joram, Joram begot Ozias. And Ozias begot Joatham, Joatham begot Achaz, Achaz begot Ezechias. And Ezechias begot Manasses, Manasses begot Amon, Amon begot Josias. And Josias begot Jechonias and his brethren at the time of the carrying away to Babylon.

And after the carrying away to Babylon Jechonias begot Salathiel, Salathiel begot Zorobabel. And Zorobabel begot Abiud, Abiud begot Eliachim, Eliachim begot Azor. And Azor begot Sadoc, Sadoc, begot Achim, Achim begot Eliud. And Eliud begot Eleazar, Eleazar begot Matthan, Matthan begot Jacob. And Jacob begot Joseph, the husband of Mary, and of her was born Jesus who is called Christ.

Let Us Pray

Grant to Thy servants, we beseech Thee, O Lord, the gift of heavenly grace, that as the birth of the Blessed Virgin was the beginning of our salvation, so the solemnity of her birth may give us an increase of peace. Through our Lord.

September 12
THE MOST HOLY NAME OF MARY

I Nocturn

From the Proverbs of Solomon, c. 8, 12 - 25 and 34 - 36; c. 9, 1 - 5

II Nocturn

Sermon of St. Bernard, Abbot

"And the Virgin's name was Mary." Let us say a few things about this name which, when interpreted, is called "star of the sea," and is admirably suitable to the Virgin Mother. She is, in fact, very appropriately compared to a star, because just as a star without any loss to itself shoots forth its ray, so the Virgin, too, without injury to her virginity gave birth to her Son. And as the ray from the star does not diminish its brilliance, neither did the Son lessen the integrity of His Mother.

She is, then, that noble star sprung forth from Jacob, whose ray brightens the whole world, whose splendors both shine in heaven and penetrate into hell; spreading, likewise, over the earth and warming both minds and bodies, it fosters virtue, and purifies from vice. She, I say, is a glorious and most wonderful star, of necessity raised above this great and broad sea, glittering with her merit, and giving light by her example.

O you, who realize that in the rushing tide of this world you are bobbing about amid storms and tempests rather than walking on land, turn not your eyes away from the light of this star if you do not wish to be lost in the storm. If the winds of temptations blow up, if you are running over mountains of tribulations, look up to this star; call on Mary! If you are being tossed about on the waves of pride, of ambition, of detraction, of envy, look up to this star; call on Mary! If wrath or avarice or the snare of the flesh shall strike against the ship of the mind, look up to Mary! If, when overwhelmed by the immensity of your crimes, when ashamed by the ugliness of your conscience, when frightened by horror for the Judgment, you begin to sink into the depths of sorrow, into the abyss of despair, think of Mary!

In dangers, in trials, in matters of doubt, think of Mary; call on Mary! Let her not depart from your mouth; let her not leave your heart, and, that you may gain the help of her prayer, do not forsake the example of her life. In following her, you will not stray; praying to her, you will not despair; when thinking on her, you will not be in error. If she holds you, you will not fall; in her protection, you will have no fear; with her as your leader, you will not faint in the way; through her kindness, you will arrive at port; and then you will realize yourself how deservedly it was declared: "And the Virgin's name was Mary." —This venerable name, being indeed already honored by a special rite in certain sections of the Christian world, the Roman Pontiff, Innocent XI, in memory of the victory obtained at Vienna in Austria under the protection of the same Virgin Mary over that awful tyranny of the Turks which had weighed on the necks of the Christian people, commanded this same name to be venerated every year throughout the universal Church as a lasting monument to such a great favor.

℟. Thou art blessed, O Virgin Mary, who didst bear the Lord, Creator of the world: * Thou didst bring forth Him who made thee, and thou remainest a Virgin forever. ℣. Hail, Mary, full of grace: the Lord is with thee. Thou didst. Glory. Thou didst.

III Nocturn

The reading of the holy Gospel according to St. Luke

At that time, the angel Gabriel was sent from God to a town of Galilee called Nazareth, to a virgin betrothed to a man named Joseph, of the house of David, and the virgin's name was Mary. And so forth.

Homily of St. Peter Chrysologus

You have heard today, dearest brethren, the Angel conferring with a woman about mankind's redemption. You have heard that it was to be effected that man should return to life over the same course by which he had fallen to his death. He takes counsel, an Angel takes counsel with Mary with regard to the salvation of man, because an Angel had plotted with Eve for his ruin. You have heard the Angel laying out, in his indescribable way, from the clay of our flesh a temple for the Divine Majesty. You have heard that God is to be placed on earth, and man in heaven through an incomprehensible mystery. You have heard that, in an unheard of manner, God and man are to be joined in one body. You have heard that the frail nature of our flesh is to be strengthened through the Angel's exhortation so as to support all the glory of the Godhead.

Finally, lest the fine sand of our body should give way in Mary to the great burden of the heavenly structure, and in the Virgin the tender shoot which was to bear the fruit of the whole human race be broken, the Angel's word, in order to put all fear to flight, immediately anticipates it by saying: "Fear not, Mary."

Through her name the dignity of the Virgin is announced before its cause, for *Mary* in the Hebrew language is translated *Queen* in ours. Consequently the Angel calls her *Queen* so that the fear of a slave's condition should depart from the Mother of our Lord, whom the very authority of her Offspring caused and ordered to be born and to be called *Queen*. "Fear not, Mary, for thou hast found grace with God." It is true that one who has found grace knows no fear. "Thou hast found grace."

Blessed is she who alone among all mankind merited, in preference to all women, to hear: "Thou hast found grace." How great a grace? He had told her just before how great it was. "Full!" And wholly full of that grace which in a profuse shower was to pour forth upon, and into all creation! "Thou hast found grace with God." When he spoke these things, the Angel himself wondered either at the fact that only a woman, or all men through a woman, had merited life; the Angel was astonished that the whole God, for whom all creation together was too limited, should come into the narrow confines of a Virgin's womb. Hence it is that the Angel tarries; hence it is that he fittingly calls her *Virgin,* speaks to her of grace, scarcely explains the mystery to her, but after many anxious moments calms her soul, that she may the better understand.

℟. All generations shall call me blessed, * Because the Lord who is mighty hath done great things to me, and holy is His name. ℣. And His mercy is from generation unto generations to them that fear Him. Because. Glory. Because.

✠ Continuation of the holy Gospel according to St. Luke.—
At that time the angel Gabriel was sent from God to a town of Galilee called Nazareth, to a virgin betrothed to a man named Joseph, of the house of David, and the virgin's name was Mary. And when the angel had come to her, he said, "Hail, full of grace, the Lord is with thee. Blessed art thou among women." When she had seen him she was troubled at his word, and kept pondering what manner of greeting this might be.

And the angel said to her, "Do not be afraid, Mary, for thou hast found grace with God. And behold, thou shalt conceive in thy womb and shalt bring forth a son; and thou shalt call his name Jesus. He shall be great, and shall be called the Son of the Most High; and the Lord God will give him the throne of David his father, and he shall be king over the house of Jacob forever; and of his kingdom there shall be no end."

But Mary said to the angel, "How shall this happen, since I do not know man?"

And the angel answered and said to her, "The Holy Spirit shall come upon thee and the power of the Most High shall overshadow thee; and therefore the Holy One to be born shall be called the Son of God. And behold, Elizabeth thy kinswoman also has conceived a son in her old age, and she who was called barren is now in her sixth month; for nothing shall be impossible with God."

But Mary said, "Behold the handmaid of the Lord; be it done to me according to thy word."

Let Us Pray

Grant, we beseech Thee, O almighty God, that Thy faithful may always rejoice under the protection of the most holy name of the Virgin Mary, and by her loving intercession be freed from all evils on earth and merit to come to the eternal joys in heaven. Through our Lord.

September 14

EXALTATION OF THE HOLY CROSS

I Nocturn

From the Book of Numbers, c. 21, 1 - 9

II Nocturn

Chosroes, King of the Persians, having in the last days of the reign of the Emperor Phocas invaded Egypt and Africa, captured Jerusalem, where he killed thousands of Christians and took away to Persia the cross of our Savior which Helena had placed on Mount Calvary. The successor of Phocas, Heraclius, because of the hardships and outrages caused by the war, sought to make peace, but Chosroes, carried away by a desire for conquest, would not grant it, even upon unjust terms. Heraclius, therefore, placed in this very uncomfortable position, earnestly begged help from God by prayer and fasting. By divine inspiration he raised an army, met the enemy in battle, and overcame three of Chosroes' generals and their armies.

Crushed by these defeats, Chosroes fled, and when about to cross the Tigris, he proclaimed his younger son Medarses co-ruler of his kingdom. This excited envy in the heart of the elder son, Siroes, who then formed a conspiracy to murder his father and brother. Soon after they had come home he carried out his plan, and obtained the kingdom from Heraclius under certain conditions, the first of which was that he should return the true cross of Christ the Lord.

The cross was thus received back after having been in the hands of the Persians for fourteen years. Heraclius came to Jerusalem, bearing the cross in solemn procession to the Mount unto which Christ had borne it. This event was marked by a wonderful miracle. For Heraclius, richly adorned with gold and jewels, was forced to stop at the gateway which leads to Mount Calvary, and the more he tried to go forward the more he seemed to be held back.

Heraclius and all those present were greatly amazed. Then Zacharias, the Patriarch of Jerusalem, said: "Consider, O Emperor, how little you imitate the poverty and humility of the Savior by carrying the cross in triumphal robes." Heraclius then cast away his princely garments and took off his shoes from his feet, and, dressed in a mean garment, he easily completed the rest of the way. Thus the cross was once more set on Calvary in the same place whence the Persians had carried it away. The commemoration of this occasion when the cross had been replaced by Heraclius in the same spot where it had been planted by our Lord caused the feast of the Exaltation of the Holy Cross, which from that day was celebrated annually, to acquire a more illustrious significance.

℟. It behooveth us to glory in the Cross of our Lord Jesus Christ, in whom is our salvation, life, and resurrection: * By whom we have been saved and delivered. ℣. We adore Thy Cross, O Lord, and we remember Thy glorious Passion. By whom. Glory. By whom.

III Nocturn

The reading of the holy Gospel according to St. John

At that time Jesus said to the multitudes of the Jews: "Now is the judgment of the world; now will the prince of the world be cast out." And so forth.

Homily of St. Leo, Pope

At the lifting up of Christ upon the cross, dearly beloved, there comes to the mind's eye not only the image which was in the eyes of those wicked men to whom it was said by Moses: "And thy life will be hanging before thine eyes, and thou wilt fear day and night, and thou wilt have no trust in thy life." For these men were able to think of nothing concerning the crucified Lord save their own crime, having not that fear whereby true confidence is justified, but that whereby a wicked conscience is tormented.

But may our understanding, which the Spirit of truth enlightens, accept with a clean and cheerful heart the glory of the cross that shines over heaven and earth; and with spiritual insight may it see what it was that the Lord, speaking of the approach of His Passion, said: "Now is the judgment of the world, now shall the prince of this world be cast out. And I, if I be lifted up from the earth, will draw all things to myself." O wondrous power of the cross, O unspeakable glory of the Passion, in which there is at once the Lord's tribunal, the judgment of the world and the power of the Crucified. For, O Lord, Thou hast drawn all things to Thyself; and when all the day long Thou didst stretch forth Thy hands to a people unbelieving and gainsaying Thee, the whole world received understanding to praise Thy Majesty.

Thou, O Lord, hast drawn all things to Thyself, when in execration of the Jews' crime all the elements gave one sentence: the lights of heaven were overcast; day turned to night; the earth too was shaken with unaccustomed tremors, and all creation denied its service to the impious. Thou, O Lord, didst draw all things to Thyself, for with the rending of the Temple veil the Holy of Holies was taken from unworthy priests, that thus the figure might be turned into the truth, prophecy to its fulfillment, and the Law to the Gospel.

Thou, O Lord didst draw all things to Thyself, that what was hidden under shadowy symbols in the one temple of Judea might be devoutly celebrated in every place as a full and open reality. For now the order of Levites is nobler, the dignity of the Elders is ampler, and the anointment of priests more sacred; for Thy cross, the fount of all blessings, is the cause of all graces. By it is given to those who believe, strength in their weakness, glory in their shame, life in death. Now that the diversity of animal sacrifices is ended, the one offering of Thy body and blood fully supplies for the variety of sacrifices. For Thou art the true Lamb of God, who takest away the sins of the world; and so in Thyself dost Thou fulfill all mysteries, that as there is a single sacrifice for all the victims, so there will be but one kingdom from every tribe and kindred.

℞. As Moses lifted up the serpent in the desert, so must the Son of Man be lifted up: * That whosoever believeth in Him may not perish, but may have life everlasting. ℣. For God did not send His Son into the world to judge the world, but that the world might be saved by Him. That. Glory. That.

✠ Continuation of the holy Gospel according to St. John.—At that time Jesus said to the multitudes of the Jews: "Now is the judgment of the world; now will the prince of the world be cast out. And I, if I be lifted up from the earth, will draw all things to myself." Now he said this signifying by what death he was to die. The crowd answered him, "We have heard from the Law that the Christ abides forever. And how canst thou say, 'The Son of Man must be lifted up'? Who is this Son of Man?" Jesus therefore said to them, "Yet a little while the light is among you. Walk while you have the light, that darkness may not overtake you. He who walks in the darkness does not know where he goes. While you have the light, believe in the light, that you may become sons of light."

Let Us Pray

O God, who on this day dost gladden us by the annual feast of the Exaltation of the Holy Cross, grant, we beseech Thee, that we who understand its mystery upon this earth may merit the reward of its redemption in heaven. Through the same Jesus Christ.

September 15

SEVEN DOLORS OF THE BLESSED VIRGIN MARY

I Nocturn

From Jeremias the Prophet, Lam., c. 1, 2 and 20 - 21; c. 2, 13 and 15 - 18

II Nocturn

Sermon of St. Bernard, Abbot

The Virgin's martyrdom is marked both in the prophecy of Simeon and in the very account of our Lord's Passion. He "is set (so the holy old man speaks of the Child Jesus) for a sign which shall be contradicted; and thine own soul a sword shall pierce"—this he said to Mary. Verily, O blessed Mother, it has pierced thy soul; for only in passing through thy soul could it enter the flesh of thy Son. And, in fact, after thy Jesus had breathed forth His spirit, the cruel lance which opened His side did not in the least touch His soul; rather, it pierced thy soul. His soul, to be sure, was no longer there, but thine could not in the least be wrenched from its place.

Thus the force of sorrow transfixed thy soul, so that we do not in the least undeservedly call thee a martyr, in whom the spiritual suffering of compassion wholly exceeded the sense of bodily suffering. Was not that word, "Woman, behold thy son," indeed a sword, truly piercing thy soul and reaching even to the separation of thy soul and spirit? What an exchange! John is given to you in place of Jesus; the servant for the Lord, the disciple for the Master, the son of Zebedee for the Son of God, a pure man for the true God! How could this utterance not pierce thy most affectionate soul when the bare remembrance cleaves our hearts, though they are of stone, though they are of iron?

Do not be astonished, brethren, that Mary is declared to have been a martyr in soul. He is to be wondered at who does not remember having heard Paul recalling that among the greatest crimes of the Gentiles was the fact that they were without affection. This was far from Mary's heart; may it be far from her unworthy servants.

Yet someone may perhaps say: "Did she not know that He was to die?" Undoubtedly! "Did she not hope that He would arise forthwith?" Most confidently she did! "Despite these things, does she grieve over Him when crucified?" Yes, vehemently! On the other hand, who are you, my brother, or whence your wisdom that you should marvel more at Mary's suffering with Him, than at the Son suffering for Mary? He could truly die in body; was not she able to die with Him in heart? Charity, "greater than which no man hath," accomplishes the one thing; charity, like to which no other had after her, likewise effects the other.

℟. Jesus, bearing His own cross, went forth. * And there followed Him a company of women who bewailed and lamented Him. ℣. Daughters of Jerusalem, weep for yourselves and for your children. And there followed. Glory. And there followed.

III Nocturn

The reading of the holy Gospel according to St. John

At that time there were standing by the cross of Jesus his mother and his mother's sister, Mary of Cleophas, and Mary Magdalene. And so forth.

Homily of St. Ambrose, Bishop

There stood by the cross His Mother, and, though the men fled away, she stood there unafraid. Behold how the Mother of Jesus, without changing her disposition of soul, was able to put aside her natural timidity.

With loving eyes she gazed upon the wounds of her Son, through which she knew redemption would come to all men. The Mother who was unafraid of the executioner looked upon the not inglorious sight. The Son hung on the cross, the Mother offered herself to the persecutors.

Mary, the Mother of the Lord, stood by the cross of her Son. No one but St. John the Evangelist has taught me this. The other Evangelists have recorded that when the Lord suffered the earth quaked, the heavens were veiled in darkness, the sun was hidden, the thief, after a good confession, was received into paradise.

John has taught us what the others have not: how, hanging upon the cross, He addressed His Mother. It is reckoned by John of greater importance that He, the Conqueror of suffering, should have tendered this consideration of filial piety to His Mother than that He bestowed the Kingdom of Heaven. For if it was a pious act that pardon was granted to the thief, it is a sign of a far more fruitful piety that the Mother is honored by her Son with so much affection.

℟. What were thy feelings, O Mother of sorrows, * When Joseph wrapped thy Son in linen and laid Him in the sepulchre? ℣. Attend and see if there be any sorrow like to my sorrow. When. Glory. When.

✠ Continuation of the holy Gospel according to St. John.—At that time there were standing by the cross of Jesus his mother and his mother's sister, Mary of Cleophas, and Mary Magdalene. When Jesus, therefore, saw his mother and the disciple standing by, whom he loved, he said to his mother, "Woman, behold thy son." Then he said to the disciple, "Behold thy mother." And from that hour the disciple took her into his home.

Let Us Pray

O God, in whose Passion, according to prophecy of Simeon, the sword of sorrow pierced the most tender soul of the glorious Virgin Mother Mary, mercifully grant that we who devoutly venerate her sorrows may receive the blessed fruits of Thy Passion: who livest and reignest with God the Father.

September 20

VIGIL OF ST. MATTHEW, APOSTLE

The reading of the holy Gospel according to St. Luke

At that time Jesus saw a publican, named Levi, sitting in the tax-collector's place, and he said to him, "Follow me." And so forth.

Homily of St. Ambrose, Bishop

The call of a publican, whom He orders to follow not by bodily steps, but with the affection of his mind, is mystical. And so he, who before was greedy for gain and turned the labors and dangers undergone by seamen to his own profit, called by a word, he who stole the goods of others, now leaves his own. Relinquishing that vile seat, he follows after the Lord with his whole mind. He also makes preparations for a great feast; for he who receives Christ in the dwelling of his soul is fed with the greatest delights and the most sublime joys.

And so the Lord willingly enters and reclines in the affection of him who has believed. But again the envy of the wicked is aroused and an image of future punishment shown. For while the faithful are feasting and reclining in the Kingdom of Heaven, the wicked will be tormented with hunger. At the same time it is shown how great is the difference between those zealous for the Law and those zealous for Grace, because those who follow the Law will suffer an eternal hunger for spiritual food; those, however, who have received the word in the interior of their soul, refreshed by an abundance of heavenly food and drink, can neither hunger nor thirst.

And therefore those who fasted in their souls murmured, saying: "Why doth he eat and drink with publicans and sinners?" This is the voice of the serpent. For the serpent first spoke thus, saying to Eve: "Why hath God commanded you that you should not eat of every tree?" Therefore they who say, "Why doth he eat and drink with publicans and sinners?" spread abroad the poison of their father. Therefore, since the Lord ate with sinners, He did not forbid us to eat with pagans, for He said, "They who are in health need not a physician, but they who are sick."

September 21

ST. MATTHEW, APOSTLE AND EVANGELIST

I Nocturn

From the Book of Ezechiel the Prophet, c. 1, 1 - 13

II Nocturn

Matthew, known also as Levi, an Apostle and Evangelist, being called by Christ as he sat in the custom-house at Capharnaum, followed Him immediately; likewise he invited Him with the rest of His disciples to a banquet. After Christ's Resurrection, and before journeying to the province which had been allotted to him to evangelize, Matthew first wrote in Judea (because of those of the circumcision who had believed) the Gospel of Jesus Christ in Hebrew. Soon afterwards, going into Ethiopia, he preached the Gospel and confirmed his preaching with many miracles.

Thus, particularly through the miracle in which he brought the king's daughter back to life, he converted her father, the king, and his wife, together with the whole province, to belief in Christ. But when the king died, Hirtacus, his successor, who had desired that Iphigenia, the king's daughter, be given to him in marriage, commanded that Matthew, by whose instigation she had vowed virginity to God and remained faithful in her holy promise, be slain while celebrating the Mysteries at the altar. Thus on September 21, he consummated his apostolic office by a glorious martyrdom. His body, which was carried to Salerno and afterwards placed by Pope Gregory VII in a church dedicated in his name, is there honored by many people and with great esteem.

From the Commentary of St. Gregory, Pope, on the Prophet Ezechiel

The four sacred animals which were foreseen in the spirit of prophecy as future beings are described in an ingenious manner where it is said: "Every one had four faces, and every one four wings." What is expressed by the face, except knowledge? And what by the wings, but a soaring flight? For truly everyone is known by his face, while by means of their wings the bodies of the birds are carried on high. Thus the face pertains to faith; the wings, to contemplation. For by faith are we known by Almighty God, as He Himself declares of His sheep: "I am the good shepherd; and I know mine, and mine know me." A little further on He says: "I know whom I have chosen."

But, by contemplation, through which we are raised above ourselves, we are, as it were, lifted into the air. So "everyone had four faces"—because, if you inquire what Matthew thinks in regard to our Lord's Incarnation, he thinks precisely the same as Mark, Luke, and John. If you ask what John thinks, it is, beyond doubt, the same that Luke, Mark, and Matthew think. If you ask what Mark thinks, it is the same that Matthew, John, and Luke think. If you inquire about Luke, he thinks the same as John, Matthew, and Mark.

℟. Blessed are ye when men shall revile and persecute you and speak all that is evil against you, untruly, for My sake: * Be glad and rejoice, for your reward is very great in heaven. ℣. When men shall hate you and when they shall separate you and reproach you and cast out your name as evil, for the Son of Man's sake. Be glad. Glory. Be glad.

III Nocturn

The reading of the holy Gospel according to St. Matthew

At that time Jesus saw a man named Matthew sitting in the tax-collector's place, and said to him, "Follow me." And so forth.

Homily of St. Jerome, Priest

The other Evangelists, because of their veneration and honor for Matthew, did not want to call him by his common name, so they said *Levi;* and hence he is known by a double name. But Matthew (according to that which was said by Solomon: "The just man is the accuser of himself in the beginning of his speech"; and in another place: "Declare your sins that you may be justified") called himself *Matthew* and *a publican,* that he might show to his readers that no one ought to despair of salvation if he is converted to better ways, since he himself was suddenly changed from a publican to an Apostle.

Although such great miracles and such great signs preceded their calling—and there is no doubt that the apostles saw them before they believed—Porphyrius and Julian Augustus asserted concerning this passage either the ignorance of a lying historian or the folly of those who immediately followed after the Savior, as if they might have followed without reason any man at all who had called to them.

Certainly the splendor itself and the majesty of the hidden Divinity which shone even in His countenance could have drawn from the first glance those who beheld it. For if it is declared that in a magnet-stone and in amber rods there is such strength that they draw to themselves rings, straws, and splinters, how much more could the Lord of all creatures draw to Himself those whom He called!

"And it came to pass, as he was sitting at meat in the house, behold, many publicans and sinners came and sat down with Jesus and his disciples." They saw that a publican had been turned from his sins to better ways, that he found the way of penance, and for that reason they also did not despair of salvation. Still, they did not come to Jesus while remaining in their former sins, as the Pharisees and Scribes murmured, but doing penance, as the following word of our Lord shows, saying: "I will have mercy, and not sacrifice. For I am not come to call the just, but the sinners." Our Lord attended the banquet of sinners so that He might have occasion to teach and might offer spiritual food to those who had invited Him.

℟. These are the holy men whom the Lord hath chosen in charity unfeigned, and hath given them everlasting glory: * Whose teaching enlightens the Church, as the sun does the moon. ℣. By faith the Saints conquered kingdoms and wrought justice. Whose. Glory. Whose.

✠ Continuation of the holy Gospel according to St. Matthew.— At that time Jesus saw a man named Matthew sitting in the tax-collector's place, and said to him, "Follow me." And he arose and followed him. And it came to pass as he was at table in the house, that, behold, many publicans and sinners came to the table with Jesus and his disciples. And the Pharisees seeing it, said to his disciples, "Why does your master eat with publicans and sinners?" But Jesus heard it, and said, "It is not the healthy who need a physician, but they who are sick. But go, and learn what this means: 'I desire mercy, and not sacrifice.' For I have come to call sinners, not the just."

LET US PRAY

May we be assisted by the prayers of Thy blessed Apostle and Evangelist Matthew, we beseech Thee, O Lord, that what we cannot obtain by our own merits, may be given to us through his intercession. Through our Lord.

September 29
DEDICATION OF ST. MICHAEL THE ARCHANGEL
I Nocturn
From the Book of Daniel, c. 7, 9 - 11; c. 10, 4 - 14
II Nocturn
Sermon of St. Gregory, Pope

We say there are nine choirs of angels, because we know as a matter of fact by the testimony of the Sacred Word that there are Angels, Archangels, Virtues, Powers, Principalities, Dominations, Thrones, Cherubim, and Seraphim. Almost all the pages of Holy Scripture testify that there are Angels and Archangels; the books of the prophets, as is known, often make mention of the Cherubim and Seraphim. The Apostle Paul also enumerates to the Ephesians the names of four choirs, saying: "Above all Principality and Power and Virtue and Domination." Again, when writing to the Colossians, he declares: "Whether Thrones or Powers or Principalities or Dominations." If, therefore, to the first four, which he spoke of to the Ephesians, the Thrones are added, there are five choirs, and when the Angels and Archangels, the Cherubim and Seraphim are joined to these, without doubt there are found to be nine choirs of angels.

However, we should know that *angel* is the name of their office, not of their nature. For these holy spirits of the heavenly fatherland are indeed ever spirits, but by no means can they always be called angels, for they are angels only when something is announced through them. Whence it is also said by the Psalmist, "He made the spirits his angels," as if he would clearly state, "Those whom He ever has as spirits, He also makes angels when He desires."

Those, however, who announce less important things are called angels, and those who announce the special things, archangels. Hence it is that to the Virgin Mary an angel was not sent, but the Archangel Gabriel. For it was certainly fitting that for this ministry the greatest Angel should come to announce the greatest of all things. For that reason they are also entitled with individual names, so that by these names it may be designated what they do. For Michael means: *Who is like unto God;* Gabriel. *Fortitude of God;* and Raphael: *Medicine of God.*

And as often as some wonderful mystery is enacted, Michael is shown to be sent, in order that from his act and his name it might be given to be understood that no one can do what God is able to perform. Wherefore, even the old enemy, who through his pride desired to be like unto God, saying, "I shall ascend into the heavens; I shall raise my throne above the stars of the sky; I shall be like to the Most High," when he will, according to revelation, be left at the end of the world in his own strength to be crushed in the utmost misery, will wage battle with the Archangel Michael, as it is declared by John: "A battle was waged with the Archangel Michael." Gabriel also, who is called *Fortitude of God*, was sent to Mary. He came indeed to announce Him who, to destroy the ethereal spirits, deigned to appear as a lowly man. Likewise, Raphael is interpreted *Medicine of God*, as we have said, for when he touched the eyes of Tobias, as it were through the office of healing, he brushed away the darkness of his blindness.

℟. The Archangel Michael, to whose care God had entrusted the souls of the blessed, came with a multitude of Angels, * To lead them to the joys of Paradise. ℣. From heaven, O Lord, send forth Thy Holy Spirit: the Spirit of wisdom and of understanding. To lead. Glory. To lead.

III Nocturn

The reading of the holy Gospel according to St. Matthew

At that time the disciples came to Jesus, saying, "Who then is greatest in the kingdom of heaven?" And so forth.

Homily of St. Jerome, Priest

After the stater had been found and the tribute paid, what is it that is sought by this unexpected question of the apostles: "Who, thinkest thou, is the greater in the kingdom of heaven?" Since they had seen the same tribute paid for Peter as for the Lord, they concluded from the equality of the price that Peter, who had been equal to the Lord in the payment of the tribute, was preferred to all the apostles; therefore they asked who would be greater in the Kingdom of Heaven. And Jesus, seeing their thoughts and knowing the source of their error, by the contrast of humility wished to cure their desire for glory.

"And if thy hand or thy foot scandalize thee, cut it off and cast it from thee." It must needs be that scandals come, but woe to that man who, although it must be that scandal be in the world, yet by his own sin causes it to come. Therefore let every affection be cut off and every dangerous relation be avoided, lest by reason of their affection all believers should be exposed to scandals.

If, He says, someone is as closely joined to you as your hand, foot or eye, and is of service, and solicitous, and quick in judgment, but causes scandal to you, and by the perversity of his morals draws you into hell, it is better that you be without his friendship and carnal services, lest while you wish to profit by your relatives and friends, you find the cause of your ruin.

"I say to you, that their angels in heaven always see the face of my Father." He said before, in the figure of the hand, the foot and the eye, that all relationships and friendships which might cause scandal must be cut off; then He moderates the austerity of this sentence by adding the counsel, saying: "See that you do not despise one of these little ones." I command severity, He says, recalling at the same time that mercy is to be united with it, "because their angels in heaven always see the face of my Father." Great is the dignity of souls, that each one should have from the very hour of birth an angel delegated to guard it. Hence we read in the Apocalypse of St. John: "To the angel of Ephesus (and of the rest of the Churches) write these things." The Apostle also ordered that the heads of women be covered in churches because of the angels.

℟. The Archangel Michael came to the help of God's people: * He stood to defend the souls of the just. ℣. The Angel stood at the altar of the temple having a golden censer in his hand. He stood. Glory. He stood.

✠ Continuation of the holy Gospel according to St. Matthew.— At that time the disciples came to Jesus, saying, "Who then is greatest in the kingdom of heaven?" And Jesus called a little child to him, set it in the midst of them, and said, "Amen I say to you, unless you turn and become like little children, you will not enter the kingdom of heaven. Whoever, therefore, humbles himself as this little child, he is the greatest in the kingdom of heaven.

"And whoever receives one such little child for my sake, receives me. But whoever causes one of these little ones who believe in me to sin, it were better for him to have a great millstone hung around his neck, and to be drowned in the depths of the sea.

"Woe to the world because of scandals! For it must needs be that scandals come, but woe to the man through whom scandal does come! And if thy hand or thy foot is an occasion of sin to thee, cut it off and cast it from thee! It is better for thee to enter life maimed or lame, than, having two hands or two feet, to be cast into the everlasting fire. And if thy eye is an occasion of sin to thee, pluck it out and cast it from thee! It is better for thee to enter into life with one eye, than, having two eyes, to be cast into the hell of fire.

"See that you do not despise one of these little ones; for I tell you, their angels in heaven always behold the face of my Father in heaven."

Let Us Pray

O God, who dost wonderfully arrange the duties of both Angels and men, mercifully grant that our life here upon earth may be protected by those who always serve Thee in heaven. Through our Lord.

October 2

THE HOLY GUARDIAN ANGELS

I Nocturn

From the Book of Exodus, c. 23, 20 - 23 and from Zacharias the Prophet, c. 1, 7 - 11 and 13 - 16; c. 2, 1 - 5

II Nocturn

Sermon of St. Bernard, Abbot

"He hath given his angels charge over thee." O wonderful bounty and truly great love of charity! Who? For whom? Wherefore? What has He commanded? Let us study closely, brethren, and let us diligently commit to our memory this great mandate. Who is it that commands? Whose angels are they? Whose mandates do they fulfill? Whose will do they obey? In answer, "He hath given *his* angels charge over thee, to keep thee in all thy ways." And they do not hesitate even to lift thee up in their hands.

So the Supreme Majesty has given charge to the angels. Yes, He has given charge to His own angels. Think of it! To those sublime beings, who cling to Him so joyfully and intimately, to His very own He has given charge over you! Who are you? "What is man that thou art mindful of him? or the son of man that thou visitest him?" As if man were not rottenness, and the son of man a worm! Now why, do you think, has He given them charge over thee?—To guard thee!

With what great reverence should you treat this word! What devotion should you proffer it; what great confidence should you place in it. Reverence because of their presence; devotion because of their benevolence; confidence because of their solicitude. Walk carefully, in all thy ways, as one with whom the angels are present, as He has given them charge. In every lodging, at every corner, have reverence for thy Angel. Do not dare to do in his presence what you would not dare to do if I were there. Or do you doubt that he is present whom you do not behold? What if you should hear him? What if you should touch him? What if you should scent him? Remember that the presence of something is not proved only by the sight of things.

In this, therefore, brethren, let us affectionately love His angels as one day our future coheirs; meanwhile, however, as counselors and defenders appointed by the Father and placed over us. Why should we fear under such guardians? Those who keep us in all our ways can neither be overcome nor be deceived, much less deceive. They are faithful; they are prudent; they are powerful; why do we tremble? Let us only follow them, let us remain close to them, and in the protection of the God of heaven let us abide. As often, therefore, as a most serious temptation is perceived to weigh upon you and an excessive trial is threatening, call to your guard, your leader, your helper in your needs, in your tribulation; cry to him and say: "Lord, save us; we perish!"

℞. In all their affliction He was not troubled: * And the Angel of His presence saved them. ℣. In His love and in His mercy He redeemed them, and He carried them and lifted them up all the days of old. And the Angel. Glory. And the Angel.

III Nocturn

The reading of the holy Gospel according to St. Matthew

At that time the disciples came to Jesus, saying, "Who then is greatest in the kingdom of heaven?" And so forth.

Homily of St. Hilary, Bishop

The Lord teaches that only those who become children again can enter the Kingdom of Heaven; that is, the vices of our souls and bodies must be renounced by our practice of childlike simplicity. Now He has labelled as children all those who believe in Him with the faith they have from hearing His words. For children follow after their father, they love their mother, and they have no will to do evil to their neighbor; nor have they solicitude for the high opinion of others; they are not haughty; they neither hate others, nor tell lies; they believe what is told them, and what they hear they consider true.

Therefore we must turn our attention to the candor of infants, because with our attention centered on it, we will mirror the submissiveness of our Lord. "Woe to this world because of scandals." The abjectness of the Passion is a scandal to the world. For human ignorance is to the greatest extent fettered in this, that it does not wish to receive the Lord of eternal glory under the deformity of the cross. And what is so dangerous to the world as not to accept Christ?

On this account He says that it must needs be that scandals come, because to accomplish the mystery of regaining eternity for us the full humiliation of the Passion had to be fulfilled in Him. "Beware lest you despise one of these little ones who believe in me." The Lord has imposed the most excellent bond of mutual love towards those especially who have truly believed in Him. "For (because the Son of Man came to save what was lost) the angels of the little ones daily see God."

Therefore the Son of Man saves, the angels see God, and the angels of children are given charge of the prayers of the faithful. There is absolute proof that the angels have charge of them. Hence, the prayers of those saved through Christ are daily offered to God by the angels. Accordingly, he is with danger despised whose requests are carried to the eternal and invisible God by the eager service and ministry of the angels.

℞. In the sight of the Angels * I will sing unto Thee, O my God. ℣. I will worship towards Thy holy temple and give glory unto Thy name. I will sing. Glory. I will sing.

✠ Continuation of the holy Gospel according to St. Matthew.—At that time the disciples came to Jesus, saying, "Who then is greatest in the kingdom of heaven?" And Jesus called a little child to him, set it in the midst of them, and said, "Amen I say to you, unless you turn and become like little children, you will not enter the kingdom of heaven. Whoever, therefore, humbles himself as this little child, he is the greatest in the kingdom of heaven.

"And whoever receives one such little child for my sake, receives me. But whoever causes one of these little ones who believe in me to sin, it were better for him to have a great millstone hung around his neck, and to be drowned in the depths of the sea.

"Woe to the world because of scandals! For it must needs be that scandals come, but woe to the man through whom scandal does come! And if thy hand or thy foot is an occasion of sin to thee, cut it off and cast it from thee! It is better for thee to enter life maimed or lame, than, having two hands or two feet, to be cast into the everlasting fire. And if thy eye is an occasion of sin to thee, pluck it out and cast it from thee! It is better for thee to enter into life with one eye, than, having two eyes, to be cast into the hell of fire.

"See that you do not despise one of these little ones; for I tell you, their angels in heaven always behold the face of my Father in heaven."

Let Us Pray

O God, who in Thy wonderful providence deignest to send Thy holy Angels to protect us, grant that those who pray to Thee may be defended on earth by Thy Angels and rejoice for all eternity in their company. Through our Lord.

October 5
ST. PLACID AND COMPANIONS

I Nocturn

*From the Epistle of St. Paul the Apostle to the Romans,
c. 8, 12 - 19 and 28 - 39*

II Nocturn
Sermon of St. Augustine, Bishop

Just as often as we celebrate, dearly beloved brethren, the solemnities of the holy martyrs, let us so expect to obtain from the Lord, through their intercession, temporal blessings, that we may, by imitating them, merit to attain to things eternal. For the joys of the holy martyrs' feasts are solemnized in truth by those persons who follow the example of these blessed ones.

The holy feasts of the martyrs are an exhortation to martyrdom, in that one should not be loathe to imitate what he loves to celebrate. We wish to rejoice with the saints, yet do not want to endure the suffering of this world with them. But, in fine, the one who does not will to imitate the holy martyrs, in so far as he is able, cannot arrive at their happiness.

The Apostle Paul likewise tell us this, saying: "As you are partakers of the sufferings, so shall you be also of the consolations." And our Lord in the Gospel states: "If the world hate you, know ye that it hath hated me before you." He refuses to live in the Body who does not wish to endure hatred with its Head.

Maybe someone will say: "And who is the man that can follow in the footsteps of the blessed martyrs?" To such a one I answer that we can imitate not only the martyrs, but even, with His aid, our Lord Himself, if we want to. Listen not to me, but to the Lord Himself, crying out to the human race: "Learn of me, because I am meek and humble of heart." And listen to the Apostle Peter telling you: "Christ ... suffered for us, leaving us an example that we should follow His steps."

℟. As gold in the furnace the Lord hath proved His chosen ones, and as a victim of a holocaust He hath received them; and in time there shall be no respect had to them, * For grace and peace is to the elect of God. ℣. They that trust in Him shall understand the truth, and they that are faithful in love shall rest in Him. For. Glory. For.

III Nocturn

The reading of the holy Gospel according to St. John

At that time Jesus said to his disciples: "Amen, amen, I say to you, unless the grain of wheat fall into the ground and die, it remains alone." And so forth.

Homily of St. Augustine, Bishop

Your faith recognizes the seed which falls into the earth, dies, and is multiplied. I say that your faith recognizes this seed because it dwells in your minds. What Christ has said concerning Himself applies also to the Christian. But evidently from that seed which has died and was multiplied, many seeds were scattered abroad over the earth. Moreover, we have the happiness of seeing, rejoicing, and of being among the harvest which that scattered seed has yielded, but only if we enjoy the grace of being gathered into the barns. The rain is indeed used for nourishment by all until the wheat gets ripe. But not all that grew so well is fit to be gathered, though it all grew in the same field and was ripened by the same air.

But now comes the reaping time, and the separation of the wheat from the chaff. Just as the grain is cleansed when thrown into the air, so let there be a separation in our lives of the good from the bad habits before the Eternal Reaper comes. Listen to me, ye holy grains, for I do not doubt that you are such; for if I doubt, neither shall I myself be a grain; hear me therefore, listen to the Chief Grain who speaks through me. You should not love your lives in this world. If you have loved them, love them no longer; so that by not loving your lives you may serve Him better and love Him more. "He that loveth his life in this world shall lose it." Thus speaks the Grain which has fallen into the earth and died in order to be multiplied. Hear Him, for He lieth not. What He admonishes us to do, He Himself has done; what He has taught by His commandments, He has surpassed by His example. Christ did not love His earthly life, because for this very reason did He come, to give it up, to lay it down for us. And when He so willed, He took it up again.

Surely we all, dearest brethren, desire life and truth. Yet, where shall we find them? Where shall we search for them? By whatever way we may go—although we cannot attain to actual possession, but only have them in our mind by faith—yet we always stretch forward towards the Life and Truth. Now this is Christ. Do you want to know the way? "I am the Way," He says. To whom do you want to go? "I am the Truth and the Life." Behold, this is what the martyrs loved, and this is why they despised present and transitory things. We need not wonder at their fortitude, because love conquers all pain. Therefore, following the footsteps of the martyrs and our eyes intently fixed upon their Head, Christ, let us not fear this hard path if we truly desire to come to so great a good. He who has promised it cannot deceive us, for He is truth and fidelity itself.

Let us therefore show a clean conscience: "Because of the words of Thy mouth, O Lord, I have kept on hard ways." Why do you fear hard ways, sufferings and trials? He Himself has trod them. You answer: "But He was God." The Apostles have trod them. You answer: "But they were Apostles." Granted, but I reply: Many men have trod them after them, and women also. Blush therefore. If you have passed through suffering in your old age, fear not death, for you are already near to it. If you are young, many youths also, both boys and girls, who had hoped to live, have passed through it. How, then, does the way which so many have marked out for us still seem hard? Hence on this feast day I most earnestly admonish you not to celebrate the feasts of these martyrs in vain. But what we celebrate in their feasts out of love, we must also strive to imitate and be like in faith and practice.

℟. The souls of the just are in the hands of God, and the torments of death shall not touch them: In the eyes of the unwise they seemed to die: * But they are in peace. ℣. God tried them and found them worthy of Himself. But. Glory. But.

✠ Continuation of the holy Gospel according to St. John.— At that time Jesus said to his disciples: "Amen, amen, I say to you, unless the grain of wheat fall into the ground and die, it remains alone. But if it die, it brings forth much fruit. He who loves his life, loses it; and he who hates his life in this world, keeps it unto life everlasting. If anyone serve me, let him follow me; and where I am there also shall my servant be. If anyone serve me, my Father will honor him."

Let Us Pray

O almighty and eternal God, who dost make us glad by the many feasts of Thy Saints, grant that we may be protected by those Saints in whose memory we rejoice. Through our Lord.

October 7
THE MOST HOLY ROSARY
I Nocturn
From the Book of Ecclesiasticus, c. 24, 11 - 22 and 24 - 31
II Nocturn

When the Albigensian heresy was impiously spreading throughout the region of Toulouse and daily sinking its roots more deeply, Saint Dominic, who had just laid the foundations of the Order of Preachers, became intent on rooting it out. That he might more powerfully promote this cause, he sought in earnest prayer the aid of the Blessed Virgin, whose dignity was impudently attacked by these errors, and to whom it is given to destroy all heresies in the whole world. When he was admonished by her to make known the Rosary to the nations as a signal defense against heresies and vices, it is wonderful with how much fervor of soul and with what happy success he executed this duty enjoined upon him. Now the Rosary is a definite formula of praying, in which we distinguish fifteen decades of *Hail Marys*, interspersed with the *Our Father*, and for each decade we recall by holy meditation a mystery of our Redemption. Hence, since that time this holy method of praying began to be promulgated and wonderfully increased through the efforts of Saint Dominic, whom the holy Pontiffs from time to time have affirmed in Apostolic letters to have been the institutor and author of this devotion.

Furthermore, innumerable fruits from this salutary institution have spread through all of Christendom, among which is reckoned rightly that victory which the most holy Pontiff, Pius V, and the Christian princes spurred on by him, gained over the most powerful Turkish tyrant at Lepanto. For since that victory was won on the very day on which the Confraternities of the most holy Rosary throughout the whole world were offering their usual supplications and were pouring forth their prayers according to their custom, the victory obtained is deservedly accorded to these prayers. Indeed, when Gregory XIII had also attested to this fact, in order that for so singular a blessing yearly thanks might be rendered everywhere in the world to the Blessed Virgin under the invocation of the Rosary, he proclaimed that in all churches in which there should be erected an altar of the Rosary, this Office should be perpetually celebrated with a double major rite. Other Popes also have granted almost innumerable indulgences to those who recite the Rosary and to the Confraternities of the Rosary.

Clement XI, however, considering the fact that in 1716 a similarly great victory over the innumerable forces of the Turks was gained in the kingdom of Hungary by Charles VI, emperor-elect of the Romans, on that day on which the feast of the Dedication of Our Lady of the Snow was celebrated, and that almost at the same time the Confraternity of the most holy Rosary was offering public and solemn prayer in the holy city, in which an immense concourse of people were taking part and with great devotion were pouring forth fervent prayers to God for the overthrow of the Turks and humbly imploring the powerful assistance of the Virgin Mother of God for the help of Christians, owing to all this, devoutly held the opinion that that victory, as also the relief a short time afterwards of the island of Corcyra, which was being besieged by those same Turks, was to be ascribed to the intercession of that same Blessed Virgin.

Wherefore, in order also that there might be an unceasing yearly reminder and thanksgiving for so extraordinary a favor, he extended this feast to the universal Church to be celebrated with the same rite. All these things Benedict XIII ordered to be inserted into the Roman Breviary. Moreover, Leo XIII, at a very stormy period in the history of the Church when for a long time a tempest of most pressing evils had raged, by a succession of Apostolic letters earnestly exhorted all the faithful of the world to the frequent use of the Rosary of Mary, more especially during the month of October, and also increased the rank of the rite of the annual feast and added the invocation of "the Queen of the most holy Rosary" to the Litany of Loretto; he also granted to the universal Church a proper office for the same solemnity. Let us, therefore, ever honor the most holy Mother of God by this devotion, which is so very acceptable to her, that she who, when called upon in the prayers of the Rosary, has so many times, for the sake of Christ's faithful, given their earthly enemies to destruction and ruin, may likewise grant that they may overcome the powers of hell.

℟. A great sign appeared in heaven: a woman clothed with the sun, and the moon under her feet, * And on her head a crown of twelve stars. ℣. Increase of graces shall be given to thy head, and a noble crown shall protect thee. And on. Glory. And on.

III Nocturn

The reading of the holy Gospel according to St. Luke

At that time the angel Gabriel was sent from God to a town of Galilee called Nazareth to a virgin betrothed to a man named Joseph, of the house of David, and the virgin's name was Mary. And so forth.

Homily of St. Bernard, Abbot

In commendation of her grace and for the destruction of human wisdom God deigned to take His body of a woman, who was also, however, a virgin, in order that He might render like to like, heal the contrary by contrary, pluck out the noxious thorn, and destroy the most powerful bond of sin.

Eve was the thorn; Mary appeared as the rose. Eve was the thorn by wounding; Mary, the rose in assuaging the desires of all. Eve was the thorn, inflicting death upon all; Mary, the rose, offering the lot of salvation unto all. Mary was a dazzling white rose through her virginity, a dark red rose because of her charity. Dazzling white in flesh, ruddy in mind; white by her pursuit of virtue, ruddy by crushing vice. Pure white through purifying her affections, ruddy by mortifying her flesh; dazzling white with love of God, ruddy with compassion of neighbor.

"The Word was made flesh," and dwells now among us. He dwells in our memory; He dwells in our thought, because He has condescended even unto the scope of our imagination. In what manner, do you say? Truly, lying in the crib, resting in the virginal lap, preaching on the mountains, spending the night in prayer, hanging on the cross, becoming pallid in death, being free among the dead, and ruling in hell; and even rising on the third day, and showing the place of the nails, the signs of victory, to the apostles; lastly, ascending before them to the mysteries of heaven. Which of these things cannot be considered truthfully, lovingly, holily?

On whichever of these mysteries I think, I think of God, and He is my God through all things. And so I have called it wisdom to meditate upon these things, and I judged it prudence to bring forth the memory of their sweetness, because from kernels of this sort the sacerdotal rod—which Mary, drawing out from heavenly fountains, has watered so copiously for us—has flowered forth in abundance. For she who received the Word from the very heart of the Father is indeed in heaven and above the angels.

℟. Arise, make haste, my love; for winter is now past, the rain is over and gone; * The flowers have appeared in our land. ℣. The Lord will give goodness, and our earth shall yield her fruit. The flowers. Glory. The flowers.

✠ Continuation of the holy Gospel according to St. Luke.— At that time the angel Gabriel was sent from God to a town of Galilee called Nazareth, to a virgin betrothed to a man named Joseph, of the house of David, and the virgin's name was Mary. And when the angel had come to her, he said, "Hail, full of grace, the Lord is with thee. Blessed are thou among women." When she had seen him she was troubled at his word, and kept pondering what manner of greeting this might be.

And the angel said to her, "Do not be afraid, Mary, for thou hast found grace with God. And behold, thou shalt conceive in thy womb and shalt bring forth a son; and thou shalt call his name Jesus. He shall be great, and shall be called the Son of the Most High; and the Lord God will give him the throne of David his father, and he shall be king over the house of Jacob forever; and of his kingdom there shall be no end."

But Mary said to the angel, "How shall this happen, since I do not know man?"

And the angel answered and said to her, "The Holy Spirit shall come upon thee and the power of the Most High shall overshadow thee; and therefore the Holy One to be born shall be called the Son of God. And behold, Elizabeth thy kinswoman also has conceived a son in her old age, and she who was called barren is now in her sixth month; for nothing shall be impossible with God."

But Mary said, "Behold the handmaid of the Lord; be it done to me according to thy word."

Let Us Pray

O God, whose only-begotten Son has merited for us by His Life, Death and Resurrection the rewards of eternal life, grant, we beseech Thee, that honoring these mysteries in the holy Rosary of the Blessed Virgin Mary, we may both imitate what they contain and receive what they promise. Through the same Jesus Christ.

October 11

MATERNITY OF THE BLESSED VIRGIN

I Nocturn

From the Book of Ecclesiasticus, c. 24, 5 - 23

II Nocturn

Sermon of St. Leo, Pope

A royal virgin of the tribe of David was chosen, who, in order to become pregnant with the holy Offspring, conceived the divine and human Infant in mind first rather than in body; and lest she, unacquainted with the celestial plan, be troubled at this unwonted communication, she learned by converse with the Angel what was to be accomplished in her through the Holy Spirit, nor did she consider it a loss of her maiden honor that she was soon to become the Mother of God. For why should she, to whom the efficacious power of the Almighty had been promised, despair concerning the novelty of her conception? Moreover, the faith of her who believed is confirmed even by the witnessing of a foregoing miracle. Elizabeth is granted an unexpected fecundity in order that it would not be doubted that He who had given pregnancy to the barren would also grant it to a virgin. Thereupon the Word, the Son of God, who in the beginning was with God, through whom all things were made and without whom nothing was made, was made man for the purpose of liberating mankind from everlasting death.

Jesus Christ our Lord, coming down from His throne in heaven, enters these lowest circumstances of human nature, and not departing from the Father's glory, is begotten in a new order by a new nativity. In a new order because, being invisible in His own nature, He became visible in ours; the Incomprehensible wished to be comprehended; abiding before time, He began to exist in time. By a new birth was He begotten—that is, conceived by a Virgin, born of a Virgin, without the concupiscence of a father's flesh, without injury to the mother's purity—because such a birth was becoming to the future Savior of men, who possessed in Himself the nature of human substance yet did not know the reproaches of human flesh. His birth is dissimilar to any other human birth, but His nature is identical; He is free, as we believe, from human necessity and intercourse; but it depended upon the divine power that a virgin should conceive, that a virgin should give birth, and that she should remain a virgin.

From the Acts of Pope Pius XI

When in 1931, amid the acclamations of the entire Catholic world, was celebrated the fifteenth centenary of the Council of Ephesus in which, during the pontificate of Pope Celestine, the Blessed Virgin Mary, of whom was born Jesus, had been proclaimed by the Fathers—contrary to the heresy of Nestorius—the Mother of God, the Supreme Pontiff, Pius XI, wished to perpetuate the memory of this most happy event by an enduring testimony of his love. Therefore, because there was already in the city a noble monument of the Ephesian pronouncement, out of his own munificence he had restored, together with the transverse wing of the Basilica, the triumphal arch in the Basilica of St. Mary Major on the Esquiline, which had been adorned by his predecessor Sixtus III with a marvelous mosaic, but which was being deteriorated by the ravages of time.

And since her true qualities were described by the encyclical letter of the Ecumenical Council of Ephesus, the unspeakable privilege of divine motherhood has reverently and profusely shed glory on the Blessed Virgin Mary, so that the doctrine of such a lofty mystery has set itself very deeply in the minds of the faithful. At one and the same time the doctrine proposes for our imitation Mary, the Mother of God, blessed among all women, and the Family of Nazareth as the noblest and supreme example of the dignity and sanctity of chaste wedlock, and of the care to be religiously expended on the education of youth. Finally, in order that a liturgical monument be not wanting, the Holy Father ordered that the feast of the divine maternity of the Blessed Virgin Mary together with the proper Mass and Office be celebrated yearly by the universal Church under the rite of a double of the second class.

℟. Blessed art thou among women and blessed is the fruit of thy womb: * Whence is this to me that the Mother of my Lord should come to me? ℣. He hath regarded the lowliness of His handmaid, and He that is mighty hath done great things to me. Whence. Glory. Whence.

III Nocturn

The reading of the holy Gospel according to St. Luke

At that time, when they were returning, the boy Jesus remained in Jerusalem, and his parents did not know it. And so forth.

Homily of St. Bernard, Abbot

Mary calls the God and Lord of angels her son, saying: "Son, why hast thou done so to us?" What angel would dare do this? It suffices for them, and they consider it a great thing that, although in their ordinary state they are spirits, nevertheless, by grace they have become and are called angels, as David testifies: "Who maketh the spirits His angels (messengers)." But Mary, knowing herself to be His mother, with confidence calls this Majesty, whom the angels serve with reverence, her Son. Nor did God disdain to be called that which He deigned to become. For shortly afterwards the Evangelist adds: "And he was subject to them." Who? To whom? God subject to man? God, I say, to whom the angels are subject, whom the Principalities and Powers obey, was subject to Mary.

Be filled with wonder at both, and decide which to wonder at most: the most benign condescension of the Son or the most excellent dignity of the Mother; each is an amazing thing, each a miracle. That God should obey a woman is humility unprecedented, and that a woman should command God is something sublime and without an equal. In the praises of virgins it is strikingly sung that they follow the Lamb whithersoever He goes. Of how great praise do you not think she is deserving who even precedes the Lamb? Learn, O man, to obey! Learn, slime of the earth, to be humbled! Learn, O dust, to give up thy will! The Evangelist, speaking of the Maker, says: "And he was subject to them." Blush, proud ashes; God humbles Himself, and dost thou exalt thyself? God has subjected Himself to men, and dost thou, in an effort to dominate men, place yourself above your Creator?

O happy Mary, to whom was wanting neither humility nor virginity. And indeed an unusual virginity which fecundity did not destroy, but rather made more glorious. Nor less outstanding was that humility which fruitful virginity did not take away, but increased. Truly incomparable in every way was that fecundity which both virginity and humility accompanied. Which of these facts is not admirable? Which not beyond compare? Which not outstanding? It is indeed a thing to wonder about if, in your consideration of these mysteries, you are not perplexed as to which of the two you should judge more worthy of your admiration: that is, whether fecundity in the Virgin or integrity in the Mother is more to be wondered at; the exalted dignity of the child, or, with such exalted dignity, humility; unless, of course, you consider the fact that doubtlessly all of these taken together are to be preferred to any one of them taken singly, and that it is incomparably a more excellent and a happier choice to ponder all together than just a few.

And what is there strange if God, whom we see and read to be wonderful in His saints, should show Himself yet more wonderful in His Mother? Venerate, therefore, ye spouses, this bodily *integrity* in corruptible flesh; and you, consecrated virgins, this *fecundity* in the virgin; imitate, all ye mankind, the *humility* of the Mother of God.

℟. Blessed art thou, O Virgin Mary, Mother of God, who hast believed the Lord: those things were accomplished in thee that were spoken to thee. * Therefore hath God blessed thee forever. ℣. Grace is poured forth on thy lips: intercede for us with the Lord our God. Therefore. Glory. Therefore.

✠ Continuation of the holy Gospel according to St. Luke.— At that time when they were returning, the boy Jesus remained in Jerusalem, and his parents did not know it. But thinking that he was in the caravan, they had come a day's journey before it occurred to them to look for him among their relatives and acquaintances. And not finding him, they returned to Jerusalem in search of him.

And it came to pass after three days, that they found him in the temple, sitting in the midst of the teachers, both listening to them and asking them questions. And all who were listening to him were amazed at his understanding and his answers. And when they saw him, they were astonished. And his mother said to him, "Son, why hast thou done so to us? Behold, thy father and I have been seeking thee sorrowing."

And he said to them, "How is it that you sought me? Did you not know that I must be about my Father's business?" And they did not understand the word that he spoke to them. And he went down with them and came to Nazareth, and was subject to them

Let Us Pray

O God, who hast willed that Thy Word should become Man in the womb of the Virgin Mary at the message of an Angel, grant that Thy servants who truly believe she is the Mother of God may be aided by her intercession with Thee. Through our Lord.

October 18
ST. LUKE THE EVANGELIST

I Nocturn

From the Book of Ezechiel the Prophet, c. 1, 1 - 13

II Nocturn

From the Book of St. Jerome, Priest, on Ecclesiastical Writers

Luke, a physician from Antioch, who, as his writings show, was not ignorant of the Greek language, was a follower of the Apostle Paul, and his companion on all his travels. He wrote the Gospel of which Paul says: "We have sent also with him the brother, whose praise is in the Gospel, through all the churches." And to the Colossians, "Luke, the most dear physician, saluteth you." Also to Timothy, "Only Luke is with me."

Likewise, he published another wonderful volume which bears the title *Acts of the Apostles*. Its narratives continue up to the two years spent by Paul at Rome, that is, up to the fourth year of Nero's reign. From it we learn that the book was composed in that city. Hence we are to relegate the journeys of Paul and Thecla and the complete tale of the lion's baptism to the apocryphal writings. For how is it that among all the rest of Paul's deeds, Luke, the sole companion of the Apostle, should be ignorant of this alone?

Even Tertullian, who lived close to that time, tells us that a certain priest in Asia, a lover of the Apostle Paul, when charged by John to be the author of the book, confessed that he had done it out of his love for Paul, and he had forthwith fallen dead on the spot. Certain ones suspect that as often as Paul says in his Epistles, "according to my Gospel," he refers to Luke's work.

That Luke had learned the Gospel not only from Paul, who had not been with our Lord in the flesh, but from the rest of the apostles, he himself declares at the beginning of his book, saying: "According as they have delivered them unto us, who from the beginning were eye-witnesses and ministers of the word." Consequently, he wrote the Gospel as he had heard it, while he composed the Acts of the Apostles according as he had himself seen. He lived eighty-four years, having no wife; he is buried at Constantinople, to which city, in the twentieth year of Constantine's reign, his bones were transferred from Achaia, together with the remains of the Apostle Andrew.

℟. I saw men standing together, clad in shining garments; and the Angel of the Lord spoke to me, saying: * These holy men became the friends of God. ℣. I saw a mighty Angel of God, flying through the midst of heaven, crying out with a loud voice and saying. These holy men. Glory. These holy men.

III Nocturn

The reading of the holy Gospel according to St. Luke

At that time the Lord appointed seventy-two others, and sent them forth two by two before him into every town and place where he himself was about to come. And so forth

Homily of St. Gregory, Pope

Our Lord and Savior, dearly beloved brethren, admonishes us sometimes by words and sometimes by works. For His very deeds are precepts; for even when He does anything without speaking, He lets us know what we ought to do. Behold, He sends His disciples two by two to preach, because two are the commandments of charity—namely, the love of God and the love of neighbor—and because between less than two charity cannot be had.

No one properly speaking is said to have charity towards himself, but, that it may be charity, love tends towards another. For look, the Lord sent the disciples by two's to preach, in order to show us without sound of words that he who does not have charity towards his neighbor ought by no means to take up the office of preaching.

But it is well said that He sent them before His face into every city and place whither He Himself was to come, for the Lord follows His preachers; the preaching comes first; and then, when the words of exhortation have gone before, the Lord comes to the dwelling-place of our mind; and by this means truth is received into the soul.

Hence Isaias says to these same preachers: "Prepare ye the way of the Lord; make straight the paths of our God." Hence also the Psalmist says to the people of God: "Make a way for him who ascendeth upon the west." Indeed the Lord hath risen upon the west; for as He set, as it were, in His Passion, He rose in greater glory in His Resurrection. To be sure, He rose upon the west, for by rising again He trampled under foot that death which He had suffered. For Him, therefore, who rose upon the west do we prepare the way when we preach His glory to your minds, so that He Himself, coming afterwards, may enlighten them by the presence of His love.

℞. These are the holy men whom the Lord hath chosen in charity unfeigned, and hath given them everlasting glory: * Whose teaching enlightens the Church, as the sun does the moon ℣. By faith the Saints conquered kingdoms and wrought justice. Whose. Glory. Whose.

✠ Continuation of the holy Gospel according to St. Luke.— At that time the Lord appointed seventy-two others, and sent them forth two by two before him into every town and place where he himself was about to come. And he said to them, "The harvest indeed is abundant, but the laborers are few. Pray therefore the Lord of the harvest to send forth laborers into his harvest.

"Go. Behold, I send you forth as lambs in the midst of wolves. Carry neither purse, nor wallet, nor sandals, and greet no one on the way. Whatever house you enter, first say, 'Peace to this house!' And if a son of peace be there, your peace will rest upon him; but if not, it will return to you. And remain in the same house, eating and drinking what they have; for the laborer deserves his wages. Do not go from house to house. And whatever town you enter, and they receive you, eat what is set before you, and cure the sick who are there, and say to them, 'The kingdom of God is at hand to you.'"

Let Us Pray

We beseech Thee, O Lord, may blessed Luke Thy Evangelist intercede for us, who, for the honor of Thy name, always bore the sufferings of the Cross in his own body. Through our Lord

Last Sunday of October
FEAST OF OUR LORD JESUS CHRIST THE KING

I Nocturn
From the Epistle of St. Paul the Apostle to the Colossians,
c. 1, 3 - 23

II Nocturn
From the Encyclical Letter of Pope Pius XI

Inasmuch as the Holy Year has offered more than one occasion of making better known the kingdom of Christ, we consider that we shall do something eminently agreeable to our Apostolic office, if, yielding to the prayers of a great part of the college of Cardinals, of the Bishops and of the faithful—whether brought to us singly or collectively—we close this year by inserting into the Church's liturgy a proper feast of our Lord Jesus Christ the King. For it has long been customary that Christ should be called King, though in a metaphorical sense, on account of the supreme merit by which He stands forth among all created things. For so it is that He is said to reign "over the minds of men," not only because of His keen mind and the extent of His knowledge, but because He is Himself the Truth, and from Him we mortals must receive and obediently accept that truth; likewise, He reigns "over the wills of men," not only because the perfect integrity of the human will is in complete submission to, and accord with, the holiness of the divine will in Him, but also because He communicates it to our free will through His own inspiration and encouragement, whereby we burn in desire for all the most noble things. And finally, Christ is acknowledged "King of hearts" on account of His "charity which surpasseth all knowledge," His meekness, and His kindness which allures men's minds. For never has it come to pass that anyone ever has been so loved by the whole of mankind, nor will it ever come to pass hereafter.

But—to go into the matter more deeply—no one can fail to see that the name and power of king, in the quite proper sense of the word, should be asserted and defended for Christ the man. For except as He is man, He cannot be said to have received from the Father "power and honor and kingdom"; for indeed the Word of God, whose substance is one with the Father, inevitably has with this Father all things in common, and therefore has over all created things a complete and entire dominion. And on what basis this dignity and power of our Lord rests, Cyril of Alexandria aptly notes: "Over all creatures, in a word, He holds sway—not by seizure and violence nor otherwise usurped power, but in virtue of His own essence and nature"; His principality is founded on that marvelous union—hypostatic, as it is called.

Whence it follows that Christ must not only be adored by angels and by men as God, but also that both angels and men are to obey and be subject to His rule as man; so that in the name of the hypostatic union alone Christ holds dominion over all creatures. But—in order to emphasize the strength and nature of His sovereignty—that this sovereignty is maintained by a threefold power scarcely needs to be said, in so far as, if this power is lacking, His rule is with difficulty understood. This same fact the testimonies regarding the universal reign of our Redeemer which are selected and produced from the Sacred Writings more than sufficiently attest, and in the holy Catholic Faith it must be believed that Christ Jesus was given to men as the Redeemer in whom they are to trust and also as the Lawgiver whom they must obey. For the Gospels do not only tell that He established laws, but they present Him in the very act of making them; whosoever, indeed, keeps these commandments, the same are said by the Divine Master both to prove their love for Him and to dwell in His love. Likewise, when the Jews accused Him of violating the Sabbath rest by the remarkable cure of the paralytic, Jesus Himself affirms that the power of judging has been bestowed on Him by His Father: "For neither doth the Father judge any man, but hath given all judgment to the Son." By this it must also be understood (for this cannot be separated from the power of judging) that by His right He metes out rewards and penalties to men while they are yet alive. And further, that power which men call executive must also be attributed to Christ, in so far as it is obligatory that all must obey His mandate, and that there are truly things prescribed for the rebellious in the meting out of punishments which no one can escape.

That a kingdom of this kind is in a certain special way spiritual and pertains to spiritual matters, those passages which we selected above from the Scriptures show in the first place most clearly, and in the second place, Christ our Lord confirms by His own manner of acting. Thus on more than one occasion—when the Jews, yea, even the apostles themselves, through misunderstanding, were of the opinion that He as Messias was about to liberate His people and restore the Kingdom of Israel—He destroyed and overturned their foolish hope; He refused to be declared as King by the surrounding multitude of admirers by fleeing both title and honor and hiding Himself; He gave witness before the Roman Judge that His kingdom was not "of this world." This kingdom is proposed in the Gospel to be such into which men may expect to enter by performing penance, but into which they cannot enter except by faith and Baptism which, although it is an external rite, nevertheless represents and effects an interior regeneration: it is opposed only to the kingdom of Satan and to the power of darkness, and demands from its lieges not only that, with a mind free from riches and earthly matters, they should prefer delicacy in their habits, and hunger and thirst after justice, but also that they deny themselves and take up their cross. Yet, since Christ has both as Redeemer purchased His Church with His Blood and as Priest offered Himself as Victim for sins and offers Himself perpetually, to whom does it not seem that His regal dignity should assume and participate in the nature of each of these offices? In other words, he would err shamefully who would take away from the Man-Christ dominion over all civil matters, since He received from the Father such an absolute power over things created that all were placed in His judgment. Therefore, by our Apostolic authority, We have ordained that the feast of our Lord Jesus Christ the King must be celebrated yearly throughout the world on the last Sunday of the month of October, that, namely, which immediately precedes the solemnity of All Saints. Likewise do We command that each year on that day the dedication of the human race to the Most Sacred Heart of Jesus be renewed.

℟. He must reign, for God hath put all things under His feet · * That God may be all in all. ℣. When all things shall be subdued unto Him, then the Son Himself shall also be subject unto the Father. That God. Glory. That God.

III Nocturn

The reading of the holy Gospel according to St. John

At that time Pilate said to Jesus: "Art thou the king of the Jews?" Jesus answered, "Dost thou say this of thyself, or have others told thee of me?" And so forth.

Homily of St. Augustine, Bishop

What great thing was it for the King of ages to become King of men? For Christ is not King of Israel in order to exact tribute, or to equip an army with the sword and to vanquish His enemies visibly; but He is King of Israel in that He rules minds, looks out for their eternal destinies, and leads those who believe, hope, and love Him into the Kingdom of Heaven. Therefore the fact that the Son of God equal to the Father, the Word through whom all things were made, wished to be the King of Israel is a condescension, not an advancement; it is an indication of mercy, not an increase of power. For He who on earth was called the King of the Jews is in heaven the Lord of the angels. But is Christ King only of the Jews, or of the Gentiles also? Yea, also of the Gentiles! For when He had said in prophecy, "But I am appointed by him King over Sion, his holy mountain, preaching the commandment of the Lord," lest anyone should say because of those words, "over Mount Sion," that He had been appointed king over the Jews alone, He immediately added: "The Lord hath said to me: Thou art my Son; this day have I begotten thee. Ask of me and I will give thee the Gentiles as thy inheritance and the utmost parts of the earth as thy possession."

Jesus answered: "My kingdom is not of this world. If my kingdom were of this world, my servants would certainly strive that I should not be delivered to the Jews: but now my kingdom is not from hence." This is what the good Master wished us to know, but first we had to be shown the foolish opinion held by men, whether the Gentiles or the Jews from whom Pilate had heard it, about His kingdom—as if He ought to have been punished with death because He had striven for a kingdom opposed to the law, or, because rulers generally are jealous of those who are rising to power, it was necessary, as it were, to be on their guard lest His kingdom should be in opposition either to the Romans or to the Jews.

Our Lord could have answered, "My kingdom is not of this world," to the first query of the governor when he said to Him: "Art thou the king of the Jews?" but instead, asking Pilate whether he spoke this of himself or had heard it from others, He wished to show to Pilate by his own answer that this (His being king of the Jews) had been charged against Him by the Jews as a crime. Thus Christ laid bare to us the thoughts of men which He knew, "for they are vain." And after Pilate's reply to these words, He then answers both the Jews and the Gentiles more fittingly and to the point, saying: "My kingdom is not of this world."

The twelfth lesson is taken from the first paragraph of the Homily of the occurring Sunday.

℞. The kingdom of this world is become the kingdom of our Lord and of His Christ: * And He shall reign forever and ever. ℣. All the kindreds of the Gentiles shall adore in His sight; for the kingdom is the Lord's. And He shall reign. Glory. And He shall reign.

✠ Continuation of the holy Gospel according to St. John.— At that time Pilate said to Jesus: "Art thou the king of the Jews?" Jesus answered, "Dost thou say this of thyself, or have others told thee of me?" Pilate answered, "Am I a Jew? Thy own people and the chief priests have delivered thee to me. What hast thou done?" Jesus answered, "My kingdom is not of this world. If my kingdom were of this world, my followers would have fought that I might not be delivered to the Jews. But, as it is, my kingdom is not from here." Pilate therefore said to him, "Thou art then a king?" Jesus answered, "Thou sayest it; I am a king. This is why I was born, and why I have come into the world, to bear witness to the truth. Everyone who is of the truth hears my voice."

Let Us Pray

O almighty and eternal God, who hast willed to re-establish all things in Thy beloved Son, the King of all, mercifully grant that all the families of the nations, torn away by the wound of sin, may be subjected to His gentle rule: Who liveth and reigneth with Thee.

October 27
VIGIL OF SS. SIMON AND JUDE

The reading of the holy Gospel according to St. John

At that time Jesus said to his disciples: "I am the true vine and my Father is the vine-dresser." And so forth.

Homily of St. Augustine, Bishop

This passage of the Gospel, brethren, where the Lord calls Himself the vine and His disciples the branches, speaks of the fact that He is the Head of the Church, the Mediator of God and men, the man Christ Jesus, and we are His members. The vine and the branches are, of course, of one nature. For this reason, then, since He was God, of whose nature we are not, was He made man, in order that the human nature in Him might be the vine of which we men might be the branches.

What, then, does this mean: "I am the true vine"? Since He added the word "true," did He refer this saying to that vine from which this similitude is taken? For He is called *vine* by similitude, not in the strictness of speech; just as He is called *sheep, lamb, lion, rock, corner-stone,* and other things of this sort, which objects themselves are rather the true things from which these metaphorical, not literal, appellations are taken.

But when He says, "I am the true vine," He distinguishes Himself from that vine to which it is said: "How art thou turned into bitterness, O strange vine!" For how can that be the true vine, which, when expected to bring forth grapes, bore thorns? "I am," He says, "the true vine, and my Father is the husbandman. Every branch in me that beareth not fruit he will take away; and every branch that beareth fruit, he will purge it, that it may bring forth more fruit."

October 28
SS. SIMON AND JUDE, APOSTLES
I Nocturn
From the Catholic Epistle of St. Jude the Apostle, c. 1, 1 - 13

II Nocturn

Simon the Chanaanite, who is also called Zelotes, and Thaddeus, who is called Jude, the brother of James in the Gospel, and the author of one of the Catholic Epistles, traveled, the former throughout Egypt and the latter throughout Mesopotamia, preaching the Gospel. Upon meeting in Persia, after they had borne innumerable sons in Jesus Christ and had spread abroad the faith among the barbarous inhabitants in these very extensive parts, through their doctrine and miracles, and finally through a glorious martyrdom, together they gave glory to the most sacred name of Jesus Christ.

Sermon of St. Gregory, Pope

It is written: "The spirit of the Lord adorned the heavens." For the ornaments of the heavens are the virtues of its preachers, which adornments Paul enumerates, saying: "To one indeed, by the Spirit, is given the word of wisdom; to another, the word of knowledge, according to the same Spirit; to another, faith in the same Spirit; to another, the grace of healing in one Spirit; to another, the working of miracles; to another, prophecy; to another, the discerning of spirits; to another, diverse kinds of tongues; to another, interpretation of speeches. But all these things one and the same Spirit worketh, dividing to every one according as he will."

Therefore as many as are the virtues of the preachers, so many are the ornaments of the heavens. Hence it is again written: "By the word of the Lord the heavens were established." Now the Word of the Lord is the Son of the Father. But in order that at the same time the complete Holy Trinity be shown to have formed these same heavens, that is, the holy apostles, it is immediately added in reference to the divinity of the Holy Spirit: "And all the power of them by the Spirit of his mouth." Therefore the power of the heavens is drawn from the Spirit; because they would not have dared to withstand the powers of this world unless the fortitude of the Holy Spirit had confirmed them.

We know what sort of men the founders of holy Church were before the coming of the Holy Spirit, and we also see the great fortitude they had after His coming. Indeed, the servant-maid who kept the door testifies regarding the great weakness and timidity of the chief pastor of the Church, near whose body we are gathered, before the coming of the Spirit. Struck by one word of the woman, fearing death, he denied the Life.

℟. These are the conquerors and the friends of God, who, despising the orders of princes, merited an everlasting reward: * Now they are crowned, and they receive the palm. ℣. These are they who have come out of great tribulation, and have washed their robes in the Blood of the Lamb. Now. Glory. Now.

III Nocturn

The reading of the holy Gospel according to St. John

At that time Jesus said to his disciples: "These things I command you, that you love one another. If the world hates you, know that it has hated me before you." And so forth.

Homily of St. Augustine, Bishop

In the reading of the Gospel which immediately precedes this the Lord had said, "You have not chosen me, but I have chosen you, and have appointed you that you should go and should bring forth fruit, and your fruit should remain; that whatsoever you shall ask of the Father in my name he may give it you." Then He says here, "These things I command you, that you love one another." And by this we should understand that this is our fruit, concerning which He said, "I have chosen you that you should go and should bring forth fruit, and your fruit should remain."

And because He added, "That whatsoever you shall ask the Father in my name he may give it you," He shall certainly then grant it to us if we love one another, since He, who has chosen us who had no fruit because we had not chosen Him, and has appointed us that we should bring forth fruit, that is, that we should love one another, has Himself given us this assurance. Charity, therefore, is our fruit, which the Apostle defines as being from a pure heart, a good conscience, and an unfeigned faith. In this way do we love one another; in this way do we love God; for we would not love one another with a true love unless we loved God. For everyone loves his neighbor as himself only if he loves God, because if he does not love God, neither does he love himself, for on these two precepts of charity depend the entire Law and the Prophets. This is our fruit.

Therefore, giving us command concerning the fruit, He said, "These things I command you, that you love one another." Whence the Apostle Paul, when he wished to commend the fruits of the spirit in contradistinction to the works of the flesh, puts this in the first place: "The fruit of the spirit," he says, "is charity." And then he enumerates all the rest, namely, joy, peace, longanimity, benignity, goodness, faith, mildness, continence, chastity, as springing from and being joined to this source.

But who can really rejoice who does not love the good over which he rejoices? Who can have true peace unless with him whom he truly loves? Who is persistently patient and persevering in doing a good work unless he fervently loves? Who is kind but he who loves the man he helps? Who is good but he who becomes such by loving? Who is full of saving faith unless he has that faith which works through charity? Who is profitably gentle if love does not control him? Who refrains from that which is sordid but he who loves that which is honest? Justly, then, does the good Master often commend love just as if it were the only thing to be commanded, without which other good things can avail nothing, and which cannot be possessed without at the same time possessing all those good things by which a man becomes good.

℟. Blessed are ye when men shall revile and persecute you, and speak all that is evil against you, untruly, for My sake: * Be glad and rejoice for your reward is very great in heaven. ℣. When me shall hate you, and when they shall separate you, and shall reproach you, and cast out your name as evil, for the Son of Man's sake. Be glad. Glory. Be glad.

✠ Continuation of the holy Gospel according to St. John.—At that time Jesus said to his disciples: "These things I command you, that you love one another. If the world hates you, know that it has hated me before you. If you were of the world, the world would love what is its own. But because you are not of the world, therefore the world hates you. Remember the word that I have spoken to you: No servant is greater than his master. If they have persecuted me, they will persecute you also; if they have kept my word, they will keep yours also. But all these things they will do to you for my name's sake, because they do not know him who sent me. If I had not come and spoken to them, they would have no sin. But now they have no excuse for their sin. He who hates me hates my Father also. If I had not done among them works such as no one else has done, they would have no sin. But now they have seen, and have hated both me and my Father; but that the word written in their Law may be fulfilled, 'They have hated me without cause.'"

Let Us Pray

O God, who didst bring us to a knowledge of Thy name by Thy blessed Apostles Simon and Jude, grant us to celebrate their eternal glory by increasing in virtue, and by celebrating this feast to really increase in virtue. Through our Lord

October 31

VIGIL OF ALL SAINTS

The reading of the holy Gospel according to St. Luke

At that time Jesus, coming down from the mountain, took his stand on a level stretch, with a crowd of his disciples, and a great multitude of people from all Judea and Jerusalem, and the sea coast of Tyre and Sidon, who came to listen to him and to be healed of their diseases. And so forth.

Homily of St. Ambrose, Bishop

Pay close attention to everything—how Jesus ascended with the apostles, and how He descended to the crowds. For how should the multitude behold Christ unless in a lowly man? They do not follow Him to the loftier heights, nor do they ascend to the sublimer things. Again, when He descended, He found the infirm, for the infirm could not be with Him on high.

From this Matthew also teaches that the weak are healed in low places. For each one must first be healed in order that, as his strength gradually increases, he may be able to ascend the mountain. And therefore whomsoever He heals in the low places, that is, recalls from sensuality, escapes injury from blindness. He comes down to our wounds, in order that by a certain application and power of His nature, He may make us partakers of the heavenly Kingdom.

"Blessed are the poor: for theirs is the kingdom of God." St. Luke puts down only four of the beatitudes of the Lord, while St. Matthew lists eight; still, in those eight of St. Matthew there are the four of St. Luke, and in these four are those eight. For the one, St. Luke, embraces, as it were, the four cardinal virtues; the other, St. Matthew, in those eight retains a mystical number. Many psalms are entitled "for the octave"; and when you are commanded to give a portion to eight, perhaps this may signify the beatitudes. For as the octave is the perfection of our hope, so is it also the sum of all virtues (namely, the beatitudes).

Queen of All Saints,
Pray for us!

November 1
FEAST OF ALL SAINTS

I Nocturn.
From the Book of the Apocalypse of St. John the Apostle,
c. 4, 2 - 8; c. 5, 1 - 14

II Nocturn
Sermon of St. Bede the Venerable, Priest

Today, dearly beloved, in one joyful solemnity we celebrate the feast of all the saints, in whose company heaven exults, by whose protection earth is made glad, by whose triumphs holy Church is crowned; their confession of Faith is so much the more glorious in honor as it was the more patient in suffering, because while the struggle increased, the glory of those fighting also increased, and, while the triumph of martyrdom is adorned with many kinds of suffering, the more grievous the torments, the greater also the reward.

Since holy mother Church, which is spread far and wide through the whole world, has in her Head, Christ Jesus, been taught not to fear insults, crosses and death, being strengthened more and more not by resisting, but by suffering patiently, she has inspired by the glory of triumph all whom the prisons inclosed as a glorious army to carry on the battle with an equal and like love of virtue.

O truly blessed mother Church, whom the honor of Divine Majesty so illumines, whom the glorious blood of the conquering martyrs crowns, whom the pure virginity of an unstained confession invests! Neither roses nor lilies are wanting to her. To attain the fullest dignity, dearly beloved, let everyone strive now for one or the other honor: either the lucid crown of virginity or the purpled one of martyrdom. In the heavenly camps both peace and warfare have their flowers with which the soldiers of Christ are crowned.

For the unspeakable and immense goodness of God has also provided this: that the period of labors and agony should not be prolonged, nor made long and everlasting, but brief and, as it were, momentary, so that in this short and fleeting life there should be pains and toils, but in the other life the diadems and rewards of merit; so that, likewise, the hardships might be ended quickly, but the rewards of merit endure forever; that after the darkness of this world they might behold the most pure Light, and might attain to happiness greater than the bitterness of all sufferings; to this likewise, the Apostle bears witness when he states: "The sufferings of this time are not worthy to be compared with the glory to come, that shall be revealed in us."

℟. In the sight of the Angels I will sing praises to Thee, * And I will worship towards Thy holy temple and give glory to Thy name, O Lord. ℣. For Thy mercy and Thy truth: for Thou hast magnified Thy holy name above all. And I will worship. Glory. And I will worship.

III Nocturn

The reading of the holy Gospel according to St. Matthew

At that time, seeing the crowds, Jesus went up the mountain. And when he was seated, his disciples came to him. And so forth

Homily of St. Augustine, Bishop

If it is asked what the mountain signifies, we answer that it is rightly understood to mean the more important precepts of justice; for those were lesser ones which had been given to the Jews. Yet the one and only God, through His holy prophets and servants, and according to a wonderfully arranged distribution of times, gave the lesser precepts to that people which yet had to be held in check by fear; and, through His own Son, He gave the greater precepts to that people which it now behooved to be set free by charity. Moreover, when the lesser precepts are given to the people of a lesser dignity, and the greater to the greater, they are given by Him who alone knows how to bestow on the human race a remedy suitable to the times.

Nor is it astonishing that, by the same God who made heaven and earth, greater precepts are given for the Kingdom of Heaven and lesser ones for the kingdom of earth. Concerning that greater righteousness it is said by the Prophet: "Thy justice is as the mountains of God." And this in turn explains well why this justice is taught on the mountain by the one Master who alone is capable of teaching such high matters.

Being seated as becomes the dignity of His office, He teaches. And the disciples came unto Him that they might also be nearer bodily for the hearing of His word, as they approached in spirit to fulfill His precepts. "And opening his mouth he taught them, saying." This circumlocution which is here written, "And opening his mouth," perhaps indicates by the mere pause that this sermon will be a somewhat longer one, unless perchance it means that now He is said to have opened His own mouth, whereas in the old Law He was accustomed to open the mouths of the prophets.

What then does He say? "Blessed are the poor in spirit for theirs is the kingdom of heaven." We have read what is written concerning the desire for temporal things: "All is vanity and presumption of spirit." Now this presumption of spirit signifies boldness and bride. Even in common language the proud are said to have great spirits, and rightly, since the wind is also called spirit. But who does not know that the proud are said to be puffed up, as if filled out by the wind? Whence it is written: "Fire, hail, snow, ice, stormy winds." Whence also is that saying of the Apostle: "Knowledge puffeth up, but charity edifieth." For this reason, the poor in spirit are here understood to be the humble and God-fearing, that is, those who have not the spirit that puffeth up.

℞. The Precursor of the Lord cometh, of whom He, the Lord, giveth testimony: * Amongst those born of women there is not a greater than John the Baptist. ℣. He is a prophet and more than a prophet, of whom the Savior said. Amongst. Glory. Amongst.

✚ Continuation of the holy Gospel according to St. Matthew.—At that time seeing the crowds, Jesus went up the mountain. And when he was seated, his disciples came to him. And opening his mouth he taught them, saying, "Blessed are the poor in spirit, for theirs is the kingdom of heaven. Blessed are the meek, for they shall possess the earth. Blessed are they who mourn, for they shall be comforted. Blessed are they who hunger and thirst for justice, for they shall be satisfied. Blessed are the merciful, for they shall obtain mercy. Blessed are the pure of heart, for they shall see God. Blessed are the peacemakers, for they shall be called children of God. Blessed are they who suffer persecution for justice' sake, for theirs is the kingdom of heaven. Blessed are you when men reproach you, and persecute you, and, speaking falsely, say all manner of evil against you, for my sake. Rejoice and exult, because your reward is great in heaven."

LET US PRAY

O almighty and eternal God, who dost grant us to honor the merits of all Thy Saints in one feast, we beseech Thee, that increasing the number of our intercessors, Thou wouldst also increase Thy mercy for which we long. Through our Lord.

November 2
COMMEMORATION OF ALL THE FAITHFUL DEPARTED
I Nocturn
From the Book of Job, c. 7, 16 - 21; c. 14, 1 - 6; c. 19, 20 - 27
II Nocturn
From the Book of St. Augustine, Bishop,
on care to be had for the Dead

The attention given to a funeral, the condition of the burial, the display accompanying the obsequies are more a consolation to the living than a help to the dead. But it does not follow that the bodies of the departed are to be cast aside and despised, especially the bodies of good and faithful men, which their souls have used holily as organs and instruments of all their good deeds. For if the garment or ring of a father, or such like things, are so much the dearer to those whom they leave behind as the affection of these same for their parents is the greater, the bodies themselves are by no means to be neglected, for they are more closely united to us than any garment. For one's body is not merely an ornament or an external aid, but is a part of man's very nature. Thus also in former times the funerals of just men were piously cared for, their obsequies were dutifully celebrated and their sepulture provided for. Often they themselves, while yet alive, gave strict orders to their children concerning the burial, or even the translation of their bodies.

The affection of one who remembers and prays for the deceased without doubt profits those who, during life on earth, merited that such things should profit them after death. Even if some emergency should prevent the burial of bodies, either at all or in holy places, nevertheless the supplications for the souls of the dead should not be forgotten. The Church has taken it upon herself to make these supplications for all who have departed in Christian and Catholic fellowship, without mentioning their names, by a general commemoration, so that those who do not have parents, children, or any relatives or friends to pray for them may benefit from the suffrages of the one pious mother who is common to all. But if such supplications, made piously and in good faith for the dead, are not had, I do not think that the place of burial profits anyone, no matter how holy it may be.

Since these things are so, let us not think that anything aids the dead for whom we are solicitous except that which we solemnly offer by sacrifices either of the Altar or of prayers or of alms Neither do these offerings profit all for whom they are made but only those who, during life, merited that they should be profitable to them. But since we cannot discover who these are, it is fitting that we offer them for all those who have been baptized, that no one may be overlooked who can and ought to receive these benefits. For it is better that these things be superfluous to those whom they neither aid nor injure, than that they be wanting to those whom they can aid. Each one, however, does these things more diligently for his own close friends in order that they may do the same for him. But whatever is done to the corpse itself avails nothing towards salvation, but is done out of respect and results from that affection according to which no one ever hates his own flesh. Therefore it is fitting that he take whatever care he can of the corpse of his neighbor, when he who bore it has passed away. And if they who do not believe in the resurrection of the flesh do these things, how much more ought they who do believe to do the same; so that such an honor bestowed upon a body which, though dead, is to rise again and to remain for all eternity, may be, in some way, a testimony of the same faith.

℟. O Lord, when Thou shalt come to judge the earth, where shall I hide myself from the face of Thy wrath? * For I have sinned exceedingly in my life. ℣. I dread my misdeeds, and blush before Thee: do not condemn me, when Thou shalt come to judge. For. Eternal rest give unto them, O Lord: and let perpetual light shine upon them. For.

III Nocturn

From the first Epistle of St. Paul the Apostle to the Corinthians

Now if Christ is preached as risen from the dead, how do some among you say that there is no resurrection of the dead? But if there is no resurrection of the dead, neither has Christ risen; and if Christ has not risen, vain then is our preaching, vain too is your faith. Yes, and we are found false witnesses as to God, in that we have borne witness against God that he raised Christ —whom he did not raise, if the dead do not rise. For if the dead do not rise, neither has Christ risen; and if Christ has not risen, vain is your faith, for you are still in your sins. Hence they also who have fallen asleep in Christ, have perished. If with this life only in view we have had hope in Christ, we are of all men the most to be pitied. But as it is, Christ has risen from the dead, the first-fruits of those who have fallen asleep. For since by a man came death, by a man also comes resurrection of the dead. For as in Adam all die, so in Christ all will be made to live.

All Souls

But someone will say, "How do the dead rise? Or with what kind of body do they come?" Senseless man, what thou thyself sowest is not brought to life unless it dies. And when thou sowest, thou dost not sow the body that shall be, but a bare grain, perhaps of wheat or something else. But God gives it a body even as he has willed, and to each of the seeds a body of its own. All flesh is not the same flesh, but there is one flesh of men, another of beasts, another of birds, another of fishes. There are also heavenly bodies and earthly bodies, but of one kind is the glory of the heavenly, of another kind the glory of the earthly. There is one glory of the sun, and another glory of the moon, and another of the stars; for star differs from star in glory. So also with the resurrection of the dead. What is sown in corruption rises in incorruption; what is sown in dishonor rises in glory; what is sown in weakness rises in power; what is sown a natural body rises a spiritual body.

Behold, I tell you a mystery: we shall all indeed rise, but we shall not all be changed—in a moment, in the twinkling of an eye, at the last trumpet. For the trumpet shall sound and the dead shall rise incorruptible and we shall be changed. For this corruptible body must put on incorruption, and this mortal body must put on immortality. But when this mortal body puts on immortality, then shall come to pass the word that is written, "Death is swallowed up in victory? O death, where is thy victory? O death, where is thy sting?" Now the sting of death is sin, and the power of sin is the Law. But thanks be to God who has given us the victory through our Lord Jesus Christ. Therefore, my beloved brethren, be steadfast and immovable, always abounding in the work of the Lord, knowing that your labor is not in vain in the Lord.

℟. O Lord, judge me not according to my deeds: for I have done nothing worthy in Thy sight: therefore I beseech Thy majesty, * That Thou, O God, mayest blot out my iniquity. ℣. Wash me, O Lord, yet more from my injustice, and cleanse me from my sin. That Thou. Eternal rest give unto them, O Lord: and let perpetual light shine upon them. That Thou.

Let Us Pray

O God, the Creator and Redeemer of all the faithful, to the souls of Thy servants and of Thine handmaidens grant the pardon of all their sins, that through our devout prayers they may rejoice in the full forgiveness for which at all times they have hoped: who livest and reignest with God the Father.

November 3
III DAY WITHIN THE OCTAVE OF ALL SAINTS
From a Sermon of St. Bede the Venerable, Priest

Then there shall never be any discord, but all things shall be in accord, all in agreement, because there shall be the perfect harmony of all the saints; all peace and joy shall hold sway. All things are tranquil and in repose. Perpetual is the glory, not that which now is, but so much the more brilliant than the present as it is the more joyful, because, as it is declared, that city shall have no need of the light of the sun, but the Almighty Lord shall enlighten it and the Lamb is the lamp thereof. There the saints shall shine like the stars for all eternity, and they who have taught many shall be as the splendor of the sky.

Wherefore no night shall be there, nor darkness, nor gathering of clouds, neither any oppression of cold or of heat, but such will be the disposition of things as "neither the eye hath seen, nor the ear heard, neither has it entered into the heart of man," except of those who are found worthy to enjoy it, "whose names are written in the book of life," who have also "washed their robes in the blood of the Lamb," and "are before the throne of God, and serve him day and night." For old age is not there, nor the misery of old age, as all come unto perfect manhood, unto the measure of the age of the fullness of Christ.

But above all these things is the being associated with the assemblies of Angels and Archangels; to enjoy likewise the Thrones and Dominations, the Principalities and Powers, and the companies of all the celestial and supernal Virtues; to behold the hosts of the Saints shining more brightly than the stars, of the patriarchs resplendent in their faith, of the prophets joyful in their expectation, of the apostles judging the world in the twelve tribes of Israel, of the martyrs decked with the purple crowns of victory; to look on the choirs of Virgins, too, wearing white robes.

November 4
IV DAY WITHIN THE OCTAVE OF ALL SAINTS
From a Sermon of St. Bede the Venerable, Priest

But of the King who presides in the midst of these saints no word can say enough, for He defies all description; and this comeliness, this beauty, this power, this glory, this magnificence, this majesty surpasses all understanding of the human mind. For it is beyond all the glory of the saints to look upon His Majesty. For we ought to bear torments daily and even to endure hell itself for a short time in order that we might be worthy to see Christ coming in glory and to be associated in the number of His saints! Would it not be fitting to suffer all that is disconcerting in order that we may be reckoned partakers of so great a good and of such great glory?

What will be, dearly beloved brethren, the glory of the just, how intense the gladness of the saints, when each countenance shall shine as the sun, when the Lord has begun to number His people in their proper ranks in the kingdom of His Father, and to bestow the promised rewards for the merits and works of each one; to replace heavenly things for things mundane, eternal for temporal, and an abundance for mere handfuls; to lead the saints into the presence of the paternal glory, and to make them sit in the midst of the heavenly company, that God may be all in all, and to give eternity and immortality to His lovers; and finally, to bring back to paradise those whom He has restored by His life-giving blood, and in the fidelity and truth of His promise to open the Kingdom of Heaven?

May these things cling firmly to our senses, may they be understood with great faith, may they be loved with the whole heart, may they be acquired by the generosity of untiring labors. This reward is placed within the power of him who works, "for the kingdom of heaven suffereth violence." This reward, O man, namely, the Kingdom of Heaven, demands no other price save thyself; it is worth as much as you. Give yourself and you will have it. Why are you disturbed over the price? Christ delivered up Himself that He might gain you as a kingdom for His Father; so too, give yourself that you may be His kingdom; and let not sin reign in your mortal body, but the Spirit unto the obtaining of life.

November 5

V DAY WITHIN THE OCTAVE OF ALL SAINTS

From a Sermon of St. Bede the Venerable, Priest

And may it be a delight to us to arrive at this palm of salutary deeds. Let us strive for it with a will and with zest; let us all run in the contest of justice while God and Christ look on; and let us not slacken our pace by any temporal desire, we who even now begin to be superior to time and to the world. If the last day shall find us free from all attachment, if it shall find us running in duty's contest, God will never fail to be the Rewarder of our merits.

He who in the time of persecution shall bestow a purple crown for martyrdom, shall also grant to those who conquer in time of peace a dazzling white crown for the merits of their justice. For neither Abraham nor Isaac nor Jacob was slain, and yet, honored for the merits of their faith and justice, they have achieved first place among the patriarchs, at whose banquet everyone who is faithful, just, and worthy of praise is found. We should be mindful that we are to perform not our own, but God's will, because he who does His will shall abide forever, just as He Himself will abide forever.

Wherefore, dearly beloved, with an upright mind, a firm faith, a robust spirit, and a perfect charity, let us be prepared for every design of God, guarding the mandates of the Lord with bravery, our innocence with humility, our zeal with good order; let us preserve our watchfulness by giving aid to those in distress, our mercy by serving the poor, our constancy by defending the truth, our caution by the strict observance of discipline, lest there be anything lacking in us by way of example of good deeds. These are the footsteps which all the saints left for us as they returned home, in order that we might, by clinging to their steps, attain also to their joys.

November 6

VI DAY WITHIN THE OCTAVE OF ALL SAINTS

Sermon of St. Bernard, Abbot

Since we celebrate today the festive memory of all the saints, which is most worthy of all devotion, I think it worth while, with the help of the Holy Spirit, to say a word for your sake concerning their common beatitude in which they already enjoy delightful rest, and concerning the future consummation which they await. Indeed, it is a faithful saying and worthy of all acceptance that those whom we honor with solemn veneration we should also imitate by a similar manner of life; that we should run with all eagerness towards the happiness of those whom we call most happy; that we should be supported by the patronage of those in whose praises we delight.

Of what avail to the saints, therefore, is our praise? Of what avail is our veneration? Of what avail is this, our very celebration? What are earthly honors to them, whom the heavenly Father honors, fulfilling the truthful promises of the Son? What are our commendations to them? They are filled. This is precisely the case, dearly beloved: the saints have no need of our goods, nor is anything bestowed on them by our devotion. Evidently it is our concern, not theirs, that we venerate their memory. Do you wish to know how much it concerns us? Through their memory I confess that I feel a vehement desire arise within me, and this desire is threefold.

It is commonly said: "What the eye does not see, the heart does not desire." My eye is my memory, and to meditate on the saints is, in a certain way, to see them. Thus, our portion is in the land of the living, nor is it a small portion, if, as is fitting, love be joined to memory. So I say, "our conversation is in heaven." However, our conversation is not just as that of the saints; for they are in heaven substantially; we, only by desire; they are there by their presence; we, by our memory.

November 7
VII DAY WITHIN THE OCTAVE OF ALL SAINTS
Sermon of St. John Chrysostom

He who with a holy love wonders at the merits of the saints, and with frequent praise proclaims the glories of the just, ought to imitate their saintly manners and uprightness, for he whom the merit of some saint delights ought to rejoice equally because of the honor shown to God. Therefore he ought either to imitate the saint if he praises him, or he should not praise if he declines to imitate; so that he who praises another may make himself praiseworthy, and he who admires the merits of the saints may himself become known for the holiness of his life. For if we love the just and the faithful because of the fact that we behold in them uprightness and fidelity, we also can be what they are, if we do what they did.

For it is not difficult for us to imitate what has been accomplished by them when we see such things to have been performed by the ancients even without a preceding example; they themselves were not made emulous of others, but they showed themselves to us as an example of virtue to be striven for, that, while we profit from them and others profit from us, Christ may always be praised in His holy Church in the person of His servants, of whom, from the beginning of the world, the innocent Abel was murdered; Henoch, who pleased God, was carried away; Noe was found just; Abraham was proved faithful; Moses was distinguished for his meekness; Josue, for his chastity; David, for his gentleness; Elias was made acceptable; Daniel, holy; and the three holy youths, constant and victorious.

The apostles and disciples of Christ are held as the teachers of those who believe; instructed by them, the confessors fight most bravely; the martyrs triumph completely; and the Christian forces, armed by God, war against the devil. In these are always kindred virtues, varied trials, and glorious victories. Why have you proclaimed yourself to be a Christian soldier if you think you can conquer without fighting, and triumph without a skirmish? Exhibit your powers, contend valiantly, fight zealously in this warfare. Think of the agreement, remember the terms, study the troops: the agreement you promised, the conditions under which you joined up, the army in which you enrolled.

November 8

OCTAVE DAY OF ALL SAINTS

I Nocturn

Lessons from the occurring Scripture

II Nocturn

From the book of St. Cyprian, Bishop and Martyr, on Mortality

It must be observed, dearly beloved, and now and then meditated upon, that we have renounced the world, though we yet spend a short time here as strangers and pilgrims. Let us cherish the day which restores to Paradise and the heavenly Kingdom, our true home, each one of us who has been snatched thence and ensnared in worldly dissipation. Who does not, when he is abroad, hasten with all speed to return to his own country? Who is there, when hastening to set sail for his dear ones, who does not more earnestly desire a favorable wind so that he may soon be permitted to embrace those whom he loves?

We regard paradise as our home country; the patriarchs we have begun to consider as our parents. Why then do we not hasten and run that we may soon see our fatherland and salute our parents? A great number of these dear ones await us there: parents, brothers, children; a great and numerous throng long for us; already certain of their own immortality, they are still solicitous about our salvation.

How great will be our joy and theirs when we come into their sight and embrace? What unspeakable delight there in that heavenly Kingdom, where there is no fear of dying, but life eternal! What supreme and perpetual happiness! There the glorious choir of apostles, the number of exulting prophets, the innumerable throng of martyrs—all are crowned for their victory over temptation and passion.

There triumphant are the virgins who by the strength of continence overcame the concupiscence of the flesh and body. There the merciful are rewarded who performed works of justice by giving food and largess to the poor, and who, keeping the commandments of the Lord, transferred their earthly patrimony into heavenly treasures. To these, dearly beloved brethren, let us hasten with an eager desire, and let us hope soon to be with them, so that we may sooner come to Christ.

℟. In the sight of the Angels I will sing praise to Thee, * And I will worship towards Thy holy temple and give glory to Thy name, O Lord. ℣. For Thy mercy and for Thy truth; for Thou hast magnified Thy holy name above all. And I will worship. Glory. And I will worship.

III Nocturn

The reading of the holy Gospel according to St. Matthew

At that time, seeing the crowds, Jesus went up the mountain. And when he was seated, his disciples came to him. And so forth.

From a Homily of St. Augustine, Bishop

"Blessed are you," He says, "when they will curse and persecute you, and say every evil thing against you unjustly because of me. Rejoice and exult, for your reward is great in heaven." Whoever seeks for the delights of this world and an abundance of temporal things in the Christian name, let him consider that our beatitude is interior, as it is said of the soul of the Church by the mouth of the Prophet: "All the glory of the king's daughter is from within."

For exteriorly there are promised curses and persecutions and detractions, for which, nevertheless, there is in heaven a great reward, which is sensed within the hearts of those suffering, who already can declare: "We glory in tribulations, knowing that tribulation worketh patience; and patience, trial; and trial, hope; and hope confoundeth not: because the charity of God is poured forth in our hearts, by the Holy Ghost, who is given to us."

Just to endure these things is not profitable, but it is profitable to bear them for the name of Christ, not only with a tranquil mind, but even with joy. For many heretics, deceiving their souls by the name *Christian*, suffer as many such things; yet they are still excluded from this reward, because it was not only said, "Blessed are they that suffer persecution," but it is added, "for justice' sake."

For where there is not a sound faith, there cannot be justice, "because the just man liveth by faith." Nor may schismatics promise to themselves anything of this reward, because, similarly, where there is not charity, there cannot be justice. "The love of neighbor worketh no evil," and if the schismatics had this love, they would not dismember the body of Christ, which is the Church.

℟. This is the true brotherhood which can never be violated by strife: the saints have given their blood for Christ and have followed Him. * They have despised the glitter of this world and have therefore come to the heavenly kingdom. ℣. Behold how good and how pleasant it is for brethren to dwell together in unity. They have despised. Glory. They have despised.

✠ Continuation of the holy Gospel according to St. Matthew.— At that time, seeing the crowds, Jesus went up the mountain. And when he was seated, his disciples came to him. And opening his mouth he taught them, saying, "Blessed are the poor in spirit, for theirs is the kingdom of heaven. Blessed are the meek, for they shall possess the earth. Blessed are they who mourn, for they shal be comforted. Blessed are they who hunger and thirst for justice, for they shall be satisfied. Blessed are the merciful, for they shall obtain mercy. Blessed are the pure of heart, for they shall see God. Blessed are the peacemakers, for they shall be called children of God. Blessed are they who suffer persecution for justice' sake, for theirs is the kingdom of heaven. Blessed are you when men reproach you, and persecute you, and, speaking falsely, say all manner of evil against you, for my sake. Rejoice and exult, because your reward is great in heaven."

Let Us Pray

O almighty and eternal God, who dost grant us to honor the merits of all Thy Saints in one feast, we beseech Thee, that increasing the number of our intercessors, Thou wouldst also increase Thy mercy for which we long. Through our Lord.

November 9

DEDICATION OF THE BASILICA OF THE MOST HOLY SAVIOR

I Nocturn

From the Book of the Apocalypse of St. John the Apostle, c. 21, 9 - 18

II Nocturn

The blessed Pope Sylvester I instituted the rites which the Roman Church observes in consecrating churches and altars. For although from the ages of the apostles places had been dedicated to God—which by some were called *oratories*, by others, *churches*—where assemblies were held every Sabbath, and the Christian people were accustomed to pray, to hear the word of God, and to receive the Holy Eucharist, yet those places hitherto had not been consecrated by a solemn rite, and up to the time of Sylvester an altar was not erected under title, which, anointed with chrism, symbolizes our Lord Jesus Christ, who is our Altar, our Victim, our Priest.

But when the Emperor Constantine obtained health and salvation through the sacrament of Baptism, then for the first time, by an edict published by him, the Christians throughout the world were permitted to build churches; he himself encouraged this holy building by his own example, as well as by this edict. For in his own Lateran palace he dedicated a church to the Savior and founded adjacent to it a Basilica, under the title of John the Baptist, on the very spot where he had been baptized by St. Sylvester and cleansed from the leprosy of unbelief. This basilica the same Pope consecrated on November 9, and the memory of this consecration is celebrated today, when, for the first time, a church was publicly consecrated at Rome, and there appeared to the Roman people an image of the Savior depicted on the wall.

Although later on, at the consecration of the altar of the Prince of the Apostles, St. Sylvester decreed that thenceforward all altars should be built of stone, yet the altar of the Lateran Basilica was built of wood. This is not surprising. For since, from St. Peter down to Sylvester, because of persecutions, the Pontiffs could not dwell in any fixed abode, they offered the Holy Sacrifice wherever necessity compelled them, whether in crypts or in cemeteries, or in the homes of the faithful, upon a wooden altar which was hollow like a chest.

When this altar had been placed in the first church, the Lateran, and when peace had been restored to the Church, St. Sylvester decreed that from that time on, no one except the Roman Pontiff should celebrate Mass upon it, in honor of the Prince of the Apostles—who is said to have offered the Holy Sacrifice upon it—and of the rest of the Popes who had been accustomed to use it. This same church, having been injured and destroyed by fires, pillagings, and earthquakes, and repaired by the laborious effort of the Supreme Pontiffs, was afterwards rebuilt anew, and Pope Benedict XIII, a Dominican, consecrated it on April 28, 1726, by a solemn rite, and ordered the commemoration of this celebration to be kept on this date. And what Pius IX had ordered to be done, Leo XIII carried out, namely, that the principal apse, threatening to fall through age, be lengthened and enlarged by a great addition; that the old mosaic, which had already been partly renewed before, be restored to its ancient figure and transferred to the new apse which was magnificently and richly decorated. He likewise ordered the transept to be embellished by a renewal of the fretted ceiling and of the vaults, while a sacristy, a house for the Canons, and a connecting portico were added to the Baptistry of Constantine during the year 1884.

℟. If they pray in this place, * Forgive the sins of Thy people, O Lord, and show them the good way wherein they should walk and give glory in this place. ℣. Give ear, O Thou that rulest Israel, Thou that leadest Joseph like a sheep, Thou that sittest upon the Cherubim. Forgive. Glory. Forgive.

III Nocturn

The reading of the holy Gospel acocrding to St. Luke

At that time Jesus entered and was passing through Jericho. And behold there was a man named Zacchæus; and he was a leading publican, and he was rich. And so forth.

Homily of St. Ambrose, Bishop

Zacchæus was a man of small stature, that is, not eminent for the worth of any inborn nobility, wanting in merit just as the Gentiles. When he heard of the coming of the Lord and Savior, whom His own had not received, he wished to see Him. However, no one easily gazes upon Jesus; no one attached to the earth can behold Jesus. And since he had neither the Prophets nor the Law as a natural recommendation, he climbed a sycamore, trampling underfoot as it were the vanity of the Jews, and amending the mistakes of his past life. Hence he hospitably received Jesus into the intimacy of his house.

And well did he climb into a tree in order that, as a good tree, he might bear good fruit, and thus, cut off from the natural wild olive, and contrary to nature, engrafted on the good olive, he might bear the fruit of the Law. For the root was holy, even though the branches (the Jews) were barren, whose unfruitful glory the race of the Gentiles surpassed by faith in the Resurrection, signified, in a certain manner, by the uplifting of his body.

Zacchæus, then, was in the sycamore; the blind man, along the road. For one of them the Lord stops and shows mercy; the other He makes famous by the renown of His visit. He questions the one and heals him; to the other's house He betakes Himself uninvited. For He knew how rich would be the reward of His visit. And though He had not heard any word of invitation, nevertheless, He already saw his desire.

But lest we seem, as though from disdain for the poor, to have quickly left the blind man and to have passed on to the rich, let us wait for him, for our Lord also waited for him; let us question him, for Christ, too, questioned him. Let *us* ask because we are ignorant; *He* questioned, though He knew. Let *us* question him so that we may know how he was cured; *He* asked so that through one, many of us might learn how we may merit to see the Lord. *He* questioned him that *we* might believe that no one can be saved except he acknowledge and praise God.

℟. All thy walls are of precious stones, * And the towers of Jerusalem shall be built up with jewels. ℣. The gates of Jerusalem shall be built of sapphire and of emerald, and round about the walls thereof of precious stones. And the towers. Glory. And the towers.

✠ Continuation of the holy Gospel according to St. Luke.—At that time Jesus entered and was passing through Jericho. And behold there was a man named Zacchæus; and he was a leading publican, and he was rich. And he was trying to see Jesus, who he was, but could not, on account of the crowd, because he was small of stature. So he ran on ahead and climbed up into a sycamore tree to see him, for he was going to pass that way.

And when Jesus came to the place, he looked up and saw him, and said to him, "Zacchæus, make haste and come down; for I must stay in thy house today."

And he made haste and came down, and welcomed him joyfully. And upon seeing it all began to murmur, saying, "He has gone to be the guest of a man who is a sinner." But Zacchæus stood and said to the Lord, "Behold, Lord, I give one-half of my possessions to the poor, and if I have defrauded anyone of anything, I restore it fourfold." Jesus said to him, "Today salvation has come to this house, since he, too, is a son of Abraham. For the Son of Man came to seek and to save what was lost."

LET US PRAY

O God, who each year dost renew the day on which Thy holy temple was consecrated and dost continue to bring us safely to the Sacred Mysteries, hear the prayers of Thy people and grant that all who enter this temple to ask Thy favors may rejoice in the obtaining of all their petitions. Through our Lord.

November 13
ALL SAINTS OF THE BENEDICTINE ORDER
I Nocturn
From the Book of Ecclesiasticus, c. 44, 1 - 15
II Nocturn
From a Sermon of St. John Damascene

Blessed and thrice blessed are they who glow with the love of God, and for love of Him have held all things as nothing. They indeed have shed many tears, and day and night they have spent in sorrow that they might receive everlasting consolation In this life they have humbled themselves so that in heaven they might be exalted. With hunger and thirst and vigils they have afflicted their flesh, that there the delights and exultation of paradise might take possession of them.

They were tabernacles of the Holy Spirit by the purity of their hearts, as it is written: "I will dwell in them and walk among them." They have crucified themselves to the world that they might stand at the right hand of Christ. They girded their loins in truth and always had their lamps in readiness, awaiting the coming of the immortal Spouse. For they were gifted with eyes of the mind, and continually contemplated that terrible day, and kept the consideration both of future goods and of future suffering so fixed in their hearts that they were never distracted from it. They strove to labor here that they might be partakers of eternal glory. Free of all disquietude, they were not unlike the angels, and now they form a chorus with them whose life they have imitated.

Blessed and thrice blessed are they, for they have considered the vanity of present things and the uncertainty and inconstancy of human prosperity. And having rejected these, they have laid up for themselves eternal goods, and have laid hold of that life which never ends, and which is not interrupted by death.

Hence, let us, even though unworthy and contemptible, strive to imitate these admirable men. We scarcely comprehend the supereminence of their heavenly life; but in accord with the measure of our infirmity and poor ability, we show forth their life by our imitation. We also wear their habit, even though we may not match their deeds. For we truly perceive that this divine profession wards off sin, and is a companion and handmaid of that incorruption granted to us through divine Baptism.

℟. Ye priests of God, bless the Lord * O ye holy and humble of heart praise God. ℣. Ye spirits and souls of the just, sing a hymn to our God. O ye holy. Glory. O ye holy.

III Nocturn

The reading of the holy Gospel according to St. Matthew

At that time Peter addressed Jesus, saying, "Behold, we have left all and followed thee; what then shall we have?" And so forth?

Homily of St. Bernard, Abbot

Brethren, you have just heard our Lord making a promise to His disciples, saying to them: "You shall sit on seats, judging the twelve tribes of Israel." Behold, the restfulness of being seated and the honor of passing judgment are promised. Now our Lord Himself was unwilling to receive these rewards except by humility and labor. Wherefore He was condemned to a most shameful death, loaded with torments, filled with opprobrium. So has He done, together with all who imitate Him in journeying on the way, in order that the enemy might be confounded. He it is, O wicked creature, He it is who will be seated on the throne of His Majesty, like to the Most High and equal to Him. The angels considered this when, at the fall of the evil one, they did not consent to his apostasy, thereby leaving us an example that as they chose to serve, so should we.

Let those who fly labor and seek honor know that they imitate him who sought for himself power and majesty; and if the devil's crime does not terrify them, his punishment should. The saints of God, who indeed will be seated in judgment, have given us an example of prudence in avoiding these vices. They, I say, in their own esteem, wretched worms of the earth, will sit in judgment. "Do you not know," says the Apostle, "that we shall judge even the angels?" They indeed who went forth weeping, sowing their seed, will come with joy carrying their sheaves. They who have sown labor and humility reap honor and rest. Because "for their double confusion and shame they will receive double in their land." Wherefore also a certain one has said: "Behold my lowliness and sorrow."

Not only that life itself, but also the promises of eternal life, and the eager anticipation of it, are a joy for the just, and a joy so great that anything to be desired cannot be compared with it. At the time when the followers of the wisdom of this world, which is indeed foolishness in God's sight, and of the prudence of the flesh, which worketh death and is inimical to God, withdrew from Christ, the holy apostles, when they clung to our Lord, sowed for us the seed of prudence. Manifestly, the martyrs sowed fortitude; the confessors followed justice throughout their lives. The same comparison exists between the martyrs and confessors as between Peter leaving all things, and Abraham using the wealth of this world for good purposes. For as the martyrs, having become perfect in a short time, filled out for a long time, so did the confessors endure long and varied martyrdoms. Plainly, the virgins who thus trod upon lust sowed temperance.

Our heavenly father, guide, master, and legislator, Benedict, also instructs us in this doctrine and directs our steps along the way of peace. Moreover, he strengthens and animates us for a life of justice in such a way that we are so much the more impelled to practice what he taught as we are certain that he taught not otherwise than he acted. The example of works is indeed a living and effective sermon, since it makes what is spoken most persuasive, showing that that which is urged is possible. In this regard his sanctity comforts us, his piety instructs us, his justice strengthens us. With what great piety was he not animated who provided not only for his children present, but was also solicitous for those of the future! He nourishes us by his life, his teaching, and by his intercession. Being always thus helped, dearly beloved, become fruitful; since for this were you appointed, "that you should go and bring forth fruit." Let us imitate him, because for this end he came, that he might give us the example and show us the way.

℟. O most holy Confessor of Christ, St. Benedict, Father and guide of monks: * Intercede for the salvation of ourselves and of all men. ℣. Help thy devoted people with thy holy intercession, that aided by thy prayers, they may attain to the heavenly kingdom. Intercede. Glory. Intercede.

☩ Continuation of the holy Gospel according to St. Matthew.—At that time Peter addressed Jesus, saying, "Behold, we have left all and followed thee; what then shall we have?" And Jesus said to them, "Amen I say to you that you who have followed me, in the regeneration when the Son of Man shall sit on the throne of his glory, shall also sit on twelve thrones, judging the twelve tribes of Israel. And everyone who has left house, or brothers, or sisters, or father, or mother, or wife, or children, or lands, for my name's sake, shall receive a hundredfold, and shall possess life everlasting."

Let Us Pray

Grant, we beseech Thee, O almighty God, that the examples of the holy Monks may urge us to a better life, that we may imitate the virtues of those whose solemn feast we celebrate. Through our Lord.

November 17
ST. GERTRUDE OF OUR ORDER, VIRGIN
I Nocturn
From the Canticle of Canticles, c. 2, 1 - 5; c. 8, 1 - 7
II Nocturn

The virgin Gertrude, born at Isleben, in the neighborhood of Mansfield, of most noble parents, at the age of five consecrated her virginity to Christ, to whom she was already mature and marriageable, in the monastery of the Order of our holy Father Benedict in the city of Rodard. From her very entrance into the religious life she began a form of angelic life, and being educated in the more advanced and divine studies, she came to that perfection of doctrine which the most erudite reasonably look upon with admiration. Outstanding was her contemplation, through which, being illumined with many revelations and heavenly visions by God, she wrote under His inspiration books full of divine wisdom.

Although she shone with such great gifts of nature and grace, although she enjoyed divine colloquies and was distinguished by the gift of prophecy and by many miracles, nevertheless, she so belittled herself that, among the outstanding wonders of the Divine Power, she believed this one to be singular—that the earth should sustain her, the most unworthy sinner, as she often called herself. When she was thirty years old, she was elected Abbess, first of the monastery where she made her profession, and then of Heldefs, or as they call it, Helfta. She exercised this office for forty years with charity, prudence, and perfect regularity of discipline, so that the community seemed to be the house of God, in which angels lived in human form under their mistress Gertrude, who, although she was mother of all, yet showed herself to be the servant of all.

The heavenly Spouse placed His delights in her purest heart, on which the divine Lover also branded the stigmata of His own wounds with the burning lance of love. From that time on she spoke of nothing but Christ whom she carried in her heart, and who declared that He would nowhere be found more at home than in the Sacrament of the Altar, and, after that, in the heart and soul of His beloved one. He attested to the holiness of this same dearest spouse by a word from His own divine mouth when He made it known that, at that time, there was no soul living which was closer to Him, or more pleasing and acceptable.

She venerated with an especial love the Virgin Mother of God, given to her in a particular way by Christ as mother and protectress, whom, together with other citizens of heaven, she frequently beheld. She was so permeated with a burning love and gratitude toward the most holy Sacrament of the Eucharist and the Passion of Christ, that she wholly melted away in tears. By daily suffrages and constant prayers she freed souls subjected to the flames of purgatory. She burned continually with zeal to promote the divine honor and to win salvation for her neighbor. And so, when she languished rather from her most fervent love of God than from sickness, Christ, accompanied by His most holy Mother, the beloved disciple, and a most beautiful choir of virgins, came to her, and led her soul, freed from the bonds of the body and taken into the secret recesses of His Heart by a marvelous opening in His breast, to the heavenly bridal chamber.

℞. With Christ I am fixed to the cross: * For I bear the marks of the Lord Jesus in my heart. ℣. I live now, not I, but Christ liveth in me. For. Glory. For.

III Nocturn

The reading of the holy Gospel according to St. Matthew

At that time Jesus spoke to his disciples this parable: "The kingdom of heaven will be like ten virgins who took their lamps and went forth to meet the bridegroom and the bride." And so forth.

Homily of St. Augustine, Bishop

Let us understand, dearly beloved, that this parable refers to all of us, that is, to the universal Church: not only to the hierarchy, nor to the people alone, but rather to all. These five plus five virgins are all the souls of Christians. But, if we may tell you what we feel, with God's inspiration, they are not just any souls whatsoever, but such as have the Catholic faith, and seem to perform good works in the Church of God. And yet, five of them are prudent, and five are foolish.

Let us see first why *five* are named, and why *virgins*. Every soul in a body is indicated by the number five, because it uses five senses. Whoever, therefore, refrains himself from illicit sight, illicit hearing, illicit smell, illicit taste, illicit touch receives, on account of that *integrity* the name virgin. But if it is good to abstain from illicit acts of the senses—and for this reason every Christian soul receives the name *virgin*—why are five admitted, and five rejected?

They are also virgins, and yet are rejected. It is a small thing that they are virgins and have lamps. They are virgins because of abstinence from illicit use of the senses; they have lamps because of their good works, of which the Lord says, "Let your works shine before men." Likewise He says to His disciples, "Let your loins be girt, and lamps burning in your hands." By girded loins is signified virginity; by burning lamps, good works. If therefore abstinence from illicit things is good, whence virginity receives its name, and if good works, which are signified by the lamps, are praiseworthy, why are five admitted, and five rejected?

The ones He called prudent, the others, foolish. By what shall we judge? How shall we distinguish? By the oil. Oil signifies something great, and very great. Do you not think it *charity?* We speak inquiringly; we do not rashly make definitions. I will tell you why it seems to me that charity is designated by the oil. The Apostle says: "I show unto you yet a more excellent way. If I speak with the tongues of men and of angels, and have not charity, I am become as sounding brass, or a tinkling cymbal." This is the more excellent way, that is, charity, which is rightly symbolized by oil, for oil excels all liquids.

℟. With an eternal love the Lord loved Gertrude, therefore He drew her from her very infancy and led her into His solitude * And He spoke to her heart. ℣. He espoused her to Himself in faith and in mercy forever. And. Glory. And.

☩ Continuation of the holy Gospel according to St. Matthew.— At that time Jesus spoke to his disciples this parable: "The kingdom of heaven will be like ten virgins who took their lamps and went forth to meet the bridegroom and the bride. Five of them were foolish and five wise. But the five foolish, when they took their lamps, did not take oil with them; but the wise took oil in their vessels with the lamps. Then as the bridegroom was long in coming, they all became drowsy and slept. And at midnight a cry arose, 'Behold, the bridegroom is coming, go forth to meet him!' Then all those virgins arose and trimmed their lamps. And the foolish said to the wise, 'Give us some of your oil, for our lamps are going out.' The wise answered, saying, 'Lest there may not be enough for us and for you, go rather to those who sell, and buy for yourselves.'

"Now while they were away buying, the bridegroom came; and those who were ready went in with him to the marriage feast, and the door was shut. Finally there came also the other virgins, and said, 'Sir, sir, open the door for us!' But he answered and said, 'Amen I say to you, I do not know you.' Watch therefore, for you know neither the day nor the hour."

Let Us Pray

O God, who in the most pure heart of blessed Gertrude Thy virgin didst prepare a pleasing dwelling for Thyself; by her merits and intercession mercifully cleanse our hearts from all stain of sin that we also may merit to become a worthy temple of Thy divine Majesty. Through our Lord.

November 18
DEDICATION OF THE BASILICAS OF SS. PETER AND PAUL

I Nocturn
From the Book of the Apocalypse of St. John the Apostle, c. 21, 18 - 27

II Nocturn

Among the sacred places which have been honored from ancient times by the Christians, the best known and most highly honored were those where the bodies of the saints were buried, or where there was some trace or relic of the martyrs. Among these sacred places, that on the Vatican Hill, which is called the Confession of St. Peter, has always been one of the most noteworthy. To this place Christians from all parts of the world come as to the rock of faith and the foundation-stone of the Church, and they honor with reverence and love the spot consecrated by the tomb of the Prince of the Apostles.

To this place the Emperor Constantine came on the eighth day after his Baptism, and having removed his crown, cast himself on the ground and wept profusely. He then took a spade and began to dig up the earth, taking away twelve basketfuls in honor of the twelve apostles, and upon that spot he built a church which was to be the Cathedral church of the Prince of the Apostles. Pope Sylvester consecrated this church on the eighteenth day of November as he had done to the church of the Lateran on the ninth of the same month. In this church Pope Sylvester set up an altar of stone, pouring ointment upon it, and decreeing that thenceforth no altar might be built except of stone.

Constantine also built a magnificent church on the Ostian way, named in honor of the holy Apostle Paul, which was also dedicated by the same blessed Sylvester. These churches were enriched by the Emperor who gave grants of much land, and adorned them with very rich gifts. In the course of time, the church of St. Peter upon the Vatican Hill fell into ruins. It was rebuilt from the foundations, enlarged, and ornamented through the zeal of many Popes. Pope Urban VIII solemnly consecrated it anew on this same recurring day, November 18, 1626.

The Basilica of St. Paul on the Ostian way was almost entirely consumed by fire in 1823, but was yet more splendidly rebuilt by the untiring zeal of four Popes. In the year 1854, Pius IX, making use of the happy occasion when the doctrine of the Immaculate Conception of the Blessed Virgin Mary, which he had just proclaimed, had brought to Rome many Bishops and Cardinals from all parts of the Catholic world, solemnly dedicated this new church in their presence on the tenth of December of the year mentioned above. He ordered that the annual feast in commemoration of that dedication should be kept on this day, which is the same as that of the Dedication of the church of St. Peter.

℟. My house shall be called the house of prayer, saith the Lord; therein everyone that asketh, receiveth; and he that seeketh, findeth; * And to him that knocketh it shall be opened. ℣. Ask, and it shall be given you; seek and you shall find. And to him. Glory. And to him.

III Nocturn

The reading of the holy Gospel according to St. Luke

At that time Jesus entered and was passing through Jericho. And behold there was a man named Zacchæus; and he was a leading publican, and he was rich. And so forth.

Homily of St. Gregory, Pope

If we are seeking to be truly wise and to contemplate Wisdom itself, let us humbly acknowledge that we are stupid. Let us forsake harmful knowledge; let us learn of praiseworthy foolishness. To this end, indeed, it is written: "The foolish things of the world hath God chosen that he may confound the wise." Hence it is said again: "If any man among you seem to be wise in this world, let him become a fool, that he may be wise." For this reason, the words of the Gospel account testify that Zacchæus, since he could see nothing because of the crowd, climbed into a sycamore tree that he might behold the Lord as He passed by. The sycamore, in fact, is called the "foolish fig-tree."

So Zacchæus, who was a little man, went up into the sycamore and saw the Lord, because those who, in humility, choose the foolishness of the world shall, in their astuteness, contemplate God's wisdom. Likewise does a crowd prevent our small stature from seeing the Lord, for the tumult of worldly cares presses down the weakness of the human mind lest it should give heed to the light of the Truth.

But we shall prudently climb the sycamore if we shall carefully hold in our mind that foolishness which is divinely commanded. For in this world what is more stupid than not to hunt for things lost, to let go of possessions to thieves, to return no harm for injuries received, even more, to show patience when other injuries are added? Our Lord has ordered us, as it were, to climb the sycamore when He declared: "Of him that taketh away thy goods ask them not again." And again: "If any one strike thee on the right cheek, offer him also the other."

From the sycamore the Lord is beheld passing by, because by this wise folly, although not as yet completely, the wisdom of God is, nevertheless, seen as it were in passing, through the light of contemplation; which wisdom they who seem to themselves to be wise cannot perceive, for, being immersed in the haughty crowd of their thoughts, they have not as yet found a sycamore from which to behold the Lord.

℟. Bless, O Lord, this house which I have built unto Thy name: of those who shall come unto this place * Hear Thou the prayers from the throne of Thy glory on high. ℣. O Lord, if Thy people shall turn and pray towards Thy sanctuary. Hear. Glory. Hear.

✚ Continuation of the holy Gospel according to St. Luke.—At that time Jesus entered and was passing through Jericho. And behold there was a man named Zacchæus; and he was a leading publican, and he was rich. And he was trying to see Jesus, who he was, but could not, on account of the crowd, because he was small of stature. So he ran on ahead and climbed up into a sycamore tree to see him, for he was going to pass that way.

And when Jesus came to the place, he looked up and saw him, and said to him, "Zacchæus, make haste and come down; for I must stay in thy house today."

And he made haste and came down, and welcomed him joyfully. And upon seeing it all began to murmur, saying, "He has gone to be the guest of a man who is a sinner." But Zacchæus stood and said to the Lord, "Behold, Lord, I give one-half of my possessions to the poor, and if I have defrauded anyone of anything, I restore it fourfold." Jesus said to him, "Today salvation has come to this house, since he, too, is a son of Abraham. For the Son of Man came to seek and to save what was lost."

Let Us Pray

O God, who each year dost renew the day on which Thy holy temple was consecrated and dost continue to bring us safely to the Sacred Mysteries, hear the prayers of Thy people and grant that all who enter this temple to ask Thy favors may rejoice in the obtaining of all their petitions. Through our Lord.

November 21
PRESENTATION OF THE BLESSED VIRGIN
I Nocturn
From the Proverbs of Solomon, c. 8, 12 - 25 and 34 - 36; c. 9, 1 - 5
II Nocturn
From the Book of St. John Damascene on the Orthodox Faith

Joachim joined himself in marriage to the most excellent and highly praiseworthy lady, Anne. Just as the Anne of ancient time gave birth to Samuel through her prayer and promise, although she was afflicted with sterility, in the same way, this Anne, too, by her supplication and promise, received the Mother of God from God, so that not even in this regard should she yield place to any of the illustrious mothers. Thus, grace (for the name *Anne* denotes this) brought forth the Queen (for that is what the name *Mary* means), because she was truly made Queen of all things created when she became Mother of the Creator.

She is brought into light in Joachim's home near the sheep pond, and taken to the temple; and from then on, being planted in the house of God and fathered by the Spirit, she is made the abode of all virtues, like to a fruitful olive tree, so that she, who had truly withdrawn her mind from every desire of this life and of the flesh, might likewise keep her soul virginal, together with her body, as was befitting her who was to receive God within her bosom.

From the Book of St. Ambrose, Bishop, on Virgins

Mary was such that her life alone is a model for everyone. If, then, it is not boresome to you, let us examine the matter, that whatever woman seeks Mary's reward for herself may imitate her example. What a great splendor of virtue shines forth in one Virgin! The reserve of her modesty, the standard of her faith, the service of her devotion! A Virgin within her home, a companion to the priesthood, a mother in the temple! O how many virgins does she aid! How many are those whom she draws in her embrace to the Lord, saying: "This virgin has guarded the marriage bed of my Son; this one has in her immaculate purity watched over His bridal chambers."

Why, therefore, should I proceed to speak of her frugality in food, of her relentless industry at her duties, the latter above nature's capacity, the former almost below nature's needs; her labor knowing no rest, her fast continuing two days at a time? And if at times the desire for refreshment prevailed, the food at hand was often such that it would stave off death, but would not serve for pleasure. She had no desire for sleep, except in so far as necessity demanded it. And indeed, when the body did rest, the mind kept watch; for often while asleep, she either repeated what she had read, or continued what had been interrupted by sleep, or reviewed what had been accomplished, or anticipated what was yet to be done.

℟. Truly happy art thou, O holy Virgin Mary, and worthy of all praise: * For from thee hath dawned the Sun of Justice, Christ, our God. ℣. Pray for the people, meditate for the clergy, intercede for all devout women; may all experience thy help who celebrate thy holy Presentation. For from thee. Glory. For from thee.

III Nocturn

The reading of the holy Gospel according to St. Luke

At that time, as Jesus spoke these things to the multitude, a certain woman lifted up her voice from the crowd, and said to him, "Blessed is the womb that bore thee, and the breasts that nursed thee." And so forth.

Homily of St. Bede the Venerable, Priest

This woman is shown to be of great devotion and faith, who, while the Scribes and Pharisees are trying our Lord and at the same time blaspheming Him, better than anybody else, understands the Incarnation so well and proclaims it with such confidence, that she puts to shame the slanderous attack of the leaders there present, as well as the faithlessness of future heretics. For as the Jews then, by blaspheming the works of the Holy Spirit, denied that the Son of God was the true Son of, and consubstantial with, the Father, so afterwards have heretics, by denying that Mary ever a Virgin, through the operation of the power of the Holy Spirit, furnished the matter for His flesh when the Only-Begotten of God was to be born with human members, declared that the Son of man must not be acknowledged the true Son of, and consubstantial with, His mother.

But, if the flesh of the Word of God is pronounced independent of the flesh of the Virgin Mother, the womb which bore it and the breast which nourished it are called blessed without a reason. Moreover, the Apostle says: "God sent his Son, *made* of a woman, made under the Law." And they are not to be listened to who conjecture that it should be read: "*born* of a woman, made under the Law, but it is "*made* of a woman," because, when conceived in the virginal womb, Christ did not draw His flesh out of nothing, nor from any other place, but from the body of His

Mother; otherwise, He who would not have His origin from man should not be truly called the Son of Man.

And so, having directed these facts against Eutychius, let us raise our voice with the Catholic Church, whose type this woman was; let us raise our mind also from the midst of the multitudes, and let us declare: "Blessed is the womb that bore thee, and the breasts which nourished thee." For truly is that Mother blessed "who," as someone has said, "didst bring forth the King who ruleth heaven and earth forever and ever."

"Yea, rather, blessed are they who hear the word of God, and keep it." In a beautiful manner the Savior assents to the woman's avowal, asserting that not only she who had merited to give birth to the Word of God in body was blessed, but that all, too, who strive to conceive the same Word in a spiritual way through the preaching of the Faith, and to bring it forth and, as it were, to foster it, whether in their own, or in the heart of their neighbors, are also blessed, because the Mother of God herself was, on the one hand, indeed blessed by the fact that she was made the temporal minister of the Incarnation of the Word; but, on the other, she is far more blessed by the fact that she remained the everlasting protectress of the same Word who must be loved always.

℟. All generations shall call me blessed * Because the Lord who is mighty hath done great things to me, and holy is His name. ℣. And His mercy is from generation unto generation to them that fear Him. Because. Glory. Because.

✠ Continuation of the holy Gospel according to St. Luke.— At that time, as Jesus spoke these things to the multitude, a certain woman lifted up her voice from the crowd and said to him, "Blessed is the womb that bore thee, and the breasts that nursed thee." But he said, "Rather, blessed are they who hear the word of God and keep it."

LET US PRAY

O God, who didst decree that on this day the blessed Mary ever Virgin, the temple of the Holy Spirit, shouldst be presented in the temple, grant, we beseech Thee, that through her intercession we may merit to be presented in the temple of Thy glory Through our Lord... in the unity of the same Holy Spirit.

ALPHABETICAL INDEX OF FEASTS

All Saints	496
All Saints of the Benedictine Order	512
All Souls	499
St. Andrew, Apostle	292
Annunciation of the Blessed Virgin	346
Ascension of Our Lord	162
Assumption of the Blessed Virgin	440
St. Barnabas, Apostle	375
St. Bartholomew, Apostle	449
St. Benedict, Confessor	342
St. Benedict, Solemnity of	403
Circumcision of Our Lord	35
Commemoration of St. Paul, Apostle	389
Corpus Christi	194
Conversion of St. Paul	321
Dedication of the Basilica of the Holy Savior	508
Dedication of the Basilicas of SS. Peter and Paul	518
Dedication of St. Mary Major	429
Dedication of St. Michael the Archangel	467
Epiphany of Our Lord	41
Exaltation of the Holy Cross	457
Finding of the Holy Cross	366
St. Gertrude, Virgin	515
St. Gregory the Great	337
Holy Guardian Angels	470
Holy Innocents	27
Holy Name of Jesus	37
Holy Name of Mary	454
Holy Relics	372
Holy Rosary	476
Immaculate Conception of the Blessed Virgin	295
St. James the Greater, Apostle	421
SS. James and Philip, Apostles	362
SS. Joachim and Anne	424
St. John, Apostle and Evangelist	25
St. John before the Latin Gate	369
St. John the Baptist, Nativity of	379
St. Joseph, Spouse of the Blessed Virgin	340
St. Joseph, Solemnity of	352
SS. Jude and Simon, Apostles	491
St. Lawrence, Martyr	436

Alphabetical Index of Feasts

St. Luke, Evangelist	483
St. Mark, Evangelist	349
St. Matthew, Apostle and Evangelist	464
St. Matthias, Apostle	334
St. Maurus, Abbot	311
Maternity of the Blessed Virgin	479
St. Meinrad, Martyr	315
St. Michael the Archangel	467
Nativity of Our Lord	16
Nativity of the Blessed Virgin	452
Nativity of St. John the Baptist	379
Our Lady of Einsiedeln	409
SS. Paul and Peter, Apostles	386
St. Paul, Commemoration of	389
St. Paul, Conversion of	321
Pentecost Sunday	178
SS. Peter and Paul, Apostles	386
St. Peter's Chains	427
St. Peter's Chair	331
SS. Philip and James, Apostles	362
St. Placid and Companions, Martyrs	473
Precious Blood of Our Lord	392
Presentation of the Blessed Virgin	521
Purification of the Blessed Virgin	325
Resurrection of Our Lord	132
Sacred Heart of Jesus	207
St. Scholastica, Virgin	328
Seven Dolors of the Blessed Virgin	461
SS. Simon and Jude, Apostles	491
St. Stephen, First Martyr	22
St. Thomas, Apostle	308
Transfiguration of Our Lord	432
Trinity Sunday	191
Visitation of the Blessed Virgin	395

INDEX OF THE TEMPORAL CYCLE

I Sunday of Advent	1
Ember Days of Advent	9
Nativity of Our Lord	16
Circumcision of Our Lord	35
Holy Name of Jesus	37
Epiphany of Our Lord	41
Septuagesima Sunday	68
Ash Wednesday	77
I Sunday of Lent	81
Passion Sunday	118
Easter Sunday	132
Rogation Days	160
Ascension of Our Lord	162
Pentecost Sunday	178
Ember Days of Pentecost	186
Trinity Sunday	191
Corpus Christi	194
Sacred Heart	207
IV-XI Sundays after Pentecost	
Lessons of the II Nocturn	223
I Sunday of August	232
I Sunday of September	238
Ember Days of September	241
I Sunday of October	246
I Sunday of November	251
IV-XXIV Sundays after Pentecost	
Homilies, Gospels and Prayers	257